A NEW HISTORICAL GEOGRAPHY OF
ENGLAND AFTER 1600

A NEW HISTORICAL GEOGRAPHY OF ENGLAND AFTER 1600

Edited by
H. C. DARBY

CAMBRIDGE UNIVERSITY PRESS

CAMBRIDGE

LONDON   NEW YORK   MELBOURNE

Published by the Syndics of the Cambridge University Press
The Pitt Building, Trumpington Street, Cambridge CB2 IRP
Bentley House, 200 Euston Road, London NW1 2DB
32 East 57th Street, New York, NY 10022, USA
296 Beaconsfield Parade, Middle Park, Melbourne 3206, Australia

© Cambridge University Press 1973, 1976

First published as part of *A New Historical Geography of England*, 1973
First published separately, 1976

Printed in Great Britain at the University Printing House, Cambridge
(Harry Myers, University Printer)

Library of Congress Cataloguing in Publication Data
Darby, Henry Clifford, 1909-
A new historical geography of England after 1600.
The last 6 chapters of the editor's
A new historical geography of England
Includes bibliographical references and index.
1. England – Historical geography.   I. Title
[DA600.D36 1976]   942   76-26029
ISBN 0 521 29145 3 paperback
(*A New Historical Geography of England*, ISBN 0 521 20116 0 hard covers)

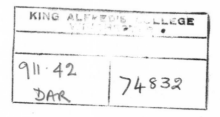

CONTENTS

[v]

MAPS AND DIAGRAMS

[vi]

PREFACE

In 1936 the Cambridge University Press published *An historical geography of England before A.D. 1800*. It has been reprinted a number of times but clearly the moment has come not for a further reprint nor for a new edition but for an entirely new volume based upon the enormous amount of work that has been done since 1936, and especially since 1945. Much of the new work has appeared in the pages of three journals, *The Economic History Review*, *The Agricultural History Review* and the *Transactions and Papers of the Institute of British Geographers*. Moreover, the English Place-Name Society has continued to produce its scholarly volumes year by year; the Domesday Book has been analysed geographically, so have the Lay Subsidies of 1334 and 1524–5. Our views of agriculture and industry in later times have also been modified by a variety of monographs.

Not only has there been much exploration of sources, but also much discussion about the method of historical geography. In particular, a contrast has often been drawn between the reconstructions of past geographies and the study of geographical changes through time, between the so-called 'horizontal' and 'vertical' approaches. This present volume seeks to combine both, and the combination was suggested by J. O. M. Broek's *The Santa Clara Valley, California: a study in landscape changes* (Utrecht, 1932).

The new work begins with the coming of the Anglo-Saxons in the belief that so far as there ever is a new beginning in history, that event was such a beginning. It continues beyond the eighteenth century, up to 1900 or so, but this has not been taken as a rigid date because 1914, rather than 1900, marks the effective end of the nineteenth century. In contemplating the result, one can only be very conscious of what remains to be done. As far as sources are concerned, although much recent work has been done on the Tithe Returns of the 1840s, a comprehensive treatment has yet to appear. There have also been interesting studies on enclosure, but no large-scale attack on a geographical basis. Or, to take another example, even so obvious a source as the Census Returns, from 1801 onwards, still awaits comprehensive analysis and interpretation. As far as method is concerned, much further enquiry is needed to see to what extent statistical techniques and locational analysis can be applied to historical data of varying quality and coverage.

In another generation or so the materials for an historical geography of England will not be as we know them now. A wider range of sources will have been explored and evaluated. Fresh ideas about method will have prepared the way for a more sophisticated presentation. And by that time we and our landscape will have become yet one more chapter in some other *Historical Geography of England*.

I am greatly indebted to my fellow contributors for their co-operation and patience. All of us must thank the staff of the Cambridge University Press for their skill and care. We must also thank Mr G. R. Versey. He has not only drawn all the maps and diagrams but has compiled many of them and has also given much general assistance at all stages of the work.

H. C. DARBY

KING'S COLLEGE
CAMBRIDGE

Candlemas, 1973

NOTE TO TWO-VOLUME EDITION

This edition consists of the last six chapters of *A new historical geography of England* (1973). The text remains the same but the opportunity has been taken to make a few minor corrections. To this there is one exception. A new page (page 2) has been added and on this there is a new map (Fig. 1). The subsequent pages and figures have been renumbered and the Index has been adjusted to meet the needs of the volume. An Introduction has been added to explain the thinking behind the work as a whole.

H. C. D.

KING'S COLLEGE
CAMBRIDGE
St Basil's Day, 1976

INTRODUCTION

An account of the geography of a past age that aims to explain as well as to describe should, like one of the present-day, take into consideration the relevant circumstances of earlier times. But when we contemplate a chronological series of cross-sections, we are at once faced with more complicated considerations. Two very different methods of treatment can be envisaged. If, on the one hand, each cross-section in a sequence aims at being a balanced geographical account, compounded of description and explanation, there will, of necessity, be much repetition and varying degrees of overlap as each cross-section ranges backwards to satisfy its own needs. If, on the other hand, each cross-section is limited strictly to its own contemporary materials, a valid criticism might be that the sequence constitutes a series of static pictures that ignore the process of becoming.

It is possible to compromise between these two extremes in a way suggested by J. O. M. Broek in *The Santa Clara Valley, California: a study in landscape changes* (Utrecht, 1932). Here, four cross-sections are separated by three studies of the economic and social forces that led to successive changes in the landscape. The device of separating the explanatory narrative from the description of a landscape at each period serves not only to explain each landscape but also to provide connecting links between the successive views. For *A new historical geography of England* the choice consists of six narratives and six cross-sections as follows:

The choice of dates for the various cross-sections depends partly on the march of events, and also (let us admit it) upon the availability of sources of information. Even so, such a choice can only be an individual one, and the thinking that lies behind it must now be described.

The work as a whole begins with the coming of the Anglo-Saxons 'in the belief that so far as there ever is a new beginning in history, that event was such a beginning'. This is not to imply that pre-Saxon contributions were unimportant. Clearly, continuity between Roman Britain and Anglo-Saxon England was much greater than was at one time believed, and further work may strengthen this belief. But this does not affect the fact that the coming of the English to England was a new beginning – with all it meant in the peopling, the language and the institutions of much of these islands. When the Normans arrived in 1066, the villages they encountered bore names that were certainly not Celtic – except in Cornwall. Part of Britain had become England.

The period between the end of Roman rule and the year of the Norman Conquest was one of great fluidity, and the sources are so limited that it is difficult for the pen to catch the scene. Yet it was a formative period of the greatest importance for the landscapes of later times. Anglo-Saxons and Scandinavians covered Roman Britain with their new villages, and proceeded rapidly to clear its woodland. No later invasion of peoples significantly modified the Anglo-Scandinavian pattern; the Norman Conquest was the transposition of an aristocracy and not a folk movement of new settlers on the land. Twenty years after their coming, the Normans instituted the enquiry that resulted in Domesday Book. Its unique character as a source enables us to survey the results of the centuries of migration and settlement and to present a view of England in 1086.

In the years after the Conquest, the countryside continued to be cleared and towns grew and prospered. But this expansive movement did not continue uninterruptedly throughout the Middle Ages. In places it slowed down; in others it ceased; and in yet other places the frontiers of cultivation even retreated, and the populations of towns may have declined. Certainly in England, as in most of Western and Central Europe, medieval agrarian and commercial effort had reached a peak by 1300, and the great age of expanding arable and trade was succeeded in the fourteenth and fifteenth centuries by one of stagnation and recession. The decline was especially marked during the hundred years between 1350 and 1450. The early fourteenth century seemed therefore suitable for another view of England. Moreover for this critical period a convenient and unique source is at hand – the lay subsidy of 1334. It is convenient coming as it did before the full impact of the recession of the later Middle Ages was felt. It is unique because the assessment agreed upon in that year continued to be the basis for later subsidies until 1623. This means that although the rolls of 1334 (as for other years) have not entirely survived, the missing figures can be recovered from later rolls. It is possible, therefore, to achieve a reasonably complete cover from which to construct a general framework for delineating the geographical and economic condition of the country as a whole.

A possible date for a cross-section at the end of the Middle Ages might be 1500. But although Henry Tudor had won the throne of England in 1485, the years around 1500 had yet to see the recession of the later Middle Ages merge into the full flowering of the sixteenth century, a flowering reflected in the writings of such men as Leland and Camden, in the maps of Saxton and Norden, and in Speed's *Theatre of the Empire of Great Britaine* (1611) which aimed at presenting 'an exact geography' of the realm. The Tudors, in the words of Charles Whibley, 'recognized that the most brilliant discovery of a brilliant age was the discovery of their own country', and in so doing helped to provide material that makes 1600 rather than 1500 a more suitable moment for another cross-section. That the Tudor dynasty came to an end with the death of Queen Elizabeth in 1603 did not determine the choice, but, at any rate, made it not inappropriate.

The choice of dates for cross-sectional views in the modern period can also be argued. Macaulay chose 1685 as the basis for the famous third chapter in his *History of England* (1848), but this is too near 1600 in the present scheme. Another date that might have been chosen is some year in the 1720s. Scotland had been united with England in 1707, the War of Spanish Succession was over in 1714, and Daniel Defoe's *Tour* appeared in 1724. This latter date was used by G. M. Trevelyan in his *England Under Queen Anne* (1930), and, like Macaulay's choice, was appropriate in the context of his own work. Other conceivable dates might have been 1760, at the beginning of the canal age, or even 1780 when the annual rate of industrial growth was first greater than 2%, but both dates are too near 1800 which for many reasons appeared as an ideal date for a cross-section in the full work. The first Census was taken in 1801; this was also the year of the so-called Acreage Returns for different crops; furthermore, between 1793 and 1815 appeared the *General Views* of each county issued by the Board of Agriculture. Taken together they yield a remarkable body of information which reinforces the choice of the year 1800.

Thus it was that the span of years from 1600 to 1800 was covered in one chapter. The clearing of the wood may have been the great epic of the Middle Ages but now, after 1600 came other epics – the draining of the marsh, the reclamation of the heath, the enclosure of the arable, the spread of landscape gardens and the beginning of the later seats of industry. And so the changes of these two centuries were brought together under the title 'The Age of the Improver'.

After 1800 it is clear that the time-intervals between the cross-sections need to be shorter. Not only was the pace of change accelerating, but the written evidence about it was increasing prodigiously. J. H. Clapham chose 1820 and 1886–7 as dates for describing what he called 'the face of the country'; both were suitable for the development of the themes of his *Economic history of modern Britain* (1926–38). But for us 1820 is too near 1800; and 1886–7 is too near 1900. We chose the year 1850 because it may be said to mark the end of 'the early railway age', some of the results of which were indicated in the census of 1851. As for agriculture, the tithe surveys of the 1840s, and the county reports in the *Journal of the Royal Agricultural Society* (1845–69) together provided the only detailed picture since the *General Views* of the Board of Agriculture. Moreover, mid-century, on the eve of the Great Exhibition of 1851, seemed a suitable moment at which to pause.

The years after 1850 saw the full development of Britain as an industrial state. Towns became the birthplaces of the major part of the population, and agriculture declined to a subordinate position in face of overseas competition. The final cross-section is tied to the year 1900. We might have chosen 1910 or 1914 which marked the effective end of the nineteenth century; the last two chapters certainly do not hesitate on occasions to reach towards these dates. Rightly or wrongly, we chose 1900 for the title of the last chapter. At any rate when Queen Victoria died on 22 January 1901 many felt that a great epoch had closed.

H. C. D.

Chapter 1

THE AGE OF THE IMPROVER: 1600–1800

H. C. DARBY

When the Tudor dynasty came to an end in 1603, the changes that were to transform the medieval landscape had already begun. Not only had they begun, but information about them was becoming increasingly abundant with the dissemination of the printed word. The tradition of English topographical writing inaugurated by Leland, Camden and Speed was soon to grow to great dimensions. As the seventeenth and eighteenth centuries progressed, there emerged a clearer picture of the differences in soil to be found in the various English counties. Compare, for instance, the description of Dorset by John Coker early in the seventeenth century with that by John Hutchins in 1774. The former referred generally to the difference between clayland and chalkland, but the latter drew much more definite pictures of the three divisions of the county – 'the down, the vale and the heath'.[1] This is not surprising in view of the increasing attention given to agricultural improvement. The Tudor husbandries of Fitzherbert and Tusser were the precursors of a large number of works concerned with the advancement of agriculture. The flow of treatises continued to increase throughout the eighteenth century when the name of Arthur Young came to dominate all others.[2]

Just as in agriculture the impulse to improve was widespread, so in industry was the impulse to contrive and invent – especially in the iron industry, in the textile industry and in coalmining. Reports and pamphlets began to multiply, and they dealt not only with machines but also with roads and canals. During these years, too, the first detailed maps of England were made. An outstanding example was John Rocque's map of Middlesex in 1754 (Fig. 1) which was on a scale of about 2 inches to one

[1] H. C. Darby, 'Some early ideas on the agricultural regions of England', *Agric. Hist. Rev.*, II (1954), 30–47; F. V. Emery, 'English regional studies from Aubrey to Defoe', *Geog. Jour.*, CXXIV (1958), 315–25.

[2] G. E. Fussell: (1) *The old English farming books from Fitzherbert to Tull, 1523 to 1730* (London, 1947); (2) *More old English farming books from Tull to the Board of Agriculture, 1731 to 1793* (London, 1950).

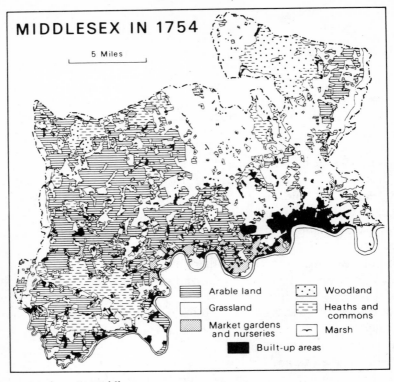

MIDDLESEX IN 1754

5 Miles

Arable land   Woodland
Grassland   Heaths and
                     commons
Market gardens   Marsh
and nurseries
Built-up areas

Fig. 1. Land use in Middlesex, 1754.
Based on J. Rocque, *A topographical map of the county of Middlesex* (London).

mile and which indicated land use by conventional symbols. There was
also a number of atlases of England with 'accurate' or 'new improved'
maps of each county. Not least among these was John Cary's *New and
correct English atlas* (1787) which ran into at least nine editions, together
with a number of reprints. These years also saw the work of William
Smith, the so-called 'father of English geology'. His first geological map,
covering the country around Bath, appeared in 1799, and in 1815 came
his large geological map of England and Wales as a whole, on a scale of
5 miles to one inch. It comprised 15 sheets engraved by John Cary and
was accompanied by a memoir dealing with the geological and physical
features and the soils of each county. The prospectus referred to support
from, among other bodies, the Board of Agriculture. From 1759 until
1809 the Royal Society of Arts (founded in 1754) offered awards for
county maps on a scale of one inch to a mile, and so stimulated the produc-

tion of maps based upon original surveys and often showing details of land utilisation.[1] In the meantime the Ordnance Survey had been constituted in 1791, and its first one-inch sheet of Kent and part of Essex appeared on 1 January 1801.[2]

There was also a whole new body of writing about the features and problems of the changing economy of the time. Political economy and 'political arithmetic' emerged as distinct enquiries, and were exemplified in the works of such men as John Graunt (1620–74), Sir William Petty (1623–87) and Gregory King (1648–1712), some of whom were members of the Royal Society founded in 1660. Gregory King attempted estimates of the categories both of population and of land use. Towards the end of the following century there appeared Adam Smith's *The wealth of nations* in 1776 and T. R. Malthus's *Essay on...population* in 1798. The England of 1800 was not only two hundred years older than that of 1600. It was a different world with new landscapes and new problems.

These developments took place in the context of more general changes. In the middle of the seventeenth century, English life had been disrupted by the Civil War of 1642–8, but thereafter freedom from domestic warfare provided a background for continuous development. The political changes following the Civil War culminated in the Restoration in 1660, which, it has been said, 'has a better claim than most dates to be regarded as the economic exit from medievalism'.[3] Moreover, the realm was strengthened by union with Scotland. The two crowns had been worn by the same king since 1603, but legislative union was not realised until 1707 when the United Kingdom of Great Britain was created to the advantage of both countries. There were also wider changes. The eviction of the Hanse in 1598 and the formation of the East India Company in 1600 were 'symptomatic of the changing character of English trade at the end of the sixteenth century'.[4] Furthermore, tentative overseas expansion was accelerated by the maritime wars of the eighteenth century which extended British interests into the markets of the world. Not only the impulse to improve and invent, but also the impulse to expand was a powerful force transforming the geography of the kingdom.

[1] J. B. Harley, 'The Society of Arts and the surveys of English counties 1759–1809', *Jour. Roy. Soc. Arts*, CXII (1963–4), 43–6, 119–24, 269–75, 538–43.
[2] C. Close, *The early years of the Ordnance Survey* (Chatham, 1926); reprinted with an introduction by J. B. Harley (Newton Abbot, 1969).
[3] C. H. Wilson, *England's apprenticeship, 1603–1763* (London, 1965), 236.
[4] W. E. Minchinton (ed.), *The growth of English overseas trade in the seventeenth and eighteenth centuries* (London, 1969), 2.

POPULATION

A number of attempts have been made to estimate the population of England and Wales about 1600, based upon such sources as parish registers, muster rolls and hearth tax returns. Apart from a low figure of 2.5 million produced by Thorold Rogers, estimates range between 3.6 million and 5.0 million. A reasonably acceptable figure might lie somewhere between 4.0 and 4.5 million. Nearly one hundred years later, a contemporary estimate by Gregory King, in 1695, put the total at 5.5 million, and this has been more or less supported by D. V. Glass who would, however, reduce it to 5.2 million.[1] John Rickman, who was in charge of the first Census of 1801, attempted to argue backwards on the basis of the births, deaths and marriages entered in parish registers. For 1700, he produced a final figure of 6.0 million; for 1750 it was 6.5 million which Deane and Cole revised to 6.1 million; and for 1780 it was 7.5 million. With the first Census itself we are on firmer ground, with its total of 8.9 million, but Rickman himself later revised this to 9.2 million (including 0.6 million for Wales).[2] In looking at these figures, it must be remembered that subsequent research has shown how uncertain any estimates based upon parish registers must be; compulsory registration by Act of Parliament did not come until 1838.[3] Even so, we may reasonably conclude that the rate of growth was slow before 1750; that it rose during the next 30 years; and that it became rapid after 1780. Here was a demographic revolution, a 'population explosion'.

Traditionally, the main cause of the increase was assumed to be a rapidly falling death rate, largely the result of advances in medical knowledge.[4] But the emphasis on medical advance has been challenged by two medical

[1] D. V. Glass, 'Gregory King's estimate of the population of England and Wales, 1695', *Population Studies*, III (1950), 358.

[2] P. Deane and W. A. Cole, *British economic growth, 1688–1959* (Cambridge, 2nd ed., 1967), 98 *et seq.* For a summary of various estimates see B. R. Mitchell with P. Deane, *Abstract of British historical statistics* (Cambridge, 1962), 5.

[3] For general summaries of the problem, see M. W. Flinn, *British population growth, 1700–1850* (London, 1969). See also P. Deane, 'The demographic revolution', being ch. 2 (pp. 20–35) of *The first industrial revolution* (Cambridge, 1965); D.V. Glass and D. E. C. Eversley (eds.), *Population in history* (London, 1965). A number of the key papers are reprinted with an introduction in M. Drake (ed.), *Population in industrialization* (London, 1969).

[4] E.g. G. T. Griffith, *Population problems of the age of Malthus* (Cambridge, 1926); M. C. Buer, *Health, wealth and population in the early days of the industrial revolution* (London, 1926).

historians who point to the lack of new drugs, to the high death rate in hospitals, to the continued dangers of midwifery and surgery before the days of anaesthetics and antiseptics, and to the unlikelihood that inoculation against small-pox had much effect.[1] P. E. Razzell, however, has thrown doubt on this view as far as inoculation for small-pox was concerned. Inoculation was first introduced into England in 1721 and mass inoculations became common after about 1760; this alone, says Razzell, 'could theoretically explain the whole of the increase in population'.[2] There are also other possible explanations for a decline in the death rate. Part of the answer might lie in the natural history of endemic and epidemic disease. Why, for example, did plague, 'the greatest single agent of mortality', disappear from England after the outbreak of 1665–7?[3] Or again part of the answer might lie in a generally improved standard of living, including a better and more varied diet associated with improvements in agriculture and transport. Certainly life seemed to have become less precarious when Gilbert White, looking back over ten years or so, wrote in 1774, 'Such a run of wet seasons a century or two ago would, I am persuaded, have occasioned a famine.'[4]

Some scholars, however, have doubted whether the death rate did substantially fall during the later decades of the eighteenth century, and they have concluded that a rising birth rate was 'the major cause' of population growth at this time.[5] It could have been associated with an earlier age of marriage and with greater economic opportunity, but both these possibilities are matters of controversy. The relation of birth rate and death rate, and the dynamics of population growth in general, have prompted much ingenious discussion. Given both a falling death rate and a rising

[1] T. McKeown and R. G. Brown, 'Medical evidence related to English population changes in the eighteenth century', *Population Studies*, IX (1956), 119–41.

[2] P. E. Razzell, 'Population change in eighteenth-century England. A reinterpretation', *Econ. Hist. Rev.*, 2nd ser., XVIII (1965), 312–32.

[3] K. F. Helleiner, 'The population of Europe from the Black Death to the eve of the vital revolution', being ch. 1 of E. E. Rich and C. H. Wilson (eds.), *The Cambridge economic history of Europe*, IV (1967), 95.

[4] Gilbert White, *The natural history of Selborne* (Everyman's Library), 151. See E. L. Jones, *Seasons and prices. The role of the weather in English agricultural history* (London, 1964), 55, 109 and 146.

[5] J. T. Krause, 'Changes in English fertility and mortality, 1781–1850', *Econ. Hist. Rev.*, 2nd ser., XI (1958), 52–70. See also: (1) K. H. Connell, 'Some unsettled questions in English and Irish population history, 1750–1845', *Irish Historical Studies*, VII (1951), 225–34; (2) H. J. Habakkuk, 'English population in the eighteenth century', *Econ. Hist. Rev.*, 2nd ser., VI (1953), 117–33; and (3) P. Deane and W. A. Cole, 122 *et seq.*

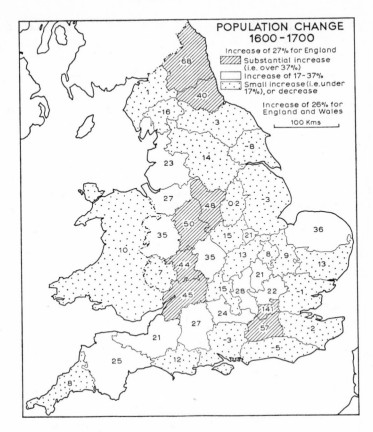

Fig. 2 Population change, 1600–1700
Based on John Rickman's estimates in *Census of 1841: Enumeration Abstract*, 36–7 (P.P. 1843, xxii).

birth rate, the discussion has then centred around which was the more effective in inaugurating a sharp and continued increase in population, and also around the precise period in which this happened. Finally, we must add that it is not possible to say to what extent the movement of people into and out of the country affected the rate of increase. There was certainly immigration from Ireland and Scotland, and also a stream of newcomers who came from Europe in connection with the new industries such as the manufacture of paper, glass and silk. Against this must be set the movement of Englishmen overseas, but we do not know to what extent one balanced the other.

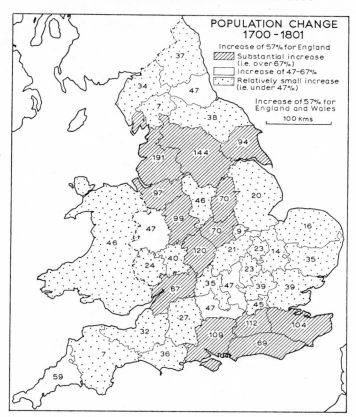

Fig. 3　Population change, 1700–1801

Based on: (1) John Rickman's estimates in *Census of 1841: Enumeration Abstract*, 37 (P.P. 1843, xxii); (2) P. Deane and W. A. Cole, *British economic growth, 1688–1959* (Cambridge, 2nd ed., 1969), 103.

Whatever be the doubts about the beginnings and causes of the increase of population, we know that it did not take place evenly over the kingdom, as may perhaps be seen from Fig. 2 (for 1600–1700) and Fig. 3 (for 1700–1801), based upon Rickman's figures modified (for 1700–1801) by Deane and Cole who point to the inevitable limitations of the evidence.[1] Any interpretation of the figures can only be unsatisfactory, and all one can hope for is a very general picture.

[1] P. Deane and W. A. Cole, 101–6. For an earlier attempt at mapping, see E. C. K. Gonner, 'The population of England in the eighteenth century', *Jour. Roy. Stat. Soc.*, LXXVI (1913), 261–303.

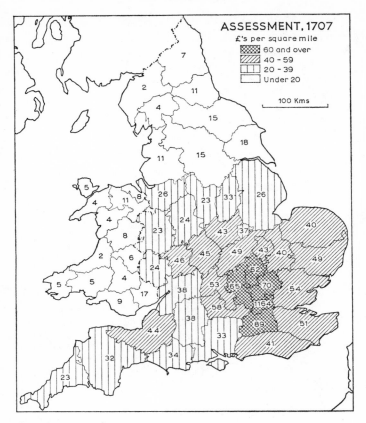

Fig. 4   The assessment of 1707
Based upon A. Browning, *English historical documents, 1660–1714* (London, 1953), 317–21.

As an alternative, one can construct maps showing the distribution of wealth on the basis of tax assessments, but these, again, have many limitations.[1] Such a map is Fig. 4 for the 1707 assessment,[2] and, at any rate, it bears out Defoe's statement that England south of the Trent was 'the most populous part of the country, and infinitely fuller of great towns, of people, and of trade' than the northern part of the realm.[3] By the first

[1] Examples of maps appear in: (1) A. Browning, *English historical documents, 1660–1714* (London, 1953), 458–9; (2) J. H. Andrews, 'Some statistical maps of Defoe's England', *Geog. Studies*, III (1956), 44.

[2] Based on the figures in A. Browning, 317–21.

[3] Daniel Defoe, *A tour through England and Wales* (Everyman's Library), I, 253.

Census of 1801 we are on more certain ground. Fig. 5 shows that there had been great changes. Except for Middlesex and Surrey, which reflected the growth of London, the most populous county was Lancashire. Considerably below it came the West Riding, Warwickshire and Staffordshire, the areas of growing industry. Not far below these, were Gloucestershire (with the port of Bristol) and Worcestershire (with saltworks at Droitwich and ironworks in the north). But the more rural counties had also shared in the general increase to varying degrees.

To what extent was the emergence of areas of dense population the result of natural increase or of immigration into them? Deane and Cole have attempted tentatively to distinguish between natural increase and net immigration for each county, again on the basis of Rickman's figures.[1] Considering the evidence as a whole, two points emerge. In the first place, a large number of migrants went to the London area, particularly to Middlesex and Surrey, but also to Essex and Kent; immigration rather than natural increase accounted for their increasing populations, and so for the growth of London. In the second place, immigration into the rising industrial areas played a surprisingly small part in their growth. Lancashire even showed a net loss of migrants during 1751–81, and Warwickshire during 1781–1801. Staffordshire and the West Riding showed a consistent loss throughout the century. It was not until after 1800 that net immigration into these counties became important. What gave these four counties their respective accumulations of population before 1800 were birth rates considerably above the national average. Unlike the London area, they had grown largely through natural increase, not only by attracting immigrants. The table on p. 10 includes the period 1801–30 in order to show how the trends continued.

We must ask why natural increase was a more important element in the growing populations of Staffordshire and the West Riding than in those of Lancashire and Warwickshire. The answer may lie in the more rapid development of large towns in the latter counties. Liverpool and Manchester between them accounted for nearly 25% of the population of Lancashire in 1801. Birmingham and Coventry accounted for about 40% of that of Warwickshire. On the other hand, Leeds and Sheffield accounted for only about 14% of the population of the West Riding (and

---

[1] P. Deane and W. A. Cole, 106–22. For a criticism see: (1) M. W. Flinn, 28–9; (2) L. Neal, 'Deane and Cole on industrialization and population change in the eighteenth century', *Econ. Hist. Rev.*, 2nd ser., XXIV (1971), 643–7; and (3) W. A. Cole, 'Rejoinder', *ibid.*, 648–51.

Table 1.1   *Annual rates of migration and natural increase, 1701–1830*
(rates per 1,000 of population)

	Net migration			
	1701–50	1751–80	1781–1800	1801–30
Lancashire	+3.0	−1.2	+11.6	+6.2
Warwickshire	+2.2	+6.5	−3.8	+3.4
Staffordshire	−4.4	−4.3	−0.9	+0.3
West Riding	−3.4	−0.8	−0.6	+1.6
Middlesex	+15.8	+14.0	+12.2	+12.2
Surrey	+11.2	+18.1	+13.4	+10.3
	Natural increase			
Lancashire	+2.7	+10.6	+13.4	+16.0
Warwickshire	+2.8	+5.3	+13.3	+11.9
Staffordshire	+6.9	+14.4	+13.8	+17.1
West Riding	+8.1	+14.6	+12.6	+15.9
Middlesex	−15.6	−9.3	−1.2	+4.1
Surrey	−10.8	−4.8	+3.3	+8.8

Source: P. Deane and W. A. Cole. *British economic growth, 1688–1959* (Cambridge, 2nd ed., 1967), 115.

less than 10% if sixteen of the townships within the large parish of Leeds be excluded). Wolverhampton (the town, not the parish) and Stoke on Trent together had only about 12% of the population of Staffordshire. There is, moreover, an accidental element in any figures for migration based upon counties, because the migrants ignored county boundaries. Birmingham, on the margins of Warwickshire, drew many of its immigrants not only from its own county but from neighbouring Staffordshire and, to a less extent, from Worcestershire and Shropshire;[1] so must Manchester from the West Riding; whereas Leeds, centrally placed in the West Riding, was less likely to attract immigrants from outside its county.

Whatever the complications and imperfections of these figures, it would seem that industrial expansion as such was associated with high rates of natural increase and that urban expansion as such (especially in

[1] R. A. Pelham, 'The immigrant population of Birmingham, 1686–1726', *Trans. Birmingham Archaeol. Soc.*, LXI (1937), 45–80. See also W. H. B. Court, *The rise of the Midland industries, 1600–1838* (Oxford, 1938), 48–50.

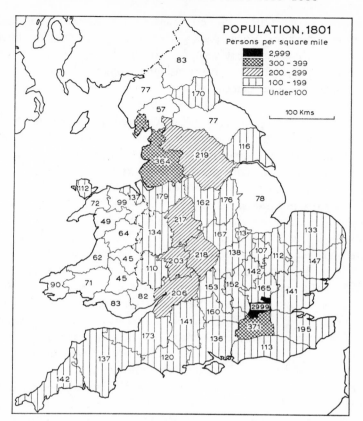

Fig. 5   Population in 1801 (by counties)
Based on *Census of 1801: Enumeration*, 451, 496 (P.P. 1802, vii).
For the distribution by registration districts, see Fig. 83 on p. 393 below.

view of high urban death rates) was associated with migration. Contemporary writers, such as J. Massie in 1758, pointed to the continual movement of population from the country districts and smaller towns to the larger towns;[1] and Arthur Young in 1774 exclaimed: 'Let any person go to Glasgow and its neighbourhood, to Birmingham, to Sheffield, or to Manchester...how then have they increased their people? Why, by emigrations from the country.'[2] Most of the Sheffield apprentices, for example between 1624 and 1799, 'sons of yeomen, farmers and labourers',

[1] J. Massie, *A plan for the establishment of charity houses* (London, 1758), 99.
[2] A. Young, *Political arithmetic* (London, 1774), 63.

came from villages within fifteen miles of the town.[1] The Board of
Agriculture report on Warwickshire (1793) in speaking of the effects of
enclosure, said that 'the hardy yeomanry of the country villages have been
driven for employment into Birmingham, Coventry and other manufacturing towns'.[2] The Leicestershire report also spoke of depopulation
for the same reason and of families having to 'migrate into towns'.[3]
Other county reports contain similar statements.[4] It must be remembered,
however, that the relationship between enclosure and population change
was much debated at the time and has also been much debated since then.[5]
There was, moreover, considerable short-distance mobility 'in local
populations in several areas in the south and east of England', that is
outside the growing industrial centres.[6]

It is not surprising that the phenomena of the time were being discussed
by contemporaries. The first edition of T. R. Malthus's *Essay on the*
principle of population appeared in 1798 and it explained the growth of
population as a response to economic opportunity. But looking backwards,
the relationship between the two is seen to be extremely complicated.
Can we be sure that the rise in birth rate did not precede the period of
rapid industrial growth? H. J. Habakkuk has formulated a number of
pertinent questions. 'Did the Industrial Revolution create its own labour
force? Or did the vagaries of disease and weather produce an additional
population that either stimulated an Industrial Revolution or had the luck
to coincide with one independently generated?'[7] Attempts to answer such
questions are impeded by uncertainty about the chronology of population
growth in relation to economic growth. Moreover, the continuous inter-
action between the two makes it difficult to separate cause from effect.
We may be clearer about these matters when there are more local studies

[1] E. J. Buckatzsch, 'Places of origin of a group of immigrants into Sheffield, 1624–
1799', *Econ. Hist. Rev.*, 2nd ser., II (1950), 306.

[2] J. Wedge, *General view of the agriculture of the county of Warwick* (London, 1794),
40.

[3] W. Pitt, *General view of the agriculture of the county of Leicester* (London, 1809), 16.

[4] T. Davis, *General view of the agriculture of the county of Wiltshire* (London, 1794),
88; J. Holt and R. W. Dickson, *General view of the agriculture of the county of Lan-*
cashire (London, 1815), 393.

[5] J. D. Chambers, 'Enclosure and labour supply in the industrial revolution', *Econ.*
Hist. Rev., 2nd ser., V (1953), 319–43.

[6] E. J. Buckatzsch, 'The constancy of local populations and migration in England
before 1800', *Population Studies*, V (1951–2), 62–9.

[7] H. J. Habakkuk, 'The economic history of modern Britain', *Jour. Econ. Hist.*,
XVII (1954), 500.

along the lines of those by J. D. Chambers, D. E. C. Eversley, E. A. Wrigley and others.[1]

THE COUNTRYSIDE

The new husbandry

Convertible husbandry. The eighteenth century has often been hailed as the great century of agricultural improvement, but many of its ideas and practices had long been anticipated. Not only were these ideas described by the numerous agricultural writers of the seventeenth century, but documentary evidence shows that they, or many of them, were being put into practice in a large number of localities throughout the country. Indeed it has been claimed that 'the agricultural revolution took place in England in the sixteenth and seventeenth centuries and not in the eighteenth and nineteenth'.[2] An important feature of the agriculture of these earlier centuries was the introduction of what has been variously described as convertible, alternate, field-grass or up-and-down, husbandry, that is what a later age was to call ley farming. Under this system, arable land was put under grass for a period in order to rest, and pasture land was ploughed up. Here was a breakthrough in farming techniques. The advantages of this for those with enclosed land had been described by Fitzherbert as early as 1523,[3] and they were set out at some length by Walter Blith about 1650.[4] By this time the practice had become widespread.

The impact of these new ideas upon open-field agriculture was also considerable because the routine of unenclosed farming was much more flexible than writers of the nineteenth and twentieth centuries sometimes supposed it to have been. In the sixteenth century there were Midland parishes where some strips in the open fields were put under grass for a few years, and where an intermixture of arable and ley could be en-

---

[1] J. D. Chambers, 'The vale of Trent, 1670–1800: A regional study of economic change', *Econ. Hist. Rev.*, Supplement, No. 3, 1957; D. E. C. Eversley, 'A survey of population in an area of Worcestershire from 1660 to 1850 on the basis of parish registers', *Population Studies*, x (1957), 230–53; E. A. Wrigley, 'Family limitation in pre-industrial England', *Econ. Hist. Rev.*, 2nd ser., XIX (1966), 82–109.

[2] E. Kerridge, *The agricultural revolution* (London, 1967), 15. See also E. L. Jones (ed.), *Agriculture and economic growth in England, 1650–1815* (London, 1967) For a convenient review with a useful bibliography, see D. Woodward, 'Agricultural revolution in England, 1500–1900: a survey', *Local Historian*, IX (1971), 323–37.

[3] J. Fitzherbert, *The boke of husbondrye* (London, 1523).

[4] W. Blith: (1) *The English improver* (London, 1649); (2) *The English improver improved* (London, 1652).

countered in each of three fields.[1] Different farmers grew different crops in the same field, and the introduction of leys enabled a more efficient use of fallow. On parts of some fallow fields, catch or 'hitch' crops were sometimes grown, leaving the fields bare for only part of the year; such hitch crops usually comprised peas, vetches and lentils. Thus Robert Loder of Harwell in Berkshire, in 1610–20, 'hitched' about a quarter of his fallow field every year.[2] The right of common grazing on the fallow fields did not prevent innovation, and village agreements indicate how local arrangements were devised to meet particular opinions and needs. Studies of such counties as Leicestershire,[3] Lincolnshire[4] and Oxfordshire[5] show how frequent were such arrangements by the early seventeenth century. In seventeenth-century Leicestershire, for example, 'within certain broad limits, the open-field farmer could do what he liked with his own strips'.[6] Such possibilities were aided by the exchange and consolidation of strips. It is true that on the eve of enclosure in the eighteenth century there were villages where, in William Marshall's phrase 'the spirit of improvement' lagged behind,[7] and where a fairly rigid open-field system persisted unaltered from medieval times; moreover, fallowing was still necessary on many heavy wet clays.[8] But there were also many open-field villages where rotations were flexible, where ley farming was important and where change and progress were very evident. Marshall's account of the Midland counties in 1790 set out clearly the advantages of current practice 'in keeping the land in grass and corn alternately'.[9]

New crops. The advance of convertible husbandry in the seventeenth and eighteenth centuries was bound up with the increasing range of field crops available to the farmer. Two main groups of crops provided possibilities of change – roots, on the one hand, and clover and grasses on the other.

[1] E. Kerridge (1967), 194 *et seq.*; J. Thirsk, *The agrarian history of England and Wales*, vol. IV, 1500–1640 (Cambridge, 1967), 178.

[2] G. E. Fussell (ed.), *Robert Loder's farm accounts, 1610–1620*, Camden Soc., 3rd ser., 53 (London, 1936), 11, 41, 91–8, 103–4.

[3] W. G. Hoskins, *The Midland peasant* (London, 1957), 152 *et seq.*

[4] J. Thirsk, *English peasant farming* (London, 1957), 99 *et seq.*

[5] M. A. Havinden, 'Agricultural progress in open-field Oxfordshire', *Agric. Hist. Rev.*, IX (1961), 73–83.

[6] W. G. Hoskins, 'The Leicestershire farmer in the seventeenth century', *Agricultural History*, XXV (1951), 9–20.

[7] W. Marshall, *The rural economy of the West of England*, I (London, 1796), 106–7.

[8] E. Kerridge (1967), 27–8.

[9] W. Marshall, *The rural economy of the Midland counties*, I (London, 1790), 184, 187.

Both groups of crops had been mentioned by Barnaby Googe in a book (1577) which was largely a translation of a work by Conrad Heresbach of the Low Countries, where the most advanced farming in Europe was to be found.[1] The new field crops enabled a greater number of stock to be carried through the year, an important fact in an age without efficient fertilizers. The number of sheep, in particular, greatly increased. More animals meant more manure for the more flexible rotations. Root crops were of value to the land as clearing crops; and clover and the leguminous grasses added nitrogen to the soil and so further increased its fertility.

Carrots and turnips had already been grown in gardens in England, and there are references to both as garden crops grown by Dutch immigrants after 1565 outside the city of Norwich.[2] About 1600 there are indications that carrots were grown in fields in the Suffolk Sandlings; and, after about 1670, another centre of carrot growing developed in the vale of Taunton Deane in Somerset.[3] Carrots also spread elsewhere but not to the same degree. Turnips, on the other hand, became widespread over much of south-eastern England. They appeared as a field crop relatively suddenly in High Suffolk in the middle of the seventeenth century.[4] They extended into Norfolk and into the Chilterns long before 1700; and in 1724 Daniel Defoe could speak of turnip cultivation as being 'spread over most of the south and east parts of England'.[5] By the middle of the eighteenth century the turnip had reached the Midlands and the north, although it was not extensively cultivated. On heavy soils, dwarf rape or cabbages formed an alternative to turnips; they also had appeared as field crops before 1700. Another alternative was swedes, but not until well into the eighteenth century.

In the meantime, about 1650, Sir Richard Weston of Sutton Court in Surrey, who had travelled in the Low Countries, was advocating the field cultivation not only of turnips but of clover and grasses.[6] Weston's

---

[1] Barnabe Googe, *Foure bookes of husbandrie by M. Conradus Heresbachius....Newly Englished and increased by B. Googe* (London, 1577).

[2] K. J. Allison, 'The sheep-corn husbandry of Norfolk in the sixteenth and seventeenth centuries', *Agric. Hist. Rev.*, v (1957), 27.

[3] E. Kerridge (1967), 268–9.

[4] E. Kerridge, 'Turnip husbandry in High Suffolk', *Econ. Hist. Rev.*, 2nd ser., VIII (1955–6), 390–2.

[5] Daniel Defoe, *Tour*, I, 58.

[6] R. Weston, *A discours of husbandrie used in Brabant and Flanders, shewing wonderful improvement of land there* (London, 1605). The imprint date seems to be an error, maybe for 1650.

advocacy was continued by Andrew Yarranton of Worcestershire, famous as a political economist. He wrote in 1663 on 'the great improvement of lands by clover', and said that since Weston's day some clover was sown 'in most counties', but that it had not become more popular owing to ignorance and mismanagement.[1] Even so, mixtures of varieties of clover with perennial rye-grass and other grasses became increasingly common as the seventeenth century passed into the eighteenth. A specialised treatise of 1671 on one of the grasses – sainfoin – was attributed to Sir John Pettus, and was described on its title page as 'being useful for all ingenious men'.[2] The advantage of turnips, clover and the grasses were set out by a variety of agricultural writers, by, for example, John Worlidge in a book first published in 1669 and reprinted with additions many times up to 1716.[3] The Royal Society of Arts, in the 1760s, attempted to encourage the improvement of clean grass seed by offering prizes;[4] and in 1790 William Curtis, a prominent botanist, wrote an account of British grasses which ran into several editions.[5]

The cultivation of other crops was also advocated by the writers of the time.[6] Among them were flax, hemp, woad, madder, saffron, liquorice, weld, rape, and they were grown locally to a greater or less degree. One new crop deserves special mention – the potato.[7] First introduced from the New World into Ireland in the 1580s, it was at first grown only in gardens. John Forster set out its many advantages in 1664;[8] it appeared as a field crop in rotations on the mosslands of Lancashire before 1700, but its spread beyond the northern parts of the realm was slow. By 1800 it seems to have been little cultivated in the south, except in gardens – in the market gardens of Middlesex and Essex, for example. This 'valuable

---

[1] A. Yarranton, *The improvement improved, by a second edition of the great improvement of lands by clover* (London, 1663). For this edition see G. E. Fussell (1947), 75.

[2] Anon., *St Foine improved: a discourse showing the utility and benefit which England hath and may receive by the grasse called St Foine* (London, 1671). No author's name appears on the title page, but the book has been attributed to Sir John Pettus.

[3] J. Worlidge, *Systema agriculturae* (London, 1669).

[4] H. T. Wood, *A history of the Royal Society of Arts* (London, 1913), 119.

[5] W. Curtis, *Practical observations on the British grasses* (London, 1790).

[6] J. Thirsk, 'Seventeenth-century agriculture and social change', *Agric. Hist. Rev.*, XVIII (Supplement, 1970), 148–77.

[7] R. Salaman, *The history and social influence of the potato* (Cambridge, 1949), 434 *et seq.*

[8] J. Forster, *Englands happiness increased... by a plantation of the roots called potatoes* (London, 1664).

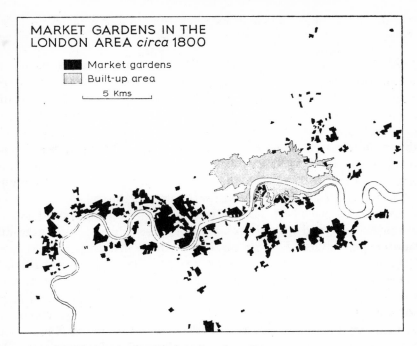

Fig. 6 Market gardens in the London area *circa* 1800
Based on T. Milne, *Plan of the cities of London and Westminster, circumjacent towns and parishes etc, laid down from a trigonometrical survey taken in the years 1795–1799* (London, 1800).

root', as William Marshall called it, had to wait until the nineteenth century for its wider cultivation.

Around London, in particular, agriculture was beginning to take on a suburban character, and market gardening spread to help feed the growing population. According to Samuel Hartlib, it 'began to creep into England' from Holland and Flanders around about 1600. In 1651 old men could still remember the first gardeners who came to Fulham and other places to grow a variety of vegetables – cabbages, cauliflowers, turnips, carrots and parsnips among them.[1] At the end of the eighteenth century, the Board of Agriculture reports on Middlesex and Surrey gave interesting accounts of the market gardens enriched by plentiful supplies of manure from London, and employed in raising vegetables for the

[1] S. Hartlib, *Legacie, or an enlargement of the discourse of husbandry used in Flanders and Brabant* (London, 1651), 9.

London market,[1] and Thomas Milne's map of 1798 shows how widespread
they had become (Fig. 6).

Fertilisers. The spread of new methods and new crops was not paralleled
by the discovery of new fertilisers. Writers, and the farmers they wrote
about, were well aware of the importance of manuring the soil, but the
substances they advocated and used were very largely the traditional ones.
Most important was the dung of the sheepfold and the farmyard, but
other manures were also in use, including oxblood, soot, peat, offal,
bones, seaweed, soap ashes with the growth of soap-boiling, sea-shells,
sheep's trotters, furriers' clippings and all kinds of waste and refuse
including rags and old leather, but only rarely night-soil. Sir Hugh Plat
in 1594 enumerated a large number of fertilising agents;[2] a second edition
appeared in 1653, and many other writers of the seventeenth and eighteenth
centuries also discussed the properties of various manures.

With the use of manures may be grouped the improvement of soils
by the application of marl and of lime and chalk. Thin and sandy soils
were improved by a dressing of clay marl while clay soils gained from
a dressing of lime. These were not new practices, but they appear to
have become increasingly current in the seventeenth century, and there
was much discussion about methods in the literature of the time. Men like
John Evelyn in 1675 were distinguishing between different kinds of soil
and the treatment appropriate for each.[3] The progress that had been made
by the end of the eighteenth century may be seen from the county reports
of the Board of Agriculture, each of which, in a chapter headed 'Improvements', devoted a section to the problems of manuring, marling and
liming.

But in spite of this discussion, and although in the 1790s bones were
being ground instead of being crushed before being applied to the land,
there was no fundamental advance in methods of fertilising because the
limits to such an advance were set by contemporary knowledge of
chemistry. As early as 1756 Francis Home had emphasised the dependence
of agriculture upon chemistry in a book that was reprinted in 1759 and

---

[1] J. Middleton, *A view of the agriculture of Middlesex* (London, 1807), 328–38;
W. Stevenson, *General view of agriculture of the county of Surrey* (London, 1809), 414–19.
For a 'general view of the former and present state of market gardens' within twelve
miles of London, see D. Lysons, *The environs of London*, 5 vols. (London, 1795–1810),
IV, 573–6; V, 446–8.

[2] H. Plat, *The jewel house of art and nature* (London, 1594).

[3] J. Evelyn, *Terra: a philosophical discourse of earth* (London, 1675).

in 1776.[1] George Fordyce's book on the same subject was published in 1765[2] and its fifth edition appeared in 1796, the year in which the newly formed Board of Agriculture published his account of different kinds of manure.[3]

New implements. The spirit of improvement that was abroad in agriculture in the seventeenth and eighteenth centuries did not greatly manifest itself in the invention of new tools and machines. As with fertilisers so with implements, the pace was slow. A wide variety of traditional ploughs remained in use, but only here and there can improvement be discerned. About the year 1730 the so-called Rotherham plough, based upon Dutch designs, was developed at Rotherham in Yorkshire, and came into use in the north and east. Then in 1784 there appeared James Small's treatise on ploughs, one of a number of such treatises in the seventies and eighties; it described an improved design and remained a standard work for the next generation or so.[4] But such improvements, and there were others, came only slowly into general use. It was not until the closing years of the eighteenth century that iron ploughs were replacing wooden ones.[5]

The common method of sowing seed for long remained that of broadcasting. Various suggestions were made for 'setting' or drilling seed at regular intervals, in order both to avoid waste and to benefit the ensuing crop – by Sir Hugh Plat in 1600,[6] by Edward Maxey in 1601,[7] by Gabriel Plattes in 1639[8] and by Josiah Worlidge in 1669.[9] There were various patents for mechanical sowers but they too came to little or nothing. Then about 1701 Jethro Tull invented a drill to sow seeds in evenly spaced rows sufficiently wide apart to allow the soil between them to be pulverished and cleared of weeds; but an account of his work was not published until 1731, after which there were many editions.[10] Tull thought that a combination of drilling and weed control would do away with the

[1] F. Home, *The principles of agriculture and vegetation* (Edinburgh, 1756).

[2] G. Fordyce, *Elements of agriculture and vegetation* (Edinburgh, 1765).

[3] G. Fordyce, *Plan for ascertaining the effects of different sorts of manures* (London, 1796).

[4] J. Small, *Treatise of ploughs and wheel carriages* (Edinburgh, 1784).

[5] C. Culpin, *Farm machinery* (London, 1938), 59–60.

[6] H. Plat, *The new and admirable arte of setting of corne* (London, 1600).

[7] E. Maxey, *New instruction of plowing and setting of corne* (London, 1601).

[8] G. Plattes, *A discovery of infinite treasure* (London, 1639).

[9] J. Worlidge, *Systema agriculturae; the mystery of husbandry discovered* (London, 1669).

[10] J. Tull, *The new horse-houghing husbandry* (London, 1731).

necessity of using a manure, and his work was followed by much controversy; but, whatever may be said, the fact remains that many have regarded his drill as the most important agricultural invention of the eighteenth century. Originally designed for grass and other light seeds, it came to be of especial value for sowing turnips. Improved varieties of drills followed, James Cooke's drill of 1783 being the most important;[1] but, if we may judge from the Board of Agriculture county reports, drills, although widely known, were not in general use even by the end of the century.

Improvements in threshing machines were suggested at various times in the eighteenth century; one of the most successful was Andrew Meikle's design of 1786, but it was not widely in use in the south until after 1800. In the meantime, with the quickening temper of the last two decades of the eighteenth century, numerous patents were taken out not only for sowing and threshing machines, but for harrows, winnowers, scarifiers, reapers, chaff-cutters, turnip-slicers and a variety of other mechanical aids.[2] But the fruits of this enterprise were not commonly available in 1800.

The improvement of livestock. The new fodder crops made possible the carrying of greater numbers of breeding stock than hitherto, and it is clear that in the seventeenth century many farmers were attempting to improve the quality of their sheep and cattle by importing rams and bulls from elsewhere. Although they worked with empirical methods, the care taken in selective breeding may be seen from the activities of men like Henry Best about 1640[3] and John Franklin about 1670.[4] By the early 1700s there were a number of well-known successful breeders of livestock, and in the 1720s Daniel Defoe could speak of the rich graziers of Leicestershire and of the Midlands generally.[5]

It is against this background that the work of Robert Bakewell (1725–95) must be viewed. He began his experiments at Dishley in Leicestershire

[1] J. Cooke, *Drill husbandry perfected* (Manchester, 1784); J. Horn, *The description and use of the new invented patent universal sowing machine, for broadcasting or drilling every kind of grain, pulse and seed* (Canterbury, 1786).

[2] R. E. Prothero, 'Landmarks in British farming', *Jour. Roy. Agric. Soc.* 3rd ser., III (1892), 27–8.

[3] C. B. Robinson (ed.), *Rural economy in Yorkshire in 1641, being the farming and account books of Henry Best of Elmswell* (Surtees Society, 1875), I, 12, 20, 27–8, 75–6.

[4] T. B. Franklin, *British grasslands* (London, 1953), 90.

[5] Daniel Defoe, *Tour*, II, 89.

in 1745. Hitherto, improvers of livestock had tried to obtain the qualities they wanted by outcrosses; Bakewell's method was to inbreed. His cattle became famous and his sheep – the New Leicester breed – even more so. He also experimented with the improvement of pigs and farm-horses. Dishley soon became a centre that attracted agriculturalists from all over the country. Although he left no account of his methods, his name became one of the best known in the history of British agriculture; and before his death others were applying the new methods of selective breeding to the various regional breeds of livestock in Britain.[1]

The strides made by animal husbandry, and indeed by agriculture in general, was reflected in cattle shows, sheep-shearings and ploughing matches. The Bath and West of England Agricultural Society was founded in 1777, and a large number of counties started experimental farms and societies for improvement; that many were short-lived does not alter the fact that their foundation bore witness to the new energy in the closing years of the eighteenth century.[2] In 1793, the Board of Agriculture was established, and its county reports published between 1793 and 1815 enable us to obtain an idea of recent improvement and of the state to which British agriculture had reached.[3]

Enclosing the arable

The enclosure that aroused so much opposition in the fifteenth and sixteenth centuries continued into the seventeenth.[4] There was an enquiry in 1607, into enclosure and depopulation within Leicestershire, Northamptonshire and five nearby counties.[5] The year 1630 saw another enquiry covering five of the Midland counties, and commissions were again appointed in 1632, 1635 and 1636 to restrict enclosure and to halt depopulation. Unrest was also reflected in the pamphlet literature of the time – in such tracts as Robert Powell's *Depopulation arraigned* (1636) and John Moore's *The crying sin of England* (1653) which was none other than 'such as doth unpeople towns and uncorn fields'. But the arguments

---

[1] R. Trow Smith, *A history of British livestock husbandry, 1700–1900* (London, 1959), 45–69.

[2] Lord Ernle, *English farming past and present* (4th ed., 1927), 209.

[3] R. Mitchison, 'The old Board of Agriculture (1793–1822), *Eng. Hist. Rev.*, LXXIV (1959), 41–69.

[4] E. M. Leonard, 'The inclosure of common fields in the seventeenth century', *Trans. Roy. Hist. Soc.*, XIX (London, 1905), 101–46.

[5] E. F. Gay, 'The Midland revolt and the inquisitions of depopulation of 1607', *Trans. Roy. Hist. Soc.*, n.s., XVIII (1904), 195–244.

against 'the decay of tillage' and 'depopulating enclosures' began to lose
their force in the latter half of the seventeenth century. Friendly arrangements for enclosure became more frequent and its advantages more clear.
The last anti-enclosure bill was rejected by the House of Commons
in 1656, and in the same year Joseph Lee was showing how many
Leicestershire villages had been enclosed without decay of tillage and
without depopulation.[1] Writers of the new age began to find virtues in
enclosed land. Samuel Fortrey in 1663 argued that only by enclosure
could land be put to the use for which it was best suited, and other
arguments in favour of enclosure were set out by such writers as John
Worlidge (1669), John Mortimer (1707) and John Lawrence (1726).[2]

The enclosure that took place during these years was by private agreement under which the body of commoners in a village appointed commissioners and surveyors to allot the new holdings. Confirmation of the
agreement was then sought from the Court of Chancery or Court of
Exchequer. Such a procedure required the unanimous consent of all
commoners concerned. It was sometimes possible to buy out individuals,
but not always; and to overcome this difficulty, recourse was made to
private Acts of Parliament, which became increasingly numerous from
the 1720s onwards. These differed from decrees in Chancery in that they
could initiate enclosure and compel dissentients to agree.[3]

At this point in time, on the verge of the great changes brought about
by parliamentary enclosure, we may pause to ask what had been the effect
upon the landscape of the enclosing activity of the years since, say, 1450. In
view of the outcry about depopulation in the Midland counties, and in view
of the flood of pamphlets, the sustained legislative activity and the many
deserted villages, it may seem strange to find that, after all, the Midlands
was the main area of parliamentary enclosure. The counties which had
produced such a volume of complaint in Tudor times were the very ones
in which open fields flourished triumphantly right on into the eighteenth
and even into the nineteenth century. How is the paradox to be explained?

It is to be explained by the fact that much of England outside the
Midlands had already been enclosed before the fifteenth and sixteenth

---

[1] J. Lee, *A vindication of a regulated enclosure* (London, 1656).

[2] S. Fortrey, *England's interest and improvement* (Cambridge, 1663); John Worlidge,
Systema agriculturae (London, 1669); John Mortimer, *The whole art of husbandry*
(London, 1707); John Laurence, *A new system of agriculture* (London, 1726).

[3] See E. C. K. Gonner, *Common land and inclosure* (London, 1912), 51 *et seq.*;
W. E. Tate, *The English village community and the enclosure movements* (London, 1967),
46 *et seq.*

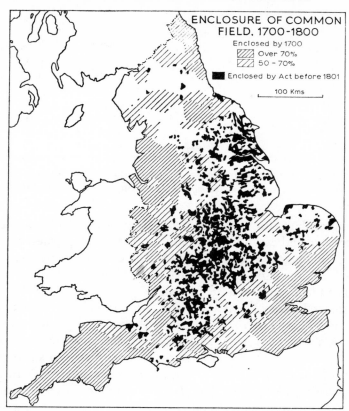

Fig. 7   Enclosure of common field, 1700–1800
Based on: (1) E. C. K. Gonner, *Common land and inclosure* (London, 1912),
map C; (2) G. Slater, *The English peasantry and the enclosure of common fields*
(London, 1907), 73.

centuries, and that these 'old enclosures', and the economy they expressed,
often went back to much earlier times. The agrarian changes of 1450–
1650 thus brought little or no depopulation to such counties as Essex,
Kent, Devon, Hereford and Worcester. That these changes, on the other
hand, brought 'serious suffering and disturbance' to the grain counties of
the Midlands did not mean that all the Midland open fields had disappeared.[1]
It was in fact far otherwise. A variety of contemporary evidence shows
that much, indeed most, of the Midlands was still in open field at the
beginning of the eighteenth century. John Morton, the historian of

[1] R. H. Tawney, *The agrarian problem in the sixteenth century* (London, 1912), 265.

Table 1.2   *Parliamentary enclosure of open fields*

Before 1750	64	1800–09	574
1750–59	87	1810–19	422
1760–69	304	1820–29	101
1770–79	472	1830–39	75
1780–89	150	1840–49	84
1790–99	398	1850 and after	106

The number of acts for each decade is calculated from G. Slater, *The English peasantry and the enclosure of common fields* (London, 1907), 268–313.

Northamptonshire, for example, wrote in 1712 that 'the enclosures lie dispersedly up and down in the county. . . Yet far the greatest part of the county is still open'.[1] The same could be said of other counties. It was not until well into the eighteenth century that enclosure began to transform the Midland landscape on a broad scale (Fig. 7).

The general pace of open-field enclosure, decade by decade, can be seen from Gilbert Slater's figures which are certainly underestimates.[2] There was a total of at least 2,800 such acts, and about one half of these had been passed by 1800. An attempt has been made to show that the intensity of enclosing activity was associated with variations in interest rates and agricultural prices; the 1780s, for example, was largely a decade of high interest rates and difficult conditions of borrowing and also one of relatively little enclosure.[3] But such correlations must not be pressed too closely.[4]

The physical operation of enclosure must often have been a most complicated one. To survey one, two or three thousand interlocking places, noting the varying title of each; to value and then to redistribute; to set out roads; to reorganise the drainage of the fields; to settle conflicting claims; and finally to proclaim an award – all involved long effort that sometimes stretched out over five or six years or more.[5] It was,

[1] J. Morton, *The natural history of Northamptonshire* (London, 1712), 15.

[2] W. E. Tate, 88.

[3] T. S. Ashton, *An economic history of England: the eighteenth century* (London, 1955), 40–1.

[4] J. D. Chambers and G. E. Mingay, *The agricultural revolution, 1750–1880* (London, 1966), 82–4; R. A. C. Parker, *Enclosures in the eighteenth century* (Hist. Assoc., London, 1960), 5.

[5] M. W. Beresford, 'Commissioners of enclosure', *Econ. Hist. Rev.*, XVI (1946), 137.

moreover, an expensive operation.[1] What the enclosure commissioners did for a village was to lay out its territory anew and so recreate much of its geography. The effect upon the scenery of much of England may be summed up under two main headings – the conversion of arable to pasture and the spread of the hedgerow.

Not all enclosures meant conversion to pasture, but many did. The changes in one locality as compared with another depended upon a variety of local circumstances and upon local initiative, but it was enclosure that provided opportunities for land to be used in the way best suited to its soil and climate.[2] The transformation that took place in the vale of Belvoir, in Leicestershire, is instructive. Gabriel Plattes, in 1639, had described it as the best corn land in Europe,[3] yet in 1809 the Board of Agriculture county report could say: 'the richest land in the vale, formerly tillage, has been laid to grass; and the poorer land up the hills, and the skirtings of the vale, formerly a sheep-walk, have been brought into tillage'.[4] The enclosure of twelve parishes in the vale had taken place between 1766 and 1792, and their stiff Lias clay soils were now proving most profitable under grass, while the light Marlstone soils of the bordering upland were taking on a new value with the agricultural advances of the time. What was true of the vale of Belvoir was true of Leicestershire as a whole. It was, wrote William Marshall in 1790, 'not long ago an open arable county including a proportion of cows and rearing cattle; now a continued sheet of greensward'.[5] What was true of Leicestershire was true of the Midland counties in general. As Arthur Young wrote in 1774:

The fact is this; in the central counties of the kingdom, particularly Northamptonshire, Leicestershire and parts of Warwic, Huntingdon and Buckinghamshires, there have been with 30 years large tracts of the open field arable under that vile course, 1 fallow, 2 wheat, 3 spring corn, inclosed and laid down to grass, being much more suited to the wetness of the soil than corn.[6]

Much of England came to look greener than before.

[1] J. M. Martin, 'The cost of parliamentary enclosure in Warwickshire', *Univ. of Birmingham Hist. Jour.*, IX (1964), 144–57. Reprinted in E. L. Jones (ed.), *Agriculture and economic growth in England, 1650–1815* (London, 1967).

[2] E. C. K. Gonner, 329; see also 236–7.

[3] G. Plattes, *A discovery of infinite treasure, hidden since the world's beginning* (London, 1639).

[4] W. Pitt, *General view Leicester* (1809), 14–15.

[5] W. Marshall, *Rural economy of the Midland counties*, 2 vols. (London, 1790), I, 193.

[6] A. Young, *Political arithmetic* (London, 1774), 148.

The Board of Agriculture reports made many references to these changes. The Norfolk report, after referring to the new husbandry on the light soils, went on to speak of 'the wonderful improvements' also to be found on clays and loams which sometimes became twice as valuable in pasture as they could ever be in arable; such improvements, the report added, were especially striking in the Midland counties.[1] The Northamptonshire report also referred to the new order; when enclosed, the lighter lands of the county were 'kept more in tillage' but the strong, heavy lands were 'generally laid down to permanent pasture'.[2] Or again, 'many of the open fields' of Warwickshire had been enclosed and 'converted into pasture', thus needing 'much fewer hands to manage them than they did in their former open state'.[3] Other county reports also mentioned depopulation.[4] There was much debate at the time about depopulation and the social effects of enclosure, and modern enquirers have continued the argument at length.[5]

Enclosure changed the appearance of the Midland landscape in yet another way. To our eyes the unenclosed countryside would have looked bare; there was little or nothing to break the sweep of the wind across the ploughed earth. With enclosure came the need for permanent fences, and the most convenient form of fence was the hedgerow made by planting quick or live cuttings usually of hawthorn. The enclosure acts laid down that new allotments of land were to be, as one act put it, 'well and sufficiently hedged and ditched' within an appointed time. The details varied from place to place, and the county reports of the Board of Agriculture, around about 1800, frequently devoted a good deal of space to the methods and problems of fencing. One result of the planting of hedgerows was to give the countryside the appearance of being much more wooded than it really was. As William Marshall put it in 1787, 'the eye seems ever on the verge of a forest, which is, as it were by enchantment, continually changing into inclosures and hedgerows'.[6] In some localities, in the Cotswolds or

---

[1] N. Kent, *General view of the agriculture of the county of Norfolk* (London, 1794), 73–4.

[2] J. Donaldson, *General view of the agriculture of the county of Northampton* (London, 1794), 5.

[3] J. Wedge, *General view Warwick* (1794), 20.   [4] See p. 312 above.

[5] See, for example: (1) J. D. Chambers (1953), 319–43; (2) J. D. Chambers and G. E. Mingay, *The agricultural revolution, 1750–1880* (London, 1966), 77–105. For a convenient summary, with bibliography, see G. E. Mingay, *Enclosure and the small farmer in the age of the industrial revolution* (London, 1968).

[6] W. Marshall, *The rural economy of Norfolk*, 1 (London, 1787), 4.

the Isle of Purbeck for example, hedgerows were replaced by stone walls built from the readily available material.

Sixteenth- and seventeenth-century topographers had drawn a distinction between the 'woodland' and the open or 'champaign' parts of England, between the old enclosed counties such as Essex, Kent, Devon, Worcestershire and the open unhedged counties of the Midlands. This distinction was now being obliterated by parliamentary enclosure, but not completely so because the layout of the new hedgerows, and of the fields they bounded, often presented a somewhat different aspect from that of the lands of old enclosure. In the latter were to be found small circular or irregular shaped fields. In the former, on the other hand, the fields were usually larger and were often bounded by straight lines. They bore the mark of conscious planning and of the surveyor with his chain. It is interesting to reflect what the English landscape would look like had wire fencing been available during the age of parliamentary enclosure.

Changes in the woodlands

The clearing that had taken place in the Middle Ages still left England with much woodland, but its extent was getting smaller, and the demands upon it were multiplying with the increase in population and the quickening of economic activity.[1] One great devourer of trees was industry. The lead and copper mines of the Lake District and the tin mines of Cornwall, for example, needed pit props for mining and charcoal for smelting. Glass-making, too, involved 'a continuale spoile of woods'; so did tanning, salt-making and a host of other industrial activities. Perhaps the greatest demand was that made by the iron industry of the Weald, the west Midlands and the Forest of Dean. There were many attempts during the seventeenth century to use coke instead of charcoal for smelting; and, after the success of Abraham Darby at Coalbrookdale in Shropshire about 1709, the iron industry began to free itself from dependence on wood.

Other demands on wood, however, were increasing. The expansion of England's mercantile marine, and the development of the navy, depended upon an adequate supply of oaks for the hulls of ships; fir trees for masts had to be imported from the Baltic and also from New England.[2] Of the

[1] H. C. Darby, 'The clearing of the English woodlands', *Geography*, XXXVI (1951), 71–83; H. G. Richardson, 'Some remarks on British forest history', *Trans. Roy. Scottish Arboricultural Soc.*, XXXV (1921), 157–67; XXXVI (1922), 174–97.

[2] R. G. Albion, *Forests and sea power* (Cambridge, Mass., 1926), especially ch. 3, 'England's diminishing woodlands' (pp. 95–138).

many royal forests, the three main ones upon which the navy relied were the Forest of Dean, the New Forest and Alice Holt Forest in north-eastern Hampshire. The woods of private landowners were at times important suppliers, but they formed a somewhat uncertain source. The expansion of arable and pasture constituted another demand; and, about 1650, Walter Blith could speak of former woodlands 'which now inclosed are grown as gallant cornfields as be in England', and he mentioned western Warwickshire, northern Worcestershire together with Staffordshire, Shropshire, Derbyshire and Yorkshire.[1]

A number of Acts of Parliament in the sixteenth century had already tried to restrict the cutting of timber; but they do not seem to have been very effective, and by 1600 there were many complaints about the loss of woodland. Arthur Standish, in 1611, complained about the destruction during the preceding twenty or thirty years and about the fact that no replanting was taking place.[2] Many of these complaints may well have been exaggerated, and it has been argued that 'the universal timber and fuel crisis cannot have appeared very formidable over much of England by 1600 or even 1630'.[3] The situation seems to have grown worse in the decades that followed, and the outbreak of civil war in 1642 served to encourage indiscriminate destruction; those royalists who were fined had frequently to sell their oaks to meet the penalties; and woods on sequestrated estates were often sold to settle claims.[4] Camden's *Britannia*, in 1610, described the hills of Oxfordshire as clad with woods, but when Edmund Gibson edited that work a century or so later, in 1695, he added: this 'is so much alter'd by the late Civil Wars, that few places (except the Chiltern-country) can answer that character at present'.[5] It is clear that by the Restoration in 1660 the amount of woodland in England had been much reduced; that the reduction was continuing may be seen from the fact that between 1660 and 1667 over 30,000 trees were cut down in the Forest of Dean to feed the iron furnaces.[6]

[1] W. Blith (1649), 83.
[2] A. Standish, *The commons complaint, wherein is contained two special grievances: the first the general destruction and waste of woods in this kingdom*... (London, 1611), p. 1.
[3] G. Hammersley, 'The crown lands and their exploitation in the sixteenth and seventeenth centuries', *Bull. Inst. Hist. Research*, XXX (1957), 155. See p. 363 below.
[4] C. H. Firth (ed.), *Life of William Cavendish, Duke of Newcastle* (London, 1886), 149.
[5] W. Camden, *Britannia*, ed. by E. Gibson (London, 1695), 257.
[6] Evidence given in *Journals of the House of Commons*, XLIII (1787–8), 564–5; see R. G. Albion, 132.

The Navy Board, in their alarm over the timber shortage, consulted the Royal Society which had been founded in 1660; and this in turn asked a member of its council, John Evelyn, to examine the problem. His report, which appeared in 1664, surveyed the destruction of wood due to the demands of shipping, industry and tillage; and it appealed to the landed gentry to plant trees.[1] The book ran into many editions, and in that of 1679 Evelyn went so far as to claim that millions of trees had been planted as a result of his advocacy. To what extent Evelyn's claim was true has been debated, but it is clear that the trees planted during these years came to maturity in time to sustain the British navy through the wars of the eighteenth century, but the problem always remained acute. At the end of the Seven Years' War (1756–63) a Liverpool shipwright named Roger Fisher painted a very gloomy picture; many counties, he wrote, had only a quarter or even a tenth of the woods they had possessed forty years earlier.[2] Fir trees for masts were increasingly imported from the Baltic and North America. Concern for naval timber continued throughout the eighteenth century. In 1787, commissioners were appointed to enquire into the state of the royal forests and their seventeen reports were issued between 1787 and 1793. Most of them dealt with separate forests but some were of a general character, especially the eleventh (1792).[3] Its conclusion was that cultivation was crowding out woodland, that the woods were approaching general exhaustion, and that the government should plant in the royal forests.

In the middle of the Seven Years' War, in 1758, the Royal Society of Arts had begun to offer gold and silver medals to encourage the planting of timber.[4] The first recipient was the duke of Beaufort who was awarded a gold medal for sowing 23 acres in Gloucestershire with acorns. Awards continued to be made up to 1835, and, as a result, it has been estimated that well over 50 million trees were planted. One feature of the planting of the time was the widespread use of new species. The traditional timbers of England were the hardwoods – oak, ash, beech, elm – but, now, softwoods were introduced, although not to everyone's liking – the Scots pine, the larch, the spruce, and varieties of fir from abroad. Some of this planting was not for utility but for the adornment of the landscape parks

---

[1] J. Evelyn, *Sylva: or a discourse of forest trees, and the propagation of timber in His Majesty's dominions* (London, 1664).

[2] R. Fisher, *Heart of oak, the British bulwark* (London, 1763).

[3] R. G. Albion, 135–6 and 439.

[4] H. T. Wood, *A history of the Royal Society of Arts* (London, 1913), 145–50.

that were becoming such a feature of the eighteenth-century landscape. Very often, ornament and utility were combined. A general picture of what Arthur Young called 'the modern spirit of planting'[1] at the end of the century may be obtained from the sections dealing with 'Woods and Plantations' that appeared in the Board of Agriculture county reports. In Northumberland, for example, we are told that 'plantations, on an extensive scale', were 'rising in every part of the county', adding greatly to its 'ornament and improvement'.[2] It was the same in the south of the realm, and in Gloucestershire there were numerous planters 'who have skreened the bleak spots of the Cotswolds, and have improved the general face of the county'.[3]

Many of the county reports that tell of this new planting, tell also of the grubbing up of trees for cultivation. The author of the Gloucestershire report noted that 'in every year many acres of beech woods are destroyed and given up to the plough'.[4] Arthur Young had witnessed similar operations in Suffolk and thought that corn and grass were of much more value than timber.[5] Thomas Preston of Suffolk was equally emphatic: 'The scarcity of timber ought never to be regretted, for it is a certain proof of national improvement.'[6]

The making of water-meadows

Meadowland had always formed an important element in the economy of the countryside, and an acre of meadow was usually much more valuable than an acre of arable. That riverside meadows received much benefit from the overflowing of their streams was generally recognised; but in the late sixteenth and early seventeenth centuries an innovation in the management of meadows greatly increased the benefits of such inundation. This was the artificial flooding of meadows at appropriate times by irrigation channels so as to stimulate the growth of grass. The resulting crop of hay

[1] A. Young, *General view of the agriculture of the county of Norfolk* (London, 1804), 381.

[2] J. Bailey and G. Culley, *General view of the agriculture of the county of Northumberland* (London, 1794), 15.

[3] T. Rudge, *General view of the agriculture of the county of Gloucester* (London, 1807), 243.

[4] *Ibid.*

[5] A. Young, *General view of the agriculture of the county of Suffolk* (London, 1804), 166.

[6] *Journals of the House of Commons*, XLVII (1792), 343; see R. G. Albion, 119.

supported a large number of sheep, and these in turn provided substantial amounts of manure.[1]

Long known in Italy, artificial water-meadows were said to have been made in England by that curious Elizabethan figure, Sir Horatio Pallavicino, who had bought an estate at Babraham to the south of Cambridge.[2] Early in the following century Rowland Vaughan published an account of the water-meadows he had made over some years in the Golden Valley in Herefordshire. The sight of 'a spring breaking out of a mole-hill with the grass very green where it ran' gave him, so he said, the idea that controlled flooding would be very good for grass, and he advocated the general adoption of the practice.[3] Vaughan's book was dedicated to the earl of Pembroke, and it may be more than chance that it was soon adopted on the Pembroke estates in Wiltshire.[4] The seventeenth-century topographer of Wiltshire, John Aubrey, said that water-meadows had been constructed in the valleys of the Wylye and the Ebble about 1635, and in those of the Kennet and the Avon about 1646.[5] The technique spread to other downland valleys, not only in Wiltshire but in the nearby counties of Berkshire, Dorset and Hampshire. It became an essential feature of chalkland farming, and was integrated into the 'sheep and barley' husbandry of the district. Fed by day on the meadow, the sheep were folded at night on the arable and greatly enriched it with their manure.

Water-meadows were also to be found elsewhere in the first half of the seventeenth century. About 1638 Sir Richard Weston of Sutton in Surrey described how he obtained great crops of hay from irrigated meadows.[6] Other writers, too, were advocating the new system. Walter Blith, about 1650, set out instructions for improving land by 'floating or watering'.[7] In 1669 John Worlidge of Petersfield in Hampshire could say that the practice had become 'one of the most universal and advantageous

[1] E. Kerridge (1) 'The sheepfold in Wiltshire and the floating of the watermeadows', *Econ. Hist. Rev.*, 2nd ser., VI (1954), 282–9.

[2] W. Gooch, *General view of the agriculture of the county of Cambridge* (London, 1813), 258.

[3] R. Vaughan, *Most approved and long experienced waterworkes, containing the manner of winter and summer drowning of meadow and pasture* (London, 1610).

[4] J. Thirsk (1967), 182.

[5] John Britton (ed.), *The natural history of Wiltshire by John Aubrey, F.R.S. (written between 1656 and 1691)* (London, 1947), 93 and 104.

[6] R. Weston, *A discours of husbandrie used in Brabant and Flanders, showing wonderful improvement of land there* (London, 1605). The imprint date seems to be in error, maybe for 1650.   [7] W. Blith (1649), 2.

improvements in England within these few years'.[1] We certainly hear of
water-meadows in such counties as Worcester,[2] Warwick and Leicester
where Robert Bakewell constructed some at Dishley,[3] but they were
never very common in the east or the north of the country.

From the seventeenth right through the eighteenth century, water-
meadows formed an important element in the agriculture of many areas,
especially in that of the chalk country. Towards the end of the eighteenth
century a number of treatises on 'the art of floating land' appeared;[4] and
in the last decade or so an account of it was included under the heading of
'improvements' in many of the county reports of the Board of Agriculture.
The outstanding description was in Thomas Davis's report on Wiltshire.
As he said: 'none but those who have seen this kind of husbandry, can
form a just idea of the value of the fold of a flock of ewes and lambs,
coming immediately with bellies full of young quick grass from a good
watermeadow, and particularly how much it will increase the quantity and
quality of a crop of barley.'[5]

The writers of the time distinguished two main types of water-meadow
– the flowing or 'floated' meadow and the catchwork meadow. The
former type was characteristic of alluvial valleys across which channels
were made to carry water from the main stream and then back to it at
a lower level, the circulation being controlled by a system of hatches and
weirs. The system varied in complexity according to the lie of the land,
but Fig. 8 shows the kind of network encountered in the valley of the
Avon below Salisbury.[6] Thus it was that many valleys, particularly those
of the chalkland, became criss-crossed by a network of channels. The
catchwork meadow was to be found on hillsides. Water from a spring or
small stream was led by a new cut with but a slight fall along the side of

[1] J. Worlidge (1669), 16–17.

[2] R. C. Gaut, *A history of Worcestershire agriculture and rural evolution* (Worcester,
1939), 123–4.

[3] W. Marshall (1790), I, 284–6.

[4] G. Boswell, *A treatise on watering meadows* (London, 1770; also 1790, 1792, 1801);
T. Wright, *An account of the advantage and method of watering meadows by art as
practised in the county of Gloucester* (Cirencester, 1789; also 1790); T. Wright, *The art
of floating land as it is practised in the county of Gloucester* (London, 1799); T. Wright,
On the formation and management of floated meadows (Northampton, 1808); W. Smith,
Observations on the utility, form and management of water meadows (Norwich, 1806).

[5] T. Davis, *General view Wiltshire* (1794), 30–1.

[6] H. P. Moon and F. H. W. Green, 'Water meadows in southern England' in
F. H. W. Green, *Hampshire* in 'The land of Britain', ed. by L. D. Stamp, pt. 89
(London, 1940).

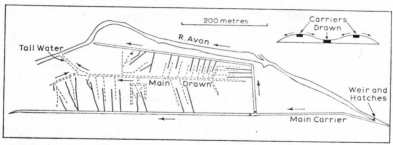

Fig. 8   Water-meadows along the River Avon (Hampshire)
Based on H. P. Moon and F. H. W. Green, 'Water meadows in southern England' in F. H. W. Green, *Hampshire* (L. of B., pt. 89, London, 1940), 375. Meadows are flooded by means of 'carriers' and then drained by means of 'drawns'.

a hill, and then allowed to escape, thus watering the slope before rejoining the stream below.

The draining of the marshes

The General Draining Act of 1600, 'for the recovering of many hundred thousand acres of marshes', not only marked the end of some decades of experiment, but was, in a sense, a promise of changes to come. Of all the many stretches of marsh in the kingdom, that of the peatland of the southern Fenland saw the most spectacular transformation.[1] At first, there was great opposition from those with vested interests in the fen pastures and in the fen streams. Many proposals were made in the early years of the seventeenth century, but nothing effective was done until in 1630–1 the fourth earl of Bedford, together with thirteen 'co-adventurers' contracted to drain the peat areas of the southern Fenland. They secured the services of the Dutch engineer, Cornelius Vermuyden, who had been at work upon the marshes of Hatfield Chase and Axholme to the north.[2] Under his direction, cuts, drains and sluices were made, the most important works being the two Bedford rivers that form so prominent a feature of the countryside today. Their activities were interrupted by disputes and by the Civil War, so that it was not until 1652 that the area now known as the Bedford Level was finally declared to be drained.

[1] H. C. Darby, *The draining of the Fens* (Cambridge, 3rd ed., 1968); L. E. Harris, *Vermuyden and the Fens* (London, 1953); R. L. Hills, *Machines, mills and uncountable costly necessities* (Norwich, 1967).

[2] J. Thirsk, 'The Isle of Axholme before Vermuyden', *Agric. Hist. Rev.*, I (1953), 16–28; L. E. Harris, 41–53.

The completion of the work was followed by great success, and on the newly reclaimed land there was not only 'all sorts of corne and grasse'[1] but also such crops as rape, onions, flax, hemp, mustard, chicory and woad. But in spite of this 'deluge and inundation of plenty',[2] it was evident before the end of the century that all was not well. Neither Vermuyden nor his associates seemed to have realised that, as soon as it was drained, the surface of the peat would rapidly become lower, due partly to shrinkage and partly to the wasting of the peat owing to bacterial action. The result was that the peat surface was soon below the levels of the channels into which it was supposed to drain. Complaints about flooding became frequent; what had seemed a promising enterprise in 1652 had become a tragedy by 1700. The solution lay in the introduction of windmills for pumping, and it was this that saved the situation as the seventeenth century passed into the eighteenth. Windmills became increasingly frequent; and in the eighteenth century they, in their hundreds, gave a distinctive character to the fen landscape.

But the windmill was to prove unsatisfactory. It was at the mercy of gale and frost and calm, and as the peat surface became increasingly drier and lower, windmill drainage became more and more ineffective. The irony was that improved drainage only caused the peat surface to sink more rapidly, and therefore become increasingly liable to flooding. There was also difficulty over the outfalls of the fenland rivers. Observers at the end of the eighteenth century were shocked at the 'misery and desolation' before them. Large stretches of country were relapsing into 'waste and water' as may be seen on Vancouver's map of 1794.[3] A solution was not to appear until the use of steam-driven pumps about 1820.

In the meantime there had been much cutting of drains and embanking of land in other parts of England, but success was often only partial and was frequently followed by deterioration. A brief view of conditions in some other marshland areas must serve to give an idea of the state of affairs by 1800. There had been various improvements in the Fenland to the north of the Bedford Level but some had been only temporary; and, in spite of much discussion and activity especially after about 1760, East, West and Wildmore Fens in Lincolnshire were still stretches of marsh

---

[1] Sir William Dugdale in 1657; quoted in H. C. Darby (1968), 280.

[2] T. Fuller, *History of the University of Cambridge* (London, 1655), section v.

[3] C. Vancouver, *General view of the agriculture of the county of Cambridge* (London, 1794).

and water at the beginning of the nineteenth century.[1] Holderness and the Hull valley, again in spite of much activity after about 1760, remained subject to persistent flooding.[2] The Somerset Levels, after various vicissitudes, had been greatly improved during the last decades of the eighteenth century, as we may read in John Billingsley's county report for 1798, but his map shows that stretches of undrained bogs still remained,[3] and the area as a whole was for long subject to inundation.[4] Although there had been much piecemeal activity in Lancashire, a large-scale map of the county in 1786 could still indicate considerable stretches of coastal marsh and mossland.[5] But changes were afoot; thus in 1780 Rainford Moss was reclaimed and planted with potatoes; and other mosslands were soon to disappear under the terms of various enclosure acts. The draining of Trafford Moss was almost over by 1800, but that of the larger expanse of Chat Moss still remained uncompleted in 1800.[6] Along the coast, Martin Mere in the Fylde had been drained (not for the first time) in the 1780s, only to be reflooded in 1789.[7] Marton Mere to the east of Blackpool was also still a lake, but an act for its reclamation was passed in 1798. The meres of northern Shropshire, which were such a feature of John Rocque's map of 1752,[8] were also soon to disappear (Fig. 9). Joseph Plymley, in 1803, could report that much progress had taken place over the preceding twenty years,[9] and in 1801 had come an act for 'inclosing, draining and improving' yet other Shropshire moors.[10]

On the other side of the country the area of the Ouse–Trent lowland is of particular interest because not only draining but another operation

[1] W. H. Wheeler, *A history of the fens of south Lincolnshire* (Boston and London, 2nd ed. 1896).

[2] J. A. Sheppard: (1) *The draining of the Hull valley* (York, 1958); (2) *The draining of the marshlands of south Holderness and the Vale of York* (York, 1966).

[3] J. Billingsley, *General view of the agriculture of the county of Somerset* (London, 1798).

[4] M. Williams, *The draining of the Somerset Levels* (Cambridge, 1970).

[5] J. B. Harley (ed.), *William Yates's map of Lancashire, 1786* (Historic Society of Lancs. and Cheshire, 1968).

[6] J. Holt, *General view of the agriculture of the county of Lancaster* (London, 1794), 86–103.

[7] H. Brodrick, 'Martin Mere', *Eighth report of the Southport Society of Natural Science, 1902–1903* (Southport, 1903), 5–18.

[8] J. Rocque, *Actual survey of the county of Salop* (London, 1752).

[9] J. Plymley, *General view of the agriculture of the county of Shropshire* (London, 1803), 223.

[10] E. J. Howell, *Shropshire* (L. of B., pt. 66, London, 1941), 288–9.

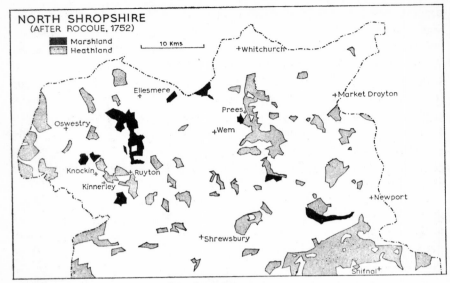

Fig. 9 Marsh and heath in north Shropshire, 1752
Based on John Rocque, *Actual survey of the county of Salop* (London, 1752).

– that of warping – was employed to make new land. The West Riding report, in 1799, said that warping had been tried to the west of Goole about fifty years earlier but that it had not been common for 'more than 20 or 25 years'.[1] Arthur Young, in the same year, described the process in some detail, and extolled the 'vast fertility' of the soil yielded by the silt-laden waters of the Humber.[2] Warping involved the controlled flooding of embanked areas at high tides; after depositing its silt the water was allowed to run off at low tides. When the salt had been leached out, the new soil yielded rich crops of wheat, beans and potatoes. The practice of artificial warping, Young said, was peculiar to this part of Britain, and could be extended with enormous profit to other districts.

This brief catalogue must stand for all the stretches of marsh in England where changes were afoot. We can generalise and say that the earlier half of the seventeenth century had seen a great burst of activity of which the Bedford Level was the chief triumph. The latter half of the eighteenth

[1] R. Brown, *General view of the agriculture of the West Riding of Yorkshire* (Edinburgh, 1799), 167.
[2] A. Young, *General view of the agriculture of the county of Lincoln* (London, 1799), 276–88. See (1) R. Creyke, 'Some account of the process of warping', *J.R.A.S.*, v (1844), 398–405; (2) J. Thirsk (1957), 230–1, 289–90.

century saw a quickening of intensive local activity, but this effort, too, was limited by the technical expertise of the time.

Under-draining the claylands

For the greater part of their history, the claylands of England were ill-drained, and water could often be seen standing upon their impervious stiff soils in winter (Fig. 81). Some drainage of surface water was secured by the furrows of the ridged-up fields,[1] but the general impression conveyed by Arthur Young's *Tours*, and by much writing of the eighteenth century, is that of countrysides water-logged in winter, and parched and cracked in summer.

The possibility of transforming this state of affairs, and of giving the claylands a new value – whether as arable or as pasture – was provided by under-draining.[2] By this practice, parallel trenches were cut across fields, bushes or stubble or loose stones were placed along the bottoms of the trenches which were then filled up with earth. The date at which such under-draining began to be practised is uncertain. It was not mentioned in Thomas Tusser's *Five hundreth pointes of good husbandry* in 1573, but in 1649 Walter Blith described how to make covered drains with the aid of stones and bushes.[3] Richard Bradley, in 1727, gave an account of a similar method of 'hollow ditching or draining' which he described as a recent invention 'chiefly practised in Essex'.[4] Arthur Young, in 1769, said that he had found the practice 'scarce any where but in Essex and Suffolk',[5] but it is clear that before 1750, and even earlier, it was also to be found at least in the nearby counties of Hertford and Norfolk.[6]

During the latter part of the eighteenth century, from about 1764 onwards, Joseph Elkington, a Warwickshire farmer, drained his sloping fields by means of trenches up to 5 feet below the surface of the

---

[1] E. Kerridge, 'A reconsideration of some former husbandry practices', *Agric. Hist. Rev.*, III (1955), 26–40.

[2] H. C. Darby, 'The draining of the English claylands', *Geographische Zeitschrift*, LIV (1964), 190–201.

[3] W. Blith (1649), 23–4.

[4] R. Bradley, *A complete body of husbandry* (London, 1727), 133–4.

[5] A. Young, *A six weeks tour through the southern counties of England and Wales* (London, 1768), 209; see also 67.

[6] P. Pusey et al., 'Evidence on the antiquity, cheapness, and efficacy of thorough draining, or land-ditching, as practised throughout the counties of Suffolk, Hertford, Essex and Norfolk', *J.R.A.S.*, IV (1843), 23–49.

ground;[1] and in 1797 he was awarded a grant of £1,000 for his work by Parliament. Even so, the principles of underground drainage were far from being understood, particularly in near-level fields of impervious clay.

An alternative method of draining heavy clay was by means of 'mole drains' which Stephen Switzer had described how to make as early as 1724.[2] By this method a trench was dug some 18 inches deep, and a rod of wood or a length of rope was laid along it; the trench was filled with clay, and the rod or rope was then withdrawn to leave an underground channel along which water could run. An improved way of making such channels was by means of a mole plough, and various types of mole ploughs were produced towards the end of the eighteenth century. These were drawn by horses or by means of a windlass and cable, and their purpose was to cut a channel below the surface of the ground by means of a sharp metal plug or 'mole' which had been inserted into a hole dug at the commencement of each drain.[3]

Drainage was very much in the minds of agriculturalists by the end of the century. The county reports of the Board of Agriculture included sections on 'Draining' in their chapter on 'Improvements'. The topics discussed included the proper depth of the drains, the distance between them, the most suitable material for filling them, and the various types of mole ploughs. The general tenor of the accounts is that while much had been done, still more remained to be done. As the Warwickshire report said: 'There is no improvement that can be made on land, productive of more salutary effects than that of draining.'[4]

The reclamation of the heathlands

The new crops and new methods of husbandry that were becoming common in the seventeenth century were of especial importance to the inherently infertile light soils of many parts of England. Turnips fed on the ground to sheep enabled the barren sands to be manured and also con-solidated by treading; marling further improved the loose soil. Among the questions asked in 1664 by the 'Georgical Committee' of the newly formed

[1] J. Johnstone, *An account of the most approved mode of draining land: according to the system practised by Mr Joseph Elkington* (Edinburgh, 1797).

[2] S. Switzer, *The practical fruit-gardiner* (London, 1724), 25–6.

[3] A. Young, *General view of the agriculture of the county of Essex*, II (London, 1807), 194–201.

[4] A. Murray, *General view of the agriculture of the county of Warwick* (London, 1813), 147.

Royal Society was: 'And who they are if there be any in your County that have reduced *Heaths* into profitable Lands?'[1] No quantitative measure of the amount of reclamation that took place is possible, but we can obtain a broad picture.

Turnip husbandry appeared on the Norfolk heathlands during the years 1670–80, and by this time sainfoin and clover had also become common there.[2] By 1700 they were to be found in a variety of places, and references to the new husbandry became frequent in the topographical literature of the time. In Cambridgshire in 1701 Robert Morden was noting how sainfoin 'does wonderfully enrich the Dry and Barren Grounds of that county', presumably on the heathy chalk belt that stretches across the south of the county from Royston to Newmarket.[3] The same feature was to be found on other downlands.[4] In 1724 Daniel Defoe referred more than once to the change that had taken place in Hampshire, Wiltshire and Dorset. It was remarkable, he wrote, 'how a great part of these downs comes by a new method of husbandry, to be not only made arable, which they never were in former days, but to bear excellent wheat, and great crops too', all of which was done, he added elsewhere, by the folding of sheep upon the ploughed land.[5] As Thomas Davis wrote of Wiltshire at the end of the eighteenth century: 'The first and principal purpose of keeping sheep is undoubtedly the *dung of the sheepfold*.'[6]

The changes in Norfolk have received more attention than those elsewhere, due in part to the writings of Arthur Young. Here were the estates of Viscount Townshend (1674–1738) at Raynham, of Sir Robert Walpole (1676–1745) at Houghton,[7] and of Thomas Coke (1697–1755) at Holkham;[8] the last-name is not to be confused with that of his kinsman

[1] R. Lennard, 'English agriculture under Charles II: Evidence of the Royal Society's "Enquiries"', *Econ. Hist. Rev.*, IV (1932), 25.

[2] E. Kerridge (1967), 273, 279, 283.

[3] R. Morden, *The new description and state of England* (London, 1701), 13.

[4] E. L. Jones, 'Eighteenth-century changes in Hampshire chalkland farming', *Agric. Hist. Rev.*, VIII (1960), 5–19.

[5] Daniel Defoe, *Tour*, I, 187, 282, 285.

[6] T. Davis, *General view Wiltshire* (1794), 20.

[7] J. H. Plumb: (1) 'Sir Robert Walpole and Norfolk husbandry', *Econ. Hist. Rev.*, 2nd ser., V (1952), 86–9; (2) *Sir Robert Walpole* (London, 1956).

[8] C. W. James, *Chief Justice Coke and his descendants at Holkham* (London, 1929); R. Parker, 'Coke of Norfolk and the agricultural revolution', *Econ. Hist. Rev.*, 2nd ser., VIII (1955–6), 156–66.

Thomas William who succeeded to the estate in 1776. We must now recognise these not so much as innovators but as powerful advocates of 'the agriculture to which the general epithet of Norfolk husbandry peculiarly belongs'.[1] The name of 'Turnip Townshend' is particularly associated with the development of the so-called 'Norfolk Four Course' in which wheat, turnips, barley and clover followed one another in succession; but this was only one of a number of variant systems that involved turnips and seeds.[2]

The new rotations coupled with increased marling produced spectacular results. Arthur Young, in 1768, was loud in his praise:

All the country from Holkham to Houghton was a wild sheep-walk before the spirit of improvement seized the inhabitants; and this glorious spirit has wrought amazing effects; for instead of boundless wilds, and uncultivated wastes, inhabited by scarce anything but sheep, the county is all cut into inclosures, cultivated in a most husband-like manner.[3]

Allowance must be made for the exaggeration of enthusiasm, but other evidence also bears witness to great changes. Some idea of these can be gained from the diary of the François de la Rochefoucauld who visited East Anglia in 1784. At Massingham, reclamation had taken place 'within the last thirty or forty years', and the owner had made 'immense sums'. At Dunton there was a prosperous farm of 1,600 acres which fifty years earlier had lain all uncultivated; the same was true of other farms, and la Rochefoucauld could only exclaim: 'The fertility of this land is wholly artificial.'[4] To this north-western area of Norfolk, Arthur Young gave the name of 'Good Sand', and this was adopted by many as a convenient regional designation (Fig. 10). It was 'good' in contrast to the infertile sandy area to the south, which was later known as the Breckland, and which stretches from Norfolk into Suffolk.[5]

Striking changes had also taken place during the eighteenth century on the light soils of Lincolnshire (Fig. 12). A picture of the transformation on the chalk wolds is given in the agricultural reports of Thomas Stone

[1] A. Young, *General view Norfolk* (1804), 3.

[2] N. Riches, *The agricultural revolution in Norfolk* (Chapel Hill, N.C., 1937), 76 *et seq.*

[3] A. Young (1768), 21.

[4] J. Marchand and S. C. Roberts (eds.), *A Frenchman in England, 1784* (Cambridge, 1933), 221, 228, 230.

[5] The word 'Breckland' was coined by W. G. Clarke in 1894 – see W. G. Clarke, *In Breckland wilds* (Heffer, Cambridge, 2nd ed., 1937), 1 and 174.

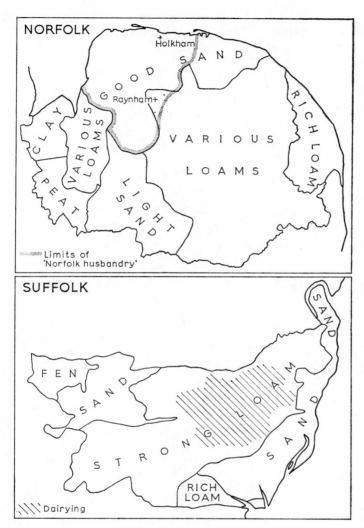

Figs. 10 and 11 Soil regions of Norfolk and Suffolk, 1804

Based on: (1) A. Young, *General view of the agriculture of the county of Norfolk* (London, 1804), map; (2) *General view of the agriculture of the county of Suffolk* (London, 1804), map and (for dairies) p. 199.

It is impossible to provide an accurate scale.

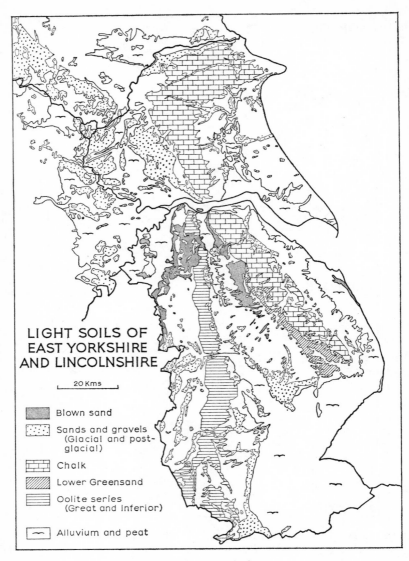

Fig. 12 Light soils of east Yorkshire and Lincolnshire
Based on *Geological Survey Quarter-Inch Sheets* 8, 12; *One-Inch Sheets* (*New Series*), 31–5, 39, 40–4, 50–5, 59, 60, 62–5, 67–73, 76–8, 85–7, 100; *One-Inch Sheets* (*Old Series*), 70, 83, 85, 86.

in 1794 and Arthur Young in 1799. 'Forty years ago', wrote Young, 'it was all warren from Spilsby to beyond Caistor; and by means of turnips and seeds, there are now at least twenty sheep kept to one before.' Elsewhere, he spoke of 'the immense and rapid progress turnips had made' in transforming 'the bleak wolds and heaths'. Even so, as he said, much warren still remained.[1] The oolitic belt that ran for forty miles north and south of Lincoln had also been changed. In the 1770s it was a tract of heath and gorse given over largely to rabbits; by 1799 it was a countryside of 'profitable arable farms' with turnips and seeds much in evidence,[2] although Young's account must be tempered by that of Thomas Stone who pointed time and again to poor management.[3] To the north, there were also changes on the Yorkshire Wolds, made especially by Sir Christopher Sykes who died in 1801. One local historian of 1798 was able to report that 'the land which formerly presented to the eye a dreary and uncultivated waste, now wears the appearance of an hospitable region'.[4]

Many other stretches of light soil elsewhere in the kingdom were also transformed in the eighteenth century. Samuel Rudder, the historian of Gloucestershire, could describe in 1779 how 'within the last forty years prodigious improvements' had taken place on the Cotswolds;[5] and Thomas Rudge summed up the changes of the century by describing how 'many thousand acres' of 'little more than furze and a few scanty blades of grass' had been turned into arable with the aid of turnips and seeds together with the 'treading and excrements of the sheep' folded upon them.[6] A similar story could be told, for example, of patches of glacial sand in northern Shropshire (Fig. 9), of the 'turnip soils' of Northumberland, and of parts of the Bunter and Keuper sandstone outcrops in the Midlands. Much of the 'Sandlings' in eastern Suffolk (Fig. 11) had become arable by 1784 with the help not only of turnips but also of carrots, for which the district became well-known.[7]

But there were limits to the magic of the new husbandry, and many tracts of barren hungry land remained unreclaimed. Such, for instance, were the Breckland with its blowing sands, the Dorset heathlands around

[1] A. Young, *General view Lincoln* (1799), 6, 225, 115, 382, 390, 393, 224, 12.

[2] *Ibid.*, 78, 136.

[3] T. Stone, *General view of the agriculture of the county of Lincoln* (London, 1794), 15, 32, 38, 46.

[4] T. Hinderwell, *The history and antiquities of Scarborough* (York, 1798), 263.

[5] S. Rudder, *A new history of Gloucestershire* (Cirencester, 1779), 21.

[6] T. Rudge, *General view Gloucester* (1807), 89, 133.

[7] J. Marchand and S. C. Roberts, 179–83.

Poole harbour, parts of the Suffolk Sandlings, stretches of the sandy outcrops in Kent, Sussex and Surrey, and many other like areas, all 'calling loudly for improvement', as one county report of the Board of Agriculture put it.[1] Even near London there were considerable stretches of heath, rough grazing and commons. Nathaniel Kent could say in 1775 that 'within thirty miles of the *capital*, there is not less than 200,000 acres of waste land'.[2] Hounslow Heath and Finchley Common, notorious haunts of highwaymen, were only two of such tracts marked on William Faden's map of 1802.[3]

Landscape parks and gardens

In so far as they owed their character to human effort, most of the landscapes of England, as elsewhere, were but the incidental by-products of economic activity. But in some ages and in some localities people consciously aimed at producing certain kinds of scenery. Such were the ornamental gardens of the seventeenth and eighteenth centuries.[4] Gardens, it is true, were not new in England. The Elizabethan period had seen a considerable increase in the study and practice of making gardens with flowers, fruit herbs and mazes, and early in the next century (1625) Francis Bacon's essay 'Of Gardens' described the ideal form of a great garden which should cover not less than thirty acres.[5] With the Restoration in 1660 this interest was not only greatly quickened but given a new accent.

When, in the 1690s, Celia Fiennes toured England on horseback, she found a large number of newly built houses surrounded by gardens and parks. A park with 'fine rows of trees' was coming to be regarded as a necessary element in the dignity of a county seat.[6] Stimulated by John Evelyn's *Sylva* (1664) people were planting not only for profit but for ornament. Early in the next century, Daniel Defoe was struck by this new

---

[1] A. Young, *General view of the agriculture of the county of Sussex* (London, 1793), 8.

[2] N. Kent, *Hints to gentlemen of landed property* (London, 1775), 101.

[3] For this and John Rocque's map of 1754, see E. C. Willatts, *Middlesex and the London Region* (L. of B., pt. 79, London, 1937), 283 *et seq.*

[4] General accounts include: (1) H. F. Clark, *The English landscape garden* (London, 1948); (2) R. Dutton, *The English garden* (London, 2nd ed., 1945); (3) M. Hadfield, *Gardening in England* (London, 1960); (4) C. Hussey, *English gardens and landscapes, 1700–1750* (London, 1967); (5) H. C. Prince, *Parks in England* (Shalfleet, I.O.W., 1967).

[5] Francis Bacon, *Essayes or Counsels* (Everyman's Library), 137–43.

[6] C. Morris (ed.), *The journeys of Celia Fiennes* (London, 1947), 55, 67, 68, 151, 233 *et al.*

addition to the variety of the English scene. 'The alteration is indeed wonderful thro' the whole kingdom', he wrote. The fine houses 'surrounded with gardens, walks, vistas, avenues' were giving 'a kind of character to the island of Great Britain in general'.[1]

The gardens that were coming into being were of a very formal character. André le Nôtre (1613–1700), who planned the layout at Versailles, had many followers in England, and the influence of his geometrical designs was very evident. Avenues and walks were laid out in straight lines, frequently radiating from one point, parterres were arranged in stiff and symmetrical patterns, trees were cut and clipped with precision, geometry triumphed over Nature. Some of these formal layouts are well seen in the engravings of Johannes Kip, Thomas Badeslade and others around 1700.

Early in the eighteenth century many were beginning to criticise this formality. Joseph Addison, in 1712, in *The Spectator* essays poured scorn upon gardens 'laid out by the rule and line'; he preferred an 'artificial rudeness' to 'neatness and elegancy'.[2] In 1728, Batty Langley could think of nothing 'more shocking than a stiff regular garden'.[3] Such criticism was symptomatic of a new inspiration in gardening design. The restrictions of the formal style were being broken down, and the irregular garden was in turn to develop into the landscape park. The new fashion owed much to the long procession of travellers who made the Grand Tour over the Alps to Italy. They began to look around through the eyes of the Italian school of landscape painters; and they admired the wild scenery painted by Salvator Rosa, and the classical landscapes of Claude Lorraine and Gaspard Poussin with their ruined temples and broken columns.[4]

It was, apparently, the poet William Shenstone (1714–63) who invented the term 'landscape gardener', and said that 'the landskip painter is the gardiner's best designer';[5] his own ornamental farm at The Leasowes in Worcestershire attracted many visitors.[6] Alexander Pope (1688–1744), an important advocate of the new style, said that 'all gardening is landscape

---

[1] Daniel Defoe, *Tour*, I, 167.

[2] J. Addison, *The Spectator*, Essay 414 (1712).

[3] B. Langley, *New principles of gardening* (London, 1728), iv.

[4] E. W. Manwaring, *Italian landscape in eighteenth century England* (New York, 1925).

[5] W. Shenstone, 'Unconnected thoughts on gardening', an essay printed in *The works in verse and prose of William Shenstone Esq.*, II (London, 1764), 129.

[6] A. R. Humphreys, *William Shenstone* (Cambridge, 1937), *passim*.

painting';[1] and, towards the end of the century, Horace Walpole put it clearly: 'an open country is but a canvass on which a landscape might be designed'.[2] The making of a landscape park thus became an exercise in which stretches of grass, clumps of trees and expanses of water were important elements. Something of this new vogue can be seen in the works of Sir John Vanbrugh (1664–1726) and Charles Bridgeman (d. 1738), but the new freedom was brought to its fullest expression in the works of three great gardeners of the eighteenth century, William Kent (1685–1748), Lancelot Brown (1715–83) and Humphry Repton (1752–1818).

William Kent had been a painter, had spent several years in Italy and was a collector of Italian landscape paintings.[3] He turned from painting and, according to William Mason, 'worked with the living hues that Nature lent, and realised his landscapes'.[4] He used Bridgeman's device of the 'ha ha' or sunk fence to abolish the separation of garden and park, so bringing the latter right up to the walls of a house. He began the destruction of avenues; he replaced formal canals by serpentine streams; and he relieved large stretches of open lawn and grass by the planting of trees in clumps; he has been described as the inventor of the clump which was to feature so prominently in the English scene.[5] He introduced temples, colonnades and obelisks, often to terminate a vista. But alongside this freedom, there was still an element of formality in Kent's designs. They represented not so much Nature herself but, to use Horace Walpole's phrase, Nature 'chastened or polished'.[6]

Elegant informality was carried a step further under the leadership of Lancelot Brown.[7] Some 188 major landscape parks have been attributed to him and they included such magnificent examples as those around the great houses of Blenheim, Chatsworth and Luton Hoo. When consulted, he had the habit of saying: 'I see great capability of improvement here',

[1] J. Spence, *Anecdotes, observations, and characters, of books and men* (London, 1820), 144.

[2] H. Walpole, *The history of the modern taste in gardening*, first appeared in 1771, reprinted frequently. The reprint used here appears in I. W. U. Chase, *Horace Walpole: gardenist* (Princeton, 1943), and is accompanied by an essay; the quotation is from p. 37.

[3] M. Jourdain, *The work of William Kent* (London, 1948).

[4] W. Mason, *The English garden: a poem in four books* (London, 1782).

[5] H. F. Clark, plate 3.

[6] I. W. U. Chase (ed.), 27.

[7] D. Stroud, *Capability Brown* (London, 1950).

THE PARKS OF SOUTHERN
BUCKINGHAMSHIRE
(AFTER A.BRYANT, 1824)

5 Kms

Fig. 13 The parks of southern Buckinghamshire, 1824
  Based on *Map of the county of Buckingham, from an actual survey by A. Bryant
  in the year 1824* (London, 1825).
  The scale of the original is 1½ inches to 1 mile.

and became known as 'Capability Brown'. Serpentine walks, stretches of
water, plantations and clumps of exotic as well as native trees now became
the fashion. The romantic style also appeared in other ways – in garden
temples, arches, obelisks, grottoes and follies of various kinds and in ruins
which, if they did not already exist, were constructed in a Gothic manner.
There was also another source of inspiration. Increasing contacts with the
East were reflected in the new vogue of chinoiserie, stimulated by Sir
William Chambers (1726–96) who wrote an account of oriental gardening in 1772.[1] Pagodas, Chinese temples and lattice-work bridges were
added to the embellishments of the English park. It was Chambers who
designed the ruined arch, the classical temple and the pagoda that can still

[1] W. Chambers, *A dissertation on oriental gardening* (London, 1772).

be seen in Kew Gardens; his Turkish mosque, Moorish alhambra and Gothic church have disappeared. Here, too, must be mentioned the introduction to the English scene of new shrubs, such as the magnolia in 1688, the hydrangea in 1736, the buddleia in 1774, the fuchsia in 1788, and varieties of rhododendron between 1736 and 1763.[1]

Capability Brown's style, his broad 'shaven lawns' and his repetitious rounded clumps, provoked criticism, which became loud after his death in 1783. Many people came to prefer not nature made elegant and 'beautiful', but what William Gilpin called the boldness and roughness of nature herself;[2] and the new mode of the rugged and the 'picturesque'[3] was advocated by such writers as Sir Uvedale Price (1747–1829)[4] and Richard Payne Knight (1750–1824).[5] Amidst much contending discussion, the third great gardener of the eighteenth century, Humphry Repton, tried to steer a middle course between elegance and the picturesque.[6] His work can be seen from his handsomely bound manuscript 'Red Books' which discussed and showed landscapes before and after 'improvement'.[7] Over some thirty years he 'improved' no fewer than 220 places, including Regent's Park in London, and echoes of his work occur in Jane Austen's *Mansfield Park* published in 1815.

Whatever the artistic differences among the landed gentry and professional gardeners of the eighteenth century, the consequences of their work were very great for the English landscape. As Uvedale Price wrote in 1794, these embellishments were giving 'a new and peculiar character to the general face of the country'.[8] The effect was to be seen not only around the great palaces of the realm – Blenheim, Chatsworth, Stowe and the like, but also around what the county gazetteers were in the habit of calling 'a neat mansion pleasantly situated in a park'. Small men as well as great had followed Joseph Addison's advice and made 'a pretty

---

[1] A. M. Coats, *Garden shrubs and their histories* (London, 1963), *passim.*

[2] W. Gilpin, *Observations relative chiefly to picturesque beauty, made in the year 1772, on several parts of England* (London, 1786), I, xv.

[3] C. Hussey, *The picturesque: studies in a point of view* (London, 1927).

[4] U. Price, *An essay on the picturesque, as compared with the sublime and the beautiful* (London, 1794).

[5] R. P. Knight, *The landscape, a didactic poem* (London, 1794).

[6] H. Repton: (1) *Sketches and hints on landscape gardening* (London, 1795); (2) *The theory and practice of landscape gardening* (London, 1803); (3) *Fragments on the theory and practice of landscape gardening* (London, 1816).

[7] D. Stroud, *Humphry Repton* (London, 1962).

[8] U. Price, I.

landskip' of their possessions.[1] The county maps of the time, such as those by Bryant, Jeffreys, Faden and others, bear witness to the widespread distribution of these parks. In the Chilterns, for example, they were numerous (Fig. 13) but not more so than in some other districts (Fig. 28).

Mountains and moorlands

Topographical writers of the seventeenth century continued to echo William Camden's descriptions of the highland regions of England. Much of the Pennines, for example, was 'wild, solitary and unsightly', and Exmoor was 'a filthy barren ground'. Other adjectives included desolate, rugged, rocky and bleak. In 1696 Gregory King gave the following estimate of land use in England and Wales in millions of acres:[2]

Arable land	11
Pasture and meadow	10
Woods and coppices	3
Forests, parks, commons	3
Barren land etc.	10
Houses, gardens, churches etc.	1
Water and roads	1
	39

The true area of England and Wales is 37.3 million acres and his total was therefore some 2 million too great; but it would seem that about one quarter of the country comprised what he described as 'heaths, moors, mountains and barren land'. We cannot apportion this between upland and lowland, but there is no doubt that by far the greater part of it consisted of upland country. Daniel Defoe in the 1720s made many references to waste, wild, barren, desolate uplands and frightful mountains.[3]

Fifty years or so later, Arthur Young drew attention to the many barren tracts in the realm, especially in the north:

From the most attentive consideration, and measuring on maps pretty accurately, I am clear there are at least 600,000 waste acres in the single county of Northumberland. In those of Cumberland and Westmoreland, there are as many

[1] J. Addison, *The Spectator*, Essay 414 (1712).

[2] Gregory King, *Natural and politicall observations and conclusions upon the state and condition of England* (1696). Reprinted in G. E. Barnett (ed.), *Two tracts by Gregory King* (Baltimore, 1936), 35.

[3] Daniel Defoe, *Tour*, e.g. I, 259, 263, 267 (Devon); II, 176 (Derbyshire), 185 (Yorkshire), 271 (Westmorland).

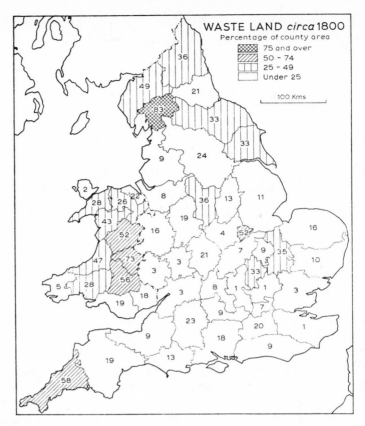

Fig. 14 Waste land *circa* 1800
Based on *General report on enclosures drawn up by order of the Board of Agriculture* (London, 1808), 139–41.

more. In the north and part (*sic*) of the west riding of Yorkshire, and the contiguous ones of Lancashire; and in the west part of Durham are yet greater tracts: you may draw a line from the north point of Derbyshire to the extremity of Northumberland, of 150 miles as the crow flies, which shall be entirely across waste lands; the exceptions of small cultivated spots, very trifling.[1]

He also found 'immense' tracts of waste in Devonshire and Cornwall.

During the eighteenth century, as earlier, there was much nibbling around the edges of the waste land, and old farms were being enlarged

[1] A. Young, *Observations on the present state of the waste lands of Great Britain* (London, 1773), 37.

Table 1.3   *Estimated enclosure of common pasture and waste*

Period	Acts	Acres (in 1,000s)
1700–60	56	75
1761–1801	521	752
1802–44	808	939
1845 and after	508	335
Total	1,893	2,101

or new ones created.[1] Here and there, improvement had taken place as a result of paring, burning and liming to produce good grass and even arable. Some 'taking in' of the waste was but temporary; tracts were tilled for a few years and then allowed to revert to rough pasture. Much of the moorland was used for grazing in summer, and came to be, in the latter part of the century, divided by miles and miles of drystone walls that brought a new element to upland landscapes.[2] Arthur Young, for example, described how a farmer at Dalton in the North Riding improved 'an extensive moor' during 1755–66. 'His first business was the inclosure, which he did by walling; the surface of the moor yielded, in some places, a sufficiency of stones for this work, but in many others pits were sunk for them.'[3] Or again in 1777, William Bray wrote of enclosure near Malham in the West Riding: 'Many of these pastures, which are of great extent, have been lately divided by stone walls.'[4] It seems that while enclosure of open fields was most rapid before 1800, enclosure of commons and waste was most rapid after 1800. Even so, Gilbert Slater's figures in table 1.3 show that at least some 800,000 acres or so of common waste land had been enclosed by 1801, mostly after 1760, and his figures are on the low side.[5]

[1] E.g. W. G. Hoskins, 'The reclamation of the waste in Devon, 1550–1800', *Econ. Hist. Rev.*, XIII (1943), 80–92; S. R. Eyre, 'The upward limit of enclosure on the East Moor of north Derbyshire', *Trans. and Papers, Inst. Brit. Geog.*, No. 23 (1957), 61–74.
[2] A. Raistrick, *The story of the Pennine walls* (Clapham, Lancaster, 1946).
[3] A. Young, *A six months tour through the north of England*, II (London, 1770), 433.
[4] W. Bray, *Sketch of a tour into Derbyshire and Yorkshire etc.* (London, 2nd ed., 1783), 308.
[5] For the figures in the table see: (1) G. Slater, *The English peasantry and the enclosure of common fields* (London, 1907), 267; (2) A. H. Johnson, *The disappearance of the small landowner* (London, 1909), 90; (3) W. E. Tate, *The English village community and the enclosure movements* (London, 1967), 88.

The Board of Agriculture, established in 1793, began at once to enquire into the condition of the waste lands, and each county report contained a chapter on 'Wastes'. Arthur Young summarised this information in 1795[1] and again in 1799.[2] These estimates were modified a little in a further report produced in 1808.[3] The total area of waste land was put at 7.8 million acres (6.2 in England and 1.6 in Wales), and its distribution among the counties is shown on Fig. 14. The overwhelming predominance of waste in those counties with much land over 800 feet above sea-level is very apparent. In the meantime, Sir John Sinclair had presented two reports in 1795 and 1797 on 'the means of promoting the cultivation and improvement of the waste, uninclosed, and unproductive lands of the kingdom'.[4] It was hoped that part at any rate might be turned into arable land, part into good grazing and part into woodland. But in spite of local changes, the uplands continued to be areas of rough grazing and peat bog. There were limits to 'the spirit of improvement' that so characterised the eighteenth century.

Although of little economic value, parts of the upland area were acquiring a new interest in the eyes of many travellers. The cult of the 'picturesque' which flourished in the latter part of the eighteenth century brought with it an appreciation of wild and rugged scenery. To the Lake District, in particular, came many writers and artists. The poet Thomas Gray had written a journal of his visit in 1769, and its publication in 1775 did much to make the district a fashionable tourist area. The first *Guide to the Lakes*, by Thomas West, appeared in 1778 and reached its seventh edition in 1799. By this time the district had been described by many others, including such well-known writers as William Gilpin, Thomas Pennant, Arthur Young and Mrs Ann Radcliffe.[5] But the writer who did most to give the Lake District a special place in English Literature was William Wordsworth, born in 1770 at Cockermouth nearby. His 'Guide to the Lakes' first appeared anonymously in 1810, and has been hailed by successive generations as a classic of geographical description.[6]

[1] A. Young, 'Waste lands, by estimation in Great Britain', *Annals of agriculture*, XXIV (1795), 10–17.

[2] A. Young, 'Waste lands', *Annals of agriculture*, XXXIII (1799), 12–59.

[3] *General report on enclosures drawn up by order of the Board of Agriculture* (London, 1808), 139–41.

[4] *Reports from Committees of the House of Commons*, IX (1803), 201–25.

[5] C. Hussey, 107, 126; E. W. Manwaring, 175, 181–3, 192–5; W. G. Collingwood, *Lake district history* (Kendal, 1928), 155–60.

[6] W. W. Merchant (ed.), *A guide through the district of the Lakes...by William Wordsworth* (London, 1951).

INDUSTRY

The industrial revolution

The term 'industrial revolution' was given currency by Arnold Toynbee, who placed the beginnings of the movement at about the year 1760.[1] Later writers, with thoughts of the continuity of history in mind, challenged the idea of any sudden and dramatic changes. Paul Mantoux, as early as 1906, held that 'in spite of the apparent rapidity of its development, the industrial revolution sprang from far-distant causes'.[2] The year 1660, rather than 1760, has been hailed as marking the turning point in economic growth and industrial expansion;[3] some writers have placed it even in the sixteenth century.[4] A number of studies of individual industries and individual regions have shown the continuity of eighteenth-century changes and their relation to those of the seventeenth century.[5] It would seem, as Herbert Heaton said in 1932, that 'a revolution which continued for 150 years and had been in preparation for at least another 150 years may well seem to need a new label'.[6]

The application of statistical enquiry to historical generalisation has produced more exact estimates of the period of greatest change. W. G. Hoffmann, in calculating the rate of growth of total industrial output from 1700 onwards, came to the conclusion that the year 1780 was 'the approximate date at which the annual percentage rate of industrial growth was first greater than 2, a level at which it remained for over a century' .The change was 'so definite that it clearly marks an epoch in the evolution of Britain's economy'.[7] T. S. Ashton also concluded that 'after 1782 almost every statistical series of production shows a sharp upward turn'.[8] W. W. Rostow advanced the view that the breakthrough, the

---

[1] A. Toynbee, *Lectures on the industrial revolution in England* (London, 1884).

[2] P. Mantoux, *The industrial revolution in the eighteenth century* (London, 1928), 25. English translation of French edition of 1906.

[3] C. Wilson, *England's apprenticeship, 1603–1763* (London, 1965), 185–205.

[4] E.g. J. U. Nef, 'The progress of technology and the growth of large-scale industry in Great Britain, 1540–1640', *Econ. Hist. Rev.*, v (1934), 3–24.

[5] E.g. A. P. Wadsworth and J. de L. Mann, *The cotton trade and industrial Lancashire, 1600–1780* (Manchester, 1931); W. H. B. Court, *The rise of the Midland industries* (Oxford, 1938).

[6] H. Heaton, 'The industrial revolution', *Encyclopedia of the Social Sciences*, VIII (New York, 1932), 5.

[7] W. G. Hoffmann, *British industry, 1700–1950* (Blackwell, Oxford, 1955), 30–2.

[8] T. S. Ashton, *An economic history of England: the 18th century* (London, 1955), 125.

'take-off into self-sustained growth', belonged in England to the years
1783–1802.[1] Others have viewed the acceleration as a two-phase process,
beginning in the 1740s with a 'considerably sharper upward trend in the
1780s and 1790s'.[2] Yet others have suggested modifications of these
dates.[3]

Not only the dates of 'the industrial revolution' but also its causes
have produced a variety of opinion. They have been viewed as connected
with agricultural change, with population growth, with the expansion
of trade, with increasing demand, with the lowering of the rate of
interest, with technological invention or with religious dissent. Clearly,
the process of growth was complex, and the search for any single group
of causes is fruitless. Many circumstances were involved, interrelated
maybe but varying in importance at different times.[4]

Deane and Cole found 'little evidence of growth in the first four
decades' of the eighteenth century.[5] To contemporaries it did not seem so.
Daniel Defoe in the 1720s saw, or seemed to see, rapid economic development: 'New discoveries in metals, mines, minerals; new undertakings
in trade; inventions, engines, manufactures, in a nation, pushing and
improving as we are: these things open new scenes every day, and make
England especially shew a new and different face in many places.'[6] To
the early years of the century belong the Newcomen engine (1705–6),
the smelting of iron by coke (1709), Kay's flying shuttle (1733), although
one must distinguish between invention and its use in economic enterprise.
Whatever the causes, the great period of technological change did not
come until after 1760. In addition to the inventions of Hargreaves (1764),
Arkwright (1769), Watt (1769), Crompton (1779) and Cort (1784), there
were many other innovations by forgotten men who improved one

---

[1] W. W. Rostow, 'The take-off into self-sustained economic growth', *Economic
Journal*, LXVI (1956), 25–48; *The stages of economic growth* (Cambridge, 1960); *The
economics of take-off into sustained growth* (London, 1963).

[2] P. Deane and W. A. Cole, 58 and 280; P. Deane and H. J. Habakkuk, 'The
take-off in Britain', being ch. 4 (63–82) of W. W. Rostow (1963).

[3] E.g. R. M. Hartwell, *The industrial revolution in England* (Hist. Assoc., London,
1966), 11.

[4] Convenient summaries may be found in the following: P. Deane, *The first
industrial revolution* (Cambridge, 1965); C. Wilson, *England's apprenticeship, 1603–
1763* (London, 1965); M. W. Flinn, *The origins of the industrial revolution* (London,
1966); R. M. Hartwell (ed.), *The causes of the industrial revolution in England* (London,
1967); R. M. Hartwell, *The industrial revolution and economic growth* (London, 1971).

[5] P. Deane and W. A. Cole, 280.

[6] Daniel Defoe, *Tour*, II, 133.

device or added to another. The number of patents sealed in each decade of the eighteenth century show the increase after 1760 and the acceleration after 1780.[1]

1700–9	22	1750–9	92
1710–19	38	1760–9	205
1720–9	89	1770–9	294
1730–9	56	1780–9	477
1740–9	82	1790–9	647

The interpretation of these figures, and the relationship between science and technology in general, have given rise to much discussion.[2] Many patents were of little or no value; others were followed by time-lags before they led to development; but at any rate, in T. S. Ashton's words, they 'may serve perhaps as a rough index of innovation'.[3]

Improvements and increased production were manifested in a whole range of miscellaneous industries – in the non-ferrous industries such as copper, brass, lead and tin; in the manufacture of sugar, candles, paper, soap and glass; in the making of pottery, when Josiah Wedgwood opened his works at Burslem in 1759; in brewing; in the chemical industries; and in salt-making, for rock salt had been discovered in 1670 during explorations for coal at a depth of about 100 feet near Northwich in Cheshire.[4] But the take-off into sustained growth between 1780 and 1800 was marked by outstanding developments in three sectors – the textile industry, the iron industry and the coal industry in association with the steam engine. Each of these three developments must be examined separately. Taken together they profoundly changed the material appearance of England.

The textile industries

Taking a broad view, the distribution of the woollen and worsted industries during the seventeenth and early eighteenth centuries was still

---

[1] B. R. Mitchell with P. Deane, 268.

[2] See the interesting collection of studies in A. E. Musson (ed.), *Science, technology, and economic growth in the eighteenth century* (London, 1972).

[3] T. S. Ashton, 'Some statistics of the industrial revolution in Britain', *The Manchester School*, XVI (1948), 214–34; the quotation is from the reprint of extracts in A. E. Musson (1972), 117.

[4] A. E. Musson and E. Robinson, *Science and technology in the industrial revolution* (Manchester, 1969); A. and N. L. Clow, *The chemical revolution* (London, 1952); L. Weatherhill, *The pottery trade and north Staffordshire, 1660–1760* (Manchester, 1971).

very much the same as in the later Middle Ages – that is they were carried on in most parts of the country, but pre-eminently in three districts, East Anglia, the West Country and Yorkshire. A picture of this distribution in the 1720s may be obtained from Daniel Defoe's *Tour* (Fig. 15). In East Anglia there were two main textile districts – north-east Norfolk and the Suffolk–Essex border. In the former, the weavers of Norwich employed 'all the country round in spinning yarn for them'; ᴸikewise in the latter district, the weavers of Colchester, Sudbury and other places were sustained by the spinning wheels of the villagers nearby. In the West Country there were a large number of towns 'principally employ'd in the clothing trade', and between them were 'innumerable villages, hamlets, and scattered houses, in which, generally speaking, the spinning work of all this manufacture is performed'. In Yorkshire, the industry was also dispersed over the countryside, several settlements merging into one another to give, in Defoe's words, the impression of 'one continued village' in the neighbourhood of Halifax.[1]

Some of the outlying textile centres declined during the seventeenth and eighteenth centuries. Salisbury and its woollen manufacture, for example, was said by Yarranton in 1677 to be 'much decayed of late years'; so was the industry of Worcester, Kidderminster and Bewdley,[2] and the textile workers of Reading were also reduced to 'a very small number' by 1695.[3] In Kent, Defoe tells us, the once 'very considerable cloathing trade' was 'quite decay'd'.[4] The same could be said of some other places. There were also changes within the three main textile districts themselves. The early product of the West Riding was a coarse cloth, but towards the end of the seventeenth century worsted cloth also began to be made there,[5] and the subsequent advance of the industry was reflected in the growth of Leeds, Bradford, Huddersfield, Wakefield and Halifax, all noted by Defoe.[6] By 1772, the value of the worsted cloth made in the West Riding equalled that made in Norwich and Norfolk generally.[7] Even so, the production of fine quality worsteds in the latter area was increasing most of the time, and absolute decline did not begin until the

[1] Daniel Defoe, *Tour*, I, 61, 17, 279–80; II, 194.

[2] A. Yarranton, *England's improvement by sea and land* (London, 1677), 207, 146, 162.

[3] W. Camden, *Britannia*, ed. by E. Gibson (London, 1695), 152.

[4] Daniel Defoe, *Tour*, I, 115.

[5] H. Heaton, *The Yorkshire woollen and worsted industries* (Oxford, 1920), 257, 263–8.   [6] Daniel Defoe, *Tour*, II, 185–204.

[7] J. James, *History of the worsted manufacture* (London, 1857), 285; E. Lipson, *The history of the woollen and worsted industries* (London, 1921), 241.

early decades of the nineteenth century.[1] To the south, however, the textile manufacture of the Suffolk–Essex towns and villages had definitely decreased before the middle of the eighteenth century. Philip Morant, the historian of Essex, said in 1748 that the trade of Colchester had 'removed in a great measure into the west and northern parts of this kingdom where provisions are cheaper, the poor more easily satisfied, and coals are very plentiful'.[2] West Country industry was also beginning to run down in the eighteenth century. Its serges could not stand competition from the Norwich 'stuffs', and unemployment began to appear in a number of centres about 1750 or so.[3] Then towards the end of the century, competition from Yorkshire began to be felt. J. Collinson, for example, the historian of Somerset, writing in 1791, could point to the decline of woollen manufacture in many places – Milverton, Yeovil, Taunton and others.[4]

There had long been some small-scale textile manufacturing on the western side of the Pennines. Woollens were made in the upland valleys of east Lancashire and linens on the plain to the west; the latter were originally based on locally grown flax but were relying on Irish yarn by the sixteenth century. In the years around 1600 or so, the making of fustian became established between the woollen and the linen districts in an intermediate belt running through Bolton and Blackburn.[5] Fustian, made of linen warp and cotton weft, had been introduced from the Continent as part of the 'new draperies' in the sixteenth century, but had never flourished in East Anglia. In Lancashire, on the other hand, the fustian area extended at the expense of the woollen area. Moreover, cotton yarn began to be used increasingly in the making of other types of cloth until cotton manufacture soon became an industry in its own right, and Lancashire cottons began to challenge imported cotton fabrics from India. Progress was steady but slow until about the middle of the seventeenth century, after which the industry began to develop much more rapidly.

[1] J. H. Clapham, 'The transference of the worsted industry from Norfolk to the West Riding', *Econ. Jour.*, XX (1910), 195–210.

[2] P. Morant, *The history and antiquities of Colchester* (London, 1748), 75.

[3] W. G. Hoskins, *Devon* (London, 1954), 128–9; E. A. G. Clarke, *The ports of the Exe estuary, 1660–1860* (Exeter, 1960), 102 *et seq.*; J. de La Mann, *The cloth industry in the west of England from 1640 to 1880* (Oxford, 1971), 32 *et seq.*

[4] J. Collinson, *The history and antiquities of the county of Somerset*, I (Bath, 1791), 13, 204, 226.

[5] A. P. Wadsworth and J. de L. Mann, *The cotton trade and industrial Lancashire, 1600–1780* (Manchester, 1931), 11–25. See also G. W. Daniels, *The early English cotton industry* (Manchester, 1920).

An important element in this growth after 1750 or so was a series of inventions which transformed the making of textiles. These inventions were as relevant to wool as to cotton, but they were earlier and more readily adopted by the latter industry. They may be summarised as follows:

(1) The speed of weaving was greatly increased by the invention of John Kay's flying shuttle, patented in 1733, and widely adopted in the 1750s and 1760s. It upset the balance between weaving and spinning in that the capacity of the greatly improved weaving looms exceeded the amount of yarn that was being produced.

(2) Successive improvements in spinning came from the spinning jennies of Lewis Paul (1738) and James Hargreaves (1764) and especially from the water-frame of Richard Arkwright (1769). Arkwright's machine took its name from the fact that it could be operated by water power; and it hastened the transition from domestic to factory spinning. Samuel Crompton's spinning mule of 1779 marked a further advance, and the rate of cotton spinning now outstripped that of weaving. Subsequent modifications adapted the spinning machines for other fibres such as wool and flax.

(3) An attempt to redress the balance between spinning and weaving was made by Edmund Cartwright, whose powered weaving loom was patented in 1785. Various difficulties, however, prevented the successful use of power-driven looms until the early years of the following century. In 1789 Cartwright patented a wool-combing machine, but this likewise did not come into general use until after 1800.

Not only wool and cotton but two other branches of the textile industry were also involved in the changes of the eighteenth century. As early as 1589 William Lee of Calverton near Nottingham had invented a mechanical knitting frame which imitated the movements of hand-knitting in the making of stockings, but it met with opposition and Lee took refuge in France. After his death in about 1610, his companions returned to Nottingham with their frame-knitting machines. The industry spread into the adjoining counties of Derby and Leicester, and there was also a substantial development of frame-knitting in London.[1] The London industry began to decline, but that of the Midlands, aided by cheaper wage rates, expanded during the eighteenth century. There were also a number of innovations. In 1730, Nottingham was first making cotton stockings from imported Indian yarn.[2] Lee's frame was improved, especially by Jedediah Strutt of

[1] E. Lipson, *The economic history of England*, II (2nd ed., London, 1934), 104–9.
[2] J. D. Chambers, *Nottinghamshire in the eighteenth century* (London, 1932), 95, 114.

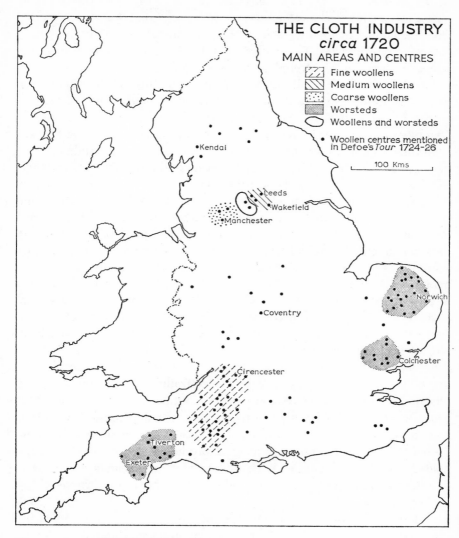

Fig. 15 The cloth industry *circa* 1720
 Based on: (1) Daniel Defoe, *A tour through the whole island of Great Britain* (London, 1724–7); (2) P. J. Bowden, *The wool trade in Tudor and Stuart England* (London, 1962), 49.

Belper who made ribbed stockings in 1758; and there was also 'a multiplicity of smaller technical innovations'.[1] Richard Arkwright, coming from Lancashire in 1768, erected his first cotton-spinning mill, driven by horses, at Nottingham. Then, after patenting his water-frame in 1769, he started his first water-powered factory at Cromford in Derbyshire in 1771. Others were built a few miles away at Belper and Milford before his return to Lancashire in 1777. By this time, the London industry was surpassed by that of the Midlands where it was marked by a degree of specialisation – woollen stockings at Leicester, cotton at Nottingham and silk at Derby.

In the meantime, there had been developments in the silk industry. Its growth had been helped by Flemish weavers in the late sixteenth century and by the application of the knitting frame in the manufacture of silk hose. Its expansion was accelerated after the Restoration in 1660, and then through the skill of Huguenot refugees from France after the Revocation of the Edict of Nantes in 1685. A considerable colony of Huguenots settled at Spitalfields in the east end of London, but there were also others at Coventry, Macclesfield, Norwich and elsewhere. The manufacture was extended after 1717 when John and Thomas Lombe introduced water-driven silk-making machinery from Italy, and set up a factory on the banks of the Derwent at Derby. This large establishment has been regarded as the precursor of the factory system, and it anticipated Arkwright's use of water power. 'Thomas Lombe was to silk what Richard Arkwright half a century later was to cotton.'[2] But the market for silk was limited by its luxury nature and by the difficulty of exporting it to the older silk-manufacturing centres on the Continent and elsewhere. The great expansion of the textile industries was in the manufacture of woollens and, more especially, that of cotton.[3] Indian calicoes and muslins had long been in demand in Britain, and the home-produced version found a ready-made market. In competition with other textiles such as linen and silk, the woollen and cotton markets soon widened to massive proportions.[4]

The various inventions, and the successive improvements upon them, had marked consequences not only for the growth of the textile industries but also for their geographical distribution. Spinning machines increasingly driven by water power were located along rivers, especially along the

[1] J. D. Chambers (1932), 35.

[2] E. Lipson, II (1934), 103.

[3] P. Deane (1965), 84–99.

[4] M. M. Edwards, *The growth of the British cotton trade, 1780–1815* (Manchester, 1967).

Table 1.4   *Water-driven spinning mills, 1788*

Lancashire	41	Hertfordshire	1
Derbyshire	22	Leicestershire	1
Nottinghamshire	17	Worcestershire	1
Yorkshire	11	Gloucestershire	1
Cheshire	8	Isle of Man	1
Staffordshire	7		
Westmorland	5	Flintshire	3
Berkshire	2	Pembrokeshire	1
Cumberland	1		
Surrey	1	Scotland	19

Source: Anon., *An important crisis in the callico and muslin manufactory of Great Britain, explained* (London, 1788).

steeply graded Pennine streams. As we have seen, the first was installed at Cromford in Derbyshire in 1771. A list of 1788 shows a total of 120 water-driven cotton-spinning mills in England, 4 in Wales and 19 in Scotland. There was a heavy concentration in Lancashire, with which may be grouped Cheshire, and there were appreciable numbers in Nottinghamshire, Derbyshire and Yorkshire.[1] It is not absolutely clear why the cotton industry should have been thus concentrated in Lancashire, although a number of reasons have been advanced – the linen–fustian background, the damp climate, the lime-free water and the availability of imports.

The water-power phase with its rural distribution was soon challenged by steam power.[2] The first steam engine to be used for cotton spinning seems to have been at Manchester in 1783 – at Richard Arkwright's cotton mill. A number of modified Savery and Newcomen engines were soon used to drive spinning mills in the 1780s and 1790s. In the meantime the first Boulton and Watt engine was used for spinning at Papplewick near Nottingham in 1785.[3] In the following year one was installed for the Cark Cotton Company in north Lancashire; the first in Manchester seems to have been installed in 1789, and in the following years its superiority began to be appreciated in spite of its expense. By 1800 there were 42

---

[1] *An important crisis in the callico and muslin manufactory of Great Britain, explained* (London, 1788). This anonymous and scarce pamphlet is discussed in P. Mantoux, *An industrial revolution in the eighteenth century* (London, 1928), 253–4; Mantoux, however, gives the table inaccurately.

[2] A. E. Musson and E. Robinson, 393–426.

[3] E. Baines, *History of the cotton manufacture in Great Britain* (London, 1835), 226.

Boulton and Watt engines employed in the Lancashire cotton industry.[1]
But they had not yet succeeded in replacing the older types, and, moreover,
many engineers pirated various features of Watt's patents to produce
their own engines. Boulton and Watt engines probably numbered not
more than one-third of the total steam engines in the county by 1800.
'Steam-powered mechanization was proceeding more rapidly in Lancashire in the late eighteenth century than has hitherto been supposed.'[2]
The application of power to weaving, however, was slow. Edmund
Cartwright patented a power loom in 1785. His small factory at Doncaster
in 1787 was worked at first by animals, and his attempt to introduce steam
power here (1789) and at Manchester (1791) was defeated largely owing
to the opposition of the weavers.[3] It was not until the early years of the next
century that power-driven weaving looms were successfully established.

The water-power phase in the woollen industry came later than in the
cotton industry; and it was of shorter duration because by the time that
machines were established in the 1790s, steam was the obvious source of
power. Thus the way was open for the full development of the factory
system, and for the close association of the textile industries with coalfields,
particularly with those of Lancashire and Yorkshire (Figs. 29 and 30).
The success of the Lancashire industry can be measured by the eightfold
increase in the import of raw cotton during 1780–1800.[4] Within a quarter
of a century or so, it had become one of the most important industries in
the country, and in the early years of the nineteenth century, the annual
value of its production was to outstrip that of the woollen industry. In
1795, the growth of the industry was described as 'perhaps absolutely
unparalleled in the annals of trading nations'.[5] W. W. Rostow has
viewed it as the 'original leading sector in the first take-off' for the
industrial revolution.[6]

The iron industry

In 1600 the most important iron-producing area was the Weald with 49
blast furnaces, but there were also eleven in the west Midlands, another

[1] J. Lord, *Capital and steam power* (London, 1923), 167–71.
[2] A. E. Musson and E. Robinson, 426.
[3] P. Mantoux, 247–8; E. Lipson (1921), 166.
[4] P. Deane and W. A. Cole, 183.
[5] J. Aikin, *A description of the country from thirty to forty miles around Manchester*
(London, 1795), 3.
[6] W. W. Rostow (1960), 53.

eight in Yorkshire and Derbyshire, and a few others scattered elsewhere.[1] Curiously enough, the traditional iron centre of the Forest of Dean lagged behind. The monopoly of the 'free miners' of the Forest had hindered the adoption of the blast furnaces, and the first was not erected until the 1590s; but others soon followed in the early decades of the next century.[2] In the meantime, here as elsewhere, the old-fashioned bloomeries were disappearing.

The available statistics are unreliable, but there seems to have been a decline in iron production between about 1620 and 1660, especially in the Weald. The traditional view was that this general decline continued for another hundred years,[3] but it has been argued that this was not so, judging by the erection of new furnaces and forges between 1660 and 1760 in areas almost entirely outside the Weald.[4] Even so, the growth in output must have been very limited, in view of the competition of cheap iron from abroad, particularly from Sweden. The older view also attributed the postulated decline to a scarcity of wood for charcoal,[5] but, again, it has been argued that the scarcity has been much exaggerated.[6] Ironworks were very selective in their use of timber; the best charcoal was made from coppice timber of 20 years or less, and systematic coppicing in the seventeenth and eighteenth centuries ensured the continuation of the industry.[7]

The distribution of the industry in the early eighteenth century can be seen from the list of furnaces and forges compiled by John Fuller in 1717.[8] His total of 60 furnaces and 114 forges is probably not complete, but it may well provide a fair picture (Fig. 16). Most furnaces were located

[1] H. R. Schubert, *History of the British iron and steel industry from c. 450 B.C. to A.D. 1775* (London, 1957), 175.

[2] *Ibid.*, 183–8.

[3] T. S. Ashton, *Iron and steel in the industrial revolution* (2nd ed., London, 1951), 13.

[4] M. W. Flinn, 'The growth of the English iron industry', *Econ. Hist. Rev.*, 2nd ser., XI (1959), 144–7.

[5] T. S. Ashton (1951), 15; H. R. Schubert, 218–22.

[6] G. Hammersley, 'The Crown Lands and their exploitation in the sixteenth and seventeenth centuries', *Bull. Inst. Hist. Research*, XXX (1957), 136–61; see also M. W. Flinn (1959), 148–53.

[7] H. R. Schubert, 222.

[8] E. W. Hulme, 'Statistical history of the iron trade of England and Wales, 1717–1750', *Trans. Newcomen Soc.*, IX (1929), 12–35; B. L. C. Johnson, 'The charcoal iron industry in the early eighteenth century', *Geog. Jour.*, CXVII (1951), 167–77; H. G. Roepke, *Movements of the British iron and steel industry – 1720 to 1951* (Urbana, Illinois, 1956).

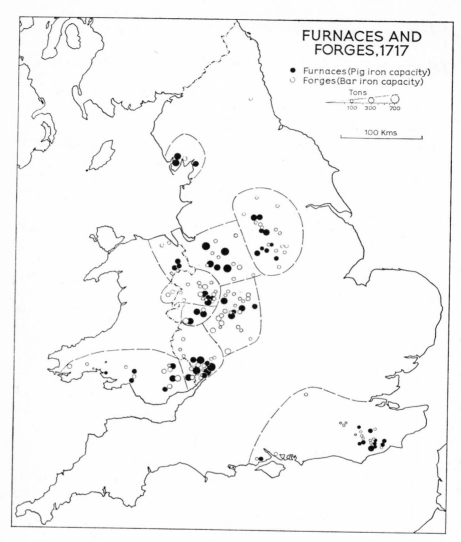

Fig. 16 Iron furnaces and forges, 1717

Based on: (1) E. W. Hulme, 'Statistical history of the iron trade of England and Wales, 1717–1750', *Trans. Newcomen Soc.*, IX (1930), 12–35; (2) B. L. C. Johnson, 'The charcoal iron industry in the early eighteenth century', *Geog. Jour.*, CXVII (1951), 168.

The areas are those named on Fig. 17.

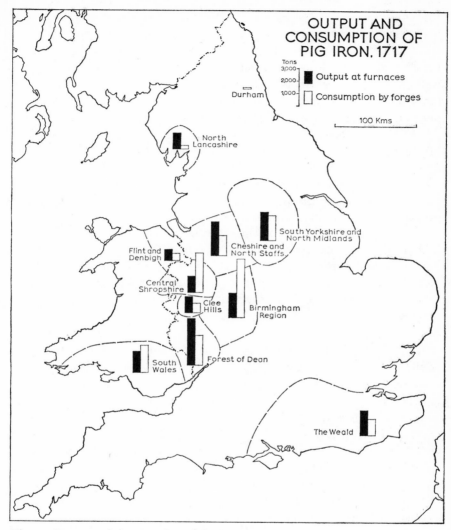

Fig. 17 Output and consumption of pig-iron in 1717
　　Based on B. L. C. Johnson, 'The charcoal iron industry in the early eighteenth
　　century', *Geog. Jour.*, CXVII (1951), 168.

fairly near supplies of iron ore, and, rivalling the Wealden ironstones, were now the Coal Measure ironstones of Yorkshire and Derbyshire, of Staffordshire and Shropshire, and of Monmouthshire and South Wales, and also the haematite areas of the Carboniferous Limestone in north Lancashire and the Forest of Dean itself. As well as ironstone and wood, water power for the furnace bellows and forge hammers was an important localising factor. Not all furnaces produced for local forges. Surpluses of high-quality pig-iron from the haematite areas of north Lancashire and the Forest of Dean were exported by sea and up the Severn to west Midland forges. The relative output and consumption of pig-iron, district by district, is shown on Fig. 17.

Many attempts were made to find an alternative to charcoal as a fuel in blast furnaces. The earliest patent for the use of coal in iron-making was granted as early as 1589. Others followed, among them being that granted in 1621 to Dud Dudley who claimed to have made iron of good quality with coal.[1] But no great advance was made until about 1709 when Abraham Darby was smelting with coke at Coalbrookdale in Shropshire. Not all types of coal were found to be suitable, and years of experiment followed before coke successfully and generally replaced charcoal. In 1760 there were only seventeen coke furnaces in blast in England and Wales (none in Scotland).[2] In the meantime another advance was made in the 1740s when Benjamin Huntsman, at Handsworth on the outskirts of Sheffield, devised a method of making good quality cast steel, but the great expansion in the use of steel had to await the inventions of the latter half of the nineteenth century.

It has been said that until 1775 the output of iron increased on average not more than one per cent per annum. 'The year 1775, in fact, marks more clearly than most dates selected as boundary-stones the end of one economic period and the beginning of another.'[3] About this time James Watt was developing an improved steam engine able to generate a strong blast and so increase the efficiency of smelting by coke.[4] The wider application of steam power not only opened up new possibilities for the manufacture of iron and ironwares, but, in turn, created a greater demand for them. Then, in 1783–4 Henry Cort patented processes which enabled high-grade wrought-iron to be made with coke. The forge-masters were now freed from their dependence upon wood, just as the furnace owners had been after 1709; not only was the charcoal-based industry finally outmoded,

[1] E. Lipson, II (1934), 159–60.   [2] H. R. Schubert, 332–3.
[3] T. S. Ashton (1951), 60.   [4] P. Deane (1965), 106.

but imported ore was no longer needed except for the manufacture of the best steel.[1]

In 1774 there were 31 coke furnaces in blast in Britain as a whole (including 5 Scottish). By 1790 there were 81 (including 12 Scottish) as compared with 25 charcoal furnaces (including 2 Scottish).[2] Cort's patent was confiscated in 1789, and the way was open for iron-masters to introduce improvements without having to pay royalties. Moreover, the continental wars from 1793 onwards provided a stimulus. By 1806 the coke furnaces in blast numbered 162 (including 18 Scottish) as compared with 11 charcoal furnaces 'still in use in different counties'.[3] Not only had the number of coke furnaces increased, but the output of each had become very much greater. The increase in the total annual output of pig-iron in tons between 1717 and 1806 was as follows, always remembering that the figures can only be approximate:[4]

	England and Wales	Scotland
1717	18,000	?
1788	61,000	7,000
1796	109,000	16,000
1806	235,000	23,000

The 1806 grand total of 258,000 included only 7,800 tons from charcoal furnaces. The transition from charcoal to coke was all but complete.

In the meantime there had also been profound geographical changes. The coke-based industry had become associated with the coalfields of the Midlands, Yorkshire, Derbyshire, South Wales and Scotland – those areas with Coal Measures that include ironstone as well as coal (Fig. 31). The coalfields of Northumberland and Durham and of south Lancashire, with little or no ironstone, on the other hand, had but few blast furnaces. The Wealden industry had all but disappeared; at Ashburnham the last furnace closed down about 1812 and the last forge about 1828.[5] The Forest of Dean industry survived longer, and the failing supply of

[1] T. S. Ashton (1951), 87 et seq.; A. Birch, The economic history of the British iron and steel industry, 1784–1879 (London, 1967), 22–44.

[2] H. Scrivenor, A comprehensive history of the iron trade (London, 1841), 359–61; H. R. Schubert, 333.

[3] H. Scrivenor, 97.

[4] H. Scrivenor, 57, 87, 95 and 97; W. E. Hulme, 22; T. S. Ashton (1951), 98.

[5] E. Straker, Wealden iron (London, 1931), 369; H. R. Schubert, 169, 366.

iron ore in the eighteenth century was made good by importation. Coke for smelting was not introduced until late in the eighteenth century. A few blast furnaces lingered on until the last was closed down about 1890.[1]

Even in the days of charcoal fuel, the coalfields had already attracted much iron manufacture. Coal Measure ironstone was available for the charcoal blast furnaces, and these produced pig-iron for the forges which in turn produced bar-iron for the smiths. Although not employed in smelting, coal was used by the smiths in the making of their wares. By the end of the seventeenth century the development of such activities was marked in three areas – the west Midlands, south Yorkshire and north Durham.

The west Midland smiths were already well known,[2] and in 1677 Andrew Yarranton described how the iron manufactures of Stourbridge, Dudley, Wolverhampton, Sedgley, Walsall and Birmingham were 'diffused all England over'.[3] Nails and edge-tools were of especial importance; guns and fire-arms increased the variety. The local iron was of low-grade quality, and the forges drew much of their supplies from elsewhere, especially from the Forest of Dean by way of the Severn;[4] the imbalance between furnaces and forges can be seen from Fig. 16. The introduction of brass in the eighteenth century gave promise of the remarkable diversification that came to be a feature of the metal trades of Birmingham – buttons, buckles, toys, jewellery and plated goods of all kinds.[5] The Soho Manufactory established by Matthew Boulton at Handsworth just outside Birmingham in 1761 soon achieved a national reputation as a 'nursery of ingenuity'.[6] After 1775, the partnership of Boulton and Watt at Soho resulted in the design and construction of steam engines which were to have so marked an effect upon the course of industrial change. To the west, in the Coalbrookdale area, the construction of the first iron bridge (across the Severn) in 1779 was a portent of things to come. A boat made of cast-iron plates was launched on the Severn in

---

[1] R. Jenkins, 'Iron-making in the Forest of Dean', *Trans. Newcomen Soc.*, V (1926), 42–65; F. T. Baber, 'The historical geography of the iron industry of the Forest of Dean', *Geography*, XXVII (1942), 54–62; C. Hart, *The industrial history of Dean* (Newton Abbot, 1971), 152.

[2] W. H. B. Court, 33 *et seq.*

[3] A. Yarranton, *England's improvement by sea and land* (London, 1677), 56–9.

[4] B. L. C. Johnson, 169.

[5] H. Hamilton, *The English brass and copper industries to 1800* (London, 2nd ed., 1967), 260–73.

[6] W. Hutton, *An history of Birmingham* (Birmingham, 1781), 271.

1787, and in the following year the Coalbrookdale works provided 40 miles of cast-iron pipes for the water supply of the city of Paris.[1]

A second important area of iron manufacturing was the south Yorkshire coalfield with local iron and wood and with power from the tributaries of the Don. Forges had long supplied iron for smiths and toolmakers in the neighbourhood of Sheffield, Rotherham and Barnsley. Continued progress is indicated by the Act of Parliament in 1624 which empowered the company of the Cutlers of Hallamshire to make bye-laws. Local iron was supplemented by imports, through Hull, from Sweden, and about 1724 Daniel Defoe could write of 'the continued smoke of the forges' at Sheffield which were always at work making 'all sorts of cutlery-ware'.[2] It was at Handsworth, just outside Sheffield, in the 1740s, that Benjamin Huntsman devised a method of making high-quality steel with coke, and nearby at Masborough another large ironworks was coming into existence.[3] Sheffield grew more slowly than Birmingham, but the variety of its products was almost as great, and included such articles as knives, shears, scissors and sickles.

A third iron manufacturing district – in north-east Durham – had different origins from those of the other two districts. There was hardly any ironstone in its Coal Measures, and no blast furnaces appear in lists of the eighteenth century. But there was wood and coal, and Newcastle was a centre for importing Swedish iron. It was at Sunderland in 1682 that Ambrose Crowley, a smith of Greenwich, established an ironworks with the aid of continental workmen; it was more economical to send iron to the north than to bring coal to the forges of the Weald.[4] In 1690, the factory was moved to Swalwell and Winlaton near Newcastle upon Tyne, and a variety of ironwork was produced in the eighteenth century – anchors, chains, nails, chisels, hammers, agricultural implements; Defoe in 1724 spoke of the considerable manufacture of hardware here 'lately erected after the manner of Sheffield'.[5] In 1770 Arthur Young

[1] P. Mantoux, 315.   [2] Daniel Defoe, *Tour*, II, 183.

[3] M. W. Flinn and A. Birch, 'The English steel industry before 1856, with special reference to the development of the Yorkshire steel industry', *Yorks. Bull. Econ. and Soc. Research*, VI (1954), 163–77; A. Raistrick and E. Allen, 'The south Yorkshire ironmasters (1690–1750)', *Econ. Hist. Rev.*, IX (1938–9), 168–85; A. Raistrick, 'The south Yorkshire iron industry, 1698–1756', *Trans. Newcomen Soc.*, XIX (1940), 51–86.

[4] M. W. Flinn: (1) 'Sir Ambrose Crowley, Ironmonger, 1658–1713', *Explorations in Entrepreneural history*, V (Cambridge, Mass., 1953), 162–80; (2) *Men of iron: the Crowleys in the early iron industry* (Edinburgh, 1962).

[5] Daniel Defoe, *Tour*, II, 252.

described the works as 'supposed to be the greatest manufactory of its kind in Europe'.[1] Whether this was true or not, it is clear that north-east Durham had become the scene of important and unusual activities.

Coalmining

The substitution of coal for wood as domestic fuel, begun in Tudor times, continued at an ever-increasing rate during the seventeenth century. Contemporary references bear witness to the widespread use of coal, and there was some working on almost every British coalfield. The total production in Britain in 1700 has been estimated at about 3 million tons, of which about 700,000 tons were produced in Scotland and Wales. By 1800, the total exceeded 10 million tons, including 2.4 million in Scotland and Wales.[2] Some coal from Northumberland and Durham was exported overseas, but the greater part went to swell the coastwise traffic to London and other ports of the east coast and the English Channel (Fig. 19). The smaller coalfields of the north-west and of Wales also shipped increasing quantities to Ireland and southwards to the English Channel and some-times even to London and beyond.[3] The increasing volume of coal was distributed inland from the coastal ports by river, by the Thames, the Severn, the Trent and other navigable waterways, and also by carts and pack-horses.[4] Coal from the Midland fields also went by inland waterways and by road. The development of a network of canals after 1760 greatly facilitated its wider distribution and transformed the possibilities for wider industrial change (Fig. 18).

Coal was being used not only as a domestic fuel but more and more for industrial purposes. By 1600 it had become 'almost the universal fuel for the innumerable lime kilns' that produced lime for mortar and for agri-culture.[5] It was also used in metal working of all kinds – iron, lead, copper and silver. It was taking the place of wood in the manufacture of salt, sugar and soap, in the making of glass, starch and candles, in the production of bricks and tiles, and in dyeing and brewing. After about 1709 it was used in the smelting, as well as in the forging, of iron. Later in the century,

[1] Arthur Young (1770), 13.

[2] J. U. Nef, *The rise of the British coal industry*, 2 vols. (London, 1932), I, 19–20.

[3] J. U. Nef, I, 90–1; T. S. Willan, *The English coasting trade, 1600–1750* (Man-chester, 1938), 55–69.

[4] J. U. Nef, I, 95–108; T. S. Willan, *River navigation in England, 1600–1750* (Oxford, 1936), 123–5.

[5] J. U. Nef, I, 205.

after the inventions of Henry Cort in 1783–4, 'integrated iron and coal concerns sprang up on all the more important coalfields'.[1]

A revolution in coalmining began early in the eighteenth century. Until then, the extraction of coal had been mainly by means of bell-pits and adits, although there were some shafts in Northumberland as deep as 400 feet.[2] The main difficulties in the development of mining operations were proper ventilation and adequate drainage. Underground workings were easily flooded, and various devices were used for pumping; but a great advance came with the inventions by Thomas Savery and Thomas Newcomen of their steam engines worked by coal. Savery was a Cornishman familiar with the difficulties of mining copper. His first patent was taken out in 1698, and he described it in a pamphlet of 1707 entitled 'The Miner's Friend'. Newcomen's engine appear in 1705–6, and was another advance. By 1720 it had been improved and was soon widely in use not only for mining but for pumping purposes generally. The new steam engine not only made deeper mining possible but was itself a great consumer of coal.

A further advance took place in 1769 when James Watt patented a much improved steam engine which worked on a different principle and used less coal. The patent was extended in 1775 for another 25 years, and in 1781 Watt took out another patent for rotary motion by which his steam engine ceased to be merely a pump but could be adapted for driving machinery of all kinds. 'From that moment the whole field of industry was thrown open to it.'[3] The adoption of the Boulton–Watt engine for pumping in coalmines was slow because the saving of coal was of little advantage to colliery owners.[4] It has been estimated that by 1800 about 500 Boulton and Watt engines were in use in England and Wales,[5] but this can only have been a fraction of the total number of steam engines at work.[6] In the first place, the old Savery and Newcomen engines had been adapted by John Smeaton and others for many general uses as well as for pumping, and some were 'still in use' in the 1820s.[7] In the second

[1] T. S. Ashton and J. Sykes, *The coal industry of the eighteenth century* (Manchester, 1929), 6.

[2] *Ibid.*, 10.

[3] P. Mantoux, 340.

[4] T. S. Ashton and J. Sykes, 40.

[5] H. W. Dickinson, *A short history of the steam engine* (2nd ed., ed. A. E. Musson, London, 1963), 88.

[6] A. E. Musson and E. Robinson, 393–426.

[7] J. Farey, *A treatise on the steam engine* (London, 1827), 422.

place, there were 'pirate engines' constructed by rival engineers who infringed Watt's patents, and whose activities gave rise to much litigation in the 1790s. Altogether, it has been estimated that about 1,200 steam engines were at work by 1800.[1] They were used in a wide variety of industries – not only in the textile, iron and mining industries but in corn mills, potteries, glassworks, breweries and for pumping in connection with canals and waterworks.[2] The application of the steam engine to traction and haulage was soon to come.

In this way, the preliminaries for the development of large-scale industry were over, and the age of steam had begun. But it must be emphasised that the coalfields were already centres of industry – of textile manufacturing associated with water power, and of metal working associated with the presence of iron as well as coal. But coal, by means of the steam engine, was now providing a source of power that dwarfed all other sources. It was capable of a thousand applications far outside the coalfields, but it was on those fields themselves that its effects were most dramatically to be seen. As Arthur Young wrote in 1791, 'all the activity and industry of this kingdom is fast concentrating where there are coal pits'.[3]

TRANSPORT AND TRADE

Transport by road

An Act of Parliament in 1555 had made each parish responsible for the upkeep of the roads within its boundaries.[4] Various other acts in the early half of the seventeenth century attempted to make this system of maintenance more effective; but, in the absence of any central organisation, very little was achieved; moreover, the methods of making and repairing roads were very primitive. In the meantime, the growing volume of traffic increased the need for improvement, particularly for the improvement of the roads leading from London. A new step was taken in 1663

[1] J. R. Harris, 'The employment of steam power in the eighteenth century', *History*, LII (1967), 131–48.

[2] J. Lord, 175.

[3] A. Young, *Annals of agriculture*, XVI (London, 1791), 552.

[4] General accounts include: (1) S. and B. Webb, *English local government: the story of the king's highway* (London, 1913); (2) W. T. Jackman, *The development of transportation in modern England*, 2 vols. (Cambridge, 1916); W. Albert, *The turnpike road system in England, 1663–1840* (Cambridge, 1972). For a convenient short account, see B. F. Duckham, *The transport revolution, 1750–1830* (Hist. Assoc., London, 1967).

when an act enabled the justices of the three counties of Hertford, Hunting-don and Cambridge to levy tolls for the repair of the section of the Great North Road that passed through them; the first tollgate or turnpike was erected at Wadesmill to the north of Ware in Hertfordshire. The act was intended to continue in force for eleven years, and in 1664–5 this term was extended to twenty-one years for Hertfordshire only. Both acts, however, were allowed to expire and the tollgates were removed; before the end of the century the road had again become 'dangerous and impassible'.[1]

The setback was only temporary. Within a few years a new system of maintenance by which those who used roads were made to pay for their upkeep was introduced. Tollgates were again authorised in 1695 on a stretch of the London–Harwich road. The increasing awareness of the importance of roads in the national life had already been indicated by the publication in 1675 of John Ogilby's *Britannia*, which set out the principal roads of England and Wales in strips or bands, incorporating notes, on either side about the roads themselves and various features to be en-countered along them. Its 102 plates were the result of a systematic measurement 'by the wheel', and it became the prototype for a large number of road books.

By 1700 only seven turnpike acts had been passed, but during the next fifty years they averaged nearly ten a year. From 1750 onwards, interest and activity greatly increased, and the average was soon 40 acts a year, reaching over 50 a year in the decade 1790–1800. The typical turnpike trust was small in scope, intended to meet a local need. It only supple-mented, and did not replace, the parish system of maintenance which remained in force until 1835. The new turnpike trusts were particularly numerous in the rapidly growing industrial areas – in Lancashire and the West Riding, in Midland counties such as Warwickshire and Staffordshire, and in the counties around London. The trusts frequently met with opposition, and bands of raiders at night destroyed many tollgates and burned the houses of the toll collectors.

Daniel Defoe in the 1720s devoted much space to the new roads. Turnpikes, he said, were 'very great things'. Roads formerly dangerous and scarce passable in winter had become firm, safe and 'easy to travellers, and carriages as well as cattle'. The effect upon trade was frequently 'incredible'. Some roads were 'exceedingly throng'd' with 'a vast number of carriages' carrying malt, barley, grain or cheese, with 'infinite droves of black cattle, hogs and sheep', and with pack-horses, mail, and ordinary

[1] W. T. Jackman, I, 63.

'travellers on horseback'. But much remained to be done, and Defoe dwelt at length upon the horrors of 'the deep clays' of some Midland counties where chalk or stones were not available for repairs. Stretches of roads in the Weald were also very bad.[1]

The evidence for the latter part of the eighteenth century varies. In 1767, Henry Homer could say; 'It is probable that there is no one circumstance which will contribute to characterize the present age to posterity so much as the improvements which have been made in our public roads.'[2] On the other hand, there were often complaints about this or that stretch of road, especially about their condition in winter. Arthur Young, travelling in the 1760s and 1770s, described some stretches, even of turnpike roads, as terrible, infamous or execrable.[3] Many trusts gave poor service and they all suffered from the lack of a central administration.

It must be emphasised that from a technical point of view, turnpikes marked no advance. Roads were still made by piling up loose material, and there was no attempt to provide a firm well-drained basis for the road surface. In order to prevent the formation of deep ruts, various acts tried to enforce the use of broad wheels, and some of this legislation was consolidated in the General Highway Acts of 1766 and 1773. But by this time the technique of road-making was beginning to improve. John Metcalfe (1717–1810) was one of the first engineers to pay attention to solid foundations and to drainage in the making of roads. Thomas Telford (1757–1834) and J. L. McAdam (1756–1836) followed, and the name of the latter has been preserved in the word macadam. Better coach design helped, and the speed of coach travel was improved. The journey from London to York took four days in 1754 (as it had done in 1706) but this was reduced to two days by 1774; similar improvements took place on other routes. John Palmer in 1784 persuaded the government to send the royal mail by coach, at first between London and Bristol; and the new mail coaches served as incentives for improved passenger services. Bridge-building, too, increased the speed of movement. Before 1750, large rivers were usually crossed by fords and ferries, but the early civil engineers were also bridge-builders, and in this connection must be mentioned not

---

[1] Daniel Defoe, *Tour*, II, 117–32.

[2] H. Homer, *An enquiry into the means of preserving and improving the publick roads* (Oxford, 1767), 3.

[3] E.g. A. Young (1768), 72, 90, 111, 112, 211. For the variety of opinion, see the anthology of eighteenth-century extracts in C. W. Scott-Giles, *The road goes on* (London, 1946), 104–44.

only Telford but John Smeaton (1724–92), and John Rennie (1761–1821). The first iron bridge, built across the Severn by John Wilkinson and Abraham Darby in 1779, pointed the way to further possibilities.[1]

Transport by water

In spite of these improvements there were limits to the possibilities of moving heavy or bulky goods by road. It has been said that 'if Britain had had to depend on her roads to carry her heavy goods traffic the effective impact of the industrial revolution might well have been delayed until the railway age'.[2] There were, however, other means of transport available. It has been estimated that in the first half of the seventeenth century there were at least 685 miles of navigable rivers, including the great arteries of the Thames, the Severn, the Trent, the Yorkshire Ouse and the Great Ouse.[3] But rivers were often obstructed, they were subject to changes of level, and many stretches were unnavigable. The example of the Netherlands and the increasing traffic of bulky goods were in men's minds, and Acts of Parliament for the improvement of various stretches of river became increasingly frequent after 1660. Pamphleteers such as Andrew Yarranton advocated making 'rivers navigable in all places where art can possibly effect it'.[4] The Aire and Calder navigation was improved primarily for the Yorkshire woollen industry about 1700. Shortly after this, the Weaver was improved with the Cheshire salt trade in mind, and the Don was improved for the Sheffield steel manufacture.[5] Many other streams were improved during these years. T. S. Willan estimated that the mileage of navigable rivers increased from at least 685 miles in 1660 to at least 960 in 1700 and to about 1,160 miles in 1726 or so (Fig. 18).[6]

The improvement of river channels led naturally to the possibility of making new ones.[7] The idea of connecting the Severn and the Thames, and so facilitating the movement of coal from the Forest of Dean, was mooted several times in the seventeenth century, by Thomas Proctor in 1610, by John Taylor in 1641, and by others. Francis Mathew, who took up the idea in 1655, also envisaged the systematic joining of other rivers, of the Warwickshire Avon with the Welland, and of the Suffolk Waveney with the Trent and the Yorkshire Ouse by various links. In spite of many

[1] A. Raistrick, *Dynasty of iron founders* (London, 1953), 193–207.
[2] P. Deane (1965), 73.
[3] T. S. Willan (1936), 133; W. T. Jackman, 1, chs. 3 and 5.
[4] A. Yarranton, *England's improvement by sea and land* (London, 1677), 7 and 64–6.
[5] T. S. Willan (1938), 136.   [6] *Ibid.*, 133.   [7] T. S. Willan (1936), 7–10.

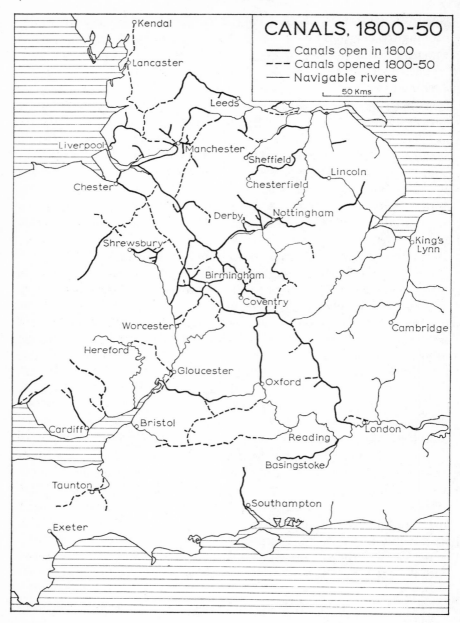

Fig. 18 Canals and waterways, 1800–50
Based on C. Hadfield, *British canals: an illustrated history* (2nd ed., Newton Abbot, 1966).
See also Fig. 44, p. 205 below.

pamphlets and much parliamentary activity, work was confined to improving old channels rather than making new ones until well on into the eighteenth century.

The canal age is generally regarded as beginning in 1761 with the opening of a canal connecting the coalmines at Worsley with Manchester. It crossed the Irwell by an aqueduct forty feet high, and was made for the Duke of Bridgewater by the engineer James Brindley; the price of coal in Manchester was immediately halved. Other canals soon followed in the 1760s and 1770s, not only in Lancashire but in the Midlands and elsewhere. The rate of construction slowed down during the recession associated with the American War of Independence (1775–83), but it started up again in the 1780s only to become greater than ever. The years 1792–3 saw a 'canal mania'. Speculation was rife, and many schemes remained only on paper.

Within thirty years or so inland transportation in England had been transformed (Fig. 18). Birmingham became the centre of a network of waterways. The Mersey was linked to the Severn in 1772; the Trent to the Mersey in 1777; the Severn to the Thames in 1789; the Mersey to the Trent and the Thames in 1790. Canals crossed the Pennines along three different routes. Liverpool, Hull, Birmingham, Bristol and London were linked together. The connection between London and the Midlands was improved by the making of the Grand Junction Canal in 1793–1805. So far as can be calculated, the cost of transport by canal was one quarter to one half that by road.[1] The easy transport of coal was now possible and the way was clear for the development of widespread industrial changes. Inland navigation also played its part in the agricultural improvement of the age by making possible the cheap transport of lime, manure and grain. It also carried building materials to expanding towns.

There was also another form of water transport of vital importance in the expanding economy of the age – coastwise shipping. Adam Smith could point out in 1776 that over the same period six or eight men, 'by the help of water carriage, can carry and bring back the same quantity of goods between London and Edinburgh, as fifty broad-wheeled waggons, attended by a hundred men, and drawn by four hundred horses'.[2] The Port Books reveal how varied and how widespread was the coastal traffic of the age. The commodities included butter, cheese, wool, cloth, salt, iron, glass,

[1] W. T. Jackman, II, 724–9.

[2] Adam Smith, *An enquiry into the nature and causes of the wealth of nations* (London, 1776), Book I, ch. 3.

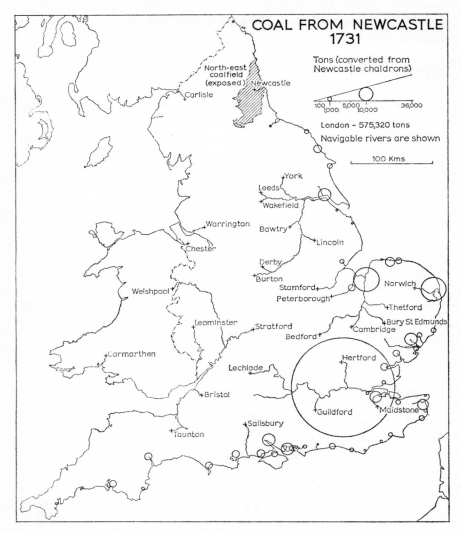

Fig. 19 Coastwise shipment of coal from Newcastle in 1731
    Based on: (1) T. S. Willan, *The English coasting trade, 1600–1750* (Manchester,
    1938), 211. The figures come from P.R.O. Exchequer K.R. Port Books 23617,
    and are for the period Christmas 1730 to Christmas 1731; (2) T. S. Willan,
    River navigation in England, 1600–1750 (Oxford, 1936), map 3.

timber and, above all, grain and coal. The London trade towered above that of any other port, but a multitude of substantial ports and small harbours also traded with one another as T. S. Willan's account so well shows.[1] Ships increased in size, and tonnage increased in amount. Cargoes of coal in three-masted square-rigged ships from Newcastle dominated the trade of the east-coast ports, and extended far along the south coast where they encountered competition from South Wales (Fig. 19). The import of coal into London rose from about 74,000 tons in 1605 to nearly half a million by 1700 and to over 1.4 million tons by 1800.[2] During these years, civil engineers were at work transforming estuaries and river moorings into docks and harbours. England's first wet dock was opened at Rotherhithe in 1700; the second was opened at Liverpool in 1715, and the third at Bristol shortly after.[3] Others followed. John Rennie (1761–1821) alone was involved in over seventy harbour schemes.[4]

Overseas trade

The improvement of harbours and the growth of ports reflected, to a great extent, the increase in England's overseas trade.[5] In 1600 English trade was almost entirely with Europe, and varieties of woollen cloth accounted for some 80% of the total exports by value. The main imports were wine from France, linen and metal-ware from central Europe via the Netherlands, together with flax, hemp, iron and timber from the Baltic lands, and cotton, raisins, dyestuffs and silks from those of the Mediterranean. After the Civil War, this pattern was transformed so much that the years 1660–1760 witnessed what has been called a 'commercial revolution', which took place in spite of, and in some ways as a result of, the many maritime wars of the age.

[1] T. S. Willan, *The English coasting trade, 1600–1750* (Manchester, 1938).

[2] J. U. Nef, II, 381–2; T. S. Ashton and J. Sykes (1929), 249–51.

[3] A. F. Williams, 'Bristol port plans and improvement schemes of the 18th century', *Trans. Bristol and Gloucs. Archaeol. Soc.*, LXXXI (1963).

[4] C. T. G. Boucher, *John Rennie, 1761–1821: the life and work of a great engineer* (Manchester, 1963).

[5] For general accounts see: (1) W. E. Minchinton (ed.), *The growth of English overseas trade in the seventeenth and eighteenth centuries* (London, 1969); (2) R. Davis, *The rise of the English shipping industry in the seventeenth and eighteenth centuries* (London, 1962). There is a convenient summary in R. Davis, *A commercial revolution* (Hist. Assoc., London, 1967). For statistics of trade, see G. N. Clark, *Guide to English commercial statistics, 1697–1782* (London, 1938), and E. B. Schumpeter, *British overseas trade statistics, 1697–1808* (Oxford, 1960).

Table 1.5   *Foreign trade, 1700–98*

(a) Totals in £000s

	England and Wales			Great Britain	
	1700–1	1750–1	1772–3	1772–3	1797–8
Imports	5,819	7,856	12,430	13,588	23,903
Domestic exports	4,468	9,123	9,739	10,195	18,301
Re-exports	2,123	3,428	5,802	6,932	11,802

(b) Geographical distribution (in percentages for each group)

	England and Wales			Great Britain	
	1700–1	1750–1	1772–3	1772–3	1797–8
Total imports from:					
Europe	61.5	46.5	34.6	34.2	29.3
Ireland etc.	4.9	8.8	10.5	10.6	13.1
North America	6.4	11.2	11.6	14.5	7.1
West Indies	13.5	18.9	24.8	23.7	25.0
East India	13.3	14.0	17.7	16.2	24.2
Africa	0.4	0.5	0.6	0.6	0.3
The Fisheries	—	0.1	0.2	0.2	1.0
Domestic exports to:					
Europe	82.1	69.4	39.9	39.2	21.1
Ireland etc.	3.2	7.6	9.4	9.9	9.0
North America	5.7	10.7	25.3	26.0	32.2
West Indies	4.6	4.9	12.0	12.0	25.2
East India	2.6	6.4	8.4	8.1	9.0
Africa	1.8	1.0	5.0	4.8	3.5
The Fisheries	—	—	—	—	—
Re-exports to:					
Europe	77.8	62.1	63.0	65.4	77.5
Ireland etc.	7.5	17.7	19.0	18.2	10.9
North America	5.0	11.2	9.0	8.7	3.1
West Indies	6.2	4.1	2.9	2.5	4.1
East India	0.5	2.0	1.2	1.0	0.6
Africa	3.0	2.9	4.9	4.1	3.7
The Fisheries	—	—	—	—	0.1

(Ireland etc. included Ireland, the Isle of Man and the Channel Islands. The Fisheries included Greenland, Iceland and the Northern and Southern Fisheries; East India implied Asia.)

Source: Calculated from P. Deane and W. A. Cole, *British economic growth, 1688–1959* (Cambridge, 2nd ed., 1967), 87.

Not only did English overseas trade greatly expand but its character fundamentally changed. To Europe now went a more diversified range of goods, but in 1750 woollens still accounted for about 46% of English-produced exports by value. By the end of the eighteenth century this share had fallen to 29%, but the export of cotton yarn and fabrics had grown from almost nothing to 24%. In return, the various parts of Europe continued to supply their different traditional products.

The outstandingly new feature of the commercial revolution was the trade with tropical lands and the development of a great English re-export trade. From the West Indies came such products as sugar, cotton and rum; and from the Middle East and Far East came tea, coffee, spices, silks and calicoes. A large part of these arrived in Britain only to be exported. Woollen goods could hardly feature in the return trade to these warm lands. To West Africa went weapons, metal goods and spirits in exchange for slaves, ivory and gold. The slaves were sold in the West Indies in return for tropical products; the ivory and gold dust went to the East in return for its products that, from the mid-seventeenth century onwards, included tea. There was also a growing varied trade with the mainland of North America. Tobacco, rice, indigo, cotton, furs and timber came in return for slaves and manufactured goods.

Something of this growing, and increasingly intricate, international network of trade can be seen from table 1.5. During the eighteenth century, re-exports came to form a large part of English overseas commerce to the great advantage of the English shipbuilding industry. This entrepôt trade lay behind the growth of Liverpool, Bristol and other ports and also behind the growth of London and its rise to be the financial centre of the world. The changes were also reflected in the general life of eighteenth-century England – in such things as the coffee-house, the drinking of tea and chocolate, the consumption of sugar and the making of mahogany furniture.

TOWNS AND CITIES

In spite of changes during the seventeenth century, the five largest towns (London apart) in the early years of the eighteenth century were still the same as in 1600 – Norwich, York, Bristol, Newcastle and Exeter; each seems to have had between ten and twenty thousand inhabitants. Daniel Defoe in the 1720s, however, could speak of some towns 'lately encreas'd in trade and navigation, wealth, and people, while their neighbours decay', and he had much to say about the rise or decline of individual towns.

Liverpool, he wrote, was 'one of the wonders of Britain' and was 'visibly' increasing in size. Manchester, too, was 'much encreased within these thirty or forty years'. Sheffield now had 'at least as many, if not more people in it than the city of York'; Coventry was 'a large and populous city'; so were Leeds and Leicester. Hull was a substantial centre of commerce, especially for the woollen goods of the West Riding. As well as Newcastle, Sunderland nearby, and Whitehaven[1] in the north-west had grown to be very considerable 'of late' by reason of the coal trade. Yarmouth, King's Lynn and Portsmouth were also thriving ports.[2] Defoe did not mention Birmingham but we know from other sources that by the 1720s it had grown tenfold since the mid-sixteenth century to over 15,000 people,[3] an increase that was helped by immigrants from the parishes around, particularly from those to the west.[4]

By the end of the eighteenth century, there had been greater and accelerating changes (see table 2.2, p. 159). Bristol alone kept its place among the first five. Although not serving a large industrial area, it had a wide agricultural hinterland and a variety of local manufactures such as soap, glass and sugar. Its coastwise trade was considerable, and its overseas connections were wide – with Ireland, Europe, the New World and Africa. Sugar, rum and tobacco became important imports and it also benefited from the slave trade. By 1801 its population had become over 60,000.[5] Norwich, it is true, had more than doubled in size since 1600 but it was no longer the largest provincial city.[6] Exeter and York had grown more slowly and now lagged behind with only about 16,000 to 17,000 inhabitants apiece. The old woollen towns of East Anglia and the West Country had been far outstripped.

The new rising centres were in the developing industrial areas. The population of Manchester–Salford had been about 12,000 or so in Defoe's day; it rose to about 30,000 by 1775 and to 84,000 in 1801. Around

[1] J. E. Williams, 'Whitehaven in the eighteenth century', Econ. Hist. Rev., 2nd ser., VIII (1955–6), 393–404.

[2] Daniel Defoe, Tour, I, 43; II, 255–6, 261–2, 183, 83, 204, 88, 242, 273; I, 65–7, 73, 136–8.

[3] M. J. Wise and B. L. C. Johnson in M. J. Wise (ed.), Birmingham and its regional setting (Birmingham, 1950), 174.   [4] R. A. Pelham, 45–80.

[5] W. E. Minchinton, 'Bristol – metropolis of the west in the eighteenth century', Trans. Roy. Hist. Soc., 5th ser., IV (1954), 69–89.

[6] P. Corfield, 'A provincial capital in the late seventeenth century: the case of Norwich', being ch. 8 (pp. 263–310) in P. Clark and P. Slack (eds.), Crisis and order in English towns, 1500–1700 (London, 1972).

Manchester–Salford, smaller centres were also growing. Oldham, for example, in 1760 was a village of not more than 400 inhabitants. The earliest factories were built there about 1776–8, and by 1801 its population had grown to about 12,000. The story of places like Bolton, Bury, Stockport and Wigan was similar.[1] It is not easy to be precise about the size of some of these places because their very large parishes included a number of separate townships, but a number of townships themselves had populations of 10,000 and over by 1801; they were large industrial villages which had yet to become corporate boroughs. Nearby, the port of Liverpool, with under 10,000 inhabitants in the 1720s, had increased to 78,000 by 1801. Its growth reflected that of its hinterland. Its exports were coal, salt and manufactured goods; and it imported raw materials such as cotton and sugar. Like Bristol it had a considerable coastwise trade and connections with Ireland and Europe. It also benefited from the notorious 'triangular trade' – exchanging goods for slaves in West Africa, selling them in the West Indies, and returning home with raw materials.[2] By the end of the eighteenth century it was larger than Bristol, and had supplanted it as the main port of the west.

Across the Pennines, Defoe had mentioned the 'vast cloathing trade' of five towns in particular – Leeds, Halifax, Bradford, Huddersfield and Wakefield.[3] Easily the largest was Leeds with some 12,000 people, more than Manchester. Its further growth was relatively slow; it seems to have had only 17,000 in 1775, but in the 1790s its rate of growth accelerated to produce, in 1801, just over 31,000, or much more if the townships within its parish are included.[4] The other four towns still had under 10,000 inhabitants each, but this is misleading because with their subsidiary townships they formed even more than in Defoe's day 'one continued village'.[5] To the east, Hull, with its first tidal basin opened in 1778, had reached 30,000 by 1801.[6] To the south, Birmingham had passed the 70,000 mark, and nearby were the lesser centres of Dudley, with just over 10,000 inhabitants, and Wolverhampton with about 13,000; but again the precise population assigned to each depends upon what townships are included; all were

[1] P. Mantoux, 367–8.
[2] F. E. Hyde, 'The growth of Liverpool's trade, 1700–1950', in W. Smith (ed.), *A scientific survey of Merseyside* (Liverpool, 1953), 148–63.
[3] Daniel Defoe, *Tour*, II, 187.
[4] P. Mantoux, 369.
[5] Daniel Defoe, *Tour*, II, 194.
[6] W. G. East, 'The port of Kingston-upon-Hull during the industrial revolution', *Economica*, XI (1931), 190–212.

joined by a web of iron-working villages into a large built-up area. In the same way the adjoining parishes and townships of the Potteries (which much later became the borough of Stoke-on-Trent) accounted for a population of about 28,000. There were also other growing centres becoming as obvious in the England of 1801 as they were important in its economy. Nottingham, with silk and hosiery, and Sheffield with cutlery, had each grown to about 30,000 inhabitants. Coventry and Leicester had over 16,000 apiece. The north-east, in spite of its long history of coalmining, was still very rural in character. Apart from Newcastle with about 28,000, Gateshead on the opposite bank of the Tyne had another 9,000; to the south, at the mouth of the Wear, was Sunderland with about 12,000 people.

Along the south coast, many small ports had long histories of coastwise and cross-Channel trade; and, in the eighteenth century, some benefited greatly from the growing trade with North America and the West Indies. Plymouth and Portsmouth also became naval centres of critical importance during the maritime wars with Holland and France in the seventeenth and eighteenth centuries. With their harbours and arsenals and dockyards they grew by 1801 to places among the ten largest provincial towns in the kingdom – Plymouth with 43,000 people and Portsmouth with 32,000. There were also naval centres along the Thames estuary, and, among these, Chatham, with its rope-walk, mast-yard and anchor works, was the largest in 1801 with 11,000. At this time, Dover, well placed as a packet station for the Continent, had grown to 15,000 people.

Centres of growth were not limited to ports and industrial areas. Many market and county towns showed a modest growth, especially towards the end of the eighteenth century, as a result partly of improving communications or partly of some local advantage, but there were not many with populations above 5,000 by 1801. One category of growing centres must be mentioned because it constituted a new element in the urban scene, and had considerable potentiality for the future – that of inland spas and seaside resorts.[1] Doctors in the sixteenth and seventeenth century were beginning to emphasise the use of waters for medicinal and curative purposes. After the Restoration in 1660, places with mineral springs began

---

[1] E. W. Gilbert, 'The growth of inland and seaside health resorts in England', *Scot. Geog. Mag.*, LV (1939), 16–35; E. W. Gilbert, *Brighton, old ocean's bauble* (London, 1954); J. A. Patmore, 'The spa towns of Britain', being ch. 2 (pp. 47–69) of R. P. Beckinsale and J. M. Houston (eds.), *Urbanization and its problems* (Oxford, 1968).

to assume a more prominent position, not only as places of medical treatment but as centres of fashion. The springs of Bath had been known in Roman times, and they began to attract attention once more in Tudor and Stuart times. Then, after the Restoration, Charles II and his court went there in 1663 and the way was prepared for the glory of the eighteenth century. The physician Dr Oliver, the architects John Wood (father and son) and the man of fashion Richard (or Beau) Nash, between them raised Bath to its pre-eminent position. Other inland resorts with springs were soon following this example – Harrogate, Epsom, Buxton, Cheltenham, Tunbridge Wells and others. Springs had been discovered at Scarborough in 1620 but its future was to be mainly bound up with sea-bathing. The practice was already common when, in 1750, Dr Richard Russell published his famous treatise on the curative properties of sea water. Soon, the inland spas were being rivalled by the coastal resorts. The Prince of Wales (afterwards George IV) began to visit Brighton in 1783; and George III began to visit Weymouth in 1789. Other seaside places were also attracting visitors – Margate and Worthing among them. All, whether inland or coastal, began to exhibit certain common architectural features such as crescents, terraces, promenades and assembly rooms. By the end of the century, Bath with its surrounding parishes, included some 32,000 people. Brighton and Scarborough had about 7,000 inhabitants each. The others were smaller, but they were to grow greatly in the nineteenth century.

In a category by itself stood London, so much larger than any other town in the country. Its exact size is a matter for argument, and any figures can convey only orders of magnitude. By 1600 it had expanded beyond the city walls and may have comprised some 250,000 people.[1] It was thus about sixteen times larger than Norwich, the greatest provincial city. It continued to grow until at the time of the Restoration in 1660 it may have included 460,000 people. The built-up area was now extending westwards over Covent Garden and Lincoln's Inn Fields. The plague of 1665 claimed perhaps as many as 100,000 victims, and, in the following year the Great Fire turned three-quarters of the old city within the walls into an expanse of smoking rubble. But these were only temporary checks. The speed of rebuilding was as remarkable as it was beneficial.[2] Houses were now of brick and stone; streets were wider; paving and drainage were better; and St Paul's Cathedral was completed in 1710. In the meantime, the

[1] N. G. Brett-James, *The growth of Stuart London* (London, 1935), 496–512.
[2] T. F. Reddaway, *The rebuilding of London after the Great Fire* (London, 1940).

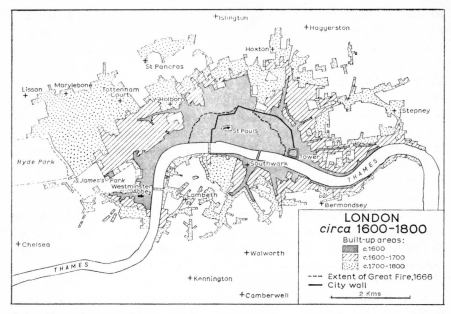

Fig. 20 London, 1600–1800
Based on: (1) N. G. Brett-James, *The growth of Stuart London* (London, 1935), maps opposite pp. 78 and 494; (2) T. Milne, *Plan of the cities of London and Westminster, circumjacent towns and parishes etc, laid down from a trigonometrical survey taken in the years 1795–1799* (London, 1800).

expansion westward had continued; the built-up areas of London and of Westminster were no longer connected only by the Strand along the north bank of the Thames, but also by the built-up area of the 'West End' around Piccadilly and St James's. The total population of this enlarged area in 1700 was over 600,000; and, as deaths greatly exceeded births, it had grown largely as a result of immigration.[1] London in its widest sense had outstripped Paris and had become the most populous unit in Europe.

To Daniel Defoe, in the 1720s, it was 'a prodigy of buildings' with 'new squares and new streets rising up every day'. Villages that had formerly stood in the country were now joined together by 'continued buildings'.[2] By 1750 its population had reached about 675,000. Within

[1] M. D. George, *London life in the eighteenth century* (London, 1930), 24 and 329–30; P. E. Jones and A. V. Judges, 'London population in the late seventeenth century', *Econ. Hist. Rev.*, VI (1936), 45–63. See also J. Summerson, *Georgian London* (London, revised ed., 1970).   [2] Daniel Defoe, *Tour*, I, 314–15.

this extensive built-up area there were many separate parts and a fairly marked differentiation into business, legal, industrial, residential and government areas.[1] Apart from ferries, London Bridge itself provided the only crossing to the south bank until Westminster Bridge was opened in 1750 and Blackfriars Bridge in 1769, after which the borough of Southwark began to grow rapidly (Fig. 20). By the time of the first Census in 1801, the population of this built-up area amounted to nearly 960,000, of which about 750,000 lived to the north of the river, and the other 210,000 or so to the south, in the counties of Kent and Surrey.[2]

Nearly one Englishman in ten was now a Londoner, and the supply of this vast and growing agglomeration constituted one of the major elements in the economic geography of seventeenth- and eighteenth-century England.[3] It had gathered a variety of industries including watch-making, silk-weaving, boot-making, brewing and distilling, and also the manufacture of soap, sugar and of a variety of items, such as anchors, associated with boat-builders' yards. The countryside around was marked by the development of market gardening and by agricultural specialisation such as dairying and the production of hay for horses.[4] But the influence of London was felt far beyond its immediate surroundings. Defoe noted more than once 'how every county in England furnish'd something of its produce towards the supply of the city of London',[5] and the general truth of this is borne out by the widespread distribution of places sending carriers to London.[6] There was also the immense volume of coastwise shipping in which the bulky imports of coal and grain stood out prominently.[7] Furthermore, after the Peace of Paris in 1763, British overseas

---

[1] O. H. K. Spate, 'The growth of London, A.D. 1660–1800', in H. C. Darby (ed.), *An historical geography of England before A.D. 1800* (Cambridge, 1936), 529–48.

[2] *Census of 1851: Population Tables, I*, vol. 1 under London (P.P. 1852–3, lxxxv). This contains a retrospective summary for 1801.

[3] F. J. Fisher, 'The development of the London food market, 1540–1640', *Econ. Hist. Rev.*, v (1935), 46–64; F. J. Fisher, 'The development of London as a centre of conspicuous consumption in the sixteenth and seventeenth centuries', *Trans. Roy. Hist. Soc.*, 4th ser., xxx (1948), 37–50; E. A. Wrigley, 'A simple model of London's importance in changing English society and economy, 1650–1750', *Past and Present*, No. 37 (1967), 44–70.

[4] G. B. G. Bull, 'Thomas Milne's land utilization map of the London area in 1800', *Geog. Jour.*, cxxII (1956), 25–30. See p. 17 above.

[5] Daniel Defoe, *Tour*, I, 265.

[6] J. H. Andrews, 'Some statistical maps of Defoe's England', *Geog. Studies*, III (1956), 33–45.

[7] T. S. Willan (1938), 141–5.

possessions and influence were world-wide, and to the port of London came a rich harvest of trade as varied as it was considerable. The river below London Bridge was crowded with vessels discharging cargoes into lighters to be landed at the quays and wharfs along the river banks. The congestion produced much discussion which led to a parliamentary committee in 1796 and to the construction in 1800–2 of the West India Dock across the neck of the Isle of Dogs.[1] It was the beginning of a new phase in the history of the port. About this time the first Census could describe London as 'the Metropolis of England, at once the Seat of Government and the greatest Emporium in the known world'.

[1] J. H. Bird, *The geography of the port of London* (London, 1957), 44–9, 76.

Chapter 2

ENGLAND *circa* 1800

H. C. PRINCE

A traveller returning to England in 1800 after many years abroad, or a Frenchman or a German seeing the country for the first time, would have been struck by one new and pervasive quality of the English countryside – its neatness. Kent, the Garden of England, a county familiar to continental visitors, exhibited the most assiduously manicured scenery, with coppiced woodlands, well-pruned orchards, elaborately trained hop-grounds, verdant water-cress beds, the smoothest downs and fields of crops that were the envy of foreign observers and the pride of returning expatriates. In many other districts the soil was cultivated to the pitch of perfection, seeds were drilled in straight rows, plants regularly spaced and clean weeded, grass closely shorn and kept uniformly green and, in the newly enclosed Midlands, fields were square and bounded by neatly cut and laid hawthorn hedges. Augustan villas which half a century earlier had been sited in the midst of barren wastes, now looked over acres of idyllic pastoral scenery, embellished with artificial lakes, rustic temples and mock heroic monuments. The distinctive characteristic of the rural landscape at that time was that it was contrived so as to give an impression of orderliness and opulence. Even so, squalor had not been banished, and some of the most wretched farms lingered in highly improved regions. But pastoral elegance was no longer a poetic ideal, and it was the ambition of many practical husbandmen to create their own *ferme ornée*.

Nor had towns escaped the tidying hand of Georgian planners. On the ashes of the City of London, over the charred remains of Blandford in Dorset, and on many other devastated and derelict sites, splendid stone buildings had arisen. London's West End terraces, malls and squares marched in measured steps across the fields of Middlesex, Bath's crescents ascended the slopes of the Avon valley, and new shopping streets and residential quarters, studiously planned and proportioned according to the classical rules, imposed a sense of order and dignity on English towns such as they had not experienced before and were not to experience again. The whole nation appeared to be engaged in reorganising its landscape, and ever-growing numbers of people were coming forward to occupy new farms, to move into new town houses and to open new businesses.

At the same time, we must remember that England in 1800 was a nation at war. It is true that in this age war did not call for the enormous organisation of twentieth-century conflicts, but it brought dislocation and the absorption of manpower and, with but two brief intervals, it continued from 1793 to 1815. In spite of high prices and financial burdens, the geographical consequences of war were not entirely negative. For agriculture, the war provided an incentive to improve methods of farming and to extend the land under cultivation; the attack on wasteland became more vigorous. For industry it meant a stimulus to shipbuilding, to iron manufacturing in the form of guns, chains and anchors, and to woollen manufacturing for clothing soldiers and sailors. Moreover, after the battle of Trafalgar in 1805, England's supremacy at sea was virtually complete, and Napoleon's attempts at blockade came to naught. Continental competitors in overseas markets were crippled and English trade with the New World flourished in spite of many vicissitudes. London's role as a financial centre was increased at the expense of Amsterdam and Paris.

POPULATION AND SETTLEMENT

On the tenth of March 1801 in every parish, township or place, enumerators were instructed to make a house-to-house enquiry to ascertain the number of inhabited houses, the number of families, the number of male and female persons, the number employed in agriculture, in trade, manufactures or handicrafts, and in other occupations. The census recorded 8,331,434 inhabitants in England and 541,546 in Wales; but these figures were defective,[1] and subsequent adjustments made retrospectively in later censuses brought the figures up to 8.6 and 0.6 million respectively.[2] In any case, the census of 1801 was incomplete. No count was taken in the Isles of Scilly, in the Channel Islands nor in the Isle of Man. For many other places the enumeration was inaccurate because the boundaries of parishes and townships were not known, and for some places no returns had been received by the time the abstract was compiled. Moreover, a large part of the population was away from home on census day. No less than 469,188 were serving in the army, navy and merchant fleet; another 1,410

[1] *Census of 1801: Enumeration*, 497 (P.P. 1802, vii).
[2] *Census of 1851: Population Tables, I*, vol., I, xxviii (P.P. 1852–3, lxxxv).

were convicts 'on board the hulks'; and an untold number of homeless vagrants, deserters and fugitives escaped the attention of the enumerators. Despite its defects and omissions the first census provided a fuller and more accurate record than the most reliable previous calculations. It marked the beginning of a statistical age.

The population was predominantly rural, and only 19% of the people in England lived in towns of over 20,000 inhabitants. If the built-up area of London, north and south of the river, be excluded from the calculation the figure becomes just over 7%. Wales had no town with over 20,000 inhabitants, and so the corresponding figures for England and Wales as a whole are reduced to $17\frac{1}{2}$% and just under 7%. Even so, England had a higher proportion of town-dwellers than any other European country, and almost twice as many people lived in London, its imperial capital and chief seaport, as in either Paris or Constantinople. But beyond London no town had more than 100,000 inhabitants, whereas in France, outside Paris, both Marseilles and Lyons exceeded that number. Not only had England few large towns but few townsmen were street-bred. Some had become townsmen as their rural birthplaces were surrounded by new buildings, while some were migrants from elsewhere. A Bolton cotton operative asked by the Factory Commission to say whence spinners were recruited at the beginning of the nineteenth century replied: 'A good many from the agricultural parts; a many (*sic*) from Wales; a many (*sic*) from Ireland and from Scotland.'[1] At Preston and other places the building of a cotton mill might create a 'sudden and great call and temptation for hands from the country, of this county and others, and many distant parts'.[2] It was, above all, from the neighbouring countryside that the factories drew their 'herds of Lancashire boors'.[3] Among Sheffield apprentices, 'sons of yeomen, farmers and labourers made up about 45% of the immigrants', most of whom came from villages within fifteen miles of the town.[4]

To an observer in 1801 the evidence for the concentration of people in northern England, for the ascendancy of industry over agriculture, and

[1] *Factories Inquiry Commission: Supplementary Report, 1834*, Pt I, 169 (P.P. 1834, xix).

[2] A. Young (ed.), *Annals of agriculture*, xv (1791), 564. Between 1784–6 the place of publication was Bury St Edmunds; between 1786 and 1815 (when it ceased), the place was London.

[3] *The callico printer's assistant* (C. O'Brien, London, 1789). B.M. 1420. b. 7.

[4] E. J. Buckatzsch, 'Places of origin of a group of immigrants into Sheffield, 1624–1799', *Econ. Hist. Rev.*, 2nd ser., II (1950), 306.

for the size of the urban population were novel and impressive findings
of the census. To a modern observer the most striking fact is the smallness
of the population. To recall what it was like to live in England at that time
we must remove three out of every four persons in the present population. We must reduce London to a centre of about 960,000 inhabitants,
shrink every provincial town to less than one-tenth of that number, de-
populate large towns in the coalfield manufacturing districts, and wipe out
almost all dormitory suburbs. Everywhere in 1800 we should have been
aware of the sights, sounds and smells of the countryside. From St Paul's
Cathedral we should have been able to view London in its entirety,
surrounded on every side by sylvan landscapes of meadows, orchards,
deer parks, woods, heaths and rutted lanes. The streets of London and
other towns were jammed with horses, carts and farmers. On the outskirts of the capital were inns that catered for the traffic of country wagon-
ners, Welsh drovers and Irish haymakers.

At the other extreme, farmers had relentlessly pushed back the edge of
cultivation across heaths and up hills. Thousands of new homesteads
clung precariously to footholds beyond the present limits of settlement.
In 1801 many places in England and Wales had more people than they
were to have in the twentieth century; they were situated in mountains
and moorlands, in the Lake District and fells of the north country, in
remote Pennine dales, in central Wales, in the south-west peninsula. In
1801, mining supported many upland communities which have since decayed. Tin mining in Cornwall was declining, but the fortunes of the
Cornish mining towns were revived by the exploitation of copper at
greater depths.[1] At the beginning of the nineteenth century Cornwall and
Devon together produced more than two-thirds of the world's copper
and the copper mine at Parys Mountain in Anglesey was the largest in
Europe. On the Carboniferous Limestones of the Peak District and of
Alston Moor, lead production had not yet reached its zenith.[2] In the
Mendip Hills veins of lead were nearly exhausted but men were busy
digging for zinc at a hundred mines.[3] Low-grade iron ore was still being
worked in Sussex and south Lancashire, and coal was dug in Pembroke-
shire and the North Riding of Yorkshire. Among the mountains of
Westmorland or wild Wales a traveller was rarely out of sight of human

[1] W. J. Rowe, *Cornwall in the age of the industrial revolution* (Liverpool, 1953), 175.
[2] A. E. Smailes, *North England* (London and Edinburgh, 1960), 148–51, 185–6,
278–9.
[3] J. W. Gough, *The mines of the Mendips* (Oxford, 1930), 175–80, 226–30.

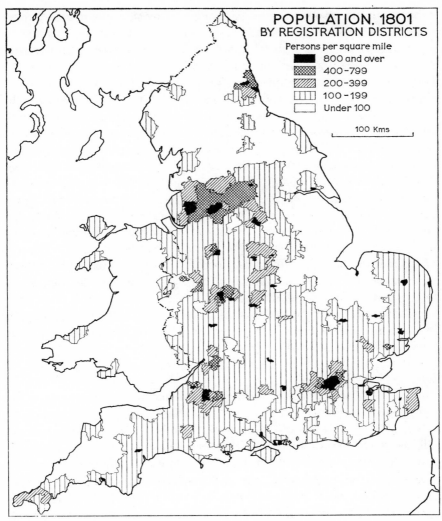

POPULATION, 1801
BY REGISTRATION DISTRICTS

Persons per square mile

■	800 and over
▨	400–799
▨	200–399
▥	100–199
□	Under 100

100 Kms

Fig. 21 Population in 1801
   Based on the retrospective evidence as given in *Census of 1851: Population Tables, I*, 2 vols. (P.P. 1852–3, lxxxv, lxxxvi).

habitations and from the edges of wolds or downs in the south country dozens of villages might be viewed at a glance.

In 1801, compared with later periods, population was evenly spread (Fig. 21). More than half the surface of England carried a density of between 100 and 200 people per square mile. The farming counties in southern and eastern England, where recently light land had been brought into cultivation, had attained average densities of population. These districts also possessed few uninhabited houses, and many villages had more families than houses to accommodate them. Towns, too, were often crowded. It was true that in Birmingham, which had grown without plan or control, every workman, so a witness said before a Select Committee, 'has a house of his own'; but in most towns, houses occupied by more than one family were common.[1] In London, an average household included a family and one or two lodgers or servants, the rookeries of St Giles and Whitechapel being more than twice as congested as the rest of the metropolis. Crowding was especially intense at spas and seaports. In many seaports every second house was shared by two families, while in Newcastle, Sunderland, Chatham, Falmouth and Plymouth there were two families for every available house. Places as far apart in distance and in character as Manchester, Nottingham, Oxford, Carlisle and Exeter were hardly less crowded.

Rural settlement

Foreigners observed many farms and solitary dwellings standing far apart, but most people lived in compact villages, in places that had been named in Domesday Book. Homes and farm buildings clustered around village greens, abutted on to village streets, stood close to churches, castles, bridges or harbours. In shape and size each village differed somewhat from every other, and was continually changing as houses were built, repaired, demolished and rebuilt. A zone in which villages predominated extended from Durham to Devon. In the north of England, memories of the 1745 campaign were still fresh and the layout of villages recalled a long history of wars and border raids. Some larger villages in east Durham, a few in Northumberland and also a few in west Cumberland were closely built around broad greens. By the beginning of the nineteenth century these open spaces were no longer used as refuges for villagers' stock but as places to hold cattle sales, race meetings and holiday festivities, 'affording a proper place for the sports of childhood,

[1] *Report of the Lords Committees on the Poor Laws, 1817,* p. 180 (P.P. 1818, v).

the recreation of youth, and even the relaxation of old age'.[1] Green villages were also common in districts far beyond the reach of marauders, in the east Midlands and close to London. Over most of the Midlands, from the Pennines to the Chilterns, it was still somewhat unusual to see a farm or cottage outside a village. Certainly, wherever open fields survived, villages were compact and isolated farms absent.

Villages varied greatly in size, in layout and in distance from one another. Considerations of shelter, security, access to water supplies, the quality of soils and differences in farming practice were all, to some extent, reflected in their siting. Southward into the chalk country, lines of small villages picked out the base of the chalk outcrop or followed the courses of streams. In Somerset, linear villages were arrayed along river banks, ridges and dunes, while circular villages ringed dry points, hilltops, and contacts of two geological formations around springs.[2] Every part of midland England displayed similar contrasts in the plans of its villages.[3]

The number of buildings in a village was sometimes controlled deliberately by the owners and occupiers of the land. Parishes in the hands of only one or two landowners were often small communities of large farmers, some of the smallest being 'closed' townships where the Poor Law was strictly enforced to prevent indigent newcomers from taking up residence and becoming charges on the rates. 'Open' townships were large rambling villages crowded with small farmers, shopkeepers, artisans and landless labourers. In the eastern counties, open villages furnished the earliest gangs employed by large farmers for stone-picking, potato-setting, singling and lifting turnips, haymaking and harvesting.[4]

West of the Severn the transition from a landscape of villages to one of hamlets was discontinuous. Outlying groups of villages appeared among hamlets and dispersed farmsteads in Herefordshire. Farther north, villages

---

[1] E. Mackenzie, *An historical, topographical and descriptive view of the county palatine of Durham*, 2 vols. (Newcastle, 1834), II, 182; H. Thorpe, 'The green villages of County Durham', *Trans. and Papers, Inst. Brit. Geog.*, XV (1949), 155–80.

[2] B. M. Swainson, 'Rural settlement in Somerset', *Geography*, XX (1935), 112–24.

[3] E.g. H. M. Keating, 'Village types of Nottinghamshire', *Geography*, XX (1935), 283–94.

[4] W. Hasbach, *A history of the English agricultural labourer* (London, 1908), 134n., 195–8; D. R. Mills, 'The poor laws and the distribution of population *c*. 1600–1800, with special reference to Lincolnshire', *Trans. and Papers, Inst. Brit. Geog.*, XXVI (1959), 185–95.

clustered on flat arable lands between Shrewsbury and Stafford, on both
sides of the Dee and Mersey estuaries, in the Fylde and around Morecambe
Bay; but the most remarkable group of villages stood over 1,000 feet
above sea-level in the Peak District. They were the highest permanent
settlements in England, preserving in stone the distinctive features of
Midland villages. Their farms crowded closely along their main streets
and beyond lay furlong upon furlong of narrow curving strip fields enclosed, small as they were, by dry stone walls.

Westward, from the Cotswolds, towards Devon, villages became
smaller, more irregular in arrangement and hamlets appeared more frequently. Devonshire, in the main, was a countryside of hamlets, of small
groups of three or four farmhouses with their yards and cottages, some
with an inn or a smithy, some dignified by the presence of a parish church.
The area was threaded with narrow winding lanes and deeply rutted
tracks leading to a multitude of hamlets. In the warm lowlands of east
Devon, and also on the bleak uplands in the west and north, compact
villages were by no means rare among the hamlets. Villages in the West
Country, unlike those in the Midlands, were surrounded by dispersed
hamlets and isolated farms, and the degree of dispersion increased
west of the Exe.[1] In west Cornwall the only compact settlements were
fishing villages, mining centres and a few inflated hamlets surrounded
by strip fields.[2] The settlement pattern was further complicated by
the presence of large numbers of solitary farms, substantial bartons
in Devon, remote trevs in Cornwall, and squatters' cottages high on
the moors.

In the Lake District, and over most of the Pennine uplands, few
settlements possessed more than twenty houses. Chapels, bridges, mills or
rows of cottages with an inn, served as centres for extensive parishes. In
remote dales the largest habitations were farmsteads, massive stone
buildings nestling in sheltered nooks on valley sides. Some were crumbling
monastic granges, some were fortified manor houses, converted castles or
peles, some were substantial and imposing farms standing alone at the
edge of the moors. In many areas the characteristic dwellings were humble
cottages, narrow windowed, squat chimneyed, slate roofed, built of rough
unhewn stone, with lichens, mosses, ferns and flowers growing in their
crannied walls. In 1810, William Wordsworth's *A guide through the
district of the Lakes* describes the long, low cottages:

[1] W. G. Hoskins, *Devonshire studies* (London, 1952), 289–333.
[2] W. G. V. Balchin, *Cornwall* (London, 1954), 35–9, 72–3, 88–92.

Cluster'd like stars some few, but single most,
And lurking dimly in their shy retreats.[1]

But these unassuming dwellings were already disappearing fast as strangers
were attracted to the mountains. Wealthy purchasers, 'if they wish to
become residents, erect new mansions out of the ruins of the ancient
cottages',[2] but old-established landowners, not to be outdone, rebuilt
their family seats and laid out model villages such as Lowther.

Hamlets and isolated farms were characteristic not only of the uplands
but also of formerly wooded districts in the English lowlands. Hamlets
predominated in Cannock Chase, in Charnwood, in the Arden district of
Warwickshire, in the Forest of Dean and in the well-wooded areas of
southern and eastern England. In the Weald, hamlets or straggling villages,
in mid-Suffolk and the Hampshire Basin scattered farmsteads, were
numerous. Where timber had once been plentiful, timber-framed or half-
timbered buildings were characteristic, sometimes weatherboarded,
sometimes hung with wooden shingles. Many old houses also had brick
chimneys and gable ends, and some occupied moated sites. In old-enclosed
country north of the Thames in Middlesex, in the Chilterns, in Essex, and
in parts of East Anglia, farms were dispersed and hamlets, loosely ranged
around spacious commons, at the edges of heaths or along roads, bore such
names as '-end' and '-green'.[3]

In many parts of England, particularly in the Midlands, new farms were
arising among old villages. In distant Northumberland, where neither
villages nor isolated houses had stood before, large farms were laid out
with huts in rows to accommodate labourers.[4] Between small villages in
the Solway lowlands and in the vale of Eden, single massive courtyard
farms were not uncommon. East of the Pennines, where reclamation had
advanced up to the edges of the moors and over the wolds, a rash of neat
pantiled-roofed farms with parlours and sash windows had broken out
in newly enclosed fields.[5] South of the Humber, on the Lincolnshire

[1] W. M. Merchant (ed.), *A guide through the district of the Lakes...by William
Wordsworth* (London, 1951), 96.

[2] *Ibid.*, 127.

[3] H. Thorpe, 'Rural settlement', being ch. 19 (pp. 358–79) of J. W. Watson and
J. B. Sissons (eds.), *The British Isles: a systematic geography* (London and Edinburgh,
1964).

[4] W. Marshall, *The review and abstract of the county reports to the Board of Agriculture:
Northern Department* (York, 1808), 40.

[5] A. E. Smailes, 156.

Wolds, on the sands of Nottinghamshire, Norfolk, Suffolk and Berkshire similar bright brick-built farmhouses and field barns were springing up in newly enclosed or improved districts.[1] Most were no more than thirty years old. Farms dating from the mid-eighteenth century were also to be found in a number of other areas – e.g. in the vale of York, in the vale of Trent, on the drift-covered wolds of Leicestershire, Northamptonshire and in the Feldon district of Warwickshire. The names of lodges, granges and farms commemorated, among other events, the colonisation of America and India, the reigning house of Hanover and the battles in the wars with France.[2] Farm building was not confined to arable districts. The Board of Agriculture reporters noted that in mid-Cheshire modern dairy farms were as spacious and well-designed as any in the kingdom; and in the dairy land of north-west Wiltshire they were built 'on a much superior plan to those in many other counties', while in Middlesex they were asserted to be 'perfect models of their kind'.[3] Enclosure and improve-ment were imposing a new pattern of settlement on the old.

No part of England, least of all the south-east, entirely escaped the transforming hand of Georgian architects and planners. On the great roads out of London government officials and citizens of London built themselves comfortable brick boxes. Old halls and courts were replaced by porticoed country houses, and at the side of the road the paint was still fresh on new gate-lodges, toll-houses and renovated posting inns. New brickwork and stucco was to be seen far beyond a half day's journey from the City. On many estates landowners were pulling down dark hovels and putting up well proportioned cottages, but in Gloucestershire and other counties it was reported that 'the popular complaint against the dilapidation of cottages is but too well founded'.[4] In making landscape gardens, whole villages had been swept away and built anew at Nuneham Courtenay, Milton Abbas, Ickworth and other places. In the new

---

[1] A. Harris, *The rural landscape of the East Riding of Yorkshire, 1700–1850* (Oxford, 1961), 70–2; M. B. Gleave, 'Dispersed and nucleated settlement in the Yorkshire Wolds, 1770–1850', *Trans. and Papers, Inst. Brit. Geog.*, XXX (1962), 105–18; N. Riches, *The agricultural revolution in Norfolk* (Chapel Hill, N.C., 1937), 144–6.

[2] W. G. Hoskins, *The making of the English landscape* (London, 1955), 157–9.

[3] H. Holland, *General view of the agriculture of Cheshire* (London, 1808), 82; T. Davis, *General view of the agriculture of the county of Wiltshire* (London, 1811), 169; J. Middleton, *A view of the agriculture of Middlesex* (2nd ed., London, 1807), 45.

[4] T. Rudge, *General view of the agriculture of the county of Gloucester* (London, 1807), 47.

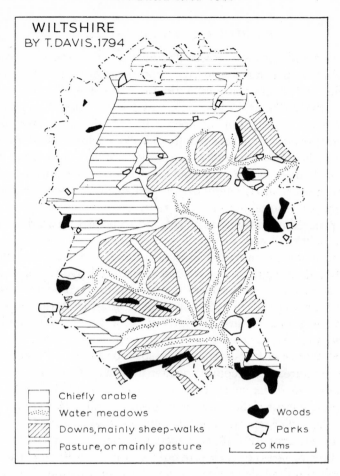

Fig. 22 The regions of Wiltshire, 1794
Based on T. Davis, *General view of the agriculture of Wiltshire* (London, 1794).

manufacturing districts factory owners commissioned model villages for their work-people at Etruria, Cromford, Styal and Mellor, and new villages were built as inland navigations extended into the Midlands. Apart from medieval churches and a few other enduring architectural monuments, most buildings and some entire villages in old England were no older than those in New England beyond the Atlantic.

THE COUNTRYSIDE

In 1800 England was more or less at midpoint in the process of parliamentary enclosure that transformed the appearance of much of the countryside. The traditional open-field agriculture of some 1,500 or so villages, largely in the Midlands, had been, or was being abolished by private Acts of Parliament (Fig. 7); but the open fields of an even greater number of villages still awaited their acts. Another kind of enclosure, that of commonable waste, had also proceeded a considerable way by private act, but, again, much open waste remained especially in the northern counties (Fig. 14). A substantial amount of non-parliamentary enclosure by mutual agreement was also taking place. In 1801, a general enclosure act simplified the proceedings leading to an act, and so helped forward the changes that were taking place.[1]

A picture of the countryside in transition is given in the county reports of the Board of Agriculture, a body established by Act of Parliament in 1793. It was not a government department in the modern sense of the term, but a society for the encouragement of agriculture, supported by government grants. Its first president was Sir John Sinclair and its first secretary was Arthur Young, and it continued until 1822, when it was dissolved. One of its first actions was to sponsor a series of 'General views' of the agriculture of each county, written upon a uniform plan. There were two editions, an earlier quarto edition for private circulation and comment, and a later and more elaborate octavo edition usually written by a different author. The earlier reports appeared between 1793 and 1796, and the later ones between 1795 and 1815. Taken together, they provide not only a view of the progress of enclosure but a conspectus of English agriculture in general, and they also contain a wealth of information on topics other than agriculture.[2]

Each report was normally accompanied by what was usually called a 'map of the soil', but very often the maps were based not so much on soil as on land use or on relief or on a combination of all three.[3] William

---

[1] G. Slater, *The English peasantry and the enclosure of common fields* (London, 1907), 140, 268–313; W. E. Tate, *The English village community and the enclosure movements* (London, 1967), 88, 130.

[2] G. East, 'Land utilization in England at the end of the eighteenth century', *Geog. Jour.*, LXXXIX (1937), 156–72.

[3] H. C. Darby, 'Some early ideas on the agricultural regions of England', *Agric. Hist. Rev.*, II (1954), 30–47.

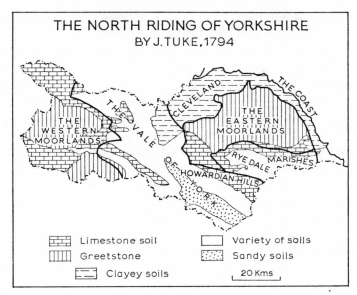

Fig. 23 The regions of the North Riding of Yorkshire, 1794
Based on J. Tuke, *General view of the agriculture of the North Riding of Yorkshire*
(London, 1794).

Smith, the so-called 'father of English geology' had produced a geological
map of the country around Bath in 1799 and a map of the geology of
England in 1801. Some of the authors of the Board's reports may have
consulted William Smith or his records, but others carried out their own
surveys. A number of authors confessed to the difficulty of delineating
complex soil variations accurately or in detail, and they sometimes solved
this problem by indicating on their maps areas of 'miscellaneous' or
'various' soils. Examples of the maps are those for Norfolk (Fig. 10),
Suffolk (Fig. 11) and Wiltshire (Fig. 22). The divisions of the first two
counties were based on differences in soil texture; that of Wiltshire upon
differences in land use. One of the most interesting was John Tuke's map
of the North Riding (Fig. 23). On a division according to soil he superimposed boundaries of districts 'each remarkable either for its climate,
soil, surface or minerals (i.e. rocks)'. Each district was distinguished 'by
the name by which it is usually known' or, if none existed, by some appropriate descriptive name. All the districts included more than one type of
soil. Only in east and south-east England did agricultural regions correspond at all closely with soil divisions.

During these years there was another attempt to delineate the agricultural variety of England. William Marshall (1745–1818) was strongly critical of the Board of Agriculture's plan for describing what he called 'the rural economy of England' in terms of counties, and he pointed to the fact that 'agricultural districts' frequently ignored county boundaries. Thus the dairy district of northern Wiltshire extended into Berkshire and Gloucestershire, and the cider country or 'fruit liquor district, of the Wye and the Severn', included parts of Herefordshire, Gloucestershire and Worcestershire; in the same way, the Fenland needed 'six county reports to treat of it'. After producing studies of various parts of England, Marshall, between 1808 and 1817 proceeded to 'review and abstract' the Board of Agriculture reports, county by county, and the five volumes of this review were re-issued as a whole in 1818.[1] These, together with Marshall's work in general, provide a valuable supplement to the Board of Agriculture's picture of England in the years around 1800.

Arable land

In 1801 estimates of acreages of land in different states of cultivation for every county in England and Wales were abstracted from the reports of the Board of Agriculture and from parliamentary accounts by Benjamin Capper,[2] and these may be compared with the estimates of W. T. Comber a few years later.[3] The total area of arable land in 1801 was estimated to be between eleven and twelve million acres. A still larger total would have been arrived at if all land in temporary grass had been added, and if the true extent of the surface area of certain Welsh and west Midland counties had been known. In constructing Fig. 24 estimates from the later Board of Agriculture reports have been used in preference to Capper's where they approximate more closely to the total surface area of a county. Whatever the defects of the figures they probably indicate the relative proportions of land devoted to different uses.

Most districts in eastern England were continuously in crops, but some western districts rarely saw a newly turned furrow, and along the western border of the West Riding it was observed that 'nearly the whole of the good land is under the grazing system, while corn is raised upon the

[1] For a summary of William Marshall's writings, see D. McDonald, *Agricultural writers, 1200–1800* (London, 1908), 215–16.

[2] B. P. Capper, *A statistical account of the population and cultivation, produce and consumption, of England and Wales* (London, 1801), 66–73.

[3] W. T. Comber, *An enquiry into the state of national subsistence* (London, 1808), 52.

Table 2.1 *Land use in England and Wales in 1801 and 1808*
(in acres)

	1801 B. P. Capper	1808 W. T. Comber
Arable land	11,350,501	11,575,000
Pasture and meadow	16,796,458	17,495,000
Total cultivated area	28,146,959	29,070,000
Woods and coppices	} 5,664,156	1,641,000
Commons and wastes		6,473,000
Buildings, roads, water etc.	3,454,740	1,316,000
Total uncultivated area	9,118,896	9,430,000
Grand total	37,265,855	38,500,000

The correct total area of England and Wales is 37,325,000 statute acres.

inferior or moorish soils'.[1] Proportions of arable and grass varied from county to county. The leading arable county, Norfolk, was about two-thirds under crops, and the leading grazing county, Leicestershire, was about three-quarters grass, but at this time there was no marked distinction, as in later times, between corn counties in the east and grazing counties in the west. In the west, tillage occupied over one half of Herefordshire, almost a half of Worcestershire and one-third of Cornwall, while in the east almost two-thirds of Surrey, Suffolk and Lincolnshire were under grass.

No less important were differences in farming enterprise and in the manner of cultivating the land. Some agricultural products took their names from and gave a unique character to particular localities. By 1800, mustard from the silt fens of Norfolk, Pontefract liquorice, Aylesbury ducks, Stilton cheese and Burton ale had achieved nation-wide renown and had entered the export market. On the other hand, neither orcharding nor hop-growing were localised. Hops were to be found in counties as far apart as Shropshire, Nottinghamshire, Cornwall and Suffolk as well as in Kent and Worcestershire.[2] Around the towns, farmers used a variety of urban refuse as manure, and supplied urban markets with perishable food-stuffs and industrial crops. The Board of Agriculture reports described in

[1] G. B. Rennie *et al.*, *General view of the agriculture of the West Riding of Yorkshire* (London, 1794), 77.

[2] D. C. D. Pocock, 'England's diminishing hop acreage', *Geography*, XLIV (1959), 14–21.

some detail the market gardens around London, dependent upon ample supplies of manure, and employed in raising vegetables for the London market.[1] Thomas Milne's map shows their extent in about 1800 (Fig. 6). Near cloth manufacturing centres in Yorkshire, East Anglia and the West Country, in addition to food and fodder crops, flax, hemp, teasles, weld, woad and saffron were grown for industrial uses. Part-time spinners and weavers in these districts brought into cultivation land yielding too little to support a family, and such part-time farmers were less attentive than full-time farmers to the finer points of husbandry. They considered farming not as a business but 'only as a matter of convenience; speak of spinning-jennies, and mills, and carding machines, they will talk for days with you'.[2] 'Never inquire about the cultivation of land or its produce within ten or twelve miles of Manchester', wrote another; 'the people know nothing about it.'[3]

The quality of farming varied greatly from one district to another, independently of the area devoted to particular farming types. Arable farming was considered 'the great object of the Hertfordshire husbandry', whereas in neighbouring Buckinghamshire, also a predominantly arable county, grasslands were praised as 'the inestimable treasures which give character to the husbandry'.[4] In Suffolk, where extensive areas were devoted to dairying and sheep farming, arable farming had achieved a high pitch of perfection while in Lincolnshire the management of arable land left much to be desired, particularly on wet clay soils, and in Shropshire large tracts of arable were wretchedly cultivated.[5] The best arable farming was to be found in Norfolk, in Kent and in parts of Hertfordshire, while the finest grassland husbandry was practised in Middlesex and Leicestershire.

The leading enterprise of most arable farms was the production of bread grain, and to that end was directed the greatest effort at improvement. Between 1780 and 1801 the price of wheat trebled.[6] Population increased

---

[1] J. Middleton, *View Middlesex* (1807), 328–38; W. Stevenson, *General view of the agriculture of the county of Surrey* (London, 1809), 414–19.

[2] R. Brown, *General view of the agriculture of the West Riding of Yorkshire* (Edinburgh, 1799), 77, 225.

[3] J. Holt, *General view of the agriculture of the county of Lancaster* (London, 1795), 211n.

[4] A. Young, *General view of the agriculture of Hertfordshire* (London, 1804), 55.

[5] A. Young, *General view of the agriculture of the county of Suffolk* (London, 1804), 46–8; A. Young, *General view of the agriculture of the county of Lincoln* (London, 1799), 92; J. Plymley, *General view of the agriculture of Shropshire* (London, 1803), 161, 348.

[6] Lord Ernle, *English farming past and present* (4th ed., London, 1927), 441.

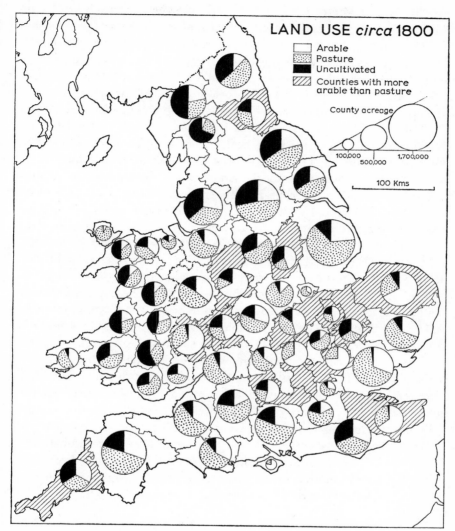

Fig. 24 Land use *circa* 1800 (by counties)
Based on B. P. Capper, *A statistical account of the population and cultivation, produce and consumption, of England and Wales* (London, 1801), 66–73; supplemented by the county *General views* of the Board of Agriculture.

rapidly, imports from enemy-held territory were restricted, and crop failures between 1794 and 1800 created an almost continuous apprehension of impending famine.[1] In 1795, wheat was severely damaged by winter frost, but it was not a bad year for spring-sown barley. In 1799 a cold wet summer was followed by an exceptionally bad harvest and in 1800, the wheat crop was again about 25% below average.[2] After 1795 several attempts were made to estimate how much grain was grown, and in 1801 the Home Office called for returns from every parish in England and Wales of the acreages growing wheat, barley, oats, potatoes, peas, beans and turnips or rape.[3] The crop returns, although they were incomplete and often inaccurate, not only provide a rough measure of the relative importance of different crops in different areas, but they enable us to locate these differences with greater precision than is possible from the Board of Agriculture reports. At a parochial scale we may identify areas where the acreage of wheat exceeded that of barley or oats or rye and also areas where other cereals were dominant. Fig. 25 provides an indication of the variations to be encountered in Leicestershire.

The total acreage growing crops in 1801 may only be guessed but there can be little doubt that over half the land in crops was sown with wheat, barley, oats and rye. The area occupied by grain crops was probably not less than six million and possibly nearer seven million acres, of which wheat perhaps occupied about three million acres, oats nearly as many, barley no more than one million and rye less than one-quarter of a million acres. Wheat not only occupied a large and increasing area; but the amount of grain yielded by each acre was also increasing more rapidly than at any previous time.[4] By the end of the eighteenth century wheat had become the almost universal bread grain of all classes and occupations.[5] The Trent, which separated wheat-eaters from the rest at the beginning of the eighteenth century, no longer marked such a dietetic boundary. In the new manufacturing districts in the north labouring families ate wheat

[1] W. F. Galpin, *The grain supply of England during the Napoleonic period* (New York, 1925), 213–19.

[2] A. Young (ed.), *Annals of agriculture*, XXXIII (1799), 129–53, 194–218, 253–74, 346–65, 518–31; *ibid.*, XXXIV (1800), 95–8.

[3] H. C. K. Henderson, 'Agriculture in England and Wales in 1801', *Geog. Jour.*, CXVIII (1952), 338–45; W. E. Minchinton, 'Agricultural returns and the government during the Napoleonic wars', *Agric. Hist. Rev.*, I (1953), 29–43.

[4] M. K. Bennett, 'British wheat yields per acre for seven centuries', *Econ. Hist.*, III (1935), 27–8.

[5] W. J. Ashley, *The bread of our forefathers* (Oxford, 1928), 1–2.

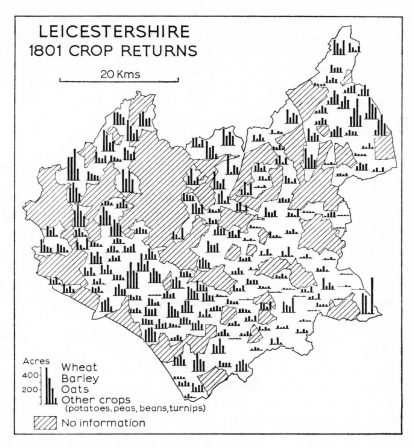

Fig. 25 Crop returns for Leicestershire, 1801
Based on W. G. Hoskins, 'The Leicestershire crop returns of 1801', being
pp. 127–53 of W. G. Hoskins (ed.), *Studies in Leicestershire agrarian history*
(Leicester, 1949); this constituted vol. XXIV of *Trans. Leicestershire Archaeol.
Soc.*

bread. In the West Riding, where in 1799 the wheat acreage was twice
that of barley, the vicar of Wakefield observed, 'the prodigious Number
of Tradesmen, Mechanics and Husbandmen, who twenty Years back
subsisted on Oat and Barley Cakes, as their favourite Diet, now consume
none but the *best* Wheaten Flour'.[1] The Board of Agriculture reports
repeatedly described wheat as a modern production. In Lancashire it had

[1] Quoted in B. P. Capper (1801), 59.

been introduced so recently that in 1775 it had 'scarcely yet acquired the name of corn, which in general is applied only to barley, oats and rye'.[1]

Rye was still grown widely in Durham, but only in southern Northumberland was it spoken of as 'the most general bread of the labouring people'.[2] In 1808 the amount of rye grown in Bedfordshire was reported to be 'much decreased of late years'; the falling demand for it as a bread grain rendered its production unprofitable on 'any soil of moderate fertility'.[3] On light sands in south-west Norfolk and on the forest sands of Nottinghamshire some rye was grown but 'scarce at all used for bread'.[4] Here, and in southern England, it was raised as spring fodder for sheep, while on the very poorest soils in Suffolk buckwheat was regarded as 'a very valuable crop'.[5] On the Welsh Border, where both rye and maslin, a mixture of rye and wheat sown together, were once widely cultivated, rye was sown 'but sparingly' and 'good wheat' was grown instead.[6] The extension of wheat growing accompanied the improvement of soils by marling and liming and the introduction of a regular course of cropping. In southwest England, where little rye was grown, the wheat acreage expanded at the expense of barley. In Cornwall most people ate barley bread. In Cheshire, in 1794, agricultural labourers still subsisted on barley bread but by 1808 wheat was the leading bread grain and little barley was cultivated.[7]

In the north, wheat was grown less extensively than oats. Even so, oats were not generally used for making bread except in the Lake District, in Craven, in the Yorkshire dales and in north Lancashire.[8] In the vale of Pickering and in north Staffordshire oatbread was baked only in times of scarcity.[9] Throughout the northern counties, however, oatmeal appeared

---

[1] T. Percival, 'Observations on the state of population in Manchester, and other adjacent places, concluded', *Philosophical Transactions*, LXV (1775), 327.

[2] J. Bailey and G. Culley, *General view of the agriculture of the county of Northumberland* (London, 1794), 80.

[3] T. Batchelor, *General view of the agriculture of the county of Bedford* (London, 1808), 386.

[4] A. Young, *General view of the agriculture of the county of Norfolk* (London, 1804), 304; R. Lowe, *General view of the agriculture of the county of Nottingham* (London, 1798), 46.

[5] A. Young, *General view Suffolk* (1804), 304.

[6] J. Duncumb, *General view of the agriculture of the county of Hereford* (London, 1805), 66; J. Plymley, *General view Shropshire* (1803), 173.

[7] H. Holland, *General view Cheshire* (1808), 298.   [8] H. C. K. Henderson, 342.

[9] J. Tuke, *General view of the agriculture of the North Riding of Yorkshire* (London, 1800), 127; W. Pitt, *General view of the agriculture of the county of Stafford* (London, 1796), 163.

in a variety of dishes such as porridge, oatcakes, crowdies or hasty puddings. In southern and eastern counties scarcely any oatmeal entered the diet, and in the south Midlands the area devoted to oats was very small. In the west, where oats were widely grown, they were used as fodder for livestock.

Beans were cultivated as a fodder crop on heavy land, particularly in the south-east. About one-fifth of the arable land in Middlesex was devoted to beans, and they were tended 'in the most clean and perfect manner'.[1] They were also extensively grown in Essex and Kent and on the strongest soils in Surrey. North and west from London they were characteristic of common-field husbandry on claylands, and were often cultivated in a slovenly manner. In Cheshire and in the north-east their acreage was increasing.

The turnip was described by Arthur Young as 'the crop which, in Norfolk, is made the basis of all others', and the advance of agricultural improvement in the north and west of the county was marked by the spread of turnip cultivation. By 1804 they were sown 'indiscriminately on all soils in Norfolk'.[2] In Suffolk they had 'changed the face of the poorer soils', and in Hertfordshire they were sown 'wherever turnips can be sown'.[3] Their cultivation had continued to spread during the closing years of the eighteenth century. In 1796 John Boys stated that in Kent, 'thirty years ago, hardly one farmer in a hundred grew any; and now there are few especially in the upland parts that do not sow some every year'.[4] In Surrey it was reported that their cultivation had 'certainly extended considerably' since 1790.[5] In Lincolnshire, wrote Arthur Young in 1799, 'thousands of acres' flourished where about thirty years earlier 'there was scarcely a turnip to be seen'.[6] On light soils in Nottinghamshire, on the Yorkshire Wolds and as far west as Cornwall they were now regularly cultivated. Fig. 26, based on information derived largely from the Board of Agriculture reports, attempts to show where turnips were grown in rotation at least once in five years. The map gives a very incomplete picture because the available information varies greatly from county to county. R. Parkinson's survey of Rutland records the course of cropping

[1] J. Middleton, *View Middlesex* (1807), 241.

[2] A. Young, *General view Norfolk* (1804), 219.

[3] A. Young, *General view Suffolk* (1804), 95; A. Young, *General view Hertfordshire* (1804), 61.   [4] J. Boys, *General view Kent* (1796), 92.

[5] W. Stevenson, *General view Surrey* (1809), 243.

[6] A. Young, *General view Lincoln* (1799), 138.

Fig. 26 References to the growing of turnips *circa* 1800
Based on: (1) the county *General views* of the Board of Agriculture; (2) Arthur
Young (ed.), *Annals of agriculture*, 45 vols. (Bury St Edmunds, 1784–6;
London, 1786–1815). (3) and the writings of William Marshall.

for each parish,[1] G. B. Worgan names only a few places in Cornwall to illustrate general observations,[2] while some localities are reported in accounts published in Arthur Young's *Annals of agriculture* (1784–1815) and in the writings of William Marshall. Notwithstanding the deficiencies of the map, it is apparent that turnip husbandry had become firmly established in East Anglia and the counties to the north-west of London.

In Essex, and in Northumberland, for example, some land appears to have already become tired of turnips and clover, while many farmers in the Midlands and in the north-west considered turnips unsuited to all but dry soils, a view shared by few observers acquainted with Norfolk practice.[3] In the Midlands, so William Marshall observed, 'not one acre in a hundred, taking the district throughout, is subjected to the turnip culture'.[4] In 1795 Edward Harries, touring through Shropshire, described a tract of arable land in the Severn valley as 'a fine sound country, chiefly arable' but with 'scarce a turnip fallow, though no land can be better adapted to that crop'.[5] In Cheshire, William Marshall complained, 'even in 1800 – *no Turnips*! – not even on the Turnip Lands, with which the County abounds'.[6] On light soils in these areas change was imminent. By 1803 turnips had appeared on the sands of eastern Shropshire, and in 1808 Henry Holland welcomed their recent arrival in the central and southern dairy districts of Cheshire;[7] but they were late in coming to some counties such as Dorset.[8]

Swedes thrived in some counties where turnips made little progress. Their introduction into the Midlands and into southern England followed, and was associated with, the replacement of grassland sheep by arable breeds.[9]

---

[1] R. Parkinson, *General view of the agriculture of the county of Rutland* (London, 1808), 45–9.

[2] G. B. Worgan, *General view of the agriculture of the county of Cornwall* (London, 1811), 55–7, 67–71.

[3] A. Young, *General view of the agriculture of the county of Essex*, II (London, 1807), 12; J. Bailey and G. Culley, *General view Northumberland* (1794), 184.

[4] W. Marshall, *The rural economy of the Midland counties*, 2 vols. (London, 1790), I, 253.   [5] A. Young (ed.), *Annals of agriculture*, XXIV (1795), 379–80.

[6] W. Marshall, *The review and abstract of the county reports to the Board of Agriculture: Western Department* (York, 1809), 7.

[7] J. Plymley, *General view Shropshire* (1803), 173; H. Holland, *General view Cheshire* (1808), 156.

[8] W. Stevenson, *General view of the agriculture of the county of Dorset* (London, 1812), 251.

[9] E. L. Jones, 'Eighteenth-century changes in Hampshire chalkland farming', *Agric. Hist. Rev.*, viii (1960), 17.

In Staffordshire it was said that 'the most material alteration that has taken place in the cultivation of this county since 1796 has been the pretty general introduction of the Swedish turnip'[1]. They were particularly successful in the Soar valley in Leicestershire, and were also advancing in Devon and Cornwall. With few exceptions they were shunned in eastern districts and in the south Midlands; and in drier localities in the east, rape and carrots were often substituted for turnips. Rape was gaining ground in the east Midlands, while carrots were favoured especially in the south and east of the country. Cabbages were also successfully brought into the root course in places as far apart as Durham, Cheshire and Suffolk.

Among the new crops none was of more importance than the potato, because it yielded large quantities of human food, serving to supplement available supplies of bread. Potatoes were raised on all well-manured dry light soils in Lancashire and Cheshire.[2] They were pre-eminent in the Fylde and their acreage was expanding in the northern counties generally. In Cornwall and Devon they produced 'certain and prolific' yields, supplying much of England from their surplus.[3] On rich sandy loams in Somerset and in Gloucestershire they were eagerly taken up, and in Herefordshire they were reported to be 'gaining ground every year: near towns in particular'.[4] In Shropshire they were still not commonly culti-vated in 1803 but their acreage was increasing annually. In the highly cultivated districts of eastern and south-eastern England, they were grown only in gardens or for feeding pigs, and in the south Midlands generally they were still hardly to be seen. Although they were rarely grown more than five miles from the metropolis they were one of the leading crops in the gardens of its immediate neighbourhood.[5]

At the beginning of the nineteenth century arable farming was pros-pering. Both landowners and farmers were spending large sums of money to bring more land into cultivation, to improve the soil, to increase productivity, to experiment with new techniques, and to venture into new enterprises. They were applying a wide range of manures in such quanti-ties as to alter the character of soils. William Stevenson, describing the

---

[1] W. Pitt, *General view Stafford* (2nd ed., 1813), 72.

[2] A. Young (ed.), *Annals of agriculture*, XIX (1793), 332–4; *ibid.*, XXIV (1795), 568–72.

[3] G. B. Worgan, *General view Cornwall* (1811), 72; C. Vancouver, *General view of the agriculture of the county of Devon* (London, 1808), 197–200.

[4] J. Duncumb, *General view Hereford* (1805), 66.

[5] W. W. Glenny in W. Page and J. H. Round (eds.), *V.C.H. Essex*, II (1907), 474–7.

soils of Surrey, asserted that 'in the strict and chemical sense of the term *clay*, no soil which has long been under cultivation has a just claim to it'.[1] And the transformation of extensive areas of light soils was no less spectacular than the conversion of clays in Surrey. From rabbit warrens and sheep-walks in west Norfolk the prosperous arable district of Good Sand had been called into existence, 'and, by dint of management', wrote Arthur Young in 1804, 'what was thus gained has been preserved and improved, even to the present moment'.[2] Other extensive agricultural regions were similarly won from the waste. In south-east England only the most obdurate, villainous tracts of heath remained for William Cobbett to reproach.

Near towns, market gardens and fields were heavily dressed with organic manures from hearths, stables, dairies, slaughter houses, fish markets and the sweepings from streets, courtyards and rubbish dumps. John Middleton estimated that Middlesex alone probably received 250,000 cart loads of London manure each year and that as much again went to neighbouring counties.[3] From manufacturing districts in the north came reports of experiments evaluating the fertilising properties of bones, blood, hair, oil cake, soap ashes, soot, rags and various composts. The great value of bones was discovered in Yorkshire but it was not until 1794 that an enterprising farmer in Lancashire began grinding them at a mill.[4] Green manuring was practised on some sandy soils with varying success, and the value of paring and burning in many different localities was keenly debated.

The texture and acidity of many soils were profoundly modified by the application of mineral manures. Enormous quantities of peat, sand, clay, limestone and marl were spread and mixed with soils of opposing characteristics. William Marshall termed marl 'the grand fossil manure of Norfolk', and manuring, chiefly with marl, was praised by Arthur Young as 'the most important branch of the Norfolk improvements, and that which has had the happy effect of converting many warrens and sheep-walks into some of the finest corn districts in the kingdom'.[5] In Lancashire, marl was declared 'the great article of fertilization, and the

[1] W. Stevenson, *General view Surrey* (1809), 20.

[2] A. Young, *General view Norfolk* (1804), 3.

[3] J. Middleton, *View Middlesex* (1807), 374.

[4] Lord Ernle, 218n.

[5] W. Marshall, *The rural economy of Norfolk*, 2 vols. (London, 1787), I, 16; A. Young, *General view Norfolk* (1804), 402.

foundation of the improvements'; it was also claimed as 'unquestionably one of the most important of the Cheshire manures'.[1] It was held in high esteem in Essex, in Hertfordshire, in the Chilterns and in some localities in south and south-west England. Chalk was extensively used on the Lincolnshire Wolds, and in 1812 it was reported to be 'coming into use' in the East Riding of Yorkshire.[2] Light drifting sands and sandy loams benefited greatly from judicious additions of marl but heavy soils were often injured by excessive applications which increased rather than relieved their tenacity.

In many districts, burnt lime was found to be cheaper and more effective than marl. In Warwickshire the effects of lime had been found 'from experience so infinitely superior to those of marl, that the last will in a short time cease to be used at all'.[3] Leicestershire farmers had learned that marl was unnecessary for their grass, and in heavily marled Lancashire it was lime that was considered 'the best manure for grass'.[4] In Derbyshire, lime was considered essential in the coal district and marling was being abandoned.[5] In Staffordshire, William Pitt thought that lime was used in a more extensive way than elsewhere and its use was still increasing.[6] In the North Riding of Yorkshire and further north, lime was superseding marl.

Burnt lime was used in many districts where marling had not been practised previously. In the Mendips it was described as 'the great article of modern improvement of these hills', and in the vicinity of Cheddington in Dorset, where no lime had been used six years earlier, it was reported in 1812 to be 'now in general use'.[7] High in the dales and on the moors of north Yorkshire, where rye had been the leading grain crop, William Marshall noted that *the alteration of the soil by liming* was such that wheat had become a more prevalent crop.[8] In the Weald of Kent some

[1] J. Holt, *General view Lancaster* (1795), 111; H. Holland, *General view Cheshire* (1808), 221.

[2] H. E. Strickland, *General view of the agriculture of the East Riding of Yorkshire* (York, 1812), 212.

[3] A. Murray, *General view of the agriculture of the county of Warwick* (London, 1813), 150.

[4] W. Pitt, *General view of the agriculture of the county of Leicester* (London, 1809), 188; J. Holt, *General view Lancaster* (1795), 124, 128.

[5] J. Farey, *General view of the agriculture of Derbyshire*, 3 vols. (London, 1811–17), I, 148.   [6] W. Pitt, *General view Stafford* (1796), 126.

[7] J. Billingsley, *General view of the agriculture of the county of Somerset* (Bath, 1798), 105; W. Stevenson, *General view Dorset* (1812), 352.

[8] W. Marshall, *The rural economy of Yorkshire*, 2 vols. (London, 1788), I, 312.

farmers used marl in 1785, but in the Surrey Weald in 1813 lime was 'almost universally used'.[1] The efficacy of liming depended upon adequate soil drainage. On waterlogged land lime was worse than useless.

In 1800, in most arable districts both marl and lime were used in smaller quantities and more frequently than hitherto. Fig. 27 shows places where applications of marl or lime were mentioned in contemporary agricultural writings; the map gives a very incomplete picture, because the information varies from county to county. Even so, the distribution illustrates some preferences of farmers largely ignorant of the chemical properties of soils and manures. Before Humphry Davy lectured on agricultural chemistry in 1803 no scientific principles governed the practice of manuring.[2] Farmers followed local traditions and learned lessons from practical experience.

About 1800 great progress began to be made in the invention, manufacture and utilisation of implements for arable farming. Lighter and more efficient harrows, horse-hoes, horse-rakes, scarifiers, chaff-cutters, turnip-slicers, drills, drill-rollers as well as reaping, mowing and haymaking machines were patented in large numbers. Norfolk led the country in the number and variety of its farm implements. The Norfolk plough, modified in detail, was adopted with enthusiasm by farmers in north-western counties. Threshing machines, widely used in Norfolk and Suffolk before 1800, were now general in northern Northumberland and were 'becoming very prevalent' in Devon.[3] Between 1794 and 1804 twenty new threshing mills were erected in Suffolk, and in 1813 the first steam engine to be used solely for agricultural purposes was installed at a farm at Haydon in Norfolk. In northern England, drill husbandry was an innovation; but in Suffolk, where drills had long been in use for sowing roots and pulses on light soils, they were now used for sowing grain on heavy land. The most rapid advances in the development of agricultural machinery were made in eastern districts, particularly for cultivating light soils, but wet lands derived no small benefit from mechanisation in speeding the sowing of seed and in the gathering of crops. In northern counties iron was employed not only in the manufacture of agricultural machinery but also

[1] A. Young (ed.), *Annals of agriculture*, II (1785), 64; W. Stevenson, *General view Surrey* (1809), 498.

[2] The substance of the lectures was published ten years later as *Elements of agricultural chemistry* (London, 1813).

[3] J. Bailey and G. Culley, *General view Northumberland* (1794), 49; C. Vancouver, *General view Devon* (1808), 121.

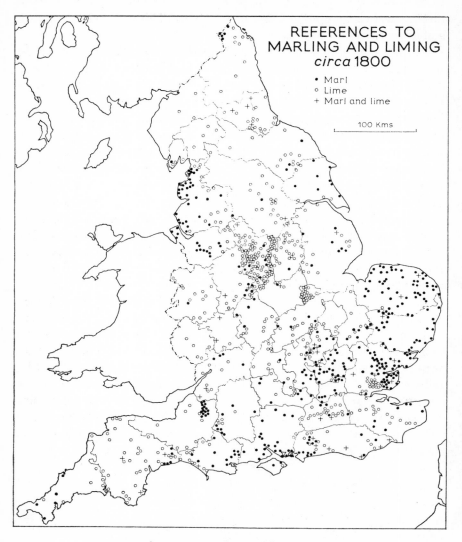

Fig. 27 References to marling and liming *circa* 1800
Sources as for Fig. 26.

in building strong gates and fences. By 1800 northern and some western districts were beginning to catch up with Norfolk in the efficiency of their arable farming.

The advance of improvement left large areas of arable land untouched. No fewer than two million acres lay fallow each summer. A large proportion of the arable land in a belt extending from Durham to Dorset was fallowed one year out of three, in some localities as often as one out of two. In such areas as the grain growing district of the West Riding bare fallows prevailed 'to a much greater extent than necessary', and in the vale of Gloucester the continuance of fallows was attributed to 'prejudice and an attachment to the practice of their forefathers'.[1] Common arable fields were not confined to the Midland belt. In Middlesex 11,000 acres out of a total of 14,000 acres of arable land remained in common fields in 1807, and fallowing was universal before the introduction of green and root crops.[2] On the heavy loam soils of north Surrey, from Carshalton to Runnymede, more than 8,000 acres lay in common fields in 1809.[3] But the area of common arable fields in both Middlesex and Surrey had been greatly reduced since 1795.

Fallowing was also widely practised on enclosed land. Kent had no common arable fields, but fallowing was generally pursued on cold stiff soils. In one large district in Essex, Arthur Young reported 'half the arable being under a dead summer fallow', and 'on all but sound dry turnip soils, it is universal'.[4] In Lancashire few open fields remained but fallowing was widespread, while in Northumberland, except where turnips were grown, 'naked fallows' still persisted, 'with an almost universal opinion that it is absolutely necessary to the fertility of the land'.[5] But there was much discussion generally among contemporaries about the value of fallowing.[6]

Grassland

In 1800 England was a grassy country, much greener than France. For every acre of arable land there were one and a half acres of grass, and the grassland acreage was expanding faster than the arable. 'The predilection

[1] T. Rudge, *General view Gloucester* (1807), 104.

[2] J. Middleton, *View Middlesex* (1807), 158.

[3] W. Stevenson, *General view Surrey* (1809), 470–7.

[4] A. Young, *General view Essex*, I (1807), 201.

[5] J. Holt, *General view Lancaster* (1795), 43; J. Bailey and G. Culley, *General view Northumberland* (1794), 62.

[6] J. C. Loudon, *An encyclopedia of agriculture* (London, 1815), 320–1, 740–2.

for *pasture* land which many years past seems to have been universally manifested', was attributed by John Billingsley to a growing demand for meat and dairy produce in London and other centres of population.[1] In the Midlands the value of many open fields when enclosed and converted into pasture was doubled; and in old enclosed districts great grain growing areas, such as the Fylde, were laid down to grass, a process which, throughout Lancashire, 'seems yearly increasing'.[2]

Both Lancashire and Cheshire were counted among the more productive grassland districts in the country; rich grazing lands were the glory of Lincolnshire; Middlesex produced some of the most valuable hay in the world; Romney Marsh fattened sheep and cattle more rapidly than any other district, and breeders and graziers in Leicestershire 'surpassed every other county in the kingdom, and I suppose every other country in the universe'.[3] In the west, each locality excelled in some branch of grassland management. Dairying dominated the broad vales of the Mersey, Dee, Severn and Avon. William Marshall observed that the western parts of the realm, apart from the hill country, were 'almost wholly applied to the produce of the DAIRY: Cheeses of different qualities being its common (or prevailing) production'.[4]

The greenest patches in the pastoral scene were picked out by ribbons of riverside meadows whose fertility was regularly restored by the silt spread over them during floods. Such were the fine grasslands of the Thames and Lea valleys and the vale of St Albans. The extensive natural meadows of Staffordshire and Derbyshire were enriched by the lime-impregnated waters of the Derwent and of the Dove, while those of Shropshire, flooded by the Severn, were 'constantly mown without any other manure being bestowed upon them'.[5] There, as in other counties, artificial channels were cut to divert silt-laden waters to places beyond the reach of natural floods. On the warplands of Lincolnshire and the Humber estuary, the silt was impounded by regulating the tidal flow. On the water-meadows of the chalk country of southern England muddy water from arable fields was floated down during the autumn. They were hot beds for grass, raising an early bite for sheep in March and April. The

---

[1] J. Billingsley, *General view Somerset* (1798), 154.

[2] J. Holt, *General view Lancaster* (1795), 71; Leicestershire and Northamptonshire are referred to in N. Kent, *General view of the agriculture of the county of Norfolk* (London, 1796), 73–4.

[3] W. Pitt, *General view Leicester* (1809), 216.

[4] W. Marshall, *Western Department* (1809), 1–2.

[5] J. Plymley, *General view Shropshire* (1803), 180.

irrigation of 20,000 acres of meadow in south Wiltshire was described as 'the greatest and most valuable of all improvements'.[1] In a few localities in Rutland, in Buckinghamshire and elsewhere, water-meadows produced only coarse rank unpalatable herbage. In many other parts of England, from the Yorkshire dales to Cornwall, meadows were watered by catchwork channels.

Almost all river valleys possessed some excellent natural and artificial meadows, but extensive areas of pasture in the grazing districts in the north and west called loudly for improvement. Even in such counties as Lancashire, Cheshire, Shropshire and Herefordshire, celebrated for their fat-stock and dairy produce, much pasture land was neglected and badly managed. In the dry eastern counties many pastures were 'certainly of inferior consideration and merit to the arable lands', and without manure and cultivation grasslands produced little or no hay.[2] Arthur Young thought the condition of grassland in Suffolk could 'scarcely be worse', but Norfolk appeared to be yet more depressing.[3] 'No where', he declared, 'are meadows and pastures worse managed.' In north-west Norfolk some irrigation had been attempted by Lord Walpole and Thomas William Coke,[4] but the practice was not widely imitated in the arable districts of England.

On heavy clays in the south Midlands, immense tracts of grass were ill-drained and infested with reeds and sedges. Draining was rudimentary or completely lacking in most areas. In Cheshire it was estimated that the value of meadows might be doubled by the provision of adequate drainage. In several Midland counties some wet and swampy land was already drained by open ditches but much remained to be done. In the Welsh borderland ditching had hardly begun; and in the south-west, the art of draining was neither widely practised nor properly understood. On all claylands the greatest need was for effective underdraining.[5] Large areas of the Midlands, once under the plough, benefited from the ridge and furrow beneath the turf, and ridging was still the most widely practised method of improving drainage on flat or gently sloping surfaces. Mole draining was successful in Huntingdonshire, Cambridgeshire and Bedford-

[1] T. Davis, *General view Wiltshire* (1811), 116.

[2] A. Young, *General view Essex*, II (1807), 94.

[3] A. Young, *General view Suffolk* (1804), 159; A. Young, *General view Norfolk* (1804), 370.

[4] A. Young (ed.), *Annals of agriculture*, XXXVII (1801), 510–12.

[5] H. C. Darby, 'The draining of the English clay-lands', *Geographische Zeitschrift*, LII (1964), 193.

shire, and was attempted further west in the vale of Oxford and in the vale of Gloucester. Hollow-draining, with stones or bushes or with bricks and tiles, was general on heavy soils in Suffolk, but there, as in mid-Norfolk and north Essex, it was carried out mostly on arable land. In 1795, hollow-draining was introduced into Lincolnshire, and in 1797 it was stated to have 'lately made its way into Northumberland'.[1] But in western districts it was still practically unknown. By 1797 Joseph Elkington's method of tapping water at its source in springs and sloughs was employed at a number of places in the Midlands. Each district perfected its own draining techniques and the results were patchy.[2]

In addition to land under permanent grass a considerable area was sown with artificial grasses in leys of more than one year. Clover and ryegrass were the two most widely grown ley crops. In the eastern counties the cultivation of clover was long established and well understood, but the rich loams of Suffolk and south Norfolk were already tired of clover, its place being taken by ryegrass, tares and vetches.[3] In Hertfordshire, on the other hand, clover had been cultivated without ill-effect, 'probably as long, or longer, than in any part of the kingdom'.[4] Clover and ryegrass were grown for one or two years in arable rotations in Lincolnshire, and the counties to the north. They were sown for short leys, but not extensively, in the Cotswolds, in the west Midlands and, to a smaller extent, in Lancashire and Cheshire. They had reached few places west of the Severn or north of the Ribble.

Lucerne and sainfoin were newly introduced as hay crops in many localities. Lucerne was not widely cultivated north of the Thames, but sainfoin was considered the most valuable of all cultivated grasses over much of the chalk country of southern England from Wiltshire to the Chilterns. It was also grown extensively on the light soils of Cambridgeshire and on the sandy soils of west Suffolk, where it was described as 'this noble plant, the most profitable of all others'.[5] On the Cotswolds artificial grasses were reckoned to be 'necessary to the very existence' of

---

[1] A. Young, *General view Lincoln* (1799), 242; J. Bailey and G. Culley, *General view Northumberland* (1794), 111.

[2] A. Young (ed.), *Annals of agriculture*, XVI (1791), 542–4, 550; J. Johnstone, *An account of the most approved mode of draining land: according to the system practised by Mr Joseph Elkington* (Edinburgh, 1797).

[3] A. Young, *General view Norfolk* (1804), 257; A. Young, *General view Suffolk* (1804), 104.

[4] A. Young, *General view Hertfordshire* (1804), 115.

[5] A. Young, *General view Suffolk* (1804), 106.

a farm, and sainfoin was cultivated 'with great success'.[1] Its cultivation spread to the well managed leys of the vale of York, but had not been successful in the Midlands.

In many districts, old grassland was never broken up. Landowners and farmers either thought it unprofitable or lacked the tools to do it. On some farms ploughing up was expressly forbidden by the terms of leases. In 1800, to promote the conversion of old pastures into tillage, the Board of Agriculture offered substantial prizes for essays describing the best methods to be followed.[2] The response was disappointing, and, apart from small patches broken up for potato growing, the area of permanent grass continued to expand.

A large part of the grassland of England and Wales, together with a considerable proportion of the arable and most of the rough grazing land, was devoted to feeding sheep. The area of land carrying or support-ing sheep at different times during the year may have been as much as three-quarters of the whole surface area of the country. About 1800 the number of sheep was variously estimated, but the most detailed calculation was that made by John Luccock, a Leeds wool-stapler.[3] County by county he examined the numbers of long- and short-woolled sheep of fourteen distinct types or breeds. The resulting total, including the number of the lamb crop and of the annual slaughter, added up to 26,150,463, or almost three times the human population. This compared well with an estimate of 25,589,214 made by Arthur Young in 1779.[4] On unimproved hill grazings there was an average of under one sheep per three acres, and some Pennine moors were overstocked at that density. At the opposite extreme, the fine pastures of Romney Marsh fattened more than five sheep per acre. On pastures of intermediate quality, on downland or on Cots-wold pasture an acre carried about one sheep.

The leading enterprise for most sheep farmers was wool production. The hardy mountain sheep of northern England and Wales were bred mostly for their fine short wools, but long-woolled varieties were estab-lished on the fells of Northumberland, on Exmoor and in other moorland areas. Hill sheep were successfully crossed with improved lowland strains to produce mutton as well as wool. On the limestone hills of central

---

[1] T. Rudge, *General view Gloucester* (1807), 174–5.

[2] *Communications to the Board of Agriculture*, III (London, 1802). The volume contains fourteen essays on the conversion of grassland into tillage.

[3] J. Luccock, *The nature and properties of wool* (Leeds, 1805), 338.

[4] A. Young (ed.), *Political arithmetick, Part II* (London, 1779), 28.

England, on the Lincolnshire Wolds and on the moors of north Yorkshire and Durham, the new crosses were well established. On the chalklands of southern England the old long-horned breeds were being displaced by fat South Downs and New Leicesters so rapidly that it seemed the old stock might 'soon be extinct'.[1] The long-woolled Lincolnshire breed held its own on the marshlands but New Leicesters were reported to be 'spreading very rapidly over the county'.[2] In Norfolk, South Downs had taken possession of all the Good Sand region, the native sheep retaining a dwindling territory in the Breckland.[3] Suffolk was now the home of the Norfolk sheep, but South Downs and New Leicesters were advancing steadily.[4] In all parts of the Midlands the New Leicesters were ousting other breeds but in the West Country they made little headway.

Apart from Romney Marsh, the best grazing lands were appropriated to cattle, but little is known about the total area used to feed them or about the numbers of stock kept. Contemporary estimates put the number at between three and a little over four million.[5] A continually changing element in the cattle population was the number of imported livestock. Each year thousands were driven on the hoof across country from Wales and from Scotland, and in 1801 no fewer than 31,543 Irish cattle were landed at English ports.[6] Some made their way to extensive fattening pastures in the vale of Trent, and on Humberside, but it was not only northern districts that received these droves. They also went to arable farms in the east Midlands and East Anglia where they outnumbered native beef-stock.

While breeders spent more energy and took greater pains to perfect strains of fat-stock than to improving the milking qualities of dairy cattle, dairying remained the most profitable enterprise for a great majority of cattle farmers. Every important livestock region produced cheese, butter, cream or fresh milk. In the north, where the emphasis was on rearing, the vale of Eden, and the Craven and Kendal lowlands sold large surpluses of butter throughout the country. In the husbandry of Lancashire the

[1] W. Marshall, *Rural economy of the southern counties of England*, 2 vols. (London, 1798), I, 347.

[2] A. Young, *General view Lincolnshire* (1799), 371.

[3] A. Young, *General view Norfolk* (1804), xv, 449.

[4] A. Young, *General view Suffolk* (1804), 209–16.

[5] A. Young, *Political arithmetick, Part II* (1779), 28, 31; G. E. Fussell, 'Animal husbandry in eighteenth century England. Part I, Cattle', *Agric. Hist.*, XI (1937), 102.

[6] G. R. Porter, *The progress of the nation* (London, 1847), 345.

dairy was the principal source of income. It not only supplied fresh milk to the populous textile manufacturing centres around Manchester and Leeds but also marketed large quantities of cheese. Cheshire, with 92,000 cows in milk, was also one of the leading dairy districts in England.[1] The claylands and clay loams of the Midlands were largely devoted to dairying, while in the vicinity of London some 8,500 cows were kept solely to supply the metropolis with fresh milk.[2] No attention was paid to the breed of the cow as long as it was a good milk producer. 'All round London,' wrote Thomas Baird, 'but particularly near Hackney, Islington, and for several miles thereabouts the cowkeepers engross every inch of land they can procure.'[3] But even in summer when grass was most abundant it was necessary to supplement the feed with grains.

Draught oxen were still to be seen ploughing strong land in the West Country. In Cornwall they were used for all kinds of work; in north Devon they were the premier draught animals, and in north Somerset they were preferred to horses for ploughing. They were also favoured on heavy soils in Herefordshire and in Shropshire. Some were kept in Gloucestershire, in Wiltshire and in Oxfordshire, but they were virtually extinct in eastern England.

Horses were being used in increasing numbers in most parts of the country. John Middleton probably over-estimated the total number at 1,800,000; but it is unlikely that there were fewer than one million.[4] In 1791, London and its environs alone used more than 31,000 horses for non-agricultural purposes. Perhaps as many as ten times that number were working in other parts of the country along canals, in wagon trains, in stage coaches, in hackney carriages. In addition, possibly a quarter of a million were kept for riding, for cavalry, for racing and for private carriages. Those working on farms were yet more numerous. Derbyshire and Leicestershire were the leading horse-breeding counties raising the finest horses for draymen and carters. The North Riding was equally famous for its saddle and coach horses, while many other localities bred farm horses. On the eve of the invention of the steam locomotive horses provided almost the sole source of motive power. Indeed, the capacity of the new machines was assessed in terms of their horse power.

[1] H. Holland, *General view Cheshire* (1808), 252.
[2] J. Middleton, *General view Middlesex* (1807), 417.
[3] A. Young (ed.), *Annals of agriculture*, XXI (1793), 112.
[4] J. Middleton, *General view Middlesex* (1807), 639.

Other livestock were relatively unimportant in England. Geese, ducks and chickens picked their way across the stubble and scratched among the winnowings in the farmyard. The pig was the universal scavenger and a usual accompaniment of the cottage garden. The population of the manufacturing districts in Lancashire and in the Midlands had little taste for pork, and in the West Riding Robert Brown complained that there were too many pigs. Only at the distilleries on the south side of London were pigs fattened in large numbers, being brought from as far afield as Berkshire, Shropshire and the East Riding. Hardly less important than domestic pigs and poultry as sources of food were the deer, rabbits and wildfowl of forest, heath and marsh.

Woods, plantations and parks

In 1800 probably no more than two million acres of woodland remained in England and Wales, now one of the least wooded of all north European nations. Most of the country within twenty miles of a seaport had been stripped of shipbuilding timber. The oakwoods along the valleys of the Tyne, Wear and Tees had been denuded not only of ship timber but also of small wood for pit props. The coastal plain of County Durham had also been cleared of its wood, so that the shipyards of Tynemouth, Sunderland and Middlesbrough now looked to the 25,500 acres of woods in the North Riding for their supplies. But much of that extensive area had already been cut over, and the shipbuilders of Whitby and Scarborough had consumed most of the available timber.[1] All that remained were slender saplings raised from the stools of timber trees.

The situation on the west coast was no better. Cheshire suffered a severe shortage of oak timber, and could not even find enough oak bark for her tanneries. Neither there nor in Lancashire had any considerable tract of ancient woodland been spared. The Lake counties possessed remnants of native woods but they were seriously deficient in oak. In Gloucestershire, the Forest of Dean, once a great storehouse of naval timber, furnished barely sufficient mature trees to repair the ships that put in at Bristol. The woods of Worcestershire had been reduced to spinneys and copses producing substantial quantities of hop poles and billet wood but little else of value.

The naval dockyards along the Channel coast were desperately short of suitable materials. The uplands of Devon and Cornwall were bare of trees, and the few oaks growing at the heads of valleys were 'wasting in

[1] J. Tuke, *General view North Riding* (1800), 187.

a most alarming manner'.[1] Timber trees had largely disappeared from the oakwoods of Dorset and Hampshire, and were no longer plentiful even in the depths of the Wealden forests. The south-east produced immense quantities of wood for hop poles, hurdles, faggots, barrel staves, charcoal and material for firing kilns and making gunpowder, but little sound timber. Essex and Middlesex had extensive areas of forest and parkland but no unexploited reserves of fully grown timber. In Norfolk and Suffolk, thousands of acres of oak, elm and ash were regularly cut for poles and billets but their mature woods 'hardly deserved mentioning'.[2]

Some of the least wooded counties were well stocked with hedgerow trees. To the west, in Devon, Somerset and Herefordshire; to the east, in Essex, Kent, Surrey and Sussex, hedgerows were both numerous and heavily timbered. The hedges of Devon were deep and rambling, whereas those of Sussex were kept 'in a state of garden cleanness'.[3] In both districts free growing oaks in field and hedge spread their branches to give shade to cattle and, when they were felled, to yield valuable pieces of curved and crooked timber. About two-thirds of the English oak used in building a man-of-war had to be curved or crooked.[4] A few hedgerow trees were specially trained to produce timber of exceptional size and shape required for the frame of a ship. Such trees were worth at least twice as much as ordinary oaks.[5]

In the centre of England were to be found the densest stands of timber. William Marshall remarked that the Midland counties, 'with little latitude, may be said to contain all the ship timber now growing in the kingdom', but as he wrote canals were 'taking off the produce of the interior'.[6] Bristol shipbuilders cleared the great timber from the lower Severn valley, made inroads into the oakwoods of Herefordshire and, working their way upstream, now drew their main supplies from 'the very fine woods of oak' left standing in Shropshire.[7] The Forest of Arden in Warwickshire still had considerable tracts of oak woods; and the forests, parks and chases

[1] G. B. Worgan, *General view Cornwall* (1811), 98; C. Vancouver, *General view Devon* (1808), 457.

[2] A. Young, *General view Suffolk* (1804), 165.

[3] A. Young (ed.), *Annals of agriculture*, XX (1793), 289.

[4] W. Marshall, *On planting and rural ornament*, 2 vols. (3rd ed., London, 1803), I, 49.

[5] R. G. Albion, *Forests and sea power* (Cambridge, Mass., 1926), 7–9.

[6] W. Marshall, *The review and abstract of the county reports to the Board of Agriculture: Midland Department* (York, 1818), 381.

[7] J. Plymley, *General view Shropshire* (1803), 212.

in Northamptonshire were abundantly wooded. Thirty years after the opening of the Trent and Mersey Canal, its industries consuming increasing quantities of wood each year, Staffordshire was 'well stocked with all kinds of timber, notwithstanding the immense quantities that have been cut down of late years'.[1] The east Midlands, on the other hand, were unremarkable for their timber resources.

Landowners planted not only oak, ash, beech and elm, but many other native, exotic, deciduous and evergreen trees. It scarcely needed the repeated exhortations of John Evelyn's *Sylva*, revised and considerably enlarged by John Hunter in 1801, or practical hints from William Marshall, or the generous prizes of the Royal Society of Arts, to induce gentlemen to 'adorn their goodly mansions and demesnes with trees of venerable shade and profitable timber'.[2] During their lifetime they had little to gain but they might expect handsome profits to accrue to their grandchildren and great-grandchildren. At Longleat, an acre of fully grown oaks and other trees was worth £1,500, and in many parts of the country plantations bearing the names of victorious admirals anticipated future glories at sea and high prices at the shipyards.[3] For the present, landowners contented themselves with the pleasure of planting; their efforts contributed more to the adornment of parks and to the mantling of bare wastes than to a solution of the immediate shortage of naval timber.

The largest estates were the most steadfast planters and the leading suppliers of merchantable timber. At Bowood in Wiltshire the earl of Shelburne planted 150,000 trees each year.[4] Much planting was of oak but the duke of Portland's estate at Welbeck also raised great quantities of beech, larch, Spanish chestnut, Weymouth pine and many other conifers.[5] On neighbouring estates in the Dukeries 'the spirit of planting' was reported to have 'prevailed much', conifers being nurtured with as much pride as oaks.[6] On the light soils of Norfolk millions of trees were planted. At Holkham alone more than two million were planted between 1781 and 1801, of which fewer than one in six were oaks. Among 48 other varieties, cherries, chestnuts, hazel, poplars, evergreen oaks, Scots pine, spruce and larch figured prominently.[7] In Lincolnshire and on the Yorkshire

[1] W. Pitt, *General view Stafford* (1796), 92.
[2] J. Hunter (ed.), *John Evelyn's Sylva*, 2 vols. (York, 1801), II, 303.
[3] *Ibid.*, II, 299; T. Davis, *General view Wiltshire* (1811), 191.
[4] A. Young (ed.), *Annals of agriculture*, VIII (1787), 76.
[5] J. Hunter (ed.), I, 89.
[6] R. Lowe, *General view Nottingham* (London, 1798), 53, 89.
[7] A. Young, *General view Norfolk* (1804), 382–3.

Wolds great mixtures of trees were propagated by Sir Joseph Banks, the duke of Ancaster and Sir Christopher Sykes, but on light soils farther north more larch was planted than any other species.

In many new plantations conifers were introduced as nurse trees. In south-east England, Scots pine and larch were sparsely disseminated among oaks and intermixed with seedlings of tender native and exotic trees in clumps and ornamental plantations. In the west and north they occupied a large proportion of the ground. In Shropshire, Joseph Plymley reported, 'many modern plantations of various sorts of firs and pine, generally mixed with different deciduous trees'.[1] In Cheshire, extensive plantations on large estates were mostly coniferous, and in 1795 the Royal Society of Arts awarded a gold medal for the planting of half a million conifers there. On high ground near Ambleside, the bishop of Llandaff attempted to establish 100 acres of mixed trees, but like most sites in Westmorland it was found to be 'too cold for any sort of wood except the fir and larch', the larch flourishing where all else failed.[2] Oak, ash, alder, birch, hazel were coppiced for billet wood and charcoal but rarely grew into tall trees. The clothing of rocky slopes with fast growing conifers was welcomed as a means of utilising and improving poor soils. The Board of Agriculture report for Cumberland, for example, referred to 'a large plantation of larches thriving exceedingly well, on the steep edge of the west side of Skiddaw'.[3]

Some writers objected to the appearance of conifers. William Wordsworth thought the scenery of the Lake District was being deformed by 'the small patches and large tracts of larch plantations that are overrunning the hill-sides'.[4] But Bailey and Culley had nothing but praise for the plantations rising in every part of northern England. In Northumberland larch more than pine or spruce was adding 'greatly to the ornament of the country'.[5] In the North Riding larch grew rapidly and produced sound timber, but in southern England Scots pine was preferred. It brought about a complete change in the appearance of the Bagshot Sands in Surrey, of the Greensand outcrops from Bedfordshire to Wiltshire, and of the sands of Hampshire and Dorset. In Cornwall and other western counties

---

[1] J. Plymley, *General view Shropshire* (1803), 212.
[2] A. Pringle, *General view of the agriculture of the county of Westmorland* (Edinburgh, 1797), 278.
[3] J. Bailey and G. Culley, *General view of the agriculture of the county of Cumberland* (London, 1794), 202.   [4] W. M. Merchant (ed.), 120.
[5] J. Bailey and G. Culley, *General view Northumberland* (1794), 109.

many different kinds of trees grew equally well, lending varied colours
and textures to the scene, breaking the harsh baldness of the skyline.

Within thirty miles of London, from 'the rich blue prospects of Kent,
to the Thames-watered views in Berkshire', the landscapes created by
Charles Bridgeman, William Kent, Lancelot Brown and Humphry
Repton had transformed the face of the countryside.[1] Hundreds of parks
lined the roads out of London; hilltops were crowned with ornamental
clumps of trees; streams tumbled over artificial cascades to spread out in
broad lakes; towers, follies, ruins and temples caught the eye at the end
of each studiously contrived vista. Grounds laid out and planted in the
early eighteenth century were now fashionable showplaces visited by
admiring tourists. Thomas Whateley's *Observations on modern gardening,*
reprinted in 1801, commended Claremont, Esher Place, Blenheim,
Caversham, the Leasowes, Woburn Farm, Painshill, Hagley, Persfield
and, above all, Stowe. Stowe epitomised all the splendour and magnificence
of the early enthusiasm for landscape gardening, but Horace Walpole's
romantic taste inclined to the subtleties of Rousham or to the alpine
savagery of Painshill, where 'all is great, foreign, and rude'.[2] By 1800 the
new rage for pictureque scenery, described in William Gilpin's *Tours,* had
reached its height, and many travellers set out to discover rugged
grandeur in the Welsh borderland, beckoned by Richard Payne Knight
'to some neglected vale'.[3]

In lowland England, thousands of acres were landscaped in the smooth
manner perfected by Lancelot Brown (Fig. 28). The elegant compositions
of shaven lawn, calm water, rounded clumps, winding drives were
repeated at many other places by Humphry Repton. Some were early
landscape gardens remodelled in detail or extended to take in fresh prospects
but some were newly created from farmland or from waste. It was,
above all, on tracts of poor soil that landscaping made its greatest impact.
Englishmen were slowly losing their fear and hatred of uncultivated land.
Much had been tamed and cultivated, but even where cultivation was
a forlorn hope it was possible to take pleasure in picturesque disorder and
perhaps to improve the scenery by judicious planting.[4]

---

[1] H. Walpole, 'History of the modern taste in gardening', in W. Marshall, *On
planting and rural ornament,* I, 242.

[2] *Ibid.,* 237.

[3] R. P. Knight, *The landscape, a didactic poem* (London, 1794), Book 3, line 235.

[4] H. C. Prince, *Parks in England* (Shalfleet, I.O.W., 1967).

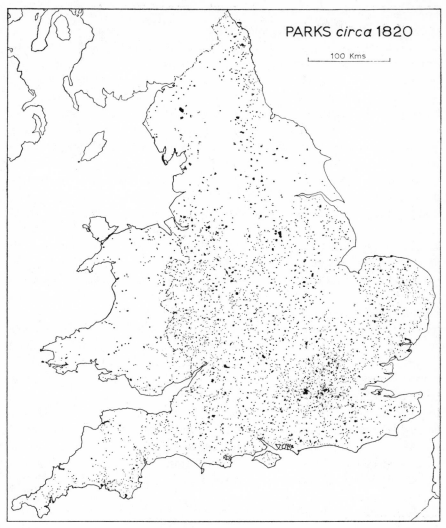

Fig. 28 Parks *circa* 1820
Based on the county maps of A. Bryant (1822–35), C. & J. Greenwood
(1817–33) and R. G. Baker (1821).

Heath, moor and marshland

If England and Wales had somewhat less wood in 1800 than at present, there was probably more unimproved and waste land. It is difficult to obtain an accurate assessment of the area of unimproved land partly because of the inherent difficulty of drawing a line between managed woodland and tumbled-down scrub, or of distinguishing downland pasture from rough hill grazing or meadow liable to flood from undrained marsh. A report of 1808 estimated the waste land at 7.8 million acres (6.2 in England and 1.6 in Wales).[1] This was higher than W. T. Comber's figure of 6.5 million for 'commons and wastes'.[2]

As well as wastes, commons and rough grazing, much cut-over woodland remained derelict awaiting improvement. Thus Delamere Forest contained nearly 10,000 acres of waste land and in well-timbered Staffordshire 9,220 acres of Needwood Forest lay 'in a state of nature'.[3] Between 1787 and 1793 the reports of the Middleton Commission, appointed to enquire into the state of the Crown forests, painted a gloomy picture of neglect. A large part of the royal forests lay treeless and idle. Vast areas were reported to be totally unproductive, yet little was being done to improve them.[4] William Gilpin's *Remarks on forest scenery*, written while he was vicar of Boldre in the New Forest, describes that pictureque waste as 'consisting of heathy land and carpet lawns interspersed with woods'.[5] On the other side of Hampshire Gilbert White described Woolmer Forest in 1789 as consisting 'entirely of sand covered with heath and fern' and without 'one standing tree in the whole extent'.[6] There were occasional improvements; thus in 1798 Robert Lowe reported that at least 20,000 acres of the forest district of western Nottinghamshire had been privately enclosed, some reclaimed for agriculture, some planted with trees.[7]

Vast stretches of desolate heath lay within a few miles of London. Surrey alone had 70,000 acres of wastes and commons, mostly on the dry

---

[1] *General report on enclosures drawn up by order of the Board of Agriculture* (London, 1808), 139–41.

[2] See p. 103 above.

[3] H. Holland, *General view Cheshire* (1808), 208. W. Pitt, *General view Stafford* (1796), 102.

[4] R. G. Albion, 135–6.

[5] W. Gilpin, *Remarks on forest scenery* (London, 1791), ed. T. D. Lander (London, 1834), I, 125.

[6] Gilbert White, *A natural history of Selborne* (Everyman's Library), 17.

[7] R. Lowe, *General view Nottingham* (1798), 51–98, 150.

sands in the western half of the county; and in Middlesex open heaths at Hounslow and Hampstead almost reached the edge of the built-up area.[1] Or, again, the improved arable husbandry of Norfolk and Suffolk scarcely touched the Breckland. In 1804 in the 16 miles from Newmarket to Thetford there were 'immense wastes', and another 18 miles as far as Swaffham deserved 'to be called a desert'.[2] There were smaller but no less dreary stretches surrendered to rabbit warrens and sheep-walks in the Sandlings of east Suffolk and in north Norfolk. In Lincolnshire much light land had already been reclaimed, but furze and broom still encumbered thousands of acres on the Wolds and along the Heath belt north and south of Lincoln. The sandy heaths of Cannock Chase and Sutton Cold-field in Staffordshire occupied more than 30,000 acres, and almost as large an area was waste in pastoral Cheshire.

A small part of the heathland was occasionally brought into cultivation. In Lincolnshire and the East Riding, 'the greater part of the Wold town-ships which remain open have a large quantity of *outfield* in ley land'.[3] About 1800, similar practices were reported in Norfolk, in Nottingham-shire, in Staffordshire, in Lancashire, in Shropshire, on the Mendips and as far west as Devon and Cornwall.[4]

Open moors over 800 feet above sea-level were rarely if ever broken up. About one-third of northern England was uncultivated mountain and moor. The economy of hill farms in these areas was almost exclusively pastoral. In the Lake District the practice of transhumance survived where cattle were kept, but when sheep replaced cattle, seasonal movement ceased and summer shielings were abandoned.[5] In the southern Pennines, hill farms bred and reared store cattle during the summer. Autumn sales provided the fattening pastures of the Midlands with one of their main sources of store animals.[6] But over most of the mountain and moorland areas of England and Wales cattle were far less numerous than sheep, and their rough grazing was devoted mostly to sheep raising.

[1] W. Stevenson, *General view Surrey* (1809), 456–70; J. Middleton, *General view Middlesex* (1807), 112–120.

[2] A. Young, *General view Suffolk* (1804), 170; A. Young, *General view Norfolk* (1804), 385.

[3] I. Leatham, *General view of the agriculture of the East Riding of Yorkshire* (London, 1794), 42.

[4] W. Smith, *An economic geography of Great Britain* (London, 1949), 17–18.

[5] A. E. Smailes, 65.

[6] R. W. Sturgess, 'A study of agricultural change in the Staffordshire moorlands, 1780–1850', *North. Staffs. Jour. Field Studies*, 1 (1961), 77–85.

At the edges of the waste, steady nibbling by cottagers and small farmers added thousands of tiny enclosures to the cultivated area. Near the woollen manufacturing districts in the West Riding of Yorkshire, on the edge of Rossendale and in Devonshire piecemeal inning was particularly active.[1] In northern Pennine dales, on the sides of the North York Moors and on the East Moor of Derbyshire, larger intakes of ten, twenty or even fifty acres were added to a few farms.[2] Patches of moorland were occasionally brought into cultivation by paring and burning the turf, by draining and by dressing the surface with lime; and a succession of oat crops was grown before the land reverted to grass. The practice was widespread in Devon and Cornwall and was also prevalent in Somerset, in parts of the Midlands and in Lancashire. But on the drier uplands of eastern England it was considered harmful.

Some of the largest remaining tracts of waste lay in the coastal marshes and peat-filled basins around the Humber, in the Fens, in the Somerset Levels and on the mosses of south Lancashire. The peatlands of eastern England had already been extensively embanked and drained; the 'carrs' and 'marishes' of the vale of Pickering, the 'carrs' of the Hull valley and the warplands of the vale of York were largely protected.[3] Ague had almost been eliminated from the Trent and Humber lowlands and, after the draining of Walling Fen, that country was now 'full of new-built houses, and highly improved'.[4] In Lincolnshire over a century of unremitting effort had brought 150,000 acres of marsh and fen into cultivation, to become 'one of the richest tracts in the kingdom'. The remaining 66,000 acres of wet land was fast disappearing, and the draining of Deeping Fen, completed in 1799, represented a 'very capital improvement'. To the north, the watery expanses of East Fen, West Fen and Wildmore Fen were drained within the next ten years.[5] In Huntingdonshire, in Suffolk

---

[1] E.g. G. H. Tupling, *The economic history of Rossendale* (Manchester, 1927), 42–69; W. G. Hoskins, 'The reclamation of the waste in Devon, 1550–1800', *Econ. Hist. Rev.*, XIII (1943), 80–92.

[2] J. Chapman, 'Changing agriculture and the moorland edge in the North York Moors', unpublished M.A. thesis, University of London, 1961; S. R. Eyre, 'The upward limit of enclosure on the East Moor of north Derbyshire', *Trans. and Papers, Inst. Brit. Geog.*, XXIII (1957), 61–74.

[3] J. A. Sheppard: (1) *The draining of the Hull valley* (East Yorks. Local Hist. Soc., No. 8, York, 1958); (2) *The draining of the marshlands of south Holderness and the Vale of York* (*Ibid.*, No. 20, York, 1966).

[4] A. Young, *General view Lincoln* (1799), 6.

[5] H. C. Darby, *The draining of the Fens* (2nd ed., Cambridge, 1956).

and in Cambridgeshire new tracts of peatlands were being reclaimed and sown with rape and clover. Among the largest, nearly 14,000 acres of Burnt Fen in Suffolk were now cultivated.[1]

By 1800 the condition of the Bedford Level, drained in the seventeenth century, was fast deteriorating. Hundreds of windmills failed to clear the water from miles of drains, dykes and lodes, and, as the peat surface shrank, windmills became less and less effective. In July 1805, surveying the country between Whittlesey and March, Arthur Young was shocked at the sight 'in all which tract of ten miles, usually under great crops of cole, oats and wheat, there was nothing to be seen but desolation, with here and there a crop of oats or barley, sown so late they can come to nothing'. He could only conclude: 'The Fens are now in a moment of balancing their fate; should a great flood come within two or three years for want of an improved outfall, the whole country, fertile as it naturally is, will be abandoned.'[2]

In Oxfordshire, Otmoor remained an undrained bog of 4,000 acres, 'the most considerable, and at the same time the most valuable waste in this county'.[3] In 1800 no part of the Somerset Levels was without a drainage system, however rudimentary, but the greatest progress had been made in the Brue and King's Sedgemoor while little had yet been done in the southern levels.[4] Draining was carried out in a piecemeal fashion and the newly reclaimed lands were inadequately protected against floods. In Devon and Cornwall small patches of coastal marsh were walled in and improved. New walls were raised along the coasts of Kent, Essex and around Morecambe Bay. In south Lancashire large areas of Trafford Moss, Rainford Moss, Bolton Moss and Bootle Moss were already growing potatoes with clover, vetches and barley sown to prepare the ground for more potatoes. The largest stretches, such as Chat Moss, remained neglected, and Cheshire still had 18,000 acres in unimproved bogs and mosses.

INDUSTRY

In 1800 the beginning of the industrial revolution, associated particularly with the invention of the steam engine and the improvement of textile machinery, left few scars on the face of England. Contemporaries marvel-

[1] A. Young (ed.), *Annals of agriculture*, XVI (1791), 463–76.
[2] A. Young (ed.), *Annals of agriculture*, XLIII (1805), 545–7.
[3] R. Davis, *General view of the agriculture of the county of Oxford* (London, 1794), 22.
[4] M. Williams, *The draining of the Somerset Levels* (Cambridge, 1970), 131–52.

led at the power of steam to drive mighty instruments of mass-production but few at that time visualised the shapes of the infernal landscapes to come. The maps of the time show no closely packed streets of houses, and no densely built towns outside Manchester, Salford, Leeds and Bradford. The manufactured products of England came from hundreds of mills, mines and small workshops scattered over the countryside.

Rural industries

Districts which, at the present time, are largely agricultural, in 1800 possessed a great variety of manufacturing activities. In addition to flour mills, bakeries, maltings, breweries, sawmills, slaughterhouses and tanneries (processing the produce of farms and forests), rural brickyards, tileries, joineries, wheelwrights' shops, cooperages, saddleries, village smithies and foundries supplied the nation with a large part of its building materials, implements and tools. The countryside teemed with craftsmen making many articles that we now do without or obtain from factories.

The Board of Agriculture reports, mentioning only the most specialised and highly localised industries, indicate how diverse those activities were.[1] Bedfordshire made osier baskets, reed mats, pillow lace; hemp spinning was nearly extinct but straw plaiting was widely practised not only there but also in Cambridgeshire, Hertfordshire and Buckinghamshire. In many villages and small towns in Suffolk, in Norfolk and in Lincolnshire, sacking, coarse linen and hempen cloth were woven, in addition to large quantities of woollen and worsted thread spun in cottages. Kent, the Garden of England, had not only oasthouses but dyeworks, saltworks, copperas works, paper mills, gunpowder mills, linen and calico printing shops. Surrey made paper, oil, snuff, leather, parchment, ironware and printed cloth. Both Sussex and Hampshire were predominantly agricultural counties but the dying charcoal iron industry of the Weald and Henry Cort's rolling mill at Fontley were situated within their boundaries. Berkshire, Oxfordshire, Gloucestershire, Wiltshire, Dorset, Somerset and Devon produced a bewildering variety of yarns and fabrics from sailcloth to silk ribbons. In most counties, a number of villages specialised in the making of pottery, glassware, hats, gloves, boots, buttons, pins, iron and brass ware, tin-plate, soap and candles. Over the whole countryside these industries were widely diffused.

In a large number of villages on the borders of Devon, Somerset and Dorset, in west Wiltshire and in the Gloucestershire Cotswolds, as much

[1] Lord Ernle, 308–12.

or more than half the population was reported in the 1801 Census to be engaged in manufacturing. These were districts where, in addition to the usual rural crafts, cloth-making was carried on in a majority of homes. Men and boys plied their looms, while women and children spun yarn. There was also a wide scatter of manufacturing households in the worsted-spinning districts of north Essex and East Anglia. But the highest proportion of the population engaged in rural and domestic textile industries outside south Lancashire and the West Riding was in the east Midlands, in southern Nottinghamshire, southern Derbyshire and western Leicestershire. Moreover the wire-drawing, nailmaking, ironmongery and hardware trades were dispersed throughout the country from the Forest of Dean through Worcestershire and Staffordshire to the Lake District, and individual firms put out work over a very wide area. Warrington file makers distributed materials to be made up by outworkers in a number of villages in south Lancashire and Cheshire; while Dudley nailmakers employed domestic workers as far afield as the Stour and Tame valleys.[1]

Although most industrial activities were highly scattered, important branches of some leading industries were rapidly concentrating in a few localities. Gunsmiths, locksmiths and button makers were increasing in hundreds of small workshops in Birmingham, watchmakers in Coventry and in Clerkenwell, and cutlers in Sheffield.[2] Salisbury cutlers still produced blades superior in workmanship to any in the country; Stafford, too, manufactured large quantities of cutlery and held a share in overseas markets, Birmingham sword-makers prospered during the wars, but the steel industry of Woodstock in Oxfordshire had lately succumbed to competition from Sheffield and Birmingham.

Industries that were growing were spreading most rapidly in one or two localities. There was an immense increase in the production of salt but most of that increase was produced in Cheshire and on Tyneside. By 1800 the Weaver navigation was carrying nearly 140,000 tons of salt a year down to the Mersey and bringing 100,000 tons of coal up to the saltworks. Cheshire salt was exported all over the world for preserving fish and meat. It was also shipped to the Potteries for glazing, and some soda was

[1] T. S. Ashton, *An eighteenth-century industrialist: Peter Stubbs of Warrington, 1756–1806* (Manchester, 1939), 9–22; S. Timmins, *The resources, products and industrial history of Birmingham and the Midland hardware district* (London, 1866), 86.

[2] J. H. Clapham, *An economic history of modern Britain: the early railway age, 1820–1850* (2nd ed., Cambridge, 1930); M. J. Wise, 'On the evolution of the jewellery and gun quarters in Birmingham', *Trans. and Papers, Inst. Brit. Geog.*, xv (1949), 57–72.

extracted.[1] About four-fifths of the salt output was exported for half a million pounds.

Glass production increased greatly as the standards of lighting in homes and workshops were improved. In 1800 its value was estimated at about one and a half million pounds.[2] A score of provincial towns and ports continued to make crown and bottle glass on a small scale. London and Southwark were still by far the largest producers of most types of glass, but the increasing demand for thick plate glass was met solely by a large new works at Ravenhead near St Helens. Large new glasshouses were rising on Tyneside to supply window glass; and at Stourbridge, already a prospering glass-making town, 'a number of very lofty and spacious glasshouses' were added at the end of the eighteenth century.[3]

The manufacture of pottery, which a century earlier had been carried on in every town in England, was fast becoming concentrated on a district of some twelve square miles containing five small towns identified simply by the name 'The Potteries'. Although the five towns retained their separate names, they had become joined together so closely by 1795 that they struck a traveller 'as but one town'.[4] Josiah Wedgwood's porcelain was more highly valued than the fine china of Derby, Chelsea, Worcester and the Delft ware of Mortlake. Cratefuls of earthenware plates and tea-cups shipped from a hundred other Staffordshire potteries were cheaper than those made in Gateshead or Barnstaple or Caughley. A large part of the two million pounds' worth of pottery manufactured in England and Wales came from this district. The great concentration of production had been achieved by a labour force of fewer than 10,000, largely without the assistance of labour-saving machines, relying upon roads and canals for the transport of the bulk of its raw materials, including much of its clay, lead and salt. By 1800 waterways linked the Potteries with Liverpool, Hull and Bristol serving distant markets.[5] In their search for economical methods of using materials, north Staffordshire manufacturers had perfected new glazes, new methods of printing, and of preparing bone paste, and in 1793 had built a steam mill to crush flints. But the scale of operations

[1] H. Holland, *General view Cheshire* (1808), 12–73, 315–24.

[2] W. Smart, *Economic annals of the nineteenth century, 1801–20* (London, 1910), 21.

[3] W. Pitt, *General view Stafford* (1796), 168.

[4] J. Aikin, *A description of the country from thirty to forty miles around Manchester* (London, 1795), 516.

[5] H. A. Moisley, 'The industrial and urban development of the north Staffordshire conurbation', *Trans. and Papers, Inst. Brit. Geog.*, XVII (1951), 149–65.

was never large. Josiah Wedgwood employed fewer workers at Etruria than William Reynolds at a new china manufactory opened in 1797 at Coalport in Shropshire which gave work to 400 people.[1]

Large commercial enterprises were taking an increasing share of the processing industries, and were flourishing in the metropolis and in other large centres of population. According to one estimate, brewing ranked third in value of output following woollen cloth and leather goods.[2] Enormous quantities of small beer were brewed at home for private consumption, and for sale at thousands of brewing victuallers' houses, but in 1800 twelve leading London firms brewed over one million barrels of porter, nearly one-quarter of all the strong beer consumed in England and Wales.[3] The great London breweries supplied most of the ale houses in Middlesex and large numbers in Kent and Surrey. They and a group of breweries on the Trent at Burton, Nottingham and Newark were the largest exporters of beer.[4] Distilling was also highly localised, more than half the spirits sold and paying duty came from London. London produced almost all the gin drunk in the country.[5]

In 1800 leather goods manufactured in England and Wales were worth more than ten and a half million pounds, their value exceeded only by that of woollen cloth. Almost every town from Berwick to Penzance had its tanners and curriers, leather being used for many articles now made from rubber, plastics and cloth. The daily wear that men and horses gave their boots, belts, saddles and straps was a good deal harder than at present. By the end of the eighteenth century many women and children of labouring families were wearing leather shoes, but many others still went barefoot or wore wooden clogs. A multitude of independent cobblers and saddlers made most of the shoes and harness worn in the country but London shops were supplied with shoes made in Stafford, Northampton, Kettering and Wellingborough. Curriers in inner north-east London and in the West End supplied glovers, bookbinders, coach trimmers and strap makers. The greatest concentration of tanneries in the country lay to the south of the Thames. About one-eighth of the nation's tanning business was transacted in Bermondsey, and a number of large tanneries were

[1] J. H. Clapham, 185; J. Plymley, *General view Shropshire* (1803), 341.
[2] W. Smart, 22–3.
[3] J. Middleton, *View of Middlesex* (1807), 583; G. R. Porter, 572.
[4] P. Mathias, 'Industrial revolution in brewing', *Explorations in entrepreneurial history*, V (1952–3), 208–24.
[5] D. George, *London life in the eighteenth century* (3rd ed., London, 1951), 40.

situated nearby in the Wandle valley from Mitcham to Croydon. Liverpool alone had a tannery larger than any in London, and hides imported from Ireland and the New World were processed in south Lancashire and Cheshire.[1] The home market consumed almost the entire output of the industry but English leather was highly valued abroad for its suppleness.

The woodworking crafts used little machinery and almost no mechanical power. A circular saw, invented in 1790, was used only in naval dockyards, and turning machines were speeding the making of chairs at High Wycombe. Shoreditch was the most important centre of furniture making. In 1800 most counties possessed one or two paper mills but the industry was concentrating on chalk streams near London, in Hertfordshire, Kent, Berkshire and Hampshire.

The woollen and worsted industries

The manufacture of woollen and worsted cloth had for long been 'supposed the sacred staple and foundation of all our wealth'.[2] It employed more workers than any other industry. The value of fabric produced for home consumption amounted to eleven million pounds, and exports were worth another eight million pounds. In 1806 a Select Committee on the woollen manufacture of England reported that production 'has been gradually increasing in almost all the various parts of England in which it is carried on; in some of them very rapidly'.[3] Exports continued to increase while the demand for wool steadily outpaced home production.

But the benefits of rising productivity were not evenly distributed. The industry brought prosperity to some areas while others were depressed. Labour-saving machines had caused widespread unemployment among spinners of woollen and worsted yarn. While spinning declined in almost all the old-established centres of the industry it boomed in the West Riding (Fig. 29). Not unnaturally, commentators blamed the new factories for depriving the rest of the country of its livelihood. In 1791, a west of England manufacturer asserted that 'Yorkshire, by dint of such machines and engines, not only use all their wool, but send down into the west country and buy it up out of the very mouths of the wool dealers

---

[1] J. Statham, 'The location and development of London's leather manufacturing industry since the early nineteenth century', unpublished M.A. thesis, University of London, 1965, 70, 81, 85.

[2] A. Young, *The farmers' letters to the people of England* (London, 1767), 22.

[3] *S.C. on the woollen manufacture in England, 1806, Report*, 3 (P.P. 1806, iii).

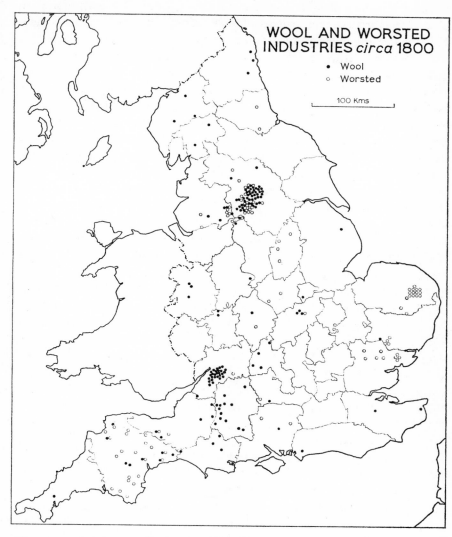

Fig. 29 Wool and worsted industries *circa* 1800
   Based on the manufacturers mentioned in: (1) *S.C. on the woollen manufacture
   in England, 1806, Report and Minutes of evidence* (P.P. 1806, iii); (2) the
   county *General views* of the Board of Agriculture; (3) Arthur Young (ed.),
   Annals of agriculture, 45 vols. (Bury St Edmunds, 1784–6; London,
   1786–1815).

and clothiers, and thereby take our trade with it'.[1] As far as the spinning of woollen yarn was concerned such complaints contained a small element of truth, but the fortunes of woollen weaving varied widely from district to district, while the state of the worsted trade was yet more complex.

The introduction of machines for spinning woollen yarn brought distress to much of Wiltshire and to neighbouring Gloucestershire. In 1796 Sir Frederick Eden learned from a clothier at Seend in Wiltshire that 'the poor, from the great reduction in the price of spinning, scarcely have the heart to earn the little that is obtained by it'.[2] Because of the decline in spinning, Stroud and other Cotswold villages, according to one observer, 'fell into decay, and almost wholly into beggary', whence colonies of mendicants poured into adjacent towns. Even where trade was active, as at Chippenham in Wiltshire in 1796, Arthur Young lamented that there were 'many begging children'. The use of spinning jennies in the home meant that families were made redundant for everyone that obtained work.

Cotswold weavers, on the other hand, successfully resisted attempts made in 1792 to install flying shuttles at Trowbridge in Wiltshire; and in south Gloucestershire few weavers were out of work, and after 1796 unemployment practically ceased. The setting up of gig-mills to dress woollen cloth appeared as a fresh threat, and in July 1802 serious riots broke out in Wiltshire. The prospect of further outrages did nothing to encourage manufacturers to adopt new machines, such as shearing frames. A witness from Bradford on Avon before the Select Committee of 1806 stated: 'if that machinery had not been instituted there would not be so many boys running about the streets without shoes or stockings on, and nearly half-starved'.[3]

Gloucestershire clothiers were not modernising their methods, but their order books were full, and unemployment was negligible in comparison with that of neighbouring counties. In Hampshire, the decay of the serge industry was attributed to the war and was optimistically 'expected to revive again on the return of peace'.[4] In Berkshire, clothiers abandoned hope of regaining the trade they had lost, while in Oxfordshire, they had resigned themselves to a 'very depressing poverty'. Even at Witney woollen manufacturing had shrunk to a point where there was

[1] H. Wansey, *Wool encouraged without exportation; or practical observations on wool and the woollen manufacture* (London, 1791), 69.

[2] F. M. Eden, *The state of the poor*, 3 vols. (London, 1797), III, 796.

[3] *S.C. woollen manufacture, 1806, Minutes of evidence*, 308 (P.P. 1806, iii).

[4] C. Vancouver, *General view of the agriculture of Hampshire* (London, 1810), 404.

'very little expectation of its ever reviving'.[1] It had also diminished in the Midlands; the country around Kettering no longer employed more than 3,000 spinners and most districts had taken up other domestic crafts.

In south-western England the decline of spinning was widespread, and severe hardship afflicted places where weaving had also declined. In north Devonshire many women were out of work, and John Collinson painted a gloomy picture of the Somerset industry in 1791. At Milverton the manufacture of serges and druggets had much declined; in the country around Keynsham they were 'now entirely dropt'; and at Pensford the industry was 'dreadfully decayed', and 'bereft of the benefit of trade, many of the houses are fallen into ruins'.[2] At Taunton, once the foremost manufacturing town in Somerset, the industry had been so reduced that it seemed unlikely to recover, and only at Wiveliscombe and Wellington were looms still active.[3] The loss of Spanish and Mediterranean markets delivered a death blow to the serge industry in south Devon, but its life was prolonged for a few years by contracts from the East India Company. As late as 1796 in Exeter itself, despite the use of many spinning jennies, there was little unemployment: 'on the contrary, they are not able to get spinners'.[4]

The most depressed textile villages in the country were in north Essex and in mid-Suffolk where not only had the spinning of woollen and worsted yarn declined but the production of Colchester baize had fallen to a quarter of what it had been before the outbreak of war in 1793. Woollen manufacturing had once been the leading industry of Essex, 'but from its long continued dwindling condition' so it was said in 1806, 'it is uncertain whether it will many years remain so'.[5] By 1803 no fewer than 38,337 persons, or 17% of the population of Essex, received poor relief.[6] Nowhere in England was so large a proportion of the population reduced to poverty as along the borders of Suffolk and Essex.

By contrast, woollen manufacturing in the West Riding was booming. Evidence submitted to the Select Committee of 1806 showed that possibly 65,000 Yorkshire people were engaged in the industry, most of whom were domestic workers living 'in villages and detached houses, covering

[1] A. Young, *General view of the agriculture of Oxfordshire* (London, 1809), 325, 328.
[2] J. Collinson, *The history and antiquities of the county of Somerset*, 3 vols. (Bath, 1791), II, 400, 429; III, 13.
[3] J. Billingsley, *General view Somerset* (1798), 296.
[4] A. Young (ed.), *Annals of agriculture*, XXVIII (1797), 634.
[5] A. Young, *General view Essex*, II (1807), 390.   [6] *Ibid.*, II, 414.

the whole face of a district of from 20 to 30 miles in length, and from 12 to 15 in breadth'.[1] The opinions of witnesses were divided about the extent to which factories had fostered the expansion of trade, but two facts are abundantly clear. Firstly that in the West Riding factories manufactured only about one-sixteenth of all the woollen cloth made in the country.[2] Secondly that the prosperity of the industry was shared by factory and domestic workers alike. In Armley, for example, the number of domestic clothiers doubled between 1786 and 1806, and comparable increases were reported in other villages around Leeds.[3] On the other hand, superfine broadcloth produced in factories was acknowledged to be both cheaper and better in quality than domestic stuff, and factory owners paid higher wages than domestic masters. Factories raised the standards for their rivals largely by the superiority of their organisation. They possessed no power looms and few mechanical aids. Power-driven machinery was first applied to the initial processes of preparing wool for spinning – to scribbling, carding and slubbing – before it was applied to spinning. But as soon as steam engines were installed, the number of spinning mules increased rapidly. In 1796 Arthur Young was informed that six or seven steam engines were working in Leeds, and by 1800 there were probably as many as twenty in the town.[4]

In 1800 much less worsted than woollen cloth was woven in England but no branch of the worsted industry was depressed. Both in Norwich and in the country around Halifax and Bradford production was rising; and elsewhere, clothiers turned from the uncertainties of the woollen trade to an assurance of modest earnings in worsteds. Mechanisation took over slowly, and not until 1800 was a steam engine used to drive a worsted spinning mill at Bradford.[5] By this time the West Riding had already surpassed Norwich in the value of its worsted manufacture. Both districts however were still increasing their output, and it is clear that Norwich produced most of the finest cloth, and that the industry gave employment directly or indirectly to about 100,000 workers in Norfolk.[6] In 1805 the stranglehold of northern competition was felt when Norwich began to buy machine-spun yarn from Yorkshire mills. By 1808 some 300 woolcombers

[1] S.C. woollen manufacture, 1806, Minutes of evidence, 9, Report, 9 (P.P. 1806, iii).
[2] Ibid., Minutes of evidence, 89.
[3] Ibid., Minutes of evidence, 16, 94, 158, 444.
[4] A. Young (ed.), Annals of agriculture, XXVII (1796), 310.
[5] J. James, History of the worsted manufacture in England (London, 1857), 592–3.
[6] J. K. Edwards, 'The decline of the Norwich textile industry', Yorks. Bull. Econ. and Soc. Research, XVI (1964), 31–41.

had departed for the West Riding. As competition stiffened, Norwich diversified its range of products, using cotton, silk, alpaca and mohair warps in an increasing proportion of its cloth. Norwich turned to the production of mixed cloths much later than most other districts.

The cotton industry

Lancashire had long been weaving fustians, half-worsteds and mixed woollen and linen cloths in addition to pure woollens, while many other districts changed from producing one type of fabric to another. Along the Bristol Avon, for example, a number of mills were converted from woollens to mixed cloths to cottons, or from cottons to worsteds.[1] In Rossendale the first steps in mechanisation were taken in the manufacture of woollens. Most water mills were spinning woollen thread and towns such as Oldham and Rochdale still produced considerable quantities of woollen goods.[2] In Lancashire and the West Riding corn mills were taken over by carders, combers and spinners, while in Derbyshire some early cotton mills were built alongside iron forges. There was a great deal of flexibility in the use to which mills were put and a diversity in the types of fabric produced, but the growing number of cotton mills in south Lancashire made a deep impression on a traveller in 1791. He reported: 'there is scarcely a stream that will turn a wheel through the north of England that has not a cotton mill upon it.'[3]

The production of cotton cloth increased more rapidly than that of other textiles. Imports of raw cotton doubled between 1790 and 1800 and more than doubled between 1800 and 1810. In 1802 the value of cotton yarn and cotton cloth exported exceeded that of woollen goods, and cotton goods became the leading export. During its first phase of expansion the industry dispersed to remote water-power sites in upland areas. About 1790 it was more widely dispersed than at any later period. A number of counties had one or more spinning mills, but the greatest numbers were located in two districts: the first comprising south Derbyshire, Nottinghamshire and parts of Leicestershire and Staffordshire; the second comprising south Lancashire, north Cheshire and north Derbyshire (Fig. 30).

The east Midlands was the birthplace of the cotton factory.[4] As long

[1] S. J. Jones, 'The cotton industry in Bristol', *Trans. and Papers, Inst. Brit. Geog.*, XIII (1947), 63–7.

[2] G. H. Tupling, 193–206.   [3] *European magazine*, XX (1791), 140.

[4] D. M. Smith, 'The cotton industry in the east Midlands', *Geography*, XLVII (1962), 256–69.

as water power dominated the industry the number of mills in Derbyshire increased. By 1807 there were 51 mills in south Derbyshire and almost as many again in Nottinghamshire, north Leicestershire and east Staffordshire. The cotton spinners of Nottingham supplied twist to domestic hosiers but the spinners multiplied their output while the hosiery trade expanded very slowly. The application of steam power to cotton spinning gave Nottinghamshire a new lead. The first Boulton and Watt engine installed in a cotton mill was at Papplewick in 1785, and by 1800 Nottinghamshire cotton mills had fifteen such engines, Leicestershire had two while Staffordshire and Derbyshire each had only one. Both Middlesex with four and Durham with three had surpassed Derbyshire in the application of Boulton and Watt engines to cotton manufacture.

It was Lancashire, however, that held an undisputed lead in cotton manufacturing. It had achieved its ascendancy very rapidly. When Arkwright founded his water-powered spinning factory at Cromford in Derbyshire in 1771, the cotton industry in Lancashire was poor and struggling, completely overshadowed by a long-established woollen industry. But by 1788 nearly twice as many water-driven spinning mills were situated in Lancashire as in Derbyshire;[1] and Lancashire advanced more rapidly than Nottinghamshire in equipping its mills with steam engines. The first Lancashire steam-powered factories were set up at Manchester, Bury, Preston, Oldham and Chorley. In 1795 Sir Robert Peel owned factories in twelve different places and employed 15,000 workers, including most of the workers in Bury. The Horrocks opened three factories in Preston, while Oldham underwent an 'extraordinary change from the scale of a mere village to that of one of the most populous towns in the kingdom'.[2] At Stockport, nearby in Cheshire, Samuel Oldknow built a steam cotton mill in 1790, and by 1795 there were twenty-three factories in the town, of which four were driven by steam.[3] But the most spectacular growth took place in Manchester. By 1795 it was pre-eminent among cotton towns. John Aikin prefaced his *Description of the country from thirty to forty miles around Manchester* with the observation that: 'The centre we have chosen is that of the *cotton manufacture*; a branch of commerce, the rapid and prodigious increase of which is, perhaps, absolutely unparalleled in the annals of trading nations'.[4] Describing the

---

[1] Anon., *An important crisis in the callico and muslin manufactory of Great Britain explained* (London, 1788). See table on p. 61 above.

[2] E. Butterworth, *Historical sketches of Oldham* (Oldham, 1849), 117–18.

[3] J. Aikin (1795), 445–6.   [4] *Ibid.*, 3.

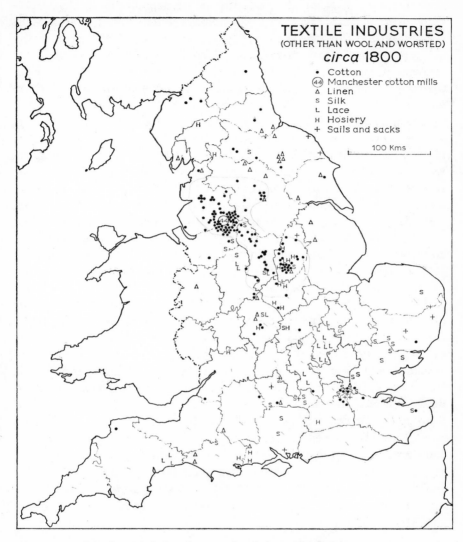

Fig. 30 Textile industries (other than wool and worsted) *circa* 1800

Based on the places mentioned in: (1) G. W. Daniels, 'Samuel Crompton's census of the cotton industry in 1811', *Econ. Hist.*, II (1930), 107–16; (2) the county *General views* of the Board of Agriculture; (3) Arthur Young (ed.), *Annals of agriculture*, 45 vols. (Bury St Edmunds, 1784–6; London, 1786–1815).

process by which Manchester outstripped its neighbours, William Rad-cliffe wrote in 1828: 'there was not a village within thirty miles of Man-chester, on the Cheshire and Derbyshire side, in which some of us were not putting out cotton warps and taking in goods, employing all the weavers of woollen and linen goods who were declining those fabrics as the cotton trade increased; in short we employed every person in cotton weaving who could be induced to learn the trade'.[1]

The application of steam power first to spinning, and later to weaving, set the seal on the supremacy of Lancashire, and above all on Manchester. In 1800 Lancashire possessed 42 out of 84 Boulton and Watt steam engines working in cotton-spinning mills in England; and these probably con-stituted not more than one-third of the total number of steam engines at work in the cotton industry of the country at this time.[2] Power-loom weaving, however, was still virtually unknown. A steam-driven loom had been set up at Manchester in 1791, but was destroyed by the hand-weavers, and it was not until 1803 that a satisfactory steam-driven loom was built at Stockport. It was improved by successive patents and was soon in use in several Lancashire towns.[3]

The other textile industries were of minor importance (Fig. 30). The fortunes of the linen industry had been submerged by the rise of cotton. Lancashire had almost entirely gone over to producing cotton goods. Leeds still produced linen thread, and linen spinning lingered in Somerset and Dorset, but hardly any progress had been made in the mechanisation of linen manufacture. The hosiery industry grew sluggishly. Between 1782 and 1812 the number of stocking frames increased from about 20,000 to 29,590, almost 85% of which were located in well-established centres, especially in Leicestershire and Notting-hamshire.[4] The cap-making and knitwear industries elsewhere stagnated, and the woollen spinners supplying them with yarn suffered much hardship. In London also, stocking frames were fast disappearing. The industry contracted at the edges and became concentrated in the east

[1] W. Radcliffe, *Origin of the new system of manufacture, commonly called power loom weaving* (Stockport, 1828), 12.

[2] A. E. Musson and E. Robinson, *Science and technology in the industrial revolution* (Manchester, 1969), 426. See p. 153 below.

[3] E. Baines, *History of the cotton manufacture in Great Britain* (London, 1835), 234; J. Wheeler, *Manchester, its political, commercial and social history, ancient and modern* (London, 1836), 107; C. Hardinck, *History of the borough of Preston and its environs* (Preston, 1857), 375.

[4] G. R. Porter, 206.

Midlands.[1] Lace-making was still a rural handicraft industry, especially in the villages of Bedfordshire and Buckinghamshire. The silk industry had moved out of Spitalfields in two directions: north-east to the depressed woollen centres of Essex and East Anglia; and also north-west to Macclesfield and Congleton in Cheshire and to Derbyshire where water-driven silk-throwing mills were established on fast flowing streams.

The iron industry

The phenomenal growth of the iron industry around 1800 clearly foreshadowed the changes that were to take place in almost every branch of industry during the nineteenth century. In 1800, iron manufacturing was of vital importance to the nation's war effort, its products were diffused, 'by numerous meandering streams, into every department of civil life', its surpluses found their way into new export markets.[2] In its various branches iron manufacturing gave direct employment to about 200,000 workers, and possibly as many more were engaged in ancillary activities such as mining ore and coal, or in engineering and distributive trades.

Not only had the total output of pig-iron doubled and doubled again in each of the last two decades of the eighteenth century but the locations of furnaces shifted during the same period. The early seats of charcoal smelting in the Forest of Dean, in the Weald and in Furness were abandoned. In 1794 it was reported that the last remaining Wealden furnace (at Ashburnham) 'blows six months in the year, and is considered as an auxiliary to the limeworks'.[3] It seems to have closed down in 1812; and the last forge, also at Ashburnham, ceased to work in 1828.[4] The Weald continued to manufacture considerable quantities of lime and charcoal.

From being widely scattered in wooded spots accessible to supplies of charcoal, the smelting of iron concentrated upon five areas: in Shropshire, in the Black Country, in south Yorkshire, in Durham and Northumberland, and, towards the end of the century, in South Wales and Monmouthshire (Fig. 31). In 1802, some forty furnaces were being built or had been

---

[1] D. M. Smith, 'The British hosiery industry at the middle of the nineteenth century: an historical study in economic geography', *Trans. and Papers, Inst. Brit. Geog.*, XXXII (1963), 125–42.

[2] From a speech in the House of Commons against the proposed duty on iron in 1806, cited in H. Scrivenor, *A comprehensive history of the iron trade* (London, 1841), 102.

[3] A. Young (ed.), *Annals of agriculture*, XXII (1794), 269.

[4] E. Straker, *Wealden iron* (London, 1931), 369.

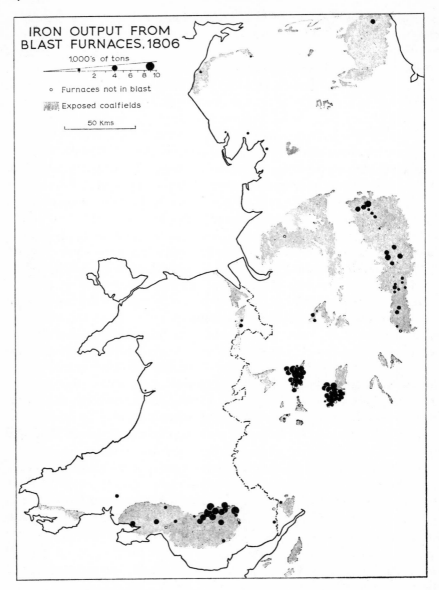

Fig. 31 Iron output from blast furnaces, 1806
Based on E. Buckley, 'Number of furnaces and make of iron in England, Scotland and Wales in the year 1806', *Report of the Commissioner on the State of Population in the Mining Districts*, Appendix, p. 25 (P.P. 1849, xxii).

completed since 1796 at places in these areas. Between 1802 and 1806 another sixty were built in the same localities.[1] In 1785 Coalbrookdale had been described by Arthur Young as 'a very romantic spot', notwithstanding 'the noise of the forges, mills, etc. with all their vast machinery, the flames bursting from the furnaces with the burning of the coal and the smoak of the lime kilns, are altogether sublime'.[2] In 1803, according to a contemporary, the number of blast furnaces in the seven miles between Ketley and Willey, in eastern Shropshire, exceeded 'any within the same space in the kingdom'.[3] The works employed some 6,000 hands and consumed 260,000 tons of coal each year. Both the Coalbrookdale Company and John Wilkinson at Bradley built hundreds of new houses to accommodate incoming workers, but the furnaces grew so fast and so thickly that there was a persistent shortage of labour.[4] A Shropshire ironmaster giving evidence before a Select Committee on the coal trade in December 1800 summed up his predicament: 'There are new furnaces for the smelting of iron constantly erecting; and it is now difficult to get pitmen to work the coals.'[5]

In the Black Country and in South Wales, furnaces were multiplying even more rapidly than in Shropshire, and by 1806 the output of pig-iron from South Wales was greater than that either from Staffordshire or from Shropshire. Attracted by high wages offered in the Welsh valleys, ironworkers journeyed from Stourbridge and other centres in the west Midlands.[6] South Wales ironmasters were quick to take advantage of the inventions of Henry Cort and Peter Onions, and forged their iron economically by puddling and rolling instead of by hammering.

In the ironworks of Shropshire and Staffordshire, Boulton and Watt steam engines were first applied to purposes other than pumping. The first engine to blow a furnace had been installed by John Wilkinson at New Willey in Shropshire, and in 1800 nearly two-thirds of the Boulton and Watt engines used in ironworks were located either in Shropshire or in Staffordshire. The need for steam coal, as well as for coke, drew furnaces towards the coal measures, but water-power sites remained important for forges and for smithies. On the Stour and its tributaries, wrote William Pitt, 'are a number of very considerable iron works, where pig iron from

[1] H. Scrivenor, 96–8.

[2] A. Young (ed.), *Annals of agriculture*, IV (1785), 168.

[3] J. Plymley, *General view Shropshire* (1803), 340.

[4] T. S. Ashton, *Iron and steel in the industrial revolution* (2nd ed., London, 1951), 199.   [5] *Ibid.*, 144.   [6] *Ibid.*, 199.

Staffordshire and Shropshire foundries, and elsewhere, is rendered malleable, and worked into bars, rods and sheet iron'.[1] Around Sheffield, the fast flowing streams were dammed to form an almost continuous succession of mill ponds for cutlers and edge-tool makers, while smelting and steel-making concentrated near the coal pits. In east Durham, the iron industry, although much smaller, made a distinctive contribution to the local economy, and produced such articles as anchors, chains and edge-tools.

In 1806 no more than one ton of pig-iron in every thirty was made in the few surviving charcoal furnaces in Cumberland, Lancashire and the Forest of Dean, and more than nine-tenths of the nation's output was smelted on five coalfields.[2] The demand for castings seemed insatiable. Cast-iron rails were fitted to tramways at Coalbrookdale, Sheffield and on Tyneside. Cast-iron beams and girders were used in factory and mine-shaft construction. Cast-iron bridges spanned the Severn and the Wear. Miles of cast-iron water pipes were laid in London and cast-iron barges sailed on the Severn. Castings also began to enter in small quantities into the construction of machinery. Wheels and pistons were cast and machines for textile manufacturing, nailmaking and for furnace bellows were fabricated to an increasing extent from iron. A mechanical engineering industry was called into existence.

Coal and steam

Advances in the techniques of mining and utilising coal had been less far-reaching than those in iron-working. The substitution of coal for wood as a domestic fuel proceeded slowly. Houses had first to be provided with adequately ventilated fireplaces and chimneys to draw off the toxic fumes; and many districts where firewood was scarce lay beyond the reach of coal. Very little was hauled overland more than five or ten miles to iron-works or steam engines. Household coal burned in London and along the coast from the Tweed to the Exe was almost entirely shipped by sea from the Tyne and the Wear. About four-fifths of the large output of North-umberland and Durham was sent away by sea. Coal was also shipped across the Irish Sea mainly from Cumberland, but also from Lancashire,

[1] W. Pitt, *General view of the agriculture of the county of Worcester* (London, 1810), 279.

[2] E. Buckley, 'Number of furnaces and make of iron in England, Scotland and Wales in the year 1806', *Report of the Commissioner on the State of Population in the Mining Districts*, Appendix, p. 25 (P.P. 1849, xxii).

from lowland Scotland and from South Wales. In the meantime, canals were extending the markets of the inland coalfields.[1]

In 1800, the age of steam had dawned but the sky was not yet darkened with the smoke of factory chimneys. Probably no more than 1,200 steam engines were at work in England and Wales.[2] Coalmining and copper mining were the industries most dependent on steam for pumping. In most manufacturing districts, however, steam engines still contributed little, if anything, to the total amount of power being used. In Sheffield in 1794, only five cutlers' wheels were driven by steam while 111 were water-powered.[3] The Soho factory in Birmingham, established by Boulton in 1761, was dependent for some years on water power, and the competition for available water was keen in the Midlands.[4] Most engineers were engaged not in building steam engines, but in constructing and improving water wheels and water-powered machines. Indeed, it has been said that 'advances in water power deserve stressing because they have been unduly overshadowed by the early development of steam engines'.[5] In almost all localities water was a greater source of power than steam, and for some types of work, such as shipping and fen draining, wind power was more important than both. Experiments with steam traction had begun on water, but on the road horses reigned supreme. The number of horses kept in London and Middlesex alone far exceeded the aggregate horsepower of all steam engines at work in England and Wales.

The location of Boulton and Watt engines (Fig. 32) broadly indicates where investment in power-driven machinery was heaviest. They made a disproportionately large contribution to driving machines in the technically most advanced factories.[6] They were most numerous in cotton mills in Lancashire, Nottinghamshire, Yorkshire and Cheshire. Ironworks in

[1] T. S. Ashton and J. Sykes, *The coal industry of the eighteenth century* (Manchester, 1929), 226–39.

[2] J. R. Harris, 'The employment of steam power in the eighteenth century', *History*, LII (1967), 131–48.

[3] A. Allison, 'Water power as the foundation of Sheffield's industries', *Trans. Newcomen Soc.*, XXVII (1949–51), 221–4.

[4] P. Mantoux, *The industrial revolution in the eighteenth century* (London, 1928), 332–3; W. H. B. Court, *The rise of the Midland industries, 1600–1838* (Oxford, 1938), 249–52; R. A. Pelham, 'The water-power crisis in Birmingham in the eighteenth century', *Univ. of Birmingham Hist. Jour.*, IX (1963), 64–91.

[5] A. E. Musson and E. Robinson (1969), 71.

[6] J. Lord, *Capital and steam power* (London, 1923), 166; for a revaluation of Lord's view see A. E. Musson and E. Robinson, 'The early growth of steam', *Econ. Hist. Rev.*, n.s., XI (1959), 418–59.

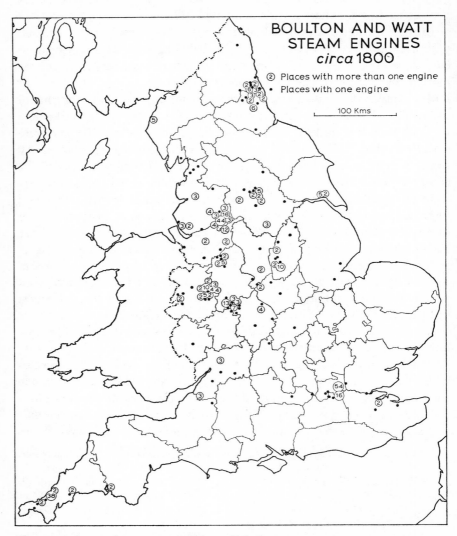

Fig. 32 Boulton and Watt steam engines *circa* 1800
Based on the Boulton and Watt Engine Book in the Boulton and Watt
Collection, Birmingham Public Library.

Shropshire and Staffordshire were well equipped with them, as were the deepest coal pits. But by far the largest number of pumping engines employed in coal mines were atmospheric engines of the Savery or New-comen type, improved by John Smeaton, James Brindley and others. Boulton and Watt engines were economical in their consumption of fuel and were preferred to atmospheric engines in districts where coal had to be imported. They were widely used in the tin and copper mines of Cornwall. The metropolitan area, also a long distance from coalfields, used Boulton and Watt engines for pumping at waterworks, breweries and distilleries. Middlesex had steam-powered corn mills, sugar mills, oil mills, cotton mills, bleacheries and dyeworks. Middlesex and Surrey together had about as many Boulton and Watt engines as Lancashire, but Boulton and Watt probably built no more than one-third of the steam engines used in Lancashire.[1] In all colliery districts Boulton and Watt engines were outnumbered, and also in such centres of manufacturing as Leeds and Birmingham. In 1802 William Reynolds reported that in Shropshire 180 steam engines were at work,[2] but at that time the firm's Engine Book records that only 43 Boulton and Watt engines had been installed in the county.

Boulton and Watt held exclusive patent rights but other manufacturers successfully pirated their inventions. The ironmaster, John Wilkinson, closely associated with the partnership, built his own engines infringing the patents. In 1800 some of the early engines were worn out, rebuilt or removed, and some were performing work different from that for which they had been intended. Pumping engines were blowing furnaces, and engines installed to grind flour were used to crush oil seeds. The Boulton and Watt Engine Book records some of the removals and changes of use. For steam engines made by other firms no comparable lists exist.

TRANSPORT AND TRADE

Transport by road

One of the greatest obstacles to the growth of manufacturing in inland districts was the high cost of transport by road.[3] Rates differed for different kinds of goods. For coal, iron ore, lime and other minerals the profitable

[1] A. E. Musson and E. Robinson (1969), 426.
[2] J. Plymley, *General view Shropshire* (1803), 340n.
[3] For a convenient short account, see B. F. Duckham, *The transport revolution, 1750–1830* (Hist. Assoc., London, 1967).

range of overland movement was rarely more than ten to twenty miles from a pit. The city of York, situated within sixteen miles of productive coal measures, obtained shipments of coal from Newcastle upon Tyne, over two hundred miles away, and the coastlands of North Wales imported coal more cheaply from South Wales than from the landlocked Flint and Denbigh coalfields.

Arthur Young and other travellers frequently remarked on the execrable condition of the roads, but these were not uniformly bad nor were parochial highways invariably worse than turnpike roads. The worst roads were often those carrying the heaviest traffic. Worst of all were the well-trodden roads between large towns, churned by herds of iron-shod cattle, by waddling geese, by lumbering wagons, by trains of mules laden with panniers of coal and by the travellers who complained. The roads that approached London were described as muddy rutted tracks, deep in filth, insufferably bad and disgraceful. In Middlesex the turnpike roads were worse than most parish roads, and in Surrey the direct roads leading to London were often impassable while the cross roads were generally good. The industrial districts of south Lancashire and the West Riding had the densest network of roadways in the country but the condition of some defied description. The turnpike roads of Lancashire were notoriously bad, rivalling those leading to the mining districts of Shropshire which, 'particularly in the clay parts of the county, are almost impassable to any but the inhabitants'.[1]

The nature of the terrain contributed to the poor state of many roads. In Surrey 'on the clays of the Weald and on the sands as well as in the low parts of the county near the Thames', the roads were 'very indifferent'.[2] In the Weald of Kent the turnpikes were 'as bad as can be imagined', but common roads, although neglected, were not so bad.[3] Steep inclines were often more difficult to negotiate than miry claylands. Even a short hill such as Highgate Hill took wagons several hours to climb, and accidents often occurred when teams of horses lost their footing. Many steep ascents and descents were the principal handicaps of roads in Devonshire, while in northern England the difficulties of crossing hill country were increased by the hazards of snow, ice, poor visibility and by waterlogged

[1] J. Plymley, *General view Shropshire* (1803), 273.
[2] W. Stevenson, *General view Surrey* (1809), 547.
[3] J. Boys, *General view Kent* (1796), 168–9. See G. J. Fuller, 'The development of roads in the Surrey–Sussex Weald and coastlands between 1700 and 1900', *Trans. and Papers, Inst. Brit. Geog.*, XIX (1953), 37–49.

mosses. Rivers were also major obstacles, especially in thinly peopled districts where bridges were far apart.

Even rugged country had some tolerably good roads where traffic was light. Turnpikes were reported to be excellent in the Lake District, and those of Northumberland and Durham were in good repair although most township roads in the north were much neglected. The rural areas of eastern England, not traversed by through traffic, were better served by roads than any other part of the country. In Norfolk, Arthur Young said, in 1804, that they had greatly improved during the preceding twenty years; in Suffolk he thought they were 'uncommonly good'; and in Essex he found it 'impossible to say too much in praise of the roads of most districts'.[1] He might have had reservations about crossing the Lea valley, but Mile End Road was by no means the worst approach to London.

The area around London and the leading industrial districts were given more attention in road improvement acts than other parts of the country, and by 1800 substantial advances had been made in Nottinghamshire, Staffordshire and Durham. Before he died in 1810 the blind John Metcalfe had improved over 200 miles of roadway in Yorkshire. Thomas Telford held the appointment of Surveyor of Public Works in the industrial county of Shropshire, while John Loudon Macadam perfected his method of giving roads a hard metalled surface near Bristol and extended his practice to thirty-four other districts. In 1808, the roads in Cheshire were 'in a state of progressive improvement', stone being brought from Mow Cop, from Flintshire and from Anglesey to lay on their surfaces.[2] Three roads out of London to Canterbury, to Bath and to Portsmouth were greatly improved and kept in excellent repair. Industry itself helped to remedy the problem it had created. Iron girders were used in the construction of new bridges designed by John Smeaton, Thomas Telford and John Rennie, while slag and cinders were incorporated in road metal. Even so, the roads of 1800 were inadequate to carry the increasing burden industry imposed upon them.

Canal and coastwise traffic

Adam Smith observed that water transport was cheaper and more efficient than land carriage as a means of opening distant markets for manufactured goods. He reasoned that 'it is upon the sea-coast, and along the banks of

---

[1] A. Young, *General view Norfolk* (1804), 489; A. Young, *General view Suffolk* (1804), 227; A. Young, *General view Essex* (1807), II, 384.

[2] H. Holland, *General view Cheshire* (1808), 302.

navigable rivers, that industry of every kind naturally begins to subdivide and improve itself'.[1] The mines of Tyneside produced more coal than those of any other district because it was profitable to ship Newcastle coal coastwise to London and to the south coast as far west as Plymouth. The inland coalfields of the Midlands were at a disadvantage until they were provided with waterways. Many inland navigations were created by dredging, widening and embanking existing streams, but the most spectacular results were achieved by cutting canals (Figs. 18 and 44). In Manchester the price of coal had been halved since the opening of the Worsley Canal in 1761, and the Birmingham Canal (opened in 1772) halved the price of coal in Birmingham. With the coming of the Soar and Erewash navigations and their southward extension to Leicester in 1794, Leicester- shire coal owners lost between 30% and 40% of their trade to Derbyshire competitors.[2] The making of the Grand Junction canal in 1793–1805 opened the way to London, but high freight rates prevented Midland coal from flooding that lucrative market. Even so, coal was easily the largest single commodity carried by canals.

In Cheshire, canals gave a new lease of life to the salt industry, and they were also of great value to farmers as a cheap means of conveying marl, lime and fuel. Benjamin Capper believed that the cutting of canals also provided fat-stock producers with an efficient means of carrying animals to market and so helped the conversion of arable land to grass in the Mid- lands.[3] The rapid growth of Birmingham, the Black Country and the Potteries as manufacturing centres was 'much promoted by canal con- veyance'.[4] Not only the trade in coal but that in iron ore, limestone, lime and manufactured goods was considerably extended. Neighbouring Shropshire was well behind Staffordshire in canal construction but made rapid progress after 1800.[5] By contrast with coalmining County Durham, which as late as 1810 had no artificial canals, some rural areas were well served by the great canals that passed through them.

As well as the new movement along inland waterways, coastwise shipping continued increasingly to integrate the economic activities of various parts of the British Isles. Even agriculture lost some of its

[1] Adam Smith, *An enquiry into the nature and causes of the wealth of nations* (London, 1776), Book 1, ch. 3.

[2] T. J. Chandler, 'Communications and a coalfield; a study in the Leicestershire and south Derbyshire coalfield', *Trans. and Papers, Inst. Brit. Geog.*, XXIII (1957), 165.

[3] B. P. Capper (1801), 37.   [4] W. Pitt, *General view Stafford* (1796), 165.

[5] J. Plymley, *General view Shropshire* (1803), 307.

parochial exclusiveness. Cast-iron rollers from the Carron works in Lanark-shire and iron-framed ploughs from Rotherham in Yorkshire were shipped to farms in Norfolk. Haymakers and harvesters crossed from Ireland and from Scotland and travelled by inland waterways to farms in the English Midlands. But agriculture was not the economic activity most deeply affected by improved coastwise transportation. Facilities for moving minerals, particularly coal, greatly expanded as ships increased in size and tonnage. More shipping was engaged in carrying coal than any other commodity, but lead, tin, bricks, building stone, slates, china clay, hard-ware and brass also bulked large.

Overseas trade

In registered tonnage of shipping, Newcastle ranked second only to London. Liverpool held third place, followed closely by the coal ports of Sunderland and Whitehaven. Bristol's fleet ceased to grow, while ships from Exeter and from King's Lynn carried diminishing shares of England's maritime commerce. Most of the tonnage was engaged in coastwise traffic. The sheer bulk of the coastal trade – particularly in coal – dwarfed that overseas. 'Foreign trade', wrote J. H. Clapham, 'had not yet com-pletely lost its primitive characteristic – the exchange of precious things.'[1] But it was increasing, and the growing industrialisation of the country was reflected in its exports.[2] Textiles were important, but with cotton goods rivalling those of wool; the products of metal manufacture, especially of iron, were becoming significant. Among imports, timber alone constituted a bulk cargo, and the import of fir from northern Europe was a consider-able item in this trade. In addition, small quantities of softwood were received from Canada, and increasing amounts of teak, mahogany and tropical hardwoods were arriving from the south Atlantic and the Indian Ocean. The growing demand for tropical products was associated with a radical reorientation of British overseas trade towards greater dependence on the New World and the Far East, and away from traditional links with Europe and the Mediterranean. Imports of raw cotton, sugar, tobacco, coffee and tea increased dramatically year by year.

More ships, of larger size and sturdier construction, were built to carry this long-distance trade. Shipyards, as a consequence, suffered from chronic shortages both of manpower and materials. The strain was increased by the demands of the navy, called upon to protect extended

[1] J. H. Clapham, 237.
[2] E. B. Schumpeter, *British overseas trade statistics, 1697–1808* (Oxford, 1960).

lines of communication, to blockade the European shores and to defeat
the hostile fleets united under Napoleon's command. The navy not only
maintained four dockyards on the lower Thames and the Medway (at
Deptford, Woolwich, Sheerness and Chatham) but also held bases on the
English Channel at Portsmouth and Plymouth. To a large extent, the
fortunes of war were decided along the south coast.

In the Irish Sea and along the shores of the North Sea, fishing, coastal
transport and, in times of peace, trade with the Baltic and with the Low
Countries, flourished. New docks were opened at Hull, but the most
spectacular transformations were those taking place in London and
Liverpool. The digging of deep-water dock basins and the building of
gigantic warehouses were tangible expressions of the opening of a new
sphere of commerce. The ships whose masts crowded the Thames and
the Mersey included some that had voyaged from distant ports throughout
the world, including the Pacific.[1] Compared with the volume of overseas
trade conducted at the end of the Elizabethan age, the quantity and variety
of goods passing through English ports at the beginning of the nineteenth
century was prodigious, and the rate of expansion was accelerating.
England had become the most prosperous mercantile nation in the world.

TOWNS AND CITIES

In 1801 the legal and political status of towns bore little relation to the
numbers of their inhabitants, to the size of their built-up areas, or to their
social and economic functions. Some cathedral cities and many ancient
corporate towns had fewer citizens than many villages. Uninhabited Old
Sarum returned a member to parliament while the 31,000 parishioners of
Sheffield were unrepresented. Of the provincial towns enumerated in the
census, five had each a population of over 50,000; another eight had each
a population of over 20,000; and yet another thirty had each a population
of over 10,000 (see table 2.2 below). The combined population of these
towns with over 10,000 inhabitants was about one million. Taking all
towns together (whether with more or less than 10,000 inhabitants each),
four categories may conveniently be distinguished: county and market
towns, ports, manufacturing centres and resorts.

The county and market towns were almost entirely built around market
places, serving extensive rural areas. Tiny Queenborough (545 inhabitants)

[1] A. M'Konochie, *A summary view of the statistics and existing commerce of the
principal shores of the Pacific Ocean* (London, 1818).

Table 2.2   *Chief provincial towns in 1801*

The table includes all those places in the 1801 Census Tables designated as 'towns' as distinguished from 'parishes', 'townships' or 'hamlets'. The populations of London, Westminster and neighbouring towns, such as Southwark and Greenwich, are excluded from this list. Figures are given to the nearest thousand.

Over 50,000		10,000–20,000 (*cont.*)	
Manchester/Salford[a]	84,000	Stockport	15,000
Liverpool	78,000	Shrewsbury	15,000
Birmingham	74,000	Wolverhampton	13,000
Bristol[b]	64,000	Bolton	13,000
Leeds[c]	53,000	Sunderland	12,000
		Oldham	12,000
20,000–50,000		Blackburn	12,000
Plymouth	43,000	Preston	12,000
Norwich	37,000	Oxford	12,000
Bath	32,000	Colchester	12,000
Portsmouth/Portsea[d]	32,000	Worcester	11,000
Sheffield	31,000	Ipswich	11,000
Hull	30,000	Wigan	11,000
Nottingham	29,000	Derby	11,000
Newcastle upon Tyne	28,000	Hundersfield[e]	11,000
		Quick[f]	11,000
10,000–20,000		Warrington	11,000
Exeter	17,000	Chatham	11,000
Leicester	17,000	Carlisle	10,000
York	16,000	Dudley	10,000
Coventry	16,000	King's Lynn	10,000
Chester	15,000	Cambridge	10,000
Dover	15,000	Reading	10,000
Great Yarmouth	15,000		

[a] Manchester, 70,000; Salford, 14,000.
[b] Bristol city, 41,000; Barton Regis hundred, 23,000.
[c] Including 17 townships within the Liberty of Leeds.
[d] Portsmouth, 8,000; Portsea, 24,000.
[e] Now in Rochdale (Lancashire).
[f] Now in Saddleworth (West Riding).

on the Isle of Sheppey held two markets each week, the city of Worcester held three, while Manchester had only one. Some towns were cathedral cities, some had medieval castles, some held assizes, some had large schools, but many had changed little in size or shape since 1600. While much new civic building was to be seen, no Georgian cathedrals had been built, no new fortresses raised, and no new universities founded. The city of York had been surpassed in population by Exeter, which had expanded its manufacturing activities, but many other cathedral cities (such as Gloucester, Lincoln and Salisbury) had fewer than 10,000 people. Much the largest cathedral city was Norwich. Almost all the built-up area of the city was contained in the square mile or so within its walls, with much open space around the castle and the cathedral. The walls were washed on the southern side by the floods of the Wensum, and sea-going wherries reached the quays of Thorpe nearby. Norwich had now reached the summit of its importance as a centre of worsted manufacturing, while its banks, its corn exchange and its posting inns served travellers from an extensive prosperous agricultural region. Its annual cattle fair, its weekly corn and cattle markets and its three market days each week set it above all other market centres in Norfolk.[1] In East Anglia, as throughout the country, there was a well-ordered hierarchy of market centres. Places of similar size were regularly spaced, provided similar services, and were very similar in their appearance and compactness.

All the leading seaports had experienced a remarkable growth in trade, in volume of shipping and in population. Bristol had grown in size but had been overtaken by Liverpool, which not only had a lion's share of the sugar and slave trades but handled most of the country's raw cotton imports. This was a very recent development. In spite of the incidents of war, the shipping using the port increased greatly in the years around 1800, and cotton began to figure prominently in imports from the West Indies. Liverpool was becoming the main supply port for the expanding industrial areas of south Lancashire and the Midlands.[2] The first docks had been dug but the waterfront itself was constantly crowded with ships, and the streets leading from the quays were among the most densely crowded in England. On the east coast, Newcastle was a much smaller town than Liverpool, but its port had a larger fleet and handled more cargo. The country's demand for coal was insatiable, and the Tyne, its leading supplier, increased production and grew wealthy. In 1801 on Tyneside nearly 40,000 people were engaged in mining and in shipping coal, while the combined population of Newcastle and neighbouring Gateshead numbered 37,000.[3] The coal trade had created more than black dirt in

[1] R. E. Dickinson, 'The distribution and function of the smaller urban settlements of East Anglia', *Geography*, XVII (1932), 22–4, 28.

[2] F. E. Hyde, 'The growth of Liverpool's trade, 1700–1950', in W. Smith (ed.), *A scientific survey of Merseyside* (Liverpool, 1953), 154–5.

[3] Anon., *A picture of Newcastle-upon-Tyne* (Newcastle upon Tyne, 1807).

Newcastle. In 1788, a Theatre Royal was opened and the Assembly Rooms were more spacious than any but those at Bath. Downstream, beyond Sandgate towards Wallsend, there was a growing industrial suburb with a multitude of glasshouses, iron foundries, lead refineries, potteries, soap-works and steam-driven flour mills.

Farther south along the east coast, the port of Hull boomed as inland navigations drew traffic from the Trent valley and the Midlands to the Humber; fishing, flour milling and the coal trade expanded.[1] The east-coast ports of Sunderland and Yarmouth, which also shared in the coast-wise coal trade, were now larger than Lynn and Boston, whose approaches were too shallow to admit large ships. A most remarkable growth in population had also taken place in the ports along the English Channel where a vast apparatus of naval armament was concentrated. Plymouth, now the sixth largest provincial town, had more than twice as many in-habitants as the city of Exeter, while Portsmouth had more than four times the population of the ancient port of Southampton. In Kent, the dock-yard towns of Greenwich and Chatham and the packet station of Dover were each larger than the city of Canterbury (with 9,000 inhabitants).

Among the five provincial towns with populations of more than 50,000 were the great manufacturing centres of Manchester–Salford and Birming-ham. In 1794, *Scholes's Manchester and Salford Directory* listed 600 streets of which 61 'were laid out but not built upon'. There was space in the town for 'handsome country houses on every hill, elegantly furnished and surrounded by as elegant pleasure grounds'.[2] But land close to the mills was crowded with tightly packed rows of cottages and with three-storey tenements whose cellars accommodated some of Manchester's 5,000 immigrant Irish. A dozen other textile manufacturing centres in Lancashire and Yorkshire each had a population of more than 10,000, but only a handful exercised the powers and privileges of incorporated towns. In the West Riding, Bradford, Huddersfield and Halifax were still only parishes, but Leeds, the first place to build a steam-driven woollen spinning mill (1792), had achieved the dignity of urban status. The textile manu-facturing conurbations of Lancashire and Yorkshire were thus only fore-shadowed on contemporary maps. The emergent Black Country, however, was recognised as 'the most populous vicinity in the kingdom out of the metropolis', employing great numbers in the manufacture of hardware,

[1] W. G. East, 'The port of Kingston-upon-Hull during the industrial revolution', *Economica*, XI (1931), 190–212.

[2] *European Magazine*, XX (1791), 216.

toys, nails, glass, iron, coke and lime. William Pitt estimated 'that a figure of 200 square miles might be marked out, having the town of Dudley near its center', which contained 'upwards of two hundred thousand people'.[1] In Birmingham, 8,000 of its 12,000 inhabited houses had been built since the coming of the canal in 1765;[2] but the road between Wolverhampton and Birmingham was still far from being continuously built-up. The Soho works were situated in green fields, and the iron furnaces between Dudley and Wednesbury stood far apart along the canal banks. The degree of dispersion was even wider in the parish of Sheffield. Unlike the west Midland centres it remained the largest and one of the most scattered villages in England, inaccessible to navigable waterways. The five fast flowing streams which plunged from the edge of the Pennines were no longer relevant to its industrial development.[3] In 1770 some 229 waterwheels had driven tilt hammers and grinding wheels, but in 1794 only 123 waterwheels were turning while steam was driving 132 grinding wheels, mostly near the centre of Sheffield.[4] Not only was the cutlery industry concentrating upon the coal seams but Huntsman's steelworks, the first modern plant of its kind, was producing steel on a large scale. Sheffield plate and Britannia plate, produced in hundreds of small workshops near the valley bottom, were competing successfully with silver ware and pewter, and contributing to the grime and congestion of the village centre.

Among the growing settlements of England were the inland spas and watering places, but only a few were, as yet, corporate towns. Bath was no longer at the height of fashion, although it remained a spacious city of tall houses, many in multiple occupation as lodgings.[5] Its broad shopping thoroughfare, Milsom Street, and the graceful crescents climbing the hillsides, commanded extensive views over the Avon valley and open country. Other inland resorts such as Tunbridge Wells, Epsom and Buxton were thriving, while Cheltenham, Leamington and Harrogate were still quiet genteel rural retreats.[6] The most novel development was

---

[1] A. Young (ed.), *Annals of agriculture*, VII (1787), 463.

[2] J. A. Langford, *A century of Birmingham life; or a chronicle of local events from 1741 to 1841*, 2 vols. (Birmingham, 1868), I, 444.

[3] R. N. Rudmose Brown, 'Sheffield: its rise and growth', *Geography*, XXI (1936), 175–84.

[4] G. I. H. Lloyd, *The cutlery trades* (London, 1913), 157, 443.

[5] R. A. L. Smith, *Bath* (London, 1944), 92.

[6] E. W. Gilbert, 'The growth of inland and seaside health resorts in England', *Scottish Geog. Mag.*, LV (1939), 22; J. A. Patmore, 'The spa towns of Britain', being

the creation of seaside resorts, following the model of Scarborough which first achieved fame as a spa. Charles Vancouver's report on Hampshire describes Lymington, Christchurch and Southampton as 'much frequented in the summer for sea-bathing'. At Southampton, the company was 'much more select than usual at such places'; and although the accommodation was dear, it was 'generally of the best sort and truly elegant'.[1] At Lowestoft and Margate, the bathing machines of London shopkeepers mingled with fishermen's boats. The king patronised Weymouth and Lyme Regis but the most extravagant of the new resorts was Brighton, frequented by the Prince of Wales. The building of the Royal Pavilion had begun in 1786, and was to continue intermittently until 1822. Of the 1,300 houses in Brighton in 1801, as many as '211 were let solely as lodging houses, and in another 208 lodgings were to be obtained'.[2] Such development did not meet with universal approval, and Arthur Young firmly disapproved of those who idled away their summer months 'in this sort of inglorious obscurity' that 'London dissipation carries in its train'.[3]

London was unique among cities, a metropolis of bewildering complexity (Fig. 20). The population of its built-up area amounted to about 960,000, of which 750,000 lived to the north of the river, and the other 210,000 to the south, in the counties of Kent and Surrey.[4] One in ten of the inhabitants of England was a Londoner. J. P. Malcolm in 1803 thought it easier 'to attempt to describe the varying form of a summer cloud, than to trace from year to year the outline of London'.[5] On the north-west, the frontier of building had reached the 'New Road', constructed in 1756–7 (now named Marylebone, Euston and Pentonville Roads). Most of Westminster and Holborn were covered with broad streets and spacious squares, and the view from Queen Square (in Holborn) to Hampstead was 'hidden by the majestic houses adorned with Tuscan pillars' which had lately been put up in Guildford Street.[6] To the south of the Thames, the roads from Westminster and Blackfriars bridges converged in St

ch. 2 (pp. 47–69) of R. P. Beckinsale and J. M. Houston (eds.), *Urbanization and its problems* (Blackwell, Oxford, 1968).

　[1] C. Vancouver, *General view Hampshire* (1810), 420, 427.

　[2] E. W. Gilbert, *Brighton, old ocean's bauble* (London, 1954), 96–7.

　[3] A. Young (ed.), *Annals of agriculture*, XXVII (1797), 118.

　[4] *Census of 1851: Population Tables, I*, vol. 1, London (P.P. 1852–3, lxxxv). This contains a retrospective summary for 1801.

　[5] J. P. Malcolm, *Londinium redivivum*, 4 vols. (London, 1803–7), I, 5.

　[6] *Ibid.*, I, 6.

George's Fields; and here, in 1814, it was said that 'with very little exception, the whole line of each road is now skirted on both sides with houses and other buildings'.[1]

This growing London consumed a large part of the country's produce. London used more bricks and tiles than any other part of the kingdom, and by night a zone of brick kilns was described by Henry Hunter as forming 'a ring of fire' and pungent smoke around the city.[2] Beyond the zone of brick kilns were the meadows that provided hay and grazing for thousands of horses and dairy cows kept by Londoners, and farther afield lay the orchards and market gardens that provided the fruit and fresh vegetables brought daily to the London markets (Fig. 6).[3] London not only had the largest fruit and vegetable markets in the country, but Smithfield was the largest cattle market, Billingsgate the largest fish market, and London merchants dominated the trade in leather, wool, precious metals and a multitude of other commodities.[4]

The years around 1800 saw a new stage in the development of the port of London. Between 1796 and 1800 a series of parliamentary committees enquired into the congestion of shipping in the Thames and made recommendations for the improvement of the port. The total quay accommodation at London was little greater than at Bristol, but the tonnages of goods entering and leaving were very much greater. Valuable and perishable cargoes, delayed in the river for weeks, were being lost through pilferage and decay. The West India Docks, across the Isle of Dogs, opened in 1802, removed hundreds of ships from the river and relieved the pressure on warehouse space in the City and Shadwell. With the opening of Commercial Road in 1803, Limehouse and Poplar became dockland settlements. At this time the masts and flags of naval artificers waved proudly above the trees in Limehouse, and the large mansions of opulent merchants looked out on fields that were being covered with miles of new streets.[5] To its supremacy in Britain, London was adding a new domination as the capital of a vast empire and the commercial and financial centre of the world.

[1] E. W. Brayley, *London and Middlesex*, 2 vols. (London, 1814), II, 86.

[2] H. Hunter, *The history of London*, 2 vols. (London, 1811), II, 2; T. Baird, 'London brick fields', in A. Young (ed.), *Annals of agriculture*, XXI (1793), 150.

[3] G. B. G. Bull, 'Thomas Milne's land utilization map of the London area in 1800', *Geog. Jour.*, CXXII (1956), 25–30.

[4] R. Westerfield, *Middlemen in English business, particularly between 1660 and 1760* (New Haven, 1915), 420.

[5] J. P. Malcolm, II, 85.

Chapter 3

CHANGES IN THE EARLY RAILWAY AGE:
1800–1850

ALAN HARRIS

Some parts of rural England still wore in 1800 an outwardly medieval aspect that had yet to be transformed by enclosure, land drainage and improved systems of farming. Even by 1850 the transformation was not complete, but James Caird's England was much nearer that of the twentieth century than the England of only fifty years earlier described by the Board of Agriculture reporters. This was also a half-century of accelerated change in the towns, many of which, in assuming new functions, acquired new dimensions, new townscapes and problems which, in scale, if not in kind, were also new. Although steam power had already proved itself a potent agent of industrial change by 1800, its greatest effects were then still to be experienced. Half a century later, despite the survival of numerous relics of an earlier order, a new industrial geography, in which communication by rail played an increasingly important part, had been largely created. In demographic history also, these were remarkable years. As G. Kitson Clark has written, 'If nothing else had happened in the first half of the nineteenth century, the growth of population alone would have secured that Victorian England was decisively different...from the Georgian England of 1800.'[1]

POPULATION

Not only were there twice as many people living in England and Wales in 1851 as half a century earlier but they showed, as the century advanced, an increasing tendency to accumulate 'in great and well-defined masses'.[2] The proportion of the total population living in towns rose progressively as the flow of labour from the rural areas gathered momentum, increased, from the 1820s onwards, by a stream of migrants from Ireland. The

[1] G. K. Clark, *The making of Victorian England* (Oxford, 1962), 66.
[2] P. Gaskell, *The manufacturing population of England* (London, 1833), 9.

Table 3.1   *Population of England and Wales, 1801–51*

(Figures in millions; population for England in brackets)

	Total	Decennial increase %
1801	8.9 (8.3)	—
1811	10.2 (9.5)	14.00
1821	12.0 (11.2)	18.06
1831	13.9 (13.0)	15.80
1841	15.9 (14.9)	14.27
1851	17.9 (16.9)	12.65

Source: *Census of 1851: Population Tables, I*, vol. 1, p. xxxiii, (P.P. 1852–3, lxxxv.)

townward movement affected first the rate of growth, and then the absolute size, of rural communities, many of which in 1851 were smaller than they had been twenty years earlier.[1] This was true, for example, of about one hundred parishes in Leicestershire and of some sixty in Dorset.[2] Many rural communities in Lancashire and Cheshire were also shrinking in size at this period, although the combined population of the two counties increased by 185% during 1801–51.[3]

In spite of local decreases, the only English county to experience a net loss of population during 1801–51 was Wiltshire, although three counties in upland Wales had also suffered in this way.[4] The rural population, still widely sustained by local crafts and industries, continued to increase in the country at large, although at a consistently lower rate than that of the great towns and manufacturing districts, especially after 1820.[5] The overall changes in England as a whole may logically be considered, first in the

[1] J. Saville, *Rural depopulation in England and Wales, 1851–1951* (London, 1957), 5.
[2] *Census of 1851: Population Tables, I*, vol. II, Leicestershire, 12–26 (P.P. 1852–3, lxxxvi); *ibid.*, vol. I, Dorsetshire, 28–40 (P.P. 1852–3, lxxxv).
[3] R. Lawton, 'Population trends in Lancashire and Cheshire from 1801', *Trans. Hist. Soc. Lancs and Cheshire*, CXIV (1963), 193; J. T. Danson and T. A. Welton, 'On the population of Lancashire and Cheshire, and its local distribution during the fifty years 1801–51', *ibid.*, X (1858), 19, 21.
[4] R. P. Williams, 'On the increase of population in England and Wales', *Jour. Roy. Stat. Soc.*, XLIII (1880), 484–5.
[5] W. Farr, 'Population', in J. R. McCulloch, *A statistical account of the British Empire* (London, 1837), 410; R. P. Williams, 466–7, 470; R. Lawton, 'Rural depopulation in nineteenth-century England', in R. W. Steel and R. Lawton (eds.), *Liverpool Essays in Geography* (London, 1967), 227–8.

context of the demographic revolution of the time, and secondly in terms of the internal redistribution of population by which it was accompanied.

The growth shown in table 3.1 underlines one of the most remarkable features of the period. The rate of increase between 1811 and 1821, even allowing for the presence of many ex-servicemen, is much the highest on record for England and Wales. Such a vast increase of population was certainly without precedent, and it is likely that the addition to the population of England and Wales in the first three decades of the nineteenth century was greater than that which had occurred between the Restoration and the first census.[1]

The study of demographic change during this period raises difficult and controversial questions.[2] The major issue is whether the more important influence on the growth of population was a rise in the birth rate or a decline in mortality. The crude death rate, according to Brownlee, fell from 28.6 per thousand in 1781–90 to 21.1 per thousand in 1811–20.[3] Brownlee's estimates have not found universal acceptance. Far from falling, J. T. Krause suggested that the death rate may actually have risen between 1780 and 1820.[4] In a re-examination of the evidence, Deane and Cole emphasised the importance of regional variations in demographic experience at this period, and concluded that while a fall in mortality was most marked in London and in the rural areas, population growth in districts that were undergoing rapid industrialisation was 'much more clearly due to an increased birth rate'.[5] Whether this resulted from earlier marriages, greater fertility, or an increase in illegitimacy is uncertain.

After 1837, when official statistics of births, deaths and marriages were first available, there is less room for dispute. From 20.9 per thousand in 1845, the lowest figure recorded since 1838, the crude death rate climbed to 25.1 per thousand in 1849, before falling sharply in 1850.[6] Both the

---

[1] W. H. B. Court, *A concise economic history of Britain from 1750 to recent times* (Cambridge, 1964), 5.

[2] M. W. Flinn, *British population growth 1700–1850* (London, 1970); M. Drake, *Population in industrialization* (London, 1969), 1–10.

[3] J. Brownlee, 'The history of the birth and death rates in England and Wales... from 1570 to the present time', *Public Health*, XXIX (1916), 232.

[4] J. T. Krause, 'Changes in English fertility and mortality, 1781–1850', *Econ. Hist. Rev.*, 2nd ser., XI (1958), 56–7, 69.

[5] P. Deane and W. A. Cole, *British economic growth, 1688–1959* (Cambridge, 2nd ed., 1967), 133.

[6] B. R. Mitchell and P. Deane, *Abstract of British historical statistics* (Cambridge, 1962), 36.

infant mortality rate and the birth rate continued at a high level. A high rate of mortality in great towns, it is widely believed, pushed up the national death rate this time.[1] Already the subject of official concern in the first *Annual Report* of the Registrar-General (1837–8),[2] the health of towns was soon to attract widespread and unfavourable comment with the publication in 1842 of Edwin Chadwick's monumental *Report on the sanitary condition of the labouring population*. At their worst, the great towns were enormous reservoirs of disease and infection:

Over half the deaths were caused by infectious diseases alone. Cruel over-crowding and malnutrition gave respiratory and other forms of tuberculosis a grotesque predominance among the fatal infections, and enabled typhus to take a steady annual toll. Infant diseases, product of dirt, ignorance, bad feeding, and overcrowding, swept one in two of all children born in towns out of life before the age of five. Other infections – smallpox, scarlet fever, and the like – lingered among the overcrowded poor, occasionally bursting into epidemic fury. And from the human and animal excrements which over-flowed from cesspools, littered streets and tainted streams...came more filth diseases like typhoid and summer diarrhoea, that clung endemic in the towns, or like Asiatic Cholera which in 1832 had killed 16,437 in its first ravaging swoop on England and Wales.[3]

William Farr's sombre figures tell a similar story. Whereas the expectation of life at birth in 1841 averaged 41.16 years for England and Wales, it was 26 years in Liverpool. Two years later the expectation of life at birth was 24.2 years in Manchester compared with 40.2 years in the country at large.[4] A comparatively high birth rate and a favourable balance of migration, however, ensured that most towns continued to grow in size.[5] Growth was most marked in the coastal resorts and the centres of mining and manufacturing industry; it was slowest in the county towns.[6] Some small towns which failed to attract railways, or whose industries were

[1] T. H. Marshall, 'The population problem during the industrial revolution', *Econ. Hist.* (1929), 429–56; reprinted in E. M. Carus-Wilson (ed.), *Essays in economic history* (London, 1954); the reference is to pp. 327–9.

[2] *Annual Report* of the Registrar-General for 1837–8 (1839), 76–8 (P.P. 1839, xvi).

[3] R. Lambert, *Sir John Simon 1816–1904, and English social administration* (London, 1963), 59.

[4] W. Farr, *Vital statistics* (ed. W. A. Humphreys, 1885), quoted in W. Ashworth, *The genesis of modern British town planning* (London, 1954), 59.

[5] A. K. Cairncross, 'Internal migration in Victorian England', *The Manchester School*, XVII (1949), 86–7.

[6] *Census of 1851: Population Tables, I*, vol. 1, p. xlix (P.P. 1852–3, lxxxv).

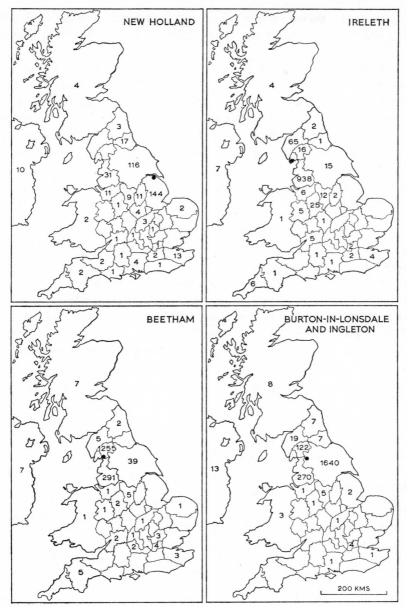

Fig. 33 County of birth of the inhabitants of four centres in 1851
Based on Public Record Office, H.O. 107/2118, 2275, 2442 and 2277.
These refer respectively to New Holland, Ireleth, Beetham, and Burton-
in-Lonsdale with Ingleton.

declining, grew little or not at all. By 1841, 29% of the population were living in towns of 20,000 inhabitants or more, compared with 18% in such places in 1811.[1]

Weavers from Bowland[2] and the linen villages near Knaresborough,[3] cloth workers from Wiltshire and Gloucestershire,[4] lead miners from Derbyshire and Alston,[5] together with agricultural workers from many counties, helped to swell the size of the towns. Much migration was local in character although, as both J. W. House and R. Lawton have observed, long-distance migration appears to have been more important than has sometimes been suggested.[6] Fig. 33 indicates that experience in this respect varied considerably from place to place. Short-distance migration to the nearest growing town and, within the large towns themselves, a movement from centre to periphery, probably accounted for a high proportion of migration at this period, just as it did later in the century.[7] The ranks of the long-distance migrants may have been recruited particularly from those who possessed some specialist skill, such as the papermakers from Kent, the puddlers and rollers of iron from Staffordshire and Shropshire and the mine captains from Cornwall who made their appearance by 1851 in the enumerators' returns for Lake District parishes.[8]

Not all areas were equally affected by the drift to the towns. On the Yorkshire Wolds, for example, the scene of much agricultural improvement after 1800, demand for labour was rising in the 1830s, and loss of

[1] A. F. Weber, *The growth of cities in the nineteenth century* (New York, 1899), 47.

[2] *Census of 1851: Population Tables, I*, vol. II, Lancashire, 46–9 (P.P. 1852–3, lxxxvi).

[3] *S.C. on Manufactures, Commerce, and Shipping*, 601 (P.P. 1833, vi); W. G. Rimmer, *Marshalls of Leeds, flax-spinners, 1788–1886* (Cambridge, 1960), 134, 163.

[4] *Census of 1851: Population Tables, I*, vol. I, Wiltshire, 22–5 (P.P. 1852–3, lxxxv); *ibid.*, Gloucestershire, 18–19, 22–5.

[5] J. P. Kay, 'Report on the migration of labourers', in *First Ann. Rep. of Poor Law Commissioners for England and Wales*, 185 (P.P. 1835, xxxv). *R.C. on Poor Laws*, Part I, Rural Queries, Appendix B, p. 98 (P.P. 1834, xxx).

[6] J. W. House, *North-eastern England: population movements and the landscape since the early 19th century* (Newcastle upon Tyne, 1954), 12; R. Lawton, 'The population of Liverpool in the mid-nineteenth century', *Trans. Hist. Soc. Lancs. and Cheshire*, CVII (1955), 108.

[7] R. Lawton, 'Population changes in England and Wales in the later nineteenth century: an analysis of trends by registration districts', *Trans. and Papers, Inst. Brit. Geog.*, XLIV (1968), 68.

[8] Public Record Office, H.O. 107/2275 and 2442 (1851); A. Harris, *Cumberland iron: the story of Hodbarrow Mine 1855–1968* (Truro, 1970), 19.

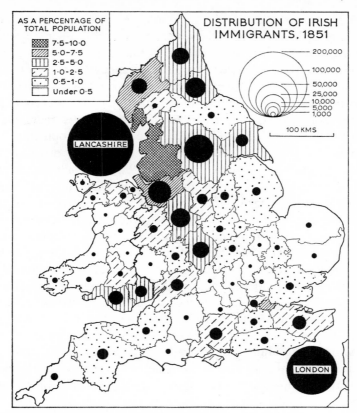

Fig. 34 Distribution of Irish immigrants, 1851
        Based on *Census of 1851: Population Tables, II*, vol. I, pp. ccxc–ccxcvi
        (P.P. 1852–3, lxxxviii, pt 1).

population appears to have been slight.[1] On the nearby claylands, on the other hand, where improvement was less marked and the effects of agricultural depression more severe, the exodus of rural labourers was considerable.[2] In several parts of the country, enclosure and land reclamation were followed by local gains in population.[3]

[1] *S.C. on Agric. 2nd Rep. and Mins. of Evidence*, 57–8 (P.P. 1836, viii, pt 1); *Census of 1851: Population Tables, I*, vol. II, Yorkshire, East Riding, 48–66 (P.P. 1852–3, lxxxvi).

[2] *S.C. on Agric. 2nd Rep. and Mins. of Evidence*, 49–53 (P.P. 1836, viii, pt 1); *Census of 1851: Population Tables, I*, vol. II, Yorkshire, East Riding, 48–66 (P.P. 1852–3, lxxxvi).

[3] A. Redford, *Labour migration in England, 1800–1850* (Manchester, 1926), 65–9.

Many recruits to the urban population were of Irish origin. To the
already familiar bands of Irish harvesters who worked their way through
the grain counties,[1] there were added, as the century advanced, tens of
thousands of poverty-stricken Irish immigrants, whose 'roaming and
restless habits appear to have carried them to every place where there was
any prospect of obtaining profitable employment'.[2] Between 1841 and
1851 the number of Irish-born in England and Wales increased from
291,000 to 520,000 or from 1.8% to 2.9% of the total population.[3] They
were to be found in many rural areas, in the mining districts and 'in
every manufacturing or commercial town',[4] but especially in and around
Liverpool, Manchester, London and Glasgow (Fig. 34). So numerous
were they in Manchester by the 1830s that their countrymen on arrival
felt 'as if they were coming to an Irish town'.[5] Here, as elsewhere, the
Irish formed closed communities, separated by both religious affiliation
and degree of poverty from most of their neighbours. They also tended
to form colonies, 'Irish' quarters,[6] which acquired the reputation of being
'the lowest, dampest, dirtiest, most unhealthy and ruinous' in their respective districts.[7] Their inhabitants served the needs of many different trades,
but mostly those in which skill either counted for little or was readily
acquired. They found work as navvies and as dock labourers and as
'hodmen' in the building trade.[8] They were also to be found in the sugar-
houses and chemical works on Merseyside and in the ironworks and coal
mines of the north-east.[9] Only a few, like Daniel Dudgeon, Controller
of Customs at Goole, attained a position of responsibility.[10]

[1] B. M. Kerr, 'Irish seasonal migration to Great Britain, 1800–1838', *Irish Hist.
Studies*, III (1943), 372–3.

[2] *Report on the state of the Irish poor in Great Britain*, 433 (P.P. 1836, xxxiv).

[3] R. Lawton, 'Irish immigration to England and Wales in the mid-nineteenth
century', *Irish Geography*, IV (1959), 38.

[4] *Rep. on Irish Poor*, 433 (P.P. 1836, xxxiv).   [5] *Ibid.*, 453.

[6] *Relief of distress of destitute poor (Ireland)*, *Papers relating to the immigration of
Irish paupers in Liverpool*, 17 (P.P. 1847, liv); R. Lawton (1955), 104; F. Beckwith,
'The population of Leeds during the industrial revolution', *Thoresby Miscellany*, XLI
(1948), 173; H. Cooper, 'On the cholera mortality in Hull during the epidemic of
1849', *Jour. Roy. Stat. Soc.*, XVI (1853), 351.

[7] *Rep. on Irish Poor*, 437 (P.P. 1836, xxxiv).

[8] *S.C. on Railway Labourers*, 501 (P.P. 1846, xiii); *Rep. on Irish Poor*, 429, 431,
433–5 (P.P. 1836, xxxiv).

[9] J. W. House, 38, 40; T. C. Barker and J. R. Harris, *A Merseyside town in the
industrial revolution: St Helens, 1750–1900* (Liverpool, 1954), 281–3.

[10] P.R.O., H.O. 107/2350 (1851), 15.

The net result of half a century of population change is shown on Fig. 35. Between 1801 and 1851 the northern industrial districts, several metropolitan counties and the west Midlands increased their share of the total population, whereas eastern, southern and north-western England declined in relative importance. A pattern that was to be familiar for many years to come had been established.

THE COUNTRYSIDE

As William Howitt remarked in 1838, with evident satisfaction, there were many corners of rural England in the early railway age where 'primitive living and primitive habits' lingered.[1] Yet even Howitt, whose interests led him to emphasise the quaint and the picturesque, felt obliged to include in *The rural life of England* a chapter on scientific farming, together with some comments on the spread of manufacturing industry to hitherto rural areas. Even as he wrote, many parts of the countryside were in a state of swift transition. Common arable fields were fast disappearing and would soon become a curiosity. Extensive areas of moor and heath were in process of enclosure and improvement. Works of land drainage were under way, and 'high farming' was becoming more general. Its influence was more evident in some districts than others, but the spirit of change was generally abroad in rural England during the first half of the nineteenth century.

In 1800 much land still awaited enclosure – both open-field arable and open common pasture and waste. Parliamentary proceedings were facilitated by a General Enclosure Act in 1801, and still further by other general acts in 1836 and 1845. It would seem that after 1800 over 1,200 acts enclosed about 1.8 million acres of arable (see table on p. 24), and another 1,300 or so acts enclosed about 1.3 million acres of common pasture and waste (see table on p. 51). But these figures are probably on the low side, and they exclude non-parliamentary enclosure.[2] Figs. 36 and 37 show, for arable and for commons and waste, the total effect of parliamentary enclosure during the eighteenth and nineteenth centuries, i.e. from the 1720s to 1870 or so.

There were also other changes of the greatest importance for the land.

[1] W. Howitt, *The rural life of England* (London, 3rd ed., 1844), 100. The first edition appeared in 1838.

[2] W. E. Tate, *The English village community and the enclosure movements* (London, 1967), 88.

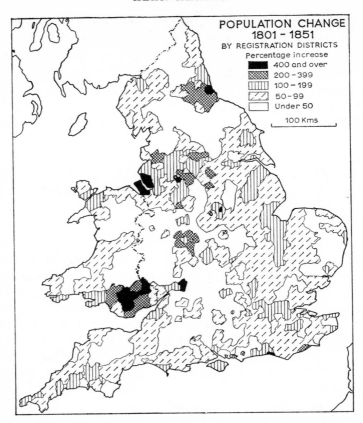

Fig. 35 Population change, 1801–51
        Based on R. Lawton in J. W. Watson and J. B. Sissons (eds.), *The British
        Isles: a systematic geography* (London and Edinburgh, 1964), 232.

The Board of Agriculture in 1803 commissioned Humphry Davy to
lecture on the connections between chemistry and plant physiology, and
the substance of these lectures was published in 1813 under the title
Elements of agricultural chemistry. Then in 1840 came an English edition
by Lyon Playfair of Justus von Liebig's *Chemistry in its application to
agriculture and physiology*. The age of chemical fertilisers was inaugurated,
and nitrate of soda, Peruvian guano and superphosphate of lime were now
added to the traditional manures. There were also improvements in the
implements of tillage – in ploughs, harrows, drills, haymakers, chaff-
cutters and other machines. A number of attempts had been made to
produce satisfactory reaping machines, and Patrick Bell's reaper in 1828

marked a great advance. Steam power was used for threshing and for other agricultural purposes in the early years of the century, but it was not applied to ploughing and cultivating until after 1850. The new spirit in agriculture could be seen in such events as the foundation of the Royal Agricultural Society in 1838, the establishment of Rothamsted Experimental Station in 1843, and the institution of the Royal College of Agriculture in 1845. Legislation also benefited agriculture; the Tithe Commutation Act was passed in 1836 and an act for the repeal of the Corn Laws in 1846. By the time of the Great Exhibition in 1851, much yet remained to be done, but agriculture had already begun to reflect the scientific and industrial changes of the century.

Enclosure of the arable

In many English counties the process of eliminating the common arable fields, which was already well advanced by 1800, had been largely completed by the end of the Napoleonic Wars. But, even so, arable land held in common still accounted in 1820 for nearly 10% of the total area of Cambridgeshire, for just over 8% of Oxfordshire, and for about 4 to 5% of Bedfordshire, Buckinghamshire and Huntingdonshire.[1] Even where the proportion of common arable land was very small, the tidying-up process sometimes involved the enclosure of many thousands of acres. In Wiltshire, for instance, about 64,000 acres, including much open arable land, were enclosed between 1815 and 1850;[2] the comparable figure for the East Riding was 45,000 acres.[3] By 1850, certainly by 1870, open fields had disappeared from all but a few rare villages (Fig. 36).

Contemporary writers were well aware of the local importance of enclosure in the years after 1815. J. A. Clarke, writing of Lincolnshire in 1851, numbered enclosure among the agricultural achievements of the preceding thirty years.[4] To C. S. Read, in 1854, the greatest improvements that had occurred in Oxfordshire farming since the appearance of Arthur Young's *General view* of that county in 1809, were 'those produced by

---

[1] E. C. K. Gonner, *Common land and inclosure* (London, 1912), 279–81.

[2] Acreage calculated from awards at the Wiltshire Record Office, Trowbridge, and from W. E. Tate, 'A hand list of Wiltshire enclosure acts and awards', *Wilts. Archaeol. and Nat. Hist. Mag.*, LI (1945). I am grateful to Miss T. E. Vernon for assistance with the Wiltshire awards.

[3] Acreage calculated from awards in the East Riding Registry of Deeds and County Record Office, Beverley.

[4] J. A. Clarke, 'On the farming of Lincolnshire', *Jour. Roy. Agric. Soc.*, XII (1851), 330.

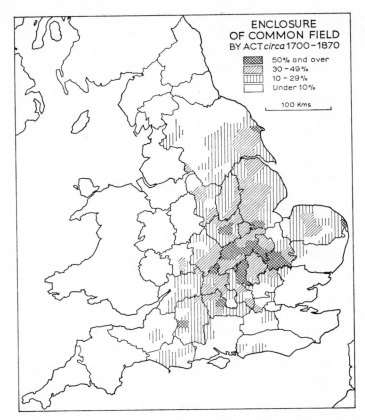

Fig. 36 Enclosure of common field *circa* 1700–1870 (by Registration Districts)
Based on E. C. K. Gonner, *Common land and inclosure* (London, 1912), map A.

the extension of enclosures'.[1] And of Cambridgeshire, where common
arable fields had survived in large numbers to annoy William Cobbett
in the 1820s,[2] Samuel Jonas declared in 1846, 'few counties, if any, have
improved more in cultivation...all the common fields have been enclosed
with the exception of five or six parishes'.[3]

In these counties, as elsewhere, the incidence of enclosure differed
greatly from one district to the next. In Wiltshire nearly 90% of the area
enclosed between 1815 and 1850 lay south of the escarpment of the

---

[1] C. S. Read, 'On the farming of Oxfordshire', *J.R.A.S.*, XV (1854), 248.
[2] William Cobbett, *Rural rides* (Everyman's Library), I, 79–80.
[3] S. Jonas, 'On the farming of Cambridgeshire', *J.R.A.S.*, VII (1846), 38.

Wiltshire Downs.[1] Or again in Lincolnshire, where 49 parishes were enclosed by Act of Parliament between 1815 and 1845, no less than 28 were in the coastal marshland of Lindsey.[2] These examples serve as a reminder of the complexity of the factors that influenced the pace of enclosure. In some districts it was the light-soiled uplands which, despite the work of earlier improvers, still awaited attention in the nineteenth century. Elsewhere it was on the claylands that the task remained largely unfinished. Open fields of high potential value in relation to the costs of enclosure sometimes survived long after similar land nearby had been enclosed. There is no simple explanation of these facts, as J. Thirsk and H. G. Hunt, among others, have demonstrated.[3] The progress of enclosure at this period, as in the past, was influenced by the distribution of landownership as well as by the nature of the soil, by local population pressure as well as by legislation which facilitated or retarded enclosure, by the extent of agricultural improvement within the framework of the open fields as well as by changing economic conditions.[4]

Enclosure of arable land was followed in some districts, particularly on the heavy claylands, by the laying of arable down to grass due to the increased profitability of heavy land for livestock as compared with grain. By 1850, the broad distinction between the arable and the grazing had been drawn, and the result was summed up in James Caird's generalisation of 1850.[5] His map showed the contrast between what he called 'the chief corn districts' of the south and east, and 'the principal grazing, green crop, and dairy districts' of the Midlands and the west (Fig. 50). In both areas market gardening continued to spread near the large towns, and particularly around London where it was fostered, as William Cobbett said in 1821, by 'the demand for crude vegetables and repayment in manure'.[6]

---

[1] Calculated from enclosure awards and from W. E. Tate (1945).

[2] J. Thirsk, *English peasant farming* (London, 1957), 292.

[3] J. Thirsk (1957), 237–40, 292–4; H. G. Hunt, 'The chronology of parliamentary enclosure in Leicestershire', *Econ. Hist. Rev.*, 2nd ser., x (1957), 265–72.

[4] M. A. Havinden, 'Agricultural progress in open-field Oxfordshire', *Ag. Hist. Rev.*, ix (1961), 73; A. Harris, *The rural landscape of the East Riding of Yorkshire, 1700–1850* (Oxford, 1961), 64–5.

[5] J. Caird, *English agriculture in 1850 and 1851* (London, 1852), frontispiece.

[6] William Cobbett, *Rural rides* (Everyman's Library), I, 47.

Reclamation and improvement

By 1850, enclosure of common arable fields was practically at an end. On the other hand, the age-old task of enclosing and improving the upland commons remained far from complete. It is perhaps hardly surprising that William Dickinson's enthusiasm for what had been achieved in Cumberland since 1815 should have been tempered with a note of regret since, according to his own estimate in 1852, at least 40,000 acres of reclaimable land in that county were still burdened with common rights.[1] In other western counties, too, much enclosure in the uplands awaited the years of 'high farming' after 1850. Even so, progress had been made by mid-century; particularly during the immediate aftermath of the Napoleonic Wars, when awards arising out of the great surge of war-time enclosure activity were still numerous; and again after 1836, though on a reduced scale, as economic conditions slowly improved and enclosure procedure was simplified and reduced in cost.

The upland counties which figure prominently on Fig. 37 do so by virtue of their unenclosed pastures. In Cumberland, for instance, the attack on the waste between 1815 and 1850 was marked by the passing of twenty private acts solely for the enclosure of commons and waste, and by a dozen enclosures under the general acts of 1836 and 1845.[2] Elsewhere in northern England, further inroads were made into the commons of Westmorland, the North and West Ridings of Yorkshire, Northumberland and Durham. In the Pennines and moors of the North Riding, for example, about 50,000 acres were enclosed between 1815 and 1850;[3] in the uplands of Durham about 23,000 acres[4] and in Northumberland 13,000 acres.[5] Farther south, the act of 1815 enclosing the enormous Forest of Exmoor

[1] W. Dickinson, 'On the farming of Cumberland', *J.R.A.S.*, XIII (1852), 289.

[2] W. E. Tate, 'A hand list of English enclosure acts and awards: Cumberland', *Trans. Cumberland and Westmorland Antiq. and Archaeol. Soc.*, n.s., XLIII (1943), 175–98.

[3] Calculated from a card-index of enclosure acts and awards relating to the North Riding, compiled by C. K. C. Andrew and kept at the County Hall, Northallerton.

[4] Calculated from a typescript list of enclosure awards at the County Record Office, Durham, and from W. E. Tate, 'Durham field systems and enclosure movements', *Proc. Soc. of Antiquaries of Newcastle upon Tyne*, 4th ser., X, no. 3 (1943), 119–40.

[5] Calculated from W. E. Tate, 'A hand list of English enclosure acts and awards: Northumberland', *Proc. Soc. of Antiquaries of Newcastle upon Tyne*, 4th ser., X, No. 1 (1942), 39–52.

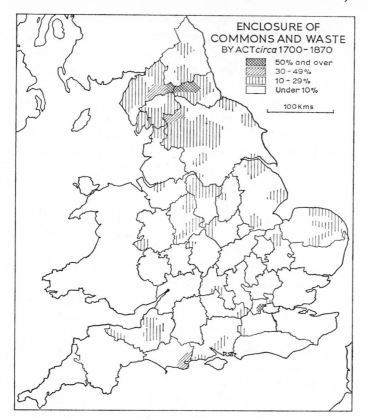

Fig. 37 Enclosure of commons and waste *circa* 1700–1870 (by Registration Districts)
Based on E. C. K. Gonner, *Common land and inclosure* (London, 1912), map B.

covered an area of about 20,000 acres mostly in Somerset.[1] The
partial reclamation of this land by the Knight family and their tenants
after 1820 was in itself an achievement on the grand scale.

   The new enclosures extended in some areas well beyond the economic
limit of cultivation, and the making of the award was not necessarily
followed by a major change in land use. Title was established, common
rights were extinguished or regulated, and miles of division fence, of
stone or earth, were laboriously erected; but the land remained under
pasture, which was sometimes 'improved' only in being freed from

   [1] C. S. Orwin, *The reclamation of Exmoor Forest* (Oxford, 1929), 20–1; W. G.
Hoskins and H. P. R. Finberg, *Devonshire studies* (London, 1952), 332.

common rights.[1] Under favourable circumstances, as in parts of Cumberland for example, oats were occasionally grown at elevations of 900 to 1,000 feet 'by way of renewing and improving the land for pasturage'.[2]

Hard-won intakes continued to be made along the moorland edge without parliamentary sanction, though their total extent is difficult to determine. According to John Watson, writing in 1845, it was usual in Cumbria and the Pennines of west Yorkshire for small landowners with large families and with little employment for one half of the year, to reclaim 'small patches of craggy ground from off their larger sheep walks'.[3] For this purpose, as Watson explained in a passage which has about it an almost timeless quality, it was necessary to hack, dig and trench, 'making use of the stones for fences, drains and roads, or otherwise stacking them up in corners, or upon the worst parts of the land; and nibbling out all and every patch that is considered worth the labour'.[4] The impression that methods of reclaiming the uplands had changed little over the years is reinforced by Stephen Glover's statement that, in upland Derbyshire, improvement involved the 'removal of surface stones, stubbing, paring, burning, draining, and the free use of Peak lime'.[5] Piecemeal enclosure was also slowly transforming the appearance of the mining districts of west Cornwall. Here, as Richard Thomas reported in 1819, 'thousands of acres of downs, commons, and wastes' were 'enclosed and improved by the miners and others on a small scale'.[6] That this activity continued locally well into the nineteenth century is borne out by descriptions in the eighteen-forties.[7] Industry and agricultural improvement were also closely associated in Cumberland and west Durham, where the London Lead Company was engaged after 1815 in draining, liming and afforesting its high moorland estate near Alston.[8] In the lead districts of Yorkshire and

[1] See B. Loughbrough, *Some geographical aspects of the enclosure of the vale of Pickering in the eighteenth and nineteenth centuries*, unpublished M.A. thesis, University of Hull, 1960, 106ff.

[2] W. Dickinson, 217.

[3] J. Watson, 'On reclaiming heath land', *J.R.A.S.*, VI (1845), 95.

[4] *Ibid.*

[5] S. Glover (ed. by T. Noble), *The history and gazetteer of the county of Derby*, 2 vols. (Derby, 1831–3), I, 162.

[6] R. Thomas, *Report on a survey of the mining district of Cornwall from Chasewater to Camborne* (London, 1819), 14.

[7] C. Redding, *An illustrated itinerary of the county of Cornwall* (London, 1842), 143; W. F. Karkeek, 'On the farming of Cornwall', *J.R.A.S.*, VI (1845), 411, 445.

[8] A. Raistrick, *Two centuries of industrial welfare; the London (Quaker) Lead Company* (London, 1938), 32.

the northern Pennines, miner-farmers were carving small intakes from the moors;[1] and in the uplands of Rossendale, the improvement of hitherto unprofitable moorland was stimulated by the presence nearby of an expanding manufacturing district.[2]

The conversion of much downland, warren and heath into arable on the sandlands and the chalk and limestone soils of lowland England continued a trend that was already under way in 1800, and that marked a further stage in the shift of cereal production from the heavy to the light lands. Enclosure, paring and burning, marling and chalking, all played a part in this transformation, but no less important was the use that was made of green crops, of 'light' manures such as bones, guano and superphosphates, of oil-cake which yielded a rich return in the form of dung, and of the closer integration of livestock and arable husbandry. To Samuel Sidney in 1848, the wolds of north Lincolnshire presented 'an unbroken succession of large farms', composed, almost 'entirely of arable land'.[3] He saw 'hundreds of sheep feeding off turnips in the fields' and 'scores of young stock feeding off cake and hay, and treading down straw in the yard'.[4] Philip Pusey, who had travelled over Lincoln Heath a few years earlier, was equally impressed by what he saw. 'Every stubble-field was clean and bright; all the hedges kept low, and neatly trimmed; every farmhouse well built. . . and surrounded by rows of high, long, saddle-backed ricks.'[5] Fifty years earlier both these districts had contained large expanses of rabbit warren and sheep-walk. On the chalklands of Yorkshire, Wiltshire, Hampshire and Dorset too, the acreage under the plough increased appreciably during the first half of the nineteenth century,[6] but not all

---

[1] R. T. Clough, *The lead smelting mills of the Yorkshire Dales* (Leeds, 1962), 21; A. Raistrick, *Mines and miners of Swaledale* (Clapham, 1955), 83–4; C. J. Hunt, *The lead miners of the northern Pennines* (Manchester, 1970), 152–9.

[2] G. H. Tupling, *The economic history of Rossendale* (Chetham Society, Manchester, 1927), 229.

[3] S. Sidney, *Railways and agriculture in north Lincolnshire: rough notes of a ride over the track of the Manchester, Sheffield, Lincolnshire, and other railways* (London, 1848), 72.

[4] *Ibid.*, 74.

[5] P. Pusey, 'On the agricultural improvements of Lincolnshire', *J.R.A.S.*, IV (1843), 287; H. C. Darby, 'The Lincolnshire Wolds', *The Lincolnshire Historian*, No. 9 (1952), 315–24.

[6] C. Howard, *A general view of the agriculture of the East Riding of Yorkshire* (London, 1835), 111; E. Kerridge in E. Crittall (ed.), *V.C.H. Wiltshire*, IV (1959), 73. J. Wilkinson, 'The farming of Hampshire', *J.R.A.S.*, XXII (1861), 290, L. H. Ruegg, 'Farming of Dorsetshire', *J.R.A.S.*, XV (1854), 437.

these districts attained the same high standards of husbandry as Lincoln-shire.[1]

Both agriculture and industry encroached upon the heathlands which, island-like, survived in many parts of the lowlands. On the Forest Sands of Nottinghamshire, on the Keuper Sandstones of mid-Cheshire, on the sandy wastes of Breckland and in the southern vale of York, enclosure, tree-planting, bone-tillage and turnip husbandry made steady progress.[2] And as the Cannock coalfield was developed, heathland there disappeared beneath sprawling mining settlements.[3] The preservation of rough land for sporting purposes, however, meant that an alternative use was not always possible.[4] Attempts to check the enclosure of commons in the vicinity of populous places also acted as a barrier to improve-ment.[5]

'As for draining,' Philip Pusey wrote in 1842, 'there is not a county, nor any large proportion of parishes, or even of farms, in which it ought not to be done.'[6] At the district level, a new drainage era had in fact opened some years earlier, in 1819–20, with the installation of a steam pump near Littleport in the Isle of Ely.[7] During the following decade steam pumping was adopted in other parts of the Fenland basin, and by 1848 it was being used 'extensively and with vast advantage' both there and in several other low-lying districts.[8] But, as J. A. Clarke ad-mitted, though considerable progress had been made by the 1840s, the task of draining this area remained unfinished, not least because more

[1] T. Walkden, 'On the advantages of ploughing-up down-land', *J.R.A.S.*, IV (1843), 83–5.

[2] R. W. Corringham, 'Agriculture of Nottinghamshire', *J.R.A.S.*, VI (1845), 2–7; W. Palin, 'The farming of Cheshire', *J.R.A.S.*, V (1844), 73; R. N. Bacon, *The report on the agriculture of Norfolk* (London, 1844), 19, 92; G. Legard, 'Farming of the East Riding of Yorkshire', *J.R.A.S.*, IX (1848), 92.

[3] M. J. Wise (ed.), *Birmingham and its regional setting* (Birmingham, 1950), 274.

[4] S. Glover, II (1833), 94, 103.

[5] F. E. Hyde, 'Utilitarian town planning, 1825–1845', *Town Planning Rev.*, XIX (1947), 157–8.

[6] P. Pusey, 'On the progress of agricultural knowledge during the last four years', *J.R.A.S.*, III (1842), 185.

[7] H. C. Darby, *The draining of the Fens* (Cambridge, 2nd ed., 1956), 222; C. T. G. Boucher, *John Rennie, 1761–1821* (Manchester, 1963), 136.

[8] *The rural cyclopedia*, II (Edinburgh, 1848), 81; W. H. Wheeler, *History of the fens of South Lincolnshire* (Boston and London, 1868), 35, 132; M. Williams, *The draining of the Somerset Levels* (Cambridge, 1970), 144, 160–1; J. Thirsk (1957), 286.

efficient drainage inevitably produced further shrinkage on the peat fens.[1] Improvement schemes were frequently accompanied by renewed efforts to rectify the deficiencies of the local rivers. In the Fenland, for instance, the Eau Brink Cut (1821) removed a great bend along the lower Ouse near King's Lynn, and a new outfall on the Nene (1830) replaced a shifting and frequently silted channel.

While steam pumps in some districts helped to bring new land into cultivation and prevented the old from reverting to fen, in others their use was still unknown in 1850. Along the Hull valley, partly drained by that year, drainage was still carried out by windmill, and ague, though rare, had not yet disappeared.[2] Or again, across the Pennines, Martin Mere, 'the Great Fen of Lancashire', received the benefit of steam drainage only in 1850.[3] Although the technical means were now available, effective drainage was too often delayed by the survival of antiquated and unco-ordinated administrative machinery, and by disagreement between those who wished to drain the land and those who, for various reasons, were opposed to change.[4] Many years were to pass in some districts before these obstacles were overcome. Outside the great levels reclamation was also proceeding, although on a less ambitious scale. Chat Moss, in Lancashire already diminished in size by drainage works, received further attention from the improvers, and by 1833 good crops of oats and potatoes were growing there on newly recovered mossland.[5] Further north, in the Wyre valley, a combination of draining and marling was turning the local moss-lands into arable land of high quality.[6] Warping and land drainage were performing a similar service for parts of the Humberhead marshes.[7]

'It is upon the lighter lands – the sandy, the loamy, the peaty soils – that the main expenditure of skill has hitherto taken place', a writer in the

[1] J. A. Clarke, 'On the Great Level of the Fens', *J.R.A.S.*, VIII (1847), 110, 112; *ibid.*, 'On trunk drainage', *J.R.A.S.*, XV (1854), 1–73.

[2] J. A. Sheppard, *The draining of the Hull valley* (East Yorkshire Local History Society, York, 1958), 21; H. Cooper, 'On the relative prevalence of diseases in Hull, and the effects of season upon disease', *Jour. Roy. Stat. Soc.*, XVI (1853), 355.

[3] H. White, 'A detailed report of the drainage by steam-power of a portion of Martin Mere, Lancashire', *J.R.A.S.*, XIV (1853), 165.

[4] J. Henderson, 'Report upon the Rye and Derwent drainage', *J.R.A.S.*, XIV (1853), 136, 140; J. A. Sheppard, 15, 18.

[5] *S.C. on Agriculture*, 187–8 (P.P. 1833, v).

[6] *Lonsdale Magazine*, I (1820), 199–204; W. J. Garnett, 'Farming of Lancashire', *J.R.A.S.*, X (1849), 24–8.

[7] R. Creyke, 'Some account of the process of warping', *J.R.A.S.*, V (1844), 398; W. Edwards, 'On dry warping at Hatfield Chase', *J.R.A.S.*, XI (1850), 180–3.

Edinburgh Review observed in 1845, and then went on to point out that 'the first great stride which England has to make in the cultivation of her arable lands, is in the adaptation of her clay soils to the alternate husbandry'.[1] The heavy clays, which without the benefit of adequate drainage were unkind to root crops and folded sheep, and which in many areas were managed on a costly and relatively inflexible system of husbandry, had not only failed to keep pace with the light lands in agricultural progress but had also become problem areas.[2] Field-drainage did something to redress the balance, and the draining methods of James Smith of Deanston in Perthshire did much to improve the heavier soils.[3] On some clayland estates draining was tackled energetically in an attempt to mitigate the worst effects of agricultural depression.[4] The strong clays of Huntingdonshire were said to be partly tile-drained in 1836 and, though erratic, some progress had by that time been made elsewhere.[5] Field-drainage was greatly accelerated during the 1840s, however, by the use of machinery which enabled first ordinary drainage tiles and later pipe-tiles to be mass-produced at low cost.[6] In some areas at least under-draining was soon followed by the extension of turnip husbandry on to land which a few years earlier had been considered too wet for it.[7] But in 1850 it was still possible to assert without serious fear of contradiction that 'if there be any land which requires improvement, it is our real heavy clays'.[8]

The changes which have been indicated were accompanied by others. Thus territorial boundaries of the various breeds of livestock continued to alter. Moorland breeds of sheep were in retreat, in upland Derbyshire and elsewhere, in the face of enclosure and reclamation,[9] and agricultural

[1] *Edinburgh Review*, LXXXI (1845), 94–5.

[2] E. L. Jones, *Seasons and prices: the role of the weather in English agricultural history* (London, 1964), ch. 9.

[3] J. Smith, *Remarks on thorough draining and deep ploughing* (Stirling, 1831).

[4] F. M. L. Thompson, *English landed society in the nineteenth century* (London, 1963), 245–55.

[5] *S.C. on Agriculture, First Report and Mins. of Evidence*, 60, 168; *Second Report etc.*, 73, 173 (P.P. 1836, viii).

[6] J. Parkes, 'Report on drain-tiles and drainage', *J.R.A.S.*, IV (1843), 372–3; H. C. Darby, 'The draining of the English clay-lands', *Geographische Zeitschrift*, LII (1964), 190–201; G. E. Fussell, *The farmer's tools, 1500–1900* (London, 1952), ch. 1.

[7] J. Grey, 'A view of the past and present state of agriculture in Northumberland', *J.R.A.S.*, II (1841), 182.

[8] P. Pusey, 'On the progress of agricultural knowledge during the last eight years', *J.R.A.S.*, XI (1850), 406.

[9] S. Glover, I (1831), 162.

improvement led to the replacement of the restless Norfolk, admirable as heath sheep, by the Southdown.[1] The Shorthorn breed of cattle had displaced the Longhorn from most parts of Westmorland by 1845 and from all Lancashire by 1849.[2] Many similar examples could be found.

Two further changes invite comment. As land was enclosed and reclaimed, many of the gaps that remained to be filled in the pattern of rural settlement were occupied by outlying dwellings. On Exmoor, in 1850, Thomas Acland found cottages and farmsteads where not long before there had been unimproved and uninhabited moorland;[3] and in the textile district of the West Riding new farmsteads, built, like their predecessors in the same area, of native gritstone, now made their appearance high up on the valley sides.[4] Locally, as on the Crown estate of Sunk Island in the East Riding, the building of farmsteads followed coastal reclamation. Other new farmsteads were the result of the enclosure of arable fields; a number of these appeared some time after the initial enclosure, as large allotments were gradually organised into new farm units. Villages also changed. Many grew substantially in size during the first three or four decades of the nineteenth century, and under this stimulus farmsteads were subdivided and rows of cottages added wherever space was available, which meant that gaps in the old village plan were now often closed by a process of infilling. Tiny cottages for landless labourers appeared side by side with elegant town-style houses which owed little or nothing to the vernacular tradition of the district.[5]

Although the age of country-house building on a grand scale was slowly drawing to a close, the eighteenth-century taste for architectural ostentation continued well into the new century. Landed aristocrats like the 5th duke of Rutland at Belvoir in Leicestershire, and the 15th earl of Shrewsbury at Alton Towers in Staffordshire, were not alone in building or refashioning great houses in the heart of the countryside, sometimes in the Classical tradition, but more frequently, as the century advanced,

[1] W. Youatt, *Sheep*, London (1837), 307–10; H. Raynbird, 'On the farming of Suffolk', *J.R.A.S.*, VIII (1847), 308.

[2] W. Youatt, *Cattle* (London, 1834), 200; F. W. Garnett, *Westmorland agriculture, 1800–1900* (Kendal, 1912), 184; W. J. Garnett, 39.

[3] T. D. Acland, 'On the farming of Somerset', *J.R.A.S.*, XI (1850), 688ff.

[4] J. C. R. Camm, *Industrial settlement in the Colne and Holme valleys, 1750–1960*, unpublished M.Sc. thesis, University of Hull, 1963, pp. 115–17.

[5] R. B. Wood-Jones, *Traditional domestic architecture of the Banbury region* (Manchester, 1963), 197–9, 288–90; W. G. Hoskins, *The Midland peasant* (London, 1957), 272–3.

in the Gothic style.[1] There were also many new settlers – retired merchants and industrialists in the Lake District afford a well-known example – who were also active in building country residences.[2] As at Edensor, on the Chatsworth estate in Derbyshire, 'improvement' sometimes involved the remodelling of a complete village;[3] or, more frequently, the landscaping of a park after the manner of Repton or in the gardenesque style of John Claudius Loudon.[4] But, as the *Quarterly Review* noted, by the middle of the nineteenth century few attempts were being made to 'improve on the extensive scale that was adopted by Brown and his school'.[5]

Apart from the planting of trees for ornament and for fox coverts or game preserves, very little afforestation took place. The English navy increasingly relied upon imported timber. It is true that the shortage during the French wars had stimulated the management of the Crown forests and the planting of oak, but not very effectively.[6] In any case, before the oaks so planted had come to maturity, the era of the wooden ship was over. Rural England, particularly lowland England, had become a countryside of grain and grass, and so it remained.

If the emphasis has been placed here on the changing elements in the rural scene that is not to deny the existence of other more permanent features. Many thousands of acres of old enclosed country must have altered little in outward appearance, though here and there hedgerows were removed and old pastures ploughed out as the burden of tithe was lifted;[7] some of these areas, denied the stimulus of enclosure, remained agriculturally backward.[8] And against the factory-farms of Northumberland with their steam-driven equipment may be set those of Middlesex where, so it was alleged in 1836, standards of land management were but little improved on those of 'our forefathers'.[9]

[1] H. M. Colvin, *A biographical dictionary of English architects, 1666–1840* (London, 1954), 730; J. C. Loudon, *An encyclopaedia of gardening* (London, 1859), 256–63.

[2] William Wordsworth, *A guide through the district of the lakes* (Malvern, Facsimile edition, 1949), 62.

[3] H. M. Colvin (1954), 506. I am indebted to the Librarian and the Trustees of the Chatsworth Settled Estates for permission to see plans of Edensor at Chatsworth.

[4] D. Clifford, *A history of garden design* (London, 1962), 173, 184; H. C. Prince, 'The changing landscape of Panshanger', *Trans. East Herts. Archaeol. Soc.*, XIV (1959), 42–58.   [5] *Quarterly Review*, XCVIII (1855), 215.

[6] R. G. Albion, *Forests and sea power* (Cambridge, Mass., 1926), 137–8, 399.

[7] G. Buckland, 'On the farming of Kent', *J.R.A.S.*, VI (1845), 301; H. Evershed, 'On the farming of Surrey', *J.R.A.S.*, XIV (1853), 412.

[8] J. Thirsk (1957), 263.

[9] *S.C. on Agriculture, First Report etc.*, 179 (P.P. 1836, viii).

INDUSTRY

Throughout the first half of the nineteenth century agriculture retained its place as the most important British industry judged in terms of employment, although its share both of the total occupied population and of the national income slowly declined as manufacturing industry and mining increased in importance.[1] Their growth was accompanied by a flood of literature, varying in character from Andrew Ure's massive *Dictionary of arts, manufacturers, and mines* (London, 1839) to Mrs Gaskell's *Mary Barton* (London, 1848). More of the 'well authenticated facts' about the country's economy called for by G. R. Porter in *The progress of the nation* (London, 1836) were gathered on a systematic basis, even though the full statistical age had not yet arrived.

Coalmining

Coal output mounted quickly between 1815 and 1850 as the demands of industry, of domestic users and of transport grew more insistent, and it may have risen from 16 million tons in 1816 to 49 million in 1850.[2] Much of the increase occurred between 1820 and 1840, when many new mines were 'sunk and worked with great rapidity and to a great extent in various parts of England'.[3]

Mining was extended in both area and depth. In Northumberland and Durham, mining activity spread into hitherto untouched or little worked districts. Slowly at first, and then with great speed as the railway network was evolved, new colliery districts were opened up in Northumberland, in south-west Durham, and in the concealed coalfield of east Durham.[4] In these areas, as elsewhere, the advent of the safety lamp and of improved techniques of winding, pumping and ventilation enabled deeper seams to be won, and by 1835 the shafts of Monkwearmouth colliery, the deepest mine in the north-east, had reached 1,590 feet.[5] Expansion of output in the

---

[1] C. Booth, 'Occupations of the people of the United Kingdom, 1801–81', *Jour. Roy. Stat. Soc.*, XLIX (1886), Appendix A; P. Deane and W. A. Cole, ch. 5.

[2] *R.C. on Coal*, 861, 883 (P.P. 1871, xviii); see P. Deane and W. A. Cole, 216. The figures relate to the United Kingdom.   [3] *Westminster Review*, XL (1843), 418.

[4] T. Y. Hall, 'The extent and probable duration of the northern coal field', *Trans. North of England Inst. of Mining Engineers*, II (1854), *passim*; A. E. Smailes, 'Population changes in the colliery districts of Northumberland and Durham', *Geog. Jour.*, XCI (1938), 222–4.

[5] [J. Holland], *The history and description of fossil fuel, the collieries and coal trade of Great Britain*, London (1835), 188–9.

north-east, from about 4.8 million tons in 1816 to about 10.5 million in 1851,[1] was accompanied by the rise of new coal ports at Seaham Harbour, at Hartlepool and West Hartlepool and on Tees-side, and by a great increase in the volume of coal shipments. By the middle of the century, however, the traffic in seaborne coal from the north-eastern ports, which for so long had dominated the London market, was entering upon a new and competitive phase. The change had been marked, in 1845, by the arrival in London of the first consignments of railborne coal. These amounted to little more than 8,000 tons in that year, but by 1851 they had reached nearly 248,000 tons.[2] The 1840s was a critical decade in the north-east.[3]

Although the northern coalfield remained in 1850 the most productive in the country, other coalfields had been growing in importance during the previous half century. Shipments of coal from west Cumberland more than doubled between 1819 and 1849, for example, and new mining districts were developed there, particularly after the construction of the Maryport and Carlisle and other railways during the 1840s.[4] Rising demand from the alkali, glass and copper industries of St Helens combined, with the Cheshire salt industry and a growing market for steam coal, to stimulate mining in south-west Lancashire.[5] Many new mines were opened to win both coal and ironstones in the Potteries,[6] in south Staffordshire,[7] along the north crop of the South Wales coalfield,[8] and in central Scotland where the era of heavy industry had begun.[9]

[1] J. W. House, 61.

[2] *R.C. on Coal*, 865–6 (P.P. 1871, xviii).

[3] A. J. Taylor, 'The third marquis of Londonderry and the north-eastern coal trade', *Durham University Journal*, n.s., XVII (1955), 22; P. M. Sweezy, *Monopoly and competition in the English coal trade 1550–1850* (Cambridge, Mass., 1938), especially ch. 10.

[4] M. Dunn, *An historical, geological and descriptive view of the coal trade of the north of England* (Newcastle upon Tyne, 1844), 133; O. Wood, *The development of the coal, iron and shipbuilding industries of west Cumberland, 1750–1914*, unpublished Ph.D. thesis, University of London (1952), 97ff., 125.

[5] T. C. Barker and J. R. Harris, ch. 15.

[6] J. Hedley, 'Mines and mining in the north Staffordshire coal field', *Trans. North of England Inst. of Mining Engineers*, II (1854), *passim*; M. W. Greenslade in J. G. Jenkins (ed.), *V.C.H. Staffordshire*, VIII (1963), 101–3, 169, 222.

[7] M. J. Wise (ed.), 232–8.

[8] J. H. Morris and L. J. Williams, *The South Wales coal industry 1841–1875* (Cardiff, 1958), 8–12; E. G. Bowen (ed.), *Wales* (London, 1957), 209–11.

[9] J. B. S. Gilfillan and H. A. Moisley in R. Miller and J. Tivy (eds.), *The Glasgow region* (Glasgow, 1958), 169–72.

The iron and steel industries

'Ingenuity furnishes endless occasion for fresh demand, while at the same time equal industry is apparent in the corresponding exertions which create the supply.'[1] Thus wrote Scrivenor of the iron trade in 1841, after several decades of erratic expansion had carried pig-iron production in England and Wales from about 220,000 tons in 1806 to 1,155,000 tons in 1840.[2] Seven years later the figure was to exceed 1,450,000 tons. Behind this progress lay the expanded gas and water undertakings of the country and new railway, engineering and shipbuilding industries. Amongst the forces influencing supply were improvements at both the furnace and the forge, which resulted in great economies in the consumption of fuel, in larger blast furnaces and in a more efficient method of puddling iron.[3]

The manufacture of iron advanced most rapidly on the coalfields of South Wales and Scotland, which together accounted for 63% of the total pig-iron output of Great Britain in 1847, compared with 40% in 1806.[4] During this period the west Midlands was surpassed by each of these districts. Yet pig-iron production multiplied more than sixfold in Staffordshire between 1806 and 1847, and in Shropshire by some 60%.[5] From south Staffordshire, where more than fifty new blast furnaces appeared between 1823 and 1847,[6] there flowed an ever-increasing variety of foundry and forge pig-iron, castings, puddled iron and finished metal goods; and the coalfield, which within living memory had retained a rural aspect, was transformed by 1846 into 'a continuous city of fire-belching furnaces and smoke-vomiting chimneys'.[7] On the Shropshire coalfield, so Thomas Smith said in 1836, 'the smoke and blackness of furnaces, forges, and foundries, give a tone to every part of the prospect'.[8] Similar changes were taking place, although on a smaller scale, in Derbyshire and

---

[1] H. Scrivenor, *A comprehensive history of the iron trade* (London, 1841), vi.

[2] B. R. Mitchell and P. Deane, 131.

[3] H. R. Schubert, 'The extraction and production of metals: iron and steel', in C. Singer *et al.*, *A history of technology*, IV (Oxford, 1958), 109–14; B. R. Mitchell, 'The coming of the railway and United Kingdom economic growth', *Jour. Econ. Hist.*, XXIV (1964), 326–8.

[4] I. L. Bell, *The iron trade of the United Kingdom* (London, 1886), 9.

[5] B. R. Mitchell and P. Deane, 131. A comparatively small output in north Staffordshire is included for 1806.

[6] H. Scrivenor (1854 ed.), 135, 295.

[7] H. Miller, *First impressions of England and its people* (Edinburgh, ed. 1857), 49.

[8] T. Smith, *The miner's guide* (Birmingham, 1836), 114.

Yorkshire.[1] In steel production, however, Yorkshire was pre-eminent: the output of blister and cast steel from Sheffield rose swiftly after 1830 as new markets for steel goods were found outside the local cutlery trades.[2] The coalfields of Warwickshire and Lancashire, which were poorly endowed with both ironstones and coal of high coking quality, failed to share in the general growth of the iron industry.[3] Its development was tardy and of limited extent also in Northumberland and Durham.[4] By mid-century, however, the iron industry of the north-east was about to pass through a period of accelerated change which ultimately affected the metal trades of districts far removed from the local region. The haematite ores of Cumberland and Furness were exported mainly to Scotland and South Wales; there was very little local iron manufacturing owing to the unsuitability of the local coal for coking.[5]

The textile industries

The continued growth of the cotton textile industry was one of the marvels of the age. Its 'rapid growth and prodigious magnitude', the *Edinburgh Review* commented in 1827, were 'the most extraordinary phenomena in the history of industry'.[6] The output of cotton textiles increased steadily from the middle of the 1820s, and by 1835 at least 185,000 mill hands and perhaps 200,000 hand-loom weavers were engaged in the industry.[7] Three

[1] K. Warren, 'The Derbyshire iron industry since 1780', *East Midland Geographer*, II, No. 16 (1961), 19–21; J. F. W. Johnston, 'The economy of a coal-field', *Proc. Geological and Polytechnic Society of the West Riding of Yorkshire*, I (1849), 50.

[2] M. W. Flinn and A. Birch, 'The English steel industry before 1856 with special reference to the development of the Yorkshire steel industry', *Yorks. Bull. Econ. and Soc. Research*, VI (1954), 173–4; J. C. Carr and W. Taplin, *A history of the British steel industry* (Oxford, 1962), 11.

[3] M. J. Wise (ed.), 295–6; S. H. Beaver, 'Coke manufacture in Great Britain: A study in industrial geography', *Trans. and Papers, Inst. Brit. Geog.*, XVII (1952), 135, 138; A. Birch, 'The Haigh Ironworks, 1789–1856: a nobleman's enterprise during the industrial revolution', *Bull. John Rylands Library*, XXXV (1952–3), *passim*.

[4] I. L. Bell, 'On the manufacture of iron in connection with the Northumberland and Durham coal-field', *Trans. North of England Inst. of Mining Engineers*, XIII (1864), 111–24.

[5] J. D. Kendall, 'Notes on the history of mining in Cumberland and north Lancashire', *Trans. North of England Inst. of Mining and Mechanical Engineers*, XXXIV (1885), 92–4; A. E. Smailes, *North England* (London and Edinburgh, 1960), 183–4.

[6] *Edinburgh Review*, XLVI (1827), 1.

[7] E. Baines, *History of the cotton manufacture in Great Britain* (London, 1835), 383, 394; R. C. O. Matthews, *A study in trade-cycle history: economic fluctuations in Great Britain, 1833–1842* (Cambridge, 1954), especially 127–8 and ch. 9.

years later the number of mill workers had risen to almost 220,000 and by 1850 to 292,000, though the number of hand-loom weavers meanwhile had fallen sharply.[1]

The face of the principal cotton-manufacturing areas quickly changed. The altered appearance of the district following the building of numerous cotton mills during the twenties and thirties formed the subject of much contemporary comment in south Lancashire.[2] The number of cotton mills at work within the township of Manchester rose from 44 in 1820 to 63 in 1826,[3] and in Heaton Norris, nearby, from about a dozen in 1825 to 20 in 1836.[4] Mills and printworks were crowded into the valleys of the Irwell and its tributaries, which in the vicinity of Manchester quickly became little more than open sewers. For a time new mills also continued to appear in outlying centres of the industry such as Carlisle, Lancaster and Bristol.[5] In Hull, a port without any tradition of textile working but in control of nearly 70% of the country's export trade in cotton twist and yarn, the industry gained for itself new territory in 1838.[6]

Although most of the new growth took the form of steam-driven factories, the older water-powered mills were slow to disappear (Figs. 38 and 39). Thus more than half the horse-power employed in the Derbyshire cotton industry in 1850 was derived from water-wheels.[7] Even in Lancashire, where conversion to steam was far advanced by the 1830s, water remained an important source of power in the valleys of Rossendale

---

[1] *Factory Returns, 1838,* 59, 205, 295 (P.P. 1839, xlii); *Factory Returns, 1850,* 470 (P.P. 1850, xlii); G. A. Wood, 'The statistics of wages in the nineteenth century – XIX, The cotton industry', *Jour. Roy. Stat. Soc.,* LXXIII (1910), 594–6.

[2] J. Butterworth, *A history and description of the towns and parishes of Stockport, Ashton-under-Lyne, Mottram-Longden-Dale, and Glossop* (Manchester, 1827), 60–1.

[3] E. Baines, 395.

[4] E. Butterworth, *A statistical sketch of the County Palatine of Lancaster* (London, 1841), 90.

[5] W. Parson and W. White, *History, directory and gazetteer of Cumberland and Westmorland* (Leeds, 1829), 118, 152; M. M. Schofield, *Outlines of an economic history of Lancaster, Part II 1680–1860* (Lancaster, 1951), 111–15; S. J. Jones, 'The cotton industry in Bristol', *Trans. and Papers, Inst. Brit. Geog.,* XIII (1947), 73–4.

[6] J. M. Bellamy, 'Cotton manufacture in Kingston upon Hull', *Business History,* IV (1962), 92–5.

[7] A. J. Taylor, 'Concentration and specialization in the Lancashire cotton industry, 1825–1850', *Econ. Hist. Rev.,* 2nd ser., I (1949), 115; D. M. Smith, 'The cotton industry in the east Midlands', *Geography,* XLVII (1962), 264–5.

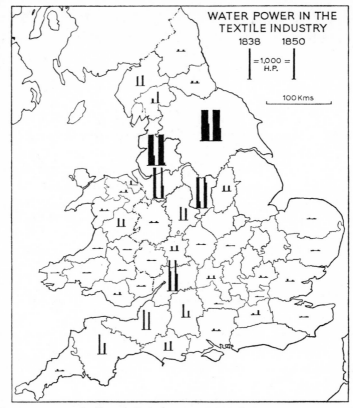

Fig. 38 Water power in the textile industry, 1838 and 1850
Based on: (1) *Factory Returns, 1838* (P.P. 1839, xlii); (2) *Factory Returns, 1850* (P.P. 1850, xlii).

and along the flanks of the uplands further south.[1] Some country mills, of which those near Ingleton in Yorkshire are an example, were able to obtain coal almost literally from underfoot.[2] Without ready access to coal, however, many remote mills were placed at a disadvantage in an age of steam, and by 1850 they had either disappeared or else had been converted to other uses.[3] The weaving of cotton by hand disappeared even more

[1] G. North, 'Industrial development in the Rossendale valley', *Jour. Manchester Geog. Soc.*, LVIII (1961–2), 17; H. B. Rodgers, 'The Lancashire cotton industry in 1840', *Trans. and Papers, Inst. Brit. Geog.*, XXVIII (1960), 138–9.

[2] A. Harris, 'The Ingleton coalfield', *Industrial Archaeology*, V (1968), 318.

[3] J. D. Marshall, *Furness and the industrial revolution* (Barrow-in-Furness, 1958), 54; J. D. Marshall and M. Davies-Shiel, *The Lake District at work, past and present* (Newton Abbot, 1971), 18, 21.

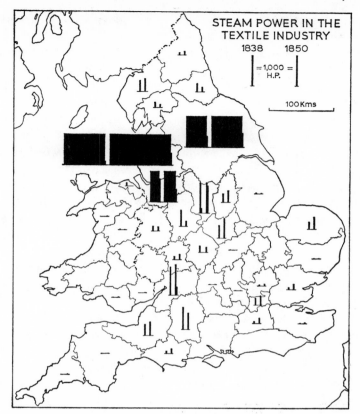

Fig. 39 Steam power in the textile industry, 1838 and 1850
Sources as for Fig. 38.

rapidly. About Oldham, Royton and Crompton, Wheeler reported in 1836, 'loom-shops have been deserted, looms sold or broken-up, and whole families have gone to the mills for employ'.[1] The number of power looms at work increased almost threefold in Lancashire between 1835 and 1850,[2] by which date the specialised power-weaving district in the north of the county was just beginning to emerge.[3]

With approximately 69% of the mill hands of the cotton industry in England and Wales in 1838, Lancashire contained by far the largest group

[1] J. Wheeler, *Manchester: its political, social and commercial history* (London and Manchester, 1836), 233.
[2] G. R. Porter, *The progress of the nation* (London, 1851 ed.), 200.
[3] H. B. Rodgers, 145–51.

of cotton workers in the country; Cheshire, with between 16% and 17%, and Yorkshire with about 6%, lagged far behind, as did the Midlands with 6.5%.[1] By 1850 geographical concentration had advanced a stage further (Fig. 40). In that year Lancashire, with 70% of the cotton mills in England and Wales, contained 74% of the employees, 73% of the spindles and 79% of the power looms engaged in the industry.[2]

The changes which overtook the worsted industry were hardly less striking (Fig. 41). Between 1838 and 1850 employment in worsted factories more than doubled, while hand-weaving of worsteds began rapidly to diminish.[3] The use of cotton warps, alpaca and mohair 'imparted a new character to the worsted industry',[4] enabling its products to compete with those of cotton in the market for cheap, light fabrics.[5] As the industry expanded, concentration within the West Riding became more marked: Yorkshire's share of the country's worsted workers rose from approximately 85% in 1838 to 90% in 1850.[6] Lancashire, Leicestershire and Norfolk, the only other counties with a substantial worsted industry, could then claim between them only some 10% of the country's worsted workers.[7] Nowhere was the quickening of activity within the Yorkshire worsted trade more apparent than in Bradford, where many new worsted mills were added between 1800 and 1830, and where the town grew rapidly and untidily.[8] Attracted by an expanding industry, worsted merchants transferred their activities to Bradford, making it the undisputed centre of the English worsted trade.[9]

The transformation of woollen manufacturing from a domestic to a factory industry proceeded relatively slowly. According to Baines, writing in 1859, even then there were as many woollen workers employed

[1] *Factory Returns, 1838* (P.P. 1839, xlii). The Midlands here include Derbyshire, Nottinghamshire, Staffordshire, Leicestershire and Warwickshire.

[2] *Factory Returns, 1850*, 456–7 (P.P. 1850, xlii).

[3] *Factory Returns, 1838* (P.P. 1839, xlii) and *1850* (P.P. 1850, xlii); E. M. Sigsworth, 'Bradford', in C. R. Fay, *Round about industrial Britain, 1830–1860* (Toronto, 1952), 119–20, 125–7.

[4] J. James, *History of the worsted manufacture in England* (London, 1857), 470–1.

[5] E. M. Sigsworth, *Black Dyke mills* (Liverpool, 1958), 43–5.

[6] *Factory Returns, 1838* (P.P. 1839, xlii) and *1850* (P.P. 1850, xlii).

[7] *Factory Returns, 1850* (P.P. 1850, xlii). But see J. K. Edwards, 'The decline of the Norwich textiles industry', *Yorks. Bull. Econ. and Soc. Research*, XVI (1964), 37–8.

[8] J. James (1857), 605.

[9] E. M. Sigsworth, 'Fosters of Queensbury and Geyer of Lodz, 1848–1862', *Yorks. Bull. Econ. and Soc. Research*, III (1951), 67.

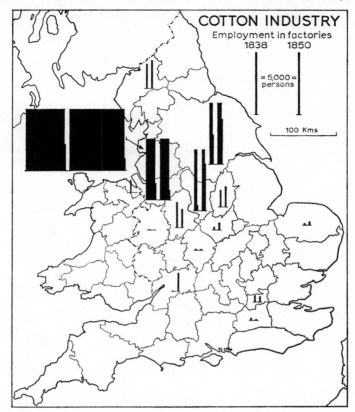

Fig. 40   Cotton industry: employment in factories, 1838 and 1850
Sources as for Fig. 38.

outside the factories as in them.[1] Mechanisation of the weaving process
was particularly slow, and the number of power looms working woollen
goods remained small until the fifties. The Yorkshire factories were largely
steam-powered by 1838, but the process of conversion was still incomplete in 1850 (Figs. 38 and 39). In several other districts, too, water
power retained its hold on the industry. In the West Country, only Wiltshire adopted steam power on an extensive scale: there steam engines
generated 64% of the power in 1838 and 77% in 1850.[2] But in Gloucestershire and Somerset steam was responsible at both dates for less than half

[1] E. Baines, 'On the woollen manufacture of England', *Jour. Roy. Stat. Soc.*, XXII
(1859), 9.
[2] *Factory Returns, 1838* (P.P. 1839, xlii) and *1850* (P.P. 1850, xlii).

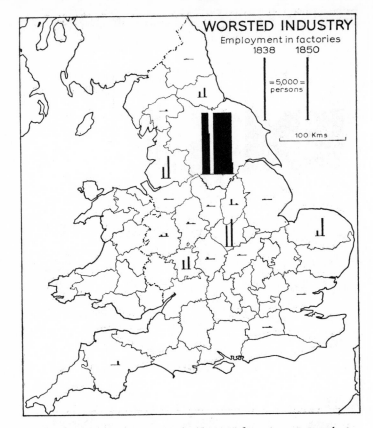

Fig. 41 Worsted industry: employment in factories, 1838 and 1850
         Sources as for Fig. 38.

the power generated. The Devonshire serge manufacturers showed even less inclination to convert to steam; the mills returned there in 1838 and 1850 were powered almost entirely by water-wheels. Yorkshire's share of the factory workers increased markedly during this period as the pace of investment in the local woollen industry gathered momentum (Fig. 42). The rate of new building in the 1830s was said to be 'immense, enough to astonish anybody',[1] and from 1833 to 1838 the number of woollen mills in the county increased from an estimated 129 to a reported 606.[2]

[1] *Report from the S.C. on Manufactures (1833)*, quoted in F. J. Glover, 'The rise of the heavy woollen trade of the West Riding of Yorkshire in the nineteenth century', *Business History*, IV (1961), 10.   [2] F. J. Glover, 10.

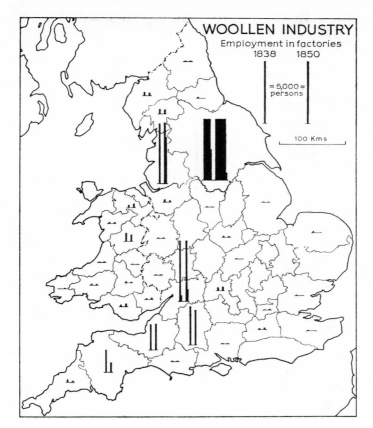

Fig. 42. Woollen industry: employment in factories, 1838 and 1850
Sources as for Fig. 38.

By 1850 the figure was 880.[1] Small valley settlements such as Slaithwaite
and Holmfirth expanded into towns.[2] And as the shoddy manufacture
emerged from its 'limited, rude and tentative' origins after 1813, the
population of Batley steadily increased, and between 1831 and 1851 almost
doubled itself.[3] Sustained by weaving, mining and quarrying, however,
many of the old upland hamlets remained small but thriving communities.[4]

The old also persisted alongside the new in other branches of the textile
industry, some of which changed but little in character during the first

[1] *Factory Returns, 1850* (P.P. 1850, xlii).   [2] J. C. R. Camm, 103–13.
[3] S. Jubb, *The history of the shoddy-trade* (London, 1860), 100.
[4] J. C. R. Camm, 114–31.

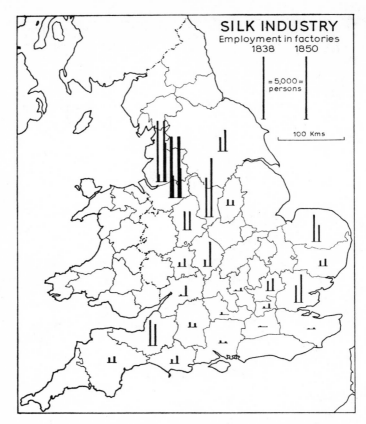

Fig. 43 Silk industry: employment in factories, 1838 and 1850
Sources as for Fig. 38.

half of the nineteenth century. With the development of machinery,
Spitalfields lost its position as a leading producer of silk to Cheshire and
Derbyshire and to the depressed woollen centres of East Anglia and Essex.
The introduction of steam power accelerated the process. The first steam
mill for spinning silk was started in Manchester in 1819–20, and the next
ten years saw a rapid increase of silk manufacture in Lancashire which had
'hardly been reckoned a silk county at all thirty years earlier'.[1] The older
silk areas in Derbyshire and Cheshire also benefited, and the latter had
a larger number of silk-factory workers by 1838 than any other county.

[1] J. H. Clapham, *An economic history of modern Britain: free trade and steel,
1850–1886* (Cambridge, 1932), 28.

New silk-spinning factories were also to be found in the traditional textile areas of East Anglia, Essex and the West Country (Fig. 43). But the weaving of silk often still remained a hand-loom domestic industry. The weaving of plain ribbons by steam power was already advanced in Derby, Leek and Congleton at a time when Coventry's fancy ribbon trade was still conducted on a domestic basis cheek by jowl with shops, warehouses and slaughter-houses.[1] Likewise in Nottingham, Leicester and Derby, hosiery and lace-making, in spite of the invention of machines, were still domestic industries, and had undergone no general technical transformation. Though the first steam-powered hosiery factories appeared in the 1840s, framework knitting remained in 1850 largely a domestic industry.[2] The introduction of steam-powered flax-spinning machines into Leeds about 1820 made it the centre of the English linen industry, and factory weaving had also made much progress by 1850. But with developments in Scotland, linen was ceasing to be an important English industry.

Other industries

Several extractive industries other than coal and iron also contributed significantly to the changing scene: quarrying, in such widely differing areas as the Lake District and the industrial Pennines;[3] and the working of china clay in Cornwall[4] and of brick clays in scores of townships, both rural and urban.[5] Mines and subsidence flashes were becoming increasingly numerous on the Cheshire saltfield,[6] while lead mining was responsible for considerable improvements in the road system of the northern Pennines.[7] The output of tin in Cornwall increased as deeper mining

---

[1] *Rep. Assistant Hand-loom Weavers' Commissioners*, pt 4, pp. 67, 353, 360, 363 (P.P. 1840, xxiv); J. Prest, *The industrial revolution in Coventry* (Oxford, 1960), 24, 93–6.

[2] L. A. Parker in W. G. Hoskins and R. A. McKinley (eds.), *V.C.H. Leicestershire*, III (1955), 15–16; D. M. Smith, 'The British hosiery industry at the middle of the nineteenth century, an historical study in economic geography', *Trans. and Papers, Inst. Brit. Geog.*, XXXII (1963), 141.

[3] J. D. Marshall, 45–7; J. C. R. Camm, 119.

[4] J. Rowe, *Cornwall in the age of the industrial revolution* (Liverpool, 1953), 117n.

[5] *Eighteenth Report of the Commissioners of Excise Inquiry* (on bricks), Appendix B, 166 (P.P. 1836, xxvi); H. A. Shannon, 'Bricks – a trade index, 1785–1849', *Economica*, n.s., I (1934), 301; M. Robbins, *Middlesex* (London, 1953), 48–50.

[6] *Chambers's Edinburgh Journal*, XI (1849), 181–3; K. L. Wallwork, 'The mid-Cheshire salt industry', *Geography*, XLIV (1959), 174.

[7] T. Sopwith, *An account of the mining districts of Alston Moor, Weardale, and Teesdale* (Alnwick, 1833), 8–9; L. C. Coombes, 'Lead mining in east and west Allendale', *Archaeologia Aeliana*, 4th ser., XXXVI (1958), 258–60.

became more general. Perhaps most striking of all, however, were the changes which accompanied the continued growth of the copper industry in the south-west. The output of copper ore from Cornwall and Devon soared from about 78,000 tons in 1815 to more than 150,000 in 1850,[1] a remarkable achievement which for a time made the district the world's leading producer of copper.[2] The effects of this and other local mining activities were not confined to the mineralised districts, where engine-houses and 'dead-heaps' yearly grew more numerous. For, as mineral railways were constructed to link the mines with the coast, tiny places such as Devoran and Point Quay rose to prominence as shipping points for ores and coal.[3] It was during this period, too, that the foundations were laid of a mining engineering industry which by 1850 was famous far beyond the south-west.[4] These developments were inevitably accompanied by population changes. The population of Gwennap, for example, where 30% of British copper originated between 1823 and 1832, grew dramatically during these years;[5] so did that of Tavistock between 1841 and 1851, the decade which saw the opening of Devon Great Consols mine.[6]

The development of the great staple industries on the coalfields of the Midlands and north naturally attracted much contemporary comment; but, on the other hand, the continuing importance of London as a centre of manufacturing industry was not always fully recognised.[7] Yet, sustained in large measure by 'the consumption and vast commerce' of the metropolis,[8] London's industries retained throughout the first half of the century both their collective importance and rich variety. Like the watch, clock and jewellery trades of the Clerkenwell district, many had behind them a long tradition of skilled craftsmanship. Others were still com-

[1] R. Hunt, *British mining* (London, 2nd ed., 1887), 892.

[2] D. B. Barton, *A history of copper mining in Cornwall and Devon* (Truro, 1961), 91.

[3] D. B. Barton, *The Redruth and Chasewater railway, 1824–1915* (Truro, 1960). 10–18.

[4] A. K. H. Jenkin, *The Cornish miner* (3rd ed., 1962, London), 174–7.

[5] C. C. James, *History of Gwennap* (Privately printed, Penzance, n.d. [1952]), 129, 195.

[6] D. B. Barton, *A historical survey of the mines and mineral railways of east Cornwall and west Devon* (Truro, 1964), 71–3; *Census of 1851: Population Tables, I*, vol. 1, Devonshire, 48–9 (P.P. 1852–3, lxxxv).

[7] P. G. Hall, 'The location of the clothing trades in London, 1861–1951', *Trans. and Papers, Inst. Brit. Geog.* XXVIII (1960), 155.

[8] Census of 1831, quoted by J. H. Clapham, *An economic history of modern Britain: the early railway age, 1820–1850* (2nd ed., Cambridge, 1930), 68.

paratively new in 1850. Iron shipbuilding, for example, was added to the already heterogeneous group of industries which clustered along the banks of the Thames below London Bridge; and the manufacture of cheap ready-made clothing established a foothold in the East End.[1] For a time, too, London was pre-eminent in the new and fast expanding field of mechanical engineering.[2]

TRANSPORT AND TRADE

Transport by road

The extension of the turnpike system and new techniques of road making produced very great changes in internal communications. About 18,200 miles of English road had been turnpiked by 1821.[3] By 1848, with the brief golden age of the roads already in the past, the figure stood at 19,900 miles.[4] J. L. McAdam's method of surfacing roads with small stones broken to size on a well-drained foundation was widely adopted on many of the trunk roads, first in the neighbourhood of Bristol and Bath, and later (although according to McAdam's own testimony before 1820) in 'almost every county in the south of England'.[5] By that year, he claimed, his methods were also finding favour in other parts of the country. The regional distribution of Road Acts, as calculated by W. T. Jackman, indicates that the most progressive districts lay within the Home Counties and the industrial Midlands and north.[6] By 1830, as appears from C. and J. Greenwood's *Atlas of the counties of England* (1834), the great manufacturing areas of the country and much of the area around London had been 'covered with an elaborate network of turnpike roads linking together every place that could be called a town'.[7]

[1] O. H. K. Spate, 'Geographical aspects of the industrial evolution of London till 1850', *Geog. Jour.*, XCII (1938), 426–7; J. Thomas, *A history of the Leeds clothing industry* (Yorks. Bull. Econ. and Soc. Research, Occasional Paper No. 1, 1955), 12; P. G. Hall, 165–7.

[2] A. E. Musson, 'James Nasmyth and the early growth of mechanical engineering', *Econ. Hist. Rev.*, 2nd ser., X (1957), 121–2.

[3] Anon., 'Turnpike roads in England and Wales', *Jour. Roy. Stat. Soc.*, I (1839), 542; *Abstract of Returns relative to the Expense and Maintenance of the Highways of England and Wales*, 258 (P.P. 1818, xvi).   [4] *Accounts and Papers*, 413 (P.P. 1847–8, lx).

[5] *S.C. on Turnpike Roads and Highways in England and Wales*, 315 (P.P. 1820, ii).

[6] W. T. Jackman, *The development of transportation in modern England* (London, 2nd ed., 1962), 743.

[7] G. H. Tupling, 'The turnpike trusts of Lancashire', *Manchester Literary and Philosophical Society Memoirs*, XCIV (1953), 43.

The Greenwoods' *Atlas* of 1834 also serves as a reminder that a century of turnpike activity had left many gaps in the system. Lancashire south of the Ribble, for instance, was the only part of that county with a close network of turnpike roads, which even there failed to extend to the moss-lands along the Cheshire boundary; and in east Leicestershire and the East Riding of Yorkshire, both predominantly rural and agricultural, the pattern of turnpike roads remained skeletal.[1] In fact, most counties which possessed an impressive mileage of turnpike road possessed also a very much greater mileage of other highways. Thus, although in 1848 the Yorkshire trusts controlled 1,737 miles of road, this represented little more than 18% of the total length of highways in the county.[2] The proportion was still lower in Devon, and lowest of all in East Anglia and Cornwall, where less than 10% of the mileage of highways had been turnpiked.[3] In the country as a whole, turnpike roads represented in 1838 about one-fifth of the mileage of all highways.[4]

Detailed study of almost any district will yield evidence of changes in the pattern and character of the roads at this period. Sometimes the changes were due to the Commissioners of Enclosure, 'those merciless annihilators of rural scenery',[5] who laid out many new roads and straightened countless old ones during the last phases of parliamentary enclosure. Frequently, however, the changes were on a larger scale and were of considerable regional significance. As the trans-Wealden routes between London and the coastal resorts grew in importance after 1800, for example, several new turnpike roads were constructed and a number of old ones re-aligned.[6] There were similar changes within south Lancashire where most of the roads were old highways, which had been turnpiked and repaired; others, including those between Bolton and Bury and between Bolton and Chorley were, either wholly or in part, new roads, less tortuous and more easily graded than the old routes between the same towns. In scores of places, including many along the line of Telford's improved Holyhead road, and on the main routes across the Pennines,

---

[1] P. Russell in W. G. Hoskins and R. A. McKinley (eds.), *V.C.H. Leicestershire*, III (1955), 80; A. Bryant, *A map of the East Riding of Yorkshire* (London, 1829).

[2] *Accounts and Papers*, 413 (P.P. 1847–8, lx); *Report of the Commissioners for Inquiry into the State of the Roads in England and Wales*, 631 (P.P. 1840, xxvii).

[3] *Rep. Commissioners on Roads*, 630–1 (P.P. 1840, xxvii).

[4] *Ibid.*, 630–1. The calculation is for England alone.

[5] *Quarterly Review*, XXIII (1820), 102.

[6] G. J. Fuller, 'The development of roads in the Surrey–Sussex Weald and coastlands between 1700 and 1900', *Trans. and Papers, Inst. Brit. Geog.*, XIX (1954), 46.

narrow lengths of highway were widened and 'angular turnings and un-necessary hills' eliminated.[1]

An immediate consequence of these improvements was a reduction in the journey times of many long-distance stage coaches: by the 1830s these were maintaining average speeds of nine and ten miles an hour, including stops, over such routes as those between London and Glasgow, and London and Bristol.[2] To many places, and particularly to those which lay, as did Hounslow, Newbury and Kendal, along great thoroughfares and at important staging-points, the coaches brought an air of bustling prosperity. Thirty-four coaches daily passed through Newbury in the heyday of the coaching era.[3] An improvement in the performance and frequency of coaches along the great arterial roads of the country was accompanied by the emergence, within the industrialised areas, of complex networks of coach services, no less highly organised than those of the open roads and frequently supporting a greater density of traffic.[4] Equally important were the new public transport facilities within the great towns. As these grew larger, suburb and centre were linked by means of a variety of short-stage horse-drawn vehicles. Thus a close network of omnibus routes had appeared in London by the middle of the 1830s, and embryonic networks of a similar kind were emerging elsewhere.[5]

Moreover, by the 1820s, if not earlier, the whole country was covered by a network of carrier services by wagon and van. In the larger centres of population the number of firms engaged in such activities ran into scores; in 1824 ninety-four different firms operated carrier services from Manchester alone.[6] As the volume of traffic using the roads gradually increased, acute problems of traffic congestion became apparent. They were probably most severe in central London where, despite street improvements, the difficulty of moving freely by road remained a subject

[1] E. Mogg, *Paterson's roads* (London, 1829), 179–93; W. B. Crump, *Huddersfield highways down the ages* (Huddersfield, 1949), 82–8.

[2] H. W. Hart, 'Some notes on coach travel, 1750–1848', *Jour. Transport History*, IV (1959–60), 148–9.

[3] *R.C. on Municipal Corporations*, 230 (P.P. 1835, xxiii).

[4] G. C. Dickinson, 'Stage-coach services in the West Riding of Yorkshire between 1830 and 1840', *Jour. Transport History*, IV (1959–60), 1–11.

[5] T. C. Barker and M. Robbins, *A history of London transport*, I (London, 1963), 14–40; H. J. Dyos, 'The growth of a pre-Victorian suburb: south London, 1580–1836', *Town Planning Rev.*, XXV (1954–5), 69–70; G. C. Dickinson, 'The development of suburban road passenger transport in Leeds, 1840–95', *Jour. of Transport History*, IV (1959–60), 214–15.   [6] G. H. Tupling, 54.

of constant complaint.[1] The problem was not confined to the metropolis. Thus it was said in 1829 that in Carlisle the city's Saturday market filled 'all the principal streets and many of the lanes' with a press of farmers' carts and other traffic.[2] So bad were conditions in some provincial towns that the removal of markets and fairs from the principal streets formed a major consideration in any scheme for improving local amenities.[3]

Canal and coastwise traffic

The first twenty years of the nineteenth century saw some notable changes in the pattern of English waterways. In southern England, water communication in the country between Thames and Severn was both extended and improved in 1810 with the opening of the Wilts & Berks Canal for narrow boats and the Kennet & Avon Canal for barges. After 1819, by which time the North Wilts Canal had become available, through traffic, following the older Thames & Severn Canal, could, if necessary, avoid the shallows of the upper Thames below Lechlade by using for part of the journey the Wilts & Berks and North Wilts Canals.[4] More useful as an alternative to a difficult section of river navigation, however, was the Gloucester & Berkeley Canal, which was opened in 1827, and which enabled vessels of up to 700 tons to reach Gloucester without first navigating the shoals of the Severn between that city and Sharpness.[5]

In the Midlands, the network of waterways was strengthened by the addition of the Grand Union Canal which linked the Leicestershire & Northamptonshire Union Canal at Gumley in Leicestershire with the recently finished Grand Junction Canal at Long Buckby in Northamptonshire (Fig. 44). Thus, in 1814, was completed 'the great line of canals which extended from the Thames to the Humber',[6] for the Leicestershire & Northamptonshire Union in turn provided access to the waterways of the Soar and Trent valleys. To the already complex network of canals

[1] S.C. on Metropolis Improvements, 34 (P.P. 1836, xx); T. C. Barker and M. Robbins, 10–14.

[2] W. Parson and W. White, 148.

[3] See, for example, K. J. Allison in P. M. Tillott (ed.), V.C.H., The city of York, 488–9.

[4] C. Hadfield, British canals: an illustrated history (London, 1950), 78–82.

[5] W. G. East, 'The Severn waterway in the eighteenth and nineteenth centuries' in L. D. Stamp and S. W. Wooldridge (eds.), London essays in geography (London, 1951), 108–10.

[6] Prospectus of the Grand Union Canal Co. quoted by A. T. Patterson in W. G. Hoskins and R. A. McKinley (eds.), V.C.H. Leicestershire, III, 102.

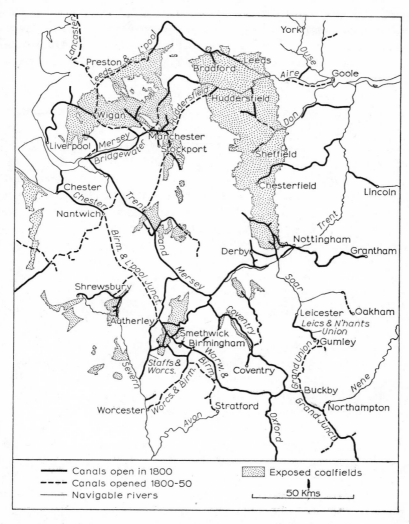

Fig. 44 Canals and waterways of the Midlands and the north, 1800–50
Based on C. Hadfield (ed.), *The canals of the British Isles*, 6 vols. (Newton Abbot, 1966).

linking the Birmingham region with the Severn was added in 1816 a connection with the Worcester & Birmingham Canal, whose flight of thirty
locks at Tardebigge lifted it through a vertical height of 217 feet at
a gradient of about 1 in 50.[1] In the north, two canals, the Huddersfield
Narrow and the Leeds & Liverpool, completed in 1811 and 1816 respectively, provided new water routes across the Pennines.

Standing apart from all these, both in time and character, was the
Birmingham & Liverpool Junction Canal, which by means of numerous
cuttings and embankments achieved in 1835 a more or less direct route
between the Staffordshire & Worcestershire Canal at Autherley and the
Chester Canal at Nantwich.[2] As an act of faith in improved canal navigation, the Birmingham & Liverpool Junction was magnificent; but it
was, nevertheless, the last of the great trunk waterways to be constructed
in this country during the canal age. It was cut at a time when efforts were
being made to increase the competitive efficiency of canals in various ways.
These involved both the introduction on a number of routes of express
services for passengers and goods, and also alterations to the canals themselves. According to Sir George Head, writing in 1835, an effective
opposition to the coaches was maintained in his day by the passage-boats
'Water Witch' and 'Swiftsure', which ran a daily service along the
Lancaster Canal between Preston and Kendal.[3] Much more enduring in
their results, however, were engineering works such as those which
shortened the length of the Oxford Canal by $13\frac{1}{2}$ miles; replaced the
summit locks of the Birmingham Canal at Smethwick by a deep cutting;
doubled the Harecastle Tunnel; and increased the capacity of the reservoirs
which served the summit locks of the Grand Junction at Tring.

A substantial amount of traffic was soon moving along some of the
newly completed waterways. The Gloucester & Berkeley carried 107,000
tons in its first year of operation (1827), and more than 390,000 tons in
1837.[4] The Kennet & Avon handled nearly 342,000 tons of traffic in 1838,
and 360,000 tons ten years later.[5] Still more intensively used was the
Regent's Canal, in London (1820), which was carrying almost half a

[1] J. H. Appleton, *The geography of communications in Great Britain* (Oxford,
1962), 6.   [2] L. T. C. Rolt, *Thomas Telford* (London, 1958), 173–86.

[3] G. Head, *A home tour through the manufacturing districts of England in the
summer of 1835* (London, 1836), 415.

[4] *R.C. on Canals and Inland Navigations of the United Kingdom, First Report*, I,
Part II, Appendix 14, p. 43 (P.P. 1906, xxxii).

[5] *Return relating to Inland Navigation and Canal Companies in England and Wales*,
680ff. (P.P. 1870, lvi).

million tons of traffic in 1828 and more than one million tons in 1848.[1] By contrast, the Bude Canal (1825), which supplied an agricultural district with sea sand for use as fertiliser, carried little more than 52,000 tons of traffic in 1848.[2] Of the other new canals at least one, the Sheffield (1819), had by 1850 attracted to its banks much heavy industry[3] and another, the Carlisle, was instrumental after 1823 in furthering the development in Caldewgate, Carlisle, of an industrial quarter near the canal basin.[4]

The most important of the new waterways formed an integral part of an already elaborate network of canals and navigable rivers, and played a vital role in the economy at large. The list of commodities handled by the Grand Junction, which carried about one million tons of traffic in 1838, reads like an inventory of industrial England. Besides coal, iron and building materials, it carried Cheshire salt, Stourbridge glass, Staffordshire pottery, Manchester textiles, a variety of metal goods, foodstuffs, agricultural produce, and much else.[5] Waterborne coal was of great importance in the industrial growth of Leicester.[6] Until the trade was disrupted by the opening of the Leicester & Swannington Railway in 1832, Leicester was supplied with coal from the Nottinghamshire–Derbyshire coalfield by way of the Erewash valley and the Loughborough and Leicester Navigations.[7] The importance of waterborne coal to a large manufacturing town may be illustrated more precisely in the case of Manchester. In 1834, 463,000 tons of coal reached Manchester by way of the Ashton, Bolton, Bridgewater and Rochdale Canals, compared with 247,000 tons by road and a mere 21,000 tons by the new Liverpool & Manchester railway.[8] The Kennet & Avon Canal acted as an important outlet for Somerset coal; by means of its feeder, the Somersetshire Coal Canal, it linked the Somerset

[1] *Ibid.*, under Regent's Canal.

[2] *Ibid.*, under Bude Canal; C. Hadfield, 'James Green as canal engineer', *Jour. Transport History*, I (1953–4), 48.

[3] A. W. Goodfellow and A. J. Hunt in D. L. Linton (ed.), *Sheffield and its region* (Sheffield, 1956), 165, 234, 236.

[4] W. Parson and W. White, 148; A. E. Smailes, *North England* (Edinburgh and London, 1960), 255.

[5] C. Hadfield, 'The Grand Junction Canal', *Jour. Transport History*, IV (1959–60), 104–5.

[6] A. T. Patterson, *Radical Leicester: a history of Leicester 1780–1850* (Leicester, 1954), 39, 40, 260.

[7] J. E. Williams, *The Derbyshire miners: a study in industrial and social history* (London, 1962), 41–2.

[8] *R.C. on Coal*: Appendix to Report of Committee E, Table 55, p. 1161 (P.P. 1871, xviii).

coalfield with markets as far east as Reading, beyond which Somerset coal competed with seaborne coal from London and coal from the west Midlands carried by way of the Oxford Canal.[1] Even on the Driffield Navigation, a minor Yorkshire waterway, coal was an important item of traffic.[2] Of all the waterways for which tonnage figures are available, none carried more than those of the Black Country. More than $3\frac{1}{4}$ million tons of traffic moved over the Birmingham Canal system in 1838, and almost 4,700,000 tons a decade later. This chiefly represented, as Joseph Priestley had observed a few years earlier, a vast flow of coal, iron ore and limestone to local ironworks, many of which occupied canal-side locations, and a movement in transit of finished and semi-finished iron goods.[3]

Writing in 1837, and thus towards the end of the period of major canal development in Britain, J. R. McCulloch claimed for England an extent of canal navigation 'unparalleled in any other country, with the exception of Holland';[4] and he devoted more attention to canals than to either roads or railways, the last of which he dismissed in a page or two. Yet, such was the pace of change, that three years later Francis Whishaw was writing at length about some of the consequences of living 'in the times of railways', not the least of which was the virtual cessation of canal building.[5]

In emphasising the role of the canal age in the developing economy of the nation, we must not forget the continuing importance of another form of water transport – coastwise traffic. The outstanding element in this was the enormous shipment of coal (some two million tons in 1830) to London, the most important consumer and chief distributor; a large number of ships worked on regular beats from north-east ports to those of the Thames estuary and elsewhere along the east and south coasts. Furthermore, there was an enormous miscellaneous traffic entering and leaving all the many harbours, great and small, around the coast. Amidst the variety of ships, a new type was beginning to make its appearance – the steamboat.

---

[1] *Ibid.*, 877–8; J. A. Bulley, 'To Mendip for coal – a study of the Somerset coalfield before 1830', *Proc. Somerset. Archaeol. and Nat. Hist. Soc.*, XCVII (1953), 55–6.

[2] *S.C. on the State of the Coal Trade*, 500 (P.P. 1830, viii); J. Priestley, *Historical account of the navigable rivers, canals, and railways, throughout Great Britain* (London, 1831), 220.

[3] J. Priestley, 228.

[4] J. R. McCulloch, 188.

[5] F. Whishaw, *Railways of Great Britain and Ireland practically described and illustrated* (London, 1840).

It is easy to lose sight of the fact that locally the established order of things had been changed by the steamboat before the advent of railways. Steamer excursions on the Thames to Richmond had assumed sufficient social importance by 1833 to find a place in the deliberations of the Select Committee on Public Walks.[1] More important still was the growth of steamer traffic downstream to Gravesend, Margate and Ramsgate.[2] Passenger traffic on the Thames steamboats was not confined to the summer months, and in 1837 it could be claimed that Gravesend owed its popularity as a residential town to the steamer services which linked it with London.[3] The effects of the steamers were felt over a wider area with the development of steam-packet services round the coast and to continental ports. Thus, innkeepers along the Great North Road complained in 1837 that, for long journeys, travellers preferred the cheaper steam packets to the coaches.[4] Since the travelling public would go out of their way 'to get to the steam', however, coach traffic on some cross routes actually benefited from the change.[5] In at least one district the introduction of steamboats led to changes of far-reaching geographical importance, as Richard Edmonds' account of the Cornish parish of Madron showed.[6] He explained in 1839 that until recently 'the early vegetables from Penzance and Mount's Bay have been principally consumed in Cornwall; but the facility of conveyance by steam-boats is now so great, that during the spring of 1838 a very considerable portion of them was sent to London and other distant markets'. Edmonds went on to predict that 'for the future Mount's Bay will most probably be the great spring-garden, not merely of Cornwall, but of all England'.

The growth of railways

Railways had their origin in the horse tramways that were in use before 1700 on many coalfields. By 1800, especially in some mining districts, they had become a well established part of both local and regional transport systems.[7] Further progress awaited Richard Trevithick's high-pressure

[1] *S.C. on Public Walks*, 362 (P.P. 1833, xv).

[2] T. C. Barker and M. Robbins, 40–3.

[3] *Report on Municipal Corporation Boundaries*, 45 (P.P. 1837, xxvii).

[4] *S.C. on Internal Communication Taxation*, 304, 309, 332 (P.P. 1837, xx).

[5] *Ibid.*, 332.

[6] R. Edmonds, 'A statistical account of the parish of Madron', *Jour. Roy. Stat. Soc.*, 11 (1839), 207.

[7] F. Atkinson, *The great northern coalfield, 1700–1900* (London, 1968), 48–52; M. J. T. Lewis, *Early wooden railways* (London, 1970), *passim*.

steam engine after 1801, and the improved design of locomotive engines, notably by George Stephenson after 1814. In 1825 the Stockton & Darlington Railway was opened, and was soon carrying passengers as well as minerals and goods. Five years later, on 15 September 1830, the Liverpool & Manchester Railway was opened, and achieved a success that surprised even its promoters. The railway age may be said to have begun.[1]

Railways multiplied after 1830, somewhat slowly at first and then with great rapidity in the years that followed the two bursts of speculative activity, from 1836 to 1837 and from 1845 to 1847, which together laid the foundations of the future railway system. Up to the end of 1838 the length of line open to public traffic was about 500 miles.[2] By July 1841 this had increased to some 1,400 miles.[3] Railway openings sanctioned during the following two years brought the total in June 1843 to about 1,700 miles.[4] In 1848 alone, more than 740 miles of new railway were opened, and at the end of that year the network of lines extended over 3,900 route miles.[5] By the close of 1849 more than 4,600 miles of railway were in operation in England and Wales, out of a total of 5,996 miles in the United Kingdom.[6] In little more than a generation the railway network of the country had evolved from a series of highly localised mineral tramways into a national system of lines carrying both goods and passengers (Fig. 60).

By the end of 1844 the outlines of a railway system had begun to emerge. 'The Great North-Western artery', 240 miles in length,

[1] The following sources have been consulted in the compilation of this section: W. M. Acworth, *The railways of England* (London, 5th ed., 1900); H. G. Lewin, *Early British railways* (London, 1925); E. Cleveland-Stevens, *English railways: their development and their relation to the state* (London, 1915); C. E. R. Sherrington, *The economics of rail transport in Great Britain*, I (London, 1928); E. T. MacDermot and C. R. Clinker, *History of the Great Western Railway* (London, 1964); H. P. White, *A regional history of the railways of Great Britain*, III *Greater London* (London, 1963); J. H. Clapham, *An economic history of modern Britain: the early railway age, 1820–1850* (Cambridge, 1930); J. H. Appleton, *The geography of communications in Great Britain* (Oxford, 1962).

[2] *R.C. on Railways*, Pt 1, p. ix (P.P. 1867, xxxviii). Unless otherwise stated, all figures refer to England and Wales. Dates appended to the name of a railway refer to the opening of the line.

[3] Anon., 'List of the railways in the United Kingdom', *Jour. Roy. Stat. Soc.*, IV (1841), 176–7.

[4] *S.C. on Railways*, 600–1 (P.P. 1844, xi).

[5] *Report of the Railway Commissioners for 1848*, 277 (P.P. 1849, xxvii).

[6] *Report of the Railway Commissioners for 1849*, 5 (P.P. 1850, xxxi).

connected London with Lancaster by means of the London & Birmingham (1838) and Grand Junction (1837) Railways and the several continuations of the latter beyond Warrington, where this north–south route met and crossed the Liverpool & Manchester Railway (1830). A steamer service linked the new town and port of Fleetwood, at the seaward end of the Preston & Wyre Railway (1840), with Ardrossan. Passengers from London could reach Darlington by using the London & Birmingham Railway as far as Rugby, and then the lines of the newly consolidated Midland Railway to Normanton, and thereafter those of the York & North Midland (1840) and Great North of England (1841) companies.

The completion of the Bristol & Exeter Railway in May 1844 extended rail communication by the broad gauge of the Great Western as far as Exeter. Lines to Folkestone, Brighton and Dover were already open, as was the South Western Railway to Southampton and Gosport. The luck-less Eastern Counties line had reached, and stopped at, Colchester, while the Northern & Eastern, even more impecunious, was struggling to reach Cambridge. Elsewhere, a number of cross-country routes had been developed: from Newcastle to Carlisle (1838), from Leeds to Selby (1834), from Selby to Hull (1840), from Manchester to Normanton (and Leeds, 1841), and from Manchester across the Pennines to Sheffield via Woodhead (1845).

No national plan lay behind this growth. 'The railways of England grew up piecemeal and haphazard in short, unconnected lengths.'[1] It will be apparent from the examples cited, however, that several trunk lines did in fact emerge at an early date; an original main line was often extended by arrangement with other companies in anything but a haphazard manner, and a process of amalgamation was already consolidating local companies into larger units. Many new lines were added to the railway map following the promotions of 1845–7; and by 1850 Scotland and England were linked by rail both by way of Carlisle and Berwick. Considerable progress had also been made in constructing lines in East Anglia and Lincolnshire; and work was under way on the Great Northern beyond Peterborough on the route between King's Cross and York. Competing lines had appeared, 'blocking lines' had been built to exclude rivals, and amalgamations had produced, *inter alia*, the London & North Western, the Lancashire & Yorkshire, the Manchester, Sheffield & Lincolnshire, and the London, Brighton & South Coast Companies.

The effects of railways were soon apparent. Coaching services along

[1] E. Cleveland-Stevens, 10.

main roads swiftly declined, though some survived until 1850, and even later, between places which were not served by rail. But by 1848, when the last of the ordinary mail and stage coaches ceased to run out of London, the days of this traffic were numbered.[1] With it went the posting trade. 'Many inns and public houses, once in full business, have disappeared', Henry Tremenheere wrote of Brentford in 1843;[2] and the same was true of other places throughout the country. For a time, however, many cross routes leading to the new railway stations were busier than ever, much to the discomfort of turnpike trustees whose gates, designed to catch a hitherto predictable flow of traffic, now proved to be badly situated.[3] The railways stimulated the growth of local passenger and carrier services, and, since these tended to use a limited number of routes within built-up areas, congestion frequently occurred.[4] In 1846 it was claimed that the rail journey between Reading and Paddington could be made in the time taken by an omnibus in travelling between Paddington and the City.[5] London's traffic problem was aggravated by the peripheral situation of the main-line railway termini north of the Thames. Excluded from the City by the Corporation of London, these generated a large volume of cross-town traffic which included heavy goods and merchandise as well as passengers. Pickford's leviathan wagons lumbered through the narrow City streets between the railway terminals and the receiving-houses of the railway companies, often situated in old coaching inns. 'One cart comes perhaps with two or three chests of tea, a waggon with a couple of tons of iron, another with a bale of goods.' The result was that many streets were completely blocked.[6]

The full weight of railway competition had fallen upon many canals by 1850, and though tonnage figures frequently showed an improvement over earlier years, receipts were falling due to the reduction of tolls. By 1847, most of those canals that were destined to be transferred to railways had already changed hands.[7] River navigations were also affected: receipts from tolls on the Yorkshire Ouse, for instance, fell from £5,108 in 1837

[1] H. W. Hart, 146.

[2] H. Tremenheere, 'Agricultural and educational statistics of several parishes in the county of Middlesex', *Jour. Roy. Stat. Soc.*, VI (1843), 126–7.

[3] *S.C. on Turnpike Trusts*, 411, 422 (P.P. 1839, ix).

[4] T. C. Barker and M. Robbins, 64–8.

[5] *Metropolitan Railway Commission*, 233 (P.P. 1846, xvii).

[6] *Metropolitan Railway Commission*, 177 (P.P. 1846, xvii). See J. R. Kellett, *The impact of railways on Victorian cities* (London, 1969), 35–40.

[7] E. Cleveland-Stevens, 91; C. Hadfield (1950), 191.

to £1,540 in 1850.[1] These, however, were only some of the more obvious effects of the coming of railways. As early as 1843, the G.W.R. was undermining the privileged position held by Middlesex farmers in the London market.[2] Henry Evershed, writing in 1853 of Surrey, noted that a new trade in milk and vegetables had been developed in the county since the completion of the South Western Railway.[3] A year earlier William Bearn had noticed fat beasts being sent from Northamptonshire to Smithfield by rail instead of, as formerly, on the hoof.[4] New coke ovens were built at Clay Cross, Camden Town and elsewhere by the railway companies for the supply of their locomotives:[5] the 'touch of the South Eastern Railway' was said to have given new life to Folkestone.[6] But the railways could also deprive. Thus, opening of railways was said to have damaged the trade of the Ingleton coalfield, which hitherto had served a large rural area on the borders of Lancashire, Westmorland and Yorkshire; 'railway coal' from south Lancashire and the main Yorkshire coalfield was in future to compete there with the local product.[7] This corner of England was no more than one of many, however, in which by 1850 'steam, the great magician of the nineteenth century', had been at work and, through railways, made its presence felt.[8]

By 1850 the railway had become a familiar part of the English scene. On every side the land had been 'bridged and cut and tunnelled',[9] and these manifestations of railway activity, together with railway inns, railway docks, railway streets and a handful of railway towns, bore ample testimony to 'the altered appearance of the country, produced by the formation of railways'.[10] In some places, notably perhaps at Euston, Chester and Newcastle, the railway station, architecturally splendid and functionally efficient, was an imposing symbol of the new age.[11] The

[1] B. F. Duckham, 'Inland waterways: some sources for their history', *The Amateur Historian*, VI (1963), 9.   [2] H. Tremenheere, 122.

[3] H. Evershed, 'On the farming of Surrey', *J.R.A.S.*, XIV (1853), 402.

[4] W. Bearn, 'On the farming of Northamptonshire' *J.R.A.S.*, XIII (1852), 47.

[5] F. Whishaw, 233, 298, 347, 423.

[6] *Illustrated London News*, XVII (1850), p. 48.

[7] *Lancaster Gazette*, 12 May 1866; *Lancaster Guardian*, 20 July 1872.

[8] S. Sidney, 21.   [9] J. H. Clapham (1930), 389.

[10] W. White, *History, gazetteer, and directory of the county of Essex* (Sheffield, 1848), 239.

[11] C. L. V. Meeks, *The railway station: an architectural history* (London and New Haven, 1957), especially 4, 35, 39; A. A. Arschavir, 'The inception of the English railway station', *Architectural History*, IV (1961), *passim*.

country station, less monumental but infinitely varied, had brought to many rural areas both a new settlement form and a new architecture.[1]

Overseas trade

In the merchant fleet, however, steam power made slow progress, and much of England's large and increasingly important overseas trade continued to be handled by sailing ships.[2] Among the imports, manufactured goods were of little importance. But from India, the West Indies and, above all, from the U.S.A. came great quantities of raw cotton; and from Germany, Spain and Australia came an increasing volume of wool. The import trade in raw materials was swollen by flax and hemp from the Baltic and by large amounts of timber from both colonial and foreign sources. In 1840, raw materials and semi-manufactured goods together were responsible for 56% by value of all imports.[3] An extensive trade in such commodities as sugar, coffee, tea, tobacco, grains and spirits – some of which were eventually re-exported – accounted for a further 40% of the total in that year.

By contrast, the export trade was dominated by manufactured goods, of which by far the most important were textiles. The greatly expanded cotton industry supplied the major share, accounting for at least 40% of the declared value of domestic exports during most of the period 1815–50.[4] In the 1840s, as in the 1820s, Europe and North America absorbed most of the country's exports, though other outlets were developed, particularly in Asia, Africa and South America.[5] New docks and warehouses in London, Liverpool, Hull and elsewhere, helped to meet the demand for more and better port facilities, while the reduction and eventual removal of tariffs during the 1840s prepared the way for free trade.

[1] J. Simmons, *The railways of Britain: an historical introduction* (London, 1961), ch. 3; M. Robbins, *The railway age* (London, 1962), ch. 7.

[2] For a general review of overseas trade see J. H. Clapham, *An economic history of modern Britain: the early railway age, 1820–1850* (Cambridge, 2nd ed., 1930), especially chs. 6 and 12. Statistics of trade and their interpretation are discussed in B. R. Mitchell and P. Deane, *Abstract of British historical statistics* (Cambridge, 1962), 274–337, and in W. Schlote, *British overseas trade from 1700 to the 1930s*, trans. and edited W. O. Henderson and W. H. Chaloner (Oxford, 1952).

[3] P. Deane and W. A. Cole, *British economic growth, 1688–1959* (Cambridge, 1964), 33. The figures refer to the United Kingdom.

[4] J. Potter, 'Atlantic economy, 1815–60: the U.S.A. and the industrial revolution in Britain', in L. S. Presnell (ed.), *Studies in the industrial revolution* (London, 1960), 259; P. Deane and W. A. Cole, 295.

[5] J. D. Chambers, *The workshop of the world* (London, 1961), 99.

TOWN AND CITIES

Not only were the large towns almost everywhere becoming substantially larger, but they were doing so at a rate that was prodigious. Thus the population of Liverpool grew by over 30% between 1811 and 1821, and by more than 40% in each of the following two decades.[1] Birmingham's population increased by more than 40% between 1821 and 1831, as did that of Manchester, Leeds and Sheffield, all of which attained their maximum rate of increase during this decade.[2] Some well-established urban communities, smaller than these but still large enough to rank among the 'large towns and populous districts', developed even faster. The population of Bradford, for example, increased by more than 60% between 1821 and 1831, making it the second most rapidly growing English city during the decade; the first place over the same period belonged to Brighton with an increase of just over 66%.[3]

In the Census of 1801, the population of London appeared as just under one million. Around it were many growing suburbs, and the metropolitan area (to be defined by the Metropolis Management Act of 1855) covered about 117 square miles and, in 1851, contained some 2.4 million people. This area corresponded fairly closely with the Metropolitan Police District which had been instituted in 1829 (and, incidentally, with the county of London to be created in 1888). But in 1839, the Metropolitan Police District was greatly extended to cover an area within 15 miles or so from Charing Cross (Fig. 79).[4] It included the whole of Middlesex and parts of Essex, Hertfordshire, Surrey and Kent; it covered nearly 693 square miles, and included a total of nearly 2.7 million people (see table on p. 373). This area within the 1839 limits came to be regarded as constituting 'Greater London'.

In 1801 no provincial city had as many as 100,000 inhabitants, but by 1851 there were seven. As in the case of London, it is difficult to define their limits in a geographical as opposed to an administrative sense, but the municipal boroughs of Liverpool and Manchester each had over 300,000 inhabitants. The other municipal boroughs with over 100,000

[1] R. P. Williams, 468–9.

[2] *Ibid.*, 486–7.

[3] E. W. Gilbert: (1) *Brighton, old ocean's bauble* (London, 1954), 97; (2) 'The growth of Brighton', *Geog. Jour.*, XCIV (1949), 38.

[4] J. F. Moylan, *Scotland Yard and the metropolitan police* (2nd ed., London, 1934), 82–3.

people were, in descending order, Birmingham, Leeds, Bristol, Sheffield and Bradford. There were thirteen other municipal boroughs each with over 50,000 people. Furthermore, nearly one million other town-dwellers lived in places with between 20,000 and 50,000. In this last group were towns as different in origin, function and appearance as Cambridge, Walsall, Wigan and York, yet all formed part of a rapidly expanding urban environment which by 1851 had come to contain about one half of the total population of England.[1] As Robert Vaughan rightly observed in 1843, the early railway age was also an 'age of great cities'.[2]

The spreading built-up areas. Such a vast and sudden accession of population could hardly fail to be accompanied by profound changes in both the extent and the character of the urban landscape. 'The increase of London since the commencement of the present century has exceeded... that of the last in celerity and extent', it was said in 1842, 'and is visible on all sides'.[3] The growth of the metropolis, a source of both pride and annoyance, amazed contemporaries, not least on account of its continuing character. Already in 1826 a vast 'province of bricks', London was growing at a rate that appeared to admit of no check.[4] 'Year by year the map of the metropolis takes new forms, and juts out in every direction fresh angles... houses are not built singly, but by wholesale.'[5] Many of the additions, as the *Illustrated London News* remarked, were big enough in themselves to rank as 'so many towns'.[6] By the late 1840s, the built-up area, that extraordinary 'admixture of the beautiful and the mean',[7] sprawled irregularly and, in places, tenuously from Hammersmith to Stratford and from Holloway to Camberwell; its salients thrust out along a host of roads, and its expanding periphery engulfed both swollen villages and open country (Fig. 78).[8] Along the river, the opening of the West India Dock in 1802 was followed by the construction of others with their associated warehouses, factories and dwellings. By 1828 there had

[1] *Census of 1851: Population Tables, I,* Vol. I, Table xxviii, p. l (P.P. 1852–3, lxxxv).

[2] R. Vaughan, *The age of great cities* (London, 1843), 1.

[3] S. Lewis, *A topographical dictionary of England,* iii (5th ed., London, 1842), 123.

[4] *Quarterly Review,* xxxiv (1826), 192.

[5] *Chambers's Edinburgh Journal,* xii (1850), 141.

[6] *Illustrated London News, Supplement,* January 1845, p. x.

[7] C. Knight, *London pictorially illustrated,* i (London, 1841), 16.

[8] *Illustrated London News, Supplement,* January 1845, p. vii; H. C. Prince, 'North-west London, 1814–1863', in J. T. Coppock and H. C. Prince (eds.), *Greater London* (London, 1964), 80–117.

come into existence the London Docks, the East India Dock, the St Katharine's Docks and the Surrey Commercial Docks.

The built-up area of Manchester also expanded steadily. J. Aston's map of Manchester and Salford, dated 1804, shows a compact built-up area that was still virtually surrounded by open country.[1] But the lines of streets, laid out but not yet fully developed, indicated the shape of things to come. Although the open countryside remained for some time within easy walking distance of much of the town,[2] the rural fringe was pushed steadily outwards, and by 1850 Greater Manchester covered about seven square miles.[3] The urban area on Merseyside, which was still relatively small and confined to the Liverpool shore of the Mersey at the beginning of the nineteenth century, received a considerable accession after 1820 with the rise of Birkenhead, that other 'glory on the Mersey's side',[4] and by the 1840s the land on both sides of the river was undergoing rapid change.[5]

An uncompromising scenic transformation was frequently effected within the space of a few years. The valley of the lower Medlock, for instance, which in 1804 presented a fringe of open country to the southern outskirts of Manchester, had become by 1836 the site of a substantial industrial suburb, 'created within a few years by the erection of factories'[6] and displaying 'forests of chimneys, clouds of smoke and volumes of vapour, like the seething of some stupendous cauldron'.[7] Fields and gardens in and around Birmingham were quickly engulfed by buildings between 1820 and 1850.[8] And in Sheffield, where a period of rapid physical expansion culminated in a building mania during 1835 and 1836, no fewer than 156 new streets were built or projected between 1831 and 1836.[9] At such times the physical results of town growth could be measured in weeks rather than years.

[1] J. Aston, *Manchester guide*, Manchester (1804).

[2] *First Report of the Commissioners on the State of Large Towns and Populous Districts*, 572 (P.P. 1844, xvii); A. Redford, *The history of local government in Manchester*, II (London, 1940), 213–15.

[3] H. B. Rodgers, 'The suburban growth of Victorian Manchester', *Jour. Manchester Geog. Soc.*, LVIII (1961–2), 4.

[4] *Illustrated London News*, X (1847), 228.

[5] R. Lawton, 'The genesis of population' in W. Smith (ed.), *Merseyside: a scientific survey* (Liverpool, 1953), 122.   [6] J. Wheeler (1836), 269.

[7] C. Redding, *An illustrated itinerary of the county of Lancaster* (London, 1842), 8.

[8] C. Gill, *History of Birmingham*, I (Oxford, 1952), 363–5; M. J. Wise (ed.), 213.

[9] G. C. Holland, *The vital statistics of Sheffield* (London, 1843), 29, 53.

Inland and seaside resorts. It was not only large and well-established towns which, in Sir John Clapham's graphic phrase, 'were growing like toad-stools'.[1] Indeed, one of the outstanding characteristics of town growth at this period was the rise to prominence of many small or hitherto in-significant places.[2] Cheltenham was one such place. In 1806 the town consisted principally of the High Street and, nearby, the first of the 'rows of white tenements, with green balconies' which were later to catch Cobbett's unfriendly eye.[3] Immediately beyond these lay open country, some of which was still cultivated in common fields. As a spa Cheltenham had enjoyed fame for some time, but its population in 1801 was barely 3,000. The discovery of new mineral springs and their skilful exploitation led to rapid growth, so that by 1831 the population had risen to 23,000. On the north side of the town, the extensive suburb of Pittville was laid out on the estate of Joseph Pitt, an M.P. who had acquired the land at the enclosure of the town fields in 1806.[4] Still unfinished when H. S. Merrett's plan of the town appeared in 1834, Pittville was the counterpart on the north of the earlier estate around the Montpellier pump room of Henry Thompson on the other side of the town.[5] Cheltenham was ceasing to be simply a 'drinking spa' and, like Bath at a somewhat earlier date, it was also becoming a fashionable residential town.[6] The growth of Leamington was even more remarkable. From 543 in 1811 the population of the parish of Leamington Priors soared to 2,183 within ten years. By the late 1820s Leamington had become 'a rich and elegant town' with stuccoed hotels, numerous boarding-houses and fashionable shops.[7] Twenty years later, by which time the population had risen to over 13,000, every road leading into the town had been 'seized upon and flanked with buildings'.[8]

Rapid and sustained growth was more common, however, in the rising seaside resorts than among the inland spas. The population of Torquay, for example, rose from 838 in 1801 to 5,982 in 1841, and to 11,474 in 1851.

---

[1] J. H. and M. M. Clapham, 'Life in the new towns', in G. M. Young (ed.), *Early Victorian England 1830–1865*, I (London, 1934), 227.

[2] W. Ashworth, 8.   [3] William Cobbett, I, 33.

[4] Hunt & Co., *City of Gloucester and Cheltenham directory and court guide* (London, 1847), 7; H. P. R. Finberg, *Gloucestershire* (London, 1955), 89.

[5] H. S. Merrett, *Plan of Cheltenham and its vicinity* (Cheltenham, 1834); scale approx. 16 in. to one mile.

[6] A. B. Granville, *The spas of England and principal sea-bathing places*, 2 vols. (London, 1841), II, 309–11.

[7] S. Lewis, III, 40; J. A. R. Pimlott, *The Englishman's holiday: a social history* (London, 1947), 99.   [8] A. B. Granville, II, 223.

The town was recommended by doctors as a winter retreat for their consumptive patients, and its growing fame was reflected in rows of elegant houses and a number of detached villas.[1] Farther north, the sea-bathing resorts along the Lancashire coast were also growing vigorously. Edward Baines estimated in 1825 that at least half the buildings in Southport had been erected within the previous four years, and observed that the resort was still expanding.[2] A few years later William Thornber, commenting on the changing face of Blackpool, noted that it was fast assuming 'the air and importance of a town'.[3]

Railway and canal towns. The fashionable seaside resorts built in the style of Belgravia-by-the-sea, and the not-so-fashionable with their variety of styles, formed an important element in the changing urban scene, but there were other, and very different, new towns, which were no less characteristic of the age. Like Middlesbrough, several towns were called into existence by new lines of communication.[4] In Yorkshire, Goole was created by the Aire and Calder Navigation Company at the seaward end of its new canal, the Knottingley & Goole completed in 1826. In the same year the first docks were opened, and on the nearby dock estate a town rose 'in point of elegance and uniformity...the handsomest in the north of England'.[5] Twenty years later, by arrangement with the Wakefield, Pontefract & Goole Railway Company, whose line reached the town in 1848, the present Railway Dock was built and further growth took place.[6] Goole had a population of 4,700 in 1851 and, in little more than twenty years, had risen from a small village 'to the dignity and importance of a considerable shipping port'.[7] The early growth of Goole was bound up with both canal and railway links, but more characteristic of the period were the new railway towns. These were created to meet the special needs of the railway companies and, like Wolverton in Buckinghamshire, were

---

[1] A. B. Granville, II, 472; W. G. Hoskins, *Devon* (London, 1954), 500.

[2] E. Baines, *History, directory, and gazetteer of the County Palatine of Lancaster*, II (Liverpool, 1825), 552; F. A. Bailey, *A history of Southport* (Southport, 1955), 59.

[3] W. Thornber, *An historical and descriptive account of Blackpool and its neighbourhood* (Poulton, 1837), 226, 230.

[4] A. Briggs, *Victorian cities* (London, 1963), ch. 7.

[5] *Hull Advertiser*, 21 July 1826.

[6] G. F. Copley, *An historical and descriptive guide to the Wakefield, Pontefract and Goole Railway* (Pontefract, 1848), 58.

[7] G. Head, 222; J. Bird, *The major seaports of the United Kingdom* (London, 1963), 145–6.

situated strategically in relation to the railway system which each was intended to serve.[1] 'Wolverton forms a remarkable example of what railway enterprise may effect', the *Railway Chronicle* wrote in 1844.[2] 'A few years since it exhibited nothing but farms and uplands; it is now the centre of a flourishing community...a colony of engineers and handicraftmen', which had grown up since 1838 around the locomotive works of the London & Birmingham Railway Company. A 'neat, brick-built, clean little town of eight or ten streets', and with a population of about 1,500, had appeared there by 1844.[3] A similar 'mechanical settlement in an agricultural district' developed after 1843 at Crewe, following the removal there from Edgehill, near Liverpool, of the workshops of the Grand Junction Railway Company.[4] But not all railway colonies were planted, as these were, in the heart of the countryside. New Swindon, for example, grew up next to the old market town of Swindon. When this happened, the physical contrast between the old and new parts of the settlement might assume considerable social as well as geographical significance.[5]

Urban order and disorder. Apart from the railway colonies, examples of ordered town development at this period were comparatively rare.[6] Where controlled development did occur, however, the results were often immediately apparent. When, for example, in 1822 the Aire & Calder Navigation Company was preparing to build houses on its Goole estate, plans and specifications were drawn up for the contractors.[7] 'The Proprietors of the Canal have laid down a plan and elevation...according to which all the buildings are to be erected of fine brick or stone, and covered with blue slates.'[8] The uniformity of appearance that resulted was much praised. But as Goole's trade prospered and the town was enlarged, rows

---

[1] B. J. Turton, 'The railway town, a problem in industrial planning', *Town Planning Review*, XXII (1961), 100; H. Perkin, *The age of the railway* (London, 1970), 127–31.

[2] *Railway Chronicle*, 1 June 1844, p. 165.

[3] *Ibid.*, 166; [F. B. Head], *Stokers and pokers* (London, 4th ed., 1849), 82.

[4] *Chambers's Edinburgh Journal*, XIII (1850), 392; W. H. Chaloner, *The social and economic development of Crewe, 1780–1923* (Manchester, 1950), 42ff.

[5] K. Hudson, 'The early years of the railway community in Swindon', *Transport History*, I (1968), 146–7, 150.

[6] W. Ashworth, ch. 2.

[7] ACN I (19), 16 December 1822, 4 August 1823 (British Transport Record Office, London).

[8] *Hull Advertiser*, 21 July 1826.

of houses of various styles appeared in close proximity to the company's estate, which formed the heart of the port. At Birkenhead, the effect of planning, though incompletely realised, was even more striking as James Law's plan of 1844 indicates.[1] On this, Paxton's Birkenhead Park, opened three years later, interposes a green barrier between the regularly formed streets of the central area and the spacious villa-dotted suburbs.[2] To the earl of Stamford, Ashton-under-Lyne owed its wide streets and good drains; Edgbaston, wholly villas in 1842, owed its character to the policies of Lord Calthorpe, the principal landowner.[3]

But for every Edgbaston there were a score of places where growth was controlled only by the prevailing state of the market for houses and by the inadequate clauses of local improvement and building acts. The well-known Blue Books of the 1840s contain a wealth of descriptive material, from which the effects of unco-ordinated and rapid town growth emerge in vivid detail. Many working-class industrial suburbs of the north were developing features similar to those of Chorlton upon Medlock where, the Health of Towns Commissioners were informed, in 1844, of houses which were built standing back to back.[4] In Hull, where standards of building were falling rapidly, there were by 1840 many congested 'courts of a very peculiar construction, a court within a court, and then another court within that'.[5] The building of working-class houses so as to 'economize the land' was not, however, peculiar to the north.[6] Extreme conditions of congestion were reached in Nottingham, where the outward expansion of the town was hampered until 1845 by the presence of common fields.[7] And filthy, overcrowded courts and alleys, some of them old but many built or re-built since 1800, could be found within a few minutes' walk of the main thoroughfares of London, Brighton and other towns. Indeed, one of the

[1] J. Law, *Plan of the township or chapelry of Birkenhead* (London, 1844).

[2] W. Ashworth, 40; H. R. Hitchcock, *Early Victorian architecture in Britain*, I (London and New Haven, 1954), 450–3.

[3] *Second Report on the State of Large Towns and Populous Districts*, Appendix 11, pp. 311, 323 (P.P. 1845, xviii); *S.C. on Buildings Regulation and Improvement of Boroughs*, 292 (P.P. 1842, x).

[4] *First Report of Commissioners on Large Towns*, *Appendix*, 60 (P.P. 1844, xvii).

[5] *S.C. on the Health of Towns*, 439 (P.P. 1840, xi).

[6] The process is effectively illustrated by M. W. Beresford, *Time and place: an inaugural lecture* (Leeds, 1961).

[7] J. D. Chambers, 'Nottingham in the early nineteenth century', *Trans. Thoroton Society*, XLVI (1943), 28–31; K. C. Edwards, 'The geographical development of Nottingham', in K. C. Edwards (ed.), *Nottingham and its region* (Nottingham, 1966), 370–1.

objects of Nash's Regent Street project (1817–23) had been to separate
untidy, squalid Soho from the fashionable estates of the West End.[1]

The appearance of towns was affected also by improvement schemes,
carried out either by local authorities or by private individuals.[2] The
cutting of New Oxford Street through the slums of St Giles's, for example,
between 1845 and 1847 swept away dilapidated courts and alleys; but
many people who were displaced by this improvement went to swell the
numbers in already crowded districts nearby, which in consequence
deteriorated still further in social status.[3] At about this time, too, Manchester and Salford opened their first public parks[4] while the former town
prohibited the building of houses back to back in 1844.[5] Elsewhere, old
streets were widened and new ones cut, markets rehoused and paving and
lighting extended by local improvement schemes; but their effect was
seldom other than piecemeal. Redevelopment on the scale of that carried
out in central Newcastle by Grainger and Dobson during the 1830s – a
scheme at once so ambitious and in its original form so aesthetically
satisfying that it has been regarded as the culmination of Georgian
urbanism – was exceptional in its scope and vision.[6]

The suburbs. As the towns grew larger, so did suburbia. It was not a new
phenomenon, but during the first half of the nineteenth century the effects
of suburban growth were becoming increasingly obvious in the vicinity
of the great towns. Those who could afford to live at some distance from
their place of work were encouraged to desert the inner areas of towns, as
a contemporary account of Manchester explains, because of the 'annoyance of smoke, the noise and bustle of business, and perhaps also the
growing value of building land, for shops and warehouses in the central
parts'.[7] Aided by better communications, Manchester merchants forsook
the central areas for Pendleton, Cheetham Hill, Higher Broughton and

[1] J. Summerson, *Georgian London* (London, 1945), 168–71; H. J. Dyos, 'Urban
transformation. A note on the objects of street improvement in Regency and early
Victorian London', *International Review of Social History*, II (1957), 261.

[2] B. Keith-Lucas, 'Some influences affecting the development of sanitary legislation
in England', *Econ. Hist. Rev.*, 2nd ser., VI (1954), 294–5; F. Clifford, *The history of
private bill legislation*, II (London, 1887), 291.

[3] H. R. Hitchcock, I, 378–80.

[4] *Illustrated London News*, IX (1846) 12, 114. F. E. Hyde, 156.

[5] A. Redford (1940), 86.

[6] A. E. Smailes (1960), 169; H. R. Hitchcock, I, 374.

[7] Quoted in T. S. Ashton, *Economic and social investigations in Manchester, 1833–
1933* (London, 1934), 37. The quotation refers to *c*. 1840.

beyond.[1] Successful cutlers sought out more attractive quarters on the western outskirts of Sheffield,[2] and Hull merchants removed to villages along the flanks of the Yorkshire Wolds, some miles outside the town.[3] Around London, suburbia advanced across the fields of Camberwell,[4] studded Lewisham with the residences of the wealthy[5] and added genteel fringes to Stepney and Hackney.[6]

The exodus of the well-to-do and the prosperous was accompanied by changes in the character of many of the older residential districts. As was said of London in 1826, 'the shopkeeper has discovered it to be most profitable in every sense to remove his family out of town; he places his stock in trade in the apartments they occupied, and employs the warehouse rent thus saved in hiring a "pretty tenement" at Islington, Knightsbridge, or Newington, where his children thrive in a purer air'.[7] In Sheffield, houses were converted into cutlery workshops;[8] and in Manchester, where the central area was said in 1842 to be 'in a state of constant alteration', buildings were modified in a variety of ways, 'sometimes to divide, sometimes to enlarge, to apply them to other uses – to convert houses into warehouses...and warehouses into workshops'.[9] In central Liverpool, as elsewhere, the coming of the railway also led to the removal of houses.[10] Still other houses in once fashionable districts were subdivided into tenements and became slums. As one class moved out, it was explained in 1846, 'a second grade go in' and eventually only 'very low parties' were attracted to such areas.[11] Many of the newcomers were themselves compelled to move in the course of time owing to the insistent pressure of commercial expansion, and by 1850 the inner areas of London

[1] E. Butterworth, 83, 87–8; H. B. Rodgers (1961–2), 5–6; T. W. Freeman, 'The Manchester conurbation', in C. F. Carter (ed.), *Manchester and its region* (Manchester, 1962), 54.

[2] S. Pollard, *A history of labour in Sheffield* (Liverpool, 1959), 6; A. J. Hunt, 'The morphology and growth of Sheffield', in D. L. Linton (1956), 228–37.

[3] G. A. Cooke, *Topographical and statistical description of the county of York* (London, n.d., c. 1820), 284.

[4] H. J. Dyos, *Victorian suburb: a study of Camberwell* (Leicester, 1961), 33.

[5] S. Lewis, III, 72.

[6] M. Rose, *The East End of London* (London, 1951), ch. 12.

[7] *Quarterly Review*, XXXIV (1826), 195.   [8] S. Pollard, 5.

[9] *S.C. on Buildings Regulation etc.*, 256 (P.P. 1842, x).

[10] T. W. Freeman, *The conurbations of Great Britain* (Manchester, 1959), 109; H. J. Dyos, 'Railways and housing in Victorian London', *Jour. Transport History*, II (1955–6), 12.

[11] *Metropolitan Railway Commission*, 214 (P.P. 1846, xvii).

and the larger provincial towns were slowly being drained of their residential population.[1] 'People do not live in the city of London', William Tite declared in 1846 with magnificent exaggeration.[2] Friedrich Engels, more careful in his choice of words, found the commercial heart of Manchester without 'permanent residents' and 'deserted at night'.[3]

Public health. Of the many problems that faced the towns none was more urgent than an adequate and unpolluted supply of water. Most towns obtained their water supply from nearby wells, springs and rivers (Fig. 45). London and Plymouth, which for many years had drawn supplies of water from distant sources, were in this respect unusual. During the first half of the nineteenth century, however, several industrial towns in northern England in turn established waterworks within the Pennines and Rossendale. Reservoirs were constructed and water was conveyed by gravity to distribution points near the towns. At Bolton the nearby uplands at Belmont provided a convenient site for waterworks,[4] but the extensive works of Liverpool and Manchester, which were initiated but not completed before 1850, were situated far from the points of consumption, at Rivington and Longdendale respectively.[5] Under the 'new system of gathering-grounds', as it was called in 1850, distant uplands sometimes acquired significance as the 'water-farms' of the expanding towns.[6]

The provision of improved supplies of drinking water was only one aspect of the sanitary problem facing the towns, as Edwin Chadwick recognised. His concern with the environmental causes of disease led him to emphasise the importance of water as a means of removing town refuse quickly and cheaply.[7] In Chadwick's view, the engineering solution to the sanitary problem lay in the provision of a constant supply of water to every house, and, he argued, that waste matter could thus be flushed from the houses through self-scouring sewers and then discharged harmlessly

---

[1] T. W. Freeman (1959), 5, 7, 32–7, 82, 109, 138, 172.

[2] *Metropolitan Railway Commission*, 64 (P.P. 1846, xvii).

[3] F. Engels, *The condition of the working-class in England in 1844*, trans. and ed. by W. O. Henderson and W. H. Chaloner (Oxford, 1958), 54.

[4] J. Black, *A medico-topographical, geological, and statistical sketch of Bolton and its neighbourhood* (Bolton, n.d., 1836), 38; *Centenary of the Bolton corporation waterworks undertaking, 1847–1947* (Bolton, 1947).

[5] B. D. White, *A history of the corporation of Liverpool, 1835–1914* (Liverpool, 1951), 56–7; A. Redford II (1940), 181–5.

[6] *Quarterly Review*, LXXXVII (1850), 498.

[7] E. Chadwick, *Report on the sanitary condition of the labouring population of Great Britain* (London, 1842), 370.

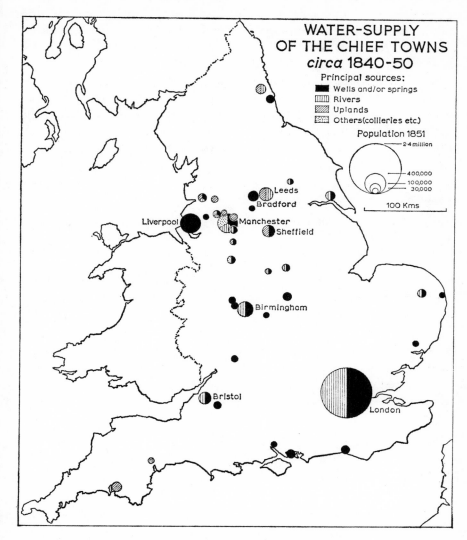

Fig. 45 Water supply of the chief towns *circa* 1840–50
Based on a variety of contemporary sources, e.g. Parliamentary Papers and
local reports.
The chief towns are those with over 30,000 inhabitants in 1851.

and profitably on the outskirts of towns.[1] In the urban, as in the rural, areas there was thus a growing awareness of the importance of land drainage. And in the person of James Smith, of Deanston, whose ideas on the drainage of cities and the construction of sewers were quoted with approval by Chadwick, skills developed in the one environment were applied to the solution of problems in the other.[2] The municipal corporations established by the Municipal Corporations Act of 1835 provided a basis for more effective local government, and by the late 1840s the need for drastic remedial measures to improve the health of the urban population was widely recognised; the Public Health Act was passed in 1848 and the sanitary reformers were hard at work.[3] But many years were to elapse before the new era of public health was reflected unmistakably in the appearance of the towns.

[1] R. Lambert, 61–2; W. H. G. Armytage, *A social history of engineering* (London, 1961), 140.

[2] E. Chadwick, 379. I am grateful to Professor John Saville for drawing my attention to this aspect of James Smith's work.

[3] R. A. Lewis, *Edwin Chadwick and the public health movement, 1832–1854* (London, 1952), especially ch. 8.

Chapter 4

ENGLAND *circa* 1850

J. B. HARLEY

The England of 1850, in the view of Sir John Clapham, 'had turned her face towards the new industry – the wheels of iron and the shriek of the escaping steam'.[1] In contemporary eyes she was now the 'workshop of the world', and the Great Exhibition of 1851 offered to all comers an unequivocal proof of her supremacy as a manufacturing nation. But amidst so much industrial reality, Léonce de Lavergne diagnosed a measure of ambivalence, a reluctance to come of age as an industrial and urban state. He felt that Englishmen harboured 'a repugnance to being shut up within the walls of the towns', and that the taste of the wealthier part of the nation was for a country life. Nor, in his opinion, was an explanation hard to find because 'in travelling through England, one cannot help being constantly impressed with the contrast between town and country. . . The largest towns, like Birmingham, Manchester, Sheffield, or Leeds, are inhabited only by workmen and shopkeepers, and the parts of the town occupied by their dwellings have a poor and melancholy appearance'.[2] If this Frenchman's short acquaintance with England led him into over simplification, he had touched correctly upon a deep dichotomy in its geography. Never, previously, had town and industry occupied so much of England, nor yet had they presented so contrasted a face to that of the countryside. The extremes had been heightened by the expansion of urban squalor and industrial dereliction on the one hand, and, on the other, by the coming to maturity of the work of the Georgian improvers, enclosers and landscape artists. Indeed, the sharply contrasted landscapes of early Victorian England mirrored vividly the deep cleavages in contemporary society: the 'two nations' were at no time more clearly portrayed than in the human geography of 1850.

[1] J. H. Clapham, *An economic history of modern Britain: free trade and steel, 1850–1866* (Cambridge, 1932), 22.

[2] L. de Lavergne, *The rural economy of England, Scotland, and Ireland* (Edinburgh and London, 1855), 120–31.

POPULATION

The distribution of population

In 1851 England was inhabited by some 16.9 million people, and Wales by just over one million. Their distribution reflected the marked quickening in the differentiation of commercial, manufacturing and mining areas from the rest of the country (Fig. 46). There were four main areas in which the average population density exceeded 800 persons per square mile. First, London was still the most crowded centre of population; when the English Registration Districts were arranged in order of magnitude of population density, the first 15 places were filled by the small but teeming London districts (a dozen of which had over 100,000 people per square mile).[1] Even the extra-metropolitan districts of Middlesex were more densely peopled than any other part of England except Lancashire. Secondly, the great coalfield concentration of people embracing east Lancashire and west Yorkshire formed the largest area of England where the population exceeded 800 persons per square mile: in aggregate it contained more inhabitants than all of London, Middlesex, Surrey and Kent.[2] The third outstanding populous area in 1851 was the west Midlands, particularly the industrial areas of Birmingham, the Black Country and the Potteries, but with smaller populations in Coventry and the east Warwickshire coalfield. Fourthly, such densities were matched, but over a lesser area, in the industrial district of Durham county. Elsewhere in England, islands of higher population density reflected smaller coalfields such as those of Bristol and Coalbrookdale, mining districts such as that of west Cornwall, and a few especially prosperous centres of rural industry.

These concentrations were directly related to migration. In 1851 'the towns, in the mass, were mainly inhabited by immigrants...Out of 3,336,000 people, of 20 years of age and upwards, living in London and 61 other English and Welsh towns in 1851, only 1,337,000 had been born in the town of their residence.'[3] The percentage varied according to local circumstances. In London there were roughly 46% native-born, in Leeds 58%, but in Manchester-Salford and Bradford this fell to just above 25% and in Liverpool below 25%. Not only the large industrial centres were thronged with strangers; Brighton had one of the largest proportions of

[1] *Census of 1851: Population Tables, I*, vol. 1, p. cxi (P.P. 1852–3, lxxxv).
[2] A. Redford, *Labour migration in England, 1800–50* (Manchester, 1926), 13.
[3] J. H. Clapham, *An economic history of modern Britain: the early railway age, 1820–1850* (Cambridge, 1926), 536.

immigrants (about 80%) for a town of its size,[1] and even Harrogate, a more staid northern spa, had 59%.[2] Many of the newcomers had come from the countryside, especially from areas adjacent to the main industrial regions; in Lancashire, for example, the largest numbers of English immigrants recorded in 1851 had originated in Cheshire, Derbyshire and Shropshire. In total, however, the most substantial influx into the towns had been from Ireland; the year 1851 marked the climax of the post-famine arrival of the Irish. They now numbered 727,000 in England, and were most numerous in the north-west,[3] where they dominated the immigrant communities of many Lancashire towns – not only the larger such as Liverpool and Manchester, but the smaller such as Ashton-under-Lyne and Wigan (Fig. 34). Frequently they had segregated into distinctive colonies; in Liverpool, behind the docks and business district; in Manchester, in areas such as 'Little Ireland' where Engels had found them in 1844; and in London in parishes such as St Giles, Shadwell and Whitechapel.[4]

These crowded immigrant quarters were only one aspect of the overall unhealthiness of urban life. The facts of medical geography in the towns often make grisly reading: at mid-century the expectation of life was low; the rates of mortality, disease and general sickness were high; and epidemics of cholera, smallpox and typhus not uncommon. Pioneer investigations of health and disease in England (in progress at mid-century) serve to underline these spatial variations in the national mortality; not only was the normal death rate higher in the towns, but also the epidemic death rate, which, as at the time of the cholera of 1848–9 and 1853–4, struck heaviest at the urban dwellers.[5] Indeed, the primary purpose of the Public Health Bill of 1848 was to improve those towns where the crude death rate exceeded 23 per thousand (the national average crude death rate stood at 21.8 per thousand in 1851–2). It is a measure of the magnitude of the problem, that, by the end of 1853, no less than 182 local health boards had been set up, some voluntarily, others compulsorily.[6] Few of the larger

[1] *Ibid.*, 537.   [2] J. A. Patmore, *An atlas of Harrogate* (Harrogate, 1963), 19.

[3] A. Redford, 137; R. Lawton, 'Irish immigration to England in the mid-nineteenth century', *Irish Geography*, IV (1959), 35–54.

[4] R. Lawton, 'The population of Liverpool in the mid-nineteenth century', *Trans. Hist. Soc. Lancs. and Cheshire*, CVII (1955), 89–120; T. W. Freeman, *Pre-famine Ireland* (Manchester, 1957), 43–7; J. H. Clapham (1926), 60.

[5] E. W. Gilbert, 'Pioneer maps of health and disease in England', *Geog. Jour.*, CXXIV (1958), 172–83.

[6] G. Slater, *The making of modern England* (London, 1919), 168.

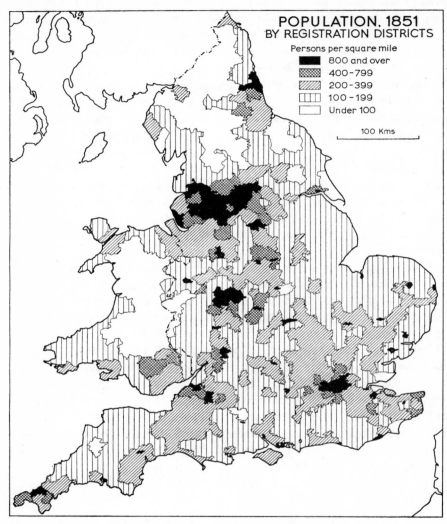

Fig. 46 Population in 1851
Based on *Census of 1851: Population Tables, I*, vol. 1, pp. cxi–cxiii (P.P. 1852–3, lxxxv).

towns were absent from this list, but smaller places could be just as unhealthy; Salisbury, for example, in the decade 1841–50 attained a mean
annual crude death rate as high as 28 per thousand.[1] On the other hand,
the rural areas with their lower death rates were still regarded as 'the
healthy reservoirs from whence the ravages amongst the town population
were repaired'.[2] Population densities lessened sharply away from the
towns and coalfields, but the countryside, too, was more crowded with
people than ever before, and large areas had densities of over 200 persons
per square mile.

Population and administrative areas

The inadequacy of an ancient system of administrative areas for the needs
of the contemporary distribution of population was much in evidence by
1850. The authors of the report on the Census of 1851 were clear in their
condemnation: 'The old division of the country into parishes, townships,
and counties, is open to many...objections...Parishes are, in many
instances, almost inextricably intermingled; and they vary in population
from single families to tens of thousands of families; in extent, from a few
hundreds of acres to many thousands of acres. The counties are also irregularly and unequally constituted.'[3] The evidence in the 1851 Census for
the size of the ancient English parish (Fig. 47) reveals the nature of this
problem more precisely. There is little to support a concept of a 'normal'
sized rural parish, and there are striking regional inequalities in parish size.
Particularly sharp is the contrast between the small parishes of parts of
southern and eastern England – averaging below 3,000 acres – and the
large parishes of north-western England – averaging over 12,000 acres.
But many smaller-scale variations were superimposed on this general
pattern. Wealden and Fenland parishes, for example, were well above the
average acreage for lowland England, while in highland counties, such as
those of the Lake District, the coastal parishes were generally much smaller
than those of the interior.

These facts hardly mirrored the realities of local government in 1850,
as they might have done at the time of the creation of the ecclesiastical
parishes. The large parishes of northern England, with their constituent
townships, had long proved too unwieldy to adminster functions such

[1] R. A. Waterhouse in R. B. Pugh and E. Crittall (eds.), *V.C.H. Wiltshire*, v (1957),
325.

[2] W. Smith, *An economic geography of Great Britain* (London, 1949), 131.

[3] *Census of 1851: Population Tables, I*, vol. I, p. lxxix (P.P. 1852–3, lxxxv).

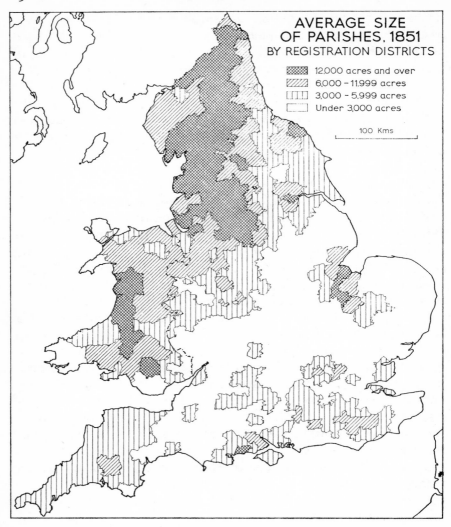

Fig. 47 Average size of parishes in 1851
Based on *Census of 1851: Population Tables, I* (P.P. 1852–3, lxxxv, lxxxvi)

as those of the poor law system; and, prior to the formation of the Poor Law Unions in 1834, this responsibility had frequently been vested in the township. The decline of the ecclesiastical parish as the smallest effective cell of local government had gone so far, that, by 1851, about a third of all the 16,000 'parishes or places' in England and Wales were separately administered townships.[1] The stronghold of these multiple-township parishes lay in the northern counties; the parish of Wigan, for example, 28,433 acres in area, contained 13 townships.[2] In southern England, although the parish was more frequently co-terminous with the township, it had not been immune from subdivision into subordinate areas such as tithings and hamlets.

Three other considerations added complexity to this chaotic patchwork of small administrative areas. First, there were still extensive areas not contained within the boundaries of any parish (they were estimated to number nearly 600), and, until an Act of 1857, these extra-parochial tracts (including areas of old royal forest and some reclaimed fens) enjoyed virtual exemption from taxation, from maintaining the poor, from the militia laws, and from repairing highways. Secondly, there were many fragmented parishes. Prior to the Divided Parishes Acts of the last quarter of the century, the number of parishes in two or more parts was nearly 1,300.[3] Thirdly, civil and ecclesiastical parishes had often ceased to be co-extensive. Boundary changes made for civil purposes had not affected ecclesiastical parishes, and, similarly, subdivisions or amalgamations of ecclesiastical parishes had been made independently by the church authorities. Such ecclesiastical areas had proliferated. Many chapelries had 'acquired boundaries as definite and generally recognised as those of the parent Parish', although their number was 'not exactly ascertainable'; furthermore, since the Church Building Acts (beginning in 1818), fragmentation had gone further with the creation around new churches of 'Ecclesiastical Districts', the boundaries of which, even to the clergy, 'unprovided with maps or plans' were uncertain.[4] Not least, the growth of non-established religions (in 1851 they claimed almost half of all church-goers),[5] with their own administrative areas, meant that the ancient parish was not even the sole territorial unit of religious life.

The consequences of these obsolete areas were most deleterious in the industrial and urban areas. The size of settlements had far outgrown the inherited administrative framework, and at mid-century there were still

---

[1] *Census of 1851: Population Tables, I*, vol. 1, p. cxvi (P.P. 1852–3, lxxxv); V. D. Lipman, *Local government areas, 1834–1945* (Oxford, 1949), 26.

[2] *Census of 1851: Population Tables, I*, vol. 11, Lancashire, 34 (P.P. 1852–3, lxxxvi).

[3] V. D. Lipman, 27, 69–72; *Guides to official sources, No. 2; Census reports of Great Britain 1801–1931* (H.M.S.O., 1951), 97.

[4] *Census of 1851: Population Tables, I*, vol. 1, pp. lxxi–lxxii (P.P. 1852–3, lxxxv).

[5] *Census of 1851: Religious Worship, Report and Tables* (P.P. 1852–3, lxxxix).

places like the town of Bury in Lancashire, with over 30,000 inhabitants, which possessed 'no more municipal organisation than that of a rural village'.[1] This state of affairs illustrates the fact that the Municipal Corporations Act (1835) was only a starting point in the creation of valid units of administration in harmony with the social geography of mid-Victorian England. In 1851, although 196 reformed boroughs had been created, places as populous as the parliamentary boroughs of London (the Tower Hamlets alone contained over half a million people), as Stoke-on-Trent, as Brighton or Huddersfield, were still without charters of incorparation.[2] And the existence of a charter did not necessarily confer the will or the capacity to cope with the problems of urban growth; at York, for example, the new corporation had done little for its citizens, although the population of the municipal borough had increased by over 10,000 between 1831 and 1851.[3] By 1850 the pattern of administrative areas was still very inchoate. The period around mid-century was characterised by the creation of a variety of authorities for special purposes – for the administration of the Poor Laws, of health and sanitation, of the highways and of education[4] – but the multi-purpose local authority areas were yet to be put on the map in the second half of the century.[5] Thus, although the ancient parish was in rapid decay as an effective cell of local government, the creation of suitable areas to replace it was still in its infancy.

THE COUNTRYSIDE

The occupation tables of the 1851 Census[6] showed that agriculture still held a position of great importance, employing no less than one-quarter of the adult males aged 20 years and over in England and Wales – a total exceeding that in the greatest of the manufacturing industries. Fig. 48 depicts the regional contrasts between the 'counties of maximum rusticity', as Clapham termed them,[7] and those where the growth of industry

[1] *Second Report of Commissioners for inquiring into the State of Large Towns and Populous Districts*, Appendix, Part II, 21 (P.P. 1845, xviii).

[2] *Census of 1851: Population Tables, I*, vol. I, pp. lxviii–lxix (P.P. 1852–3, lxxxv).

[3] E. M. Sigsworth in P. M. Tillott (ed.), *V.C.H., The city of York* (1961), 254–5, 281–3.

[4] V. D. Lipman, 34–76.

[5] K. B. Smellie, *A history of local government* (London, 4th ed., 1968), 41–70.

[6] *Census of 1851: Population Tables, II*, vols. 1 and 2 (P.P. 1852–3, lxxxviii, pts 1 and 2).

[7] J. H. Clapham (1932), 252.

had transformed the economy. Some groups of registration districts in East Anglia, in southern England, in Devon and in parts of Yorkshire had over 60% of their adult male population engaged in agriculture. On the other hand, in the registration districts surrounding London, and in the mining and manufacturing regions, below 40% (and sometimes less than 25%) were recorded as employed in agriculture. Such areas formed a broad belt stretching from Lancashire and the West Riding southwards into the west Midlands; other important outliers where the agricultural population had been eclipsed by 1851 were in Durham, west Cumberland and Cornwall.

A consideration of the actual (rather than the percentage) distribution of those employed in farming presents a somewhat different pattern (Fig. 49). The lowest densities of males per square mile employed in agriculture lay predictably upon the mountains and moorlands of northern England, and, to a less extent, in the south-west. High densities occurred, again as we might anticipate, in south-eastern England – particularly in parts of Essex, Hertfordshire, Kent and Surrey – where the rural population as a whole was most numerous. On the other hand, the continued importance of agricultural occupations – indeed their apparent intensification – upon some of the coalfields was marked. As Thomas Welton, a contemporary statistician, observed: 'The numbers employed upon the land in the midst of collieries and manufacturing towns were really surprising;...perhaps most of all in...the South Staffordshire district, where the number of agriculturalists per square mile was nearly as high as in Hertfordshire.'[1] The textile areas of Lancashire and the West Riding, which had more agriculturalists per square mile than much of rural England, were in a similar category. No doubt this was to be explained partly by ambiguities in the census classification,[2] and partly by the fact that many smallholders also worked in a factory or mine. But the conclusion is statistically inescapable, that amid furnaces and factories, men still clung tenaciously to work on the land.

By 1850, the disappearance of common-field husbandry had divested the township of its former importance as a unit of local agricultural organisation. The statistics of farm size contained in the 1851 Census are, therefore, a timely index of contemporary contrasts in the organisation of

---

[1] T. A. Welton, *Statistical papers on the census of England of Wales, 1851* (London, privately printed, 1860), 50.

[2] *Census of 1851: Population Tables, II*, vol. 1, pp. lxxviii–lxxix (P.P. 1852–3, lxxxviii, pt 1).

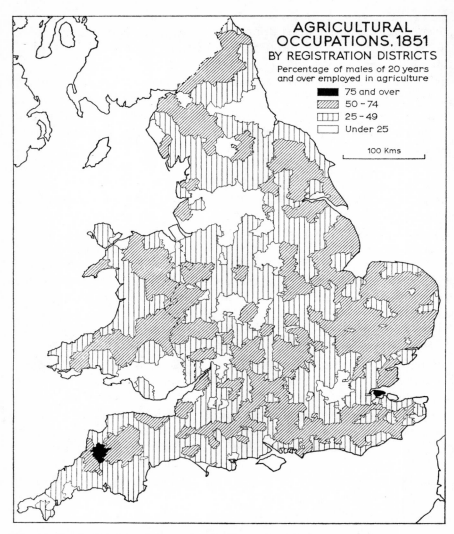

Fig. 48   Agricultural employment in 1851 (percentages)
         Based on *Census of 1851: Population Tables, II* (P.P. 1852–3, lxxxviii, pts. 1
         and 2).

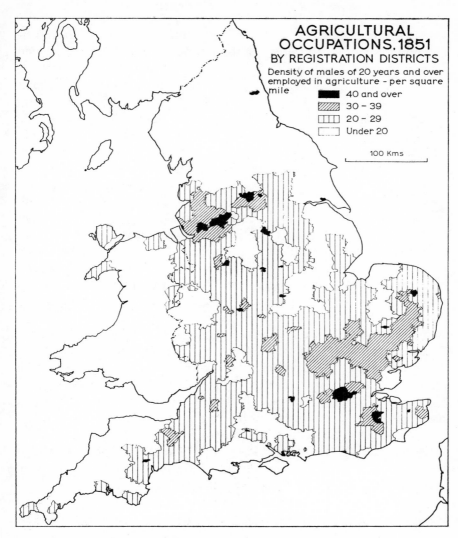

Fig. 49 Agricultural employment in 1851 (densities)
Sources as for Fig. 48.

farming. Large farms of 500 acres and over were most numerous in eastern and southern England and in Northumberland; and small farms of below 100 acres were most important in the north Midland counties, in the north-west and the south-west (although we may note that the census excluded the acreage of hill pastures). Within these general divisions there were, however, internal contrasts: in lowland England, for example, smaller farms occurred on the claylands and in the Fens, while large farms were to be found on the light-soil areas of the chalk, limestone and sandstone outcrops.[1] Around the larger towns, and particularly around London, arable farming had in places given way to market gardening to supply an increasing demand for vegetables and 'all sorts of garden produce'.[2]

Among the more ubiquitous features in the countryside of 1850, land-scape parks continued to grow in number as the railways opened fresh areas such as the Chilterns to the homes of London merchants.[3] The older creations of Lancelot Brown and Humphry Repton were sometimes re-modelled to suit the taste of the age, but they continued to exhibit a style which often transcended that of any single region. In general, however, the rural landscape is most easily described in terms of its infinite variety, and the contrasts in farming measured by the census were amply sub-stantiated by the descriptions of contemporary writers. James Caird, for example, broadly divided the English countryside into the 'Corn' and the 'Grazing' counties (Fig. 50). 'The chief commodity of the western farmer', he wrote, 'is the produce of his dairy, his cattle and his flock. The large eastern farmer looks principally to his wheat and barley.'[4] If the general validity of his distinction is clear, a twofold division is, however, inadequate for a fuller account of the English countryside.

We should be clearer about the face of England at mid-century if the tithe surveys of the 1840s had been plotted. They were made on a parish basis and cover about three-quarters of the country. 'They provide a record of the use of land; whether cultivated or uncultivated, arable or grass, orchard or hop ground, heath or marsh, wood or agriculturally un-productive.'[5] This information has been plotted for a number of districts

[1] D. B. Grigg, 'Small and large farms in England and Wales: their size and distri-bution', *Geography*, XLVIII (1963), 268–9.

[2] J. C. Clutterbuck, 'The farming of Middlesex', *Jour. Roy. Agric. Soc.*, V (1869), 18.

[3] H. C. Prince, *Parks in England* (Shalfleet, I.O.W., 1967), 10.

[4] J. Caird, *English agriculture in 1850–51* (London, 1852), 482.

[5] H. C. Prince, 'The tithe surveys of the mid-nineteenth century', *Agric. Hist. Rev.*, VII (1959), 25.

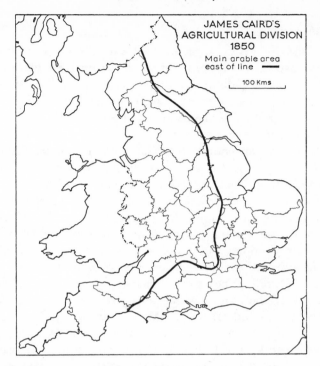

Fig. 50   Corn and grazing counties in 1850
Based on J. Caird, *English agriculture in 1850–51* (London, 1852).

and sample parishes, e.g. for the Chilterns (Figs 51 and 52); but much
work remains to be done before the full contribution of the surveys has
been extracted for the country as a whole.[1]

Both Caird and the Royal Agricultural Society (in its series of prize essays
on the agriculture of England) had used the county as a unit of description
and, within the county, a scheme of subdivisions based usually on either
geology or soil texture.[2] From these divisions within individual counties
there can be built a larger system of agricultural regions in England as a
whole. Broadly speaking there were five types of region – the sandlands, the
fens, the south-east chalk and limestone areas, the claylands and the uplands.

[1] Examples of the use of the material are to be found in many of the 92 county
reports of the Land Utilization Survey – L. D. Stamp (ed.), 'The land of Britain'
(London, 1936–46).

[2] H. C. Darby, 'Some early ideas on the agricultural regions of England', *Agric.
Hist. Rev.*, II (1954), 41–7.

The sand districts

The light lands of eastern England, long a model for improvers, had emerged by 1850 as districts of mature high farming. In western Norfolk, Caird found much to admire 'in the large, open, well cultivated fields, divided from each other by straight lines of closely-trimmed thorn hedges, and tilled with garden-like precision and cleanliness'. It was still a source of wonder to contemporaries that such abundant crops 'were growing, in many places, on an entirely artificial soil'. The Norfolk farmer was regarded as without equal in the permanent improvement of the soil by claying and marling, which, as earlier, was still widely favoured.[1] But not only in Norfolk had such practices helped to fashion a new countryside. In Cambridgeshire, for example, the 'poor and hungry lands' would have remained sterile but for high farming and enclosure which had greatly enhanced their productivity.[2] And in the western 'sand district' of Nottinghamshire comparable achievements could be reviewed; no district in England had 'undergone a greater change for the better'.[3] Large flocks of sheep replaced the rabbits which once browsed the forest lands, and fine crops of turnips and corn were harvested from large fields divided by quickset hedges. Such grand transformations had attracted substantial capital investment. Part of Delamere Forest in Cheshire, for example, disafforested and brought into cultivation in 1856, was reclaimed with the help of a light tramway to transport marl to the new fields.[4] Optimism about these areas still ran high: at least half of Cannock Chase appeared capable of cultivation to James Caird,[5] and it was regarded as out of place that it should remain untilled in a densely peopled county. On the other hand, some reclamation already embraced terrain beyond even the skill of the improver to improve. It was reported from western Suffolk that much cultivated land was 'apt to blow, that is to be driven by the wind', and it was ranked 'amongst the worst soils'; while from the contiguous district

[1] J. Caird, 163; B. Almack, 'On the agriculture of Norfolk', *J.R.A.S.* v (1844), 307; H. C. Prince, 'The origin of pits and depressions in Norfolk', *Geography*, XLIX (1964), 15–32.

[2] J. Caird, 151; S. Jonas, 'On the farming of Cambridgeshire', *J.R.A.S.*, VII (1846), 43.

[3] R. W. Corringham, 'Agriculture of Nottinghamshire', *J.R.A.S.*, VI (1845), 2–3.

[4] R. B. Grantham, 'A description of the works for reclaiming and marling parts of the late Forest of Delamere, in the county of Cheshire', *J.R.A.S.*, XXV (1864), 369–80.

[5] J. Caird, 243.

of Norfolk, C. S. Read concluded that, though improved, it 'must ever remain poor and comparatively barren'.[1]

Arable farming dominated the improved sandlands by 1850. In the Good Sand region of Norfolk, the tithe surveys reveal almost continuous cultivation in some areas. But Norfolk was, in any case, an arable county and, by mid-century, it had some 63% of its area under the plough.[2] Here, as over much of England, the arable acreage had reached its maximum extent. Similarly, on the less sterile areas of Bagshot Heath 60% was under the plough; in the upper Wey Basin in Surrey it was again the lighter soils based on the Bargate Beds, the Brick Earth and the Upper Greensand which were most cultivated (67% to 91%). The Hastings Beds, although partly clay, and the Upper Greensand of Sussex were likewise predominantly arable. Even within the 'grazing' counties, the lighter soils derived from the Triassic and Old Red sandstones and from fluvio-glacial sands and gravels, stood out at mid-century as islands of arable farming – in Warwickshire and Worcestershire and in the North Riding of Yorkshire.[3]

Increased productivity was closely linked to the better organisation of farming. Light-land farms were, in the main, relatively large and were tenanted by men of capital and of an improving zeal. Investment was reflected in the face of the countryside: in the bones, guano, nitrates and superphosphate which increased yields; in the new machinery – ploughs, drills, scarifiers, clod-crushers and steam-driven threshing machines;[4] and, here and there, in new and substantial brick buildings which were gradually replacing 'the inconvenient, ill-arranged hovels, the rickety wood and thatch barns and sheds', which Caird and others found to be widespread.[5] On the other hand, high farming had not dispensed with the armies of field labourers – male and female – who still undertook many of the seasonal tasks of farming; the abundance of cheap labour, especially in

---

[1] S. Lewis, *A topographical dictionary of England*, IV (London, 7th ed., 1848), 259–60; C. S. Read, 'Recent improvements in Norfolk farming', *J.R.A.S.*, XIX (1858), 265–6.   [2] J. E. G. Mosby, *Norfolk* (L. of B., pt. 70, London, 1938), 142–9.

[3] E. C. Willatts, *Middlesex and the London region* (L. of B., pt. 79, London, 1937), 268–70; D. W. Shave in L. D. Stamp and E. C. Willatts, *Surrey* (L. of B., pt. 81, London, 1941), 394; E. W. H. Briault, *Sussex* (L. of B., pts. 83–4, London, 1942), 498–505; A. W. McPherson, *Warwickshire* (L. of B., pt. 62, London, 1946), 789–840; K. M. Buchanan, *Worcestershire* (L. of B., pt. 68, London, 1944), 521–664; M. M. Milburn, 'On the farming of the North Riding of Yorkshire', *J.R.A.S.*, IX (1848), 499–511.

[4] C. S. Orwin and E. H. Whetham, *History of British agriculture, 1846–1914* (London, 1964), 7–10; F. M. L. Thompson, 'The second agricultural revolution, 1815–1880', *Econ. Hist. Rev.*, XXI (1968), 62–77.   [5] J. Caird, 490.

southern England, lessened the economic advantages of mechanisation. The debate continues both about the degree of diffusion of new agricultural technologies by 1850 and about the regional variations in the labour productivity of the English farm worker.[1]

As in 1800 the basis of light-land farming was a grain and sheep system with the Norfolk four-course rotation integrating its branches. Its principles were widely disseminated; it was the rotation 'most generally approved'; and examples of its adoption (often as a condition of lease) occurred from Cornwall to Northumberland. But equally, by 1850, a reaction had set in against too dogmatic an adherence to its tenets. Even in Norfolk, although the four-course was still hallowed at Holkham Park, many scientific farmers had deviated from it with success.[2] In any case, on poorer soils and in the less climatically favoured north of England, oats and rye entered the rotations; and everywhere local practice diversified the field crops from a long list of clovers, grasses and roots. Moreover, uniformity of rotation did not necessarily go hand-in-hand with identical farm economies. In Norfolk, there was an emphasis on the production of malting barley which was then shipped to London. But in many four-course districts, fat lambs and wool, and even some beef, were raised as well as cereal crops; in Cheshire, with its 'Sand-Land Dairy Farms', and in parts of Staffordshire and the West Riding, a four-course rotation was associated with dairy farming. Elsewhere, the sandy soils carried market gardens. In Bedfordshire they occupied the sandy heaths of the Lower Greensand outcrop; the sandy loams of the Lea valley were 'appropriated to market-gardening and nurseries'; and, on the blown sands behind the shore of northern Wirral, horticulture also flourished.[3]

Fenland and marsh

The Fens, despite the different challenges to improvement they had offered, may, by 1850, be grouped with the sandlands as lowland districts where men could look back on a period of remarkable progress. The Isle of Ely

[1] E. J. T. Collins, 'Harvest technology and labour supply in Britain, 1790–1870', *Econ. Hist. Rev.*, XXII (1969), 453–73.

[2] P. D. Tuckett, 'On the modifications of the four-course rotation, which modern improvements have rendered advisable', *J.R.A.S.*, XXI (1860), 258–66.

[3] W. Palin, 'The farming of Cheshire', *J.R.A.S.*, V (1844), 59–62; F. Beavington, 'The change to more extensive methods in market gardening in Bedfordshire', *Trans. and Papers, Inst. Brit. Geog.*, XXXIII (1963), 89; also W. Bennett, 'The farming of Bedfordshire', *J.R.A.S.*, XVIII (1857), 18; H. Evershed, 'Agriculture of Hertfordshire', *J.R.A.S.*, XXV (1864), 270; J. Caird, 261–3.

to Samuel Jonas was 'a wonderfully fine district, and one in which more improvement had taken place within a few years than any other'. He could see the changes wrought by the application of the steam engine to draining, and by the claying and enclosure of lands which were still in progress.[1] The countryside was already 'traversed by excellent roads and railways and...mostly freed from the overflow of floods'.[2] The present landscape was nearly fashioned. It was then, as now, an arable region specialising in the cultivation of grain crops, potatoes and vegetables. Its fertility was becoming an agricultural legend, and J. A. Clarke, reviewing its agriculture in 1848, could write of 'the abundance and luxuriance' of the fenland crops, as he looked across the 'immense plain of dark arable fields'.[3] In addition, other formerly boggy morasses, such as the Isle of Axholme, King's Sedgemoor, the Holderness carrs and the mosslands west of the Pennines, although still presenting problems,[4] were systematically becoming, with the light lands, the new granaries of nineteenth-century England.

The south-east chalk and limestone areas

James Caird caught the essence of much of the chalkland when he wrote of a bare and undulating outline, of lofty downs still untouched by the plough, of white flinty roads, of coppices and widely spaced farmsteads, and, in the valleys, of the grass of the irrigated water-meadows. There was, of course, regional variety. On the Hampshire chalklands the country was 'rather warmer' than in Dorset and Wiltshire; and the soil variations in a chalkland district were so manifold in Berkshire as to require a 'lengthened description'. The history of enclosure had also influenced the countryside: in Yorkshire, where improvement of the Wolds had begun earlier, the landscape was 'all enclosed, generally by thorn hedges, and plantations everywhere grouped over its surface'; Salisbury Plain, on the other hand, was still raw, 'the face of the country...bare and un-sheltered, with no fence dividing field from field'.[5]

Farms on the chalk were amongst the largest in England. On Salisbury

[1] S. Jonas, 62; H. C. Darby, *The draining of the Fens* (Cambridge, 2nd ed., 1956), 237–46.   [2] J. Caird, 179.

[3] J. A. Clarke, 'On the Great Level of the Fens, including the Fens of south Lincolnshire', *J.R.A.S.*, VIII (1847), 132.

[4] M. Williams, *The draining of the Somerset Levels* (Cambridge, 1970), 209–29.

[5] J. Caird, 57, 79, 92, 310; J. B. Spearing, 'On the agriculture of Berkshire', *J.R.A.S.*, XXI (1860), 9–10; E. W. H. Briault, 501; J. Thirsk, *English peasant farming* (London, 1957), 259.

Plain they ranged from 800 even up to 5,000 acres, and cultivated fields often lay two miles distant from a homestead; in Wiltshire, chalk farms ranged from 400 to 1,000 acres; in Hampshire and in Yorkshire, too, the holdings were above the average for the county.[1] They had attracted tenants with capital, who could pay high rents and invest in high farming. New barns, yards, cottages and wold ponds had appeared on the hillsides; some farmers spent a pound an acre every year on fertilisers in Lincoln-shire.[2] And yet, even in these areas there were corners of backwardness. On the Sussex Downs, Caird found ancient wooden ploughs drawn by teams of six oxen; in some areas the dilapidated farm buildings did not measure up to high farming, and labourers' cottages (notwithstanding the model dwellings described here and there with such pride) were more often than not squalid and insanitary.[3] As in many agricultural regions there were numerous instances of highly progressive and grossly antiquated farming continuing virtually side by side.[4]

The chalklands were part of arable England. Of 19 parish tithe surveys in the Yorkshire Wolds 13 revealed an arable acreage equivalent to two-thirds or more of the total farmed area, and in only one survey did the arable area fall below a half. Some parishes on the Surrey Downs had up to three-quarters of their area under the plough,[5] although in Wiltshire more extensive tracts remained un-enclosed. As on the other light lands, the mid-century marked the end of an era in land-use history, in so far as the maximum arable acreages were reached – a major consequence of the preceding agrarian revolution. A variable acreage of unimproved pasture remained as sheep-walk on most farms; and, in addition, especially in the south-western chalklands, irrigated water-meadows were still universally important. In Wiltshire, for example, these meadows covered about 20,000 acres, and had been elaborated wherever possible.[6] The variants of a staple

---

[1] J. Caird, 80–1, 85, 310; E. Little, 'Farming of Wiltshire', *J.R.A.S.*, v (1844), 62.

[2] D. B. Grigg, 'Changing regional values during the agricultural revolution in south Lincolnshire', *Trans. and Papers, Inst. Brit. Geog.* (1962), 91–103; J. B. Spearing, 33; J. Thirsk (1957), 259.

[3] J. Caird, 127–8; L. H. Ruegg, 441–5; *Report of Special Assistant Poor Law Commissioners on the Employment of Women and Children in Agriculture*, 15–25 (P.P. 1843, xii).

[4] J. D. Chambers and G. E. Mingay, *The agricultural revolution, 1750–1880* (London, 1966), 172.

[5] A. Harris, *The rural landscape of the East Riding of Yorkshire, 1700–1850* (Oxford, 1961), 102; D. W. Shave, 393.

[6] E. Kerridge in E. Crittall (ed.), *V.C.H. Wiltshire*, IV (1959), 72.

grain and sheep husbandry, as on the sandlands, prevailed. In Buckinghamshire, Dorset and Wiltshire sheep were bred and folded to enrich the
soil for crops of wheat and barley: they were the 'manure carriers' of a
specialised cereal farming, and a maxim of the husbandry was 'the greater
the number of sheep, the greater the quantity of corn'. On the Hampshire
and Berkshire downs, however, the sheep themselves received more
attention and were 'a source of profit as well as manure'. The Sussex chalk
farmer also relied on his breeding flocks of Southdown ewes.[1] Sheep were
indeed the dominant livestock along the length of the chalk outcrops.
Stocking of up to one sheep an acre was common, and such counties as
Lincolnshire (with 1,000,000 sheep) and Wiltshire (with about 600,000
sheep) had particularly dense sheep populations.[2] The principles of the
Norfolk four-course rotation were widely but not rigidly embodied.
Chalkland rotations were adapted to local soils. In Wiltshire, for example,
on the flint and chalk loams the ordinary four-course was used; on the
light flinty soils, fertilisers had enabled a longer course with an extra
grass or rape crop to be practised; on the heavy lands – often on the level
hill tops – where turnips grew with difficulty, a modified three-course was
employed in which wheat and green crops predominated; on the sand
outcrops along the edge of the downs a four-course was again followed;
while on land that had become 'clover sick' or 'turnip tired' new green
crops were substituted.[3]

Finally, of the light lands, the Jurassic Limestone shared many of the
characteristics of chalk farming. James Caird had noted this similarity when
he remarked that the heath farming of Lincolnshire much resembled that
of the wolds. The whole outcrop there was a fairly continuous arable
farming region. Contemporary descriptions of the Cotswolds (where the
arable terrains were still named 'downsy' land because they were remembered as sheep-walk), of the 'Stonebrash district' of Oxfordshire, and
of the 'Red Stony Soil' of Northamptonshire, confirm that the grain–sheep
economy had colonised much of the limestone belt. And beyond, from
Northamptonshire to Durham, on the narrow strip of the Magnesian Limestone, similar conditions were continued into the more pastoral counties.[4]

[1] J. Caird, 59, 93, 128; J. B. Spearing, 12; J. Farncombe, 'On the farming of
Sussex', *J.R.A.S.*, XI (1850), 76–80.

[2] L. H. Ruegg, 407, 432; A. Harris, 105; J. H. Clapham (1932), 276; E. Kerridge
in E. Crittall (ed.), *V.C.H. Wiltshire*, IV (1959), 72.

[3] E. Little, 162–6; E. Kerridge in E. Crittall (ed.), *V.C.H. Wiltshire*, IV (1959), 73.

[4] J. Caird, 190; J. Bravendar, 'Farming of Gloucestershire', *J.R.A.S.*, XI (1850),
132–45; C. S. Read, 'On the farming of Oxfordshire', *J.R.A.S.*, XV (1854), 189–276;

The claylands

Clayland landscapes provided a sharp contrast to the spacious appearance of the light lands. A closely knit countryside of small fields and high hedgerows was the characteristic which frequently caught the eye of contemporaries. Edward Little, writing of north Wiltshire, captured this essential difference: 'Instead of open down country... the whole consists of enclosures, some of which are very small; and in many places the hedgerows are so thickly stocked with trees as to give the appearance of an extensive plantation when viewed from a distance.'[1] But the differences were not merely visual; they were economic and technical. There were still many obstacles to high farming on these claylands, amongst them, some of the features which gave the countryside its distinctiveness. The plentiful hedgerow timber, for example, was one impediment to good farming; 'the luxuriant foliage of summer', Caird explained, must overshadow the surface, and draw from the soil much of that nutriment which fields would otherwise yield to the farmer's stock'.[2] Many agricultural writers were in agreement with him.[3] The magnitude of the problem was illustrated in Devon. Here, in 1844, ten parishes totalling 36,976 acres contained no less than 7,997 fields whose 1,651 miles of hedge occupied 7% of the area.[4] Hedge-grubbing became an approved part of high farming.[5] Only occasionally did a more conservative farmer defend his massive hedges as providing shelter for his stock, although William Johnston, on aesthetic grounds, regretted their destruction and the fact that land was regarded 'as nothing else than a manufactory of agricultural produce'.[6] Ridge and furrow was also regarded as a hindrance to improvement. In

W. Bearn, 'On the farming of Northamptonshire', *J.R.A.S.*, XIII (1852), 44–113; S. H. Beaver, *Yorkshire; West Riding* (L. of B., pt. 46, London, 1941), 180–1; J. H. Charnock, 'On the farming of the West Riding of Yorkshire', *J.R.A.S.*, IX (1848), 289–90.

[1] E. Little, 172.   [2] J. Caird, 40.

[3] J. Grigor, 'On fences', *J.R.A.S.*, VI (1845), 194–228; W. Cambridge, 'On the advantage of reducing the size and number of hedges', *ibid.*, 333–43; J. H. Turner, 'On the necessity for the reduction or abolition of hedges', *ibid.*, 479–88; R. Baker, 'On the farming of Essex', *J.R.A.S.*, V (1844), 39; J. Farncombe, 85; J. Bravendar, 128–9.

[4] J. Grant, 'A few remarks on the large hedges and small enclosures of Devonshire and the adjoining counties', *J.R.A.S.*, V (1844), 420–9.

[5] J. H. Clapham (1932), 267.

[6] W. Johnston, *England as it is, political, social and industrial*, 3 vols., I (London, 1851), 4.

some districts it was a hallmark of agricultural inertia; in Northampton-shire, the ridge and furrow lands had remained under grass, fossilising the old arable strips 'in the same state as when they were sown down at the time of enclosure'. Elsewhere, as in Cheshire, the 'butts' and 'reins' were still a customary, albeit obsolete, method of land drainage. At mid-century farmers were still reluctant to disturb their 'consecrated form' and thereby lay bare the less fertile tops of the ridges, although, as in Worcestershire, they hindered the use of new machinery. Samuel Jonas was over-optimistic when he looked forward (in western Cambridgeshire) to a not too distant day when the high backs would be 'gradually ploughed down and sized into straight uniform lands'.[1]

In 1850, poor drainage was still a major stumbling block to progress on the claylands, despite the availability of government grants for drainage, and of mass-produced tile drains from new machines.[2] In many counties, however, a start had been made. Even in Surrey, condemned by Caird for its rural backwardness, another reporter found the London Clay 'naturally stubborn to cultivate', but made productive by draining. And in Berkshire, Bedfordshire and Huntingdonshire much clayland drainage had been successfully executed.[3] On the other hand, there were many areas where drainage was urgently recommended; Philip Pusey had believed in 1842 that one-third of England required draining. The heavier the land, the slower the progress. From Devonshire to Durham, 'cold clay' farming came in for criticism as being backward or defective – its soils described variously as wet, stubborn, exhausted and sterile. A description of the Lias clays of the vale of Marshwood in Dorset as being 'a terrible rough country' probably fitted many such districts. Even in Huntingdonshire, the essayist who in one sentence had praised its farmers as managers of strong land, in the next censured 'the large extent of poor, undrained, unproductive grassland, which yet remains unimproved'.[4] Although the

---

[1] W. Bearn, 80; W. Palin, 62–3, 77–8; C. W. Hoskyns, *Talpa: or the chronicles of a clay farm* (London, 1854), 29; C. Cadle, 'The agriculture of Worcestershire', *J.R.A.S.*, 2nd ser., III (1867), 449; S. Jonas, 55.

[2] H. C. Darby, 'The draining of the English clay-lands', *Geographische Zeitschrift*, LII (1964), 190–201.

[3] J. Caird, 118; H. Evershed, 'On the farming of Surrey', *J.R.A.S.*, XIV (1853), 402; J. B. Spearing, 23; W. Bennett, 5; G. Murray, 'On the farming of Huntingdon', *J.R.A.S.*, 2nd ser., IV (1868), 266.

[4] P. Pusey, 'On progress of agricultural knowledge during the last four years', *J.R.A.S.*, III (1842), 170; H. Tanner, 'The farming of Devonshire', *J.R.A.S.*, IX (1848), 460; J. Caird, 334–6; L. H. Ruegg, 240; G. Murray, 266.

statistical evidence for the areas drained by 1850 – as later – is uncertain, it is clear that the technical mastery of the clay soils was far from complete.[1] In contrast to the light lands the heavy lands were still relatively backward and the 'agricultural revolution on the English clays', debated by some historians, was only partly under way.[2] The small size of many clayland farms, tenanted by uneducated men of insufficient capital to effect improvement, was a contributory factor in this lack of progress.[3]

Two groups of clayland enterprise can be identified: those where grassland was characteristic; and those where grass and arable were more equally intermixed. Grassland farms dominated the heavy clay vales and lowlands of the grazing counties. In southern Cheshire, for example, the tithe surveys showed a proportion of two-thirds grass to one-third (or even less) arable, and in eastern Leicestershire permanent grass sward also occupied up to two-thirds of the farm area.[4] The pasture varied from the carefully managed 'prime old grazing lands' of the vale of Aylesbury to parts of Leicestershire with 'wet, spongy, hassocky, ant-hill-covered pasture', and one critic asserted that a large proportion of English grassland needed improvement.[5] In 1850 the large towns still obtained their milk supplies mainly from suburban farms or from town cowsheds[6] and the farmers in the specialist dairying regions still manufactured either cheese – a Cheshire, a Stilton, a Gloucestershire – or butter as in Northamptonshire and western Warwickshire. In other districts, such as Corve Dale in Derbyshire and South Hams in Devonshire, the emphasis was upon the rearing and feeding of beef cattle, but a diversified livestock region such as the vale of Aylesbury relied on its dairies, its fat cattle and its flocks of ewes.[7]

---

[1] A. D. M. Phillips, 'Underdraining and the English claylands, 1850–80: a review', *Agric. Hist. Rev.*, XVII (1969), 44–55.

[2] R. W. Sturgess, 'The agricultural revolution on the English clays', *Agric. Hist. Rev.*, XIV (1966), 104–21; E. J. T. Collins and E. L. Jones, 'Sectoral advance in English agriculture', *Agric. Hist. Rev.*, XV (1967), 65–81; R. W. Sturgess, 'The agricultural revolution on the English clays: a rejoinder', *Agric. Hist. Rev.*, XV (1967), 82–7.

[3] W. J. Moscrop, 'A report on the farming of Leicestershire', *J.R.A.S.*, 2nd ser., II (1866), 293; H. Evershed (1853), 412; E. Little, 173; R. W. Corringham, 30; J. Farncombe, 81.

[4] C. S. Davies, *The agricultural history of Cheshire 1750–1850* (Manchester, 1960), 128; W. J. Moscrop, 292.

[5] J. Caird, 3; W. J. Moscrop, 337; R. Smith, 'The management of grassland', *J.R.A.S.*, X (1849), 2.

[6] E. H. Whetham, 'The London milk trade, 1860–1900', *Econ. Hist. Rev.*, XVII (1964), 369.   [7] J. Caird, 3.

The second group of farming types on the heavier soils had a higher proportion of arable. The clays, prior to the agricultural revolution on the light lands, had been the principal granaries, but by 1850, some clay districts such as the Fylde in Lancashire were rapidly changing to a grass-land husbandry.[1] Many other districts retained a strong interest in arable farming despite its higher costs of production. Thus in the 1840s some 60% of the Boulder Clay area of south-east Hertfordshire was cultivated. The Chilterns with its cover of clay-with-flints was also an arable area, with stretches of grassland confined largely to its valleys and its landscape parks, as may be seen from the tithe surveys mapped by F. D. Hartley (Figs. 51 and 52). It was matched by the extensive tracts of clayland under the plough on the Weald Clay of Surrey and Sussex, and on the London Clay of Essex.[2] Even away from south-east England, on the clay-lands of the grazing counties, many arable fields survived in 1850. They formed the basis of farm economies which combined some grain growing with the management of livestock, but, in these localities, arable farming had remained at its most backward. There were farms where green crops had only been at most partially introduced into the rotation; the old three-fold course – fallow, wheat, beans, as on the clays of the vale of York[3] – was widely practised, and crop yields were well below the national average. In the claylands the enclosure of the common arable fields had been far from a universal prelude to improvement.

The uplands

The mountains and moorlands of England (although the scene of such grand transformations as the reclamation of Exmoor)[4] were not subjected, even in the heyday of high farming, to the thorough-going improvement of the downs and heaths of lowland England. As contemporaries noted, a harsher environment had imposed certain absolute boundaries to human

[1] W. Smith, 'Agrarian evolution since the eighteenth century', in A. Grime (ed.), *A scientific survey of Blackpool and district* (London, 1936), 44–7.

[2] L. G. Cameron, *Hertfordshire* (L. of B., pt. 80, London, 1941), 329–32; D. W. Shave, 393; H. C. K. Henderson, 'Our changing agriculture: the Adur Basin, Sussex', *Jour. Min. of Agric.*, XLIII (1936), 630, 632–3; E. A. Cox, 'An agricultural geography of Essex *c.* 1840', unpublished London University M.A. thesis, 1963; E. A. Cox and B. R. Dittmer, 'The tithe files of the mid-nineteenth century', *Agric. Hist. Rev.*, XIII (1965), 12.

[3] G. Legard, 'Farming of the East Riding of Yorkshire', *J.R.A.S.*, IX (1848), 99.

[4] T. D. Acland, 'On the farming of Somersetshire', *J.R.A.S.*, XI (1850), 688–93; C. S. Orwin, *The reclamation of Exmoor Forest* (Oxford, 1929).

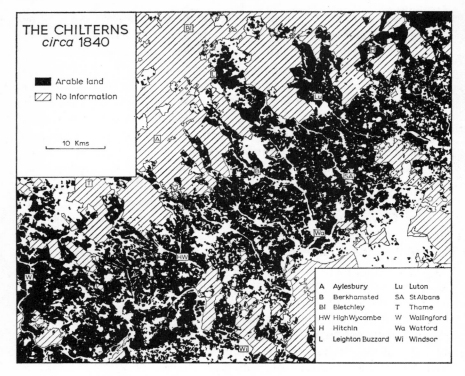

Fig. 51   The Chilterns: arable land *circa* 1840
Based on the tithe returns as plotted in F. D. Hartley, 'The agricultural geography of the Chilterns *c.* 1840', unpublished M.A. thesis, University of London, 1953.

endeavour. Cultivation was limited by altitude. On the Mendip Hills, where much of the land was between 800 feet and 900 feet above sea-level, although there were substantial patches of land cultivated intelligently by recently established farmers, T. D. Acland noted in 1851 that 'a large part of the hill must be reclaimed over again before it can be properly farmed'.[1] And farther north in Cumberland William Dickinson explained that 600 feet was the upper limit for wheat, although oats succeeded up to 800 feet and were occasionally sown at higher altitudes when land was broken up to improve the pasture. But optimism was often tempered with caution. Thus, although J. J. Rowley praised the efforts in Derbyshire to enclose

[1] T. D. Acland, 729. See M. Williams, 'The enclosure and reclamation of the Mendip Hills, 1770–1870', *Agric. Hist. Rev.*, XIX (1971), 65–81.

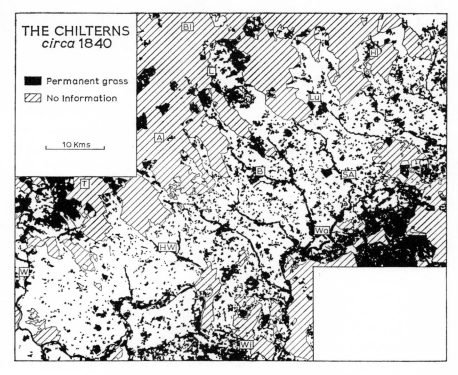

THE CHILTERNS
circa 1840

■ Permanent grass

▨ No Information

|___ 10 Kms ___|

Fig. 52   The Chilterns: permanent grass *circa* 1840
Source as for Fig. 51.
For the key to the initials see Fig. 51.

the Millstone Grit moorland, he had to admit that there were many
'difficulties and drawbacks; the seasons are critical; the winters long'.
Moreover, much upland grazing remained as unstinted common, and its
associated abuses impeded fencing and draining. The result, as the first
Ordnance Survey maps for northern England show, was that the upper
edge of cultivation was ragged, with many single enclosures detached,
here and there, from the body of the improved land. J. H. Charnock,
writing of the heather moors of the West Riding, noted that each year
saw additional examples of moorland enclosure, but he had to admit to
only partial and superficial improvement. In the lead dales of Durham and
Northumberland – where grass fields reached up to 1,500 feet and even
1,700 feet – the agricultural holdings were small and the moors 'not half
stocked'. Already, at mid-century, the farmers of Westmorland had

before them the disheartening spectacle of land cultivated in the Napoleonic Wars, but subsequently 'permanently depreciated'.[1]

Thus, the progress of moorland improvement, although much had been accomplished, must not be overestimated. Arable fields, especially on the Millstone Grits, were few and scattered as the tithe evidence for Derbyshire suggests.[2] The best pastures lay on the Carboniferous Limestone. Craven was esteemed for its 'high feeding qualities', while the 'rich' grazing valleys of the North Riding – such as Wensleydale and Swaledale – were noted for their productiveness.[3] Here, the pastoral economy of the hill farm was most prosperous and, like English farming as a whole, it depended on the populous industrial regions. The products of hill farming were summed up by Webster when he wrote: 'so long as the tall chimneys of Yorkshire and Lancashire smoke, so long will the Westmorland farmer have a never-failing demand for all his produce – beef, mutton, butter, cheese and wool'.[4]

Other forms of upland utilisation were also well established by mid-century. Reservoirs had been created in the valleys of the Pennine upland. Afforestation with larch and fir had continued in Cumbria, stimulated by the demand for pit props; and heather moorlands were rented for shooting. Tourists came to the hills in increasing numbers, and, in the Lake District, there was a new class of competitors for the ownership of the soil, 'the merchant princes of the manufacturing districts, who eagerly buy up any nook where they may escape from their own smoke, and enjoy pure air and bracing breezes, with shooting and fishing'.[5]

INDUSTRY

The Census of 1851 included the first scientific attempt to classify occupations,[6] and it has stimulated several studies of the distribution of

[1] W. Dickinson, 'On the farming of Cumberland', *J.R.A.S.*, XIII (1852), 289; J. J. Rowley, 'The farming of Derbyshire', *J.R.A.S.*, XIV (1853), 49; J. H. Clapham (1932), 259; J. H. Charnock, 299; D. Macrae, 'The improvement of waste lands', *J.R.A.S.*, 2nd ser., IV (1868), 321; T. G. Bell, 'A report upon the agriculture of the county of Durham', *J.R.A.S.*, XVII (1856), 92; C. Webster, 'On the farming of Westmorland', *J.R.A.S.*, 2nd ser., IV (1868), 7, 17.
[2] H. C. K. Henderson, 'Changes in land utilization in Derbyshire', in A. H. Harris, *Derbyshire* (L. of B., pt. 63, London, 1941), 71–4.
[3] J. H. Charnock, 300; M. M. Milburn, 514–16.
[4] C. Webster, 16.   [5] *Ibid.*, 8.
[6] *Guides to official sources*, No. 2 (H.M.S.O., 1951), 30.

industry in the mid-nineteenth century. Augustus Petermann's pioneer distribution map of occupations compiled to illustrate the Census Report, had stood the test of time sufficiently to form the basis of J. H. Clapham's analysis of the 'localisation of manufacture about the end of the early railway age', and of R. Lawton's recent study which has re-mapped Petermann's data in a more assimilable form.[1] Other accounts, such as those of C. Day and T. A. Welton, have also used this census to comment on the distribution of industry.[2]

It is clear that the boundaries of industrial England (despite the survival of much loosely distributed rural industry) were more narrowly drawn than ever before. In particular, the coalfields had consolidated their position as the premier seats of industrial activity – especially in the textile and metal manufacturing industries. But the census also revealed the danger of oversimplifying the industrial structure. In spite of the well-known specialisation between coalfields, the major industrial regions were seldom a simple amalgam of coalmining and one staple manufacture. South Lancashire, for example, not only contained concentrations of workers in the major industries such as coalmining, the metal industries and the manufacture of textiles, but also in a variety of other manufactures, such as paper making, glass and earthenware (Fig. 59). On the coalfield of north Staffordshire, the district of the Potteries was of growing importance.

The coal and iron industries

Coal and iron ore, in this classic age of the blast furnace, were the twin pillars of a number of English industrial regions. The *Mineral statistics* enumerate some 1,704 collieries which produced an unprecedented total of 47 million tons of coal.[3] The collieries varied enormously in size and layout and, moreover, many small shafts, as a scrutiny of the map evidence confirms, had no place in the early editions of the *Mineral statistics*: the figures of coal production may therefore be an underestimate. The regional totals of iron-ore production are even harder to compile. The main feature of iron-ore mining was its concentration (up to 95%) upon the Coal-Measure ores (Fig. 53); and coal and iron sometimes came from the same

[1] J. H. Clapham (1932), 22–46; R. Lawton, 'Historical geography; the industrial revolution', in J. W. Watson and J. B. Sissons (eds.), *The British Isles: a systematic geography* (London and Edinburgh, 1964), 229–38.

[2] C. Day, 'The distribution of industrial occupations in England', *Trans. Connecticut Academy of Arts and Sciences*, XXVIII (1927), 79–235; T. A. Welton, *passim*.

[3] R. Hunt, *Mineral statistics of the United Kingdom for 1853 and 1854* (Mem. Geol. Survey, 1855), 50.

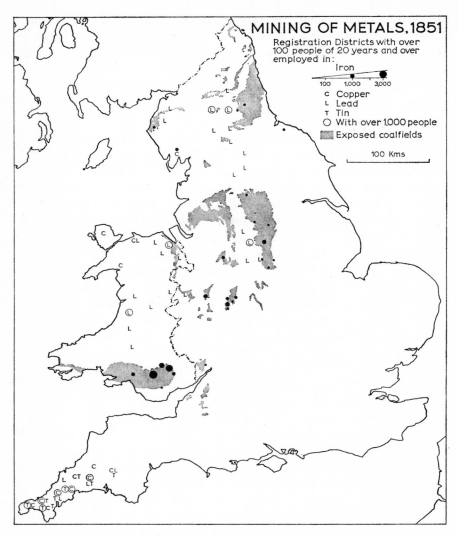

Fig. 53 Employment in iron and other metal mining in 1851
Based on *Census of 1851: Population Tables, II* (P.P. 1852–3, lxxxviii,
pts. 1 and 2).

pit, so that iron mines were not listed separately in the *Mineral statistics*. The confused topography of such an area was illustrated to the south-west of Bradford. What the Ordnance surveyors called 'coal and iron pits', were intermingled with 'collierys' and 'coal pits' in a complex mining landscape. The coal and iron pits fed a suite of blast furnaces directly by means of a tramway, the whole site providing a small epitome of the marriage of coal and iron which had virtually completed the relocation of the iron industry by 1850.[1] In Derbyshire and south Yorkshire, local coal was also used to smelt local iron. Only in Furness did a few charcoal-iron furnaces remain in production.[2]

Of the English regions where coal and iron occurred in bulk, the coke-iron industry of the Black Country outstripped all others. It ranked first in the English output of iron ore and pig-iron (1.2 and 0.75 million tons respectively) and third in coal production.[3] It is hard to visualise the intensity of heavy industry in this relatively small district – at most only 16 by 17 miles. The accounts of eye-witnesses suggest that perhaps nowhere else in England had the countryside been so transformed. A landscape was mapped out 'interspersed with blazing furnaces, heaps of burning coal in process of coking, piles of iron-ore calcining, forges, pit-banks, and engine chimneys; the country being besides intersected with canals, crossing each other at various levels; and the small remaining fields of grass or corn, intermingled with heaps of refuse of mines or of slag from the blast furnaces'.[4] Although many of its collieries were small, shallow and ill-equipped, and the scale of production of its blast furnaces was small, the Black Country was perhaps the most remarkable heavy industrial region of 1850.[5] The early industrial revolution had almost run its full course: the district was soon to reach its peak in mineral production (the productive thirty-foot coal seam was already substantially exhausted)[6] at its point of greatest national importance.

The north-eastern coalfield region, unlike the Black Country, stood on

[1] Yorkshire O.S. 6", First Edition, Sheet 216 (1852).

[2] R. Hunt, 'The present state of the mining industries of the United Kingdom', *Jour. Roy. Stat. Soc.*, XIX (1856), 317.

[3] B. R. Mitchell and P. Deane, *Abstract of British historical statistics* (Cambridge, 1962), 115–31; G. C. Allen, *The industrial development of Birmingham and the Black Country 1860–1927* (London, 1929), 84–96.

[4] *First Report of the Midland Mining Commission, South Staffordshire*, iv (P.P. 1843, xiii).   [5] *Ibid.*, civ; W. Smith (1949), 124; G. C. Allen, 145.

[6] B. C. L. Johnson and M. J. Wise, 'The Black Country, 1800–1850', in M. J. Wise (ed.), *Birmingham and its regional setting* (Birmingham, 1950), 232–4.

the threshold rather than at the climax of an industrial boom. A large-scale iron industry around Middlesbrough based on the Jurassic ores of the Cleveland Hills was being set up. Although the Skinningrove and Eston seams were newly opened only in 1850, by 1854, 59 modern furnaces were already in blast, to make the region second in English pig-iron production. Coalmining, on the other hand, had done no more than retain its ancient supremacy (Fig. 54). Northumberland and Durham had the greatest production (15.4 million tons) of any coalfield – over a quarter of the English output.[1] Moreover, many of its collieries were modern and well equipped: the pits were deeper than elsewhere, the pit engines of larger capacity, and the most modern shaft ventilation had been introduced. The results of a rapid spread of mining across the coalfield can be assessed by 1850. The expanding railway network had provided a crucial stimulus, for few collieries were, by then, without a rail link.[2] Many collieries had become the nucleus of self-contained pit-head villages planted in the open countryside. West Cramlington, on a branch of the North Eastern Railway, was not untypical of the newly colonised areas. The terraces of miners' cottages formed three sides of a square; the colliery works and railway sidings lay in the centre; and the Blue Bell Inn, the Primitive Methodist Chapel and the Mechanics Institute completed this small community. The names of the terraces of houses: 'Crank Row', 'Long Row', 'Smoky Row', 'Pump Row', 'Brick Row', 'Foreman Row', prosaic and mechanical, were resonant of the new industrial age which called them into being.[3] These hastily built rows of brick or stone cottages, sometimes with blue-slate roofs, were becoming ubiquitous in the industrial regions of north England, not only in Northumberland and Durham, but in Cleveland, where they 'appeared suddenly, like fungi' on the bleak open plateau.[4] Likewise in west Cumberland they straggled around pit-head and blast furnace in the industrial hinterland of Maryport, Workington and Whitehaven. But in these northern industrial areas the climax of heavy industry lay in the future.

The secondary metal-using trades, as the 1851 Census reveals, were more widely dispersed than the heavy iron industry (Fig. 55). Nonetheless, the outstanding concentrations (with the exception of London and south Lancashire) were associated with important areas of coal and iron

[1] R. Hunt (1855), 41, 51.

[2] A. E. Smailes, *North England* (London and Edinburgh, 1960), 165.

[3] Northumberland O.S. 6", First Edition, Sheets 80 (1864) and 88 (1864); and Durham O.S. 6" First Edition, Sheet 20 (1861).   [4] A. E. Smailes, 230.

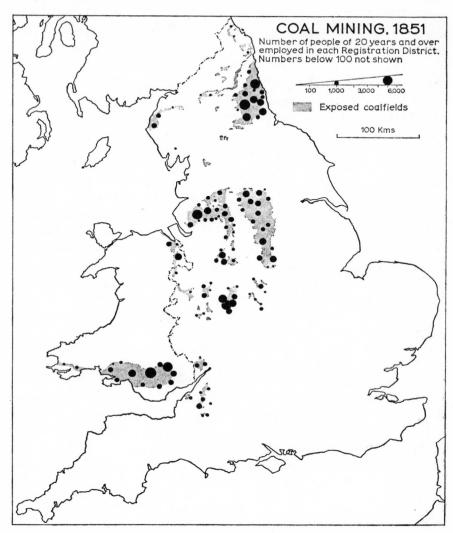

Fig. 54 Employment in coalmining in 1851
Source as for Fig. 53.

production. Many Black Country towns had developed specialist 'hardware' trades: at Wolverhampton, tinplate, japanned and holloware articles; at Darlaston, nuts and bolts; at Halesowen, Dudley and Rowley, nails; and at Walsall, saddlers' ironmongery[1] – to cite but a few. And in Birmingham, the metropolis of this metal-manufacturing region, the trades were 'so numerous and so varied...that no one could be found who would undertake to describe them all';[2] although the staple brass, gun, button and jewellery industries were located within distinctive quarters of the town.[3] The Sheffield district, coming second to the west Midlands in the metal trades, was not dissimilar in industrial organisation for it, too, lacked the large factory. Within the staple cutlery, file-making and tool-making trades, there were many firms occupying small workshops. On the eve of the introduction of the Bessemer process (when over four-fifths of the nation's small output of perhaps 60,000 tons of steel came from Sheffield) there were no less than 135 small steel-making firms in the town.[4] In the metal-using (as in most) industries, old and new processes thrived side by side; technological innovation had been sporadic in its impact; 'this was not the machine age' as W. H. B. Court put it, 'but the machine age had begun'.[5]

The textile industries

By 1850 the machine age had become most mature in the textile districts on the coalfields of east Lancashire and west Yorkshire. James Caird found that 'the evidences of a busy population everywhere present themselves'.[6] But south Lancashire was no Black Country. It was still to one observer 'like a vast city scattered amongst meads and pastures'.[7] Even in intensively mined areas, such as that around Wigan, collieries were often small by Northumberland standards; the pits were scattered and, beneath the spidery arms of small mineral railways, the ancient field patterns were

[1] G. C. Allen, 65–83.

[2] S. Timmins, *The resources, products and industrial history of Birmingham and the Midland hardware district* (London, 1866), 208.

[3] M. J. Wise, 'On the evolution of the jewellery and gun quarters in Birmingham', *Trans. and Papers, Inst. Brit. Geog.*, XV (1951), 59–72.

[4] C. Singer *et al.* (eds.), *A history of technology*, V (Oxford, 1958), 53; G. P. Jones, 'Industrial evolution' in D. L. Linton (ed.), *Sheffield and its region* (Sheffield, 1956), 156.

[5] W. H. B. Court, *A concise economic history of Britain from 1750 to recent times* (Cambridge, 1958), 178.

[6] J. Caird, 264.

[7] S. Bamford, *Walks in south Lancashire and on its borders* (Blackley, 1844), 10.

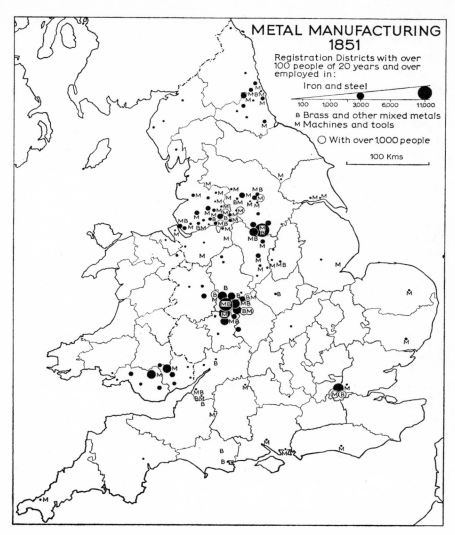

Fig. 55 Employment in metal manufacturing in 1851
Source as for Fig. 53.

not yet erased.[1] Coalmining was, however, an important strand in the south Lancashire economy. It ranked second to that of Northumberland and Durham, producing 9.9 million tons in 1854 (Fig. 54); and, moreover, this output came increasingly from deeper and more modern collieries, although, here and there, as on most coalfields, shallow drift and adit mines were to be found.[2]

But the most remarkable feature of the economic geography of mid-nineteenth century Lancashire was the extent to which the cotton industry had concentrated there (Fig. 56). Through cotton, south Lancashire had become, in the words of one contemporary 'the principal manufacturing district, not only of England, but of the world'.[3] Moreover, the boundaries of the cotton region embraced north-east Cheshire and the extreme west of Yorkshire. It was the fullest embodiment of the new factory age. Although there remained up to perhaps 50,000 hand-loom weavers, mechanisation had gone further in the cotton industry than in any other.[4] Of the steam power available to British industry at mid-century, the most important regional concentration was driving nearly a quarter of a million power looms in the cotton industry. In 1850 the number of cotton factories in England and Wales was nearly 1,800,[5] and their buildings dominated the skyline; it was from their tall chimneys that at least one traveller now took his landmarks rather than from 'church spires and monumental columns'.[6] But art as well as money had been lavished upon the new cotton mills; even in Salford, it was reported that 'some of them have a good architectural effect', and, rather fancifully perhaps, that 'were they built of stone instead of brick, when they cease to vomit forth smoke they might pass for triumphal columns'.[7] In the multi-storied spinning mills of south Lancashire there had been more scope for design than in the weaving sheds of the north, although even in remote valleys they had retained 'a forceful architectural character', in the face of the accelerating change from water to steam power.[8]

The isolated cotton mill was still important. Certainly in remote

[1] Lancashire O.S. 6″, First Edition, Sheet 93 (1849).

[2] B. R. Mitchell and P. Deane, 115; A. J. Taylor, 'The Wigan coalfield in 1851', *Trans. Hist. Soc. Lancs. and Ches.*, CVI (1954), 119.

[3] T. A. Welton, 61.   [4] J. H. Clapham (1932), 28.

[5] *Factory Returns, 1850*, 16 (P.P. 1850, xlii).

[6] C. Redding, *The pictorial history of the county of Lancaster* (London, 1844).

[7] *Ibid.*, 33.

[8] J. M. Richards, *The functional tradition in early industrial buildings* (London, 1958), 75–7.

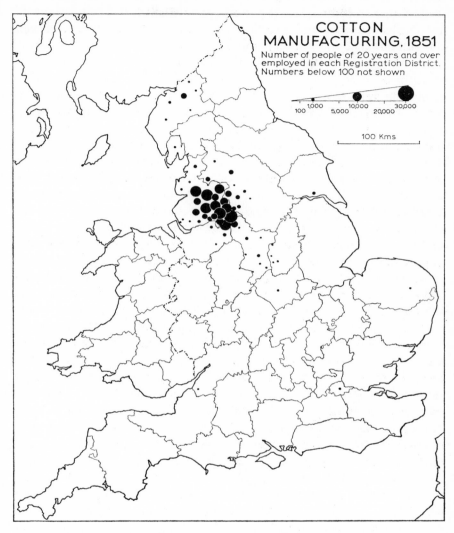

Fig. 56 Employment in cotton manufacturing in 1851
Source as for Fig. 53.

moorland valleys small water-powered mills had remained in production; while numerous bleach and dye works, printworks, and 'tenter grounds', where cloth was stretched and dried, are delineated in streamside locations on the First Edition of the six-inch Ordnance Survey Map in Lancashire. There were also steam-powered mills situated away from the stream sides in fairly open country. Hurst Cotton Mills, for example, north-east of Ashton-under-Lyne, lay within the perimeter of a landscaped park, together with a small coalpit, a terrace of cottages, a Methodist chapel and a school. Such factory villages – the equivalent, in the cotton province, of the north-eastern colliery settlements – had become a characteristic element in the industrial landscape.[1] But many erstwhile industrial villages were, by 1850, the new cotton towns. Contemporary maps captured them at a time of expansion; to the north-east of Bury, for example, around Chesham Field Cotton Mill, we can glimpse, in the half-finished rows of terraced houses and in the roads mapped out but not built along, these new units of workplace and home.[2] In many locations the paramount importance of coal and communications in the determination of site is demonstrated: factories frequently abutted on to canals, turnpike roads and railways, and were seldom far from a coalpit. Indeed, it has been argued that a cotton firm 'incurred a substantial penalty in siting a mill more than a few miles from the nearest supply, especially since many of its competitors had coal almost literally on their doorsteps'.[3] In general, therefore, with the notable exception of Preston, cotton manufacture had become concentrated on the coalfield; at the same time, the well-known geographical specialisation in the Lancashire cotton industry was largely shaped by 1850: not only was the separation of the spinning and weaving branches established, but 'every cotton town had acquired a distinctive industrial personality'.[4] Away from Lancastria the cotton industry was in relative decline and poorly adapted to the age of steam. In the east Midlands, for example, although there were 110 cotton-spinning mills in 1850, they represented only 6.5% of the total cotton mills in England (as compared with the region's 39% at the end of the eighteenth century); many were still water-powered.[5]

---

[1] Lancashire O.S. 6", First Edition, Sheet 105 (1848); S. Pollard, 'The factory village in the industrial revolution', *Eng. Hist. Rev.*, LXXIX (1964), 513–31.

[2] Lancashire O.S. 6", First Edition, Sheet 88 (1851).

[3] H. B. Rodgers, 'The Lancashire cotton industry in 1840', *Trans. and Papers, Inst. Brit. Geog.*, XXVIII (1960), 140.   [4] *Ibid.*, 146.

[5] D. M. Smith, 'The cotton industry in the east Midlands', *Geography*, XLVII (1962), 256–69.

Fig. 57 Employment in woollen and worsted manufacturing in 1851
Source as for Fig. 53.

A traveller across the Pennines in 1850 would have been struck by the similarity of the industrial landscape as he passed eastwards from the Lancashire zone of cotton, to the west Yorkshire zone of worsted and woollen manufacture (Fig. 57). These districts had much in common. In the first place, the locations had achieved stability. In the English worsted industry the decay of the Norfolk manufacture and the rise of west Yorkshire was such that, by 1850, some 87% of the spindles and 95% of the looms were installed in the latter district. In the woollen industry, although Yorkshire's share of the national manufacture was less (from 40% to 50%), the industry had likewise 'almost reached the pitch of concentration which it showed in the twentieth century'.[1] Secondly, by 1850, internal geographical specialisation in west Yorkshire matched that of Lancashire. Worsted manufacture, concentrated in the north-west, was more of an urban factory industry, prominent in large towns such as Bradford and Halifax. Woollen manufacture, in the south-east of the region, apart from the dominance of Leeds, was carried on, contrariwise, in smaller mills with riverline sites in the lesser towns or industrial villages, and the conversion to steam power was less complete. Thirdly, however, both types of factory – worsted and woollen – had spread as in Lancashire, away from the streams, and were often sited near to coalpits.

West Yorkshire, although fully in the factory age, was still a curious hybrid scene of agricultural and industrial activity. Even allowing for artist's licence, there was apparently some reality in the contemporary paintings of textile mills with rustic figures and scenes hard by the factory gate.[2] It was in this district, after all, that Caird had discovered a competent class of smallholders producing butter and milk for the local market.[3] On some parts of the major coalfields, industry had blackened and blighted the landscape; but on others, factories and collieries were set against a rural backcloth.

The dominance of cotton and woollen manufacture should not lead us to overlook the contribution of other textiles to the industrial economy of 1850. If flax had ceased to be a major English industry – although sailcloth was still made in a number of ports – silk retained third place in the textile industries in terms of the numbers employed.[4] There were silkworkers in 1851 not only in the main textile provinces of Lancastria and

---

[1] W. Smith (1949), 113; J. H. Clapham (1932), 27.
[2] E. M. Sigsworth, *Black Dyke mills* (Liverpool, 1958), 176–8.
[3] J. Caird, 286–8.   [4] J. H. Clapham (1932), 29.

Fig. 58 Employment in miscellaneous textile manufacturing in 1851
(Hosiery, lace, ribbon, silk)
Source as for Fig. 53.

Yorkshire, but also in the east Midlands and Warwickshire, in Norfolk and Essex, in London and Hertfordshire, and in the south-western counties (Fig. 58). Fully mechanised silk factories could be found in all the major textile areas, but the industry was also characterised by a widespread survival of the out-worker system and, as in other textile trades where the factory system was only partly developed, by a distinctive domestic architecture. Separate loomshops were housed in an upper storey, in extra ground-floor rooms or in out-buildings; in places there had developed an almost regional style of working-class housing.[1]

Tin, copper and lead mining

The non-ferrous mining industry, by 1851, was of great relative importance in parts of Devon, Cornwall and the northern Pennines. These districts were uniquely dependent on their mines (Fig. 53). In Devon and Cornwall, Thomas Welton calculated that mining employed 28% or over of the adult male population in ten registration districts; this figure rose to 53.9% in the Redruth District. In the north Pennine area as a whole mining was of comparable importance (28.8%), rising to 45.9% in Weardale Registration District, to 51.5% in that of Reeth and to 59.6% in that of Alston.[2] These statistics reflect both the absence of other industries and the poverty of agriculture; mining had spread over infertile moorlands to provide the only inducement to a sporadic agricultural colonisation. Such areas were also distinctive amongst industrial regions because they had attained, in general, the peak of their production (iron-ore and coal output, on the other hand, continued to rise sharply after 1850). Thus the 'Cornish Copper Kingdom', with Redruth as its capital, was soon to reach its maximum output in 1856, and the lead dales of the northern Pennines were also near their zenith. Indeed, in the latter area, some of the richest deposits were already exhausted, and in Cornwall a legacy of derelict mines remained in 1850 from earlier speculative booms.[3]

In the south-western region, different types of mine were intricately

---

[1] O. Ashmore, *The industrial archaeology of Lancashire* (Newton Abbot, 1969), 27–37; D. M. Smith, *The industrial archaeology of the east Midlands* (Dawlish, 1965), 34–50; W. J. Smith, 'The architecture of the domestic system in south-east Lancashire and the adjoining Pennines', in S. D. Chapman (ed.), *The history of working-class housing: a symposium* (Newton Abbot, 1971), 249–75.

[2] T. A. Welton, 56–7.

[3] W. J. Rowe, *Cornwall in the age of the industrial revolution* (Liverpool, 1953), 305, 323–32; J. W. House, *North-eastern England: population movements and landscape since the early 19th century* (Newcastle upon Tyne, 1954), 32.

mixed, but the salient features of the mining landscape, the engine house with its tall chimney, the ore-dressing floors and smelting houses, the waste heaps, the mineral railways, the adits and watercourses, and the groups of miners' cottages – sometimes mere hovels of cob and thatch[1] – were common to all districts. Mining was closely concentrated upon the fringe of mineralised rocks around the edge of the granite; the stream working of tin still survived, but most of the ore came from deep mines. Copper production had, however, outstripped that of tin, and the copper workings employed three-quarters of the mining population in 1851 (Fig. 53). Lead took third place in the mining activities of south-west England.

The centre of lead mining lay in Pennine England (Fig. 53) and the lead dales of Northumberland and Durham clearly surpassed those of Derbyshire and Yorkshire. The mineralised zone was richest near the head of the dales, and as a result mining had spread upwards to nearly 2,000 feet, although smelting sometimes took place down-dale.[2] The first edition of the Ordnance Survey 6″ Map, published for this area at mid-century, captured the detail of these landscapes in their economic heyday: the derelict and active pits, the old levels, the washing places for lead, the chimneys and the smelting mills – all framed by great rectangular intakes into the moorland edge. At Allenhead, for example, a fairly extensive lead-mining colony had grown up at 1,300 feet above sea-level, and mines and old workings scarred the hillside: administrative buildings, workshops and cottages, flanked by plantations, nestled below in the valley floor.[3]

Manufacturing industries outside the coalfields

Away from the coalfields there was a great variety of manufacturing industry in 1850, but it only rarely made such a spectacular contribution to the landscape as did mining, metal smelting and textile manufacture. More often than not these industries took second place to other activities: in the countryside to agriculture, in the ports, and apparently in London, to commerce and trade. And yet, although the non-coalfield industry was not outstanding in the industrial topography of the steam age, it employed, as J. D. Chambers has reminded us, many more people than did the 'great industry' of the coalfields. In 1851, there were still more shoemakers than coalminers, and more handicraft blacksmiths than men tending iron

---

[1] W. J. Rowe, 152; A. H. Shorter *et al.*, *Southwest England* (London, 1969), 164–8.
[2] A. E. Smailes, 274.
[3] Northumberland O.S. 6″, First Edition, Sheets 93 (1865) and 111 (1865).

furnaces; and those employed in the non-mechanised industries still out-numbered those in the mechanised industries by three to one.[1]

In rural England, many 'industries' were still really handicraft trades; production was for the local market so that the industrial workers were widely disseminated relative to the total population in such trades as milling, smithing, shoemaking and tailoring. As a group the handicraft industries were of most importance within two districts: in the east Midlands – stretching from Nottinghamshire south-east into Bedfordshire – and in the West Country. The first, the east Midlands, provided several examples of industries which had not migrated to steam-powered factories, and, although the countryside might be semi-industrialised, the domestic system had altered the rural landscape but little (Fig. 58). Such was the hosiery industry, surviving only in a condition of stagnation. There were, it is true, a number of hosiery factories in towns such as Derby, Leicester and Nottingham, but the majority of the framework knitters were still out-workers in converted farm buildings and cottages, where the application of power was almost unknown, and where the frame itself had re-mained practically unaltered for a hundred years or more.[2] Domestic lace manufacture was important in an area stretching from Derbyshire to London (Fig. 58); and in Bedfordshire and West Hertfordshire the craft of straw plaiting to make hats and bonnets was also organised as a domestic industry (Fig. 59). The Northamptonshire boot and shoe industry, although it had taken on a modern location, was likewise a small-scale handicraft trade, resisting mechanisation, and its workers were con-trolled by 'manufacturers' in Leicester and Northampton. In the West Country too, the industrial geography was mostly static. The Wiltshire woollen industry was exceptional in that steam was used far more than in Gloucestershire or Somerset.[3] And in Devon the woollen industry still relied on the water-wheel, and the making of gloves, lace and silk was a cottage industry. In many small country towns and villages the industrial legacy of the pre-railway era lay scarcely disturbed.

[1] J. D. Chambers, *The workshop of the world* (London, 1961), 21–2; J. H. Clapham (1932), 23–5.

[2] D. M. Smith, 'The British hosiery industry at the middle of the nineteenth cen-tury: an historical study in economic geography', *Trans. and Papers, Inst. Brit. Geog.*, XXXII (1963), 125–42; F. A. Wells, *The British hosiery and knitwear industry* (Newton Abbot, 2nd ed., 1972), 106–17; L. A. Parker in W. G. Hoskins and R. A. McKinley (eds.), *V.C.H. Leicestershire*, III (1955), 2–23; W. G. Hoskins, *Leicestershire* (London, 1957), 81.

[3] J. de L. Mann in E. Crittall (ed.), *V.C.H. Wiltshire*, IV (1959), 173.

Fig. 59 Employment in miscellaneous manufacturing in 1851
(Earthenware, glass, straw hats)
Source as for Fig. 53.

In contrast, the industries of the rapidly growing ports foreshadowed one of the more important industrial growth points after 1850, and dock-side industries, processing imported raw materials, were becoming more prominent in the waterfront scene. At Bristol, a report of 1823 advocated the establishment of a cotton industry, and a factory was built in 1837;[1] in Liverpool, in addition to oil-seed milling, sugar refining, soap and tobacco manufacturing, there were some 30 grain mills in 1845 (a quarter of them driven by steam), and more were constructed in the next decade;[2] and at Hull, too, oil-seed milling was an established industry.[3] If the forma-tion of dockside industrial zones was well under way, the foundations of a modern shipbuilding industry were only just discernible in 1850. Ship-yards building iron vessels were in production at Birkenhead on the Mersey, at Millwall on the Thames, and, in a small way, on the Tyne. But such coastal seats of industry, in comparison with those of the coalfields, were as yet in their infancy.

London was, as it had always been, the exception. It constituted by any yardstick the most important single concentration of economic activity in the whole country. Some of its metal, textile and miscellaneous in-dustries were, in terms of numbers employed in 1851, of national pre-eminence (Figs. 55, 58 and 59). In both highly specialised trades and in the more staple – including clothing, silk and printing – it had the greatest single labour force. Much of this industry was crammed into a zone in central and inner-suburban London, especially in the East End and Southwark, and in the West End.[4] It was comprised then, as now, of a chain of distinctive industrial quarters, each link housing its own trades: the silk-workers in Bethnal Green and Whitechapel (containing the parish of Spitalfields); the instrument-makers, goldsmiths and watchmakers in the parishes of Clerkenwell and St Luke; the printing trades in a quarter of the City and Finsbury; and the clothing trades, ranking as the largest metropolitan industry, in centres both in the West End (in Westminster) and in the East End (in Stepney).[5] But if no list can convey the number

---

[1] S. J. Jones, 'The growth of Bristol', *Trans. and Papers, Inst. Brit. Geog.*, XI (1946), 77.

[2] W. Smith (1949), 548–9.

[3] J. H. Bird, *The major seaports of the United Kingdom* (London, 1963), 128.

[4] P. G. Hall, *The industries of London since 1861* (London, 1962), 28–9, 37; P. G. Hall, 'Industrial London: a general view' in J. T. Coppock and H. C. Prince (eds.), *Greater London* (London, 1964), 226–35.

[5] *Ibid.*, 37–70; P. G. Hall, 'The location of the clothing trades in London, 1861–1951', *Trans. and Papers, Inst. Brit. Geog.*, XXVIII (1960), 158–78.

and complexity of these trades, we can at least point to their common characteristics. In organisation they were an urban variant of the domestic system – a complex web of small masters, apprentices and out-workers; the division of labour was accomplished by splitting the manufacturing process into a series of stages – each performed by a different group; hence, the typical unit of production was small, little mechanised, and requiring none of the space or paraphernalia of large-scale industry. These enter-prises blended unobtrusively into the urban landscape; the small workshop, often a converted house or shop, was the most typical industrial building of inner London. Perhaps, because of this, the importance of their pro-duction came to be overlooked by contemporaries.[1] Indeed, public atten-tion was so sharply focused on the great industries of the coalfields, that, in the year of the Great Exhibition, John Weale concluded that London could be regarded as a 'vast trading and commercial, rather than a manu-facturing town'.[2]

TRANSPORT AND TRADE

Road, canal, rail and coastwise transport

In 1850 we can review both the developed network of improved roads and inland waterways and, in the railways, describe a brand-new system of internal communications, challenging both turnpike road and canal. But we must not allow the more dramatic advance of the railways to over-shadow the continuing importance of the older forms of transport. As the heyday of coaching receded, the symptoms of decline were indeed written large and clear. One by one the famous stage coaches ceased to run along the main roads of the country; by 1850 the coaches of the Sleepy Leeds, the Peak Ranger, the Red Rover had all passed into the history of trans-port; some ignominiously to end their days as summer-houses.[3] The revenues of the turnpike trusts were likewise plunging sharply,[4] yet, at the same time, the total mileage of turnpike roads in 1848 was greater than at any earlier date in the century. It is true that there were marked regional differences in the extent of turnpiking (varying from about a third of the total roads of Middlesex to under 10% in Cornwall, Cumberland and

[1] P. G. Hall (1960), 158.

[2] J. Weale, *London and its vicinity exhibited in 1851* (London, 1851), 220.

[3] G. M. Young (ed.), *Early Victorian England 1830–1865*, 2 vols. (London, 1934), II, 294.

[4] H. J. Dyos and D. H. Aldcroft, *British transport: an economic survey from the seventeenth century to the twentieth* (Leicester, 1969), 223.

Norfolk),[1] but on a national as on a local scale the physical legacy of new roads was permanent. The organisation which created them was in irreversible decline, but widened, straightened and macadamised highways and reconstructed bridges remained.[2] Nor did the passing of the stage coach and of the turnpike trust presage the disappearance of other horse-drawn transport. Local directories continued to list a host of road carriers, and carts and carriages were to crowd the roads which fed the railways for many years to come.

The same was true of the canals. Much has been written about the internecine strife between canal and railway company – by 1850 nearly 1,000 miles or roughly one-fifth of the navigable waterways of Great Britain had passed into railway ownership.[3] Although the income of some canals, like that of the turnpike trusts, had collapsed, some new canals were dug to act as railway feeders or distributors. The canal mileage was to reach its greatest length in 1858. The mature system was not, however, a national network (Figs. 18 and 44). Administratively, it was an inefficient complex of competing undertakings, and parts of the system – as in the west country – were severed from the central arteries of trunk canals. But its greatest overall weakness was the varying gauges of channels and locks, and the constant changes in the permissible draught. If the narrow boat could go virtually anywhere – except on the tub canals of the west country[4] – the larger barges of the northern and southern canals were confined to their own regions.[5] Waterways, however, continued to compete in the carriage of bulky and heavy industrial commodities, especially those from factories and furnaces in waterside locations. In 1848, for example, the tonnage of goods carried by water between Manchester and Liverpool was twice that carried by rail.[6] The decay of the canals was also suspended by the initial emphasis – especially outside north-eastern England – of the railways on passenger traffic.

But the railway was the truly new feature of the age (Fig. 60). The main trunk lines radiated spoke-like from London: in the south-east, two lines to Norwich were complete, so were lines to the main towns of the south coast – Dover, Brighton, Portsmouth and Southampton; westwards, rail communication had reached Plymouth; in the Midlands, Birmingham

[1] *Ibid.*, 222.   [2] C. Singer *et al.* (eds.), V, 535.

[3] C. Hadfield, *British canals: an illustrated history* (Newton Abbot, 2nd ed., 1966).

[4] C. Hadfield, *The canals of south-west England* (Newton Abbot, 1967), *passim.*

[5] H. J. Dyos and D. H. Aldcroft, 108.

[6] W. T. Jackman, *The development of transportation in modern England* (London, 2nd ed., 1962), 741.

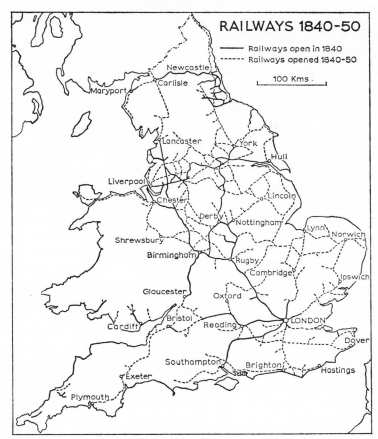

Fig. 60   Railways, 1840–50
Based on: (1) H. G. Lewin, *Early British railways* (London, 1952); (2) G.
Bradshaw, *Map of Great Britain showing the railways* (London and Man-
chester, 1850).

was soon to be served by two routes from the capital; and, in the north,
lines from London flanked the Pennines on both east and west. Many
cross-country lines had also been constructed, leaving conspicuous blanks
only in the south-west and in the north Pennines. By 1852, the most
populous English towns not yet served by a railway were Hereford,
Yeovil and Weymouth. On the other hand, the unco-ordinated schemes
of different companies had complicated the basic railway network; sometimes an exceptional gauge, such as the seven-foot of the Great Western,

had resulted; sometimes the lines of two companies both served the same town, but without a convenient interchange of traffic; sometimes a multiplicity of owners controlled a line; and, by 1850, only three companies could claim to have built a continuous stretch of railway more than a hundred miles in length.[1]

The railway builders had contributed a whole range of new features to the landscape. While the shanty towns of navvies' huts, often hastily constructed from turf, timber and tarpaulin, were ephemeral,[2] the great earthworks and engineering structures which carried the iron roads across England were prominent on an unequalled scale. There was much to look at: the dignified tunnel entrances; the viaducts built in brick, in timber, in iron, prominent against the skyline; the great cuttings gashing the countryside, some raw rock, some grass-grown; the high embankments, some newly planted with trees; the well-designed bridges of timber, stone and brick; as well as smaller features such as engine houses and water towers. Even the smallest rural station could add to landscape novelty. As temporary wooden shelters were replaced by permanent buildings, one company architect might perpetuate a traditional building style, another indulge in the exotic: on the Great Western Railway, for example, the stations between London and Reading were classical in design; to the west of Reading, they were Tudor in inspiration, but they were mainly Gothic at the far west of the line.[3] In the spate of new railway structures the aesthetic as well as the utilitarian had received consideration, and some of the English concepts of rural elegance had rubbed off on to railway architecture.

In the towns the railways had been more conspicuous and robust agents of transformation. At Stockport, the great viaduct strode over the town and 'the whole ravine in which it lies'.[4] At ground level, the incision of railways into the central areas of towns often resulted in the creation of

[1] J. Simmons, *The railways of Britain: an historical introduction* (London, 1961), 61; J. H. Appleton, *The geography of communications in Great Britain* (London, 1962), *passim*; J. A. Patmore, 'The railway network of Merseyside', *Trans. and Papers, Inst. Brit. Geog.*, XXIX (1961), 231–44; J. A. Patmore, 'The railway network of the Manchester conurbation', *Trans. and Papers, Inst. Brit. Geog.*, XXXIV (1964), 159–73; H. J. Dyos and D. H. Aldcroft, 126–45.

[2] T. Coleman, *The railway navvies* (London, 1965), 72–7.

[3] C. Barman, *An introduction to railway architecture* (London, 1950), 30–2, 61–73; C. Barman, *Early British railways* (Harmondsworth, 1950), 32–9.

[4] F. Engels, *The condition of the working class in England in 1844*, translated and edited by W. O. Henderson and W. H. Chaloner (Oxford, 1958), 52.

completely new railway quarters. In central London, road and water had barely felt the challenge of the new railways by 1852,[1] but in the north-west suburbs the building of the Euston terminus (1837) and that of King's Cross (1852) caused a great upheaval. Indeed, King's Cross had carved out a 45-acre site (erasing the old small-pox and fever hospitals and many crowded streets).[2] And around the Great Western terminus, Tyburnia or Paddington New Town had sprung up, so that here, too, the railway had 'altered the whole appearance of the place'.[3] In Liverpool, Manchester and Birmingham, as the detailed researches of J. R. Kellett have shown, the story was much the same. By mid-century, as the railway became a major urban landowner, it had initiated a cycle of demolition (often of slum clearance) and renewal; its inroads into the central business district were matched by a rise in land values, by changing land use, and also by a re-alignment of internal traffic routes. The extent of the railway's land hunger was intensified by the need of competitors each eager to acquire an urban terminus and the manner in which it was satisfied depended significantly on the pre-existing pattern of property ownership.[4] Few towns had resisted the overtures of the railways whose extravagant, often monumental, buildings, befitting the commercial power of their owners, became as nearly a symbol of the Victorian townscape, as castle or cathedral in medieval times.

Thus the importance of the railways in 1850 can hardly be exaggerated: they had not only become 'the iron veins that traverse the frame of our country',[5] but they were also growing into a major industry in terms of the work force and capital employed.[6] Many aspects of life and landscape had felt their transforming touch: towns were assuming new shapes and industry new locations; in the countryside, rural isolation was breaking down, and the farmer, as many contemporaries reported, had acquired new markets. Not least, Englishmen were given new possibilities for the enrichment of life. The railways, as E. J. Hobsbawn has put it, 'transformed the speed of movement...from one measured in single miles per hour to one measured in scores of miles per hour, and introduced the

[1] R. Clayton (ed.), *The geography of Greater London* (London, 1964), 87.

[2] J. Timbs, *Curiosities of London* (London, 1855), 639.

[3] P. Cunningham, *Handbook of London* (London, new ed., 1850), 528.

[4] J. R. Kellett, *The impact of railways on Victorian cities* (London, 1969), 14–15, 125–34, 150–60, 175–88, 244–62.

[5] J. Ruskin, *The seven lamps of architecture* (London, 1849), 182.

[6] H. Pollins, *Britain's railways: an industrial history* (Newton Abbott, 1971), prints statistics for 1850 for the United Kingdom, 49, 56, 65.

notion of a gigantic, nation-wide, complex and exact interlocking routine symbolised by the railway time-table'.[1] One could now 'breakfast in the din of the metropolis' and, by evening, walk on 'the breezy sands of the coast of Devon'.[2] Even the toiling industrial populations were now occasionally set free, by the excursion ticket, for brief, gay, hectic interludes on the occasion of a public holiday. The railways served the nation as lungs as well as arteries.

To transport by road, canal and rail, coastwise shipping must now be added. If this ancient trade had retained only a lesser share of the country's domestic commerce in the face of railway competition, in absolute terms, the volume of coastal cargoes was still increasing in 1850.[3] And, despite the motley fleet which trafficked around England's coasts, with barges, brigs, ketches, schooners and smacks[4] far outnumbering the steamboats sponsored by the railway companies,[5] the quantities handled (including the trade with Ireland) still exceeded the whole of the overseas trade proper. Most commodities were characterised by bulk and a low unit value. As well as the massive trade in coal – some five million tons were shipped annually by the 1850s from the Tyne, Wear and Tees alone[6] – raw materials such as China clay, copper ore and Welsh slate were carried by sea, as were a variety of foodstuffs, including grain and butter. Many of the lesser sea and river ports were also touched by this trade.

Overseas trade

The technological revolution, which was to result in the replacement of wooden sailing ships by iron steamships, was only in its infancy in 1850 but the merchant fleet of the United Kingdom (which totalled some 3.57 million tons at that date) already amounted to one quarter of the world's steam tonnage.[7] The striking progress in long-distance shipping was a direct response to the expansion of England's international trade which, by mid-century, was growing at a faster rate than ever before.[8] The

[1] E. J. Hobsbawn, *Industry and empire* (London, 1969), 110.

[2] M. E. C. Walcott, *A guide to the south coast of England* (London, 1859), xi.

[3] H. J. Dyos and D. H. Aldcroft, 208–10.

[4] B. Greenhill and A. Giffard, *The merchant sailing ship: a photographic history* (Newton Abbot, 1970).

[5] T. R. Gourvish, 'The railways and steamboat competition in early Victorian Britain', *Transport History*, IV (1971), 1–22.

[6] B. F. Duckham, 'The decline of coastal sail: a review article', *Transport History*, II (1969), 75.

[7] H. J. Dyos and D. H. Aldcroft, 232.   [8] B. R. Mitchell and P. Deane, 328.

statistics point not only to the country's manufacturing economy but also to its dependence on foreign trade. The leading imports in 1850, quantities of which were re-exported, were either industrial raw materials (especially cotton, dyewoods and dyestuffs, flax, silk, hemp, wool and timber) or foodstuffs. The nation could no longer feed itself from home agricultural production, and grain, sugar, tea and coffee were among the leading imports. In the export trade cotton goods had by now outpaced woollen manufactures which had for so long been dominant. The cotton export had become nearly three times as valuable as that of woollens (the second commodity) and over four times as valuable as iron and steel which occupied third place; they were followed (in descending order) by hardwares and cutlery, non-ferrous metals and manufactures, clothing and hats, silk goods, and machinery and chemicals.[1]

The robust claim made by Thomas Baines for Liverpool in 1852, that its commercial greatness reached to 'every corner of the globe',[2] could have summed up the geographical pattern of English overseas trade as a whole. In terms of value the strongest commercial links had been forged with North America, but there were also substantial trade flows to and from the underdeveloped parts of the Empire, especially India, and other tropical lands in Asia, in Latin America and Africa. England's trading relationships with the rest of the world were not, however, simply of a bilateral character between an industrial nation and a series of primary producers. There were exceptions. Not least, by 1850, a reciprocal trade in manufactured goods was growing between England and the more advanced industrial countries – especially the U.S.A., and Belgium, France and Germany. As the artificial barriers to Free Trade were dismantled – and its victory was symbolised by the repeal of the Corn Laws[3] – and as the economic structure of the trading nations became more tightly interlocked, England, with its banking, capital, insurance and shipping services, largely controlled the world market.[4]

---

[1] *Ibid.*, 297–303; the statistics, which are indivisible, relate to the United Kingdom as a whole. Much additional commentary on overseas trade appears in J. H. Clapham (1930), 237–50, and (1932), 217–31.

[2] T. Baines, *History of the commerce and town of Liverpool, and of the rise of manufacturing industry in the adjoining counties* (London, 1852), 840; an analysis of Baines' data appears in F. E. Hyde, *Liverpool and the Mersey: an economic history of a port, 1700–1970* (Newton Abbot, 1971), 48–51.

[3] N. McCord, *Free Trade: theory and practice from Adam Smith to Keynes* (Newton Abbot, 1970), 61–97.

[4] H. J. Dyos and D. H. Aldcroft, 233; E. J. Hobsbawn, 134–48.

TOWNS AND CITIES

The 1851 Census revealed how, for the first time, populations classed administratively as 'urban' and 'rural' co-existed in roughly equal numbers. The Census Commissioners found it difficult to demarcate town and country; where, for example, could proper lines be placed in the new suburbs or amidst the congeries of industrial villages? No general definition was stipulated, and in the case of ambiguity it was left to local registrars to nominate and delimit towns. In this empirical fashion the local balance between rural and urban was computed. At one end of the scale, excluding London, only in six registration counties (Lancashire, Warwickshire, Gloucestershire, Staffordshire, the East Riding and Sussex) did the enumerated urban population exceed the rural; at the other end of the scale, in eighteen counties the urban population formed only 30% or less of the total.[1]

In population totals the towns had reached new limits (Fig. 61). We can conveniently define metropolitan London in terms of the Metropolis Management Act of 1855, which covered the area later to be included in the administrative county of 1888. This metropolitan area included about 117 square miles, and contained nearly 2.4 million people (see table on p. 373). It was over six times as populous as Liverpool, the next greatest centre, and there were six other cities, each with over 100,000 people. As in the case of London, it is difficult to define, in geographical as opposed to administrative terms, the limits of these seven provincial cities, but the 1851 Census figures for their municipal boroughs were as follows:

Liverpool	375,955
Manchester–Salford	367,233
Birmingham	232,841
Leeds	172,270
Bristol	137,328
Sheffield	135,310
Bradford	103,310

Around them all, incipient conurbations had sprawled. Furthermore, the 1851 statistics relating to population within the boundaries of municipal boroughs did not, as for Liverpool and Birmingham, include the population of contiguous suburbs. Below these seven provincial cities ranged a hierarchy of smaller places; thirteen other municipal boroughs each had

[1] *Census of 1851: Population Tables, I*, vol. 1, p. l (P.P. 1852–3, lxxxv).

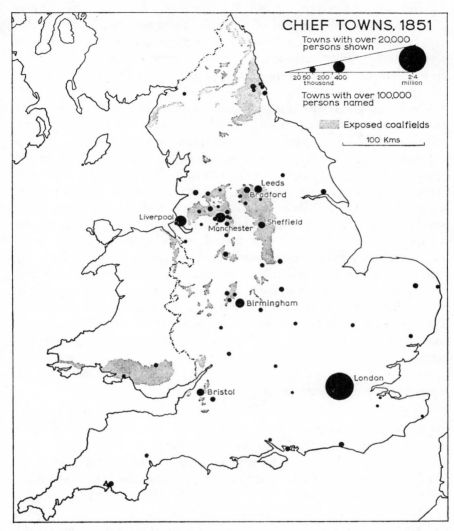

Fig. 61   Chief towns in 1851
Based on *Census of 1851: Population Tables, I*, vol. 1, pp. cciv-ccvii (P.P. 1852–3, lxxxv).
The figure for London is that of the Census division which extended into Middlesex, Surrey and Kent, and which was very similar to the later county of London.

a population of over 50,000; another thirty-two each had over 20,000 inhabitants. At the other end of the scale, there were small towns each with fewer than 2,000 people (such as the 1,707 in the municipal borough of Chippenham) but such semi-rural places were becoming far less representative of an urban centre in 1850 than were the large industrial concentrations.

The urban areas were not only extensive but infinitely complex, and there was no one 'typical' town which could epitomise the geography of urban England. Administratively, the urban areas were governed by a diverse set of local institutions; the age of buildings ranged from the many surviving enclaves of Tudor and Georgian to the 320,000 or so new houses built in England between 1841 and 1851;[1] the urban plan was often formless, but here and there the town planner had made his mark as at Middlesbrough, Ashton-under-Lyne, Crewe and Birkenhead, or in model 'villages' such as Saltaire.[2] Broadly speaking, however, the towns fell into five categories based upon occupations – country and county towns, manufacturing and mining towns, seaports, coastal and inland resorts, and, in a category by itself, London. But such a grouping can only be very imperfect, for many towns straddled two or even more categories. The larger county towns, in particular, hardly fit the scheme, and some, such as Derby, Leicester and Nottingham, were also important industrial centres.

Country towns and county towns

Rural England, in 1850, was still serviced by a close network of small market towns inherited from the pre-railway age. A number of these places had less than 2,000 inhabitants, but many more had from 2,000 to 5,000 people. The 1851 population of some of the country towns of Norfolk such as Diss (2,419), Downham Market (2,867), East Dereham (3,372), Swaffham (3,858), Thetford (4,075) and Wymondham (2,970) points to the modest scale of their activities. Frequently, their appearance had altered so little since 1800 as to give a quality of timelessness often absent in the Victorian town. The railway, when it came, was often relegated to the edge of a town, where a small station, a gas-lit railway inn and a railway terrace, were relatively unobtrusive. The buildings fronting the cobbled high street and market square were still overwhelmingly of local

---

[1] *Census of 1851: Population Tables, I,* vol. I, p. xcv (P.P. 1952–3, lxxxv).

[2] W. Ashworth, *The genesis of modern British town planning* (London, 1954), 118–31.

brick, flint, stone, cob and thatch, although by 1850 the canal and then the railway had sometimes made possible an alien peppering of mass-produced brick and Welsh slate.

Generally speaking, such towns were still in the age of the cart, the carrier, the corn exchange and the retail market, mingling town and country folk once a week in a day of jostling commerce. There were, too, periodic wholesale markets: at Chippenham for Wiltshire cheese, at Chester for cheese sold to the industrial towns of the north-west; at Aylesbury, Evesham and Banbury (to list but a few) for the cattle brought by long-distance drovers whose livelihood the railways would soon capture.[1] In the pages of contemporary trade directories the social and economic role of these towns can be glimpsed: they list not only auctioneers, dealers, innkeepers and tradesfolk, but also varied rural-based industries such as those at Thame, with its fell-mongering and tanning, brewing, basket making, coach building and chair making from beechwood.[2] Yet other craftsmen were noted in the census enumerators' books: Watlington, another small Oxfordshire market town, included braziers, saddlers, wheelwrights, millwrights, coopers and thatchers. The lists of such activities in the small towns of 1850 were very long indeed.[3]

Not surprisingly, however, a number of small towns were quietly reverting to a more completely rural economy. This was the case with six Oxfordshire market towns (Islip, Charlbury, Bampton, Burford, Woodstock and Deddington) which lost their market functions during the nineteenth century.[4] Some towns too had declined as a result of the decrease in stage-coach traffic. By 1845, for example, Staines had lost 'the appearance of bustle and prosperity'. Not half a dozen coaches passed daily instead of the former sixty-eight.[5] On the other hand, not all ancient country towns had shrunk, and many showed clear symptoms of outgrowing their semi-rural status. Market Harborough provided an example. Its inns (like those of Melton Mowbray) were still courting wealthy patrons from amongst the followers of the Quorn and Pytchley hunts; but simultaneously, the town had adopted the gasworks, the railway and some factory industry; off some of its side streets, clusters of back-to-back houses and several

[1] C. S. Orwin and E. H. Whetham, 24–8.
[2] W. Guest *et al.* in M. Lobel (ed.), *V.C.H. Oxfordshire*, VII (1962), 183–4.
[3] E. Craster in M. Lobel (ed.), *V.C.H. Oxfordshire*, VIII (1964), 233; *Guides to Official Sources*, No. 2, 28–31.
[4] A. F. Martin and R. W. Steel (eds.), *The Oxford region* (Oxford, 1954), 131.
[5] S. Reynolds in S. Reynolds (ed.), *V.C.H. Middlesex*, III (1962), 25.

narrow and unhealthy courts could be explored; its death rate was more akin to that of an industrial town – so high as to warrant a survey by a Board of Health inspector.[1] This situation was not unusual; where the inn yards, burgage plots and gardens of country towns had been infilled with inferior cottage property, the problems of congestion and sanitation were just as real as in a new cotton town. The places petitioning for the application of the Public Health Act of 1848 included not only Bradford and Dewsbury, but Diss, Eton and Ely: by mid-century, Barnsley and Barnstaple alike were awakening to the insanitary nature of an urban environment.[2]

The most acute problems belonged to those county towns with large industrial populations. Legacies from the past often obstructed modern re-planning. In Nottingham, for example, the imprisonment of the town behind its common meadows, prior to the enclosure of 1845, had resulted in a chronically overcrowded mass of courts, alleys and lanes, but not even the release of new land for building provided a quick solution to the urgent need for decent working-class housing.[3] Coventry (comparable to a large county town) was likewise still hemmed in, in 1849, by about 2,000 acres of Lammas and Michaelmas lands over which freemen and others had rights of pasturage, thus 'depriving the inhabitants from building their residences and places of business in airy situations, generally confining them to the limits of the ancient city'.[4] One result of overcrowding was that old town houses, formerly merchant residences, slid down the social scale, and then suffered swift deterioration as they were split up into workshops and tenements. The evils of dirt, overcrowding, disease and outworn housing, intensified by the urban revolution of the early railway age, were not confined to a few of the larger county towns. By 1850 it would have been hard to find exceptions; Chester, Gloucester, Shrewsbury, Exeter and York were included amongst those places singled out for attention by the Parliamentary Commissioners on the health of towns.[5]

[1] R. A. McKinley in J. M. Lee and R. A. McKinley (eds.), *V.C.H. Leicestershire*, v (1964), 142.

[2] *Returns relating to the Public Health Act of 1848*, 3–13 (P.P. 1852–3, xcvi).

[3] J. D. Chambers, *Modern Nottingham in the making* (Nottingham, 1945), 6–38; S. D. Chapman, 'Working-class housing in Nottingham during the industrial revolution' in S. D. Chapman (ed.), 135–63.

[4] *Second Report of Commissioners for Large Towns*, Appendix, Part II, 262 (P.P. 1845, xviii).

[5] *Ibid.*, Appendix, Parts I and II.

Manufacturing and mining towns

A striking aspect of the urban geography of 1850 was the existence of an inland group of giant provincial towns such as Manchester, Birmingham, Leeds, Bradford and Sheffield, each with over 100,000 inhabitants. Together with Salford, Manchester, 'the masterpiece of the industrial revolution',[1] contained over 400,000 people: the population of the area which is today defined as the Manchester conurbation already included in 1851, 1,063,000 people. Furthermore, the coalescence of nearby towns had begun: the first edition of the Ordnance Survey Map (1848) shows that a continuous line of houses flanked the eight miles of road from Manchester to Oldham; and that Ashton-under-Lyne, Hyde and Dukinfield were also fused by ribbon development.[2] Evidently this pattern of growth had become endemic in the outward sprawl of the large industrial towns. The point was well made by Robert Rawlinson describing Birmingham in 1849. 'Most of our large towns', he wrote, have 'received their increments chiefly from buildings erected along the roads branching out into the country, presenting so many streets radiating from a centre, but leaving the intervening spaces to be irregularly and imperfectly filled up at subsequent periods as change or necessity directed.'[3] In Birmingham, urban extension had, in fact, taken place across the borough boundary along routes leading out of the town by road, railway and canal; Balsall Heath, for example, had grown out from the centre as an elongated limb along Moseley Road and the Birmingham and Gloucester Railway.[4]

Within the expanded urban frontiers important changes had also taken place in the internal geography of some large towns. When Engels visited Manchester he was able to identify 'a fairly large commercial district... almost entirely given over to offices and warehouses'; the lower floors were occupied by shops, there were few permanent residents, and the main streets were congested with an enormous volume of traffic.[5] As streets were improved, as the railways intruded into the towns, and as larger civic and commercial buildings were built to reflect the new municipal status, the competition for central space had grown greater. One

[1] F. Engels, 50.

[2] T. W. Freeman, *The conurbations of Great Britain* (Manchester, 1959), 3, 135.

[3] R. Rawlinson, *Report to the General Board of Health on...Birmingham* (1849); quoted in C. Gill, *History of Birmingham*, 1 (Birmingham, 1952), 367.

[4] C. R. Elrington and P. M. Tillott in W. B. Stephens (ed.), *V.C.H. Warwickshire*, VII (1964), 16.

[5] F. Engels, 54.

result, apparent in the 1851 Census for some of the central wards of Leeds, Birmingham, Bradford and Manchester, was that the city centres were already dying as residential areas.[1]

Beyond, the more familiar image of the large industrial town was reached in the inner built-up zones where industry and poor-class houses were tightly intermixed. In Manchester, where this belt was, on average, one and a half miles in width, most of the worst features of uncontrolled expansion were to be found. Here was an area crammed with a medley of industrial premises – bone and cotton mills, gas and print works, tanneries and warehouses; it was criss-crossed by road, canal and river, and eaten into by railway sidings and goods yards; the intervening living spaces were characterised by narrow rows of cottages, a chapel here and there, a workhouse, and, in an empty corner, the paupers' cemetery.[2] The back-to-back terraces separated a labyrinth of narrow sunless alleys, cul-de-sacs and courts, where the scavenger seldom took his cart, where the water supply was deficient, and where poverty and filth ruled. Inner Manchester was not, of course, unique in all this. Central Bradford was just as 'dirty and uncomfortable', with its workers' houses at the bottom of the valley packed between high factory buildings.[3] In Leeds, too, near the flood plain of the river Aire and the Timble Beck, was a district of 'narrow, crooked and irregular' streets where 'a great number of dye houses and other manufactories' were interspersed with the dwellings of the working classes.[4] But the town was especially characterised by its disconnected rows of back-to-back houses: in the Ordnance Survey 'Five foot' plan for Leeds, published in 1850, there were no less than 360 streets where these urban cottages, 'one up and one down', often with a ground-floor space of as little as 5 square yards, had been constructed in the years since 1815.[5] And Birmingham, although it was regarded as comparatively healthy, had nonetheless developed extensive slums, built without order, slight and cheap, and only penetrated through a maze of small undrained streets and unpaved courts.[6] In most large towns such jerry-built districts had sprung up piecemeal, often the investment of little speculators,

[1] T. W. Freeman, 82, 138, 172.

[2] O.S. Plan of Manchester 1/1056, First Edition (1851).

[3] F. Engels, 49.

[4] *Second Report of Commissioners for Large Towns*, Appendix, Part II, 313 (P.P. 1845, xviii).

[5] M. W. Beresford, 'The back-to-back house in Leeds, 1787–1937', in S. D. Chapman (ed.), 95–132.

[6] R. Rawlinson, 23.

developing single fields here and there, and lacking even the rudiments of an overall plan.[1]

If the bulk of the working class were still housed near the town centres, the exodus of the well-to-do had started by 1850. Commuting by private carriage and horse omnibus – but not yet in any great numbers by main-line railway[2] – they had taken up residence in the outer suburbs. Thus Engels noted of Manchester, 'The villas of the upper classes are surrounded by gardens and lie in the higher and remoter parts of Chorlton and Ard-wick or on the breezy heights of Cheetham Hill, Broughton and Pendle-ton.'[3] In Sheffield, the larger villas were mostly located on the higher, south-facing slopes;[4] likewise, in Leeds the 'better classes' tenanted the higher parts of the town in 'cheerful open streets'.[5] And yet, although many suburbs contained individual houses laid out in an elegant and spacious manner, overall planning was almost as uncommon as in the industrial neighbourhoods. The Edgbaston estate, where the Birmingham business man carried into 'his retirement a correct taste, not only for the useful, but also for the beautiful and picturesque'[6] was an exceptional development. More characteristically, the built-up area made haphazard contact with older villages, which became the nuclei of new suburban districts, with cores of older buildings forming distinctive inliers in the new landscape. Yet farther afield, beyond the continuously built-up fringe, old agricultural villages were colonised by merchants and factory owners, wealthy and land hungry, so that by mid-century Fallowfield, Withington and Didsbury were already partly suburban to Manchester,[7] and, in effect, Chapel Allerton and Headingley were suburbs of Leeds.[8] Residential segregation by social and economic class had become firmly entrenched in the major towns.

In Bolton, by the late 1840s, there were 61 cotton factories; in Bury, in 1845, there were 12 woollen manufactories and 26 cotton mills; Oldham,

[1] D. Ward, 'The urban plan of Leeds and the factors which have conditioned its growth', unpublished Leeds University M.A. thesis (1960), 78–106.

[2] J. R. Kellett, 356–7.

[3] F. Engels, 55.

[4] A. J. Hunt, 'The morphology and growth of Sheffield' in D. L. Linton (ed.), 237.

[5] J. Smith, 146.

[6] C. Gill, 366, quoting F. White, *General and commercial directory and topography of the borough of Birmingham* (Sheffield, 1855).

[7] T. W. Freeman, 4.

[8] R. Baker, 'On the industrial and sanitary economy of the borough of Leeds', *British Association Report* (1858), 164.

too, had over 100 cotton mills, all worked by steam; and even Wigan, on the western margin of the textile district, had 26 cotton mills by 1846.[1] Appropriately enough, Engels had designated such places 'factory towns'. In east Lancashire and west Yorkshire the Ordnance Survey town plans, published after 1843 at a scale of 1/1056, show parallel rows of workers' cottages, interrupted only by textile mill, chapel and church. The buildings, and in particular the houses, bore the marks of their relatively rapid construction. In Stalybridge many streets appeared 'rather hastily and imperfectly constructed', and St Helens seemed a town 'built in a hurry'. The stone-built towns of the Pennine valleys were more solidly erected and, perhaps, less raw to the eye; but, at their worst, the factory towns were little better than casual accumulations of factories and slums.[2] Their skies were smoke-laden (so much in Lancashire as to have 'blackened the houses of red brick')[3] and there was more filth underfoot. Dr Lyon Playfair's investigations, for example, carefully illustrated with statistics and maps, had elicited many 'melancholy facts': an inadequacy of sewers, polluted streams, a lack of constant water supply, unpaved and unscavenged streets – these were some of the 'nuisances' common to many Lancashire towns.[4] Ashton-under-Lyne, 'the most elegant ordinary town in the country',[5] with its planned streets, its factories segregated from the 'new bright red cottages' gave 'every appearance of comfort',[6] but was almost unique. In the main, improvement had been confined to town centres, where newly erected town halls, mechanics institutes, public libraries and baths, gas-lighting, and a limited 'public' water supply, were now common. Even so, the textile towns remained predominantly huge working-class communities, as a recent study of Macclesfield shows.[7] They were too poorly equipped to be effective service centres; a limited range of retail shops and several score of ale houses alone served the needs of thousands.

---

[1] S. Lewis, I, 299, 456; II, 377; III, 475–6.

[2] R. Millward, *Lancashire* (London, 1955), 81–91; E. Butterworth, *An historical account of the towns of Ashton-under-Lyne, Stalybridge, and Dukinfield* (Ashton, 1842), 145; *Chambers's Edinburgh Journal*, No. 119, n.s., 11 April 1846, quoted in T. C. Barker and J. R. Harris, *A Merseyside town in the industrial revolution: St Helens 1750–1900* (Liverpool, 1954), 313; G. M. Young (ed.), I, 166.

[3] F. Engels, 49–51.

[4] *Second Report of Commissioners for Large Towns*, Appendix, Part II, *passim* (P.P. 1845, xviii).

[5] E. Butterworth, 54.   [6] F. Engels, 52.

[7] C. S. Davies, *A history of Macclesfield* (Manchester, 1961), 166–8.

The 'mining and hardware' towns were facsimiles, only in part, of other industrial towns. The ubiquitous red rash of inferior dwellings had wrapped around most of them by 1850. But they lacked the disciplined lay-out induced by the factory; a neat framework of streets could not readily be set down on land pitted with subsidence and pocked with furnace and mine. Urban disorder had resulted where houses and industry had vied for possession of the land. Thus, for example, Burslem, Hanley and Longton were reported to be built in an 'irregular and rather dispersed manner'[1] and West Bromwich parish appeared as 'a large straggling town, the buildings being scattered about without much order, but dense enough in some parts to form streets'.[2] Many of the Black Country towns were like this, and it was the same elsewhere. The local improvement acts promoted by municipal corporations – Leeds and Liverpool in 1842, Birkenhead in 1843, Manchester in 1844 and 1845, Nottingham, St Helens and Wallasey in 1845, Newcastle, Burnley and Southport in 1846, and so on[3] – had done little by 1850 to put a brake on the worst evils of urban laissez-faire.

Seaports

The relative importance of the six principal ports of England in 1850 can be seen from table 4.1 below.

Table 4.1   *Vessels, tonnage and exports for the six principal English ports, 1850*

	Inwards		Outwards	
	Ships	Tons	Ships	Tons
London	9,914	1,904,948	6,523	1,384,683
Liverpool	4,531	1,605,315	4,807	1,656,938
Newcastle	2,032	316,297	5,174	849,572
Hull	2,485	466,430	1,764	369,743
Southampton	626	152,117	603	147,519
Bristol	730	137,812	276	79,448

Note: The figures are combined totals for British and foreign ships.
Source: *Vessels and Tonnage etc., 1816–1850* (P.P. 1851, lii).

[1] *Second Report of Commissioners for Large Towns*, Appendix, Part I, 9 (P.P. 1845, xviii).
[2] S. Lewis, I, 401.
[3] S. D. Chapman (ed.), 155–6.

If we exclude London – which was more than a great seaport – the pre-eminence of Liverpool, also the largest provincial town of 1850, was un-challenged. And indeed, although the port of London handled more vessels and a slightly larger tonnage, the export trade of Liverpool, as measured by value, was over twice that of London and three times that of Hull. By 1852 Liverpool shipped over 1,000 million yards of cotton piece-goods, a quarter of a million tons of coal and 315,000 tons of iron bars, rails, hoops, rods and pig-iron[1] – all commodities reflecting its coalfield in-dustrial hinterland. The most distinctive manifestation of this economy was a complex system of massive docks and warehouses. In 1857, when the Merseyside Docks and Harbour Board assumed control of the port, it acquired no less than 15½ miles of quayside and 199 acres of enclosed water space. Many docks were newly constructed at mid-century: in 1848 alone five new docks were opened, and, by 1852, a further three;[2] a continuous granite wall impounded the Liverpool shore, to the rear of which stood massive warehouses, some six or seven storeys high, austerely built of cast iron and brick, and already dominating the waterfront.[3] The river now served a city larger than industrial Leeds or Birmingham. It contained some of the most notorious examples of overcrowding in courts and cellars, as well as of undrained and unpaved streets, and of high mortality and sickness rates;[4] at the same time many of its middle-class citizens had already deserted the old town to occupy villas in 'pleasant villages from Bootle to Aigburth', or even as far afield as Hoylake and Southport.[5]

In the other major ports the work of extensive dock improvement had begun somewhat falteringly. At Southampton, the first modern dock had opened only in 1842; and ships under sail still far outnumbered those propelled by steam. At Hull, the construction of the Railway Dock (1846) and the Victoria Dock (1850) more clearly foreshadowed the pattern of its modern dockland; the trade of the port was, moreover, rising steadily and its wharves were among the few in England (including those of Liverpool and the new railway port of Fleetwood) where the tonnage of steam vessels exceeded that of sailing ships. But in some seaports relatively little change was visible in 1850. This was so on the Tyne and the bulk of

---

[1] W. Smith (ed.), *A scientific survey of Merseyside* (Liverpool, 1953), 157.
[2] J. E. Allison, *The Mersey estuary* (Liverpool, 1949), 29–32.
[3] Q. Hughes, *Seaport: architecture and townscape in Liverpool* (London, 1964), 7–39.
[4] J. H. Treble, 'Liverpool working-class housing, 1801–1851' in S. D. Chapman (ed.), 167–220.
[5] T. Baines, *Liverpool in 1859* (London, 1859), 8.

the coal cargoes still left under sail from Newcastle – as from Sunderland and the other north-east ports. Bristol, notwithstanding its ancient importance, was likewise not keeping abreast of the newer ports serving industrial England.[1]

Apart from the six principal ports, many smaller harbours still shared in the coastal trade. They were the maritime equivalent of the country market town, and the railway ports had not yet captured all their commerce.[2] Indeed, in the statistics for 1850, it was possible to list a further 64 places in England where vessels were registered and where a quantifiable amount of shipping had 'entered and cleared Coastwise'.[3] The smallest harbours, such as Bridport, Chichester and Chepstow, had each cleared less than a tonnage of 30,000 in the year, and, moreover, like a score of other small ports in 1850, including Rye, Penzance and Scarborough, they had never been entered, so the return informs us, by a single steam vessel in the whole of that year.

Coastal and inland resorts

Seaside resorts had expanded more rapidly than any other group of English towns[4] and, in so doing, had overtaken inland spas. Symptomatic of these changes, the population of Brighton came to exceed that of Bath by 1851. A. B. Granville visited and described a number of sea-bathing places around the English coasts in 1839–40;[5] but his itinerary had its gaps, especially along the south coast where many seaside villages were fast becoming 'places of resort'. Seaside places also figured prominently in Spencer Thomson's account of the health resorts of Britain in 1860.[6] Brighton, with a population of 65,569 in 1851, stood apart, far ahead of its rivals in visitors and in built-up area.[7] But Hastings (16,966), Ramsgate (11,838) and Margate (10,099) each exceeded 10,000 inhabitants; Weymouth (9,458) and Torquay (7,903) were not far behind. On the other coasts, only Scarborough (12,915) and Whitby (10,899), which like Dover (22,244), were also small seaports, could match the importance of

[1] J. H. Bird, 30.

[2] J. D. Chambers (1961), 59.

[3] *Returns of the Number and Tonnage of Sailing and Steam Vessels*, 4–5 (P.P. 1851, lii).

[4] *Census for 1851: Population Tables*, I, vol. 1, pp. xlviii–l (P.P. 1852–3, lxxxv).

[5] A. B. Granville, *The spas of England and principal sea-bathing places*, 2 vols. (London, 1841).

[6] S. Thomson, *Health resorts of Britain; and how to profit by them* (London, 1860).

[7] E. W. Gilbert, *Brighton, old ocean's bauble* (London, 1954), 153–5.

the southern towns. The resorts of Lancashire and Cheshire were still embryonic; Southport (4,765) was the largest; Blackpool had a resident population of only 2,000, and New Brighton, recently planted among sand dunes, comprised little more than a 'few clusters of houses and villas' in a 'perfect desert'.[1] Even less developed were the remote beaches of Cornwall which received only a trickle of visitors. The image of St Ives was that of 'an ugly, narrow, dirty, dull town',[2] and Looe was still supported mainly by its pilchard fisheries. Moreover, the future of the Cornish resorts was regarded as by no means secure, and, although Spencer Thomson considered that 'the lines of rail will by degrees bring into notice other spots suited for invalid residence', he thought 'the extreme distance from the great centres of English life must prove a serious obstacle'.[3]

Each resort did its utmost to imitate Brighton,[4] and this may be one cause of the similarities between the seaside towns of 1850. Piers and promenades were becoming as ubiquitous as bathing machines had been by 1800, and even the boarding houses and hotels were often of a standard type, prompting one critic to admonish the 'interminable terraces, parades, paragons and parabolas of houses...which mere brick-and-mortar speculators have run up'.[5] For leisure, as well as for labour, urban environments had been mass-produced by the early Victorians. Notwithstanding this, almost every resort had some individual character. The varied physique of the coastline had ensured that this was so. In some towns, such as Torquay (where the building levels girdled the semi-circular bay, the lower containing shops, the middle stone-built terraces, the upper detached villas) a restricted site had closely guided the plan of the town.[6] But at others, such as Southport, the flat, sandy shores had enabled the designs of the drawing board to be transferred to the ground more easily.[7] At Bournemouth, Granville concluded that nature had done everything, and that the hand of man had only to fashion 'and suitably and judiciously to convert to its own purpose'.[8] His advice was followed, but by 1850, the future resort was little more than a coastal variant of an upper-class suburb with many detached houses shaded by trees and

[1] A. B. Granville, II, 11.   [2] M. Walcott, 544.   [3] S. Thomson, 164.
[4] E. W. Gilbert (1954), 13.   [5] A. B. Granville, II, 526.
[6] *Illustrated London News*, XVI (1850), 41–2.
[7] F. A. Bailey, 'The origin and growth of Southport', *Town Planning Rev.*, XXI (1950), 297–317; F. A. Bailey, *A history of Southport* (Southport, 1955).
[8] A. B. Granville, II, 532.

beautified by flowering shrubs.[1] Bournemouth was not alone: differences in Victorian social classes were widely reflected at the seaside as well as in the suburbs. Not only did some resorts such as Scarborough (in its new and old towns respectively) have a fashionable and unfashionable end,[2] but whole towns were already characterised by the nature of their clientele. Thus, while on the one hand, the steamer service to Gravesend had made it the resort of the Cockney trippers;[3] on the other, Brighton was more nearly 'part of the "west end" of London maritimized'.[4] Finally, by 1851, a number of seaside resorts had gained a permanent residential population; the invalid and the elderly were amongst the many who had recently migrated to the English coastal towns.

Although A. B. Granville was able to identify 70 spas in England associated with the taking of mineral waters he had to admit, in 1841, that many were 'growing out of fashion' and some of those most in repute at the beginning of the century were 'nearly forgotten'.[5] The map he compiled of these places must also be looked at with a sceptical eye for it included 'spas' such as Shap Wells in Westmorland and Houghton-le-Spring in County Durham which were little more than villages, and towns such as Clitheroe and Thetford, where the springs were a very subsidiary activity.[6] The 1851 Census, in its recognition of four principal watering places – Bath, Leamington, Cheltenham and Tunbridge Wells[7] – gave a more realistic assessment of the contribution of the inland spa to urban life, but it is helpful, in addition, to note the old-established centres of Harrogate and Buxton, which were to acquire a new lease of life with the arrival of the railways. Indeed, the major inland spas, although they were being rapidly overtaken by their coastal competitors, were by no means dead in 1850. Bath and Cheltenham were still the second and third largest of all English resorts and the rate of increase of the major spas was still above the national average for all towns.

The landscape of the spa town was largely a response to medical and social fashion. The focus of its activities were the springs, thermal or chalybeate, and their locations had guided the layouts of their towns. In

---

[1] C. H. Mate and C. Riddle, *Bournemouth, 1810–1910* (Bournemouth, 1910), 64 *et seq.*

[2] A. B. Granville, I, 176–7. [3] E. W. Gilbert (1954), 18.

[4] A. B. Granville, II, 565. [5] A. B. Granville, I, xxxv.

[6] The places recognised by Granville are mapped in J. A. Patmore, 'The spa towns of Britain' in R. P. Beckinsale and J. M. Houston (eds.), *Urbanization and its problems* (Oxford, 1968), 48.

[7] *Census for 1851: Population Tables*, I, vol. I, p. xlix (P.P. 1852–3, lxxxv).

Harrogate, for example, there were two distinct settlements, High and Low Harrogate, centred on different groups of springs; but at Cheltenham, where the springs were scattered over a considerable area, no less than seven separate spas had left a legacy in the fabric of the town. As well as taking the waters in pump rooms, in saline baths or in 'hydros', visitors were caught up in a social round, manifest in formal parades, in assembly rooms, in large hotels and in public gardens. By 1850, the developments at Leamington provided a coherent expression of these needs. The new town, laid out in 1808, was in its heyday; its spacious streets and dignified squares had matured; and its newly created gardens on the banks of the river Leam were also patronised by a leisured class of visitor. In a different architectural idiom, it had much in common with Bath, the great eighteenth-century spa; both clung to a concept of urban elegance which was fast disappearing from the English scene.[1]

London

Two outstanding characteristics were often emphasised by eyewitnesses of London's geography in 1850. In the first place, there was the simple fact of its size: 'this huge magnitude which drives every other feeling out of mind'[2] was the reaction of one American. Indeed, it was a popular diversion to rise above the great metropolis in a balloon,[3] and look down on the growing city. It filled the Victorian Englishman with pride, albeit occasionally tinged with anxiety, for hardly a day passed without some 'new street takes the place of the green field'.[4] The metropolitan area as defined by the Metropolis Management Act of 1855 (the same, incidentally, as the county of London to be created in 1888) covered some 117 square miles and included a population of nearly 2.4 million. Beyond lay the limits of the Metropolitan Police District up to a radius of 15 miles or so from Charing Cross (Fig. 79); the extent of this 'Greater London' covered some 693 square miles and included a total population of 2.7 million (see table on p. 373). On the north bank, the three components of historic London, the City, the West End and the East End, now formed a solid mass of houses for over six miles from east to west; and extensive development on the south bank had given the capital a breadth of four miles from north to south. Beyond, its suburban arms extended, octopus-

---

[1] J. A. Patmore (1968), 62–5.
[2] W. Ware, *Sketches of European capitals* (Boston, Mass., 1851), 252.
[3] J. H. Banks & Co., *A balloon view of London*: folding map (London, 1851).
[4] J. Weale, 59.

like, creeping into the countryside along main roads and railways (Fig. 78). Places such as Kilburn, Tottenham, West Ham, Lewisham and Balham had now been grafted on to the body of London, as improved public transport – including omnibus, steamboat and train – made a quicker journey to work possible for the growing tide of daily commuters.[1] In the spaces between the ribbon development, detached suburbs, such as Finchley, Norwood and Plaistow (separated by shrinking patches of park and common, woodland and marsh, pasture fields and brick-fields) were only a stone's throw from the new urban boundary.

In the second place, the internal complexity of London was the subject of frequent comment. A bewildered German visitor had decided that 'no other town presents so strong a contrast between its various quarters'.[2] Indeed, the metropolis was a loose aggregate of contrasting settlements. According to one contemporary, by 1850 it had 'swallowed the episcopal city of Westminster, the boroughs of Southwark and Greenwich, the towns of Woolwich, Deptford and Wandsworth, the watering places of Hampstead, Highgate, Islington, Acton, Kilburn,...the fishing town of Barking' and many 'once secluded and ancient villages'.[3] These older nuclei of the conurbation still administered their own affairs; Greater London, outside the City, was governed by no fewer than 300 bodies, many of parish status.[4] Muddle, mismanagement and local self-interest prevailed; it was 'a province covered with houses'; and a Royal Commission of 1854 concluded that 'its diameter...is so great...its area is so large that each inhabitant is in general acquainted only with his own quarter'.[5]

In so far as London was made up of distinctive communities, each could form the subject of a separate description. But in its diversity London also mirrored the rest of England. In the narrow sense of urban architecture, for example, contemporaries regarded it as a truism that most of the 'distinctive peculiarities' of the provincial towns were present 'in one unnoticed corner or other of the vast metropolis'.[6] But in a broader sense the essence of early Victorian England was distilled in its capital. The

[1] T. C. Barker and M. Robbins, *A history of London Transport: passenger travel and the development of the metropolis* (London, 1964), I, 25–68; J. R. Kellett, 365–71.

[2] M. Schlesinger, *Saunterings in and about London*, English ed. by Otto Wenekstern (London, 1853), 13.

[3] J. Weale, 60.

[4] G. M. Young (ed.), I, 204.

[5] Quoted in A. Briggs, *Victorian cities* (London, 1963), 332–3.

[6] J. Weale, 450.

remodelling of parts of central London from its foundations symbolised the vitality of the mid-century scene; new, grander buildings for government, finance, religion, clubs, City gilds, museums and art galleries were daily altering the skyline. The City, deserted by resident merchants and already beginning to empty of poorer-class population, was the commercial hub of the manufacturing nation – although still set in narrow streets and cramped counting houses. The port of London, a rich 'commerical Aladdin's cave', its docks growing quickly down-river, was England's window to the world, a direct manifestation of expanding imperial and international status. On the other hand, the preservation of the royal parks in London suggested rather a national nostalgia for the older, the more elegant and more rural way of life which Lavergne noted in 1855 – even in the city environment.[1] And in suburbia too, by 1850, the urgent need 'to snatch a clear piece of country from the general fate, and to provide a belt of pure air'[2] around London was recognised. In the final analysis, however, London best epitomised the character and problems of England in this age, by bringing wealth and poverty so sharply together. At one extreme, in the vicinity of the parks, amidst 'a velvety luscious green' stood houses 'like palaces with stone terraces and verandas',[3] but at the other were the squalid rookeries of inner London,[4] the Agar Town so vividly described by Dickens;[5] and the widespread mediocrity of urban environment condemned by Ruskin: 'the pitiful concretions of lime and clay...about our capital'.[6] Indeed, the naked facts of London's health problem, marshalled in a string of parliamentary reports,[7] were startling enough: such facts as the 80,000 houses (inhabited by 640,000 people) unsupplied with water, or, the subsoil sodden with decaying sewage, were soon to motivate reform. Meanwhile, the London of 1850, like the nation at large, was testimony to aspiration and indifference, to innovation and conservatism, to solid achievement and abysmal failure – it was a vivid mosaic of black and white. Such were the half-secure foundations from which the geographical changes of the rest of the Victorian age had to spring.

[1] L. de Lavergne, 133.   [2] J. Weale, 465.   [3] M. Schlesinger, 13–14.

[4] G. M. Young (ed.), I, 175.   [5] *Household Words* (1851).   [6] J. Ruskin, 165.

[7] G. M. Young (ed.), I, 201–2, lists these; see also A. S. Wolh, 'The housing of the working classes in London, 1815–1914' in S. D. Chapman (ed.), 15–54.

Chapter 5

THE CHANGING FACE OF ENGLAND:
1850–*circa* 1900

J. T. COPPOCK

It was not so much 1900 as 1914 that marked 'the real economic terminus of the nineteenth century'.[1] Over the span of years since 1850 no revolution transformed the face of England as the enclosure movement and the industrial revolution had done during the preceding hundred years; rather there were changes of degree and of emphasis. Nevertheless, they were on a considerable scale: the population doubled, despite large-scale emigration; living standards almost doubled, generating new demands; industrial production quadrupled and became more diversified; and the number of people living in towns trebled. England was becoming increasingly an urban and industrial society.

If an octogenarian alive in 1911 had reflected upon the changes in the landscape of his youth he would have noticed chiefly changes of scale and degree. In the towns he would recall considerable improvements in the quality of the urban environment; streets had been lit, paved and drained; the centres of cities had been extensively rebuilt; and the quality of the new housing had been improved even if in an uninspiring fashion. Schools, churches, public buildings and public parks were all more numerous, although, around the city centres and in stagnating towns, slums remained. Above all, he would have been struck by changes in the scale of urbanisation, by the vast expanses of slate roofs which met his eye. The differences in the countryside would not have been so obvious to him; yet a less prosperous and less well-tended air, a greener landscape, a spatter of derelict fields, occasionally an abandoned farmstead or cottage, some new orchards and plantations would all have indicated quite fundamental changes.

[1] W. Smith, *An economic geography of Great Britain* (2nd ed., London, 1953), 63.

POPULATION

Perhaps the most widespread of all the changes of the age was the re-distribution of population. According to the decennial censuses, the population of England and Wales rose from 17.9 million in 1851 to 36.1 million in 1911, but the number living in rural districts fell from 8.9 million to 7.9 million, and their share of population from about 50% to 22%; at the same time, the urban population, as defined in the census reports, rose by 19.3 million, or 218%, to reach 28.1 million in 1911.[1] These figures underestimate the scale of both rural depopulation and urban growth, for the failure of administrative boundaries to keep pace with changes in the distribution of population resulted in the inclusion of urban populations within so-called rural districts. From a careful examination of the census data, C. M. Law has calculated that the true urban population was underestimated by almost 700,000 in 1851 (and the rural population correspondingly overestimated) and by more than 2,300,000 in 1911.[2]

Rural population. This redistribution was largely due to widespread migration from the countryside, encouraged by improved communications, better opportunities for employment elsewhere, and the changing structure of agriculture.[3] Fig. 62 shows the net changes in population density, although this too minimises the extent of areas where population was decreasing; for a rising population in many enumeration districts merely indicates that gains in the towns within those districts exceeded losses in their rural areas.

This loss of population was neither uniform nor continuous; in some districts numbers were already falling by the 1850s and continued to do so in each succeeding decade. More generally, the downward trend began in the 1860s or 1870s and was sometimes reversed by suburban development or by the construction of a new railway line. In south-east England and in the industrial districts of the Midlands and northern England, numbers increased in each decade, although the population of the remoter parishes often declined.

Where the population in rural districts grew, this was due primarily to the expansion of towns beyond their administrative boundaries, and to the

[1] C. M. Law, 'The growth of urban population in England and Wales', *Trans. and Papers, Inst. Brit. Geog.*, XLI (1967), 126.

[2] *Ibid.*, 126, 130.

[3] R. Lawton, 'Rural depopulation in nineteenth century England' in R. W. Steel and R. Lawton (eds.), *Liverpool essays in geography* (Liverpool, 1967), 247–55.

development of dormitory settlements. In Sussex, increasing numbers of those working in the towns chose to live in rural areas; and in Cheshire cottages were tenanted by workers in neighbouring industries.[1] Mining, too, greatly affected numbers in some rural areas. The production of coal was expanding throughout the period, and new pits were being sunk, often among farmland, and new settlements created, for example, north of the Tyne and in east Durham. Ironstone mining similarly contributed to the growth of population in rural parts of the east Midlands. In contrast, the lead dales of the Pennines, and the tin and copper mining districts of Cornwall, were affected by the falling demands for their products in the face of overseas competition. Lead mining was generally expanding in the 1850s and production reached a peak in the early 1880s; thereafter, both employment and output declined, although the blow was softened by the fact that miners with smallholdings could and did become full-time farmers.[2] Production of copper and tin reached their peaks in the 1850s and 1870s respectively and thereafter their mining communities began to decline.[3]

Migration from rural areas was a near-universal feature of this period, irrespective of whether populations were increasing or declining, although the rate of migration fell at the turn of the century as fertility declined and there were fewer potential migrants.[4] Moreover, it was selective, in that it was predominantly a movement of young people between the ages of 15 and 35, in that more women migrated than men (except from areas where mining was declining), and in that employees were more likely to move than employers.[5] Employment in the countryside was generally less well paid than in the towns; industrial wage rates were some 50% higher than agricultural rates throughout the period, and opportunities for employment in rural areas were not only fewer but were declining.[6] For young

[1] *Report on the Decline in the Agricultural Population of Great Britain, 1881–1906*, 24 (P.P. 1906, xcvi); *R.C. on Labour*, vol. 1 (England), pt. 4, *Reps. by Mr Roger C. Richards*, 97 (P.P. 1893–4, xxxv).

[2] B. R. Mitchell with P. Deane, *Abstract of British historical statistics* (Cambridge, 1962), 166; J. W. House, *North-eastern England: population movements and the landscape since the early 19th century* (Newcastle upon Tyne, 1959), 33–4.

[3] B. R. Mitchell with P. Deane, 155, 159; G. R. Lewis in W. Page (ed.), *V.C.H., Cornwall*, 1 (1906), 563–70.

[4] A. K. Cairncross, *Home and foreign investment 1870–1913* (Cambridge, 1953), ch. 4.

[5] J. Saville, *Rural depopulation in England and Wales 1851–1951* (London, 1957), chs. 2 and 3; Lord Eversley, 'The decline in number of agricultural labourers in Great Britain', *Jour. Roy. Stat. Soc.*, LXX (1907), 275.

[6] J. R. Bellerby, 'Distribution of farm income in the United Kingdom 1867–1938', *Jour. of Proceedings, Agricultural Economics Soc.*, X (1953), 135; J. Saville, 20–30.

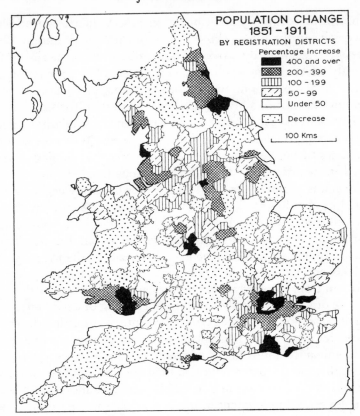

Fig. 62   Population change, 1851–1911
Based on R. Lawton in J. W. Watson and J. B. Sissons (eds.), *The British Isles: a systematic geography* (London and Edinburgh, 1964), 232.

women domestic service often provided an escape, and young men were drawn to the mines, the railways, the factories and to the increasing range of other occupations, such as the police force; some emigrated overseas.[1] Change of occupation did not necessarily mean migration, for labourers were attracted to rural industries such as the Peterborough brickworks and to local employment on the railways; but frequently it did. E. G. Ravenstein showed that migrations often took place over short distances and suggested a wave-like sequence of movements; but, while his general thesis is probably correct, there were certainly migrations over long distances.[2]

[1] *Ibid.*, 31–2.
[2] E. G. Ravenstein, 'The laws of migration,' *Jour. Roy. Stat. Soc.*, XLVIII (1885),

Agriculture remained the principal occupation in rural areas, although its share of male employment fell from a quarter in 1851 to a tenth in 1911, and migration was largely confined to agricultural labourers; for despite agricultural depression, numbers of farmers remained remarkably constant.[1] Owing to ambiguities in the census, and uncertainty about the number of farm workers who described themselves as general labourers, it is not possible to say accurately how many labourers moved out of agriculture, although there is no doubt that there was a considerable migration. One careful analysis has suggested a decline of nearly half a million in the number of adult male agricultural labourers in England and Wales between 1861 and 1911, but there was also a reduction in casual labour and a decline in the importance of harvest gangs.[2] To reinforce the attractions of the towns, fewer labourers were required in agriculture; mechanisation of harvesting and haymaking, almost universal by 1906, widespread laying of land to grass, and economy on farm maintenance – all reduced the demand for labour except in areas such as the vale of Evesham where intensive systems of farming were being more widely adopted.[3] There seems to be no clear relationship between agricultural prosperity or type of farming and the scale of rural migration which appears to have been remarkably uniform, affecting both pastoral and corn-growing areas and occurring in times of both agricultural prosperity and depression.[4]

It is not possible to determine the relative importance of the attraction of towns and the falling demands for labour in the countryside. Supply and demand seemed to have kept roughly in balance, although some labourers complained that farmers were deliberately using less labour than the land required.[5] The Assistant Commissioners who reported on agricultural labour to the Royal Commission on Labour in the early 1890s found the supply of labour adequate in 27 of the 38 districts they visited, although there were local difficulties.[6] What is certain is that without migration

198–9; H. C. Darby, 'The movement of population to and from Cambridgeshire between 1851 and 1861', *Geog. Jour.*, CI (1943), 118–25.

[1] 'The agricultural population', *Jour. Board of Agric.* (1904–5), 274; A. L. Bowley, 'Rural population in England and Wales: a study of the changes of density, occupation and ages', *Jour. Roy. Stat. Soc.*, LXXVII (1914), 610; Lord Eversley (1907), 275.

[2] F. D. W. Taylor, 'United Kingdom: numbers in agriculture', *Farm Economics*, VIII, No. 4 (1955), 39; R. Lawton, 249.

[3] *Rep. on Decline in Agric. Pop., 1881–1906*, 14 (P.P. 1906, xcvi).

[4] A. L. Bowley, 616.

[5] *R.C. on Labour*, vol. 1 (England), pt. 2. *Reps. by Mr Cecil M. Chapman*, 53 (P.P. 1893–4, xxxv).   [6] Lord Eversley (1907), 282.

there would have been widespread unemployment in rural areas. Two
other changes contributed to a falling demand for labour in the countryside; the displacement of local manufactures by factory-made products
and the decline of the country craftsman. In many parts of the country the
incomes of farm labourers had been supplemented by the earnings of their
families in industries such as straw plaiting and lace manufacture, as well
as by casual employment in agriculture. The extension of factory employment and the importation of cheaper goods led to a falling demand for
many of these products, and the introduction of compulsory schooling
and the migration of young people reduced the potential labour force.
Lace manufacture in Buckinghamshire was almost extinct by 1884 and was
in decline in Bedfordshire, and straw plaiting in Essex had ceased to
provide employment by 1901.[1] In the Luton area, the employment of
outworkers making hats with imported plait in place of straw plaiting
survived much longer, but generally such industries were in decline,
although some were increasingly factory industries, such as boot and
shoe manufacture in Northamptonshire and hosiery manufacture in
Leicestershire.[2]

Development of a national market for factory-made goods, and the
increasing ease and cheapness of travel to large cities, also affected the
demand for the services of local craftsmen; thus, the number of tailors
in Rutland fell from 173 in 1851 to 63 in 1911 and that of shoemakers from
236 to 138.[3] Fewer people needed fewer services, and economic and technological changes, such as the disappearance of the stage coach, further
diminished the demand for local products and local craftsmen; these losses
were not offset by new opportunities for employment in rural areas as
policemen, postmen, school teachers and the like.

Population changes also affected rural housing. Modification of the
Poor Law in 1863 had encouraged the building of cottages, and by the
1880s the standard of rural housing was said to be much improved.[4] Nor
did building cease with the onset of depression, for new cottages were

[1] C. Jamison in W. Page (ed.), *V.C.H. Buckinghamshire*, II (1908), 107; A. Ransom
in W. Page (ed.), *V.C.H. Bedfordshire*, II (1908), 123–4; M. Christy in W. Page and
J. H. Round (eds.), *V.C.H. Essex*, II (1907), 377.

[2] *V.C.H. Bedfordshire*, II, 107, 121; J. H. Clapham, *An economic history of modern
Britain: machines and national rivalries, 1887–1914* (Cambridge, 1938), 179–82.

[3] J. Saville, 74.

[4] J. H. Clapham, *An economic history of modern Britain: free trade and steel, 1850–
1886* (Cambridge, 1932), 507–8; R.C. *Agric. Depression, Minutes*, Evidence of Read,
Q. 16,189 (P.P. 1894, xvi, pt. 2).

necessary to retain tenants and labourers. Conditions seemed to have varied with the material used, the severity of depression, and the size of estate. Cottages were said to be best on the estates of large landowners; thus, in the Thakeham Poor Law Union in Sussex there were excellent cottages built in recent years on the estates of the Duke of Norfolk and Lord Leconfield.[1] But in other villages where many of the cottages had been built and occupied by their owners, in areas which were severely hit by depression, and in those where wattle and daub were the usual materials, conditions were often wretched; and on the Cambridge–Sandy road, for example, cottages were rotting away.[2] Depopulation may also have eased the pressure on accommodation, although in some areas surplus cottages were demolished, as on the Bedford estate, where three cottages were said to have been pulled down for each one erected.[3]

Urban population. In 1851 every other Englishman was a townsman, by residence if not by birthright; by 1911 the proportion had increased to four out of every five in a population which had doubled in size.[4] These changes in the urban population were closely associated with the changing urban geography, and interpretation is complicated by the variations in the census returns (four different definitions of urban areas being used between 1851 and 1911), and by the time-lag in adjusting administrative boundaries to keep pace with urban expansion. The rate of urban growth was not uniform throughout this period, for it was only to be expected that it would decline after a century of rapid urban expansion. The urban population increased by more than 20% in each decade between 1801 and 1881, but although the population classified as urban continued to rise, the rate of growth fell to 18.8% in 1881–91, to 17.5% in 1891–1901, and to 12.2% in 1901–11.[5]

Nor was the rate of urban growth uniform throughout the country, although the patterns of distribution did not change greatly during this period (see pp. 355–7 below). In the main, the large towns in 1911 were those that had been large in 1851, but the contrast between large and small

---

[1] *R.C. on Labour*, vol. 1 (England), pt. 5, *Rep. by Mr Aubrey J. Spencer*, 15 (P.P. 1893–4, xxxv); *Ibid.*, *Rep. by Mr William E. Bear*, 59 (P.P. 1893–4, xxxv).

[2] *R.C. on Labour*, vol. 1 (England), pt. 3, *Rep. by Arthur Wilson Fox*, 16–17 (P.P. 1893–4, xxxv); H. R. Haggard, *Rural England*, 2 vols. (London, 1902), II, 59.

[3] *R.C. on Labour*, vol. 1 (England), pt. 1, *Rep. by Mr William E. Bear*, 21 (P.P. 1893–4, xxxv).

[4] C. M. Law, 126.

[5] *Ibid.*, 130.

towns tended to increase during these decades; for while the large towns continued to grow, the population of many small towns in rural areas changed little or even declined, especially where they were not served by a railway or were remote from the main centres of population. C. M. Law's adjustments of the census data to correspond with built-up areas show that the number of towns with populations of 50,000 or more rose from 25 to 79 between 1851 and 1911, and their share of the urban population from 56.5 to 65.6%, while the number with populations between 2,500 and 20,000 rose only from 457 to 764 and their share fell from 30.3 to 21.2% (though this decline was relative and their total population also increased).[1]

THE COUNTRYSIDE

Although the contribution of agriculture and forestry to the national income fell from a fifth in 1851 to barely a twentieth in 1911, changes in the countryside were certainly the most widespread of all the changes in the geography of England in the second half of the nineteenth century.[2] In part they were due to the growth of towns and industry, which both attracted the agricultural labourer and provided new and expanding markets for the farmer; but they were largely a consequence of improvements in international transport and falling freight rates which brought English farmers increasingly into competition with overseas producers farming better land or under better climates. The volume of wheat imported trebled between 1850 and 1875 and doubled again between 1875 and 1914; imports of maize and other feeding stuffs also increased sharply, and those of meat and animals, which had been only a seventh by value of cereal imports in 1854, were nearly as large by 1900.[3] Enforced adjustment to this changed situation was the keynote of rural change.

From an agricultural viewpoint, the period can broadly be divided into three: (1) mid-century until the late 1870s, when the impact of rising imports was delayed by a combination of circumstances; (2) the late 1870s to the mid-1890s, when prices, especially of cereals, were falling and sectors of the agricultural economy were acutely depressed; (3) the years from the 1890s to the First World War, when prices made some recovery,

---

[1] *Ibid.*, 130, 135, 141.

[2] J. D. Chambers and C. E. Mingay, *The agricultural revolution 1750–1880* (London, 1966), 210.

[3] B. R. Mitchell with P. Deane, 298–300.

although many of the trends established in the previous twenty years continued. For this analysis, therefore, the last two periods will be treated together.

Reclamation and improvement, 1851–circa 1875

In many ways the 1850s and 1860s formed an Indian summer in English arable farming, and are sometimes spoken of as the era of high farming. In these two decades the physical resources of English agriculture were raised to their highest level, especially through land drainage and, to a lesser extent, through the re-equipment and re-organisation of farms. Between 1847 and 1870, some twelve million pounds was advanced under various statutory schemes of land improvement, three-quarters of it for drainage; and James Caird estimated that private landowners provided a much larger sum.[1] The Duke of Northumberland alone spent £992,000 on his estates between 1847 and 1878, a sum raised entirely out of estate revenue; and other great landowners invested large sums, although the movement was by no means universal.[2]

Reclamation in the sense of bringing into agricultural use land formerly not used for farming must have played only a limited part. Fen and bog still made their contribution, although on a small scale. Whittlesey Mere was successfully drained in 1851 and crops were growing in 1853 where there had been water only two years before.[3] Very little mossland remained in Lancashire by 1880, and improvements ranged from the large-scale reclamation of Chat Moss to that of the farmer at St Michael's on Wyre, who reclaimed 30 acres of moss on his 160-acre holding in the course of his tenancy.[4] Other reclamation was taking place along the coast; on the Norfolk side of the Wash, for example, various additions to the cultivated area were made between 1858 and 1882.[5] According to the Ordnance Survey, 35,444 acres had been added to the total land area of England and Wales between successive surveys, covering some thirty-five years, and 4,692 acres had been lost by coastal erosion; but there was no record of the

[1] J. Caird, *The landed interest and the supply of food* (London, 1878), 83, 87.

[2] F. M. L. Thompson, *English landed society in the 19th century* (London, 1963), 250.

[3] W. Wells, 'The drainage of Whittlesea Mere', *Jour. Roy. Agric. Soc.*, XXI (1860), 141.

[4] *R.C. on Agriculture, Reps. of Assistant Commissioners: Mr Coleman's reports*, 30, 33, 40 (P.P. 1882, xv).

[5] J. E. G. Mosby, *Norfolk* in L. D. Stamp (ed.), 'The land of Britain', pt. 70 (London, 1938), 237.

acreage brought into agricultural use.[1] Still more agricultural land was created through the clearing of woodland. Some of the most extensive areas reclaimed in this way were a product of disafforestation. The best known example is Hainault Forest, disafforested in 1851, where large areas, including the King's Wood, were grubbed up and converted into farmland to yield the Crown a revenue eight times that from the woodland it replaced.[2] Woods in other counties were similarly cleared to provide new farm land; thus 1,970 acres of Wychwood Forest in Oxfordshire were cleared in 1856–8, and converted into seven new farms.[3]

More usually, reclamation meant the improvement of downland, heath, moor or other rough land already grazed by livestock. It is clear that extensive areas were being improved in this way, although it is debatable whether these gains offset the losses to towns and railways. On Salisbury Plain, a large area of maiden down was said to have been broken up, much of it in the 1860s, to result in the 'bakelands' whose cultivation was to prove so difficult when seasons were bad and prices low.[4] In Sussex, large tracts of the high chalk downs were ploughed up, and in the Breckland much land was also brought into cultivation in the 1850s.[5] In the uplands, too, moorland was being improved, and on Exmoor the years from 1851 to 1866 were a period of active reclamation as rough pasture was converted to permanent grass.[6] Moorland in Yorkshire was being reclaimed at £16 per acre, but reclamation did not necessarily mean ploughing.[7]

Reclamation of rough land often accompanied the enclosure of commons and manorial waste, although the two processes were not synonymous; while some enclosures led to arable cultivation or to improved grazing, others involved little more than a re-organisation of existing uses, and in others land was withdrawn from agriculture to be planted with woods or to provide sites for houses. The great bulk of arable enclosures

[1] *R.C. on Coast Erosion, Reclamation of Tidal Lands and Afforestation in the U.K., Final Report*, 43 (P.P. 1911, xiv).

[2] Lord Eversley, *Commons, forests and footpaths* (rev. ed., London, 1910), 83.

[3] C. Belcher, 'On the reclaiming of waste land as instanced in Wichwood Forest', *J.R.A.S.*, XXIV (1863), 274.

[4] *R.C. Agric. Depression, Rep. by Mr R. Henry Rew on the Salisbury Plain District of Wiltshire*, 13 (P.P. 1895, xvi).

[5] H. C. K. Henderson and W. H. Briault, *Sussex* (L. of B., pts. 83–4, London, 1942), 502; *R.C. Agric. Depression, Rep. by Mr R. Henry Rew on the County of Norfolk*, 11 (P.P. 1895, xvii).

[6] C. S. Orwin, *The reclamation of Exmoor Forest* (Oxford, 1929), 83.

[7] *R.C. on Agriculture, Reps. by Assistant Commissioners*, 228 (P.P. 1881, xvi).

had been completed by 1850, but there were still probably between two and three million acres of unenclosed common land remaining in England and Wales, of which less than 250,000 acres were common arable.[1] Some 618,000 acres were enclosed between 1852 and 1888 under the General Enclosure Acts, and small additions, totalling 30,751 acres were made between 1878 and 1914 under the Commons Act of 1876.[2] An unknown acreage was also enclosed privately. The acreage of awards approved by the Inclosure Commissioners averaged some 45,000 acres a year between 1852 and 1861, but only some 33,000 acres between 1862 and 1871. From 1868 onwards the Commissioners deliberately discouraged further proposals in expectation of new legislation, and after 1876 it became increasingly difficult to enclose.[3]

Without detailed examination of the enclosure awards it is not possible to say how much of the land enclosed was arable, how much meadow and how much waste, although the location and size of the enclosures and the description in the Commissioners' reports give some indication. According to Gilbert Slater, awards involving the enclosure of common arable in England after 1845 totalled 139,517 acres, or about a fifth of all land so enclosed.[4] The acreages enclosed under individual awards varied widely, ranging from 8 acres in Bromsberrow (Gloucestershire) to 15,200 acres in Dent (West Riding), and in general enclosures were larger in predominantly upland counties; for example, the average in Cumberland was 1,322 acres, compared with 120 acres in Kent.[5] Enclosures were widespread, but there were large concentrations in Devon, in the central Pennines, in Surrey and in Norfolk. Enclosures of common fields were largely confined, as they had been earlier, to the counties extending across the Midlands from the East Riding to Dorset, while enclosures of waste were numerous in the uplands and on some of the poorer soils of the lowlands.

The precise effects of such enclosures must await further investigation. In many instances in the lowlands, as at Totternhoe (Bedfordshire), enclosed in 1892, regular fields bounded by hedges or fences appeared, but in some parishes, particularly those on lights soils or where enclosure came late and ownership had been concentrated into a few hands, there was

---

[1] *Inclosure Commissioners: Thirtieth Ann. Rep.*, 3 (P.P. 1875, xx).
[2] Calculated from the annual reports of the Inclosure Commissioners.
[3] *Ann. Rep. of proceedings under the Tithe etc. Acts, 1914*, 24–5 (P.P. 1914–16, v).
[4] G. Slater, *The English peasantry and the enclosure of common fields* (London, 1907), 191.
[5] *H. of C. Papers*, Nos. 359, 360 and 363 of 1906 (P.P. 1906, xcviii).

little outward evidence of change and the landscape remained open.[1] In the uplands the pattern was more variable. Enclosure might mean new roads, new farmsteads and rectilinear fields, as at High Bishopside (West Riding), or merely the subdivision of moorland into large enclosures separated by straight fences, often of post and wire, as on the moors on either side of Dentdale in the same county.[2]

By far the most important improvement to the land itself during this period was the extension of sub-soil drainage. James Caird, in evidence before the Lords' Committee on Land Improvement in 1873, had said that about two million acres had probably been drained; while another witness estimated the figure at three million acres out of twenty million requiring drainage.[3] Whatever the truth, the area drained was large.

Other improvements were also taking place. New farmsteads and cottages were being built, fields enlarged and field boundaries straightened. Wire fencing was almost unknown in the 1860s, but it had become common by the 1880s; sometimes it was barbed. There was said to be a vigorous campaign against unnecessary hedgerows, and on one farm at Cricklade in Wiltshire five miles of hedges were removed and thirty-six fields reduced to nine.[4] But none of these changes appears to have been on a sufficient scale to transform any extensive area of the countryside.

Although there were annual fluctuations, the 1850s and 1860s were generally years of prosperity, when rents were being increased to pay for improvements, when the benefits of mechanisation were beginning to make themselves felt, and when prices were generally more favourable than they had been since the Napoleonic Wars. The steam plough had been introduced in the 1850s, though only some 200,000 acres were thought to be cultivated by it in 1867; and an improved reaper-binder had appeared in 1850, so that by the 1860s most of the bigger farmers at least had their hay and corn cut by machine.[5] In many localities the railway was beginning to affect the pattern of agricultural activity as the droving of livestock for fattening disappeared, as crops and livestock products began to move to market by rail, and as it became possible for the fertility of

[1] Evidence from successive editions of Ordnance Survey 6″ maps.
[2] *Ibid.*
[3] *Rep. S.C. of the House of Lords on the Improvement of Land, Report*, iii; *ibid.*, *Minutes*, Evidence of Caird, Q. 4,125–6; Evidence of Denton, Q. 830 (P.P. 1873, xvi).
[4] J. H. Clapham (1932), 267, 503; R. Molland in E. Crittall (ed.), *V.C.H. Wiltshire*, IV (1959), 86.
[5] J. H. Clapham (1932), 268; see, for example, H. Evershed, 'Agriculture of Hertfordshire', *J.R.A.S.*, xxv (1864), 299.

light soils to be improved by large quantities of manure which were transported 50 miles or more from the great cities, especially from London. Transport was thus coming to play a much more important role in agriculture, both by permitting agricultural produce to move more freely within the country and also, with more serious consequences for agriculturalists as a whole, by abolishing the protection against overseas competition which distance had formerly provided.

Agricultural changes, 1875 – circa 1914

Although in mid-century James Caird urged that livestock should play a more important role, and although livestock products probably did increase in importance, many farmers and landowners retained an almost mystical attachment to wheat.[1] Although the proportion of foreign wheat in the nation's bread supply rose steadily from a quarter in 1850 to three-quarters in 1894, and although the price of wheat was falling, it was not until a succession of bad harvests in the late 1870s that the changed situation was made dramatically clear, even though unfavourable seasons distracted attention from the need for fundamental adjustment in the farming systems themselves.[2] A Royal Commission sat during 1879–82 to investigate the situation and, when cereal prices continued to fall and then those of livestock and livestock products, a second Commission was appointed in 1893. The reports and evidence of these Commissions provide a mine of information, but they are often coloured by the assumption that depression was universal.

At first, the burden of lower prices and poor harvests was largely absorbed by landowners who granted remissions of rent and then permanent reductions from the high values of the 1860s and 1870s; but, as prices continued to fall, more fundamental adjustments had to be made. The report of the Assistant Commissioners made it clear that the situation was worst on heavy land or on poor light land in the eastern part of the country, where crops were less reliable, alternative systems of farming less easily adopted, and cultivation difficult, at least on heavy land. But in western and northern counties, where wheat occupied a minor place in farming systems, in areas easily accessible by rail from large cities or with local markets, as in the colliery villages of the Durham coalfield, depressed conditions either did not exist or were much less severe, although rents

---

[1] J. Caird, *English agriculture in 1850–51* (London, 1852), 476, 480–9.
[2] J. H. Clapham (1932), 3; C. S. Orwin and E. H. Whetham, *History of British agriculture 1846–1914* (London, 1964), 259.

were usually reduced, if on a smaller scale. The crisis affected above all the arable farmer for whom wheat was the lynch-pin of his system. Thus in north Devon there had often been no reductions in rent by the 1890s; in Cumberland, rents fell between 15–25%; while in Norfolk the fall, even on the best land, was 25–35%, reaching 40–60% on land of medium quality.[1] Yet even within the eastern counties, location could make a critical difference; at Much Hadham, in Hertfordshire, rents in 1901 ranged from 30s. an acre on the best land in a good position to between 7s. 6d. and 10s. on land more than three miles from a station.[2]

There can be little doubt that depressed conditions did exist widely in the periods 1879–82 and 1893–5, and that depression was most acute in 'the corn growing counties', although it is often difficult to separate the special and temporary difficulties presented by bad seasons from the long-term trends. Comparison of returns of the gross annual value of land in 1879–80 and in 1894–5 show a marked contrast between eastern counties, where reductions reached 39.9% in Suffolk and 39.7% in Essex, and northern and western counties such as Cheshire and Cornwall, where the reductions were only 6.4 and 6.6% respectively.[3] There were numerous reports of land falling out of cultivation in both periods, and special returns were made in 1884 and 1887 of abandoned farms and abandoned land, although their usefulness is impaired by uncertainties among farmers about their meaning. In the Breckland, fields did tumble down to grass and were soon overrun by heather; and in Essex and Cambridgeshire fields had been invaded by thorn, briar and bramble;[4] but more commonly land 'out of cultivation', was arable land which had become covered with coarse self-sown grass, and Pringle's 'terrible map dotted thick with black patches' of south-east Essex showed such land which had either been put down as temporary pasture or had sown itself (Fig. 63).[5] Some land may have been let go simply to avoid payment of rates and tithes, and such

[1] R.C. on Agric. Depression. Rep. by Mr R. Henry Rew on North Devon, 12 (P.P. 1895, xvi); ibid., Rep. by Mr Wilson Fox on the County of Cumberland, 25 (P.P. 1895, xvii); ibid., Rep. by Mr R. Henry Rew on the County of Norfolk, 19 (P.P. 1895, xvii).

[2] H. R. Haggard, I, 535.

[3] R.C. Agric. Depression, Statement showing the Decrease and Increase in the Rateable Value of Lands, 1870–1894, 10 (P.P. 1897, xv).

[4] R.C. Agric. Depression, Minutes, Evidence of Read, Q. 16,042 (P.P. 1894, xvi, pt. 2); ibid., Rep. by Mr R. Hunter Pringle on the Ongar...Districts of Essex, 129 (P.P. 1894, xvi, pt. 1); H. R. Haggard, II, 59.

[5] J. H. Clapham (1938), 79; R.C. Agric. Depression, Rep. by Mr R. Hunter Pringle on the Ongar...Districts of Essex, 48, 129 (P.P. 1894, xvi, pt. 1).

self-sown pasture was often let at rents of a shilling or two per acre as sheep run, particularly on heavy clay or on very light soil.[1] The Breckland and south-east Essex illustrate the nadir of depression. In the Breckland in the 1890s many farms were unlet and large areas had been let go, with only a few fields around the house still cultivated; in Essex, an enormous area was said to be worthless and covered with coarse herbage.[2] In other areas of light or heavy land in lowland England there were similar difficulties; farms could be had for nothing on the Cotswolds by a tenant willing to pay rates; on Salisbury Plain the tops of the farms had gone out of cultivation, and C. S. Read thought that all the land there that had been reclaimed in his lifetime had gone back.[3] Tenants changed frequently, and many farms were taken in hand either because no tenants could be found or to prevent further damage to the land by those who had lost heart or resources, although it was usually said that tenants could be found for good farms or good land; at one time Lord Wantage had 13,000 acres in hand which he farmed as a single unit.[4] Even where land was not out of cultivation, standards of farming had fallen; for labour costs were the most important item of expenditure and the one which could be most easily reduced. Economy ruled in farm management, and land went out of high cultivation, hedges and ditches were neglected and the appearance of farms was allowed to deteriorate.[5]

As the evidence of rent and land values has shown, the situation was very different in areas which did not depend on arable farming. Few farms were unlet, rent reductions were smaller and, although agriculturalists often complained about depression, there was little evidence of it; Cornwall had not suffered as elsewhere; practically no farms were unlet in

[1] R.C. Agric. Depression, Rep. by Mr Jabez Turner upon the Frome District of Somerset and the Stratford-on-Avon District of Warwickshire, 28 (P.P. 1894, xvi, pt. 1); ibid., Rep. by Mr R. Hunter Pringle on the Counties of Bedford, Huntingdon and Northampton, 5, 22 (P.P. 1895, xvii).

[2] R.C. Agric. Depression, Rep. by Mr Wilson Fox on the County of Suffolk, 31, 51 (P.P. 1895, xvi); ibid., Minutes, Evidence of Read, Q. 16,032 (P.P. 1894, xvi, pt. 2); ibid., Minutes, Evidence of Pringle, Q. 8,610 (P.P. 1894, xvi, pt. 1).

[3] R.C. Agric. Depression, Minutes, Evidence of Adams, Q. 41,950 (P.P. 1894, xvi, pt. 3); ibid., Rep. by Mr R. Henry Rew on the Salisbury Plain District of Wiltshire, 15 (P.P. 1895, xvi); ibid., Minutes, Evidence of Read, Q. 16,031 (P.P. 1894, xvi, pt. 2).

[4] Lady Wantage, Lord Wantage, V.C., K.C.B., A memoir (London, 1907), 377–9.

[5] J. H. Clapham (1938), 83; R.C. Agric. Depression, Rep. by Mr R. Henry Rew on North Devon, 14 (P.P. 1895, xvi); R.C. on Labour, vol. 1 (England), pt. 2, Reps. by Mr C. M. Chapman, 52 (P.P. 1893–4, xxxv).

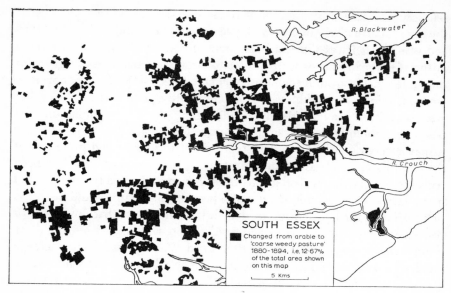

Fig. 63 Abandoned arable land in south Essex, 1894
Based on *R.C. Agric. Depression, Report by Mr R. Hunter Pringle on the Ongar...Districts of Essex*, map (P.P. 1894, xvi, pt. 1).

Devon; there was good competition for farms in Northumberland, and little visible sign of depression in Cumberland.[1]

Neglect, economy, and remission or reduction of rent were spontaneous reactions, but it gradually became clear that fundamental changes in farming systems would have to be made. Such changes had often been anticipated and many were pioneered by migrants from other parts of the country, notably from Scotland and south-west England, who brought with them new systems and new attitudes. To the farmers from Ayrshire, the low rents and ease with which farms could be got made farming in southern England attractive, and agents, anxious for good tenants, advertised vacant farms in Scottish newspapers.[2] The Ayrshire farmer

---

[1] *R.C. Agric. Depression, Minutes*, Evidence of Collins, Q. 37,162 (P.P. 1894, xvi, pt. 3); *ibid., Rep. by Mr R. Rew on North Devon*, 14 (P.P. 1895, xvi); *ibid., Minutes*, Evidence of Scott, Q. 30,141 (P.P. 1894, xvi, pt. 2); *ibid., Rep. by Mr Wilson Fox on the County of Cumberland*, 22 (P.P. 1895, xvii).

[2] *R.C. Agric. Depression, Rep. by Mr R. Hunter Pringle on the Ongar...Districts of Essex*, 43 (P.P. 1894, xvi, pt. 1); P. Connell, 'Experiences of a Scotsman on the Essex clays', *J.R.A.S.*, 3rd ser., II (1891), 311.

brought a knowledge of dairying (and sometimes even his herd of Ayr-shires) and of the cultivation of temporary grass and the potato; one such farmer in Essex had 247 acres of temporary grass and only 71 acres of tillage on a 636-acre farm that fifteen years before had nearly all been cropped.[1] Although he had many lessons to learn, the Scottish farmer often did well, in part at least because he depended largely on family labour and worked hard and lived hard.

Such migrants came in considerable numbers. On one Hertfordshire estate Scots outnumbered English, and so numerous were the newcomers when Rider Haggard made his survey of Hertfordshire that he was led to ask 'But where are the home people?'[2] On the Essex clays in 1894 there were about 120–130 Scots, and one witness claimed that this migration was the chief reason for Essex becoming a dairy county.[3] Other farmers migrated from Devon and Cornwall, bringing with them a knowledge of grassland husbandry and stock farming, and they and the Scots were found throughout southern England.

Conversion to pasture. Perhaps the most widespread agricultural change was the laying down of land to permanent grass, both because such farm-ing was less expensive of labour and because livestock products were less affected by falling prices. An increase in grassland had been advocated in the 1850s and, although land was generally being ploughed up in this period, there is some evidence that arable was being converted to pasture even in the 1860s and 1870s; on the Raby Castle estate in County Durham, for example, 100–150 acres a year had been laid to grass between 1860 and 1880.[4] From the late 1870s, however, arable land was being laid to grass throughout the country. Some of this was land which had tumbled down to grass and become permanent pasture by default; some was sown as a ley and allowed to remain in the hope that conditions would improve. The agri-cultural returns show an increase in both the acreage and the proportion of arable in temporary grass in the 1880s and 1890s, and a subsequent reduc-

[1] *R.C. Agric. Depression, Rep. by Mr R. Hunter Pringle on the Ongar... Districts of Essex*, 45 (P.P. 1894, xvi, pt. 1).

[2] *R.C. Agric. Depression, Rep. by Mr Aubrey Spencer on the Vale of Aylesbury and the County of Hertford*, 14 (P.P. 1895, xvi); H. R. Haggard, 1, 510.

[3] *R.C. Agric. Depression, Rep. by Mr R. Hunter Pringle on the Ongar... Districts of Essex*, 44 (P.P. 1894, xvi, pt. 1); *ibid., Minutes*, Evidence of Strutt, Q. 13,890 (P.P. 1894, xvi, pt. 1).

[4] F. M. L. Thompson, 255; J. Caird (1852), 480–9; *R.C. on Agriculture, Reps. by Assistant Commissioners*, 226 (P.P. 1881, xvi).

tion in the 1900s as such grass came to be reclassified as the permanent grass it had in fact become. Much of it was therefore of poor quality.

There were both natural and physical obstacles hindering this change. The drier conditions in the eastern parts of the country, where the need to reduce costs was greatest, were thought to make the establishment of good permanent pasture difficult; and it was claimed that up to fourteen years might be necessary for the making of a good sward.[1] Light soils presented particular difficulty and neither on Salisbury Plain nor on Lincoln Heath was it easy to establish good pasture; similar difficulties were also experienced on some heavy land.[2] The high cost of establishing good pasture was also an obstacle to both tenant and owner, although wealthy landowners such as the dukes of Bedford and Northumberland could help by laying down grass for their tenants on a large scale.[3] Another difficulty was the obligation to restore land to arable on the expiry of a tenancy, although this was unlikely to be enforced; for in many areas only farms with a considerable proportion of pasture could be let.

It is impossible to know exactly how much land was converted to permanent pasture. The evidence of the agricultural statistics shows an increase of two million acres in the acreage returned as permanent pasture between 1875 and 1900 and of a further half million by 1914; but the amount of permanent pasture had almost certainly been understated in the statistics by at least a million acres in 1875,[4] and there was a considerable withdrawal of land from agricultural to urban and industrial uses during this period. In view of the confusion between permanent and temporary grass it is probably wisest to examine the decline in the acreage under tillage, which was near-universal, with only Lancashire and Cheshire recording an increase. This anomaly was possibly due to the use of local units of measure in earlier years; for although depression was not serious, land was certainly laid to grass in both counties, and the expansion of towns alone might have been expected to lead to a reduction in the area

[1] J. A. Caird, 'Recent experience in laying down land to grass', *J.R.A.S.*, 2nd ser., XXIV (1888), 148–9.

[2] *R.C. Agric. Depression, Rep. by Mr R. Henry Rew on the Salisbury Plain District of Wiltshire*, 16 (P.P. 1895, xvi); *ibid., Minutes*, Evidence of Epton, Q. 36,138 (P.P. 1894, xvi, pt. 3); *R.C. Agric. Depression, Rep. by Mr R. Hunter Pringle on the Ongar... Districts of Essex*, 62 (P.P. 1894, xvi, pt. 1).

[3] Duke of Bedford, *A great agricultural estate* (London, 1897), 197; F. M. L. Thompson, 313.

[4] R. H. Best and J. T. Coppock, *The changing use of land in Britain* (London, 1962), 73.

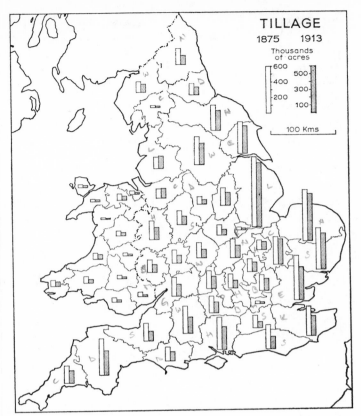

Fig. 64   Tillage in 1875 and 1913
Based on: (1) *Agricultural Returns, 1875* (P.P. 1875, lxxix); (2) *Agricultural Statistics, 1913* (P.P. 1914, xcviii).

under tillage crops. The relative reduction in the acreage under tillage was greatest in those western counties where arable land had been least important and in those Midland and southern counties where there were large acreages of heavy land (Fig. 64). Within any farm, it was generally the most difficult soils and the least accessible fields which were laid to grass.

On the diminished area of ploughed land there were also changes in cropping. Restrictive covenants governing rotations were usually incorporated in farm leases, but it is difficult to know how far they had been enforced under high farming. Whatever the practice, it seems likely that rotations now became more flexible; for only by allowing considerable

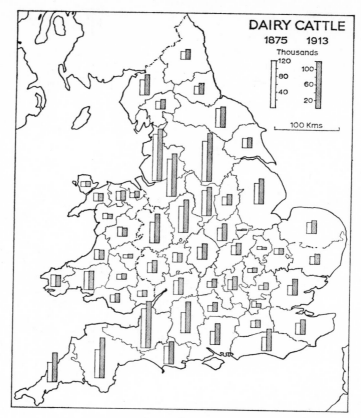

Fig. 65   Dairy cattle in 1875 and 1913
Sources as for Fig. 64.

latitude could landowners retain tenants.[1] The proportion of tillage devoted to wheat fell steadily and its place was largely taken by oats; the change was proportionately greatest in those western and northern counties where little wheat was grown. With the exception of the potato, labour-demanding root crops also became less important, although the mangold gained ground at the expense of the turnip. The growing of potatoes increased on deep friable soils and where communications were good, although competition from both foreign and other domestic producers was felt towards the end of the century.

While the replacement of arable by pasture was primarily due to the

[1] J. H. Clapham (1932), 275.

need to reduce costs, it also implied changes in livestock, although numbers of livestock increased relatively more slowly than the acreage of grass, perhaps in consequence of the reduced resources of farmers and the poor quality of much of the new grass. Most of the livestock on arable farms had either been cattle fed in yards to produce manure, or sheep folded on the arable to consolidate and improve the soil; but the former were now unprofitable and the latter expensive of labour. Consequently the rearing and fattening of cattle on grass became more important, and fewer sheep were kept throughout the lowlands, especially in areas of light arable land.

Dairying. The principal change in livestock farming was the expansion of dairying which enjoyed a large measure of natural protection (Fig. 65). In the 1850s the production of milk for sale had largely been confined to stall-fed cows in town dairies and to the immediate periphery of towns; most of the other dairy cattle were kept in the traditional dairying areas of Cheshire, Derbyshire and Somerset, where they provided milk for the making of butter and cheese. By the early 1860s milk was already being sent by rail to London from more distant farms, although the quantity was small and the quality supposedly inferior.[1] The cattle plague of 1865, which reduced the cattle population of the London cow houses from some 24,000 to 14,000 made it immediately necessary to bring supplies from farther afield and the gallonage supplied increased rapidly, much of it by the diversion of milk from butter and cheese production.[2] A growing urban population, an improved railway network, falling costs of transport, and an increasing area of grassland stimulated both the spread of dairying to new areas and the further diversion of milk from cheese and butter making in the traditional dairy districts. In detail, dairying was encouraged by local markets, such as the colliery villages of County Durham, or by good rail communications to large cities; it was hindered by the absence of suitable buildings, by inadequate supplies of drinking water and by the belief of some landowners that dairying harmed the soil.[3]

The most striking changes were those resulting from the need to supply London with milk. Even before the onset of depression the quantity of milk reaching London by rail had risen from 7 million gallons in 1866 to

---

[1] E. H. Whetham, 'The London milk trade, 1860–1900', *Econ. Hist. Rev.*, XVII (1964–5), 370; D. Taylor, 'London's milk supply, 1850–1900: a re-interpretation', *Agric. History*, XLV (1971), 33–8.

[2] F. A. Barnes, 'The evolution of the salient patterns of milk production and distribution in England and Wales', *Trans. and Papers, Inst. Brit. Geog.*, XXV (1958), 179–80.   [3] P. McConnell, 312.

20 million in 1880, and the radius within which supplies were drawn had increased to 100–150 miles.[1] The provision of depots at stations by wholesalers, and the introduction of fast milk trains, facilitated the switch from butter or cheese making to supplying the urban milk market, and permitted farmers in new areas to take up dairying. Farmers in Dorset, north Wiltshire and Berkshire began to deliver milk to the station instead of the factory, and milk churns could be seen at every station between Maidenhead and Faringdon.[2] The catchment area was gradually extended, especially to the west, and by 1892 some 83% of London's milk was thought to come by rail; the maximum regular journey on the Great Western network (which carried more milk than any other line) was 130 miles, but consignments came from much farther afield, especially in cooler weather.[3]

Although London was the biggest single market and probably the greatest influence on the growth of dairy farming, milk production extended in response to other markets, either by the diversion of milk from butter and cheese making, as with Manchester's supplies from north Cheshire, or by the adoption of dairying as a new enterprise. Dairying developed on the small farms of the industrial Pennines in east Lancashire and around the colliery villages and industrial towns of north-east England.[4] Milk was sent from Leicestershire to Leeds and Newcastle as well as to London; there was even a summer market for milk in the growing holiday resorts, such as Margate and the Lake District.[5]

The Scots and West Country farmers played an important part in encouraging the extension of dairying; so did the railways and, increasingly, the wholesale companies. Although there were many complaints about prices and railway charges, dairying provided many farmers with a welcome

[1] E. H. Whetham, 372.

[2] R.C. Agric. Depression, Rep. by Mr R. Henry Rew on the County of Dorset, 22 (P.P. 1895, xvii); E. H. Whetham, 374–5; P. H. Ditchfield and W. A. Simmons in P. H. Ditchfield and W. Page (eds.), V.C.H. Berkshire, II (1907), 337.

[3] R. H. Rew, 'An inquiry into the statistics of the production and consumption of milk and milk products in Great Britain', Jour. Roy. Stat. Soc., LV (1892), 265; E. A. Pratt, The transition in agriculture (London, 1906), 11–12.

[4] R.C. on Agriculture, Reps. of Assistant Commissioners, Mr Coleman's Reports, 54 (P.P. 1882, xv); T. W. Fletcher, 'The great depression in English agriculture, 1875–1896', Econ. Hist. Rev., XIII (1961), 23; R.C. Agric. Depression, Rep. by Mr R. Hunter Pringle on South Durham etc., 23 (P.P. 1895, xvi).

[5] C. Whitehead, 'A sketch of the agriculture of Kent', J.R.A.S., 3rd ser., X (1899), 451; R.C. Agric. Depression, Rep. by Mr Wilson Fox on the Garstang District of Lancashire etc., 9 (P.P. 1894, xvi, pt. 1); ibid., Minutes, Evidence of Rolleston, Q. 13,315 (P.P. 1894, xvi, pt. 1).

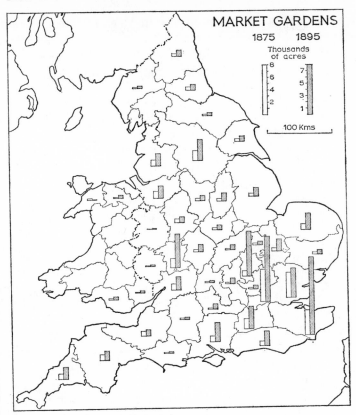

Fig. 66   Market gardens in 1875 and 1895
Based on : (1) *Agricultural Returns, 1875* (P.P. 1875, lxxix); (2) *Agricultural Returns, 1895* (P.P. 1896, xcii).
The negligible amounts for Rutland, Westmorland and a number of Welsh counties cannot be shown. It must be remembered that part of the increase was due to differences in definition and interpretation between 1875 and 1895 – see R. H. Best and J. T. Coppock, *The changing use of land in Britain* (London, 1962), 60–1.

relief from falling cereal prices. In Wiltshire, where milk was successfully challenging the traditional sheep and corn on Salisbury Plain, one farmer sent 1,500 gallons daily to London and another near Winchester said that milk was his most profitable enterprise.[1] Although there were fears of over-production, farmers with easy access to a station fared better than

[1] *R.C. Agric. Depression, Rep. by Mr R. Henry Rew on the Salisbury Plain District of Wiltshire*, 18, 28 (P.P. 1895, xvi); *ibid., Minutes*, Q. 6,464 (P.P. 1894, xvi, pt. 1).

many others; for, as one Scots farmer in Hertfordshire put it, to lack communications was 'agricultural death'.[1] Numbers of dairy cattle increased everywhere (although this was partly due to better enumeration), with the highest percentage increases around London (Fig. 65).

The growing of fruit and vegetables. The growing of fruit, vegetables and flowers was also adopted as a means of combating falling prices, although, as with milk-selling, the increase in production began before the onset of depression. Fruit and vegetables had long been grown in and around the large cities, notably around London, where orchards and market gardens were gradually being displaced outwards as the built-up area expanded; but flower growing was largely a new undertaking. The acreage under fruit and vegetables increased partly by planting in and around existing areas and partly by the rise of new centres (Fig. 66). Here, too, good communications were essential, both to carry produce to market and to bring back supplies of town manure to areas of light soil such as mid-Bedfordshire, where a rapid expansion of horticulture followed upon the opening of the Great Northern line in 1850; so critical was access by rail in this area that market gardening gave way to ordinary farming at distances greater than two miles from a station.[2] In the vale of Evesham, where there were only 500 to 600 acres of market gardens in the 1850s, the five railway stations provided a similar stimulus, and the acreage under market-garden crops trebled between 1883 and 1908, when it was estimated at 15,000 acres.[3] In Kent, where market gardening was also expanding rapidly, there were thought to be some 20,000 acres of vegetables and flowers in 1890; transport of produce by road was still important near London, and manure and produce also travelled by water to and from coastal areas.[4]

While market gardening was increasing around the larger towns, as on the mosslands of Lancashire, new centres were also developing farther afield and the urban markets were coming to draw their supplies from a much wider range of both home and foreign producers. Growers in Kent began to send produce to Midland England and Evesham became

[1] H. R. Haggard, I, 511.
[2] F. Beavington, 'The change to more extensive methods in market gardening in Bedfordshire', *Trans. and Papers, Inst. Brit. Geog.*, XXXIII (1963), 89; H. Evershed, 'Market gardening', *J.R.A.S.*, 2nd ser., VII (1871), 432.
[3] J. Udale, 'Market gardening and fruit growing in the vale of Evesham', *J.R.A.S.*, LXIX (1908), 95.
[4] C. Whitehead (1899), 431.

a major supplier of Manchester.[1] The railways offered new possibilities in the Fens, where first-class soils had helped farmers to weather the depression, and where flowers, and vegetables such as carrots, were beginning to be grown by both smallholders and large farmers, and in Cornwall, where special trains transported vegetables (especially broccoli) to London, the Midlands and north England.[2] In some of these new centres the stimulus to expansion was provided by migrants from established horticultural areas, for example at Wisbech by a fruit grower from Kent.[3] Personal links were also important in marketing, and the expansion of carrot growing around Chatteris was said to owe much to Chatteris men in the London market.[4]

Two other, though quite different, systems of growing flowers and vegetables were also developing. In the main arable areas farmers began to grow vegetables on a field scale as part of a rotation, as with the production of green peas in Essex; and it became so difficult to distinguish between market gardening and the growing of horticultural crops by arable farmers that the collection of the acreages of market gardens was abandoned in 1897.[5] The second development was a rapid increase of greenhouses, especially around Worthing and in the Lea valley; growth here also owed much to individuals, such as the Rochford family who owned 86 acres of glass in the late 1890s, a quarter of the acreage in the Lea valley.[6] Tomatoes, grapes and flowers were the chief crops, a clear indication of the influence of the growing urban markets.[7]

Parallel to, and often associated with, the spread of market gardening and of the growing of flowers and vegetables was an increase in the production of fruit (Fig. 67). The acreage recorded under orchards rose from 141,000 acres in 1873 to 237,000 in 1914, and that under small fruit from 33,000 to 76,000 acres between 1888 and 1914, although both of

[1] *Ibid.*, 469; *Departmental Cttee on the Fruit Industry of Great Britain, Minutes*, Evidence of Wise, Q. 4,979 (P.P. 1906, xxiv); J. Page, 'The sources of supply of the Manchester fruit and vegetable markets', *J.R.A.S.*, 2nd ser., XVI (1880), 476–7.

[2] *R.C. Agric. Depression, Rep. by Mr Wilson Fox on the County of Cambridge*, 5 (P.P. 1895, xvii); E. A. Pratt, 171.

[3] J. E. G. Mosby, 182.

[4] *R.C. Agric. Depression, Rep. by Mr Wilson Fox on the County of Cambridge*, 5–6 (P.P. 1895, xviii).

[5] E. A. Pratt, 127; R. H. Best and J. T. Coppock, 61.

[6] W. E. Bear, 'Flower and fruit farming in England', pt. 2, *J.R.A.S.*, 3rd ser., IX (1898), 528; *ibid.*, pt. 4, *J.R.A.S.*, 3rd ser., X (1899), 268, 283.

[7] *Ibid.*, pt. 4 (1899), 286.

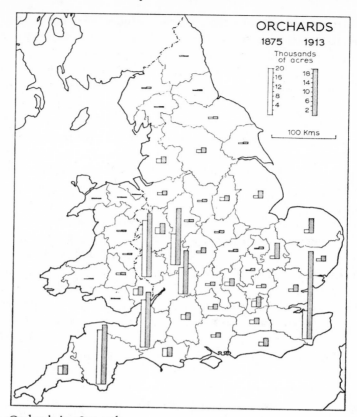

Fig. 67   Orchards in 1875 and 1913
Sources as for Fig. 64.
The negligible amounts for Rutland and a number of Welsh counties cannot
be shown. It must be remembered that part of the increase was due to differences in definition and interpretation between 1875 and 1913 – see R. H. Best
and J. T. Coppock, *The changing use of land in Britain* (London, 1962), 60–2.

these increases were in part due to better enumeration.[1] Much of the large
acreage of cider and perry orchards in the West Country was in poor condition and, although there was some planting of cider orchards in Herefordshire, western counties were little affected by the expanding market for
fruit.[2] New orchards were largely confined to the eastern counties. The

[1] All unattributed acreages are derived from the annual volumes of agricultural
statistics.
[2] *Deptl Cttee Fruit Industry, Minutes,* Evidence of Pickering, Q. 4,045 (P.P. 1906,
xxiv); J. H. Clapham (1938), 91.

biggest gain was in Kent, where the acreage under orchards rose by 200% between 1875 and 1913, and that under small fruit by 92% between 1888 and 1914; and there was also a large increase in the Evesham district.[1] New areas were also developing; there were only a few orchards around Wisbech in 1880, but as many as 6,000 acres by 1899; and some 3,000 acres of fruit were grown within a ten-mile radius of Histon, Cambridgeshire, twenty-one years after the opening of Chivers jam factory in 1875, two-thirds of it attributable to the market offered by the factory.[2] The jam factory at Tiptree in Essex likewise seems to have acted as an incentive to fruit growing in that locality.[3] The growing of small fruit was often associated with orchards, although in some localities, such as the strawberry-growing area of Hampshire, small fruit alone was produced. Small fruit was also sometimes introduced as a field crop by arable farmers.

The growing of hops provides an interesting example of a short-lived and highly localised development.[4] By the 1850s, hops were largely confined to the west Midlands and south-east England. The removal of hop duty in 1861 led to a rapid rise in the acreage under hops, which reached a maximum of 71,000 acres in 1878.[5] This expansion was often achieved by planting on less suitable sites, and, in the face of rising imports and higher yields from the home crop, the trend was almost immediately reversed. In Kent, the leading county, the distribution of hop growing reverted to its previous pattern and many hop fields were converted into orchards; in Worcestershire, by contrast, the gains of the 1860s and 1870s were maintained.[6]

The expansion of fruit, flower and vegetable growing added further variety to the pattern of farming and helped arable farmers to find alternative cash crops in place of wheat. It was not all gain, for in some areas the development of new centres harmed local producers, as in Cheshire, where farmers growing early potatoes faced severe competition from growers in Cornwall and the Channel Isles who could now compete with

[1] W. E. Bear, 'Flower and fruit farming in England', pt. 3, *J.R.A.S.*, 3rd ser., x (1899), 63.

[2] *R.C. Agric. Depression, Rep. by Mr Wilson Fox on the County of Cambridge*, 6 (P.P. 1895, xvii).   [3] W. E. Bear, pt. 3 (1899), 71–2.

[4] D. M. Harvey, 'Locational changes in the Kentish hop industry and the analysis of land-use patterns', *Trans. and Papers, Inst. Brit. Geog.*, XXXIII (1963), 123–44.

[5] D. C. D. Pocock, 'England's diminished hop acreage', *Geography*, XLIV (1959), 14.

[6] A. D. Hall and E. J. Russell, *The soils and agriculture of Kent, Surrey and Sussex* (H.M.S.O., 1911), 28; C. Whitehead, 'Fifty years of hop farming', *J.R.A.S.*, 3rd ser. I (1890), 325.

them;[1] but in general the greater acreages under field vegetables and soft fruit were a major benefit to the arable farmer.

Other changes. There were also changes in the structure of farming, although the evidence is conflicting. In areas of light soil it seems likely that large farms were increasing in importance as individuals created farming empires out of farms which could not be let; one of the most striking examples was a holding of 14,000 acres in Wiltshire which was rented from seven landowners.[2] Elsewhere, there is evidence of both amalgamation and subdivision; for while larger farms were often difficult to let, many occupiers of smallholdings lacked resources and suffered severely. In localities which depended on horticultural crops, such as the vale of Evesham, many more smallholdings were created.[3] Smallholdings were the subject of much discussion, but legislation that enabled local authorities to provide such holdings had little effect before the Act of 1908.

Evidence about the land itself is ambiguous. While investments in improvement certainly diminished, they did not cease; new buildings were necessary for new systems of farming, especially for dairying, and new cottages were required to retain agricultural labourers. There is evidence, too, of land reclamation 'in the hilly districts', but its location and extent are unknown, for statistical data are absent or unsatisfactory and map evidence uncertain; comparison of successive editions of the Ordnance Survey 6″ maps suggests that, if anything, improved land was reverting. What is certain is that the agricultural area as a whole was diminishing; between 1851 and 1871 it was thought that some 700,000 acres of land went out of agricultural use in England and Wales as a result of the growth of towns and the railway network, and losses must have continued at similar rates in succeeding decades.[4]

Woodland

The fate of the woods and forests during these years is even less certain; there are few contemporary references and statistical data are scanty and unsatisfactory. The principal change in the 1850s and 1860s, at least in the

[1] *R.C. on Agriculture, Reps. by Assistant Commissioners, Mr Coleman's Reports,* 63 (P.P. 1882, xv).

[2] *R.C. Agric. Depression, Rep. by Mr R. Henry Rew on the Salisbury Plain District of Wiltshire,* 28 (P.P. 1895, xvi).

[3] *R.C. on Labour,* vol. 1 (England), pt. 2, *Rep. by Mr Aubrey J. Spencer,* 95–6 (P.P. 1893–94, xxxv).

[4] *Inclosure Commissioners: Thirtieth Ann. Rep.,* 3–4 (P.P. 1875, xx).

lowlands, appears to have been the conversion of woodland into agricultural land. Yet in some localities, such as Sherwood Forest, the area under woods was increasing and in the uplands, too, there was afforestation; in Teesdale, for example, a good deal of planting was said to have been done in years before 1881.[1] Some of the proposals for enclosure recommended by the Inclosure Commissioners also referred to the possibility of afforestation, as at Loweswater Common in Cumberland, where it was claimed that the land would be 'much improved' by planting.[2]

In the remaining decades, afforestation seems to have been the general rule, although the statistical evidence is not very reliable. From 1871 the acreage of woodland in each parish was recorded at intervals by the inland revenue officers responsible for the collection of the agricultural returns, the source of information being at first the rate books and subsequently enquiry among landowners. The acreages so recorded rose from 1,314,000 acres in 1871 to 1,683,000 in 1905.[3] These increases are unlikely to be an accurate measure of any change, for it is probable that the estimates became progressively more complete; but the remarks of observers and the evidence of the Ordnance Survey maps suggest that the trend they indicate was real. It was generally recognised that the state of British woodlands was unsatisfactory and that this was due in part to the abolition of duty on imported timber and to the impoverishment of landowners;[4] but some professional foresters often blamed the high esteem in which field sports were held, claiming that this handicapped the proper management of woodland.[5] Consideration of visual amenity also affected the use of private woodlands, and some, such as Burnham Beeches and Epping Forest, were now being acquired for public recreation.[6] The acreage of private parkland was also increasing and probably reached its maximum extent during this period.[7]

Yet, despite these criticisms, Lord Ernle could claim that at last British woodlands were coming to be treated commercially.[8] There were many

---

[1] R.C. Agriculture, Reps. by Assistant Commissioners, 229 (P.P. 1881, xvi).

[2] Special Rep. of Inclosure Commissioners, 1861, 4 (P.P. 1861, xx).

[3] Agricultural Returns, 1871, 55 (P.P. 1871, lxix); Rep. on census of woodland, 1924 (H.M.S.O., 1928), 6.

[4] C. E. Curtis, 'The management and planting of British woodlands', J.R.A.S., LXIV (1903), 16.

[5] E. P. Stebbing, Commercial forestry in Britain (London, 1919), 35–7.

[6] Lord Eversley (1910), 46.

[7] H. C. Prince, Parks in England (Shalfleet, I.O.W., 1967), 10.

[8] R. E. Prothero (later Lord Ernle), English farming past and present (1st ed., London, 1912), 383.

reports of new plantings, often on poorer land thrown out of cultivation. At Langham, in Essex, woods of larch and fir had recently been planted when Rider Haggard made his tour in 1901–2.[1] In Surrey there had been extensive afforestation with larch and pine on poor land, and on the Hampton Lodge estate near Farnham, for example, a considerable area had been planted between 1880 and 1905, chiefly with Scots pine, but with some Douglas fir, Corsican pine, spruce and larch.[2] These woods were mainly for ornamental and sporting purposes, but large tracts of Scots pine had been planted on adjacent areas to supply hop poles.[3] Comparison of successive editions of Ordnance Survey maps reveals numerous plantings in other areas, often in small plots on difficult terrain, as on steep slopes in the Oxfordshire Chilterns, or on poor soils, as on the Greensand outcrop in Bedfordshire, where 666 acres were planted on the Woburn estate between 1897 and 1907.[4] The evidence of the large-scale maps also suggests that some lowland heaths and commons were being colonised by trees, although the different styles of the first and second editions of the six-inch maps make comparison difficult. Large tracts of Hindhead Common, which were bare of trees in 1871, were shown as woodland in 1894–6 and, not far away, on Witley Common scattered trees had become more numerous; but the trend was by no means universal and trees had apparently disappeared from some commons. Afforestation must also have continued in upland areas, where the planting of catchments was being encouraged, while on the Grizedale Hall estate in Lancashire, oak coppice was being converted into high forest by allowing single saplings to grow and cutting back the remainder.[5]

What is clear from the Ordnance Survey maps, from contemporary accounts and from the 1924 census of woodland, is that many of the trees planted were conifers, although interpretation of the census data is complicated by extensive fellings during the First World War. The abnormal age structure of the broadleaf forest shows that it was not being replaced by new plantings, while conifers accounted for a much higher proportion of the woodland planted between 1884 and 1914 than their share of the mature high forest would warrant; coniferous high forests represented

[1] H. R. Haggard, I, 445–6.
[2] J. Nisbet in H. E. Malden (ed.), *V.C.H. Surrey*, II (1905), 576, 578.
[3] *Ibid.*, 578.
[4] J. C. Cox in W. Page (ed.), *V.C.H. Bedfordshire*, II (1908), 146.
[5] W. Farrer in W. Farrer and J. Brownhill (eds.), *V.C.H. Lancashire*, II (1908), 465–6.

only 26% of high forest in England, but accounted for 45% of new plant-ings, and for more than 50% in such different counties as Buckingham-shire, Surrey and Westmorland.[1] Whatever the ambiguities of the data, afforestation, much of it with conifers, was certainly taking place; but its scale was small, and the English woodlands remained some of the least extensive and least productive in Europe.

Other rural land uses

Agriculture and forestry were not the only activities in rural areas. In addition to mining, other demands were increasingly made on rural land. Some of these, like field sports, were long-established; but most were new, at least in the form in which they appeared, as with water-gathering in the uplands and with public recreation. Hunting, shooting and fishing had long been features of rural life, but they were generally the preserve of landowners and their friends, and involved little in the way of land manage-ment. From the middle of the nineteenth century the shooting of driven grouse became an increasingly important aspect of land management on heather moor, and the renting of shootings became fashionable. Some indication of the changing importance is given by the increase in the size of bag on the duke of Devonshire's 14,000 acres of grouse moor at Bolton Abbey, where the average bag of grouse increased from less than 200 brace a year between 1800 and 1850 to over 3,600 brace by the end of the century.[2] In the lowlands, too, the impoverishment of both landowners and land, and the rise of a wealthy, non-landowning clientele, led to the commercial letting of shootings and often of a landowner's residence.[3] This trend was particularly marked in areas of poor land such as the Breckland, where shooting became the principal activity and where land was kept in cultivation as much for game birds as for its agricultural output; the partridge was said to have been 'the salvation of Norfolk farming' and an estate such as that of Lord Iveagh near Thetford became principally a sporting property.[4] Large stretches were given up to game and rabbits and many owners were no longer resident, but had let their houses to

[1] *Rep. on census of woodland, 1924* (H.M.S.O., 1928), 33.

[2] A. S. Leslie (ed.), *The grouse in health and disease* (London, 1911), 384.

[3] *R.C. Agric. Depression, Rep. by Mr R. Hunter Pringle on the Ongar . . . Districts of Essex*, 72 (P.P. 1794, xvi, pt. 1); H. R. Haggard, II, 2.

[4] *R.C. Agric. Depression, Rep. by Mr R. Henry Rew on the County of Norfolk*, 58 (P.P. 1895, xvii); H. R. Haggard, II, 2.

shooting tenants.[1] Other poor land which had tumbled down was let for sport as well as for rough grazings.[2]

A middle-class counterpart of these interests in field sports was the growing concern throughout the second half of the nineteenth century with outdoor recreation and with what was coming to be called amenity, the visual quality of the countryside. The General Enclosure Act of 1845 had made provision for the allotment of land for recreation, but by 1876 only 1,742 acres had been allotted out of a total of 618,800 acres enclosed under this Act.[3] Problems were arising over the management of commons around London, and there was a growing feeling, epitomised by the formation in 1865 of the Commons Preservation Society, that the remaining commons ought not to be enclosed but kept for public recreation. Attention was mainly concentrated on commons near towns, but there was also resistance to encroachment on rural commons, dramatised in 1866 by the train load of labourers brought out by night to remove the iron fences erected around Berkhamsted Common in Hertfordshire.[4] The Metropolitan Commons Act of 1866 provided machinery for the regulation of commons within fifteen miles of Charing Cross and the Enclosure Act of 1876 laid much greater stress on the recreational needs of the public at large, although in practice it was not as effective as the Commons Preservation Society would have wished.[5] In addition there were several special acts, such as that for the preservation of the Malvern Hills. Finally the Enclosure Act of 1899 made provision for regulated commons, to which the public could be granted access, and some large rural commons were opened to the public in this way. Attempts to provide rights of access to all moorland areas were unsuccessful, although the growing concern with amenity gained a further outlet with the formation of the National Trust in 1895.

The uplands were also being required to provide water for the growing towns around their flanks. The first considerable reservoirs had been those begun by Manchester Corporation in the Longdendale valley in the 1840s, but gradually all suitable areas in the southern Pennines were taken for gathering grounds and towns had to look farther afield:[6] to the north of the Wharfe, where Leeds and Bradford established reservoirs in the

---

[1] R.C. Agric. Depression, Rep. by Mr Wilson Fox on the County of Suffolk, 31, 38 (P.P. 1895, xvi).

[2] Rep. on Decline in Agric. Pop., 1881–1906, 35 (P.P. 1906, xcvi).

[3] E. C. K. Gonner, 93.   [4] Lord Eversley (1910), 46.   [5] Ibid., 198.

[6] R. C. S. Walters, The nation's water supply (London, 1936), 99.

Washburn and Nith valleys respectively; to the Lake District, where Manchester acquired Thirlemere; and to Wales, which supplied Birmingham and Liverpool. Other upland areas were required to make their contribution and by 1904 the gathering grounds, mostly moorland, held by local authorities in England amounted to at least 82,050 acres and in Wales to at least 6,350 acres.[1]

Another, though more localised, feature of the countryside was the diversion of land to military use, and in the 1890s the War Office acquired a large tract of land on Salisbury Plain for training grounds.[2] Heathland on the Surrey–Hampshire border was also purchased and extensive barracks and rifle ranges constructed; in Pirbright parish, for example, nearly three-quarters of the parish was military land.[3]

INDUSTRY

The broad features of the industrial geography of England which had emerged by 1850 were still recognisable at the outbreak of the First World War in 1914 and, with the exception of iron and steel and shipbuilding, no major changes in the location of the different branches of industry occurred in the intervening period. The most obvious development was the growth of industry, whether measured by the size of the industrial population, which doubled, or by the volume of output, which increased fourfold between 1851 and 1911.[4] It is true that the character of existing industry altered, that new industries developed and that several new industrial towns appeared on the map of England, but the principal centres of the various branches of manufacturing industry were those established during the industrial revolution; the chief differences were that they were bigger and more complex.

Unfortunately, the data available for the study of changes in the industrial geography of this period are very unsatisfactory, particularly for the new, expanding and technically complex industries such as engineering. Classifications of occupations in the decennial censuses, which are the main (and in many instances the only) source, were frequently changed and, although comparisons can be made between the censuses of 1851, 1861 and 1871 and between those from 1881 to 1911, no reliable view of

---

[1] *Reconstruction Cttee, Forestry Subcttee: Final Report*, 93 (P.P. 1917–18, xviii).
[2] C. R. Clinker in E. Crittall (ed.), *V.C.H. Wiltshire*, IV (1959), 290.
[3] D. M. Sprules in H. E. Malden (ed.), *V.C.H. Surrey*, III (1911), 363.
[4] B. R. Mitchell with P. Deane, 60, 271–2.

changes over the period as a whole is possible. Even if data were comparable the use of the occupational tables as a basis for comparison would be unsatisfactory, as changes in productivity varied widely from industry to industry and throughout the period, so that the longer the time-scale the broader and less certain must any conclusion be. Because of their complexity and the lack of data about their distribution, many branches of manufacturing industry will be under-represented in the account which follows.

Comparisons between different industries are particularly difficult, but Hoffman's coefficients of growth for the United Kingdom for the period 1855–1913, which, if acceptable, must broadly reflect conditions in England as a whole, show above-average values in the making of paper, furniture, cotton piece-goods, tobacco and woollen cloth among consumer goods and of aluminium, zinc, rubber products, iron and steel manufactures, timber and copper products among producer goods.[1] Some industries, on the other hand, such as silk manufacture and lead production, declined, and others grew more slowly than industry as a whole. Production by machinery in factories extended its hold, and most remaining kinds of domestic industry were eliminated; by 1901, handwork and outwork, which had been characteristic of hosiery, boot and shoe, nail and cutlery manufacture and many other industries in 1850, were largely confined to the tailoring and clothing trades.[2]

Coalmining

Coal was the principal source of power throughout these decades, although latterly electricity, gas and oil became alternatives, and increasing efficiency in the use of coal was weakening the pull of the coalfields. Nevertheless, coal remained a major factor in industrial location, and coalmining was itself one of the principal growth industries; output of the English fields rose fairly steadily from some 48 million tons in 1854 (the first year for which complete figures are available) to 185 million in 1913.[3] Not all coal was consumed by industry; increasing quantities were taken by railways and householders, and the share of exports rose from little more than a twentieth in 1850 to a fifth in 1903 and nearly a third by 1913.[4]

[1] W. G. Hoffmann, *British industry, 1700–1950* (Oxford, 1955), 69, *passim*.

[2] *Rep. S.C. on Home Work*, 238 (P.P. 1907, vi).

[3] *Return of the Quantities of Coal etc.*, 2 (P.P. 1856, lv); *Mines and Quarries: General Report, with Statistics, for 1913*, 220 (P.P. 1914–16, lxxx).

[4] J. H. Clapham, *An economic history of modern Britain: the early railway age, 1820–1850* (Cambridge, 1926), 430, 484; J. H. Clapham (1938), 63; W. Smith, 275.

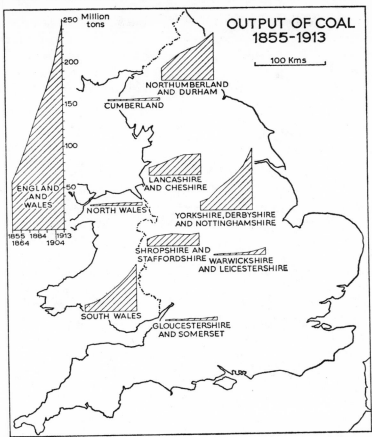

Fig. 68   Output of coal, 1855–1913
Based on: (1) R. Hunt, *Mineral statistics, 1855* (Mem. Geol. Survey, 1856);
(2) *Mines and Quarries: General Report with Statistics for 1913* (P.P. 1914–16,
lxxx).
The negligible output for Kent in 1913 (59,000 tons) cannot be shown.

Only one new field was discovered, the concealed Kent coalfield, and
this was only on the verge of production in 1913, but there were major
changes in the share of output from different coalfields and in the distribution of mining within each field (Fig. 68).[1] In 1850, Northumberland
and Durham, with their considerable sea-coal trade to London, had been
the principal sources of coal, but although their output rose steadily, they
were overtaken in the 1890s by the most extensive and most easily worked

[1] J. H. Clapham (1938), 166–7; B. R. Mitchell with P. Deane, 115–16.

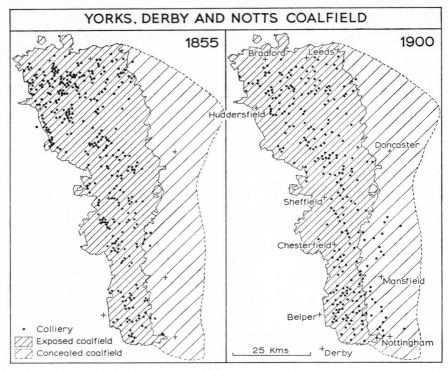

Fig. 69 Yorks, Derby and Notts coalfield in 1855 and 1900
Based on: (1) R. Hunt, *Mineral statistics, 1855* (Mem. Geol. Survey, 1856);
(2) *List of mines, 1900* (H.M.S.O., 1901).

of the coalfields – that of Yorkshire, Derbyshire and Nottinghamshire. Industrial growth, the increasing concern of the coastal fields with the export trade, the development of the railway network, and competition between the railway companies for the coal trade, were considerably extending the markets of the interior fields. At the same time, the coal resources of some of the old and smaller fields were either approaching exhaustion (with contemporary standards of technology), or becoming more difficult to work; in the south Staffordshire field, the working out of the more accessible seams of the famous 'thick coal' and difficulties of drainage led to an increasing reliance on mines in Cannock Chase, which accounted for a third of joint output of both fields in 1880 and a half in 1900.[1] The relative, and after 1872 the absolute, decline of production on

[1] M. J. Wise, 'The Cannock Chase region', in M. J. Wise (ed.), *Birmingham and its regional setting* (Birmingham, 1950), 279–80.

the south Staffordshire coalfield also stimulated the expansion of mining in east Warwickshire, which had good rail and canal communications with Birmingham and the Black Country.[1]

Changes in the distribution of mining within individual fields were less striking. Many additional shafts were sunk in existing areas and some pits reorganised or deepened, but the most interesting changes geographically were the abandonment of small shallow pits in the outcrop of the Coal Measures, and the increasing number of deeper shafts sunk through over-lying strata to reach concealed fields. This trend may be illustrated by the Yorkshire, Derbyshire and Nottinghamshire field, where many mines along the western margin went out of production between 1855 and 1900, although some of these were very small pits producing only ganister (Fig. 69). Expansion into the concealed field was most marked in Notting-hamshire where the first deep shaft was sunk in 1859 and where sixteen pits were opened between 1870 and 1880.[2] Developments elsewhere were similar but in some fields there were technical difficulties; in south-east Durham, extension of mining was hindered by the difficulty of penetrating water-bearing sands, but a technique of freezing was employed after 1900 to permit the sinking of new shafts into the concealed field.[3] In other areas, new markets or communications extended mining; there was a considerable expansion of mining in the Ashington area of Northumberland, following the development of the port of Blyth, where coal shipments rose from 150,000 tons in 1883 to 4,730,000 tons in 1913.[4]

The iron and steel industries

Iron-ore mining. The distribution of iron-ore mining underwent a much more radical transformation and, by contrast with coal, home production faced increasing competition from imported, high-grade ores (especially from Spain). Imports, which were negligible in 1850, had reached 7.4

---

[1] J. C. Mitcheson in M. J. Wise (ed.), 296.

[2] G. D. B. Gray, 'The south Yorkshire coalfield', *Geography*, XXXII (1947), 113–31; K. C. Edwards, 'Coal', in K. C. Edwards (ed.), *Nottingham and its region* (Nottingham, 1966), 279–80.

[3] G. Poole and A. Raistrick, 'Extractive industries', in P. C. G. Isaac and R. E. A. Allan (eds.), *Scientific survey of north-eastern England* (Newcastle upon Tyne, 1949), 88–9.

[4] A. E. Smailes, *North England* (London and Edinburgh, 1960), 174; J. H. Clapham (1938), 388.

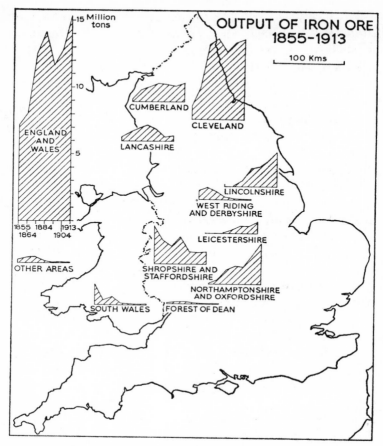

Fig. 70   Output of iron ore, 1855–1913
          Sources as for Fig. 68.
          'Other areas' include Cornwall, Devon, Durham, Northumberland, Somer-
          set, Warwick, Wiltshire, Worcester, North Wales and, in some years,
          Cheshire, Hampshire, Nottingham and Westmorland.

million tons by 1910.[1] The principal internal change was the decline in the
production of Coal Measure ores and the exploitation of those not associated with the coalfields (Fig. 70). In 1850, the Coal Measure ores were
estimated to provide 95% of output, but by 1913 they contributed only
10% of a much larger total of domestic ore.[2] Their place was taken mainly

[1] H. G. Roepke, *Movements of the British iron and steel industry 1720 to 1951*
(Urbana, Illinois, 1956), 61.   [2] *Ibid.*, 61, 63; W. Smith, 120, 322.

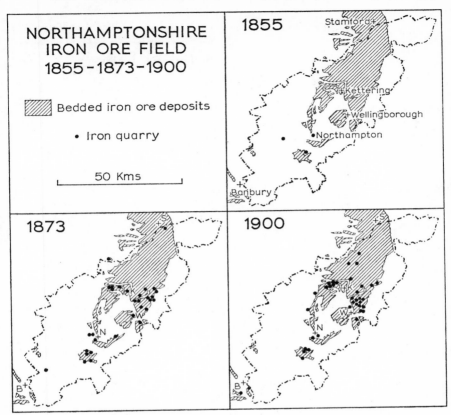

Fig. 71 Northamptonshire ironfield in 1855, 1873 and 1900
Based on: (1) R. Hunt, *Mineral statistics, 1855* (Mem. Geol. Survey, 1856);
(2) R. Hunt, *Mineral statistics, 1873* (Mem. Geol. Survey, 1874); (3) *List of quarries, 1900* (H.M.S.O., 1901).

by the rich haematite of Cumberland and north Lancashire and by the low-grade bedded ores which occur in the Jurassic rocks between Oxford-shire and the North Riding, although other ore bodies played a part, such as the magnetite of Rosedale in the North York Moors.[1]

Mining of haematite was given a strong stimulus by the demand for non-phosphoric ores for Bessemer steel. The output of ore expanded sharply between 1850 and 1870, especially in the Barrow area where a large ore body had been discovered in 1850; but from the 1880s difficulties of mining, competition from imported haematite, and the exploitation of

[1] J. C. Carr and W. Taplin, *History of the British steel industry* (Oxford, 1962), 13.

Fig. 72   Blast furnaces in 1855
         Based on R. Hunt, *Mineral statistics, 1855* (Mem. Geol. Survey, 1856).
         Only furnaces in blast are shown.

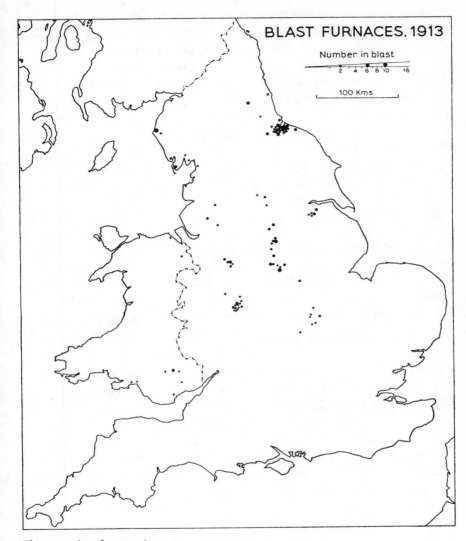

Fig. 73   Blast furnaces in 1913
Based on *Mines and Quarries: General Report with Statistics for 1913* (P.P. 1914–16, lxxx).

more easily worked Jurassic ores, led to a decline in production.[1] The existence of ores in the Jurassic rocks had been known much earlier, but they began to be worked extensively only from mid-century. In Cleveland, following the opening of mines at Eston in 1850, there was a rapid expansion of output until the peak year of 1883; thereafter output stagnated, and increasing quantities of ore were imported for steel production on Teeside.[2] Following the rediscovery of ironstone beds in Northamptonshire, a consignment was sent to Staffordshire in 1852, although at first the Midland ironmasters were said to be prejudiced against these ores.[3] By 1864 their prejudices had been overcome, and output grew rapidly in the next decade, reaching nearly 1½ million tons in 1873; the ore was worked in both mines and quarries and, although a steam navvy was introduced in 1895, production was mainly by hand until after the First World War.[4] The Lincolnshire ores, similarly rediscovered, were mined from 1859, and production had reached 2.6 million tons by 1913.[5] Output from east Midland fields accounted for a rising proportion of home production and, by 1913, 43% of the output of domestic ores came from these sources.[6] Changes in the location of mines and quarries within fields was much more narrowly confined than in coalmining; only in Northamptonshire was there any great extension of the area affected by mining (Fig. 71).

Pig-iron production. Between 1855 and 1913 the quantity of pig-iron made in England rose from 1½ to 8 million tons, and there were also changes in the location of pig-iron production. These resulted from developments in mining, and also from the changing demand for its products (Figs. 72 and 73).[7] The major feature was the declining importance of sites on the coalfields and the rise of new centres on the orefields and at the coast. In 1852 three-quarters of all pig-iron was made in the west Midlands, but output was already declining in 1865 when the number of blast furnaces reached its peak.[8] As local ores were exhausted there was an increasing

[1] *Ibid.*, 12; B. R. Mitchell with P. Deane, 129–30.

[2] H. G. Roepke, 54, 63; J. H. Clapham (1932), 48; B. R. Mitchell with P. Deane, 129–30.

[3] S. H. Beaver, 'The development of the Northamptonshire iron industry 1851–1930', in L. D. Stamp and S. W. Wooldridge (eds.), *London essays in geography* (London, 1951), 34.   [4] *Ibid.*, 38–9, 49.

[5] D. C. D. Pocock, 'Stages in the development of the Frodingham ironstone field', *Trans. and Papers, Inst. Brit. Geog.*, XXXV (1964), 105; H. G. Roepke, 64–5.

[6] *Ibid.*, 66.   [7] *Ibid.*, 64–5.

[8] B. R. Mitchell with P. Deane, 131; B. L. C. Johnson and M. J. Wise in M. J. Wise (ed.), 237.

reliance on ores from other domestic fields, especially from the east Midlands, but this was only a temporary phase, for economies in the use of coal and the high cost of iron manufacture on coalfield sites were reducing their advantages. It is true that some ironmasters were acquiring leases of orefields in the east Midlands, but production of pig-iron on the coalfields gradually declined.[1] By 1911 there were only two major and eleven smaller furnaces remaining in south Staffordshire, and there was a similar, though somewhat later, decline in the production of pig-iron on other coalfields. In north Staffordshire and west Yorkshire the peak was reached in the 1870s, and by 1913 the number of furnaces in blast on the former field had declined from thirty-six to thirteen.[2]

The most successful of the new areas was Teesside. Its initial advantages of easily worked ore and close proximity to Durham coke were reinforced by the larger size and greater efficiency of the Teeside furnaces compared with older plant elsewhere, and by its estuarine site when Spanish ore began to be imported in 1861, although Cleveland ore still accounted for 84% of the ore used in 1883 and 60% in 1913.[3] The first furnaces were blown in 1852 and by 1869 there were 92; production expanded rapidly, rising to nearly 248,000 tons in 1860, and to 766,000 tons in 1870.[4] For a brief period iron-making spread more widely in the North Riding, but many of the works outside the Tees valley did not survive long, and nearly all pig-iron was produced at estuarine sites. By 1913, some 2,639,000 tons were being made.[5]

Elsewhere on the Jurassic outcrop, the development of pig-iron making came later and the industry grew more slowly; for these fields were much less accessible to sources of coking coal and to the ports, and the ores were not suitable for steel making until the development of the basic process. At first all the Northamptonshire ore was sent to furnaces on the coalfields, but in 1853 pig-iron was made at Wellingborough from local ores; thereafter, the number of blast furnaces increased steadily, although half

[1] S. H. Beaver (1951), 43.

[2] B. L. C. Johnson and M. J. Wise in M. J. Wise (ed.), 243; S. H. Beaver, 'The Potteries', *Trans. and Papers, Inst. Brit. Geog.*, XXXIV (1964), 17; F. J. Fowler, 'West Yorkshire', in J. B. Mitchell (ed.), *Great Britain, geographical essays* (Cambridge, 1962), 364.

[3] J. C. Carr and W. Taplin, 51, 152; J. H. Clapham (1932), 50; W. Smith, 327.

[4] A. A. L. Caesar in J. B. Mitchell (ed.), 445; B. R. Mitchell with P. Deane, 131–2 (the figures are for the North Riding).

[5] B. R. Mitchell with P. Deane, 132. For the north-east coast, the figure was 3,869,000.

the ore continued to be sent to other areas.[1] Pig-iron was first made at Scunthorpe in 1864.[2]

The sequence of events in north-west England was different again, although this area was also handicapped by its remoteness from both markets and supplies of coke, despite the opening of a line from the Durham coalfield in 1861.[3] At first, all ore was sent elsewhere, but a blast furnace was blown at Barrow in 1857, and the increased demand for an iron suitable for Bessemer steel led to a sharp rise in the output of pig-iron between 1865 and 1870; production reached its peak of nearly 1.6 million tons around 1900.[4]

Steel manufacture. In the third quarter of the nineteenth century most pig-iron was still made into wrought or puddled iron, with the Midlands, Sheffield and, increasingly, north-east England as the major centres.[5] Between 1860 and 1875 the number of finished-iron works and puddling furnaces grew but, although puddled iron was able to hold its own for a while, it faced increasing competition from steel.[6] From 1882 both the output of puddled iron and the number of puddling furnaces declined steadily, the industry surviving longest in those areas, such as the west Midlands, where there was a large local market for its products; but even there iron was giving way to steel.[7]

Until the revolutions in steel making associated with the names of Bessemer and Siemens made steel competitive with wrought-iron, steel manufacture was on a small scale and was almost entirely confined to Sheffield, which became, until 1879, the principal area for both Bessemer and open-hearth steel.[8] The Bessemer process was the first to be developed commercially, in 1856, although until the invention of the Thomas–Gilchrist basic process, whereby phosphorus was eliminated from phosphoric ores, the ores in the Jurassic rocks were unsuitable for steel making. The Siemens brothers' 'open-hearth' furnace for steel making, though

[1] J. C. Carr and W. Taplin, 89; S. H. Beaver (1951), 39, 41.

[2] D. C. D. Pocock, 'Iron and steel at Scunthorpe', *East Midland Geographer*, III, pt. 3 (1963), 125; H. G. Roepke, 69, 71.

[3] A. E. Smailes, 184.

[4] J. C. Carr and W. Taplin, 12; H. G. Roepke, 77.

[5] J. H. Clapham (1932), 52, 57.

[6] J. C. Carr and W. Taplin, 38.

[7] J. H. Clapham (1932), 52.

[8] J. C. Carr and W. Taplin, 11; K. Warren, 'The Sheffield rail trade', *Trans. and Papers, Inst. Brit. Geog.*, XXXIV (1964), 131.

patented in 1861, was not in commercial use until 1868, but because of the better control which this method offered and its ability to use scrap, open-hearth steel gradually replaced Bessemer steel; 80% of the steel made in Great Britain in 1880 was Bessemer steel, but by 1900 the proportion was only 36%.[1] With the successful development of the Thomas–Gilchrist process in 1880, an increasing proportion of the steel made by both methods was basic steel.

Accompanying these technical changes were changes in the geography of steel making. The first major market for steel was in the manufacture of rails, where it gradually displaced iron during the 1870s.[2] Rail making was concentrated in Sheffield, which had seventeen of the forty-nine Bessemer converters producing steel in 1869, and in south Lancashire, which had twenty.[3] The suitability of the haematite ores of Cumberland and Lancashire for Bessemer acid steel led to a rapid expansion of steel making in the north-west, where Barrow had, for a while, the largest steelworks in the country.[4] This area accounted for two-fifths of all steel made in England in 1880, but it was handicapped by the high cost of mining the ore and by the lack of both coking coal and a major local market for its steel; although its output had risen to over 700,000 tons by the 1890s, its share of English production declined steadily, to less than a tenth in 1913.[5]

The development of steel making on the north-east coast, especially on Teesside, was delayed by the large investment which had been made in the iron industry since 1850, by the unsuitability of the local ores for acid Bessemer steel, by the large local market for wrought iron, and by unfavourable experience with steel in shipbuilding.[6] Nevertheless, it rapidly became a major centre for Bessemer steel and established an early lead in the production of basic Bessemer; with the widespread acceptance of both the open-hearth process and of sheet steel for ship plates, the north-east became the major centre for steel production in England, accounting for over 2 million tons in 1913, or nearly half the total output.[7]

The west Midlands were slow to adopt Bessemer steel, largely because

---

[1] *Ibid.*, 34; W. A. Sinclair, 'The growth of the British steel industry in the late 19th century', *Scottish Jour. of Polit. Econ.*, VI (1959), 44–5; H. G. Roepke, 85.

[2] J. C. Carr and W. Taplin, 34.

[3] H. G. Roepke, 84.

[4] *Ibid.*, 83; J. C. Carr and W. Taplin, 84.

[5] H. G. Roepke, 83. The figure for Great Britain was 5%.

[6] *Ibid.*, 28; D. L. Burn, *The economic history of steel-making 1867–1939* (Cambridge, 1940), 173–4.

[7] W. A. Sinclair, 35; H. G. Roepke, 83. The figure for Great Britain was 27%.

of the region's heavy commitment to the wrought-iron trades, and never became a major steel-producing area; for it lacked both good coking coal and ready access to either domestic or imported ore.[1] Production in Sheffield rose almost threefold between 1880 and 1913 to reach 879,000 tons, although its share declined from a third to a fifth.[2] The only new centre to appear was Scunthorpe, where steel production began in 1890; but, unlike continental Europe, there was no major development on the Jurassic orefields, mainly because of the ease with which high-grade ores could be imported and the lack of readily accessible supplies of coking coal.[3]

Engineering industries. Users of iron and steel were often to be found in the same localities as blast furnaces and steelworks, and the steel-rail trade in particular was closely associated with steel making. But there were differences; the old-established districts such as the west Midlands and Sheffield continued as important centres for the manufacture of iron and steel products, but no large iron- and steel-using industries developed inland along the Jurassic outcrop, and the market for iron and steel was much more widely dispersed than their manufacture. Engineering, which had been largely confined at mid-century to the making of textile machinery, stationary steam-engines, locomotives and rolling stock, now became increasingly diversified, especially after 1875.[4] Marine engineering from the 1850s, the manufacture of gas engines from the 1870s, electrical engineering and cycle making from the 1880s – all provide examples of branches of engineering which rose to prominence in this period; and each in turn required the making of machine tools, which were becoming increasingly important for mass production of articles like guns and sewing machines.[5] Not all were widely distributed, although the increasing use of electrical and gas engines enlarged the choice of possible sites; marine engineering was mainly associated with shipbuilding, especially in north-east England, agricultural machinery with towns such as Ipswich and Lincoln in the leading arable districts and the cycle industry with the west Midlands. The manufacture of motor cars, which began in 1896 with

[1] W. K. V. Gale in M. J. Wise (ed.), 208; G. C. Allen, *The industrial development of Birmingham and the Black Country* (London, 1929), 238–43; J. C. Carr and W. Taplin, 79.   [2] H. G. Roepke, 83. For Great Britain, from 28% to 11%.
[3] J. H. Clapham (1938), 147; J. C. Carr and W. Taplin, 156; D. C. D. Pocock, 129.
[4] J. B. Jefferys, *The story of the engineers 1800–1945* (London, n.d.), 52; G. C. Allen, *British industries and their organisation* (London, 4th edn., 1959), 135.
[5] G. C. Allen (1959), 135.

the formation of the Daimler Motor Company, was established in the west Midlands partly by accident, although an area with such varied manufactures, especially in small metal trades, had obvious attractions for an assembly industry of this kind. Employment in car making rose from 151 in 1900 to 34,000 in 1913, partly in newly established firms and partly in firms which had turned to car manufacture from cycle production, and by 1913 the two industries had become the largest single trade in the west Midlands.[1]

The increasing scale of operation, and the mechanisation of many branches of engineering, led to larger factories and to some changes in location; for example, the hand-made nail trade of the Black Country rapidly declined in face of competition from factory nail-making established in Leeds and elsewhere.[2] The major locational change in engineering was in shipbuilding. Before iron was commonly used in the construction of ships, shipbuilding had been widespread, with London and the Thames estuary as the leading area.[3] When iron and, after 1880, steel became the chief material, and increased quantities of coal were needed in shipbuilding, London was at a disadvantage, and the organisation of the industry on Thames-side also helped to raise costs of production.[4] The cheaper classes of ships came to be made in increasing numbers in northern shipyards on the Clyde, the Tyne, the Wear and the Tees, and the Admiralty also began to place orders there. London's share declined both relatively and absolutely, and it became dependent on ship-repairing and the making of expensive or experimental ships.[5] Between 1854 and 1914, employment in shipbuilding on the north-east coast increased tenfold, and by 1914 some 87% of the tonnage launched in England was built in this area.[6]

Textile industries

The distribution of the textile industries underwent no fundamental change, although their relative importance declined as other branches of manufacturing were developed, and their share of total employment almost halved between 1851 and 1911.[7] Employment in cotton manufactures

[1] *Ibid.*, 174; G. C. Allen (1929), 297; S. B. Saul, 'The motor industry in Britain to 1914', *Business History*, V (1962–4), 24.

[2] G. C. Allen (1929), 227, 272–4.

[3] S. Pollard, 'The decline of shipbuilding on the Thames', *Econ. Hist. Rev.*, 2nd ser., III (1950–1), 72.   [4] *Ibid.*, 72; G. C. Allen (1959), 157.

[5] S. Pollard, 76, 78, 85.   [6] A. E. Smailes, 182; W. Smith, 391.

[7] B. R. Mitchell with P. Deane, 60.

grew, as did the number of spindles, and factories increased in size and productivity; thus, the average cotton weaver managed 1.6 looms in 1850 and 2.2 in 1882.[1] Lancashire's dominant role remained unchallenged, but between 1841 and 1884 the two main branches of the cotton industry became segregated into a southern spinning district, based on Oldham, and a northern weaving district, based on Blackburn, largely as a consequence of the earlier development of spinning as a factory industry in south Lancashire and the co-existence of suitable physical resources and a large reserve of workers with experience of textiles among the hand-loom weavers of Rossendale and east Lancashire when weaving was being mechanised.[2] By 1884, 62% of the looms were in northern districts and 78% of the spindles in southern districts, and this regionalisation, which was accompanied by specialisation of plant, subsequently became more marked.[3]

Employment in the woollen and worsted industries changed relatively little, although the number of power looms more than doubled between 1856 and 1874 and the consumption of wool trebled between 1850–4 and 1909–13.[4] Wool was not predominantly a factory industry until about 1860 and the concentration of manufacturing into factories was not completed until the last quarter of the nineteenth century.[5] Yorkshire, which already accounted for 70% of employment in wool and worsted in 1851, remained the leading area;[6] indeed, worsted weaving became even more concentrated in the West Riding, until by 1904 more than 93% of looms were to be found there. In the early years of the twentieth century, however, worsted spinning was growing rapidly in the east Midlands to meet the needs of hosiery knitters, although its share of output remained small.[7] Most of the remaining outliers of woollen manufacture were gradually eliminated, with the exception of the Gloucestershire industry based on Stroud, and even this declined. Increasing specialisation by area was also a feature of the Yorkshire textile industry, but this was based, not upon function (as in Lancashire), but on product, with worsted manufacture concentrated in the north-west around Bradford and Halifax, and woollens

[1] J. H. Clapham (1932), 82; J. H. Clapham (1938), 175.

[2] J. Jewkes, 'The localisation of the cotton industry', *Economic History*, II (1930), 95–6; W. Smith, 474–5.

[3] J. Jewkes, 96; S. J. Chapman and T. S. Ashton, 'The sizes of business, mainly in the textile industries', *Jour. Roy. Stat. Soc.*, LXXVII (1914), 491–2.

[4] B. R. Mitchell with P. Deane, 198; G. C. Allen (1959), 254.

[5] *Ibid.*, 253.   [6] W. Smith, 135.   [7] *Ibid.*, 435, 449, 451.

in the south-east between Huddersfield and Wakefield; there was also a contrast in organisation, with the great majority of firms in the woollen industry combining spinning and weaving, while those in worsted manufacture exhibited a high degree of specialisation.[1]

The silk industry became a less important branch of textile manufacture after the abolition of protective duties in 1861; in the town of Derby, for example, the twenty-one manufacturers of silk in 1864 had been reduced to two in 1912, and the number of employees from 4,760 in 1851 to 300 in 1911.[2] Artificial silk did not take its place until 1885, and the first important factory was opened only in 1900.[3] On the other hand, the hosiery industry grew steadily and was transformed from an almost entirely domestic craft into a factory industry. In 1860, domestic workers, scattered in Leicestershire villages, outnumbered factory workers by more than twelve to one, but between 1850 and 1892 there was a tenfold drop in the number of hand-frames, although some 5,000 remained in 1892 and there were still 25,000 outworkers in 1907.[4] The transformation of the clothing trade from a domestic craft to a factory-based activity was also in progress during this period, especially in the main textile areas; in Leeds, for example, there were some 7 or 8 factories in 1881 and 54 in 1891.[5] Nevertheless, clothing remained the branch of manufacturing industry with the largest number of outworkers; in 1901 these constituted 80% of all those working at home.[6]

Other industries

Boot and shoe manufacture also became a factory industry in this period, although for several decades the industry remained heavily dependent on outwork, and much of what was done in factories was not mechanised. In the 1850s the making of boots and shoes was a widespread rural craft, although it already gave employment to proportionately four times as many people in Northamptonshire as in the country as a whole.[7] Its development in this county was helped by the decline of other domestic

---

[1] *Ibid.*, 440–7.

[2] D. M. Smith, 'The silk industry of the east Midlands', *East Midland Geographer*, III, pt. 1 (1962), 29.

[3] J. H. Clapham (1938), 181.

[4] J. H. Clapham (1932), 85–6; J. H. Clapham (1938), 178–9.

[5] J. H. Clapham (1938), 183.

[6] *Rep. S.C. on Home Work*, 238 (P.P. 207, vi).

[7] P. R. Mounfield, 'The footwear industry of the east Midlands: (iii) Northamptonshire, 1700–1911', *East Midland Geographer*, III, pt. 8 (1965), 434.

crafts and by the absence of competing industries. Factories were built in Northampton and subsequently in other towns, notably in the Ise valley.[1] Leicestershire also became an important industrial county, especially for lighter footwear, although here the predominance of a single centre, Leicester, was more marked.[2] In 1871, 71% of those working in boot- and shoe-making were still outworkers, but by 1904, most of those employed in this trade were working in factories.[3]

The chemical industry, which roughly doubled its labour force between 1851 and 1911, also rose to prominence, although its great diversity and the lack of satisfactory statistical data make it difficult to measure changes.[4] New branches, such as that of dyestuffs, came into being, and old branches, such as soap-making, were transformed; but the principal regional change was the decline of the established heavy chemical industry in north-east England and the development of alkali manufacture in Lancashire and Cheshire. In 1867 more than half the output of alkali was manufactured on Tyneside by the Leblanc process and production of chemicals here was at its maximum in 1880; by 1895 only four works survived out of the twenty-five which had been in production in the early 1870s.[5] By 1864, there were already twice as many chemical factories in Lancashire and Cheshire as on Tyneside, and the granting of a licence for the Solvay process to the firm of Brunner Mond and Company gave this area an added advantage, for this was replacing the Leblanc process; the growth of Widnes provides a striking example of industrial specialisation.[6] Production of salt from the Cheshire brine fields, on which both areas depended, grew rapidly until the 1880s, but the Tees-side field, although discovered in 1859, was not worked until 1881, too late to save the chemical industry in the north-east.[7]

Many other new and old-established industries grew in this period. Rubber manufacture, which had developed under the protection of the textile industry, was greatly stimulated by the demand for insulating

---

[1] *Ibid.*, 437.

[2] P. R. Mounfield, 'The footwear industry of the east Midlands: (iv) Leicestershire, 1700–1911', *East Midland Geographer*, IV (1966), 9, 17.

[3] J. H. Clapham (1932), 119; J. H. Clapham (1938), 181.

[4] J. H. Clapham (1938), 171.

[5] P. C. G. Isaac and R. E. A. Allan (eds.), 162; L. F. Haber, *The chemical industry during the 19th century* (Oxford, 1958), 152.

[6] J. H. Clapham (1932), 106; S. Gregory *et al.* in W. Smith (ed.), *Scientific survey of Merseyside* (Liverpool, 1953), 255.

[7] K. L. Wallwork, 'The mid-Cheshire salt industry', *Geography*, XLIV (1959), 174; J. H. Clapham (1932), 515; L. F. Haber, 155.

material and for bicycle and car tyres. Its labour force grew fourteen-fold between 1851 and 1901, and it became increasingly localised in Lancashire and Cheshire, which provided less than a fifth of all employment in 1871 and more than a third in 1901.[1] The repeal of paper duties in 1861 gave a fillip to paper manufacture and production increased eightfold between 1865 and 1907, with the Home Counties and Lancashire as the chief centres. Paper box and bag manufacture also grew rapidly.[2]

Many new industries were concerned with the making or processing of foodstuffs, often at ports. One of the most important and interesting geographical changes was in flour milling. In 1851, milling, largely in wind and water mills, had been widely distributed in the grain-growing counties, and half the mills each employed only one or two people.[3] New methods of milling, using metal rollers, made large mills more economical to run, and the increasing volume of imports of hard wheats for bread-making favoured the erection of large mills at the ports, especially London, Liverpool, Hull and Bristol.[4] By 1912, port mills produced nearly two-thirds of all flour used in the country, and, although some inland mills, such as those at Cambridge and York, were saved by mechanisation, many of the older mills were abandoned.[5] In the country as a whole there was only one mill grinding wheat in 1906 for every nine in 1884; and in Colchester, where there were twelve windmills in 1866, only one survived in 1906.[6]

Although the economies of the coalfield industrial regions continued to be dominated by the staple industries in which they had specialised, manufacturing became more widespread and more diversified, especially in Greater London, which retained its position as the largest single centre of manufacturing industry, and in the west Midlands, with industries, like those of London, which had long been very varied. The size of plant also tended to grow and large industrial empires, embracing a range of manufactures in different parts of the country, were appearing, especially in engineering.[7] Yet, although employment in manufacturing industry

[1] W. Woodruff, *The rise of the British rubber industry during the 19th century* (Liverpool, 1958), 118.

[2] A. D. Spicer, *The paper trade* (London, 1907), 100, 104, 173.

[3] J. H. Clapham (1932), 34, 88; J. H. Clapham (1938), 185.

[4] J. H. Clapham (1932), 89.

[5] W. Smith, 552; J. H. Clapham (1938), 185.

[6] *The Tariff Commission*, vol. 3, *Rep. of the agricultural committee* (London, 1906), para. 323; W. Marriage in W. Page and J. H. Round (eds.), *V.C.H. Essex*, II (1907), 447.   [7] J. H. Clapham (1938), chap. 4.

continued to grow and its share of all employment rose slightly, it ceased to be the only or, in some instances, the major cause of urban expansion; for employment in service industries was rising rapidly.

TRANSPORT AND TRADE

In the growth of the economy, and especially in its geographical manifestations, improved communications played a major part, internally by speeding the flow of goods and services, chiefly through the extension of the railway system, and externally by the development of the steel steamship, which brought both markets and sources of raw materials closer in time. Changes in the geography of communications chiefly concerned the development of the railway net, for the canal and the turnpike had already been eclipsed by 1850 and, while the tram provided effective competition within the larger towns towards the end of the century, the motor vehicle was not a potential threat until after 1900.

Railways

Except along the Welsh Borderland and in the south-west, the main outlines of the railway net had already been established by 1850, and the subsequent activities of railway companies were largely concerned with its elaboration and intensification (Fig. 74). The scale of these later changes can too readily be minimised; the route mileage in England and Wales (separate figures are not available) rose from 5,132 miles in 1850 to 11,789 miles in 1875, an increase of 130%, and reached 16,223 miles in 1912 (216%).[1]

The pattern of growth was extremely complex. Railways were promoted for a variety of reasons by many companies, and the details were often to be explained by quite ephemeral local circumstances;[2] but a number of large companies with much wider perspectives came increasingly to predominate. By the early 1860s, the North Eastern Railway had acquired a territorial monopoly in Durham and the East and North Ridings; and in 1862 amalgamation in East Anglia led to another regional enterprise, the Great Eastern, which also enjoyed a virtual monopoly of the

[1] *Rep. of the Commissioners of Railways for the year 1850*, VII (P.P. 1851, xxx); *General Rep. by Captain Tyler in regard to...Railway Companies*, 2 (P.P. 1876, lxv); *Railway Returns...for the year 1912*, xxi (P.P. 1913, lviii).

[2] J. H. Appleton, 'The railway network of southern Yorkshire', *Trans. and Papers, Inst. Brit. Geog.*, XXII (1956), 169.

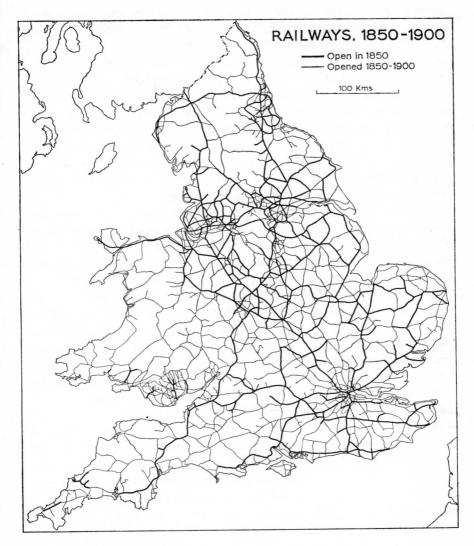

Fig. 74   Railways, 1850–1900
Based on: (1) G. Bradshaw, *Map of Great Britain showing the railways* (London and Manchester, 1850); (2) J. G. Bartholomew, *The survey atlas of England and Wales* (Edinburgh, 1903), plates 6 and 7.

territory it served.[1] Elsewhere, other groupings emerged – the Great Western, the London & South Western, the London & North Western, the Midland, and the Great Northern, although their predominance was in part achieved indirectly through the leasing of running rights over other lines, which they had often been instrumental in promoting, or through representation on the boards of nominally independent companies. No single company emerged in the south-east where there were three smaller groups, the London, Chatham & Dover, the South-Eastern and the London, Brighton & South Coast, although the last also enjoyed a local monopoly within its more limited area. Competition between them was most acute where they came into contact in areas which still awaited development or which provided lucrative traffic.

The role of competition should not be exaggerated, since there were increasingly informal agreements and understandings, but it undoubtedly played a major part in shaping the railway network by encouraging the construction of alternative routes and stations. Central London's sixteen terminal stations, several of them in close proximity, Manchester's five, Salisbury's three and Tunbridge Wells' two, were largely the product of such competition. Rivalry between the Great Western and the London & South-Western, which was aggravated by a difference in gauge, led to alternative routes from London to Plymouth, both of them completed after 1850; while competition between the South-Eastern and the London, Chatham & Dover similarly provided alternative routes between London and Dover.[2] Duplications were most striking at the local scale, as in the Leen valley (Notts.) which carried three rival lines, or in the Avon valley downstream from Bath, where there were two.[3] Some lines were built primarily to thwart competitors, as with the Hurstbourne–Fullerton line, constructed by the London & South-Western to prevent the Didcot, Newbury & Southampton Railway from reaching Bournemouth.[4] Others were intended to make routes shorter and more competitive, such as the South-Eastern line through Sevenoaks which was built (despite a two-mile tunnel and deep cuttings through the chalk) to reduce the time of the journey to Dover, formerly reached via Redhill.[5] Some lines were

[1] C. E. R. Sherrington, *Economics of rail transport in Great Britain* (London, 1928), 123; J. Simmons, *The railways of Britain* (London, 1961), 22.

[2] J. Simmons, 24; H. P. White, *A regional history of the railways of Great Britain*, II (*Southern England*), (London, 1961), ch. 3.

[3] J. H. Appleton, *The geography of communications in Great Britain* (Hull, 1962), 158–9.   [4] H. P. White, 143.   [5] *Ibid.*, 44.

promoted because services were considered poor or expensive in the absence of competition, as with the Hull, Barnsley & West Riding line.[1]

The reasons for the construction of lines were legion and often local. Only four acts, all before 1850, had authorised the laying of more than a hundred route-miles by a single company, and many main lines were created piecemeal at different dates by a variety of promoters; the Paddington–Penzance line was built by eight companies in fifteen instalments spread over sixty-eight years.[2] Between 1850 and 1870, many of the main lines in the west Midlands and south-west England were completed, as well as a large number of branch lines. In 1868 a further trunk route from London was opened from St Pancras to Bedford, promoted by the Midland Railway to overcome congestion on the Great Northern lines from Hitchin to King's Cross, and by the mid-1870s no important English town was without a reasonably direct route to London.[3] Subsequent additions were mainly branch lines or cut-offs, designed to speed traffic by avoiding some of the now-unnecessary meanderings of the earlier routes, such as the Sway line, opened in 1888 to shorten the journey from London to Bournemouth, or the Badminton cut-off, linking Paddington more directly with South Wales via the Severn Tunnel, which had been opened in 1886.[4] Other gaps were filled by light railways, of which 1,542 miles were authorised between 1896 and 1914, to carry agricultural produce, minerals and passengers (although this figure also includes some tramways).[5] Two further trunk lines were also constructed, the one promoted by the Midland Company between Settle and Carlisle and opened in 1876 to provide a third route to Scotland, the other, the Great Central, opened in 1899 and following a circuitous route from St Marylebone to Sheffield.[6] By 1914, only the remote moorland areas of the west and north lay more than five miles from a railway.

Few lines were initially built to carry passengers for short distances, and the spacing of stations, on the main lines at least, was often too great for them to fulfil this need; thus, West Drayton, 13¼ miles from Paddington, was for some time the first station west of the terminus.[7] As demand grew

[1] J. H. Clapham (1932), 183–4.   [2] J. H. Appleton (1962), 160–1.

[3] C. E. R. Sherrington, 97–8; C. H. Ellis, *British railway history*, 2 vols. (London, 1959), II, 13.

[4] H. P. White, 161; C. H. Ellis, 230

[5] C. Klapper, *The golden age of tramways* (London, 1961), 35.

[6] C. E. R. Sherrington, 99, 134.

[7] H. P. White, *A regional history of the railways of Great Britain*, III (*Greater London*), (London, 1963), 110.

around London, other stations were added and new lines constructed to produce an elaborate network.[1] Electrification was introduced on surface lines in south London in 1906, and 109 miles had been electrified and 127 miles partly electrified by 1912.[2] Other less complex suburban networks developed around the northern cities, notably Liverpool, Manchester and Newcastle, and some of these lines, too, were electrified between 1903 and 1906.[3]

The extension of the railway network was not a continuous process; the rate of activity was determined both by the state of the economy and by the financial circumstances of individual companies. Lines were sometimes left uncompleted for several years, as that between Basingstoke and Salisbury, and gaps, such as that between Horsham and Leatherhead, lay unfilled for long periods.[4] Lines were also closed as better routes were developed, as amalgamation removed competition, as traffic declined, or simply in recognition of the fact that too many railways had been provided; but while some lines were closed in almost every year between 1850 and 1914, the total mileage affected was comparatively small.[5]

The creation of new routes was not the only way in which the railway's influence extended; additional track capacity was also important. Many lines were opened with only a single track, a second being added as demand grew. Physical difficulties sometimes caused delay; doubling of the Great Western line from Exeter to Plymouth was not completed until 1905 for this reason.[6] On the broad-gauge lines, doubling sometimes accompanied the conversion to standard gauge, and the opportunity was also taken to straighten or improve routes; thus several stretches of the original line from Plymouth to Penzance were abandoned.[7] As traffic increased on busy lines, additional tracks were laid, among the earliest being a third track from Bletchley to London, opened in 1859.[8] By 1900, most of the trunk lines out of London had four tracks, at least in part, and on

[1] *Ibid.*, 82.

[2] P. Hall in J. T. Coppock and H. C. Prince (eds.), *Greater London* (London, 1964), 66; *Railway Returns...for the year 1912*, 96 (P.P. 1913, lviii).

[3] C. E. R. Sherrington, 107, 125.

[4] H. P. White (1962), 105, 156.

[5] J. A. Patmore, 'Railway closures in England and Wales 1836–1962', *Trans. and Papers, Inst. Brit. Geog.*, XXXVIII (1966), 107.

[6] D. St J. Thomas, *A regional history of the railways of Great Britain*, I (*The West Country*), (London, 1960), 54.

[7] *Ibid.*, 106.

[8] C. E. R. Sherrington, 90.

very busy sections there were as many as six. On the Great Western route from Paddington, four tracks had been laid to Southall by 1877, to Maidenhead by 1884 and to Didcot by 1889.[1] On the Great Northern route from King's Cross the need for additional tunnels handicapped quadrupling, but much of the line to Peterborough had four tracks by 1900.[2] Where additional tracks were not possible a new line was sometimes constructed, for example south of Croydon.[3] Along a few routes, diminished traffic led to a reduction in the number of tracks, but in general track mileage increased nearly as fast as route mileage.[4] Intermediate stations were also opened to tap additional traffic.

The railway network did not grow haphazardly, but more lines were constructed than were required on economic grounds, and routes were often excessively tortuous because they were conceived in a variety of local circumstances. Its development was not only of economic significance; it represented one of the major landscape changes of the period, whether in imposing structures such as Brunel's bridge at Saltash or Scott's St Pancras station, or unobtrusively, as along many rural lines which, mellowed and blending with the countryside, no longer merited Wordsworth's protest against the 'rash assault'.[5]

Canals and roads

Railways dealt a heavy blow to canal promoters, for the canals' share of traffic fell steadily (although the total tonnage carried changed little). Individual canals often fared very differently. On some, such as the Aire and Calder, trade expanded; on the dense network of the industrial Midlands it held its own; but on most rural canals it declined. On the Oxford Canal, for example, receipts halved between 1848 and 1858, and on the Kennet & Avon the tonnage carried fell to less than one half between 1858 and 1898.[6] Statistics submitted to the Royal Commission on Canals in 1905 showed that there had been 3,162 miles of canal open in 1898 (the latest available returns), and that several hundred miles of canal had been

---

[1] E. T. MacDermot, *History of the Great Western Railway*, II (London, 1931), 322–93.

[2] H. P. White (1963), 160; C. E. R. Sherrington, 129.

[3] H. P. White (1963), 80.

[4] D. St J. Thomas (1960), 138.

[5] A. J. George (ed.), *The poems of Wordsworth* (Boston and New York, 1932), 778.

[6] *R.C. on Canals and Inland Navigations of the United Kingdom*, Appendix 1, statement 1 (P.P. 1906, xxxii); C. Hadfield, *British canals* (London, 1950), 194; C. Hadfield, *The canals of southern England* (London, 1955), 299.

closed; but an official witness admitted that the latter figure included only those canals for which a certificate of abandonment had been issued, and many more miles must have been neglected, or under-used, or illegally abandoned.[1] Some canals were converted for use by the railways, and lines were constructed along their banks; at least one, the Bude Canal, was adapted for water supply.[2] Some canals had been opened after the beginning of the railway age, but only one major canal was constructed, the 35½ mile Manchester Ship Canal which, opened in 1894, transformed Manchester into a major seaport.[3]

The railways quickly acquired the long-distance passenger traffic which the turnpikes had carried, and from 1860 dis-turnpiking was actively pursued; only 184 trusts remained in 1881 and the last disappeared in 1895.[4] The care of the turnpikes then reverted to the parish, which had long been responsible for the much greater mileage of unturnpiked roads. Standards of maintenance were uneven, but the roads were generally neglected and the best turnpikes were the first to deteriorate.[5] In 1888, responsibility for main roads passed to the new county councils and there was some improvement, although not all turnpikes became main roads.[6] Yet there was no national road network; the roads carried only local traffic and, until motorists became numerous, there was no powerful lobby to press for their improvement.[7]

Matters were different in the towns where granite setts and other improved surfaces appeared, where the first experiments in tarred surfaces were made, and where new roads were built, such as Shaftesbury Avenue and Charing Cross Road in central London.[8] In the large towns, trams, at first horse-drawn, began to compete with the long-established horse buses and, later, with short-distance travel by rail.[9] Their use was facilitated by the 1870 Tramways Act and by various technical developments; horses were replaced by steam power and, in the 1890s, by electric traction, and

---

[1] R.C. on Canals, Evidence of Jekyll, Qs. 14, 76, 86; ibid., Appendix 1, statements 2 and 5 (P.P. 1906, xxxii).

[2] C. Hadfield (1955), 321, 327.

[3] C. Hadfield (1950), 226.

[4] S. and B. Webb, English local government: the story of the king's highway (London, 1920), 222.

[5] R.C. on Transport, Final Report, 1931, 10 (P.P. 1930–31, xvii).

[6] C. J. Fuller, 'The development of roads in the Surrey–Sussex Weald and coastlands between 1700 and 1900', Trans. and Papers, Inst. Brit. Geog., XIX (1953), 47.

[7] Ibid., 49; R.C. on Transport, Final Report, 11 (P.P. 1930–31, xvii).

[8] J. H. Clapham (1938), 375; P. Hall (1964), 57.   [9] H. P. White (1963), 79.

the tramway mileage in England and Wales increased from 194 in 1878 to 1,187 in 1902 and had reached 2,213 by 1913–14.[1] From 1903 motorbuses began to replace horse-drawn vehicles. In 1905 the London General Omnibus Company had 70 motorbuses out of its 1,417 buses, and had a further 700–800 on order; elsewhere, changes were inhibited by the fact that local authorities had dual roles as tramway operators and as vehicle-licensing authorities.[2]

Outside the towns there was little mechanised transport, although some trams ran between towns in north England, for example between Leeds and Wakefield.[3] Approximately two thousand miles of new roads had been made under enclosure awards after 1845, but little was done to the existing routes.[4] Improvements in rural road surfaces came only with the development of motor transport, and then only slowly. Although most motor vehicles were restricted to a maximum of four miles per hour before 1896, to twelve between 1896 and 1903 and to twenty thereafter, their numbers grew rapidly, reaching 175,588 in 1911–12.[5] They created so much dust that tarred surfaces became essential; by 1908 there were thought to be 1,269 miles of tarred roads in England, and by 1913 there was a larger mileage of dustless roads than in any other country.[6]

These developments in transport were not the principal changes in the geography of England after 1850; nevertheless, by facilitating and cheapening the movements of both goods and people, they played a major part in the agricultural, industrial and population changes, weakening the barriers of distance and allowing a wider separation of produce and market, mine and factory, residence and workplace.

Maritime trade, coastwise and overseas

Railways were also challenging the immemorial traffic by sea around the coasts of Britain. By 1880, over 60% of the coal imported into London arrived by railway and not by coastal collier; but the challenge was met by faster and larger colliers and by improved unloading facilities along the Thames estuary. 'All in all,' concludes one study, 'coastal shipping

---

[1] *Return of street and road tramways and light railways, 1914*, 4 (P.P. 1914, lxxvii).

[2] *Rep. R.C. on Motor Cars*, vol. I, p. 6 (P.P. 1906, xlviii), J. H. Clapham (1938), 376–7.

[3] J. H. Clapham (1938), 375; C. Klapper, 125.

[4] *Inclosure Commissioners, Thirty-second Ann. Rep.*, 4 (P.P. 1877, xxvi).

[5] *Rep. R.C. on Motor Cars*, vol. I, pp. 2–3 (P.P. 1906, xlviii); K. G. Fenelon, *The economics of road transport* (London, 1925), 22.

[6] J. W. Gregory, *The story of the road* (London, 1931), 254; S. and B. Webb, 248.

withstood railway competition exceptionally well. It accounted for a falling proportion of the country's internal trade from 1845 onwards but in absolute terms its volume increased, particularly in the forty years after 1865.'[1] Even so, it was the larger ports that benefited. The coming of the railway and the increasing size of ships meant the decline of many smaller harbours serving local hinterlands; ports such as Whitby, Boston, King's Lynn and Rye were falling into reduced circumstances.[2] Moreover, the railways themselves were entering the port and shipping business, and came to be large dock owners in such ports as Grimsby, Hull and Southampton, ports with growing overseas connections.

Vital for the economy of the country as a whole was the growth in foreign trade and the developments in shipping which had made 'transport costs little heavier between continents than they had once been between counties'.[3] In 1833 sailing ships had accounted for 94% of British merchant tonnage, but while the tonnage under sail remained constant between 1850 and 1885, that of steamships rose by 4 million, and their capacity had become twice that of the whole merchant fleet in 1850.[4] By the end of the century virtually all ships were being built of steel and powered by steam; such extra capacity was needed to carry a greatly expanded volume of trade, which rose approximately sevenfold between 1850 and 1913.[5] Throughout the period most imports were of food and raw materials, but these contributed a declining proportion; by 1913 manufactures accounted for a quarter by value, for Great Britain was no longer the workshop of the world.[6] The share of manufactures in exports declined, largely because of the rise in shipments of coal, which accounted for 80% of all exports by weight in 1913, and was also a major contributor to coastwise trade.[7]

London remained the leading port, though its share of trade declined (Figs. 76 and 77). In 1843 it had accounted for over half the customs receipts, but it handled only a third of imports in 1913, and the value of its export trade was exceeded by that of Liverpool, the second port. Hull

[1] H. J. Dyos and D. H. Aldcroft, *British transport: an economic survey from the seventeenth century to the twentieth* (Leicester, 1969), 210.

[2] J. H. Clapham (1932), 522–3.

[3] J. H. Clapham (1938), 73.

[4] J. H. Clapham (1932), 519; J. H. Clapham (1938), 158–9.

[5] A. G. Kenwood, 'Port investment in England and Wales', *Yorks. Bull. Econ. and Soc. Research*, XVII (1965), 156.

[6] W. Smith, 169.

[7] *Ibid.*, 636.

had reached third place, assisted by the railways, the coal trade and the increasing size and number of steam trawlers, but it handled little more than a tenth.[1] Such a large increase required heavy investment at both new and established ports.

TOWNS AND CITIES

Between 1851 and 1911 the area occupied by towns in England and Wales almost certainly increased more rapidly than the population they contained. As living standards improved, new communications were developed and new activities were undertaken in towns; the urban area is estimated to have reached two million acres by 1900.[2] This expansion was achieved mainly by the growth of existing towns; and at both dates most of the larger towns were to be found in the industrial areas established on or near the coalfields on the Pennine flanks, in north-east England, in the west Midlands and around the coast. Throughout the period, London was by far the largest centre, with 2,685,000 inhabitants in 1851 within what was later to be defined as the conurbation, and 7,252,000 in 1911 within the same boundary, an increase of 170%.[3] The most striking feature of Fig. 75, which shows changes in the distribution of towns with 20,000 or more inhabitants in 1911 (as listed in the census reports), is the development of towns with between 20,000 and 50,000 inhabitants in locations away from the coalfields, notably on Tees-side, in the east Midlands, in the Home Counties, and around the coasts; for by 1880 the powerful pull of the north had weakened.[4] Outside these areas were to be found mainly stagnating market towns and decaying ports.

Expansion and redevelopment

The most obvious physical expression of urban expansion was the extension of the built-up areas of existing towns, although its complexities are such as almost to defy generalisation; for each town, and each development in it, was a special case, in which personal initiative and personal preference played a large part. Small towns grew by accretion, by the addition of single houses and small estates around their boundaries, and on land left undeveloped in earlier periods. This process has been studied in detail in the Northumberland town of Alnwick, where 349 houses covering 64

[1] *Ibid.*, 165, 170.   [2] R. H. Best and J. T. Coppock, 229.
[3] J. T. Coppock in J. T. Coppock and H. C. Prince (eds.), *Greater London* (London, 1964), 34.
[4] W. Ashworth, *The genesis of modern British town planning* (London, 1954), 88.

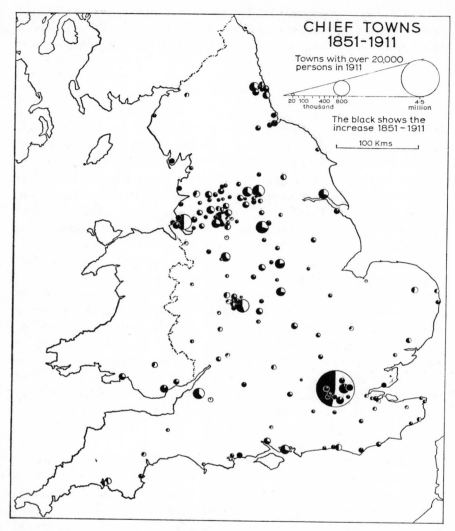

Fig. 75   Chief towns, 1851–1911
Based on: (1) *Census of 1851: Population Tables, I* (P.P. 1852–3, lxxxv, lxxxvi); (2) *Census of 1911*, vol. I, pp. 10–40 (P.P. 1912–13, cxi). The smaller symbols within that for the county of London represent the Greater London boroughs that lay outside the county. Two provincial towns (Bath and Macclesfield) decreased in population, and are accordingly represented by incomplete circles.

acres were built between 1851 and 1891 in developments ranging in size from a single house to 70 houses, although the population remained at about 7,000 throughout the period.[1] In the larger towns, urban expansion was more complex and was greatly affected by the revolution in transport. Towns which grew rapidly in the early phase of the industrial revolution had remained compact, for modes of transport and standards of living had dictated that most people should live near their places of work. The cab and the horse-drawn omnibus, which became common in the 1830s, were essentially forms of transport for the middle classes, and major changes came only when the railways and tramways (and later the motor-driven omnibus) began to provide cheap travel for a working population whose standards of living were also rising. This was especially so in London and in the great provincial cities of the Midlands and north England, where the tramways permitted long ribbons of housing to develop along the main roads and so link surrounding towns and villages.

Changes in housing standards and housing tastes also affected the outward spread of towns and cities. A substantial villa with half an acre or more of ground increasingly became the aim of the professional or business man, and even the terrace house of the clerk or skilled worker had a garden, however small. But as the tide of building spread outwards, more intensive use was often made of land, and the small parks established earlier were sometimes subdivided to accommodate smaller houses at higher densities. After the Public Health Act of 1875, local authority byelaws, although not universal and often inadequately enforced, prescribed maximum densities and affected street layouts. From this period date many of the rows of terrace houses laid out in grid pattern which are particularly well shown in rapidly growing industrial towns such as Middlesbrough. Such houses, however unattractive aesthetically, represented a great advance on the back-to-back housing of the early phases of the industrial revolution. Their uniformity was accentuated by the increasing use of similar materials, for the railways enabled builders to use other than local materials, and roofs of Welsh slate were very common in houses built during this period; but the uniformity of buildings should not be exaggerated, for areas were often developed piecemeal in a variety of styles, even if the differences were largely superficial. Building by local authorities, though possible after 1851, was not important, and, although they built more houses in the 1890s than in the four previous decades, the total

[1] M. R. G. Conzen, *Alnwick, Northumberland, Trans. and Papers, Inst. Brit. Geog.*, XXXVII (1960), 49, 75, 82–5.

remained small.[1] New churches, shops, schools and other public buildings also contributed to the enlargement of the built-up area; thus, fifteen new churches and chapels were built in Oldham between 1870 and 1888.[2]

Although outward extension into farmland was the most obvious feature of urban growth, it was complemented by extensive redevelopment in the older parts of towns as houses were replaced by shops, offices, warehouses, theatres, hotels, railway stations and the like, and as some slum clearance was begun. Like suburban development, this was especially a feature of the larger towns. The railways were a major cause of redevelopment for, while a railway station could be placed on the outskirts of a small settlement and new building take place around it, as in St Albans and Watford, the already large size of London, Manchester and other great cities made this impossible and houses had to be cleared; thus, a new goods station at Manchester involved the destruction of some 600 houses.[3] The construction of both roads and railway lines also contributed to urban redevelopment, as did the erection of civic buildings, especially in the northern industrial towns; for example, many halls were built in the 1880s and 1890s. Even in established residential areas land had also to be found for the new schools required by the 1870 Education Act.

Such redevelopment was accompanied by the dispersal of other activities such as private schools, charitable institutions and the like, which demanded space and which were unable to compete with industry and commerce for valuable land in the centre of cities. Redundant churches and ancient burial grounds were similarly converted to other uses: in central London, for example, nine churches were sold between 1860 and 1894.[4] Nevertheless, residential accommodation was the principal loser from the redevelopment of central areas, and the scale of destruction was considerable; thus in Liverpool more than 20,000 houses were demolished between 1873 and 1911.[5] Furthermore, many of the houses which remained were converted to other uses, especially offices and workshops. Slum clearance also contributed to the loss of houses and Birmingham provided one of the earliest and largest examples of municipal slum clearance in the nineteenth century.[6] Yet such clearance was expensive and was never undertaken on

1 W. Ashworth, 91, 93.
2 R. Millward, *Lancashire* (London, 1955), 86.
3 T. W. Freeman, *The conurbations of Great Britain* (Manchester, 1959), 138.
4 W. Besant, *London in the nineteenth century* (London, 1909), 249.
5 J. P. Lewis, *Building cycles in Britain's growth* (London, 1965), 134.
6 W. Ashworth, 97.

a very large scale in this period; large areas of slums remained and in Birmingham, for example, there were still 43,366 back-to-back houses in 1913.[1] It is not, therefore, surprising that the centres of all the larger cities began to lose population at a faster rate than it was replaced by natural increase. In Birmingham, Leeds, Liverpool and Manchester, population in the central areas began to fall during the 1840s, in Newcastle during the 1850s and in Bradford between 1871 and 1881.[2]

The rate of housebuilding varied more widely than that of population growth, although the latter was clearly a major factor. Transport developments (especially in London), the level of industrial activity, rates of emigration, and household formation were other major causes of fluctuations in the rate of building. House construction reached a peak in the late 1870s and again around the turn of the century; in the intervening troughs it proceeded at only half the peak rates.[3] There were, however, regional variations; in Bradford, for example, the earlier peak occurred in the late 1860s and early 1870s, in Liverpool in the late 1870s and early 1880s, and in Newcastle in the late 1880s.[4] The expansion of an urban area was clearly not an even or continuous process; nevertheless, between 1851 and 1911, there was a net addition of 4,118,000 to the stock of houses in England and Wales, 3,332,000 of them in urban registration districts.[5]

All these developments tended to promote social segregation within towns, although few areas could house only a single class; for middle-class residents required shops and other services, and accommodation was needed in working-class areas for doctors and other professional men. Nevertheless, both rebuilding and urban growth led to particular areas being occupied by different social groups. As the wealthy moved out to new suburbs and beyond, the houses they left were often occupied by those with lower incomes, and were subdivided into flats and tenements.

The growing towns

Although most of the major towns were established by the 1850s, urban growth was not uniform and there were several cases of very rapid urbanisation, of which Barrow-in-Furness, Crewe, Middlesbrough and Swindon were among the most striking examples. The development of Barrow and Middlesbrough was chiefly associated with changes in sources of iron ore, the discovery of a body of haematite near Barrow and the rediscovery of the low-grade Jurassic ores in Cleveland. Dependence on

[1] T. W. Freeman, 85.   [2] *Ibid.*, 82, 172, 179, 187.   [3] J. P. Lewis, 316–17.
[4] *Ibid.*, 323.   [5] *Ibid.*, 332.

local supplies was short-lived; but, whereas Middlesbrough continued
to expand and to rely on an increasing volume of imported ore, the fate of
Barrow, in a cul-de-sac some distance from its source of coking coal, lay
for long in the balance. Barrow's expansion began in the 1850s and it was
claimed by one observer that not even in America was there another town
which grew as fast.[1] The opening of a steelworks in 1858, of a rail link to
the Durham coke supplies in 1861, and the building of one of the most
modern shipyards, led to a rapid development and its population had
reached nearly 18,000 by 1871. Unfortunately its prosperity did not last;
ore began to run out, the market for its rails collapsed, and it survived
only because of financial support from the duke of Devonshire.[2] In
Middlesbrough, the need for imported high-grade ore for Bessemer steel
and the increasing importance of shipbuilding led to a concentration of
activity around the estuary of the Tees and population rose from 18,992
in 1861 to 91,302 in 1901.[3] On a smaller scale, Scunthorpe provided
another example of rapid growth resulting from developments in the iron
and steel industry.[4]

The development of both Crewe and Swindon was closely linked with
the location of railway workshops. Unlike continental Europe, the railway
age in England followed industrialisation, and the railways served to link
and strengthen established towns rather than to create new ones; the chief
exceptions arose from the building of workshops and the creation of what
were, in effect, company towns. By the 1850s, Crewe, where a company
village had been established in the 1840s, had become not only a major
railway junction but also an important manufacturing centre.[5] A rail
rolling mill was opened in 1853, the construction of the London & North
Western's locomotives was localised there in 1857, and a Bessemer steel
plant erected in 1864.[6] At this time the company had more than 3,000
workers on its pay roll, but as population grew from 4,500 in 1851 to
42,000 in 1901, there was increasing industrial diversification.[7] Swindon
was chosen by the Great Western Company as the site for the interchange

[1] S. Pollard, 'Barrow in Furness and the seventh duke of Devonshire', *Econ. Hist. Rev.*, 2nd ser., VIII (1955–6), 125.

[2] S. Pollard (1955–6), 216–17.

[3] R. H. Best and J. T. Coppock, 200–2.

[4] D. C. D. Pocock (1963), 124–38.

[5] W. H. Chaloner, *The social and economic development of Crewe 1780–1923* (Manchester, 1950), 44.

[6] *Ibid.*, 69–71.

[7] T. W. Freeman, 138.

of engines, and it came to house the principal locomotive workshops of the company.[1] The village which arose around the workshops gradually expanded to link with the old town of Swindon and the two became an administrative whole in 1900, with a population of more than 45,000, and with four-fifths of its working population in the company's employ.[2] Ashford, Darlington, Derby and, on a smaller scale, Wolverton were other towns where rapid growth was stimulated by the opening of railway workshops.

Another type of settlement to experience rapid growth during this period, particularly in south-east England, was the dormitory settlement, which was made possible by the improvements in rail transport, although long-distance commuting predates the railway age, and the heyday of the dormitory town came after 1918. The distinction between a dormitory settlement and a dormitory suburb is somewhat arbitrary, for many suburbs began as separate settlements and were later absorbed into the adjacent city; but the wide separation of workplace and residence certainly became more common in the sixty years after 1850. Long-distance commuting was actively promoted by some of the railway companies, for example, the London & North Western, which offered a free first-class season for a year to all who bought houses of more than £50 rateable value in certain towns served by the company and lying between ten and thirty miles from London (though the railway companies did not generally concern themselves with estate development).[3] Provided land was available for building, and this was not always the case, the opening of a railway station often led to the erection of large detached and semi-detached houses, especially if there was easy access to place of work. Sometimes there was a considerable delay; at Radlett in Hertfordshire, for example, there was little development between 1868 and 1894, after which improvements in rail services and a changed attitude on the part of landowners led to rapid expansion.[4] Such dormitory settlements were often grafted on to existing small towns, such as Dorking and Sevenoaks, but their development is most striking where no previous building had occurred, as at Three Bridges in Sussex or at Amersham on the Hill in Buckinghamshire. Similar settlements developed on a smaller scale around other cities, as at West Kirby in Wirral or at

[1] L. V. Grinsell *et al.*, *Studies in the history of Swindon* (Swindon, 1950), 99–100.
[2] *Ibid.*, 124; T. W. Freeman, 280.
[3] E. Course, *London railways* (London, 1962), 199; H. Pollins, 'Transport lines and social divisions', in R. Glass (ed.), *London: aspects of change* (London, 1964), 42.
[4] J. T. Coppock (1964), 281.

Altrincham in Cheshire. As in the suburbs, the residents of such dormitory settlements sometimes opposed improvements in services or the introduction of cheap fares because they feared the social changes that might result.[1]

Holiday resorts also expanded rapidly during this period.[2] Some had already been established by the middle of the nineteenth century, notably Brighton, with a population of 65,569 in 1851 which reached 131,237 by 1911; but others grew almost from nothing or from small ports and fishing villages.[3] Here, too, the railways played an important part. One of the most striking examples of rapid growth was Bournemouth, which had been planned as a resort, but which had acquired a population of only 691 by 1851; its development was particularly marked after the opening of a direct line to London in 1870, and by 1881 its population had reached 16,859, which grew further by 1911 to 78,674.[4] Blackpool and Southport provided interesting examples of the effect of landownership on development, for the former's rapid growth was facilitated by the subdivision of an estate into numerous lots, while Southport's more orderly expansion was largely under the control of a single estate which planned its development as a garden city.[5]

Other new or greatly expanded settlements were to be found in the mining areas, as larger and deeper pits were sunk in the concealed coalfields, and as mining moved into rural areas as in mid-Northumberland, south Nottinghamshire, Cannock Chase, and in east Durham where four mining settlements came into being between 1850 and 1900.[6] But such settlements often remained little more than villages, with most of their populations dependent on a single industry.

An interesting category of settlement comprised experiments in new styles of urban living. These derived their inspiration from the enlightened industrialists who built model villages for their workpeople, or from the prophets of the garden city movement, personified by Ebenezer Howard, and given expression in the First Garden City Company, which promoted the building of Letchworth on an almost virgin site in 1904.[7] Such

[1] H. Pollins, 43–5.

[2] E. W. Gilbert, *Brighton, old ocean's bauble* (London, 1954), ch. 2.

[3] E. W. Gilbert, 'The growth of inland and seaside health resorts in England', *Scot. Geog. Mag.*, LV (1939), 17–35.

[4] C. H. Mate and C. Riddle, *Bournemouth 1810–1910* (Bournemouth, 1910), 98, 136–7.   [5] R. Millward, 86, 102–3.

[6] A. E. Smailes, 173.   [7] W. Ashworth, 141–3.

developments might either form completely new settlements or take their place among the suburbs surrounding existing towns and settlements. Sir Titus Salt's Saltaire was the first example of an industrial village after 1850; on a site near Bradford he built a model village which had grown to 820 dwellings by 1871 and which included chapel, church, school, dispensary, bath-house, club and institute, as well as a 14-acre park.[1] Other examples include Port Sunlight, begun in 1888, Bournville, begun in 1879 and in effect an essay in town planning rather than a company village, and Hampstead Garden Suburb (although work on this did not begin until 1907).[2] By 1914 there were over fifty schemes for garden suburbs building or in being.[3]

Railway towns, dormitory settlements, seaside resorts and mining villages were among the fastest growing settlements. Between 1851 and 1911 the population of mining settlements increased by 1,194% and that of resorts by 291%, compared with an average urban growth rate of 213%.[4] Established industrial towns also continued to expand, although their rate of growth depended on their earlier industrial history and on their industrial structure, so that averages are misleading. A town might temporarily lose population, as did Coventry in the 1860s after the decline of the silk trade, only to expand again with a change in its industrial structure.[5] Development in the smaller industrial towns was often piecemeal, with new plant being established, and speculative builders or the industrial firms themselves providing housing nearby. In the cotton towns, where the first half of the century had been the main period of expansion, growth was comparatively slow and some of the smaller towns were even losing population at the close of the century; in the chemical district of south Lancashire and north Cheshire, on the other hand, the rapid growth of the industry was paralleled by rapid expansion of towns, epitomised by Widnes, which doubled in population between 1865 and 1875.[6]

Many ports, too, grew rapidly, stimulated by the great expansion of trade and the increasing importance of processing imports, although the establishment of improvement commissions and the activities of the railway companies also played a part (Figs. 76 and 77). Grimsby, for example, owed its rapid rise after 1850 to the activities of the Manchester, Sheffield & Lincolnshire Railway Company, which built new docks and

[1] *Ibid.*, 126–8.   [2] *Ibid.*, 132–4, 160–3.   [3] *Ibid.*, 163.
[4] C. M. Law, 139.   [5] J. H. Clapham (1932), 96.
[6] D. W. F. Hardie, *A history of the chemical industry in Widnes* (Birmingham, 1950), 63.

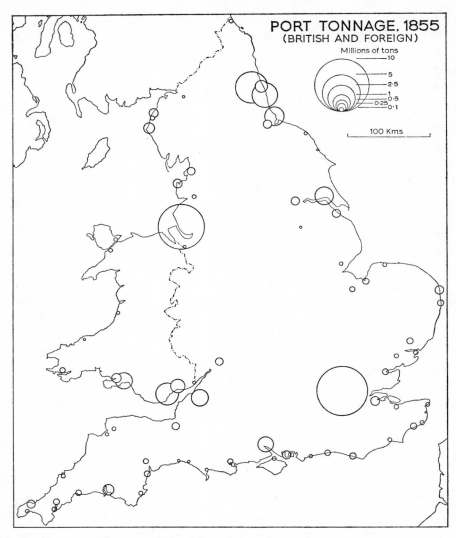

Fig. 76   Port tonnage (British and foreign) in 1855
        Based on *Trade and Navigation (U.K.), 1855* (P.P. 1856, lvi).
        The figures refer to foreign trade only and do not include coastwise traffic.

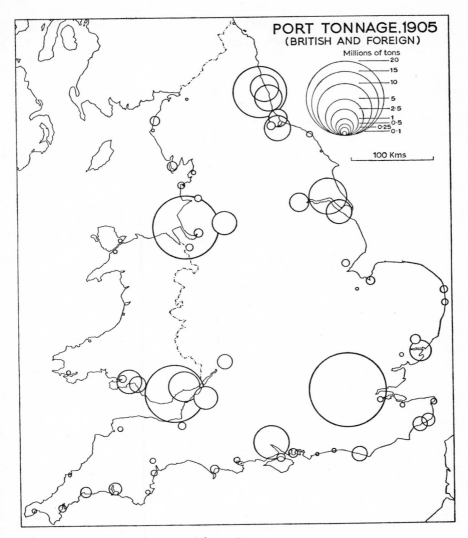

Fig. 77   Port tonnage (British and foreign) in 1905
Based on *Annual Statement of the Navigation and Shipping of the United Kingdom for the year 1905* (P.P. 1906, cxvii).
The figures refer to foreign trade only and do not include coastwise traffic.

even houses.[1] Both the packet ports, which linked railway passenger services with continental Europe, and the coal ports grew rapidly, and new docks and new industries, especially flour milling, contributed to the growth of the larger ports. The ports of north-east England, in particular, rose swiftly to prominence in this period, aided by the coal trade and by the expansion of steel making and shipbuilding.[2] By contrast, Southampton developed as a liner port with the construction of the Test and Itchen Quays and the transfer of the American Line and later the White Star Line from Liverpool; and its population rose from 60,051 in 1881 to 119,012 in 1911.[3] New or greatly expanded cargo ports also appeared. Birkenhead was transformed from little more than a dormitory settlement for wealthy Liverpool merchants into a considerable port; Avonmouth and Portishead were developed in the late 1870s to meet the problem posed by Bristol's shallow tidal access, and Manchester became a major seaport in 1894 with the opening of the Manchester Ship Canal.[4]

Never-the-less, despite all these changes, the principal feature of the urban geography of the period was the continued growth of great cities, and the development of what Patrick Geddes was to recognise in 1915 as conurbations.[5] It is true that their rates of growth were not as rapid as those of the mining settlements, of the resorts or of some of the industrial towns; but they maintained their share of the total population. Sending out tentacles of development along major routeways, absorbing surrounding towns and villages, they came to resemble 'something which has burst an intolerable envelope and splashed'.[6] Their occupational and social composition was also distinctive in the high proportion of employment in service industries and in the large number of immigrants both from elsewhere in the same region and from farther afield (although this latter feature was even more characteristic of the rapidly growing towns such as Birkenhead, 62% of whose population were immigrants in 1861, compared with 49% in Liverpool).[7]

[1] A. G. Kenwood, 156; W. Ashworth, 129–30.
[2] J. Bird, *The major seaports of the United Kingdom* (London, 1963), 345, 384.
[3] *Ibid.*, 160–2.
[4] J. H. Clapham (1932), 523–4; J. Bird, 190; A. G. Kenwood, 165.
[5] P. Geddes, *Cities in evolution* (London, 1915), 34.
[6] H. G. Wells, *Anticipations* (London, 1902), 45.
[7] R. Lawton in W. Smith (ed.), 125.

Greater London

These changes in the urban geography of England, especially those resulting from improvements in transport, were most marked in the London area, partly because of its sheer size and its disproportionate share of office and service employment (Fig. 78). The number of local journeys trebled between 1881 and 1901, but the individual railway companies differed greatly in the extent to which they promoted local travel.[1] At first, most companies were concerned only with long-distance traffic, and stations were too widely spaced to serve the needs of those wishing to travel to work; but, gradually, interest in short journeys grew, especially among those companies with a smaller share of long-distance goods and passenger traffic, and intermediate stations were opened, for example, in 1879 at South Hampstead and Queen's Park on the London & North Western line.[2] For this reason, the companies serving south London actively promoted commuter traffic, and numerous branch lines were constructed for this purpose; while those companies whose lines ran north and north-west to the Midlands were less active in this respect; commuter traffic thus grew more rapidly in the south than in the north-west. The railway companies often anticipated urban growth and extended lines 'confident that population would follow', as with the north-western extensions of the Metropolitan Railway in the 1870s;[3] but sometimes the initiative came from intending passengers, and residents in Camberwell were protesting in the 1890s at the inadequacy of rail services.[4] More commonly, speculative builders erected houses near a station, and gradually the land between this new nucleus and the outer fringes of the then built-up area would be built over. The tramways and omnibuses, with their greater flexibility in setting down and embarking passengers, and their commitment to existing roads, made for much more continuous development.

The attitudes of the railway companies and the routes taken by their lines were not the only factors guiding suburban development. Access to place of work, especially to the City, which was receiving a quarter of a million workers daily by 1891, was also important, and the smaller scale of development in north-west London can in part be attributed to the fact

[1] W. Ashworth, 151.   [2] P. Hall (1964), 64.
[3] H. C. Prince in J. T. Coppock and H. C. Prince (eds.), *Greater London* (London, 1964), 132.
[4] H. J. Dyos, *Victorian suburb: a study of the growth of Camberwell* (Leicester, 1961), 79.

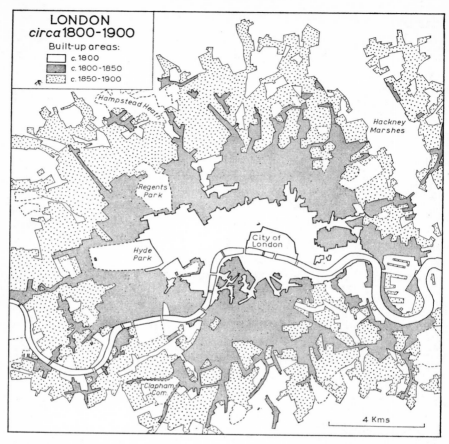

Fig. 78   London *circa* 1800–1900
   Based on: (1) T. Milne, *Plan of the cities of London and Westminster, circumjacent towns and parishes etc., laid down from a trigonometrical survey taken in
   the years 1795–1799* (London, 1800); (2) H. G. Collins, *London in 1851*
   (London, 1851); (3) Ordnance Survey, One-Inch Sheets (1894–1903).

that the City was generally less easily reached from stations along these
lines.[1] Availability of land was also a major consideration, for a necessary
requirement was a landowner willing to sell or lease and a developer
anxious to build; the country to the south-west of Hampstead long remained open because it belonged to an entailed estate.[2] It is probable that
physical conditions also had some effect, both by making some areas more

   [1] P. Hall (1964), 66.   [2] H. C. Prince (1964), 130.

attractive than others and by creating difficulties for the builder; the late development of the extensive areas in Middlesex underlain by London Clay was probably due in part to physical obstacles of this kind. Availability of water mains and trunk sewers was also increasingly important, but these, and the availability and physical character of land, affected chiefly the detailed pattern of growth; the broad strategy was determined principally by considerations of accessibility.

Travel to work by rail was at first a middle-class preserve; but the introduction of cheap workmen's fares, obligatory from the Cheap Trains Act of 1883 (though a condition of parliamentary consent to legislation affecting railways in the London area for twenty years before), made it possible for at least the clerk and the better-paid manual worker to live some distance from their places of work; but in some occupations, as in the docks, the nature of their work tied employees to the older parts.[1] By 1882, some 25,000 workmen's tickets were sold daily in the London area.[2] The Great Eastern Railway Company played a major role in this respect, and its cheap fares made possible the great expanses of working-class suburbs which were built in north-east London in the last quarter of the century; a twopenny fare on this company's lines could purchase a journey four times as long as that available for the same fare on the London & North Western Railway, and trains were more frequent.[3] Not all these working-class suburbs grew as a result of cheap fares; house-building was also a response to the development down-river of new docks and the eastward migration of noxious industries, such as the manufacture of chemicals and paint.[4] Nor must the scale of daily movement be exaggerated; less than a quarter of a large sample of trade unionists in south London in 1897 travelled any distance to work.[5] Railway policy together with the attitudes of landowners influenced the social character of new suburbs, and this, once established, tended to be self-perpetuating. Thus, the great spreads of working-class housing in Stamford Hill, Tottenham and Edmonton, which the railways had done much to promote, made these areas unattractive to middle-class families.[6] Conversely, land-

[1] H. Pollins, 42; H. J. Dyos (1961), 77; J. P. Lewis, 134.

[2] H. J. Dyos (1961), 77.

[3] P. Hall (1964), 65–6.

[4] W. Ashworth, 'Types of social and economic development in suburban Essex', in R. Glass (ed.), 63–4.

[5] H. J. Dyos (1961), 62.

[6] *R.C. on the Housing of the Working Class, Minutes,* Evidence of Birt, Q. 10,217 (P.P. 1884–5, xxx).

owners often prescribed restrictive covenants or specified the minimum value of houses to be built, and both landowners and residents could combine to resist developments which were socially unacceptable; thus the labouring classes were effectively prevented from entering St John's Wood and the residents of sedate villas in Acacia Road slept peacefully.[1]

As elsewhere, the development of the suburbs was accompanied by changes within the built-up area. H. T. Dyos has calculated that in the London area some 76,000 people were displaced by the building of termini and other railway developments between 1853 and 1901.[2] At least the houses demolished in this way were often of poor quality, as in the slums of Agar Town, pulled down in the 1860s to provide a site for the new Midland terminus at St Pancras, and it was said that the railway companies often chose routes through working-class areas to minimise costs. Certainly railway construction through middle-class suburbs sometimes involved heavy outlays in compensation and in onerous obligations to minimise damage or loss of amenity, as the directors of the Great Central Railway Company found in bringing their new trunk line to St Marylebone in the 1890s.[3] In central London, this problem was avoided by the construction of underground railways, the first of which, the Metropolitan, was opened between Paddington and Farringdon in 1863.[4] The first deep-level 'tube', the City & South London, followed in 1890, and a complex network of underground railways was soon developed to provide shuttle services within the City.[5]

London also provides some of the best examples of the contribution of road-making to urban redevelopment. The extensive programme of road-work undertaken by the Metropolitan Board of Works in the 1870s and 1880s led, through the construction of Shaftesbury Avenue and Charing Cross Road, to the replacement of the Seven Dials slums and to the erection of numerous shops and offices along the new street frontages.[6] The need for central locations for hotels, theatres, offices and shops similarly led to the destruction of older houses; for example, the Cecil, Savoy, Grand, Metropole, Victoria and Carlton hotels were erected in

---

[1] H. C. Prince (1964), 134.

[2] H. J. Dyos, 'Railways and housing in Victorian London', *Jour. Transport History*, II (1955–6), 14.

[3] P. Hall (1964), 62–3; H. C. Prince (1964), 127, 133–4.

[4] H. P. White (1963), 82.

[5] *Ibid.*, 98.

[6] P. Hall (1964), 57; T. W. Freeman, 39.

central London in the 1880s and 1890s, and many theatres in the 1890s and early 1900s.[1] Slum clearance also contributed to the loss of houses, although many of these were subsequently replaced. The Metropolitan Board of Works dealt with 22 schemes, covering 59 acres.[2]

Not all the inhabitants of these and other demolished houses were resettled elsewhere. New tenements were constructed in some areas by commercial companies, by charitable institutions and later, to some extent, by local authorities. Such rehousing was at high densities, and on the Peabody estates in London densities of 700 persons per acre were achieved.[3] Nevertheless, such rehousing was on a relatively small scale, and it is not surprising that the population of the City began to fall in the 1840s and that of the remaining central boroughs followed suit in the following decade; the area of declining population grew steadily and by 1911 even the population of the county of London as a whole had begun to fall.[4]

The port of London was also changing. Its centre of gravity shifted downstream with the opening of the Royal Victoria Dock in 1855, the Royal Albert Dock in 1880, and the Tilbury Docks in 1886; the site of this last development was far enough downstream to enable the steamships of the time to get into the docks on one tide. The Port of London Authority was constituted by Act of Parliament in 1908, and, in the following year, the Authority took over control of the entire port, together with the docks and properties of various existing companies.[5]

In the meantime, the size and complexity of this vast and expanding area was recognised by the Metropolis Management Act of 1855. This defined a metropolitan area to be administered for certain purposes by a Metropolitan Board of Works, and in 1888 the area was constituted an administrative county; thus the London County Council came into being. It included the City together with portions of Middlesex, Surrey and Kent and, in 1899, its administration was reorganised by the London Government Act. The new county now comprised the City together with 28 metropolitan boroughs, including that of Westminster which was dignified as a 'city' in 1900 (Fig. 79). The county that thus came into being covered an area of about 117 square miles, and its population in

[1] D. F. Stevens in J. T. Coppock and H. C. Prince (eds.), *Greater London* (London, 1964), 192–3.
[2] W. Ashworth (1954), 95.
[3] J. Parsons, *Housing by voluntary enterprise* (London, 1903), 49.
[4] J. T. Coppock (1964), 33–4.   [5] J. H. Bird, 345–6, 384–8.

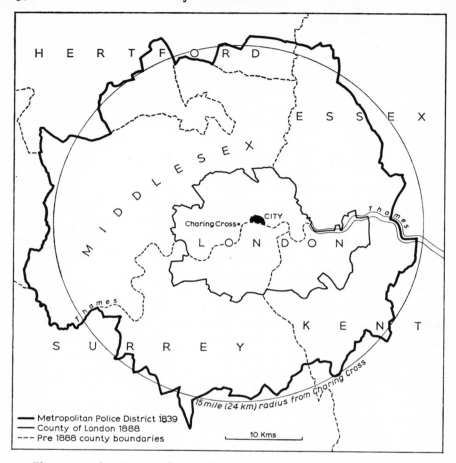

Fig. 79 London: Metropolitan Police District (1839) and County (1888)
Based on *Report R.C. on London Traffic*, plan no. 1 (P.P. 1906, xlv).

1911 was just over 4.5 million. But the built-up area had extended far
beyond the county of London to form an outer ring of suburbs in
neighbouring counties. If this 'Greater London' be defined in terms of
the Metropolitan Police District of 1839 (i.e. an area extending within
a radius of 15 miles or so from Charing Cross), it covered nearly 693
square miles, and included in 1911 a total population of 7.3 million. By
this time one Englishman in five was 'a Londoner'. Some idea of the
changes over the century as a whole may be obtained from table 5.1 in
which the figures have been adjusted to the areas indicated.

Table 5.1   *The growth of Greater London, 1801–1911*

Figures are adjusted to the county and metropolitan police area of 1911.
Figures for the county include those for the City.

	City	County	Outer ring	Greater London
Area in sq miles	1.1	117	576	693
Population in thousands				
1801	128	959	155	1,114
1851	129	2,363	322	2,685
1881	51	3,830	936	4,767
1901	27	4,536	2,045	6,581
1911	20	4,522	2,730	7,252

Source: Census of 1911, vol. I, pp. xxiii–xxiv, 646 (P.P. 1912–13, cxi); *Census of 1901, County of London*, p. 1 (P.P. 1902, cxxi).

Beyond the limits of Greater London lay a fringe of towns, not only serving their immediate countryside, but also acting as dormitory settlements for those who worked in London itself. Little wonder that contemporaries described it as 'the greatest city in the world'.[1]

[1] A. J. Herbertson and O. J. R. Howarth (eds.), *The British Isles* (Oxford, 1914), 549.

Chapter 6

ENGLAND *circa* 1900

PETER HALL

The Victorian era survived just three weeks of the twentieth century. At 6.30 in the evening of 22 January 1901 the Queen died peacefully at her beloved Osborne, and the Earl Marshal put the country into deep mourning until 6 March.[1] The news was received with gloom in Yeovil, where the staple trade was the manufacture of light tan gloves; 'the death of the late Queen', the factory inspector later reported, 'had the effect of producing unusual depression', though 'with the Coronation next year, manufacturers are looking forward to doing a brisk spring trade'.[2] The war in South Africa ground on, bringing slack times for industries which shipped to the Cape Town market; though in Bridport, on the Dorset coast, the ancient flex and twine trade revived with a flood of orders for balloon netting.[3]

POPULATION

Still in half mourning, Englishmen and English women submitted themselves to the eleventh decennial census of population on the last midnight in March. The 1901 Census had peculiar significance as an epitaph for a century and an age; for the first census had been taken in 1801, while the first reasonably reliable count by the registrars had marked the start of the Victorian era in 1841. The enumerators, 'clergymen, professional men, schoolmasters, and others of exceptional education when available',[4] counted a population that had nearly quadrupled in the century – from 8.9 million to 32.5 in England and Wales together. In absolute terms the last decade of the century had recorded the greatest increase of all: 3.6 million between 1891 and 1901. But, the Registrar-General observed, the proportionate rate of increase was one of the lowest recorded in the century.[5]

---

[1] *The Times*, 25 January 1901, p. 8, and 29 January, p. 10.
[2] *Ann. Rep. Factories, 1901*, 5 (P.P. 1902, xii).
[3] *Ibid.* [4] *The Times*, 3 January 1901, p. 5.
[5] *Census of 1901: General Report*, 15 (P.P. 1904, cviii).

[374]

This growth had been diversely spread across England to produce a very uneven distribution of population (Fig. 80). As in the previous decade, between 1891 and 1901 'the counties showing the highest rates of increase mainly include those around London, as Middlesex, Essex, Surrey, Kent and Hertfordshire; counties in which the chief industry is coal-mining, as...Northumberland, Durham..., and to some extent Staffordshire and Derbyshire; or counties which are mainly manufacturing, as Nottinghamshire, Leicestershire, Northamptonshire, the West Riding of Yorkshire and Lancashire'.[1] But ten English counties had lost population; and they were mainly agricultural.[2] Analysing the returns in more detail, the Registrar General found that the rural districts – with which he grouped the smallest urban districts, because they were mostly market towns – were increasing as a group very slowly, and that many individual districts were declining.[3]

The fact was that England had 'now been provided by the railroads with a system of veins and arteries, and by the telegraphy and penny post with a nervous organization', the inevitable result of which was 'a more rapid circulation of labour and an excessive growth of population in some parts of the kingdom at the expense of that of others'.[4] The agricultural labourer now sensed 'the contagion of numbers, the sense of something going on, the theatres and the music halls, the brightly lighted streets and busy crowds: all, in short, that makes the difference between the Mile End fair on a Saturday night, and a dark and muddy country lane, with no glimmer of gas and with nothing to do. Who could wonder that men are drawn into such a vortex, even were the penalty heavier than it is?'[5] So wrote Sir Hubert Llewellyn Smith, in Booth's great survey of the life and labour of the people in London. The statistics of migration proved him right. In his paper on the laws of migration in 1885, Ravenstein had shown that the counties of dispersion – those with enumerated populations less than the number of their natives scattered throughout the kingdom – were gathered in a great belt which ran diagonally across the agricultural heart

[1] *Ibid.*, 21.

[2] *Ibid.*

[3] *Ibid.*, 25. For an extended treatment of the pattern of rural migration losses, see R. Lawton, 'Population changes in England and Wales in the later 19th century: an analysis of trends by registration districts', *Trans. and Papers, Inst. Brit. Geog.*, XLIV (1968), 55–74.

[4] H. L. Smith, 'Influx of population (East London)', in C. Booth (ed.), *Life and labour of the people in London*, III (London, 1892), 76.

[5] *Ibid.*, 75.

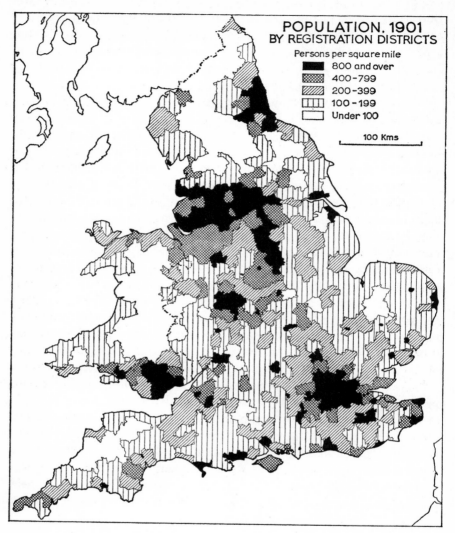

Fig. 80 Population in 1901
Based on *Census of 1901* (P.P. 1902, cxviii–cxxi).

of England from Cornwall to Lincolnshire; while the counties of absorption – those with enumerated populations greater than the numbers of their natives living elsewhere – were gathered in two great groups, one representing the northern and Midland industrial counties from Northumberland to Warwick, the other the metropolitan corner of England from Essex through to Hampshire.[1]

The most important explanation of these differences is found in later pages of the census report, which record changes in the work Englishmen did. The total agricultural population of England and Wales had been falling continuously since 1851 – from over 1.7 million to 1.2 million, or by nearly one third, in half a century.[2] Jobs in coalmining on the other hand had increased prodigiously – by 24.7% in the decade 1891–1901 alone. But this increase was highly concentrated in certain coalfields, above all in Northumberland and Durham; while some of the great coalfields of the first half of the nineteenth century, like the Black Country, were now mere shadows of their former importance.[3] Cotton, the great staple of the early industrial revolution, had shown in the last decade a decline in employment for the first time; woollens declined by no less than 13.5%, and the whole textile group showed an overall reduction.[4] Clothes makers showed only a modest increase; shoemakers hardly any at all.[5] In all these trades, workers were feeling the consequences of mechanisation; in some, foreign competition was beginning to bite. But to compensate, other industries were recording spectacular increases: paper and printing showed 26.9% in a decade, chemicals 40.9%, engineering with machine making 67.4%, general and local government 37.3%, insurance 79.4%.[6]

The trouble was that they did not really compensate because different jobs were done in different places. After two decades of agrarian depression, Englishmen were used to news of migration from the rural districts. They might remember their parents' stories about the fate of the hand-loom weavers sixty or seventy years before. But they were not yet fully familiar with the notion that long-term, secular decline in a staple industry

[1] E. G. Ravenstein, 'The laws of migration', *Jour. Roy. Stat. Soc.*, XLVIII (1885), 184.

[2] *Census of 1901: General Report*, 101 (P.P. 1904, cviii). But see p. 679 below.

[3] *Ibid.*, 105–6.   [4] *Ibid.*, 118–20.

[5] *Ibid.*, 123–4.

[6] *Ibid.*, 91, 97, 109, 115, 116. For an extended analysis of changes in employment patterns at the national level, see P. Deane and W. A. Cole, *British economic growth 1688–1959* (Cambridge, 2nd. ed., 1967), 142, and W. Ashworth, 'Changes in the industrial structure 1870–1914', *Yorks. Bull. Econ. and Soc. Research*, XVII (1965), 61–74.

could bring a whole manufacturing area into lingering depression and decay. Yet such was beginning to be the case – or at least the prospect. The decline in cotton was already a problem in some Lancashire towns; the problem was not lessened by news that chemicals were booming on the middle Mersey. Shoemakers in Leicestershire and Northamptonshire, seeing their jobs menaced by machinery, drew small comfort from the fact that office jobs were on the increase in London.[1]

These changes naturally affected urban districts of every order of size. Urban England generally was growing; and by 1901, on a rigorous basis of computation, 78% of the population of England and Wales was already urban.[2] Yet when the urban areas were grouped and analysed by the census-takers, it was discovered that the fastest-growing English towns were the medium-sized ones; the greatest cities, in contrast, were growing relatively slowly. The average rate of increase for the urban areas of England and Wales, during the decade 1891–1901, was 15.2%. But towns of between 20,000 and 50,000 people recorded 20.3%, and those of between 50,000 and 100,000 recorded 23.2%;[3] while the four biggest cities all recorded less than 10%: the county of London 7.3%, Liverpool 8.8%, Manchester 7.6%, Birmingham 9.2%.[4] Curiously, the census noted that the English towns with the highest rate of growth – East Ham with 193.5%, Walthamstow with 105.3%, Kings Norton and Northfield with 101.8% – were suburbs of either London or Birmingham;[5] so that 'a falling off in the rate of increase, or even an actual decline, in the population of a great town is not necessarily an indication of a corresponding decline in its prosperity'.[6]

Three main sets of changes, then, dominated the economic and social geography of England as recorded by the census at the outset of the twentieth century. They were:

  1. First, the agonised adaptation of English agriculture in the face of foreign competition, coupled with the continued exodus from the country-side.

  2. Secondly, the changing fortunes of the great industrial staples and of the areas which depended on them, coupled with the success or failure of these areas to adapt their industrial structures to changing demands.

[1] R. Lawton, 62–3, gives detailed evidence.
[2] C. M. Law, 'The growth of urban population in England and Wales, 1801–1911', *Trans. and Papers, Inst. Brit. Geog.*, XLI (1967), 132.
[3] *Census of 1901: General Report*, 26 (P.P. 1904, cviii).
[4] *Ibid.*, 27.   [5] *Ibid.*, 28–9.   [6] *Ibid.*, 29.

3. Thirdly, the suburban explosion which was beginning to liberate large numbers of English people from overcrowded and insanitary homes in the great cities.

THE COUNTRYSIDE

Agricultural depression

The last twenty years of the nineteenth century had witnessed an agricultural depression on a scale never before known in the English countryside. Its precise results are difficult to chart statistically, because both the figures of acreage and the figures of agricultural population are suspect. The contemporary verdict was that in the United Kingdom between 1870 and 1900 land under grain crops had fallen by 40%, and that under green crops by one sixth, while grassland had increased by nearly one third.[1] It is almost certain that the actual declines were greater than this because all the time more land was being recorded in the returns.[2] As to the agricultural population, contemporary experts differed widely. It was generally agreed that the figures for women were not to be taken seriously because before 1871 they had included farmers' wives. It was noticed, too, that the earlier figures had probably included much seasonal labour, but that since 1881 the increase in gardeners had partly helped to offset declines in the agricultural population proper.[3] The most careful estimate for England and Wales, by Lord Eversley in 1907,[4] is that the male agricultural population over 20 years of age had declined by 66,650 between 1881 and 1901, and in all by 245,120 between 1861 and 1901.[5] The general belief – it was officially expressed – was that the decline had been exceptionally severe in the arable districts.

Contemporaries were in no doubt that the great agricultural depression had borne more hardly on the arable east than on the pastoral west of England. The impact of foreign wheat had been felt earlier and more severely than the impact of foreign meat. As late as 1885–7, British farmers had supplied nearly 34% of the wheat for British bread; by 1900–2

[1] *The Tariff Commission*, vol. 3, *Report of the Agricultural Committee* (London, 1906), paras. 353–4.

[2] J. T. Coppock, 'The accuracy and comparability of the agricultural returns', in R. H. Best and J. T. Coppock, *The changing use of land in Britain* (London, 1962), 57–9 and *passim*.

[3] W. H. Bear, 'The agricultural population at the Census of 1901', *Jour. Roy. Agric. Soc.*, LXIV (1903), 123, 128, 137; and Lord Eversley, 'The decline in the number of agricultural labourers in Great Britain', *Jour. Roy. Stat. Soc.*, LXX (1907), 270–4.

[4] Lord Eversley, 275.   [5] *Ibid.*

the proportion was down to 22.5%.[1] In meat, the British farmer kept a bigger share, which was estimated at 66.0% for the first half of the 1890s and at 55.3% for the first five years of the new century.[2] Aided by transcontinental railroads, lake steamers and big ocean steamships, the price of North American imported wheat had begun to decline in Britain from about the late 1870s;[3] while the first wholly successful shipment of frozen meat from Australia had been made in 1879, regular shipments had started only in the eighties, and successful chilling of meat had not been applied on a regular reliable basis by 1901.[4]

The results were plain to see on the face of the ground. The Royal Commission of 1897 on Agricultural Depression said: 'Broadly speaking, it may be concluded that the heavier the soil, and the greater the proportion of arable land, the more severe has been the depression' (Fig. 81). In the eastern and in some of the southern counties, the situation was 'undoubtedly a grave one'. But in the pastoral areas of Great Britain, the depression was 'of a milder character'.[5]

If there was one county that had suffered more severely than any in England, in the Commission's view, it was Essex. 'Essex as a whole', an Assistant Commissioner had told them, 'is a corn growing county':[6] the soil was right and the climate was right. But on the stiff, deep, tenacious London Clay soil in the south, which was described as 'stiff, tough, numb, dumb and impervious'[7] there were 'large farms...half or threequarters of which have either been permitted to run wild or have been sown down in despair'.[8] Areas which twenty years before had grown fine crops of wheat and beans and clover were 'lying in wretched pasture, next to useless'.[9]

Rider Haggard, setting out on his tour of rural England at the turn of

[1] *R.C. on the Supply of Food and Raw Material in Time of War*, Appendix 1, Summary Table B (2), 78 (P.P. 1905, xl). For other figures which are compatible with these Board of Trade estimates see R. F. Crawford, 'An inquiry into wheat prices and wheat supply', *Jour. Roy. Stat. Soc.*, LVIII (1895), 81; and for contradictory figures, *Tariff Commission, Report* (1906), para 353.

[2] R. H. Hooker, 'The meat supply of the United Kingdom', *Jour. Roy. Stat. Soc.*, LXXII (1909), 332.

[3] *Tariff Commission, Report* (1906), para 114.

[4] J. T. Critchell and J. Raymond, *A history of the frozen meat trade* (London, 1912), 30–1, 41, 248.

[5] *R.C. Agric. Depression, Final Report*, 21 (P.P. 1897, xv).

[6] *R.C. Agric. Depression, Rep. by Mr R. Hunter Pringle on the Ongar...Districts of Essex*, 38 (P.P. 1894, xvi, pt. 1).

[7] *Ibid.*, 37.   [8] *Ibid.*, 42.   [9] *Ibid.*

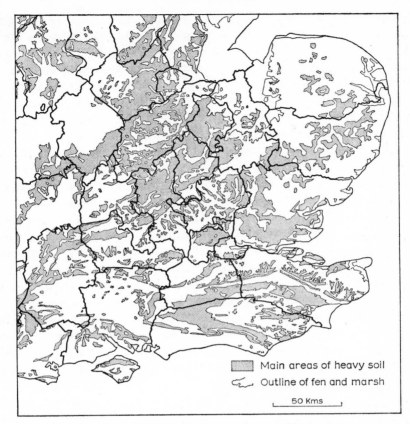

Fig. 81   Lowland England: distribution of heavy soils
Based on miscellaneous sources.

the century, told the same story. 'Between Billericay and Althorne we
saw hundreds, or rather thousands, of acres of strong corn lands which
have tumbled down to grass. I can only describe the appearance of this
land as wretched: it did not look as if it would support one beast upon ten
acres.'[1] Near Maldon, on land which a local resident called 'the finest
wheat-growing country in England', capable of yielding 40 bushels to the
acre, 'few of the fields seemed to produce a crop of grass high enough to
hide a lark; but such as it might be, that was their produce for the year'.[2]
    There were two responses to this sorry problem. Around Laindon and
Basildon in 1894, there was much cutting up of land into smallholdings of

[1] H. R. Haggard, *Rural England*, 2 vols. (London, 1902), I, 466.   [2] *Ibid.*, I, 470.

between one and ten acres.[1] Temporary and often ramshackle dwellings on the new holdings marked the process.[2] But much land suffered a better fate – argue about it as contemporaries might. As early as 1880, Scotsmen were beginning to move on to the south Essex clays, especially around Brentwood and Chelmsford.[3] Many of them came from the Kilmarnock district of Ayrshire, where the farmers understood dairying but were finding their rents too high.[4] They came south bringing their Ayrshire cattle with them;[5] and 'when we are advising a "brither Scot" who is on the outlook for land in the South, we always advise him to beware of light land, and take the heavy in preference'.[6] In the view of the Scots, the experience of the English farmers was too limited; it was not that the dairying paid better so much as that the Scots understood their trade well.[7]

Northwards in Suffolk, the Commission reported that farmers were also 'in great straits'.[8] Near Bury St Edmunds, a farmer told the Tariff Commission, a few years later, that the majority of farmers were only farming the best part of their land and leaving the other land down for three or four years' ley, and then breaking it up and substituting oats and barley.[9] In Norfolk the story was one of 'struggle to make both ends meet'.[10] In Cambridgeshire, much of the heavy land in the south of the county had 'simply tumbled down' to grass and was 'as good as abandoned';[11] while northwards, between Cambridge and Huntingdon, there was 'a deplorable state of things'.[12] 'The soil', wrote Haggard, 'is for the

---

[1] *R.C. Agric. Depression, Minutes*, Evidence of Rutter, Q. 34,288–9 (P.P. 1894, xvi, pt. 3).

[2] B. E. Cracknell, *Canvey Island: the history of a marshland community* (Leicester, 1959), 42.

[3] *R.C. Agric. Depression, Rep. by Mr R. Hunter Pringle on the Ongar . . . Districts of Essex*, 43 (P.P. 1894, xvi, pt. 1).

[4] P. McConnell, 'Experiences of a Scotsman on the Essex clays', *J.R.A.S.*, 3rd ser., II (1891), 311.

[5] *R.C. Agric. Depression, Rep. by Mr R. Hunter Pringle on Ongar . . . Districts of Essex*, 44 (P.P. 1894, xvi, pt. 1).

[6] P. McConnell, 314.

[7] *Ibid.*, 313.

[8] *R.C. Agric. Depression, Rep. by Mr Wilson Fox on the County of Suffolk*, 82 (P.P. 1895, xvi).

[9] *Tariff Commission, Report* (1906), para. 883.

[10] *R.C. Agric. Depression, Rep. by Mr R. Henry Rew on the County of Norfolk*, 23 (P.P. 1895, xvii).

[11] *R.C. Agric. Depression, Minutes*, Evidence of Fox, Q. 61,329, 61,330 (P.P. 1896, xvii).   [12] *Ibid.*, Q. 61,331.

most part a heavy clay, and much of it has gone down into an apology for pasture, often so thickly studded with wild thorns and briars, that it looks like a game covert which has been recently planted.'[1] Yet in the Fenland, observers agreed, some corn districts had hardly depreciated at all: they were fertile, easy to work, and less likely to suffer from drought.[2]

In adjacent Hertfordshire things were a little better than in south Cambridgeshire: 'Being near London and there being plenty of railway accommodation,' a witness told the Commission in 1895, 'I think it has kept up rather better than other districts of a similar character of soil.'[3] But there was depression in the more remote parts where the land was less good.[4] In 1902 Haggard came to the same conclusion: 'In Hertfordshire prosperity is, in the main, confined to the neighbourhood of a railway line. Where means of communication are lacking, as a Scotch gentleman said to me, there is "agricultural death"'.[5] Here, Scots and Cornish immigrants had moved near the railways where they could get cheap London manure for their mixed farming; native Hertfordshire men were suffering depression in the backwoods.[6]

A little to the north in the south Midland counties, the heavy soils of the Kimmeridge and Oxford Boulder Clays were in little better shape than the London Clay soils of south Essex. In the north of Bedfordshire, in much of Huntingdonshire and southern strip of Northamptonshire, for example, conditions on the clay were much the same as in Essex; always on strong clay there was 'the same sort of desperate condition'.[7] But apart from the poorest clays, these lands would carry grass and they were not suffering wholesale abandonment.[8] Nevertheless, the Commissioners concluded of this area, 'the ordeal through which the farmers of strong clay have passed ever since 1879 almost beggars description'.[9]

---

[1] H. R. Haggard, II, 58.

[2] *R.C. Agric. Depression, Rep. by Mr Wilson Fox on the County of Cambridge,* 25 (P.P. 1895, xvii); H. R. Haggard, II, 2; and for a later view, see A. D. Hall, *A pilgrimage of British farming 1901–12* (London, 1913), 76–7.

[3] *R.C. Agric. Depression, Minutes,* Evidence of Spencer, Q. 46,561 (P.P. 1896, xvii).

[4] *Ibid.,* Q. 46,614.

[5] H. R. Haggard, I, 511.

[6] *Ibid.,* I, 569.

[7] *R.C. Agric. Depression, Minutes,* Evidence of Pringle, Q. 47,508 (P.P. 1896, xvii).

[8] *Ibid.,* Q. 47,494; *R.C. Agric. Depression, Minutes,* Evidence of Brown, Q. 35,716 (P.P. 1894, xvi, pt. 3).

[9] *R.C. Agric. Depression, Rep. by Mr R. Hunter Pringle on the Counties of Bedford, Huntingdon and Northampton,* 37 (P.P. 1895, xvii).

Northwards it was the same story. In Lincolnshire, the clay lands had 'suffered both from the effects of low prices and bad seasons more than any other class of land';[1] the four-course rotation was broken, farmers let the grass seeds lie, and the grass degenerated into sheep-walk of almost no value. In Holderness, they were suffering very much more than on the Wolds; 'in fact, they are suffering more there than in any other district in Yorkshire'.[2] A farmer at Skerne, on the edge of the Wolds and the Holderness clay plain, told Haggard in 1902 that 'half of his farm was wold and half clay, and he wished he were rid of the strong land'.[3]

It was notable though that the light lands had suffered less. In Lincolnshire the Wolds, the Heath and the Cliff were in good condition.[4] At the depth of the depression 'the Wolds were as highly farmed as ever', while if the Cliff and the Heath had gone back they had not gone back far.[5] Here the witnesses contradicted each other somewhat, both before the Commission and afterwards: in 1906 the Tariff Commission found that 'corn does not pay at all to grow' and that it had not paid 'to farm highly during the last few years'.[6] On the Heath, Sir Daniel Hall was surprised that 'the output was considerable from such poor, thin-looking soil'; the secret was peas plus a two-year ley.[7] Admittedly, light land did not do well everywhere on the drier arable half of England. On the Hampshire Downs, former 'admirable sheep pasture'[8] had been broken up eighty years before during the Peninsular Wars because of high wheat prices, but now 'it would take many years to re-establish it as pasture of the same quality as that which it originally was'.[9] Yet on the Wiltshire Downs, not many miles away, 'throughout the district there was evidence of a general quiet prosperity among the farmers';[10] the holdings were big, twelve or fourteen hundred acres, and the farmers cut their expenses by having few hedges or

[1] R.C. Agric. Depression, Rep. by Mr Wilson Fox on the County of Lincolnshire, 8 (P.P. 1895, xvi).

[2] R.C. Agric. Depression, Minutes, Evidence of Riley, Q. 36,488 (P.P. 1894, xvi, pt. 3).

[3] H. R. Haggard, II, 364.

[4] R.C. Agric. Depression, Rep. by Mr Wilson Fox on the County of Lincolnshire, 6–7 (P.P. 1895, xvi).

[5] Ibid., 37.

[6] Tariff Commission, Report (1906), para. 863.

[7] A. D. Hall, 96.

[8] R.C. Agric. Depression, Minutes, Evidence of Fream, Q. 11,814 (P.P. 1894, xvi, pt. 1).

[9] Ibid., Q. 11,812.

[10] A. D. Hall, 6.

gates. In such a prairie farming system corn and sheep were the staple elements. In Gloucestershire, the Cotswolds had weathered the depression better than the heavy clays of the vale of Berkeley: the lighter lands were 'almost the only lands that can be made to pay anything at all for culti-vation', a witness told the Commissioners.[1] These were chalk and lime-stone districts. On the very lightest lands, on the sands of East Anglia or of the Weald, there was often reversion to waste. Almost all the light land in Norfolk broken up from sheep-walk and rabbit warren in the previous fifty years, a witness told the Commission in 1894, had gone back;[2] in Suffolk 'in the light lands hundreds of acres are going out',[3] though they were not entirely out of cultivation for they were still broken up every two to three years. A skilled cultivator though could cut his losses on the sandy lands. Thus the earl of Leicester, proprietor of Holkham and descendant of the celebrated Thomas Coke, explained to Haggard how he laid down the light lands to sheep-walks for as long as sixteen or twenty years, then broke them up to take four crops without manure. 'My system of tem-porary pastures is to throw the light lands out of cultivation for as long as it pleases you; if not productive of much gain, it entails no more loss beyond the rent.'[4] But according to a local Norfolk expert giving evidence to Haggard, the rentals of large light land farms had fallen by just the same amount as the rents of the stiff arable land – by no less than half – during the depression.[5]

In a wide zone of Midland claylands, arable eastern England passed almost imperceptibly into pastoral western Britain (Fig. 82). In the south, in Wiltshire and Dorset and Gloucestershire, the experience had been mixed.[6] In the Midland triangle, in Shropshire, Herefordshire, and Worcestershire, the depression had not been so severe except on the strong clays, but there the results of the depression could be dire, for strong clays in the Midlands were strong indeed. Around Stratford upon Avon, strong wheat and bean land had 'laid itself down' into grass:[7] tillage was being

[1] *R.C. Agric. Depression, Minutes,* Evidence of Stratton, Q. 34,914 (P.P. 1894, xvi, pt. 3).

[2] *R.C. Agric. Depression, Minutes,* Evidence of Read, Q. 16,032 (P.P. 1894, xvi, pt. 2).

[3] *R.C. Agric. Depression, Minutes,* Evidence of Simpson, Q. 16,775 (P.P. 1894, xvi, pt. 2).

[4] H. R. Haggard, II, 466.   [5] *Ibid.,* II, 528.

[6] *R.C. Agric. Depression, Final Report,* 16–17 (P.P. 1897, xv).

[7] *R.C. Agric. Depression, Minutes,* Evidence of Turner, Q. 11,728–9, 11,737, 11,743 (P.P. 1894, xvi, pt. 1).

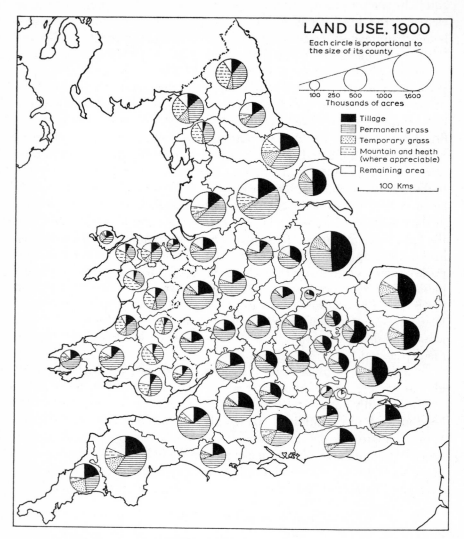

Fig. 82   Land use in 1900 (by counties)
Based on *Agricultural Returns, 1900*, 4–21 (P.P. 1901, lxxxviii).

'supplanted by bad pasture', said an Assistant Commissioner, 'simply because the yields and prices obtainable from arable land do not pay the expense of cultivation'.[1] Good red marl land produced wheat which had sold for 6s. or 7s. a bushel in 1876–7, but only for 3s. by 1893, when the owner laid it down to grass.[2] But in Leicestershire even the heaviest land, 'stiff yellow clay of a very tenacious character, and not to be ploughed except with three horses',[3] was yielding a return under grass, and it was said that many thousands of acres had been converted to grass in the last quarter-century, and that milk prices had fallen, but not as much as those for grain.[4] The farmer benefited too from cheaper manure and feeding stuffs.[5]

Northwards, around Garstang to the north of Preston, 'those who are exclusively engaged in the sale of milk have felt the depression by far the least'; farms which formerly made cheese were now selling milk direct to the big towns, which 'appear to take an unlimited supply'.[6] Northwards again, 'the position of the farmers in Cumberland', an Assistant Commissioner reported in 1895, 'is, I believe, more satisfactory than in any other upon which I have reported.'[7] The Cumberland farmer had felt the drop in cereal prices relatively little, depending as he did upon the sale of cattle, sheep, butter, cheese, poultry and eggs.

The same story was repeated in the south-west. In Devon, arable acreage had declined rapidly, and the agricultural labour force had diminished at about the same rate.[8] But, according to an Exeter auctioneer who talked to Haggard, the agricultural position was nothing like as bad as that in the eastern counties; the fall in grain prices was less crushing, and so great was the dependence on pasture that less labour was needed.[9] In Somerset,

[1] R.C. *Agric. Depression, Rep. by Mr J. Jabez Turner upon the Stratford on Avon District of Warwickshire*, 24 (P.P. 1894, xvi, pt. 1).

[2] H. R. Haggard, I, 419–20.

[3] T. Stirton, 'Select farms in the counties of Leicester and Rutland', *J.R.A.S.*, 3rd ser., VII (1896), 524.

[4] R.C. *Agric. Depression, Minutes*, Evidence of Parker, Q. 10,409, 10,609 (P.P. 1894, xvi, pt. 1).

[5] J. Bowen-Jones, 'Typical farms in Cheshire and North Wales', *J.R.A.S.*, 3rd ser., IV (1893), 618–19.

[6] R.C. *Agric. Depression, Rep. by Mr Wilson Fox upon the Garstang District (of Lancashire)*, 7 (P.P. 1894, xvi, pt. 1).

[7] R.C. *Agric. Depression, Rep. by Mr Wilson Fox on the County of Cumberland*, 28 (P.P. 1895, xvii).

[8] R.C. *Agric. Depression, Minutes*, Evidence of Harris, Q. 3,415–16 (P.P. 1894, xvi, pt. 1). [9] H. R. Haggard, I, 199.

Haggard could conclude that 'on the whole, agriculture still prospers'.[1]
Here, especially on the heavier clays, around Frome, very rapid conversion
of arable land had taken place during the eighties and early nineties, with
very varied results.[2]

Farming for stock did not pay everywhere. In Wharfedale and Airedale,
in remote north-west Yorkshire, was an area almost wholly in grass, producing butter, beef and mutton, but 'the condition of the grass land
farmers was such that some few are pretty well bankrupt'.[3] Yet, only a few
miles away, the Darlington area had not experienced severe depression, and
'the answer is in one word – "meat"'.[4] Here too, though, there was
a threat: meat prices had fallen 1s. to 1s. 6d. a stone in four years. As re-
frigerated meat came in increasing quantities into British ports, it was
brought home to farmers that in meat, as in wheat, distance no longer
afforded automatic protection.

Dairying, fruit-growing and market gardening

There was, however, one product for which refrigeration could not yet
conquer distance. From all over the pastoral half of England, reports were
coming of a switch to fresh milk production. In the northern dales of
Yorkshire, where for centuries Wensleydale cheese had been the staple
product of the small farmers, they were finding that they got a better year-
round income from fresh milk, and the Northallerton Pure Milk Society
had set up a works on the Danish model.[5] In northern Derbyshire, improved railway facilities allowed farmers to send their milk direct to the
large towns, and 'not one-twentieth of the milk that used to be made into
cheese and butter is made today'.[6] Near Macclesfield, for instance, the
staple cheese-making industry had suffered a severe blow from Canadian
competition after 1880; now the milk went to Manchester and other towns.[7]
Here, labour shortage was a powerful contributory cause: the young men
were leaving farm work and were flocking to the large towns, and 'if at

---

[1] *Ibid.*, I, 230–1.

[2] *R.C. Agric. Depression, Rep. by Mr Jabez Turner on the Frome District of Somerset*,
7–8 (P.P. 1894, xvi, pt. 1).

[3] *R.C. Agric. Depression, Minutes*, Evidence of Broughton, Q. 15,294 (P.P. 1894,
xvi, pt. 2).

[4] J. H. Dugdale, 'Select farms in the Darlington district', *J.R.A.S.*, 3rd ser., VI
(1895), 527.

[5] L. Jebb, *The small holdings of England* (London, 1907), 35–47.

[6] *Tariff Commission, Report* (1906), para. 924.

[7] *Ibid.*, para. 1230.

the present time milk had to be made up into cheese in the farmhouse as formerly, it is doubtful where the dairy maids would come from'.[1]

In all the great northern cities and towns, rising living standards and improving knowledge of nutrition were helping to increase the demand for milk. But the biggest single market was London, and this had a profound influence on the agriculture of southern England. Since much of the area around London was not natural pasture land, London's milkshed extended principally to the west, where the Great Western Railway was responsible for shipping fully half of all the milk that arrived in the capital.[2] In twelve years from 1892 to 1904, shipments by the Great Western rose by nearly two-thirds, to about $17\frac{1}{2}$ million gallons of milk a year. Most of the milk came from main and branch line stations between Reading and Chippenham, on average about 80 miles from London and at the most 130 miles away. From Swindon, the milk came by express into Paddington, 77 miles distant, in less than two hours. In cooler months the catchment area could be extended: the Great Western brought milk over 320 miles from St Erith in Cornwall to Paddington.[3] The Great Northern was more modest: it tapped the north Staffordshire producers, collecting their milk at Egginton Junction near Burton on Trent, 154 miles from King's Cross. The line which really specialised in long-distance shipments was the London & North Western; in the autumn of 1905 it was bringing milk from Goold's Cross, in County Tipperary, on the Great Southern & Western Railway of Ireland, 430 miles into Euston.[4]

Fresh milk was one special product in which the British farmer was still sure of enjoying a natural monopoly of supply. But there were other products which combined in varying measure the essential attributes of bulk and perishability; and the most dramatic developments in English agriculture at this time were found in those areas which had turned within recent years from grain or stock to the intensive production of fruit or vegetables for the urban markets. Fruit, a departmental committee could say in 1905, was 'the only form of agriculture which has exhibited any sign of progress in recent years',[5] and the reason was 'the extraordinary growth of the taste for fruit on the part of the public'.[6] The orchard acreage of Great Britain had expanded by nearly two-thirds between 1873 and 1904, almost

---

[1] W. J. Skertchly, 'Agriculture in Derbyshire', *J.R.A.S.*, LXVI (1905), 223.

[2] E. A. Pratt, *The transition in agriculture* (London, 1906), 11.

[3] *Ibid.*, 12.   [4] *Ibid.*, 13, 16.

[5] *Report of the Departmental Committee upon the Fruit Industry of Great Britain*, 2 (P.P. 1905, xx).   [6] *Ibid.*, 3.

all in England.[1] Precisely because of the bulk and perishability of the product, it was natural that most fruit-growing areas should be within easy reach of their markets; and the more perishable the product, the more evident this was. Of the big orchard counties, some were near the towns – Kent, Worcestershire, Gloucestershire, Herefordshire; but some were not – Somerset, Devon (Fig. 67). In small fruit, the leading counties were all reasonably close to the big London or Midlands markets – Middlesex, Worcestershire, Cambridgeshire, Norfolk, Hampshire, Essex.[2]

Some of the outstanding districts were naturally found where the sprawling suburbs of London ended. For fruit, Kent was outstanding. Its nearness to London gave it not only an assured market, but also – for the motor vehicle had not yet banished the horse from London streets – an assured supply of stable manure.[3] Hops for the great London breweries had been Kent's staple, and they had kept up well during most of the depression, but at the turn of the century the experience was much more mixed. At Wye, in Kent, the Tariff Commissioners were told in 1906, 'On an average the last years have been as good as any other consecutive years';[4] at Selling, the acreage had increased, and 'the last 10 years have been as profitable as the 10 previous years'.[5] But in the Tonbridge area 'the acreage under hops...has been reduced by quite one-third since 1886'[6], while around Tenterden hops were 'much reduced in acreage' and profits had 'disappeared'.[7] Some parts of Kent – like that around Swanley – were near enough to London to send their produce daily by road.[8] Here, and extending north to Erith and west to Bexley, the last thirty years had seen a great growth of forced strawberry cultivation in cold houses by small growers.[9]

West of London, conditions were much the same. 'The agriculture around West Drayton', a witness reported in 1898, 'has greatly changed during the last twenty years.'[10] Wheat had given way to fruit trees or market gardening. The west Middlesex fruit and market-garden area started as near to London as Chiswick, extending then through Brentford and Isleworth as far as the Colne Valley. It produced top fruit such as

[1] Ibid., 2.   [2] Ibid.   [3] Ibid., 6.
[4] Tariff Commission Report (1906), para. 997.
[5] Ibid., para. 1003.   [6] Ibid., para. 1021.   [7] Ibid., para. 1028.
[8] Rep. Deptl. Cttee Fruit Industry (1905), 6 (P.P. 1905, xx).
[9] W. E. Bear, 'Flower and fruit farming in England', pt. III, J.R.A.S., 3rd ser., x (1899), 300–1, 305–6.
[10] J. L. Green, The rural industries of England (London, 1895), 96.

apples, pears, plums and damsons; soft fruit such as strawberries, rasp-
berries, gooseberries and currants; roots such as potatoes, beetroot, parsnips and carrots; and every type of vegetable.[1] From here too most of the
produce went to Covent Garden by road; for 'whether it costs the same as
rail transport or not, there is less handling involved than in the transfer to
and from the railway waggons'. 'So it is that residents on the highways and
main thoroughfares leading from West Middlesex into London have to
sleep as best they can to the constant rumbling of long processions of
market-garden carts, which, leaving the farms in the evening, do their
twelve, fifteen, or twenty mile journey, and arrive at the London markets
with their loads any time between midnight and three o'clock in the
morning.'[2] This was an exceedingly labour-intensive form of farming:
a typical farm of 50 to 100 acres might employ 60 to 120 hands, compared
with a score in the old days of grain.[3]

In the same way, the Lea Valley had been opened up for market gardening since about 1880. Here, along the old road to Waltham Cross, 'a vast
and overwhelming extension of London northwards' in the preceding
twenty years had 'made of the road almost a continuous street as far as the
border of Herts'.[4] The road was the route to the London markets; the
villages along it supplied the necessary labour, the canalised river brought
in coal to heat the glasshouses; the good gravel and brick-earth soils and
the lack of strong winds made the valley ideal for the new form of farming.[5]
In Edmonton, a witness said in 1898, there were in 1870 only 10 acres
under glass in the whole parish; now there were a hundred, and land was
renting at £10 the acre while nearby farm land would fetch only £3.[6] It
was quite possible, one writer thought, that the area under glass in Ches-
hunt alone was equal to that in the whole of the rest of England and Wales
outside Middlesex and Kent.[7]

Slightly farther afield, the railway facilities became critically important.
Worthing was the capital of the Sussex glass hot-house industry, and
within the borough were 3,500,000 square feet of greenhouses.[8] Here, in
just over twenty years, the average shipments on a busy day in the season
had risen from 100 to 2,500 packages in 1906. The London Brighton &

---

[1] E. A. Pratt (1906), 99–101.   [2] *Ibid.*, 100–1.   [3] *Ibid.*, 102.

[4] H. S. Vaughan, *The way about Middlesex* (London, 1896), 22.

[5] E. C. Willatts, *Middlesex and the London region* in L. D. Stamp (ed.), 'The land
of Britain', pt. 79 (London, 1937), 222.

[6] W. E. Bear, 'Flower and fruit farming in England', pt. II, *J.R.A.S.*, 3rd ser., IX
(1898), 525.   [7] *Ibid.*, 306.   [8] E. A. Pratt (1906), 90–1.

South Coast Railway took the fruit, gathered in the morning, by a special train which got to London Bridge by 2.30 in the afternoon, and the fruit was in the markets between 4 and 5 o'clock.[1]

In mid-Bedfordshire, around Sandy and Biggleswade, the Great Northern and the Midland Railways had helped create 'a stretch of country, about fifteen miles long and four or five broad',[2] almost entirely devoted to market gardening. Originally this was poor heath country,[3] but the soils were warm, and the Great Northern line brought stable manure cheaply from London.[4] It was said, in 1906, that the output of market-garden crops – of every sort, but especially of brussels sprouts, carrots and vegetable marrows – had quadrupled in the last 20 years, principally because of increased demand from the towns;[5] and though Biggleswade sold chiefly to London, the produce from Sandy went to the north and even as far as Glasgow.[6] This was smallholders' country; the majority of holdings were 10 to 15 acres, many were only 7 or 8 and some were as little as 2 or 3 acres;[7] the smallholders were shrewd enough to have weathered the storms of competition. For even here, perishability was no necessary protection from growers just across the Channel or North Sea. The family farmers of north Holland, in the Netherlands, had crushed the Biggleswade onion trade,[8] but in its place the production of brussels sprouts was developing into a major industry.[9]

In the vale of Evesham too, fruit and market gardening were developments of the last thirty years of the century; the market-garden acreage had risen from 300–400 acres in the early years of the century to some 2,000 acres in 1870, but by the first years of the twentieth century it had become 15,000 acres.[10] This too was smallholding land: the usual farm was between 1 and 8 acres, and 75% of the gardeners had started life as labourers.[11] 'Land practically derelict 20 years ago was taken by working men at £1 per acre in 2 and 3 acre lots for growing asparagus. Many now hold 6 acres, they own their houses, and some of them have sufficient means to support them for life.'[12] The men sold much of their produce at one or two auction markets in Evesham; most of it went to Birmingham

[1] *Ibid.*, 92–5.   [2] *Ibid.*, 103–4.   [3] A. D. Hall, 424.   [4] *Ibid.*

[5] E. A. Pratt (1906), 104; L. Jebb, 84.

[6] E. A. Pratt (1906), 104; L. Jebb, 84–5.

[7] E. A. Pratt (1906), 104; L. Jebb 85.

[8] *Tariff Commission Report* (1906), paras. 938–9.   [9] E. A. Pratt (1906), 106.

[10] *Ibid.*, 134; *Tariff Commission Report* (1906), para. 956.

[11] L. Jebb, 57.   [12] *Tariff Commission Report* (1906), para. 956.

or the northern towns, very little to Covent Garden, for, said one, 'if we had to depend on London, we should soon be in the workhouse'.[1] True, there were disadvantages in the smallholding system; distribution was inefficient, the men could not easily make up the two-ton lots the railways demanded, and there was a lack of canning facilities.[2] Cooperation was the answer and by the beginning of the century it was 'becoming a distinctly active force'.[3]

Though both Biggleswade and Evesham were near big urban markets, their produce went far afield. Specialised fruit and vegetable growers necessarily sold to distinct markets. On the fertile warp soils of the Isle of Axholme, wheat had suffered a catastrophic fall in the depression,[4] but here, Haggard wrote, 'is one of the few places I have visited in England which may be called, at any rate in my opinion, truly prosperous in the agricultural sense, the low price of produce notwithstanding, chiefly because of its assiduous cultivation of the potato'.[5] The story was the same on the coastlands between Boston and Spalding. At the small village of Kirton alone, on a peak day they were sending away 95 wagon loads, with 285 tons of potatoes, mainly to London but also to Sheffield.[6] Another great staple of the Lincolnshire coastlands was celery, and in a belt sixteen miles long centred on Boston, half the total area was being given up to celery in the first years of the new century.[7] The Isle of Axholme, too, profited from celery. In the village of Haxey, in 1906, a visitor found celery being grown not only by the stationmaster but by his goods-yard foreman and the foreman's eight-year old boy.[8]

The most striking case of agricultural specialisation for a distant market was, however, to be found at the extreme south-west tip of England. The Isles of Scilly were already exploiting their climatic advantage over the rest of the country by producing potatoes for the London market by 1865. But in that year the first experimental shipment of flowers to Covent Garden had taken place; and since then, despite the heavy freightage – 8s. to 9s. 6d a hundredweight – the trade had boomed, eating into former coastland potato land.[9] In 1885, some 65 tons were dispatched, and

[1] E. A. Pratt (1906), 137.

[2] *Ibid.*, 139–40; *Tariff Commission Report* (1906), para. 1071.

[3] E. A. Pratt, *The organization of agriculture* (London, 1904), 302.

[4] *R.C. Agric. Depression, Rep. by Mr R. Hunter Pringle on the Isle of Axholme*, 16 (P.P. 1894, xvi, pt. 1).

[5] H. R. Haggard, II, 186.   [6] E. A. Pratt (1906), 126; L. Jebb, 28–9.

[7] E. A. Pratt (1906), 126.   [8] *Ibid.*, 124–5.

[9] W. E. Bear (1898), 298–300.

by 1900 this had become 575 tons.[1] And already, competitors were springing up on the mainland of England – above all in Lincolnshire, where, by the beginning of the new century, a group of villages along the railway near Spalding were virtually living on the sale of flowers.[2]

By then, the early vegetable trade had become centred at the end of the Cornish mainland, in a highly specialised and highly concentrated zone around the little village of Gulval on Mounts Bay. Here, over 300 miles from the London market, soil and aspect were critical. The best land was found about half a mile from the sea on the gently sloping southern slopes, where light soils had developed on the 'killas' or china clay slates. The smallholders, on their 5- to 15-acre plots, got two early crops a year – broccoli between Christmas and February, potatoes in May.[3] The older men here could remember the day when broccoli was sent from Hayle to Bristol by boat, but by the turn of the century the railway dominated operations here, taking the produce as far as the north of England and even up to Dundee. Reckoning the whole of west Cornwall together, over 900 trucks were sent off in a single week.[4]

By the turn of the century, then, the urban Englishman's food came from a bewildering variety of sources. Foreign produce, Haggard pointed out, 'often can be delivered in our market at a lower cost of carriage than must be incurred to despatch it from one part of England to another'.[5] Or in any case for very little more. Apples could be brought from North America to Manchester in 1897 for 35s. upwards a ton, while to bring them from Somerset cost 26s. 8d.; onions took 15s. 10d. to bring from east Yorkshire but only 17s. to bring from Egypt.[6] Here, the cheap freight for vegetables was already telling against local market gardeners. Potatoes came to Manchester at different times of the year from the Canaries, the Channel Islands, Cheshire, Scotland, Bedfordshire, Yorkshire, Worcestershire and Lincolnshire; onions from Spain, France, Holland, Germany, Portugal and Egypt.[7]

The outlook for English agriculture, as the twentieth century began, was far from good. In Haggard's verdict, 'Many circumstances combine to threaten it with ruin, although as yet it is not actually ruined'.[8] Here and there, on small enclaves of favoured land, even small men were making

---

[1] E. A. Pratt (1906), 73.   [2] *Ibid.*, 76.   [3] A. D. Hall, 341–2.
[4] E. A. Pratt (1906), 117, 121.   [5] H. R. Haggard, II, 536.
[6] W. E. Bear, 'The food supply of Manchester', *J.R.A.S.*, 3rd ser., VIII (1897), 226–7.
[7] *Ibid.*, 212–15.   [8] H. R. Haggard, II, 536.

good livings from specialised produce; here perhaps, land was actually supporting more people than it had thirty years before. But in general the prospect was one of massive and continuing migration from the land. 'Everywhere the young men and women are leaving the villages where they were born and flocking into the towns.'[1] A Herefordshire schoolmaster said that of a hundred boys who had passed through his hands in six years, not more than a dozen had stayed; those that came back to visit their friends said 'that nothing would induce them to leave what they call "town sweets"'.[2] There was too little to induce them to stay; 'England', as an Essex vicar suggested, being 'hardly merry England for the farm labourer'.[3] Many witnesses said that education was unsettling the farm labourer, and were wont to complain of the yokel who referred to a badly built haystack as 'a most egregious blunder', or to the teamster who talked of 'my colleague the cattleman';[4] but the causes were more complex. General Booth, of the Salvation Army, summed it up for Haggard: 'the smallness of the supplies, the poorness of their food, the struggle there is to make things meet, and nothing before them at the end but the probability of pauperism', coupled with education 'and the newspapers and periodicals and the glory of war. You have all these to contend with, and the railways and the telegraphs and the penny postage which are put down as such great advantages. All these things are against your keeping a man on the land, especially if he can't get enough to eat.'[5]

INDUSTRY AND TOWNS

Not long after 1900 a Royal Commission on coal supplies was discovering that the proved coal resources to a depth of 4,000 feet in the United Kingdom amounted to 100,914,668,167 tons – enough to last 435 years at current rates of consumption; some 60 thousand out of this 101 thousand million tons lay in England itself.[6] True, this coal was being won at an increasing cost; the pioneers of the early industrial revolution had reaped the benefit of the most accessible coal, and by 1900 new deeper shafts and more difficult seams were being mined.[7] The fastest expanding coalfields

[1] *Ibid.*, II, 539.   [2] *Ibid.*, I, 295.   [3] *Ibid.*, I, 493.

[4] P. A. Graham, *The rural exodus* (London, 1892), 34; see H. R. Haggard, I, 251.

[5] H. R. Haggard, I, 495–6.

[6] *R.C. Coal Supplies: Final Report: Part I, General Report (1905)*, 2–3 (P.P. 1905, xvi).

[7] J. E. Williams, *The Derbyshire miners: a study in industrial and social history* (London, 1962), 174.

tended to be the concealed coalfields of the east Midlands where large new pits were being sunk; big increases in output were taking place in central and northern Nottinghamshire and in south Yorkshire, between Mansfield and Doncaster. The Durham–Northumberland and Lancashire coalfields, which had experienced major growth only a few years earlier, were now showing much more modest increases in production, though there was expansion in Northumberland and south-east Durham. The fastest growing of all fields were small Midland fields like those in Warwickshire and Leicestershire, although the Staffordshire field was stagnating.[1]

Coal and steam power provided the basis for England's industrial strength. In the first years of the twentieth century, it was true, there were frequent reports of industries like cotton textiles turning from steam to electricity; but the electricity was produced locally on coalfields, and it would have been costly to transport even if then it had been technically feasible. Most contemporaries would have agreed with the French observer Lozé who said, in 1900, that the greatness of a nation could be measured by its coal production.[2]

Well over one half of the towns with populations of 50,000 and over were situated on or near coalfields. T. A. Welton analysed the results of the 1901 Census to discover what were the primary activities of each of these large towns.[3] By grouping the constituent towns of conurbations such as London and Merseyside he arrived at a total of 65 towns (60 in England) to which he added Oxford and Canterbury. Anticipating the modern distinction between basic and non-basic industries, he distinguished six major types of 'primary occupations' which could support the population of a town, providing it with an economic *raison d'être*.[4] Nineteen of the English towns, from London downwards, were described as basically 'commercial'; mainly ports, they also included four resort towns – Bournemouth, Brighton, Hastings and Bath. Eighteen were metal towns; they included major cities such as Birmingham, Sheffield, Newcastle upon Tyne, Leeds and, perhaps surprisingly to some of Welton's readers, Manchester. Fifteen towns, mainly in the north, depended on textiles and clothing. Three towns depended on defence – the two naval

[1] *Ibid.*, 175.

[2] E. Lozé, *Les charbons britanniques et leur épuissement* (Paris, 1900), 17.

[3] T. A. Welton, 'Memorandum on primary occupations in 1901', *Jour. Roy. Stat. Soc.*, LXVI (1903), 360–5.

[4] Welton first developed the idea in *Statistical papers based on the Census of England and Wales, 1851, and relating to the occupations of the people and increase of population 1841–51* (London, privately printed, 1860).

ports of Portsmouth and Plymouth (with Devonport) and also Canterbury which Welton described as 'a very quiet place, if the soldiers be left out of account'. One town (Wigan) depended primarily on mining. Finally, there was a sixth group of towns with manufactures, 'employing a large section of their inhabitants, which were neither metallic nor textile'. These towns contained 'special industries on a large scale': Hanley (potteries), Burton on Trent (brewing), St Helens (glass, coal and chemicals), Walsall (saddlery and metals), Reading (biscuits), and Oxford (printing). In making this sixfold grouping, Welton recognised that two types of primary occupations were 'universally present, namely the commercial and metal working divisions', and that others were often absent or nearly so, although the class of 'other manufactures' could 'hardly fail to exist in some measure'.

The census also showed how varied were the industries on each coalfield. It would be a mistake to think of a major industrial area as combining coalmining with some staple manufacture alone; each coalfield also sustained a host of varied crafts and trades. Even so, on a broad view two groups of industries were especially associated with particular coalfields – the metal industries, particularly iron and steel, and the textile industries. To these two groups must be added a third outside the coalfields. Industrial London, with its many and varied manufactures, stood in a category of its own.

The iron and steel industries

Whether expanding or not, the coalfields continued to attract the rapidly growing complex of iron, steel and engineering industries. This fact might have surprised a foreign visitor who had noticed the relative shift of iron and steel industries from Ruhr coal to Lorraine ore or Pittsburgh coal towards Duluth ore.[1] Actually, British steelmaking was also shifting away from coal; for the amount of coal needed to make a ton of pig-iron had progressively declined to 2.02 tons by 1899, and steel was a product very economical in its use of coal compared with the old wrought-iron. But there was one remarkable feature which distinguished British steelmaking and its location: it was the failure to exploit the large resources of low-grade Jurassic ores in Lincolnshire and Northamptonshire, which the Thomas–Gilchrist 'basic process' had made available after 1878, and the consequent almost complete failure of the industry to shift towards this

[1] W. Isard, 'Some locational factors in the iron and steel industry since the early nineteenth century', *Journal of Political Economy*, LVI (1948), 205, 207.

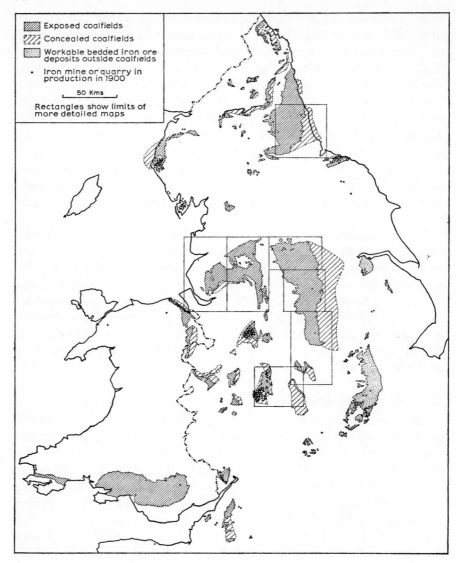

Fig. 83   Coalfields and iron mines or quarries in 1900
Based on: (1) *List of mines, 1900* (H.M.S.O., 1901); (2) *List of quarries, 1900*
(H.M.S.O., 1901).

ore.[1] The attitude of British steelmasters, indeed, remained that summed up by Sir Lowthian Bell in his comments on the Bessemer process in 1886: 'It is calculated that ore can be brought from Bilbao and converted into steel rails at Middlesbrough at the same or even a less cost than the same article can be made of iron from the ironstone of the Cleveland ores, lying almost at the gates of the rail-mills.'[2] True, as Bell pointed out, 'in Lincoln-shire and Northamptonshire the ironstone is obtained cheaply, which en-ables these districts to furnish, out of their abundance, after supplying the needs of their own furnaces, large quantities to works situated in Staffordshire, Derbyshire, etc.'[3] But these quantities were modest indeed compared with those furnished by the similar minette ores of Lorraine, despite the fact that the Jurassic ores were the cheapest to mine in the country, at a fraction of the cost of imported ore.[4] The Northamptonshire ore increased its price three times on a trip to Middlesbrough; the minette ore only doubled on its trip to the Ruhr.[5] British steelmasters reflected that 'what they gained on the ore, therefore, they might lose on the trains'.[6]

But the reasons were more complex than this, for only one fifth of British steel was of the 'basic' variety, by which advantage was taken of the Thomas–Gilchrist process. Steelmasters in the old iron districts were suspicious of 'basic steel'; they were unfamiliar with it, and they were too often incapable of the scientific methods needed to produce a high-quality product.[7] Their distrust was shared by British structural engineers, and, as a manager of Dorman Long put it in 1905, more rapid development must await the 'technical education of Great George Street'.[8] And the new Jurassic orefields only hesitantly produced a steelmaking tradition: they were making between 6% and 7% of the total make of pig-iron by the turn of the century,[9] but in steel Scunthorpe started only in 1890[10] and Northamptonshire did not produce basic steel until 1927.[11]

[1] D. L. Burn, *The economic history of steelmaking 1867–1939: a study of competition* (Cambridge, 1940), 167; and T. H. Burnham and G. O. Hoskins, *Iron and steel in Britain 1870–1930* (London, 1943), 116.

[2] I. L. Bell, *The iron trade of the United Kingdom* (London, 1886), 17.

[3] *Ibid.*, 10.   [4] T. H. Burnham and G. O. Hoskins, 110.

[5] *Ibid.*, 112.   [6] D. L. Burn, 181.   [7] *Ibid.*, 172–8.

[8] *R.C. on the Supply of Food and Raw Materials, Minutes*, Evidence of Bell, Q. 9,699 (P.P. 1905, xxxix).

[9] H. G. Roepke, *Movements of the British iron and steel industry 1720–1951* (Urbana, 1956), 64–5.

[10] D. C. D. Pocock, 'Iron and steel at Scunthorpe', *East Midland Geographer*, III (1963), 129.

[11] T. H. Burnham and G. O. Hoskins, 116–17. For iron mining in Northamptonshire

Yet it is not true simply to say that iron and steel stayed on the coalfields. Certain important coal and iron districts of the early nineteenth century, like the Black Country, were now of minor importance in iron or steel making.[1] It would have been truer to say that manufacture was being attracted to two sorts of ore supply. One was the high-grade, non-phosphoric haematite of north-west England; the Cumberland coast works made close on 18% of British pig-iron in 1900, and 13% of the steel.[2] But there the ore was said to be 'a vanishing quantity';[3] it was expensive to bring Durham coal across the Pennines,[4] and there was no local market for engineering products (Fig. 83). The other, and much more important, source was imported high-grade ore from Spain or Sweden.

The north-east (Fig. 84). The classic case of a seaboard industry dependen on imported ore was the north-east coast, which was by far the most important single steelmaking region in 1900, with 35% of the country's pig-iron production and 27% of the steel.[5] On Tees-side, seventy years before, 'scarcely a house broke the solitude from Stockton to the sea, and nothing but the smoke from the infrequent farm chimney rose up into the ether'.[6] But a description in 1888 ran: 'Now the sight in the passage up or down the river by day is startling, by night is spectacular. The clang of the riveters in the shipyards, the roar of the blast furnaces, and the thud of the steam hammers at the rolling mills and the engineering works fill the ear. A long halo of light spreads over a large part of the scene from the Tees Bridge Iron Company's works at Stockton Bridge down to the huge steel works at Eston, and tongues and darts of flame ride up into it.'[7]

All this was the work of iron; for though Middlesbrough had started life as a coal port, prosperity did not come to it until after the 1850s, when the Cleveland ore began to pour into the town's blast furnaces. At the banquet for Queen Victoria's Jubilee in 1887, it was said that 'with coal, and

see S. H. Beaver, 'The development of the Northamptonshire iron industry, 1851–1930', in L. D. Stamp and S. W. Wooldridge (eds.), *London essays in Geography* (London, 1951), 33–58; and for the manufacturing industry, F. Scopes, 'The development of Corby, Part 1 – before 1918', *Northamptonshire Past and Present*, III (1963), 125–30.

[1] H. G. Roepke, 64–5, for ironmaking. Steel was never important here.
[2] H. G. Roepke, 64–5, 83.
[3] *R.C. Supply of Food etc. Minutes*, Evidence of Milton, Q. 5,757 (P.P. 1905, xxxix).
[4] W. Isard, 212.
[5] H. G. Roepke, 64–5, 83.
[6] Anon, *Industrial rivers of the United Kingdom* (London, 1888), 252.
[7] *Ibid.*, 252–3.

without iron, Middlesbrough would not have achieved its present pre-eminence'.[1] As it was, 'the growth of the town made the first planned settlement of the "Middlesbrough Owners" seem like a tiny frontier encampment strategically placed alongside the river';[2] a railway line and station now separated it from the new town centre around the town hall and municipal buildings, which had been erected in Jubilee year. No longer did the town owe its *raison d'être* to the ore in the hills behind: throughout the nineties the orefield had been declining, and its miners were moving down into Middlesbrough to find work processing the ore that now came from Bilbao.[3]

Some miles farther north, Newcastle kept its distinctive character, preserved since Tudor times, as a coal-shipping port. Coal shipments, which amounted to over 12 million tons in a typical year in the nineties, made the port of Tyne the third port of England, after London and Liverpool, in respect of tonnage handled.[4] As the trade had increased, exports to foreign countries had steadily become more important relative to the coastwise trade, accounting for seven-twelfths of the tonnage of total exports in the 1890s; and with the growth of steam navigation, the bunkering trade had also increased prodigiously.[5] But on these unrivalled facilities for transport a great and complex manufacturing industry had also been built up. Progress had been remarkable: 'The Tyne in less than half a century,' ran one account, 'has quadrupled its coal shipments, has tripled the quantity of tonnage owned in the port, has practically created an import trade, has covered its banks with iron shipyards and engineering works, has developed the most important coal bunkering trade on the east coast.'[6] And the area had witnessed heavy immigration during the 1890s.[7]

The most distinctive Tyneside industry was representative, for it had evolved directly out of the supply of coal and iron and out of the presence of the waterway. In Palmer's Yard at Jarrow, 'coal and iron ore come in at one end of the works; ships are launched, with steam up, at the other

---

[1] *Ibid.*, 247.

[2] A. Briggs, *Victorian cities* (London, 1963), 276.

[3] J. W. House, *North-eastern England: population movements and the landscape since the early 19th century* (Newcastle upon Tyne, 1954), 34–5.

[4] R. W. Johnson, *The making of the Tyne* (London and Newcastle upon Tyne, 1895), 43–4.

[5] *Ibid.*, 197, 207.

[6] *Ibid.*, 48.

[7] A. G. Kenwood, 'Residential building activity in north-eastern England, 1853–1913', *The Manchester School, Econ. and Soc. Studies*, XXXI (1963), 121.

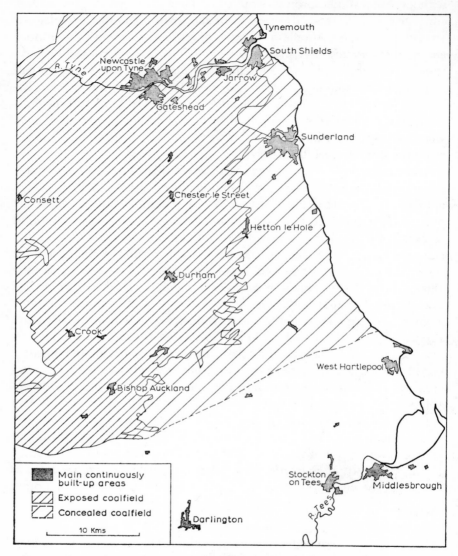

Fig. 84   The north-east: built-up areas *circa* 1900
Based on: (1) J. G. Bartholomew, *The survey atlas of England and Wales*
(Edinburgh, 1903); (2) Ministry of Town and County Planning map of
Coal and Iron (Ordnance Survey, 1945).

end'. Here, 'magnificent blast furnaces extract the iron from the ore, and deliver it in the form of pig iron. Puddlers, working half naked in front of scorching furnaces, convert the cast iron into malleable iron; steam hammers and the rolling mill turn it into plates and bars fit for shipping purposes.' Engines were made here in a large separate factory. Palmer's also made all sorts of ships, 'from the Atlantic mail-steamer down to the tiniest river-craft, from the iron-clad war ship down to the small but dangerous torpedo vessel'.[1] That was a Tyne tradition generally; though its speciality was the manufacture of moderate-sized cargo-carrying boats, which were so greatly in demand to carry the rising tide of world commerce.[2]

South Yorkshire (Fig. 85). Shipbuilding and marine engineering were natural outgrowths of the coal and iron industry on a highly productive coastal coalfield facing the markets of Europe. But in the great interior coal and metal districts of England, districts which had seen rapid development in the first decades of the industrial revolution a hundred or more years before, the process of evolution was more complex and sometimes more difficult. The two most striking examples were Sheffield and the west Midlands.

The traditional Sheffield steel trades, as was fitting before Bessemer made steel a mass product in 1855, were handicraft trades. In the typical cutlery shop could be found 'a few workmen filing, hammering, drilling and fitting parts together, with a deftness and quickness which only long practice, aided by hereditary aptitude, could give. The tools they use are old-fashioned; the shop is meagre of all appliances and aids to labour; their own manner shows surly independence and reserve.'[3] Extreme division of labour was the rule: one shop converted iron to steel by the old cementation process; another sheared it into shape; a third shop might specialise in cast-iron.[4] This handicraft trade was already beginning to give way, in the sixties and seventies, to factory production; by the 1890s table blades, scissors and files were largely made on the factory system.[5] But in Sheffield this was a relative term; in scissor grinding for instance, even in the factories, men must pay for tools, appliances and steam power.[6] Even at the beginning of the twentieth century there were 160 'tenement factories',

[1] Anon, *Great industries of Great Britain* (London, 1886), I, 24.
[2] *Ibid.*, I, 102.   [3] *Ibid.*, III, 120.   [4] *Ibid.*, III, 220–1.
[5] *R.C. on Labour, Minutes, Group A*, Evidence of Wordley, Q. 19,300 (P.P. 1892, xxxvi, pt. 1).
[6] *Ibid.*, Evidence of Holmshaw, Q. 19,394–7.

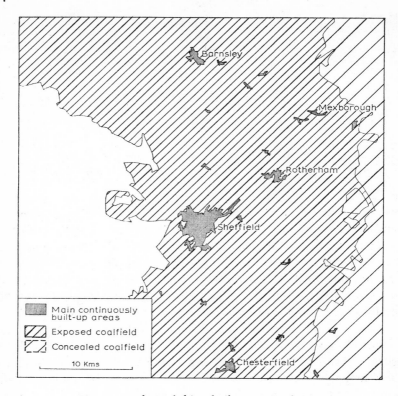

Fig. 85 South Yorkshire: built-up areas *circa* 1900
Sources as for Fig. 84.

or small flatted workshops, with about 12,000 workmen, in the city; the
number of separate tenements in the same building might vary from three
or four to seventy or eighty. Here sometimes only one occupier might be
found, but more frequently several. The grinder would rent a proportion
of a 'wheel'; there he would employ labour 'to grind, bolster, buff, glaze
or finish' the cutlery; he would provide his own grindstone and tools and
would pay for power.[1] And the system applied not merely to cutlery, but
to other 'light trades': silver polishing, scale cutting, brass turning. At the
turn of the century the progress of these light trades was uneven. Cutlery
showed no increase in volume; implements, tools and files were growing
more slowly: production of plate grew rapidly.[2]

[1] *Ann. Rep. Factories, 1902*, 78 (P.P. 1903, xii).
[2] S. Pollard, *A history of labour in Sheffield* (Liverpool, 1959), 202.

In 1900, the old hand trades were still found at the western edge of the town centre of Sheffield, where they had established themselves a hundred years before, and in the residential quarters just outside – in Hillsborough, Walkley, Crookes and Heeley.[1] But on the lower, flatter land in the Don valley to the east, in Brightside and Attercliffe, the Bessemer revolution had created a new Sheffield in the last forty years of the nineteenth century.[2] The division was not complete: 'there are grinding wheels in Brightside, which is not very bright', a witness told the Labour Commission in 1892, but 'I should decidedly say a great majority of the men are not grinders as in another part of the town...It is heavier labour, the great castings, the armour plates, and guns and armaments generally, boiler making and so on.'[3] It was this 'East End' which had witnessed a dramatic increase in industrial employment during the latter half of the century; between 1851 and 1891, employment in the heavy trades had risen over 300%, in the light trades only 30%. The cause was the Bessemer revolution; but because of the inland position of the city, the effect was different from that in other great iron and steel producing areas of England. 'Only by the high value of its steel per ton could Sheffield neutralise its unfavourable geographical position';[4] but it did so triumphantly, retaining a virtual monopoly in the special steels which were in rapidly increasing demand. Around the supply of these steels, too, developed a whole range of heavy engineering products including boilers, railway equipment, and armaments.

The west Midlands (Fig. 86). In the other great inland metal district – the west Midlands – the advent of the Bessemer process had been accompanied by rapid decline. The south Staffordshire coalfield had reached its peak as an iron-making area about 1840, when local iron and local coal united to give Staffordshire no less than 29% of total British production.[5] But the switch to imported iron dealt the area, isolated as it was from tidewater on a remote inland plateau, a particularly grievous blow. The Great Depression of the 1830s, coupled with waterlogging of the coalmines, marked the end; by the 1890s the whole of Staffordshire accounted for only about 7% of British pig-iron production.[6] In 1889 the historian of the Black Country, F. W. Hackwood, was already looking back with nostalgia on

---

[1] *Ibid.*, 89–90; A. J. Hunt in D. L. Linton (ed.), *Sheffield and its region: a scientific and historical survey* (Sheffield, 1956), 234.

[2] S. Pollard, 89–90, 159; A. J. Hunt, 234.

[3] *R.C. on Labour, Minutes*, Evidence of Holmshaw, Q. 19,556–9 (P.P. 1892, xxxvi, pt. 1). [4] S. Pollard, 159. [5] H. G. Roepke, 28. [6] *Ibid.*, 64.

the days, only thirty years earlier, when there were 155 blast furnaces in work in the area: 'To stand on Church Hill [in Wednesbury] at night and gaze around on the busy scene of myriad fires belching forth like so many volcanoes was a sight not easily forgotten. But all this has passed away now...'[1] For Hackwood the causes were not far to seek: 'The need for canals to the sea-board, and the burden of heavy royalties on nearly exhausted and water-logged mines, are cankerous problems.' But 'another form of decay' lay in the 'antiquated ideas' of the local ironmasters, who failed 'to adopt all these newer methods which characterised the strength of their new rivals and competitors who sprang up on the northern sea-boards and other favoured places'.[2] Wrought-iron had been the Stafford-shire staple and it could not withstand the competition of Bessemer steel. In fact one of the first basic Bessemer converters in Britain, using the phosphoric 'Puddlers tap' which was in such liberal supply here, opened in Wednesbury in 1882,[3] but this was an isolated exception to a dismal general rule. By the early years of the twentieth century whole plants were removing to coastal sites;[4] between 1895 and 1903 eight iron mills had 'been dismantled and three others ceased working with little prospect of restarting'.[5]

Contemporaries like Hackwood realised that the real strength of the Black Country lay in the lighter, more highly manufactured iron goods for which the area's distance from ore supplies put it at little disadvantage.[6] But even there, some of the old staples – staples on which the industrial revolution in the area had been based – were now in serious plight. The wretched hand nailers of Dudley were suffering from the competition of machine-made nails from Birmingham and (more importantly) from the north of England.[7] The same story came from Halesowen and Bromsgrove to the south, where the women were a majority in the flimsy sheds which formed the home workshops.[8] They got their materials from, and gave

[1] F. W. Hackwood, *Wednesbury workshops* (Wednesbury, 1889), 118.   [2] *Ibid.*, ii.
[3] G. C. Allen, *The industrial development of Birmingham and the Black Country, 1860–1927* (London, 1929), 239.
[4] *Ann. Rep. Factories, 1902*, 38 (P.P. 1903, xii).
[5] *Ann. Rep. Factories, 1903*, 43 (P.P. 1904, x).
[6] F. W. Hackwood (1889), *passim*.
[7] G. P. Seven, *A handbook to the industries of the British Isles and the United States* (London, 1882), 17; see also F. W. Hackwood, *The story of the Black Country* (Wolverhampton, 1902), 16.
[8] *R.C. on Labour, Minutes, Group A*, Evidence of Price, Q. 17,596; Evidence of Powell, Q. 18,409 (P.P. 1892, xxxvi, pt. 1); J. L. Green, 123–4.

their nails back, to the 'foggers' or middlemen,[1] and in the heavier branches
of the trade, such as the manufacture of 'railway dogs', their work 'is more
like blacksmith's labour than labour for females'.[2] As late as 1892 it was
estimated that there were still 6,000–7,000 hand nailers in Halesowen,
about 100 in Sedgley and 1,500 in Bromsgrove.[3] The extinction of the
trade, Hackwood judged, 'will not be matter for much regret', for it had
'never brought either profit or renown upon any locality in which it has
been seated'.[4] In the neighbouring Cradley Heath area, the staple chain-
making trade still employed a large number of equally wretched female
home workers as late as 1902.[5] Ten years earlier it was estimated that
perhaps one half the work in the area was done at home; the female
workers, perhaps a quarter of the whole labour force, all worked at home.[6]
The merchants or foggers 'have no factories, they have no machinery, and
they do not lay out anything whatever. They only simply (*sic*) buy the
iron and deliver it out to the workers, and the workers have to find their
own tools and their own firing, to manufacture the iron to chain...I do
not know that you could call them anything bad enough, they are sweaters
and foggers.'[7] Up in Gateshead they also made chains, and could claim
a higher price, because 'the carriage on the Tyne' allowed them to deliver
the work 15*s.* a ton cheaper.[8]

In Halesowen the women also worked in home workshops to forge
small bolts, fetching the iron from the sweater's workhouse, half a hundredweight at a time. Here was to be seen 'a poor woman carrying a bundle
of iron on her shoulder, or rather in her arms, a bag of work on her head,
and a child about four years of age dragging at her dress; probably she
would have to carry that iron and work a distance of half a mile'.[9] The
pay was so low in the nineties that the home workshops could still under-
cut the factory machinery.[10]

It was the same story up to the north of the Black Country, where about
nine in every ten of Britain's lock and key makers were found.[11] Of about
1,800 workers in Wolverhampton and Willenhall, about a quarter were

[1] *Ibid.*, Evidence of Price, Q. 17,628–34.   [2] *Ibid.*, Q. 17,617.

[3] *Ibid.*, Q. 17,586–8, and Evidence of Powell, Q. 18,384.

[4] F. W. Hackwood (1902), 16.

[5] *Ann. Rep. Factories, 1902*, 39 (P.P. 1903, xii).

[6] *R.C. on Labour, Minutes, Group A*, Evidence of Homer, Q. 16,918–19 and 16,927
(P.P. 1892, xxxvi, pt. 1).

[7] *Ibid.*, Q. 16,920, 17,186.   [8] *Ibid.*, Q. 17,047.

[9] *Ibid.*, Evidence of Juggins, Q. 18,067.

[10] *Ibid.*, Q. 17,817–18.   [11] *Ibid.*, Evidence of Day, Q. 18,104–10.

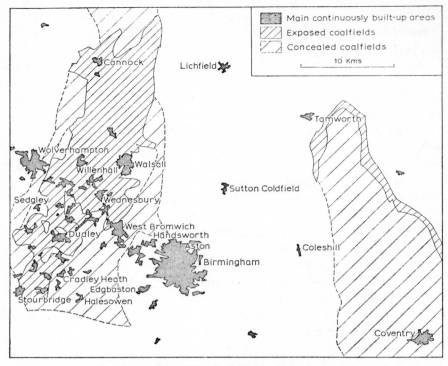

Fig. 86 West Midlands: built-up areas *circa* 1900
Sources as for Fig. 84.

outworkers, 'men who work in bedrooms occasionally, the bed at the back and the vice in the window, and in the washhouses and all about'.[1] The real homework, of this order, was associated especially with Wolverhampton; but 'instead of being ones or twos, as in those little cribs, in Willenhall it is on a greater scale';[2] the small masters provided workshops. Here, 'locks of every variety of principle and quality' were produced;[3] the rim lock, the cabinet lock, the stock or fine plate lock, the drawback lock, the dead lock, the mortice lock, the loose padlock and others. If a worker let fall the lock he was making, he never stooped to pick it up; he could make another in less time. In the 1890s, cash-box locks had been made for 1*d.* each and padlocks for 1½*d.* a dozen,[4] but employment and output were both

[1] *Ibid.*, Q. 18,128–31.   [2] *Ibid.*, Evidence of Martin, Q. 18,330.

[3] F. W. Hackwood, *The annals of Willenhall* (Wolverhampton, 1908), 161.

[4] *R.C. on Labour, Minutes, Group A*, Evidence of Day, Q. 18,195 (P.P. 1892, xxxvi, pt. 1).

declining in the face of German competition. By 1900, factory competition was making its mark: output was up, but the work force stayed about the same.[1]

In all these trades then the sweated home worker was engaged in desperate competition with the factory product, and most contemporary observers realised that he must eventually lose the battle. But meanwhile the old traditions of the small workshop offered a unique advantage in the development of new industrial traditions. Nowhere was this more evident than in the capital of the whole district. 'Birmingham, in the nineties, was poised between the town of a thousand workshops and the home of the great industries of the twentieth century. The hitherto busy activity of craftsmanship in innumerable trades was to take second place, but it provided a large body of skilled workers and a great variety of manufacturers.'[2] Contemporary observers noticed the adaptability of Birmingham industry in the face of rapid change: 'it has many different trades, and if some are depressed and slack others may be active and prosperous', wrote a chronicler of the city in 1900; 'Birmingham...is pretty smart at taking up new ideas, and does not let new manufacturing industries go begging for a home'.[3] There were clear advantages too, for the worker, who could easily find alternative employment if a factory shut its doors.[4]

Admittedly, in 1900, Birmingham's two most important staples were still doing well. Jewellery was in increasing demand from an increasingly affluent middle class, and there was a shift towards the better type of product; the brass trade, if it experienced a falling demand from the gas industry, found compensation in the new electrical and motor industries.[5] Other trades experienced varying fortunes. The manufacture of high-quality buttons had received a blow from the advent of the long tie, but the women's trade was increasing;[6] in the holloware trade, the tinplate section suffered from the multiplication of modern bathrooms, and the japanned ware section was hard hit by the increasing use of china teapots, cash registers and leather bags.[7] The demand for guns was limited by the long years of world peace and by restrictions made by foreign governments;[8] but the steel-pen trade, aided by the spread of literacy, went from

---

[1] G. C. Allen, 256–7.

[2] P. W. Kingsford, 'The Lanchester Engine Company Limited 1899–1904', *Business History*, III (1961), 107.

[3] T. Anderton, *A tale of one city: the new Birmingham* (Birmingham, 1900), 141.

[4] E. Deiss, *A travers l'Angleterre industrielle et commerciale* (Paris, 1896), 15.

[5] G. C. Allen, 251–2.   [6] *Ibid.*, 264.   [7] *Ibid.*, 261.   [8] *Ibid.*, 265–6.

strength to strength,[1] while the plating trade benefited from the rising demands of the hotel industry.[2] In general though the traditional industries were declining, or were stagnant, or at best were increasing only slowly.[3]

These traditional trades were still tightly concentrated in the inner parts of the city, and certain of them were extremely localised in industrial quarters: armaments, jewellery, copper, pens, beds, buttons.[4] Most notable was the jewellery quarter, which had been established in the Vyse Street area north of the city centre since 1865; at the turn of the century it employed some 300 master jewellers with several thousand workers.[5] But new industrial traditions were now being rapidly superimposed on the old, and from the first they tended to be factory traditions, carried on in new areas where space was available for expansion at the edge of the growing city.

The new traditions were centred around engineering. It is a myth that the industrial revolution in Birmingham was built on engineering products: the happy combination of Watt and Boulton and Murdock at the Soho works was an isolated phenomenon, and up to 1880 machine-building expertise was concentrated especially in Lancashire and Yorkshire, where the demand existed for textile machinery; in certain of the coastal coalfields, which developed a shipbuilding tradition; and in London, which had its old skills in the manufacture of precision machinery.[6] In the Black Country on the other hand there was a very limited local demand. Yet during the years between 1880 and 1914 the West Midlands became one of the most important engineering areas of Britain; and a disproportionate part of the new effort was concentrated in Birmingham. The sources of the development were technological innovation and new demands. The modern bicycle was really invented between 1885, when the first workable safety bicycle was developed, and 1888, when the pneumatic tyre appeared; Coventry at first attracted the trade, both because of personal factors and because a depression in the sewing-machine trade had produced available factory buildings. The forged parts came from Birmingham, and here the industry migrated progressively during the cycling boom of the 1890s.[7]

[1] *Ibid.*, 256.

[2] C. J. Woodward, 'Manufacturing industries', in *British Association handbook of Birmingham* (Birmingham, 1886), 203.

[3] *Ibid.*, 291.

[4] E. Lozé, 708.

[5] E. Deiss, 40; M. J. Wise, 'On the evolution of the jewellery and gun quarters of Birmingham', *Trans. and Papers, Inst. Brit. Geog.*, XV (1949), 70.

[6] G. C. Allen, 292.   [7] *Ibid.*, 294–6.

Visiting the area about 1896, Deiss noted that workshops in Coventry fell from 50 to 43 between 1892 and 1896, while in Birmingham they rose from 114 to 153.[1] By 1897 the trade in the Midlands was estimated to employ 66,000.[2] Bicycle making led naturally to motor-car manufacture, especially when combined with the tradition of gas-engine manufacture in Birmingham and Wolverhampton.[3]

An advertising brochure of 1897 could prophesy with satisfaction: 'In commenting on the merits of MOTOR CARS, we are of necessity compelled to regard them as being at present only in an experimental stage. That they are destined to become the means of conveyance in the future...is admitted without doubt by all far-seeing men...It is very satisfactory to reflect upon this fact that greater progress has been made here in Birmingham in this direction than in any other part of the world.'[4] By 1905, the big firms were 'at high pressure' and employment was 'rapidly increasing',[5] and by the outbreak of the First World War Birmingham and Coventry were together established as the first centres of the new industry in Britain.[6] In the verdict of a later historian: 'It is questionable whether apart from the desire to be near the centre of the grapevine, there were serious economic factors involved';[7] William Morris flourished outside the area though he got his components from it,[8] and there were successful firms in Scotland. The Midlands provided a suitable environment though; for many of the firms were new firms, engaged in evolving a new industrial tradition, while the light metal tradition provided necessary materials.

The manufacture of motor cars soon became a large-scale industry which needed space, and so it rapidly found itself on vacant land on the edge of Birmingham: Austins were already at Longbridge, on the Bristol Road south-west of the city, by 1906.[9] The same thing happened in

[1] E. Deiss, 10. [2] *Ann. Rep. Factories, 1896*, 36 (P.P. 1897, xvii).

[3] G. C. Allen, 297. See also G. Maxcy and A. Silberston, *The motor industry* (Cambridge, 1959), 11.

[4] Anon, *Birmingham 1837–97: a souvenir of the Diamond Jubilee Year* (Birmingham, 1897), no page number.

[5] *Ann. Rep. Factories, 1905*, 64 (P.P. 1906, xv).

[6] Evidence in S. B. Saul, 'The motor industry in Britain to 1914', *Business History*, v (1962), 30. [7] *Ibid.*

[8] *Ibid.*; see P. W. S. Andrews and E. Brunner, *The life of Lord Nuffield* (Oxford, 1955), 62, 66.

[9] M. J. Wise and P. O'N. Thorpe, 'The growth of Birmingham 1800–1950', in M. J. Wise (ed.), *Birmingham and its regional setting* (Birmingham, 1950), 226–7.

electrical engineering, where the General Electrical Company established a big plant at Witton, in the Tame valley north-east of the city, in 1901.[1] It was notable that the new industries reversed a Birmingham tradition: the older industries, like Watt's factory and foundry, had established themselves north-west of the city, adjacent to the coalfield, but now the developments were away from the coalfield,[2] as at Witton, at Longbridge, or at Cadbury's model village of Bournville, which had been established as early as 1882 on vacant land south of the city.[3]

This was the direct effect of the new industry. But both cars and electrical goods also created a vast demand for materials and components of every kind, which revolutionised the whole economy of the city and of the area around, and brought a new lease of life to many small and medium-sized firms. Bicycles demanded great quantities of weldless steel tubes; Wednesbury, which had specialised in the welded variety, failed to respond to the challenge and so remained industrially moribund,[4] but other towns were to the fore. Cars demanded not merely tubes but also sheets, wires, screws, locks, windscreens and lighting equipment.[5] Even the saddlery industry of Walsall received a new lease of life, first from bicycle saddles, then from car upholstery.[6] The tremendous demand for rubber led Dunlops to concentrate their activities in the city.[7] The electrical industry stimulated instrument making, brass founding, wire and tube making, and general engineering.[8] All these developments created a great demand for machine tools, which soon became a separate industry; power presses in particular came to be used in a great variety of industries, including the old ones which became mechanised, like locks and hollow ware and brass. Such interdependence allowed the Black Country and the city to retain their traditional small-scale form of industry, so that the motor-car industry, for instance, became a classic case of 'a great number of independent medium sized or small firms, each specializing on some single process of service and depending on a general background of metal processes and services'.[9]

[1] *Ibid.*, 224.   [2] G. C. Allen, 324.
[3] *R.C. on Labour, Report by Miss Clara E. Collet on the Conditions of Work in Birmingham, Walsall, Dudley and the Staffordshire Potteries*, 54 (P.P. 1893–4, xxxvii, pt 1); W. J. Ashworth, *The genesis of modern British town planning* (London, 1954), 132–3.
[4] J. F. Ede, *A history of Wednesbury* (Wednesbury, 1962), 271; S. J. Langley, 'The Wednesbury tube trade', *Univ. of Birmingham Hist. Jour.*, II (1949–50), 173.
[5] G. C. Allen, 298.   [6] *Ibid.*, 299.   [7] *Ibid.*, 301.   [8] *Ibid.*, 305–6.
[9] P. S. Florence, *Investment, location, and size of plant* (Cambridge, 1948), 59.

The close continuity of these plants within the city and the neighbouring area was especially economical where production was in small lots.[1]

In the Black Country engineering traditions developed on a coalfield that was well on the way to extinction. They might as easily have developed off the coalfields altogether. An observer looking for industry up the agrarian eastern side of Britain would find many examples of towns like Boston, where 'industry at the turn of the century was small scale and was related to local needs rather than national markets'.[2] He would find everywhere small market towns and village where the old rural artisans were suffering badly from the agrarian depression.[3] He would find a few examples of localised village crafts in decay, such as the straw plaiting of south Bedfordshire.[4] He would happen on small-town industries catering for a national market, which continued precariously despite their inefficiency, like the Luton straw-hat industry, 'one street in Luton being known as Rotten Row due to its number of failures'.[5] But in the bigger market towns of the eastern counties, and above all in Lincolnshire, he would find a flourishing engineering industry which in the course of a century had grown from serving purely local needs to meeting the demands of a national and even a world market.[6] The biggest centre of all was Lincoln, where six big firms specialised in traction engines: 'From the engine which drives the merry-go-round or the wild-beast show to the country fairs, to that which hauls heavy warlike and other stores in the Sudan or South Africa, every type of road locomotive is made in Lincoln.'[7]

Alike on active coalfields, on worked-out coalfields and on no coalfield at all, therefore, the new engineering industries were rapidly evolving and were already contributing to British industry its distinctive twentieth-century character. What was important, of course, was not coal or the lack

---

[1] *Ibid.*, 59–60.

[2] F. H. Molyneux, 'Industrial development in Boston, Lincolnshire', *East Midland Geographer*, III (1964), 269.

[3] L. M. Springwall, *Labouring life in Norfolk villages 1834–1914* (London, 1936), 97.

[4] J. L. Green, 57; R. Trow-Smith, *The history of Stevenage* (Stevenage, 1958), 74.

[5] J. G. Dony, *A history of the straw hat industry* (Luton, 1942), 128. On the domination of the Luton economy at this time by the hat industry, see J. Dyer *et al.*, *The story of Luton* (Luton, 1966), 170–1.

[6] R. H. Clark, *Steam-engine builders of Lincolnshire* (Norwich, 1955), *passim*; Lord Aberconway, *The basic industries of Great Britain* (London, 1927), 80–9.

[7] Lord Aberconway, 83–4.

of it, but the existence of an industrial tradition that could be transmuted: most commonly the coalfields had thrown up such a tradition, but it could readily evolve in a different environment. Lincoln showed that; Birmingham, which had never directly depended on its neighbouring coalfield, showed it too; but the best example was the capital city and chief port which still, as it had a hundred or fifty years before, dominated the industrial map of England.

The textile industries

South Lancashire (Figs. 87 and 88). By 1900 the major industrial supports of the British urban economy were experiencing very different fortunes. Reversals in fortune were just beginning to occur, and their precise significance escaped contemporary observers, whose verdicts frequently contradicted each other. Perhaps the most striking case was provided by cotton textiles. Cotton still employed one half of all the textile workers in England and Wales, or indeed one in every 25 of the recorded occupied population of the country. And, as the Registrar-General recorded in his General Report on the 1901 Census, 'The decline here shown of 3.1 per cent in the number employed in an industry of such magnitude is unquestionably a matter of serious concern.'[1] There was one part of England above all where that concern should have been manifest. Throughout the nineteenth century the cotton industry had become progressively more concentrated in Lancashire, until by the turn of the century that county counted over 80% of all the cotton workers in England and Wales.[2] Yet there was a contradiction here, which was reflected in the reports of the Lancashire factory inspectors themselves. On the one hand there was unprecedented prosperity, record dividends and boundless confidence in the future: 'The year 1900 has so far as cotton spinning is concerned in this district been one of unprecedented profit making,' was the report from Oldham.[3] In 1905, in Lancashire as a whole, 57 new mills with five million spindles were opened or in course of erection.[4] Yet in the same period, on the other hand, it could be reported that 'many women weavers have earned less than 7s. per week', and 'many cotton workers have keenly felt the pinch of poverty'.[5]

---

[1] *Census of 1901: General Report*, 119 (P.P. 1904, cviii).
[2] S. J. Chapman, *The Lancashire cotton industry* (Manchester, 1904), 148–9.
[3] *Ann. Rep. Factories, 1900*, 278 (P.P. 1901, x).
[4] *Ann. Rep. Factories, 1905*, 148 (P.P. 1906, xv).
[5] *Ann. Rep. Factories, 1903*, 101 (P.P. 1904, x).

There was one good explanation for this: increasing mechanisation and increasing productivity. Schulze-Gaevernitz, a German visitor, had been astonished in 1895 by the high productivity of the British industry in comparison with its European competitors: Oldham had 2.4 operators to a thousand spindles, but Mulhouse, in Alsace, used 5.8, and the factories in the Vosges 8.9; in weaving there was one operative to 4.6 looms, in Alsace one to 1.5.[1] Nevertheless, by the beginning of the new century there was already a cloud on the Lancashire industrialist's horizon. 'The question of the growth of cotton in the British dominions is one which is occupying the attention of the trade considerably, and is of great import-ance, looking at the large number of mills which are being erected in America, Russia, etc., every year,' remarked the superintending inspector for the north-western district in 1902.[2] And, taking the representative period 1881–1911, in east Lancashire and north-east Cheshire, 'population was stagnating in many areas, this reflecting in some measure a slackening in the rate of growth of the economy of many of the textile towns'.[3] Premonitions of future depression were thus already in the air.

Some parts of south-east Lancashire were already less concerned with cotton than in years gone by. 'Manchester is constantly becoming more and more simply the seat of the export trade,'[4] commented Schulze-Gaevernitz in 1895. An observer looking out from the new town hall tower saw no longer factories, but 'immediately around him, and receding to a considerable distance, are the business streets, made up of warehouses, banks, insurance and other offices, shops, clubs and institutes of various kinds'.[5] On a closer look, indeed, the subdivisions of the 'Manchester trade' had localised themselves in particular commercial quarters within this great commercial complex; the dealers in yarn and grey cloth were mainly round the Exchange, the calico printers were more centralised than the shippers, the home trade houses were round the infirmary.[6] Essentially, central Manchester was the great emporium for the surrounding cotton districts; its lifelines were the new Ship Canal docks or the great goods depot at London Road railway station, where 2,000 tons of goods trundled

[1] G. von Schulze-Gaevernitz, *The cotton trade in England and on the Continent* (London and Manchester, 1895), 96, 98, 208.

[2] *Ann. Rep. Factories, 1902*, 96 (P.P. 1903, xii).

[3] R. Lawton, 'Population changes in Lancashire and Cheshire from 1801', *Trans. Hist. Soc. Lancs. and Cheshire*, CXIV (1962), 197, 201.

[4] G. von Schulze-Gaevernitz, 74.

[5] J. Mortimer, *Mercantile Manchester past and present* (Manchester, 1896), 76.

[6] *Ibid.*, 95–6.

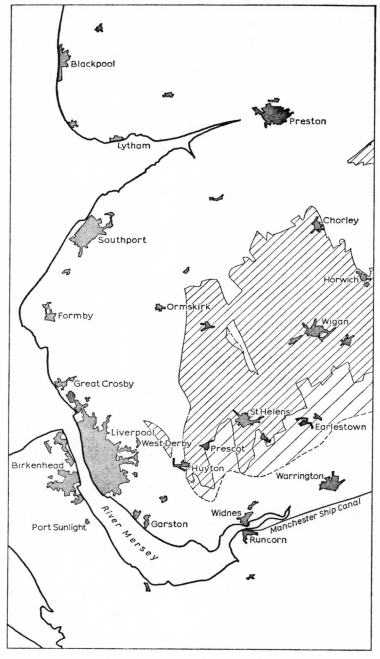

Fig. 87 South Lancashire (west): built-up areas *circa* 1900
Sources as for Fig. 84.

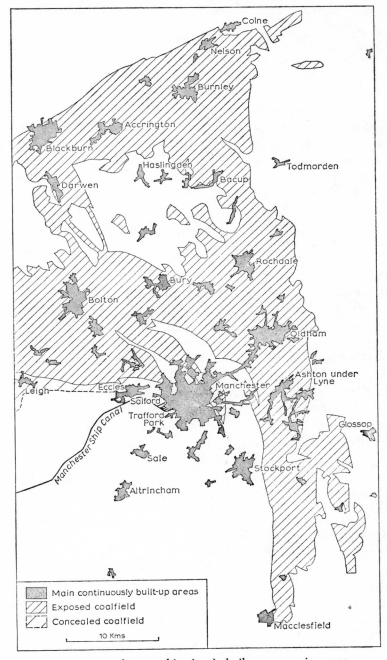

Fig. 88 South Lancashire (east): built-up areas *circa* 1900
Sources as for Fig. 84.

in or out, carried by the horse-drawn 'lurries' over the cobbles, every working day.[1]

The Ship Canal had been opened in 1894, and according to many Manchester observers that was not a moment too soon. In the newspapers of the late eighties there had been constant complaints of 'an exodus of merchant houses such as was never seen before'.[2] 'That Manchester is rapidly losing her supremacy as a distributing centre,' wrote a representative of the traders in 1890, 'will hardly be denied.'[3] 'There is no doubt that we have suffered severely from the effects of the high rates of transit, both for import and export.'[4] The Ship Canal brought a dramatic change. By 1900 the port of Manchester already had a trade of over 3 million tons, and was handling sea-going vessels of 4,000 tons upwards.[5] The railways were forced to lower their rates in competition, and one alderman estimated that the community was saving half a million pounds or more a year in reduced charges;[6] rateable values and post office business were booming.[7] The benefit extended into Salford and other surrounding towns.[8]

The Mancunian promoters of the canal were no doubt hoping that it would chiefly save their cotton trade. But one of the most immediate effects was that 'in the wake of the Canal, all kinds of industries have sprung up'.[9] Adjacent to the docks, the 1,200-acre park of Sir Humphrey de Trafford, 'until quite recently, owing to its privacy, a home for wild birds and fowl of all descriptions',[10] had been bought by a development company and was being developed by an industrial estate. The Westinghouse Company, later Metropolitan Vickers, was already building its factory at Trafford Park, thus helping powerfully to give it a distinctive character as a centre of the new, fast-growing electrical engineering industry.[11] Here indeed Manchester was following an old tradition; for the

---

[1] *Ibid.*, 108, 117–18.

[2] 'Home trader', *The home trade of Manchester* (London and Manchester, 1890), 45.

[3] *Ibid.*, 46.   [4] *Ibid.*, 59.

[5] K. Baedeker, *Great Britain* (London and Leipzig, 1901), 356.

[6] A. W. Fletcher, 'The economic results of the Ship Canal on Manchester and the surrounding district, i', *Trans. Manchester Stat. Soc.* (Session 1896–7), 92.

[7] *Ibid.*, ii (1898–9), 158–9.

[8] J. S. McConchy, 'The economic value of the Ship Canal to Manchester and district', *Trans. Manchester Stat. Soc.* (Session 1912–13), 10–12.

[9] *Ibid.*, 17.

[10] *Ann. Rep. Factories*, 1900, 279 (P.P. 1901, x).

[11] T. H. S. Stevens, *Manchester of yesterday* (Altrincham, 1958), 148; W. H. Chaloner, 'The birth of modern Manchester', in C. F. Carter (ed.), *Manchester and its region* (Manchester, 1962), 145.

city had developed a natural monopoly in textile machinery manufacture, and an important position in the making of steam engines to drive the spindles and looms, by the last two decades of the eighteenth century; by 1850 it had also become a major centre for heavy machine tools, locomotives and boilers.[1] As new demands evolved, Manchester engineers met them; the old-established textile machinery firm of Mather and Platt went into dynamos, and many small firms were just experimenting with motor-car manufacturing so that by 1914 indeed Manchester looked like becoming a major centre of the British motor industry.[2]

In 1900 Manchester, therefore, was then a textile city only in a very special sense. Its great rival, Liverpool, had never had more than a very indirect relationship with Lancashire's staple industry. Essentially Liverpool was the great commodity port for the whole of northern and much of Midland England, and because of its command of an industrial hinterland it took from London pride of place as first export port of the kingdom. Its total tonnage had risen from 450,000 tons in 1800 to well over 11 million tons at the end of the nineteenth century.[3] 'The most unimaginative individual could hardly fail to be impressed with the scene that meets his gaze when coming for the first time into the port of Liverpool by sea', wrote a Liverpudlian in 1896, welcoming delegates to the British Association meeting. 'Stretching for a distance of six or seven miles he beholds a line of the finest docks in the world, behind which rises the city, which, with its recent additions and its suburbs, contains nearly three-quarters of a million inhabitants.'[4] From the Herculaneum Dock in the south to the Hornby Dock in the north stretched 60 dock basins with 26 miles of quays.[5] At its centre, the great Landing Stage, largest structure of its kind in the world, had been extended to a length of half a mile to cater for 'the recent great development of the Atlantic passenger trade'.[6]

In the general mood of euphoria there were more cautious voices to be heard. Both in absolute and general terms, Liverpool's trade had been falling for much of the 1890s; and so, with the sole exception of Manchester,

---

[1] W. H. Chaloner, 141–2; Lord Aberconway, 129–33.
[2] W. H. Chaloner, 145.
[3] E. Deiss, 261.
[4] H. S. H. Shaw and H. P. Boulnois in W. A. Herdman (ed.), *Handbook to Liverpool and the neighbourhood* (Liverpool, 1896), 102.
[5] K. Baedeker, 346.
[6] H. S. H. Shaw in W. Herdman (ed.), 113.

had that of virtually all the Mersey ports. The ports feeding London in
contrast had gained trade.[1] Nor was Liverpool distinguished as an industrial city. In chemicals, though many important processes had first
been developed here, the city itself had 'long ceased to be the principal
seat of these manufactures';[2] they had migrated outwards to St Helens,
Widnes and Runcorn. The old eighteenth-century pottery had long since
been closed.[3] And 'the first thing which the inquirer discovers about
Liverpool is that there is no one important industry, and that there are
few large factories. . . Apart from dressmaking, tailoring, and the clothing
trade generally, by far the most important industry in Liverpool and the
neighbourhood is the manufacture of tobacco – an industry which has
greatly increased in recent years.'[4] Port industries, depending on imported
raw materials and the fact of break in bulk, were in fact Liverpool's
staples. The heavier, early stages of processing – soap making, flour
milling – were concentrated along the river, next to the docks. The later
stages, such as jam and confectionery making, tended to concentrate in
industrial areas on the outer edge of the city, often adjacent to the railways
that provided the means of distribution to regional and national markets.[5]
Unlike the textile factories of interior Lancashire, these factories employed
relatively low proportions of women, for 'it is unusual for the more
respectable working-class women to go to the factories after marriage'.[6]
And although the trade of Liverpool had given rise to an imposing commercial centre – the Exchange with its associated financial houses and
brokers' offices, and the shipping lines[7] – the contribution to the city's
employment was not impressive. The Booth Line, with its assets of half
a million pounds and profits averaging £100,000 a year, in 1900, had
a total office staff of only seventeen.[8]

Between the two giants of Lancashire, a new industrial region was in
process of developing around the tidal flats at the head of the Mersey

[1] E. D. Jordan and M. J. B. Baddeley (eds.), *Black's guide to Liverpool* (Liverpool,
1900), xv.

[2] C. A. Kohn in W. Herdman (ed.), 137.

[3] E. Deiss, 321.

[4] A. Harrison, *Women's industries in Liverpool* (Liverpool, 1904), 13.

[5] W. Smith, 'The location of industry', in W. Smith (ed.), *A scientific survey of
Merseyside* (Liverpool, 1953), 178–9.

[6] A. Harrison, 14.

[7] G. Chandler, *Liverpool's shipping: a short history* (London, 1960), 39.

[8] A. H. John, *A Liverpool merchant house: being the history of Alfred Booth and Co.,
1863–1958* (London, 1959), 104–6.

estuary. The beginnings of the chemical revolution had been felt in
Liverpool eighty years before, and soda manufacture had been a staple of
St Helens and Widnes since that time. Now, however, new technologies
were causing rapid changes in fortune. The new processes for making
caustic products – the ammonia soda and the electrolytic process – had
helped to industrialise the Cheshire saltfield and to bring prosperity to
Widnes and Runcorn, but it killed the industry of St Helens, based on the
old Leblanc process, which had migrated out from Liverpool about 1820.[1]
Glass saved St Helens: the development of new processes for window glass
and bottle manufacture allowed Pilkingtons to pull ahead of their rivals,
and, increasingly, St Helens and Pilkingtons were becoming synonymous
terms.[2] On the south side of the Mersey, in 1887, W. H. Lever had bought
the stretch of desolate waste ground which became Port Sunlight. By the
first decade of the new century here were 90-acre works, railways, sidings,
docks, wharves, and a 140-acre model village. By 1900, the factory was
turning out not only the original Sunlight soap but also Lifebuoy,
Monkey Brand soap and Sunlight Flakes – which in this year, by a happy
inspiration, Lever rechristened Lux.[3]

West Yorkshire (Fig. 89). The other great textile district of northern
England had suffered even poorer fortunes than the cotton towns in the
last years of the century. Though total employment in the woollen and
worsted industries had fallen by nearly 14% in a decade, still in 1901 over
150,000 people in the West Riding depended on it, and in the city of
Bradford, where 46,000 of them were concentrated,[4] a contemporary
observer could say: 'The foundation of Bradford is wool. It has grown
out of wool as Manchester grew out of cotton and Middlesbrough has
grown out of iron.'[5] Probably, in the estimation of this witness, at least
five-sixths of all the wool manufactured or partly manufactured in the
country was at some stage the subject of a bargain in the Bradford wool
exchange, or in some Bradford merchant's warehouse.[6] But in the last

---

[1] L. F. Haber, *The chemical industry during the nineteenth century* (Oxford, 1958),
153–9; T. C. Barker and J. R. Harris, *A Merseyside town in the industrial revolution:
St Helens, 1750–1900* (London, 1959), 444–6.

[2] T. C. Barker and J. R. Harris, 447–52.

[3] C. Wilson, *The history of Unilever: a study in economic growth and social change*, I
(London, 1954), 34–6, 56–7.

[4] F. Hooper, *Statistics relating to the City of Bradford and the woollen and worsted
trades of the United Kingdom* (Bradford, 1904), 60.

[5] A. R. Byles, 'Industries', in British Association, *Handbook to Bradford and the
neighbourhood* (Bradford, 1900), 46.   [6] *Ibid.*

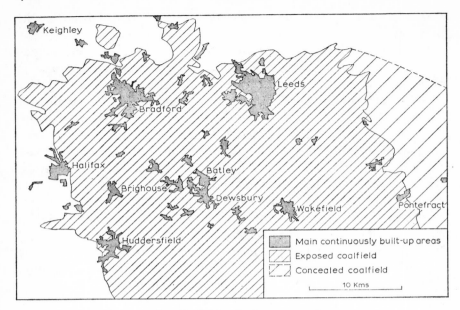

Fig. 89   West Yorkshire: built-up areas *circa* 1900
Sources as for Fig. 84.

decade of the century, wool had brought Bradford only a 14,000 increase in population. Leeds, in contrast, had evolved quite as fundamentally away from wool as Manchester had from cotton. 'At the beginning of the century a clothier in Leeds was a manufacturer of cloth,' Clara Collet could write in 1891, 'at the end of the century a clothier is a manufacturer of clothes.'[1] And the city's population was booming; between 1891 and 1901 alone it had increased by 61,000 or 14%. The secret was constant adaptation of its industrial structure to changing needs. Leeds had 'a very diversified trade', an observer could tell the Royal Commission on Labour in 1892;[2] the clothing trade had grown out of the old staple woollen and worsted trade; though the old flax and linen trades had nearly died out, Leeds was the biggest leather centre of the kingdom; above all, the engineering trades were flourishing and now provided employment for 20,000 people.[3]

[1] C. E. Collet, 'Women's work in Leeds', *Econ. Jour.*, 1 (1891), 467.
[2] *R.C. on Labour, Minutes, Group. C,* Evidence of Beckworth, Q. 15,513 (P.P. 1892, xxxvi, pt. 2).
[3] *Ibid.*, Q. 15,503–12.

The distinctive Leeds industry, by 1900, was the manufacture of ready-made clothing in factories. The sewing machine had been introduced into the city's workshops about 1855; the band-saw, which could cut many thicknesses of cloth simultaneously, about ten years later. 'By the cutting machine some two dozen double thicknesses were given out at a time for trousers, the work was fixed and given out to women to do at home.'[1] The Leeds system put a much greater proportion of the total job into factories than in London, and Clara Collet hoped that 'the factory system has such immense advantage over the domestic system that there is good ground for hoping that East London will either lose its clothing entirely, or save it by adopting the much more economical factory system'.[2] In Leeds, juvenile suits, trousers and waistcoats were made chiefly by female labour, either in factories or at home. Coats needed more skill, and, after being cut up in the factories, they went to Jewish workshops where the work was minutely subdivided, some parts – the finishing and the machining for instance – being performed by women, other parts – the buttonholing and the felling – by Jewish workmen.[3]

The Jews had started to come into Leeds in large numbers in the 1880s, probably because the city was on the way from Hull, where they landed from eastern Europe, to Liverpool, where they hoped to embark for America. Including a small number of an older generation, the Jewish population of the city was estimated at 15,000–20,000 at the start of the century,[4] and one district – the Leylands – had been taken over entirely by the immigrants.[5] Even by the year 1888 there were at least 64 Jewish clothing workshops, employing more than 2,000 people.[6] In some of these complete vertical integration of the processes had already been achieved: 'highly paid skilled designers prepare work for the costly "cutting out" guillotines, and hundreds of women guide the pieces through self-acting

[1] C. E. Collet, 467.

[2] *Ibid.*, 469.

[3] *Board of Trade, Report on the Volume and Effects of Recent Immigration from Eastern Europe into the U.K.*, 117 (P.P. 1894, lxviii); *R.C. on Alien Immigration, Minutes of Evidence*, Evidence of Marston, Q. 14,269–94 (P.P. 1903, ix); J. Thomas, *A history of the Leeds clothing industry* (Yorks. Bull. Econ. and Soc. Research, Occasional Paper No. 1, 1955), 20–3.

[4] *R.C. Alien Immigration, Minutes*, Evidence of Marston, Q. 14,327–30 (P.P. 1903, ix).

[5] *Ibid.*, Evidence of Connellan, Q. 15,018. For a description, see E. Krauz, *Leeds Jewry: its history and social structure* (Cambridge, 1964), 21–2.

[6] *B.O.T. Rep. on Immigration*, 116 (P.P. 1894, lxviii).

sewing and button-sewing machines, to be finally pressed into the "smart new suit" of the city clerk.'[1]

With an increasing number of clerks looking for a 'smart new suit', the Leeds clothing industry had a bright future. But other parts of the city's economy were already past their peak. The great complex of leather industries had reached its apogee in the 1890s, when it 'consisted of a score of tanneries, four score boot manufacturers and over four hundred boot and shoe makers'.[2] Even so, it was already on the decline due to its reluctance to adopt new techniques like tanning with hemlock bark and chrome-tanning for the new lighter shoes.[3] One part of the shoemaking trade, as in London, had passed into the hands of the Jewish immigrants; they were said to make slippers in workshops, which were also living rooms by night, at half the price of English makes.[4]

Most of Leeds' staple industries at the start of the new century, then, were outgrowths of the relatively simple technical innovations of the early industrial revolution. But less clearly evident to most contemporary visitors, another great complex of industries was rapidly growing. Leeds had developed an engineering tradition, as had Manchester, due to the local demands of the textile industry in the early nineteenth century. Already by the mid-century general machinery shops had been starting up, and in the intervening decades they had evolved into large factories with a wide range of products.[5] The firm of Greenwood and Batley was typical: founded in 1856, by the early twentieth century it already had hydraulic, steam turbine, electrical, textile, ordnance and machine tools divisions.[6] The same process of diversification into engineering was observable in this period in nearby Huddersfield.[7]

The east Midlands (Fig. 90). There was one other area of England where the textile and dress industries were a staple trade, and where these industries were suffering changes of fortune by 1900. In a belt of the east

[1] B. Webb, 'Women and the factory acts', in S. and B. Webb, *Problems of modern industry* (London, 1898), 98.

[2] W. G. Rimmer, 'Leeds leather industry in the nineteenth century', *Publications of the Thoresby Society*, XLVI (1961), 151.

[3] *Ibid.*, 155–64.

[4] *R.C. Labour, Minutes, Group C*, Evidence of Ingle, Q. 13,937 (P.P. 1892, xxxvi, pt. 2).

[5] J. Buckman, 'Later phases of industrialisation, to 1918', in M. W. Beresford and G. R. J. Jones (eds.), *Leeds and its region* (Leeds, 1967), 161–2.

[6] Lord Aberconway, 100–4.

[7] R. Brook, *The story of Huddersfield* (London, 1968), 213–17.

Midlands stretching from the mid-Nottinghamshire coalfield in the north to Northampton in the south, up to 1880 the basic industry had been the manufacture of hosiery, or footwear, or – as in Leicester and the surrounding villages – of both. In the northern part of the belt from Nottingham to Leicester, hand-knit hosiery, contracted out from the cities through middlemen, had been a basis of the economy of the village for centuries. But the new automatic knitting machinery needed mechanical power and could not be economically installed in the cottages.[1] By 1894, a Leicester witness could claim that 99% of the product was made by machinery;[2] merely a few hand looms existed for glove making.[3] Four years later a Nottinghamshire observer noted: 'The main indoor industry in and all around Arnold is frame-work knitting, which has seriously declined as an outdoor occupation. One used to hear "Clikketty, clikketty, churrrr" (the noise of the machinery) from almost every other house. Now such a sound is rarely heard, the work having passed into factories.'[4] And there the tendency, wherever possible, was to bring in cheap female labour to operate the new machines.[5]

The villages benefited from new developments. In the mid-Nottinghamshire area around Mansfield, Sutton in Ashfield and Kirkby, in the 1890s, a great deal of seaming and finishing of underclothing was done in the homes.[6] And here was an expanding trade, for plain and fancy hosiery makers were moving extensively into making up ladies' blouses, skirts and all types of ladies' and children's clothing.[7] Even before this, the hosiery trade in Leicester had been overhauled by the boot and shoe trade, which (a witness said in 1894) had been established, only some twenty-five years before but was now the biggest industry of the place.[8] Not long before this it had been a village trade, concentrated in the villages of Northamptonshire. The material had been cut up in London and then sent to North-

[1] *Ann. Rep., Factories, 1903*, 42 (P.P. 1904, x).

[2] *R.C. on Labour, Minutes, Group C*, Evidence of Oscroft, Q. 13,466 (P.P. 1892, xxxv, pt. 2).

[3] *Ibid.*, Evidence of Holmes, Q. 12,672–3.

[4] J. L. Green, 103.

[5] *Ann. Rep. Factories, 1902*, 39 (P.P. 1903, xii).

[6] *R.C. on Labour. The Employment of Women: Report by Miss May E. Abraham on the Conditions of Work in the Confectionery, Hosiery and Lace Trades*, 159 (P.P. 1893–4, xxxvii, pt. 1).

[7] *Ann. Rep. Factories, 1902*, 39 (P.P. 1903, xii); *ibid., 1903*, 42 (P.P. 1904, x).

[8] *R.C. on Labour, Minutes, Group C*, Evidence of Wates, Q. 12,526–33 (P.P. 1892, xxxvi, pt. 2).

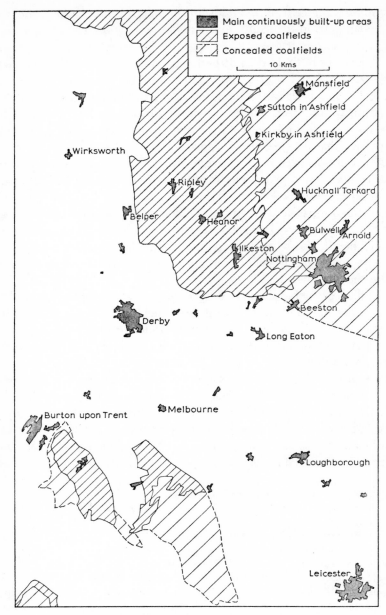

Fig. 90 East Midlands: built-up areas *circa* 1900
Sources as for Fig. 84.

ampton and the surrounding villages, where small masters with old-established skills performed the process of 'closing' before the shoes were sent
back to a London factory to be made up.[1] But by the turn of the century,
so it was said, 'the continued introduction of labour-saving machinery,
and the consequent sub-division of labour, is slowly but surely directing
the trade into the hands of large employers or limited companies, and with
them the little man has but very slight chances of competing either in the
home or foreign markets'.[2] The change was associated with the fact that,
as a union official said in 1892, 'a comparatively new class of people
entered the trade. Among the most successful manufacturers in Leicester
were hat manufacturers and so on.'[3] With increasing demand, the change
did not mean the decay of the industry in the villages. In contrast to the
Leicestershire hosiery industry, the Northamptonshire villages acquired
their own shoe factories. 'Several villages, the homes of innumerable outworkers some ten or fifteen years ago, are now the centres of large factories, quite up-to-date in every respect, and equipped with all the latest
developments of labour-saving machinery.'[4]

To the north in Nottingham, shoemaking did not become a staple industry; but here, if anything, the course of industrial evolution was even
more representative of the contemporary changes in the national economy.
At the turn of the century, hosiery and lace, which in 1851 had employed
the great majority of the Nottingham work force, were still flourishing;
lace in particular was a major industry with some 20,000 work people in
the early years of the new century.[5] But new industrial traditions were
developing, exemplified by three great enterprises which had become concentrated in the city for very varied reasons. Boots had become a manufacturing drug company in 1888, and by the end of the century had 60
shops in 28 towns; Players had come into existence in 1877 when John
Player bought the tobacco factory established fifty years earlier; the small
Raleigh Street cycle works had been taken over by Frank Bowden in 1887,

[1] S.C. *House of Lords on the Sweating System, Minutes*, Evidence of Pocock,
Q. 11,521–3 (P.P. 1888, xxi).
[2] *Ann. Rep. Factories, 1902*, 39 (P.P. 1903, xii).
[3] A. Fox, *A history of the National Union of Boot and Shoe Operatives, 1874–1957*
(Oxford, 1958), 26.
[4] *Ann. Rep. Factories, 1904*, 5–6 (P.P. 1905, x). See P. R. Mounfield, 'The footwear
industry of the east Midlands (IV), Leicestershire to 1911', *East Midland Geographer*,
IV (1966–9), 13–14.
[5] F. A. Wells, 'Nottingham industries: a hundred years of progress', in J. D.
Chambers *et al.*, *A century of Nottingham history 1851–1951* (Nottingham, 1951), 33.

just as the great boom in cycling was about to start.[1] There were good reasons why these and other new industries should have found it exceptionally easy to grow in Nottingham. The city was centrally sited, being within fifty miles of Birmingham, Coventry, Sheffield or the Potteries. The manufacturers of lace-making machinery turned readily to cycles; indeed, during the two last decades of the century more than one third of the cycle makers had earlier been occupied in making lace machinery. The tradition, long established in the lace trade, of renting a 'standing' made it relatively easy for a small man to start up in a new line.[2] The new industries helped swell the city's population by no less than 25% in the last two decades of the old century.[3] Soon, the more successful plants were finding space too constricted within the city of Nottingham itself. Beeston, a frame-knitting village to which lace making had been attracted in the late 1870s, found itself first the home of the Humber cycle works and then, just after the turn of the century, of British Ericsson telephones.[4] Despite the growth of engineering, other developments like ready-made clothing helped to preserve Nottingham's reputation as a city of women workers.[5]

Industrial London (Figs. 91 and 92). London's industrial domination would be easily missed by the casual observer. A French observer noted how London's industries, scattered in the sea of houses, did not show their importance very visibly.[6] It was not merely a matter of scatter, though; it was the lack of a clear industrial base, which confused visitors accustomed to simpler industrial traditions. 'London has no single staple industry. We find in it no dominant trade or group of trades... Ship-building may leave the Thames; silk-weaving decline in Spitalfields; chair-making desert Bethnal Green; books be printed in Edinburgh or Aberdeen; and sugar-refining be killed by foreign fiscal policy; but the industrial activity of London shows no abatement.'[7] This was the judgement of Ernest Aves in Booth's survey of *London life and labour* just before the turn of the

[1] *Ibid.*, 32; J. M. Hunter, 'Sources of capital in the industrial development of Nottingham', *East Midland Geographer*, II, No. 16 (1961), 39.

[2] J. M. Hunter, 'Factors affecting the location and growth of industry in Greater Nottingham', *East Midland Geographer*, III (1964), 338–42.

[3] R. A. Church, *Economic and social change in a Midland town: Victorian Nottingham, 1815–1900* (London, 1966), 236.

[4] D. M. Smith, 'Beeston: an industrial satellite of Nottingham', *East Midland Geographer*, II, No. 14 (1960), 48–9.

[5] H. R. Haggard, II, 281.   [6] E. Deiss, 8.

[7] E. Aves, 'London as a centre of trade and industry', in C. Booth (ed.), V (London, 1895), 48.

century. Writing in a nineteenth-century context, Aves could not help being surprised by London's success. True, it was the greatest market of the kingdom and of the Empire; it was the place where materials, machines, tools and labour were most readily found; it had unrivalled communications and the greatest port in the world.[1] But 'the disadvantages are grave, and if London had to start again, would prove insuperable':[2] London had neither coal nor iron, ample running water nor fresh air, nor sufficient light and space, nor good workers at low wages. Therefore, Aves concluded, the economic hold of London would always be weak where fuel, iron or steel entered largely into production costs; where materials were bulky or weighty; or where the processes demanded much space.[3]

The conglomeration of London trades, then, was largely a series of residual categories. Apart from purely local trades like baking, brewing and newspaper production, there were the trades where prompt execution was necessary or the direct and constant supervision of the buyer or his agent was desirable, as in jewellery or precious instruments. There were the later stages of production, especially where manufacture was associated with sales, as in the dress trades; there were the repairing trades. There was a large group depending on a pool of cheap unskilled labour – cheap furniture, ready-made clothing, boots and shoes, ropes and sacks, paper and cardboard boxes, envelope making. There was a small group dependent on local raw materials – soap, glue, size, leather. And there was a group of trades simply found in London due to inertia; it included the making of clocks, pianos, baskets, saddlery and harness, portmanteaus and leather bags, and carriages.[4]

In truth most London industries were located where they were because of a complex of reasons. Aves observed how many London industries, like those of Birmingham, were gathered in small industrial quarters, where there was economic advantage 'in grouping around the main processes of an industry those allied and subsidiary trades and processes, which, combined with adequate means of distribution, go to secure the maximum of aggregative efficiency'.[5] These quarters were to be found mainly throughout a district which ran round the northern and eastern and southern edges of the central area from the West End to Bow, east of St Paul's, and from there south of the river to Southwark and Lambeth and Battersea. Here were found the packing-case makers of the City, the carriage builders of the West End, the heavy-van makers of east and south

[1] *Ibid.*, v, 87–9.   [2] *Ibid.*, v, 90.   [3] *Ibid.*, v, 91.   [4] *Ibid.*, v, 93–5.
[5] *Ibid.*, v, 97.

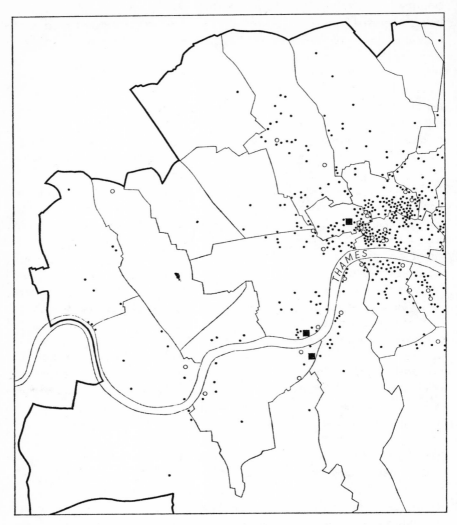

Fig. 91 Industrial London (west), 1898
Based on *Report R.C. on London Traffic*, plate F (P.P. 1906, xlii).
This map and Fig. 92 give a very imperfect view of London's industries in that they omit the large number of small workshops, e.g. for clothing in the East End. For the names of the boroughs see Fig. 94.

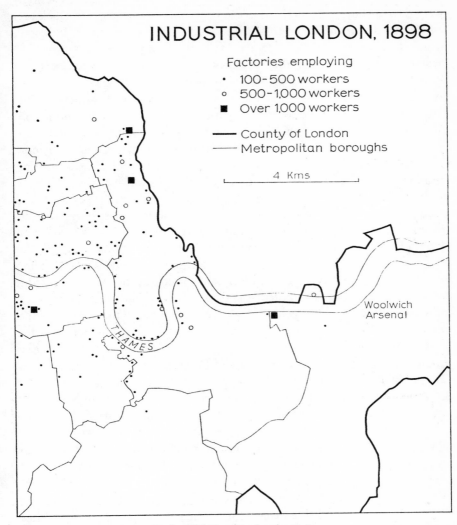

Fig. 92 Industrial London (east), 1898
For source and comment see Fig. 91.

London, the envelope makers of Southwark, the watchmakers of Clerkenwell, the furniture makers of Shoreditch, and the boot makers of Hackney.

Within this complex of trades one stood out: the clothing industry,
which (including the manufacture of footwear and fur) accounted for
nearly one third of all London's 793,000 manufacturing workers in 1901.[1]
Part of this trade – especially in dressmaking – was concentrated in the
West End, where it satisfied the whims of wealthy customers.[2] But
ready-made tailoring and footwear manufacture was the virtual monopoly
of the East End, where there had grown up 'a new province of production,
inhabited by a peculiar people, working under a new system, with new
instruments, and yet separated by a narrow and constantly shifting
boundary from the sphere of employment of an old-established native
industry'.[3] This was small-scale industry, and in the public view it was
peculiarly associated with the sweating or subcontract system. But, as
Beatrice Webb pointed out, there was no more subcontracting here than in
any trade dependent on wholesale warehouses for orders.[4] And that was the
raison d'être of the system; the great warehouses on the city's eastern edge,
outgrowth of a commercial tradition, had pioneered the transition from
second-hand clothes dealing to new, ready-made clothes making between
1840 and 1860, aided by technological innovations like the band-saw and
sewing machine. But the East End trade had reached its peak only in the
years immediately before 1900, when thousands of Jews poured into east
London from persecution in Russia and Poland. They settled in the areas
close to where they landed, which happened to be the traditional homes of
London's Jewish community since the seventeenth century; and they took
up clothes manufacture because little skill or capital was needed.[5] By the
1901 Census, of the 95,245 Russian- and Polish-born immigrants in the
United Kingdom, 53,537 were in London county, and 42,032 of these (or
45% of the total for the whole country) were in the borough of Stepney.[6]
Here 'the portion bounded on the City side by the Minories, Hounds-
ditch and Bishopsgate, north by the Great Eastern Railway and Buxton
Street, and south by Cable Street, forms the central Jewish area'.[7] They
were migrating outwards along 'the path of least resistance', along the

---

[1] Figures in G. Pasquet, *Londres et les ouvriers de Londres* (Paris, 1914), 211.
[2] *Ibid.*

[3] B. Potter (i.e. B. Webb), 'The tailoring trade', in C. Booth (ed.), IV (London,
1893), 37.   [4] *Ibid.*, IV, 56–7.   [5] *Ibid.*, IV, 60.

[6] *R.C. Alien Immigration, Report*, 14 (P.P. 1903, ix).

[7] C. Russell and H. S. Lewis, *The Jew in London* (London, 1900), xxxviii.

great radial arteries of the Whitechapel and Commercial Road.[1] Travelling incognito as a machinist in search of work, Beatrice Webb had penetrated this area in 1888. 'It is mid-day. . . For a brief interval the "whirr" of the sewing machine and the muffled sound of the presser's iron have ceased. Machinists and pressers, well-clothed and decorated with heavy watch-chains; Jewish girls with flashy hats, full figures and large bustles; furtive-eyed Polish immigrants with their pallid faces and crouching forms; and here and there poverty-stricken Christian women – all alike hurry to and from the mid-day meal.'[2]

The advantages of small-scale production in certain of the clothing trades were manifest. There was the need for rapid execution of orders; there was the limited amount of capital needed, for 'with £1 in his pocket any man may rise to the dignity of a sweater';[3] there was the possibility of introducing the division of labour principle, which the English journeyman had neglected. 'The English tailor would take one hour to put in one pocket, and the Jew tailor, with the sub-division, puts in four in 20 minutes, or four in a quarter of an hour.'[4] Of course division of labour was no monopoly of the small system, and 'the change in the character of the industry which is generally associated with Jewish labour is, in fact, due to industrial conditions which (in London) the Jew has been the first to see and take advantage of'.[5] But the proprietors of the big clothing factories of Leeds had seen and taken advantage too. Admittedly, Beatrice Webb was right in saying that the London system depended on 'a class of workers. . .*with an indefinitely low standard of life*', and that without it the trade would cease to exist.[6] But even though the immigrants might become richer and more knowledgeable and more skilled, the Leeds factories provided the guarantee that the system of divided labour would remain. This message was already plain in the east London of the early twentieth century, from the example of other trades where the factory system was already triumphing: in footwear, where the small master system of the East End was giving way before the factories of Leicester and Northampton;[7] and in furniture, where the more successful of the small shops

[1] *Ibid.*, xl.

[2] B. Potter in C. Booth (ed.), IV, 1.

[3] *Ibid.*, 60.

[4] *R.C. Alien Immigration, Minutes*, Evidence of Wright, Q. 19,722 (P.P. 1903, ix).

[5] C. Russell and H. S. Lewis, 71–2.

[6] B. Potter in C. Booth (ed.), IV, 66.

[7] P. G. Hall, 'The east London footwear industry; an industrial quarter in decline', *East London Papers*, V (1962), 3–21.

of Shoreditch and the Hackney Road were already outgrowing their cramped sites and were considering an outward move.[1]

Some of the most important trades of London's overcrowded inner industrial ring, therefore, were facing major economic challenges at the turn of the century. Particularly this was true of the engineering trades which had settled in this ring with the development of engineering itself, eighty or more years before. South of the river a pronounced concentration in Lambeth dated from that time; north of it, the watchmakers and precision-instrument makers of Clerkenwell originated in an even earlier age. But though most sections of engineering were recording rapid increases in employment, the Booth survey noted that 'for some years past the tendency throughout the engineering and metal trades has been for London to become more and more exclusively a repairing shop... Circumscribed for space, with heavier rent, rates and taxes, greater cost of labour, and in most cases more to pay for the carriage of raw material, the London manufacturer finds himself severely handicapped in competing for work with his provincial rivals of the North and Midlands.'[2] Even so, 'electrical engineering had made enormous strides; automatic machinery, from a gas-meter to a money-box, has become a craze; cycles are a requisite of youth, and no household is complete without its sewing machine'.[3] Similarly, though watchmaking had declined in Clerkenwell, due to the reluctance of the makers to adopt mass production methods, the men could readily find new work in expanding trades like electrical machinery.[4]

One of the most dramatic developments was the rise of motor engineering. In 1903, a factory inspector reported: 'The chief development in West London is I think the motor-car industry. One new factory started at the beginning of the year, and has since had to be enlarged. Another one is in course of erection and there are other factories that turn out new cars. Also almost very month we receive several notices of small new repair factories for motor cars, scattered all over the London portion of the district.'[5] In this particular year an important move occurred. Napiers, the printing machine and minting machine engineers, had been established in Lambeth since the 1830s. But in 1903, with the rapid expansion of the

[1] P. G. Hall, *The industries of London since 1861* (London, 1962), 90.

[2] J. Argyle, 'Engineering, iron-ship building, and boiler-making', in C. Booth (ed.), v (London, 1895), 294.   [3] *Ibid.*, 296.

[4] G. H. Duckworth, 'Watches and clocks' and 'Surgical, scientific and electrical instruments', in C. Booth (ed.), vi (London, 1895), 27 and 41–2.

[5] *Ann. Rep. Factories, 1903*, 8 (P.P. 1904, x).

motor-car side of their business, they moved to a new works at Acton, and by 1904 they were employing more than 500 men there.[1]

Thus the new industries could evolve in the small workshops of inner London; but the move represented by Napiers was becoming more typical, for the new type of engineering soon demanded more space. In 1901 the west London inspector reported: 'the chief things to be noted are the great increase in the use of electrical motors, and the extension of factories towards the west outside London'.[2] 'There appears to be a general tendency', it was observed, 'for the larger factories to move out of London into the country westward to Hayes, Southall, and even so far as Reading.'[3] To the north of London too, 'owing to the prohibitive rents of buildings in the City, and the increasing facilities for obtaining labour outside the centres', there was also 'a tendency to remove factories further into suburban districts'.[4]

Technological developments helped to make this possible. The increasing use of electricity in west London factories had been noticed as early as 1897,[5] and by 1902 the inspector was speculating on its effects: 'It seems probable that electricity will have nearly as important an influence in the twentieth century on the industries of this Kingdom as steam had in the nineteenth...It is to be hoped that in the new age our manufacturing towns will be able to transplant many of their industries into the country ...Surely London is big enough already without wanting to grow any more.'[6] Only four years later the north London inspector was commenting on another development: 'A few of the country factories now rely almost entirely on motor waggons for the carriage of their manufactures to their warehouses in London, etc., and this has proved so successful that it will give in the future much wider freedom of choice when fixing a site for a new factory.'[7] These years therefore saw the beginnings of the new suburban industrial areas of London, which many later observers mistakenly interpreted as a phenomenon of the interwar years of 1918–39. Between 1900 and 1914, Park Royal – a show-ground which proved unsuccessful and was redeveloped for industry – attracted nine factories, Hayes and Southall eleven, the Chiswick–Isleworth belt eleven; while the

---

[1] C. H. Wilson and W. Reader, *Men and machines: a history of D. Napier and Son, Engineers, Ltd., 1808–1958* (London, 1958), 80.

[2] *Ann. Rep. Factories, 1901,* 4 (P.P. 1902, xii).   [3] *Ibid.,* 5.   [4] *Ibid.,* 4.

[5] *Ann. Rep. Factories, 1897,* 118 (P.P. 1898, xiv).

[6] *Ann. Rep. Factories, 1901,* 3–4 (P.P. 1902, xii).

[7] *Ann. Rep. Factories, 1905,* 5 (P.P. 1906, xv).

Lea Valley, earlier established as an area of working-class housing, attracted no less than thirty-seven factories, nineteen of them migrants from inner London.[1]

THE SPREAD OF THE SUBURBS

But it was not industry alone which was seeking space in the suburbs. In 1899 Adna Ferrin Weber had published his definitive analysis of the growth of cities in the nineteenth century. Between 1881 and 1891 (and, for that matter, between 1891 and 1901), he said, the largest growth was 'in the cities of from 20,000 to 100,000 inhabitants, with the classes 100,000 to 250,000 and 10,000–20,000 in close company'. The biggest cities had increased less than the general population.[2] During the years 1880–90 of the century Liverpool appeared to have lost 6.2% of its population. 'Yet nobody believes that Liverpool is decaying; the explanation of the matter is simple enough: the growing business of the city requires the transformation of dwellings into stores and the dispossessed persons move away from the centre of business. As there is little more room within the municipal limits most of these people live in the environs, but are no longer counted in Liverpool.'[3] That was partly remedied in the decade that Weber wrote: the city took in Walton, Wavertree and some of Toxteth Park in 1895; it later took in Garston in 1902 and Fazakerley in 1904.[4] By 1914, Liverpool had jurisdiction over all the effective urban area on the Lancashire side of the Mersey, save Bootle; and she had lost Bootle only after a desperate parliamentary battle.[5]

Both in Liverpool and in Manchester, suburban growth was causing loss of population in the central cities while outer areas like West Derby or Birkenhead, and Chorlton, continued to grow. By 1900 in Manchester, 'the "cottontots" were prosperous inhabitants living in a wide range of suburbs from Victoria Park to Alderley Edge and Wilmslow, the less prosperous but solid middle classes occupied smaller houses in suburbs such as Moss Side, Withington and Fallowfield on the south or

[1] Evidence in D. H. Smith, *The industries of Greater London* (London, 1933), 41, 106–9. See also P. G. Hall (1962), 127 and 130.

[2] A. F. Weber, *The growth of cities in the nineteenth century* (New York, 1899), 50. See also J. S. Nicholson, *The relations of rents, wages and profits in agriculture and their bearing on rural depression* (London, 1906), 138. See p. 678 above.

[3] A. F. Weber, 51.

[4] B. D. White, *A history of the Corporation of Liverpool, 1835–1914* (Liverpool, 1951), 172.   [5] *Ibid.*, 175.

Cheetham Hill on the north, and were also colonising the growing sub-urban areas of Cheshire'.[1] There was progressive displacement out from the centre; the innermost ring of house property was liable to become a zone of blight as the commercial core extended outwards, but even-tually, it was said, 'as the trade continues to grow, this property rises again in value, being occupied for manufacturing purposes or for salerooms, and so recoups in large measure, if not fully, all past losses'.[2] Thus the 'conglomeration of people spreads over an unusual space, the working class here preferring small self-contained houses to barrack-like tenements, in which respect Manchester resembles Philadelphia, that huge 'city of homes'; and the houses 'extend long tentacles along the roads leading to the neighbouring towns, which often seemed to be joined to the central mass'.[3] The physical growth of the conurbation, here as elsewhere, out-ran the administrative map, which however laboured to keep up: Man-chester swallowed Harpurhey, Bradford and Rusholme in 1885, Blackley, Moston, Crumpsell, Newton Heath, Clayton, Openshaw, Kirkmanshulme and West Gorton in 1890, Withington and Moss Side in 1904.[4]

Thus in Merseyside and south-east Lancashire, the suburban spread of a central city had already produced a proto-conurbation in 1900, fully ten years before Patrick Geddes in Edinburgh coined the name to express the reality. In the very different conurbation of west Yorkshire the same process was already taking place, and the visitor, in 1900, found 'one vast manufacturing hive, in which city verges on city, and one village merges into another, so that a person travelling by night from Kildwick on the north to Holmfirth on the south would never be out of sight of the gas-lamps, with a population increased more than ten-fold in numbers and a hundred-fold in real wealth and comfort of life' since 1800.[5] Here, as elsewhere in the north, improved urban transport had brought about a great change. Until late in the nineteenth century the privately run horse trams in Leeds had catered badly for the needs of workers and had failed to colonise new suburban areas – especially the working-class ones. But in the early years of the new century the new municipal electric trams had

[1] T. W. Freeman, 'The Manchester conurbation' in C. F. Carter (ed.), 56–7.

[2] 'Home trader' (1890), 32.

[3] A. R. Hope Moncrieff (ed.), *Black's Guide to Manchester* (London, 1900), 3.

[4] A. Redford, *The history of local government in Manchester* (London, 1939–40), II, 318, 322–3; III, 18.

[5] British Association, *Handbook to Bradford and the neighbourhood* (Bradford, 1900), 49–50.

remedied this and were connecting the city centre with distant suburbs for twenty hours in the twenty-four.[1]

In the west Midlands it was the same story: 'A very large scheme is gradually being developed for covering practically the whole of the midlands with a network of tram lines, electrically equipped',[2] and already 'it might be said that the continuous roads and houses from Aston on the east to Wolverhampton on the west, covering as they do, various municipalities and urban districts, are quite as much entitled to a single name as is Greater London'.[3] Birmingham in particular was 'swallowing up its immediate suburbs',[4] and whole villages like Moseley and Handsworth were in course of being submerged in the urban flood. 'These now old villages often present some curious anachronisms. A grey old church, partly buried by a hoary fat churchyard, is surrounded by the most modern of shops and stores; and a primitive little bow-windowed cottage, with a few flower pots in the window, has, perchance, a glaring ginshop next door.'[5] Erdington, for instance, grew from a village of 2,599 people in 1881 to a major suburb with a population of 16,368 in 1901.[6] The trams were the agents of suburban growth, though Edgbaston, 'the Birmingham Belgravia', was still successfully resisting trams along the Harborne road in the early years of the new century.[7] Farther out, in the neighbourhood of Acocks Green and Northfield, the railway was the agent of colonisation.[8] In Birmingham administrative reality ran steadily behind physical reality; large areas like Aston, Erdington, Handsworth and many of the southern suburbs were not incorporated until 1911.[9] And a year after that, when the Handsworth trams were still not completely integrated physically with those of Birmingham, a historian could write that 'Perry Barr is still rural of aspect, and some of the old-world garden lore lingers there yet'.[10]

[1] G. C. Dickinson, 'The development of suburban road passenger transport in Leeds, 1840–95', *Jour. Transport History*, IV (1959–60), 219–22.

[2] *Ann. Rep. Factories, 1900*, 245 (P.P. 1901, x).

[3] *Cornish's stranger's guide through Birmingham* (Birmingham, 1902), 17.

[4] T. Anderton, 119.   [5] *Ibid.*, 116.

[6] A. Briggs, *History of Birmingham, borough and city 1865–1938*, II (Oxford, 1952), 139.

[7] T. Anderton, 89; A. Briggs, II, 140.

[8] M. J. Wise and P. O'N. Thrope in M. J. Wise (ed.), 224.

[9] A. Briggs, II, 155.

[10] F. W. Hackwood, *Handsworth: old and new* (Privately printed, Handsworth, 1908), 78.

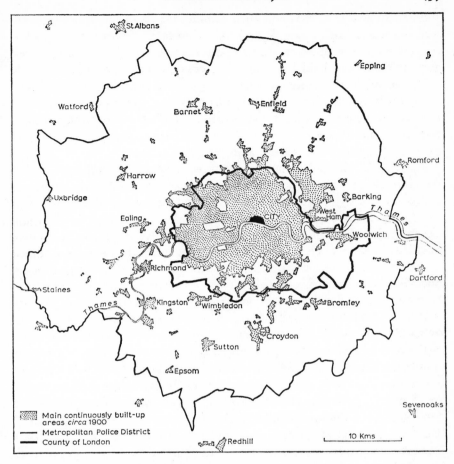

Fig. 93   Greater London: built-up area *circa* 1900
Based on: (1) Ordnance Survey One-Inch Sheets (1894–1903); (2) *Report R.C. on London Traffic*, plan no. 1 (P.P. 1906, xlv).

In a smaller city, Bristol, expansion of the old port industries had caused prodigious growth, and the citizens were bemused. 'LOST, STOLEN OR STRAYED', wrote one of them in 1902, 'an ancient city known as Bristol. Not heard of for some time. When last seen was wearing well and running uneventfully over a number of hills.'[1] Bristol had no Edgbastons; when the street tramways were promoted in the seventies, 'a few persons avowedly opposed the lines from a dread of the influx into the fashionable

[1] L. Cowen, *Greater Bristol* (Bristol, 1902), 11.

suburbs of working men and their families on holidays. The tramways were, however, sanctioned.'[1] And following this, the workmen began to penetrate the new areas on a more permanent basis. 'Several firms, such as manufacturers of tobacco, clothing, corsets, rope, etc., have recently built fine, modern factories on the outskirts of the town,' wrote the factory inspector in 1899, 'and round these factories have sprung up rows of neat cottages, in some cases built and owned by the factory proprietors, who rent them to their workpeople.'[2] The city extended itself in 1894 and again in 1897, bringing its area from 4,461 to 11,500 acres.[3]

Above all, London's suburbs continued to grow, 'stretching out into the country long and generally unlovely arms', wrote Henrietta Barnett in 1905 (Fig. 93). 'Most people have seen the homes inhabited by the middle class with their small villas side by side, their few yards of garden carefully cherished, the monotony of mediocrity unbroken by fine public buildings or large open spaces.'[4] Less familiar were 'the districts occupied by the industrial classes, with their rows and rows of mean houses, every one alike, with limited back-yards, each one only divided from the other by a wall'.[5] Foreign observers commented on the low density and the low height of London's residential areas in contradistinction to those of their own cities.[6] Between 1881 and 1901 the whole area within six or so miles of the centre had been losing by migration.[7] This area, which became the county of London in 1888, experienced a slowing down in its rate of population growth in the last thirty years of the century.[8] But that meant no diminution in the attractive power of the metropolis; outside the county, but inside the metropolitan police area, the so-called 'outer ring' had been growing at the rate of more than 50% each decade since 1861 (see table on p. 373).[9] Here the population, wrote an American observer in 1895, 'now exceeding a million and a half, may in an approximate fashion be regarded as Londoners who are dependent upon the suburban trains of the great railways, in so far as their daily work takes them from circumference to center'.[10] 'Suburbia,' as one suburban child remembered it from that time, 'was a railway state...a state of existence within a few

[1] J. Latimer, *The annals of Bristol in the nineteenth century* (Bristol, 1887), 463.

[2] *Ann. Rep. Factories, 1899*, 145 (P.P. 1900, xi).

[3] J. Latimer, *The annals of Bristol concluded, 1887–1900* (Bristol, 1902), 38, 50.

[4] H. O. Barnett, 'A garden suburb at Hampstead', *Contemporary Review*, LXXXVII (1905), 231.

[5] *Ibid.*   [6] G. Pasquet, 40–1.   [7] *Ibid.*, 23–4.

[8] A. Shaw, *Municipal government in Great Britain* (London, 1895), 295.

[9] *Ibid.*   [10] *Ibid.*

minutes walk of the railway station, a few minutes walk of the shops, and a few minutes walk of the fields.'[1] Of course it did not remain near the fields for long. By 1899, 'to all intents and purposes Croydon and London are now continuous';[2] and two years later, an observer in Middlesex noted of Hendon that 'it is hardly too much to say that it is a suburb of London'.[3] 'One may go east or north or south or west from Charing Cross,' wrote the American visitor of 1895, 'and almost despair of ever reaching the rim of the metropolis.'[4]

The new suburbs of the 'industrial classes', which Henrietta Barnett had noted, were a more recent and a more limited phenomenon. Still in 1901, some 16% of the population of the L.C.C. area was recorded as 'overcrowded', in the sense of living more than two to a room; and the worst boroughs, gathered just north and east of the centre, all recorded more than 25%[5] – Holborn, Finsbury, Shoreditch, Bethnal Green and Stepney (Fig. 94). Such a slum district 'represents the presence of a market for local casual labour. So the slums of Drury Lane are the creation of one market for casual labour – the theatres; and another market for labour which is riveted to the spot – the early work of Covent Garden.'[6] Similarly 'the fringe of misery radiating on the east and north-east of the City'[7] represented the demands of the low tailoring trade, the fur workers, the City outworkers, the small furniture trade, the match-box makers, the sack makers, and the Docks. 'If we could abolish all such casual labour,' this writer continued, 'then the poor labourer might do what the aristocracy of labour does now – migrate to the suburbs, or to outside areas like Tottenham, where there are cottages to be had with gardens.'[8] But before this could happen, redevelopment was eating into the slum areas. Land near the Bank of England was said to be running up towards £1 million an acre, and 'even a mile or two away the commercial value is so great that the residential population is steadily and rapidly vanishing'.[9] The process of displacement, said a witness in 1903, was taking place in all the boroughs adjoining the city – in Southwark, in Holborn, in Finsbury, in Shoreditch; but it was particularly serious in Stepney.[10] The effect was that

[1] J. Kenward, *The suburban child* (Cambridge, 1955), 74.

[2] E. A. Martin, *Croydon: old and new* (London, 1900), 6.

[3] J. P. Emslie, 'A walk on the banks of the Brent', *Home Counties Magazine*, III (1901), 122.

[4] A. Shaw, 231–2.   [5] G. Pasquet, 128–9.

[6] B. F. C. Costelloe, *The housing problem* (Manchester, 1899), 48.

[7] *Ibid.*, 49.   [8] *Ibid.*   [9] *Ibid.*, 53.

[10] *R.C. Alien Immigration, Minutes*, Evidence of Gordon, Q. 17,681 (P.P. 1903, ix).

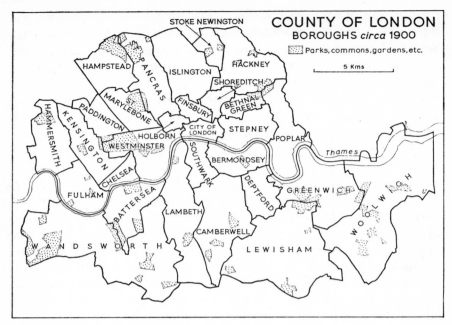

Fig. 94 The county of London and boroughs *circa* 1900
Based on J. G. Bartholomew, *The survey atlas of England and Wales* (Edinburgh, 1903), plate 80.

workmen's rents might rise 70% or 80% in a short time;[1] and analysis by
the L.C.C. showed that the average weekly rent of new working-class
houses was 3s. 3½d. in the central area but only 2s. in the areas outside the
county altogether.[2] While the price of land in the central area made it
quite uneconomic to rehouse the working classes at rents they could afford
without a loss, in the outer areas it was still possible.[3]

Charles Booth in 1901 logically argued that large numbers of the working class were not casually employed and were free to move; he urged
'a large and really complete scheme of railways underground and over-
head, as well as a net-work of tram lines on the surface', so that 'London
will spread in all directions'.[4] To some extent this was happening.

[1] B. F. C. Costelloe, 53.

[2] *R.C. on London Traffic, Report*, 9 (P.P. 1905, xxx).

[3] *Ibid.*

[4] C. Booth, *Improved means of locomotion as a first step towards the cure of the housing
difficulties of London* (London, 1901), 15–16, 17.

'Between 1877 and 1904 new building advanced in a great crescent beyond the Lea, covering the Flood Plain and Taplow Gravels from Highim (*sic*) Hill to Ilford and extending southwestwards onto the alluvium to link with Canning Town.'[1] Between 1861 and 1901 the population of Walthamstow rose from 7,137 to 95,131; on the opposite side of the Lea in Enfield it rose from 10,930 to 61,892.[2] Of course these were one-class suburbs; developed on the basis of the cheap workmen's fares of the Great Eastern Railway, they would not attract the middle class.[3] The real trouble was that there were not enough railways like the Great Eastern; the really cheap workmen's fares only served very limited areas of London. Thus in south London, while workmen's fares had become more general, they had not achieved their specific aim of decentralisation; but when a really cheap fare offered the opportunity, as along the South London where a 2*d.* fare was available, there the working class had concentrated.[4] Shortly after the turn of the century the L.C.C. statistical officer compared rents and workmen's fares in central with suburban districts; he found that by using the cheap L.C.C. trams the suburban workman gained a clear advantage, but with railways the comparison was far more evenly balanced, and indeed in some cases the central location had the advantage.[5] Small wonder then that in 1897, less than one-quarter of the trade union members of south London used public transport to get to work.[6] In London, as elsewhere, commuting in 1900 was still a phenomenon affecting only a minority.[7]

By the beginning of the twentieth century, the impact of improved transport upon the physiognomy of London was far from complete. True, the central area had been losing residential population for some time, while it gained daytime population. The decline in the night population of the City itself had begun forty years before: from 112,063 in 1861 it was down to 26,923 in 1901. But by this time the estimated daytime population was 359,940.[8] The West End was still in a state of transition: in

---

[1] H. Rees, 'A growth map for northeast London during the railway age', *Geog. Rev.*, xxxv (1945), 462.

[2] *R.C. London Traffic, Report*, 14 (P.P. 1905, xxx). [3] *Ibid.*, 15.

[4] H. J. Dyos, 'Workmen's fares in south London 1860–1914', *Jour. Transport History*, I (1953–4), 15.

[5] *Rep. London Traffic Branch of the Board of Trade*, 14 (P.P. 1910, xxxvi).

[6] H. J. Dyos, *Victorian suburb: a study of the growth of Camberwell* (Leicester, 1961), 62.

[7] J. R. Kellett, *The impact of railways on Victorian cities* (London, 1969), 95.

[8] *R.C. London Traffic, Report* 5–6 (P.P. 1905, xxx).

contrast to the City it was still a residential area, yet, here too, younger workers were beginning to commute in to work.[1] Altogether it was estimated that in inner London – embracing the City, Westminster, St Marylebone, Holborn, Finsbury, Shoreditch, Bethnal Green, Stepney, Bermondsey and Southwark as well as parts of St Pancras and Lambeth – the 'day population' was 2,427,000 and the 'night population' 1,387,960.[2] These figures are suspect because the recorded movement by public transport into the area during the morning rush period between 7 a.m. and 10 a.m. was only 419,000, of which the great majority, 326,000, came by train.[3] Including those who walked or used bicycles, perhaps between one-half and three-quarters of a million people commuted into inner London every morning.

Important as the railways were in this process, they had not yet fully realised their potential function. Though by 1901 over two million people lived in the outer ring of Greater London, between six and fifteen miles from the centre, and the entire population of that area had reached 6,600,000,[4] and though the rate of growth in the inner area (i.e. the county of London) was slowing down,[5] nevertheless the last decade of the old century still saw about two-fifths of the total population growth of Greater London taking place within the six- or seven-mile ring which represented the effective radius of horse tram or bus.[6] The railway system was still a very imperfect system for shuttling the commuter to and fro; it was particularly deficient in the West End, where the Inner Circle Line made a very wide circuit and the commuter had to rely on the horse bus, which was cheap but not very comfortable.[7] The first tube line under the West End, the Central London Line, had remedied this to some extent for east–west travellers by 1900; but it connected with only two surface termini. Even by 1905 the Royal Commission on London Traffic could estimate that the average commuter spent two hours per day in transit.[8] An improvement

---

[1] G. Kemmann, *Der Verkehr Londons mit besonderer Berücksichtigung der Eisenbahnen* (Berlin, 1892), 17. On the growth of retailing in the West End, see the useful chronological table in A. Adburgham, *Shops and shopping 1800–1914* (London, 1964), 283–7.

[2] *R.C. London Traffic, Report of Advisory Board of Engineers*, 12, 13 (P.P. 1906, xlv).

[3] *Ibid.*, 22.

[4] G. Cadoux, *La vie des grandes capitales* (Paris and Nancy, 1908), 110.

[5] See p. 740 above.

[6] T. C. Barker and M. Robbins, *A history of London transport*, 1 (London, 1963) 221–2, 272.   [7] G. Kemmann, 30.

[8] *R.C. London Traffic, Report of Engineers*, 27 (P.P. 1906, xlv).

had to await a multiplication of the tubes in central London and an electrification of the suburban surface lines; though the first was achieved rapidly between 1906 and 1910, the second had to wait until after the First World War.

Slowly, therefore, Englishmen were becoming more mobile. This was reflected not only in their pattern of work but also in their pattern of play. The turn of the century represented perhaps the golden age of the English seaside resort. Like the commuting habit, the holiday habit had been pioneered by the middle class, and until late in the nineteenth century the new resorts remained largely their preserve; but by 1900 the excursion train habit was ushering in a momentous change. 'We have occasionally heard that Scarborough is vulgar, in consequence of the numerous day excursions that run into it', complained a brochure of 1891; but there could be 'no more delightful spectacle than to witness the exuberant spirits, the ludicrous efforts at enjoyment, and the utter disregard of the proprieties and conventionalities of society. But they do not frequent the Spa Grounds, or interfere with the pleasures of genteel society.'[1] By this time, certain resorts had begun to mushroom without the patronage of genteel society. Blackpool had been built on the earnings of a new class, the skilled workmen who had benefited from the rising productivity and rising living standards of the last decades of the nineteenth century. 'Ninety per cent of these people', a Lancashire observer told Schulze-Gaevernitz on the promenade at Blackpool in 1895, 'are mill-hands...the remainder mostly machine workers...That slender, caring-for-himself man, who with his better-half came on the trip, is a mule-spinner who can earn £2 and more weekly. That stronger-looking man next to him is probably a representative of the machine-making everywhere planted alongside of the cotton industry, and then certainly a member of the well-known Amalgamated Society. That full-grown girl, who evidently places great value on herself and her outward appearance, may be one of those four-loom weavers so numerous in our town, with weekly wages of 24*s.* or more, and fair savings.'[2]

For many Lancastrians, such prosperity was recent and still not quite familiar. At a sumptuous boarding house high tea, the German observer was able to talk to an old man who could well remember a youth of bitter poverty: '"But if you want to see the true sign of this change..., it lies before you on the table, the strength of Lancashire", as he raised with

[1] Anon, *The Yorkshire health resorts illustrated* (Scarborough, 1891), 9.
[2] G. von Schulze-Gaevernitz, 198–9.

triumphant bearing a piece of wheaten bread. Cobden was a sacred being to the old man. "We fought the battle, and we have won." With these words he closed his story.'[1] Whether quite fair or not, the point was well made. Blackpool's visitors, and its residents, were the beneficiaries of half-a-century of free trade, of the policy of ruthless geographical division of labour, which had essentially been the creation of Cobden and his fellow Anti-Corn-Law campaigners. Ruining many British farmers in the process, this policy had yet made Britain the acknowledged workshop of the world. Even as the old man looked back, Germany and the U.S.A. were closely threatening this unique role. Yet as Lancashire and England played through the late Victorian and Edwardian summer, outside competition must have seemed a remote cloud in an otherwise untroubled sky.

[1] *Ibid.*, 201.

INDEX